To a friend of mine

with best wishes

NIKKI & DAVID GOLDBECK'S
AMERICAN WHOLEFOODS CUISINE

NIKKI & DAVID GOLDBECK'S AMERICAN WHOLEFOODS CUISINE

Over 1300 Meatless, Wholesome Recipes

From Short Order to Gourmet

SPECIAL TENTH ANNIVERSARY EDITION

Ceres Press
Woodstock, NY

PUBLISHER'S NOTE
The recipes found on pages 49, 263, 383, and 384 are captioned Brown
Rice-a-Roni, Stove-Top Stuffing, Giant and Individual Twinkies, and
Devil Dogs solely for the purposes of helping the reader identify the foods
being prepared and are not to be confused with the commercially available
products, which are trademarks of their respective manufacturers.

Designed by Julian Hamer

Drawings by Bob Domino

PRINTED IN THE UNITED STATES OF AMERICA

Published by agreement with Penguin USA.
For information address Ceres Press, P.O. Box 87
Woodstock, NY 12498
(914) 679-5573

Acknowledgments

We would like to express our deepest gratitude
to Molly Allen for her professional and
loving editing of this book. Also, our appreciation
to Adrienne Becker for her dedicated assistance
in helping to prepare the manuscript,
to Ellen Shapiro for the excellent index,
and to family and friends who tasted and tested,
offering much needed praise and criticism.

Contents

Introduction 1

The Wholefoods Philosophy 3
The Food Spectrums 5
The Protein Principle 5
Carbohydrates and Weight
Control 9

The New American Menu 11
Putting Together a Meal 11

COOKING IN THE WHOLEFOODS STYLE 21

Recipe Notes 23

Short-Order Cooking 26
Cold Sandwiches and Salad
Platters 27
Hot Sandwiches and Entrées 33
Side Dishes 46
Vegetable Cookery 50
Soups 54
Dressings and Sauces 56
Desserts 59

Appetizers and Hors d'Oeuvres 63
Dips 63
Relish Tray 64
Pâtés and Spreads 66
Cheese and Egg Appetizers 70
Quiche 74
Vegetable Appetizers 76
Bean Appetizers 86

Soups 89
Convenience Soups 90
Everyday Soups 92
Specialty Soups 105
Cold Soups 108

The Main Course 111
Pasta Entrées 111
Cheese Entrées 124
Egg Entrées 130

Stove-Top Vegetables 139
Baked Vegetable Entrées 149
Stuffed Vegetable Entrées 156
Tofu Dishes 166
Tempeh 173
Mainly Beans 176
Grain Mains 188
Patties, Balls, and Loaves 194
Filled Pancakes 208
Savory Pastries 218

Side Dishes 230
Vegetable Accompaniments 230
Bean Accompaniments 257
Grain, Dumpling, and Pasta
Accompaniments 262
Savory Pastry Accompaniments 279
Salads and Dressings 286

Condiments 306

Sauces and Gravies 312

Bread Baking and Cracker Making 320
Flatbreads 320
Bread Without an Oven 323
Quick Breads 325
Yeast Breads 333

Snacks 348

Desserts 354
Fruit Desserts 355
Puddings and Frozen Desserts 361
Baked Goods 366
Cookies 370
Cakes 381
Pies and Individual Pastries 394
Finishing Touches 410

Beverages 417

The Food Factory 420
Yogurt Making 420
Growing Sprouts 422
Putting Up Produce 425
Convenience Mixes 443

Planning the Menu 451
Simple Wholefoods Dinners 451
Family and Company Dinners 452

Children's Party Suggestions 454
Adult Party Suggestions 454
Barbecue Suggestions 455
Holiday Entertaining
    Suggestions 455
International Dinners 456
    The Latin Influence 456
    The Italian Kitchen 458
    French Cuisine 459
    Northern and Eastern Europe 461
    A Visit to Greece and the
        Middle East 463
    The Orient 465
    Asian Fare 466

THE FOOD READER 469

The Wholefoods Pantry 471
The Dry Pantry 471
The Condiment Pantry 473
The Refrigerator Pantry 474
The Freezer Pantry 474
The Minimal Pantry 474

Food Handling and Storage 476
Kitchen and Pantry Storage 476
Food Handling During Cooking 482

On Cooking 484
Helpful Habits 484
Basic Techniques 487
Enriching Foods 507

Kitchen Math 511
Table of Metric Equivalents 511
Baker's Math 511
Table of Food Weights and
    Measures 512

Eating Out 520
Unfamiliar Territory 520
Beyond the Menu 520
Meals en Route 522
The Wholefoods Restaurant 523

Index 525

Introduction

The discovery of a new dish does more for the
happiness of mankind than the discovery of a star.
—BRILLAT-SAVARIN

Although New Year's Day, 1970, looked and felt like many others before, it was to be the most significant of our lives. Prompted by friends and fueled by the sense of new beginning that permeates this holiday, we had resolved to experiment with our traditional "Basic Four Food Group" diet. So, on January first, with New Year's chicken molé still in our memories, we set forth to find out what life without meat and mass market foods would be like—for a week.

As two people whose diets had been omnivorous, we were prepared to be both bored and hungry. But the week's resolution quickly turned into months and then years, for we discovered simultaneously that we had a taste for the new dishes we were sampling and a flair for this style of cooking. Admittedly, we were aided by Nikki's background in nutrition and her professional work in recipe development, but it was the purely gustatory pleasure our meals brought that kept us going.

As we ventured forth, we found that we could easily go for a month or more without repeating the same menu. Boredom was no problem for us. Using basic nutrition skills we checked nutriment levels and found them more than ample. When we did need inspiration in the kitchen, we discovered that health-oriented books were of little help, for in most cases, the author's concern for health obscured aesthetics. More often it was the time- and tongue-tested ethnic cuisines that held the basis of what we were looking for.

For years we traveled and ate, accumulating recipes and concepts to broaden and enliven our table. "Why can't there be an accessible cuisine," we wondered, "that tastes good and happens to be healthy?" Over the years that

followed, we consciously attempted to synthesize the world's meatless and wholefoods dishes into a cuisine that could be accepted on its own, regardless of the health benefits—simply because we know how interesting, inexpensive, and varied this style of dining can be.

It has been a great satisfaction for us to see our attitudes and goals confirmed and even sanctioned by scientific and governmental bodies. The National Academy of Science has documented the validity of vegetarian diets, and both the U.S. Surgeon General and the Senate Select Committee on Nutrition and Human Needs have approved the benefits of decreasing the average amount of meat in the Western diet and increasing consumption of whole grains, legumes, low-fat cheeses, and fresh fruit and vegetables, foods that are the backbone of what we see as a new American cuisine. (As this book was going to press, The National Academy of Sciences issued a report, "Diet, Nutrition and Cancer," in which "for the first time" the relationship between diet and cancer was explored. Their findings are once again in conjunction with the Wholefoods Philosophy, as well as the above cited reports: to reduce the risk of cancer, eat less fat, very little salt-cured, pickled, and smoked foods; eat more vegetables, fruits, and whole grains.)

In *American Wholefoods Cuisine* we have combined our experiences to formulate a style of cooking that can serve a society in which people devote vastly different amounts of time to food preparation, have demanding taste buds, yet are thinking more than formerly about nutritional considerations. The choice of basic ingredients used in proper proportion in the diet forms the cornerstone of this cuisine. It is our well-supported belief that optimal human nourishment depends on both the wholeness and the diversity of the foods we eat. We have provided variety by offering more than 1,300 kitchen-tested recipes from all around the world, as well as convenience by relying on the abundant wholefood staples and condiments that the food system offers us ready to use.

You will not find any recipes in this book that are dependent on meat, fish, or seafood, for those areas of American cooking have already been well developed; you can, of course, add these ingredients to a recipe as you see fit. Those who feel no diet is complete without animal protein should note our modest use of eggs and dairy foods. (In the study of nutrition, eggs are used as the standard against which all protein foods are measured.) We have also provided extensive information for those interested in nutrition; however, it is not necessary to be a nutritionist before beginning in the kitchen, as the relative protein content of each recipe is indicated when appropriate, along with ample menu suggestions.

The traditional and best-prepared cooking of many cultures has been adapted here to today's practicalities, and even the sometimes ill-prepared short-order style of American cooking has been improved to suit our nutritional goals. Our adoption of America's native short-order cooking will be of particular interest to those with firmly rooted taste preferences or little time to spend in the kitchen. While the majority of recipes are geared to those with a moderate interest in cooking, there are also dishes that offer a day's entertainment for the cook.

The one dominant criterion for our recipe selection has been that the food pleases us in the purely hedonistic sense of the word. If a dish doesn't make our taste buds dance, quite frankly we're not interested in it, no matter how nutritious it is. At the same time, we are concerned that our recipes fulfill the requirements for a nourishing diet. Admittedly, there are some dishes that contain more fat, sweetening, and even sodium than we would recommend on a routine basis. They are not meant to be the focus of the daily menu, but only one part that will be balanced by others. Pecan or Lemon Meringue Pies, oozing with honey, butter, and eggs, are not desserts for everyday eating; nor are such rich foods as Fried Camembert, Steamed Artichokes with Creamy Lemon Butter, or Vichyssoise. But there is no doubt they are well worth the pleasure they give when they are used prudently to add color to the table.

Like all cuisines, the one that is represented in *American Wholefoods Cuisine* can be integrated into your present diet or it can provide you with a totally new dietary format. For us, it offers a permanent pattern of eating that holds the answers to many of our society's persistent food problems. It is a cuisine built around relatively inexpensive foods and, more importantly, those that provide good value in return for their purchase price. As an equally attractive bonus, we have found our weight easier than ever to control. Not only do staple wholefoods satisfy at moderate calorie levels, but other common dietary pitfalls —hidden salt, fat and refined carbohydrates—have been eliminated.

The Western world is at a cusp in its gustatory history in which new dietary needs must be met. The question is whether we are going to solve the call for fewer calories, less fat, increased fiber, and cheaper protein through the clever use of traditional foods or the commercial use of questionable ingredients and processes.

The Wholefoods Philosophy

The human digestive system is essentially the same one our ancestors had 50,000 years ago. It is designed to digest and utilize the foods provided by our habitat. For the most part, these basic foodstuffs were discovered by our Stone Age ancestors in a hit-or-miss fashion. Those who ate best tended to live longest, and consequently their heirs and friends followed their example. The accepted diet became the one that maintained the species, and thus you might say it is a "Darwinian diet." Additionally, as certain foods became more constant in the diet, our bodies accommodated to these choices. Witness this process in the atrophy of the appendix, an organ once needed to help digest very coarse foods, now becoming obsolete from disuse.

Just as we cannot put unleaded gasoline in our 1950 Chevy pickup and expect it to run efficiently, modern technological foods may be inappropriate for our prehistoric bodies. Processed and fragmented foods and those that add unnatural amounts of sugar, salt, and fat, as well as modern food chemicals, are still very new to our system.

We have already seen that problems can be created by the fragmentation of a wholefood. Grains afford a well-known cautionary example. In its entirety, the wheat kernel is composed of a fibrous bran, a germ rich in B vitamins and protein, and a starchy endosperm. In the production of white flour the bran and germ are discarded. Thus, the fiber and B vitamins, which are known to be necessary for the body to efficiently metabolize the remaining carbohydrate, are no longer available. Similarly, when nuts and seeds are commercially processed for oil, the inherent vitamin E is lost. By disturbing this natural balance, we lose the protection that vitamin E gives against the harmful breakdown of unsaturated fats in the body when the oil is consumed.

Scientists are only beginning to study the effect of modern foods. According to Dr. Jean Mayer, dean of the American nutrition community, there is a risk in a food supply made up of over-processed foods, which may not by themselves be toxic but which can become dangerous if they assume too large a proportion in the diet. The U.S. Surgeon General's office reinforces this position stating in its landmark study, *Healthy People,* that "because the number and amounts of additives were much less 30 to 40 years ago, and because malignancy can take that long to develop, careful scrutiny of the health effects of substances added to food is important." Thus, in our attempt to eliminate or at least limit these unknowns, foods that have been over-processed are omitted from *American Wholefoods Cuisine.* And, since we know that foods that are fresh and unfragmented are richest in nutrients, it seems logical to eat those foods that are as close to nature as possible—what we refer to as "wholefoods."

Moreover, sophisticated scientific study has begun to revise the concept of our ancestors as "rapacious and successful hunters," i.e., meat eaters, an image that has reinforced uninhibited meat consumption. According to recent findings, the prehistoric table was probably set with at least three times more plant than animal food, the reverse of what the average American currently eats. With this new understanding, the common-sense approach would be to emulate the early ratio of plant to animal foods. This includes not only fruit and vegetables, but beans, grains, nuts, and seeds.

Perhaps the most controversial area in nutrition concerns the proper diet mix, that is, what amounts of different foods are needed for maximum health. If this could be distilled into one formula, our lives would be made easier, but because there are so many variables, it is not possible. Most significant is the fact that each of us has different nutritional needs; just as our faces are different, so are our internal workings. Couple this "biological individuality" with our personal food preferences and the fact that foods themselves vary in nutritional worth, even from one orange to the next, and you have a subject that cannot be reduced to simple rules. Our pleasurable solution, then, is to try to cover our needs, both known and unknown, through diversity.

Formerly, "variety" was taken to mean eating something from each of the Basic Four Food Groups. But, as it is not uncommon to eat the same foods from each group meal after meal, this idea must be extended to include a broad selection *within* each as well. If the only grain you eat is wheat, which is not difficult since it is the main ingredient in most baked goods, you should begin to include rye, cornmeal, barley, rice, buckwheat, and millet too. It is not enough to eat just oranges or apples; an optimal diet would include all fruits in season. And this concept would hold true for all food groups.

In light of the above concerns and on the basis of the study of nutrition by various research and scientific groups, these rather broad but reasonable guidelines emerge:

• Consume sufficient calories to maintain normal growth, a high energy level, and a weight deemed to be acceptable.

• Provide a daily source of good-

THE FOOD SPECTRUMS

Length of line indicates *approximate* ideal proportions in the diet.
Foods above the ► make a positive contribution to the diet.
Foods below the ► are less advantageous.

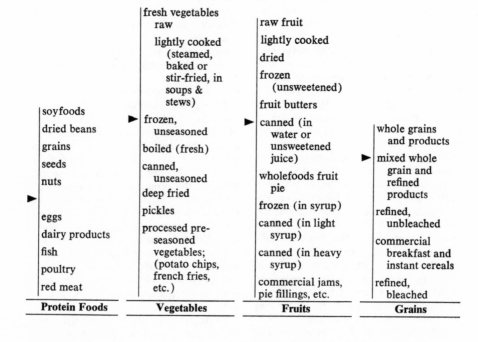

Protein Foods	Vegetables	Fruits	Grains
soyfoods	fresh vegetables raw	raw fruit	
dried beans	lightly cooked (steamed, baked or stir-fried, in soups & stews)	lightly cooked	
grains		dried	
seeds		frozen (unsweetened)	
nuts		fruit butters	
	► frozen, unseasoned	► canned (in water or unsweetened juice)	whole grains and products
	boiled (fresh)		► mixed whole grain and refined products
	canned, unseasoned	wholefoods fruit pie	
►	deep fried	frozen (in syrup)	refined, unbleached
eggs	pickles	canned (in light syrup)	commercial breakfast and instant cereals
dairy products	processed pre-seasoned vegetables; (potato chips, french fries, etc.)	canned (in heavy syrup)	
fish			
poultry		commercial jams, pie fillings, etc.	refined, bleached
red meat			

quality protein, averaging about 25 to 35 grams for young children, 55 grams for adolescent boys and men, and 45 grams for adolescent girls and women, rising to 75 grams during pregnancy.

• Indulge in a generous amount of unrefined carbohydrates found in fresh fruits, vegetables (including beans), and whole grains.

• Maintain a moderate fat intake, with emphasis on vegetable rather than animal fats.

• Limit the intake of sodium, refined sugars, refined starches, as well as substances that have no natural counterpart (food additives).

THE FOOD SPECTRUMS

We have designed the model on pages 4–5 in order to rate foods according to their ability to help meet the preceding guidelines. Its purpose is to enable you to visualize and judge your current diet in relation to the wholefoods concept. Those foods at the top of the spectrum will make a more positive contribution to nourishment, whereas those at the bottom are less beneficial and may even have a negative effect. The relative length of each spectrum indicates the approximate emphasis each group should be given in meal planning.

THE PROTEIN PRINCIPLE

The Dutch chemist who gave protein its name, from the Greek "to take first place," had no idea how prophetic this designation would be. There is no nutrient that has such strong associations (wealth, power) and is so greatly over-

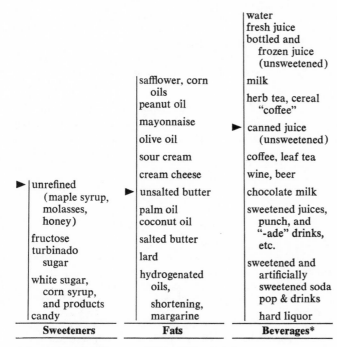

Sweeteners	Fats	Beverages*
		water
		fresh juice
		bottled and frozen juice (unsweetened)
	safflower, corn oils	milk
	peanut oil	herb tea, cereal "coffee"
	mayonnaise	canned juice (unsweetened)
	olive oil	
	sour cream	coffee, leaf tea
	cream cheese	wine, beer
unrefined (maple syrup, molasses, honey)	unsalted butter	chocolate milk
	palm oil coconut oil	sweetened juices, punch, and "-ade" drinks, etc.
fructose turbinado sugar	salted butter lard	
white sugar, corn syrup, and products	hydrogenated oils,	sweetened and artificially sweetened soda pop & drinks
candy	shortening, margarine	hard liquor

* Approximately 1½ quarts (1500 milliliters) daily

emphasized. To obtain the benefits of meatless dining we must look closely at our understanding of protein and protein foods.

One of the few nutritional lessons we ever receive is the list of complete protein foods. Ask most people what foods supply protein and they will answer, almost as a litany, "Meat, fish, eggs, and dairy." But this perspective is incomplete, formed more by commercial, historical, and social reasons than by axioms of good nutrition. The truth is that there are many other foods that contain protein which most of us do not take advantage of.

Twentieth-Century Protein

Twentieth-century Americans eat, on the average, about twice the protein their bodies need, largely through meat consumption. While superficially this sounds like glorious luxury, it is actually counterproductive. First of all, protein foods are the most expensive items in the food budget, so that a high-protein diet is a costly one.

A second fact many people do not realize is that our bodies have a limited need for protein. Once this level is exceeded, the remaining protein is used for energy (calories) or stored as body fat, often making fuel or fat at a very high price.

Protein foods of animal origin are abundant in saturated fat, which appears to accelerate heart disease. Moreover, their dominant "first place" position in our diet tends to decrease our consumption of other food groups that are equally as essential to good nourishment.

What Is Protein?

A protein molecule is a complex chemical structure composed of amino acids linked in specific patterns. Some of these amino acids can be manufactured within the body; others must be supplied by food. Those amino acids that must be provided by the diet are called "essential amino acids," and foods that contain abundant amounts of these

essential amino acids are technically referred to as "high-quality proteins" or "complete proteins."

In general, most animal products, like meat, fish, poultry, eggs, and dairy products, meet this criterion; that is, they are convenient bundles of all the essential building blocks of protein.

Vegetable foods also contain protein-building amino acids; however, although the amounts may be substantial, they do not always contain these amino acids in ideal proportions. Thus, they have been deemed of lower value than the animal foods. But, as you will soon see, beans, grains, nuts, and seeds, the primary sources of vegetable protein, can be made into "high-quality proteins," and at the same time fulfill our other dietary objectives in ways that animal foods cannot.

Since the traditional terms used to describe relative protein values are misleading—many so-called incomplete proteins do furnish all the essential amino acids, and impose a value judgment by the choice of the words "incomplete" vs. "complete," or "low-quality" vs. "high-quality," we have devised a more objective terminology for our recipes.

Major Protein indicates there are 15 or more grams of protein per average serving, ample protein for a meal.

Minor Protein indicates there are less than 15 grams of protein per average serving.

Protein Complement is used to describe dishes that should be coupled with the foods that enhance their protein value, as explained in the diagram on page 8.

The Protein Continuum

People all over the world get protein in a variety of ways. Some obtain it solely from vegetable sources; others combine vegetable proteins with dairy; a third group of nonmeat eaters, and by far the most common, are ovo-lacto vegetarians, meaning those who eat eggs as well as dairy products. There are also a few select societies that meet almost all

THE PROTEIN CONTINUUM

ANIMAL PROTEINS					VEGETABLE PROTEINS				
Red Meat	Poultry	Fish	Eggs	Dairy	Soy	Beans	Grains	Nuts	Seeds
Carnivores (all meat)		66% (Americans in the 1970s)			50% (U.S. Dietary Goals)		Vegan (Pure vegetarian)		

their protein needs from animal foods alone—the meat-eating, blood-drinking Masai, for example. Most meat eaters, however, are not exclusively carnivores and eat many meatless protein dishes as well, such as grilled cheese sandwiches, pasta, tacos, or a snack of nuts.

All of us lie somewhere along this "protein continuum" and your place on it affects the balance of your total diet. The U.S. government estimates that Americans today obtain about one third of their protein from vegetable sources, whereas at the beginning of the twentieth century this figure was closer to 50 percent which is also the current U.S. dietary goal. Where do you fit on this continuum?

Why All This Interest in Nonanimal Protein?

In addition to providing protein equal in quality to that of animal foods, vegetable proteins:
• make for more varied, interesting meals
• are a necessary part of a truly balanced diet
• cost less
• contain high levels of complex carbohydrates and dietary fiber
• provide significant amounts of iron, B vitamins, zinc, calcium, potassium, magnesium, and phosphorus plus many trace elements
• are low in fat (or if they do contain fat, as in the case of nuts, it is largely unsaturated)
• contain fewer chemical residues since environmental pollutants as well as pesticides tend to accumulate in the fat and flesh of animals as a result of the huge quantities of feed they consume over their lifetime (this is also true of the antibiotics and growth stim-

ulants used routinely in raising animals)
• aid in weight control, as these foods are self-limiting due to their high bulk and water content
• conserve the world's protein by taking advantage of the protein in its original form rather than feeding these valuable foodstuffs to animals, which actually consume more vegetable protein than they return as meat protein

Stone-Age Protein for the Twenty-First Century

Thus, what has not been commonly taught, although its basis is generations old, is that when beans, grains, nuts, seeds, and the products made from them are properly matched, they can provide protein of a quality equal to the more publicized animal protein. If you mix foods in any two of these groups, or combine any one of them with a small amount of animal protein, you will create more and better protein than if you eat them separately. This concept of combining two foods for greater protein value has been given the ungastronomic name "protein complementation."*

In most cultures where meat is eaten only in small amounts and rather infrequently, this concept has been followed for centuries. Oriental, Italian, Mexican, Mideastern, Indian, and Greek cuisines, to name only the most

* In May, 1974, the National Academy of Sciences issued a report reinforcing the adequacy of a vegetarian regime, stating: "If this mixing of plant proteins is done judiciously, combinations of lower quality protein foods can give mixtures of about the same nutritional value as high-quality animal protein foods." (*Vegetarian Diets*, A Statement of the Food and Nutrition Board, Division of Biological Sciences, National Research Council.)

obvious, are dependent on protein complementation. When the waiter in an Italian restaurant sprinkles Parmesan cheese on your pasta, he is not only providing you with good service, he is also following a nutritional principle thousands of years old—that cheese elevates the protein in grains. The same is true when Mexicans fill their corn tortillas with beans, and Arabs enhance their chick-pea fritters (falafel) with a sesame sauce (tahini). Even Americans follow this nutritional principle by pouring milk on their cereal.

Animal vs. Vegetable Protein

Animal proteins are therefore not more important in the diet than vegetable proteins. However, the two must be regarded differently in menu planning.

Animal proteins can stand alone as the protein-giving portion of a meal. Vegetable proteins must be mixed with each other, or with small amounts of animal proteins, to adequately serve this purpose.*

In line with this principle of protein complementation, you will recognize that snacking on peanuts alone is somewhat wasteful of their protein potential. However, if you mix the peanuts with cashews or sunflower seeds, you will elevate their value.

* Because amino acids are believed to be stored in the body for only a few hours, it is best to serve these complementary foods within a short time period, although they do not necessarily have to be eaten in the same dish, or even the same course. It is perfectly acceptable to have a bean soup as an appetizer and rice pudding for dessert·and realize the benefits of the combined protein in these foods.

PROTEIN COMPLEMENTS

The following diagram illustrates the foods that complement each other. To create a high-quality protein meal, simply follow the direction of the arrows, incorporating something at either end. It is especially useful when planning a meal with Protein Complement recipes; classify them according to their predominant ingredient.

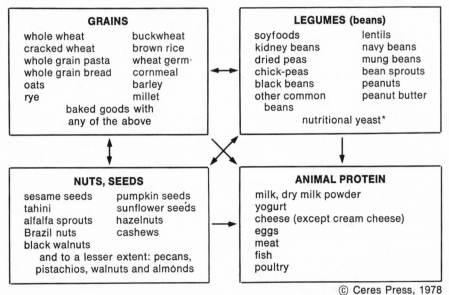

© Ceres Press, 1978

*Nutritional yeast has an amino acid pattern similar to legumes and thus can be combined with the same foods to enhance their protein value. The use of nutritional yeast in enriching foods is discussed on pages 508-509.

Of course, you need not limit the combination to two groups but could, for example, make excellent protein by combining lentils, rice, and yogurt, as in Indian cookery.

Note that there are no arrows emanating from the animal proteins. This is because they do not have to be paired with any other food.

You should be aware that the best protein in grains is in the germ portion, making unrefined grains the most reliable complements.

Classic Combinations

Here are common examples of completed protein dishes that will be familiar to you. These foods already seem to be natural companions; as you work more with protein complements, you will discover that other combinations are equally as logical in the gustatory sense.

Macaroni and cheese
Cereal and milk
Rice pudding
Pizza (cheese and a grain crust)
Spanish rice and beans
Bean tacos (beans and corn tortilla)
Manicotti (cheese and pasta)
Minestrone soup (pasta and beans)
Peanut butter sandwich (peanut butter and grain)
Falafel (chick-peas and sesame seeds in sauce)
Baked potato and cheese

Feeding Children

All authorities agree that when eggs and dairy products are included in the diet, the diet will be adequate and appropriate for all age groups, including children. Interestingly, many of the dishes children favor contain complementary proteins; peanut butter sandwiches, cereal and milk, pizza, grilled cheese, tacos, and macaroni and cheese have kept many youngsters well fed for generations.

When an infant is ready for solid foods, parents will do well to offer the regular family fare, unseasoned and ground in a baby food grinder or food processor where necessary, and moistened with yogurt, cottage cheese, or tofu. Introduce your children to the variety and richness of wholefoods cuisine early and you will find they have a more liberal palate as they grow older.

If no animal products at all are used, as in the vegan regimen, particular attention must be given to certain nutrients, notably vitamin B_{12}, calcium, and iron, but with proper food selection even this more restricted food plan can be made suitable for children.

CARBOHYDRATES AND WEIGHT CONTROL

Second only to our lack of understanding about protein foods are our misconceptions about carbohydrates. Most people believe that carbohydrates are fattening and non-nutritious, an impression that has been reinforced by many popular weight loss books.

This is only true when carbohydrates are refined. The heart of the wheat kernel, for example, which is all that is used to make white flour, supplies primarily calories. The bran and the germ, however, offer good-quality protein, fiber, and significant amounts of vitamins and minerals. Thus, when the grain is left intact, the proper balance of all these elements is retained. Moreover, the presence of bran and small amounts of fat from the germ can actually encourage weight control since these elements make wholegrain products more satisfying and thus *self-limiting*.

The following figures, taken from the United States Department of Agriculture, illustrate the nutritional advantages of whole wheat flour versus its refined white enriched and unenriched counterparts. These values carry through to all products made from wheat and for these purposes reflect the picture for other grains as well. Note the similarity in calorie value.

NUTRITIONAL ADVANTAGES OF WHOLE WHEAT FLOUR

	Whole wheat flour (1 cup)	White enriched flour (1 cup)	White unenriched flour (1 cup)
Calories	400	455	455
Protein (grams)	16	13.1	13.1
Fat (grams)	2.4	1.3	1.3
Carbohydrate (grams)	85.2	95.1	95.1
Calcium (mg.)	49	20	20
Phosphorus (mg.)	446	109	109
Iron (mg.)	4.0	3.6*	1.0
Potassium (mg.)	444	119	119
Thiamine (mg.)	0.66	0.55*	0.08
Riboflavin (mg.)	0.14	0.33*	0.06
Niacin (mg.)	5.2	4.4*	1.1

* From added nutrients
Source: USDA Handbook No. 456 (1975)

Beans are another food amply endowed with carbohydrates, but as you now know, they also provide excellent protein. Compared by weight to meat, their contribution is striking.

Remarkably, our attitudes about carbohydrates have even affected our opinion of fresh fruit and vegetable sugars. In the original package, the sugars in produce supply a modest amount of calories in conjunction with an abundance of vitamins and minerals.

It was probably nature's design to sweeten certain foods in this way to tantalize us into consuming them. However, when we extract only the sugar from cane, corn, and fruit, as is done to make common table sugar, corn syrup, and fructose, and then add this refined sugar in concentrated amounts to other foods (where they do not in many cases naturally occur), we receive only the taste and calories and none of the traditional advantages of the whole-food.

The intent of this nutrition lesson is to dispel the notion that carbohydrates detract from the diet. Actually, unrefined carbohydrates are the foundation of all good nourishment.

NUTRITIONAL CONTRIBUTION OF BEANS

	Kidney beans (1 pound)	Beef, boneless chuck (1 pound)
Calories	1,556	1,166
Protein (grams)	102.1	84.1
Fat (grams)	6.8	88.9
Carbohydrate (grams)	208.8	0
Calcium (mg.)	499	50
Phosphorus (mg.)	1,842	853
Iron (mg.)	31.3	12.7
Potassium (mg.)	4,463	1,357
Thiamine (mg.)	2.31	0.36
Riboflavin (mg.)	0.91	0.75
Niacin (mg.)	10.4	20.4

Source: USDA Handbook No. 456 (1975)

The New American Menu

With this new understanding of protein and human nourishment we have need of a new approach to menu planning as well. At present the typical American meal consists of three major elements:

1. the focal point, generally meat or fish
2. the filler, such as bread, pasta, or rice
3. the accompanying vegetable and/ or fruit

To design a more relevant menu, the emphasis in food selection should be shifted so that the former accompaniments—grains, vegetables, and fruits—are given more prominence and, conversely, many main dish foods are assigned to accompaniment or condiment status. For example, an updated meal might feature a grain- and bean-based entrée, enhanced perhaps with small amounts of meat for flavor. This meal will provide good-quality protein, a high level of complex carbohydrates, and only a small amount of saturated fat. Or, a meal may be composed of a large salad accompanied by smaller portions of cheese or egg dishes.

Several approaches to meal planning based on these principles are explored here in detail and beginning on page 451 many sample menus are provided. By using wholefoods that are similar in kind to tastes you have already cultivated, and by improving the ingredients you use in traditional recipes, you can assimilate these new concepts into your diet quite naturally. As your eating horizons broaden, you will find your repertoire of meals will follow suit.

PUTTING TOGETHER A MEAL

People approach menu planning in different ways. Some think in terms of a particular food they would like to use, while others plan around a specific dish. The following section is therefore divided into The Food Approach and The Course Approach.

The Food Approach

More Fruits and Vegetables

The one dietary guideline no one has had any argument with is the need for more fresh fruits and vegetables. This actually simplifies menu planning.

At every meal you should eat at least one form of fresh produce, and there is no upper limit. If the main dish includes substantial amounts of vegetables or fruit, you may wish to stop there. A hot vegetable plate, for example, with a high-protein sauce, accompanied by a complementary bread, can make a simple yet excellent meal. Classic examples include French Aioli with Vegetables—steamed vegetables and beans with a garlic sauce (which in our version includes yogurt), and Indonesian Gado Gado—a mixture of vegetables and tofu in a peanut sauce. Closer to home is a vegetable plate topped with cheese sauce.

You may, however, decide to include additional produce. When more than one vegetable or fruit dish appears on the menu, they should be as diverse as possible to provide the broadest taste and nutritional experience; variety of color is a good rule. Try not to repeat ingredients in several dishes; for example, don't serve stuffed mushrooms and then mushroom loaf, or tomato soup and tomato salad.

If there is ample protein on the menu, the accompanying fruit or vegetable dish can be strictly that—just fruit or vegetables. But if the main dish is somewhat scanty, a vegetable or fruit dish with nuts, cheese, crumb topping, or a protein-rich sauce or dressing will help fortify the meal.

It is also a good idea to have at least one uncooked fruit or vegetable on the menu. This may appear as an appetizer, salad, dessert, or beverage.

Plain frozen fruits and vegetables, and fruits canned in water or juice are pantry items that can fill in when needed.

Grains

Each meal should contain a whole grain in some form. Pasta, rice, cracked wheat, cornmeal, etc., may compose part of the main dish. Otherwise, the simplest way to provide this menu component is with a whole grain bread or cracker.

Muffins, biscuits, chapatis, and tortillas can all lend real character, and there are dozens of recipes for homemade baked goods in these pages, some requiring only a few minutes to put together. Many such baked goods are also available commercially, and we always make sure our freezer and pantry are well stocked with home-baked breadstuffs supplemented with the best of the commercial choices to round out any menu.

A cooked grain dish is another way to fill out the meal and is a necessity when the main dish is primarily nuts or beans. A simple bowlful of brown rice or kasha may do the job, or you may wish to choose something with more zip if there is no saucy or spicy dish to accompany it. Any of the pilaf recipes, grain-stuffed vegetables, pasta accompaniments, or cold grain salads can be incorporated here.

Soup can also be used to fulfill the grain portion of the meal and offers an outlet for leftover cooked grain or pasta.

Two dishes featuring grain are not generally suited to the same menu. Grain burgers and a grain-stuffed vegetable, for instance, would be somewhat redundant, as would a macaroni casserole with a rice pudding dessert.

If you do serve bread and a grain dish, aim for variety. Offer corn bread when rice is on the menu, rye bread or muffins to accompany a stew with barley or cracked wheat. Don't forget, crackers can be made primarily from rye, corn, oats, or rice as well as wheat.

THE VALUE OF GRAINS

In terms of *quality* of protein, grains actually rank higher than many beans, nuts, and seeds; whole grain rice and millet are both thought to contain all eight essential amino acids. The actual *quantity* of protein in grain foods, however, is low. In other words, it takes a larger serving of grains to provide as much protein as other traditional foods. For this reason, grains are more useful for increasing the value of other protein foods. Whole grain breads, corn tacos, rice, cracked wheat (bulgur), barley, millet, oats, buckwheat (kasha), pasta, etc., all serve the important function of elevating beans, nuts, and seeds to animal protein status. Moreover, the combination of these grains with milk (as in cereal, rice pudding, macaroni and cheese) is a traditional means of raising their level of protein.

Beans on the Table

Beans can be appropriate to every course in the meal, as evidenced by their international popularity in soups, dips, stews, casseroles, fritters, salads, and even sweet bean pies for dessert.

At their simplest, cooked beans can be eaten out of hand, warm or cold, as a snack or as an hors d'oeuvre. In Spain, a platter of room-temperature chickpeas liberally spiced with fresh ground pepper is as common at the cocktail hour as peanuts and pretzels in the American barroom.

Plain cooked beans can also be tossed into a salad without any embellishment. Marinated in an oil and vinegar dressing, beans become a salad in themselves or are an excellent sandwich filling, especially in pockets of the pita bread

THE VALUE OF BEANS

Beans contain only trace amounts of fat and have an abundance of complex carbohydrates, which makes them highly compatible with a diet that emphasizes fiber. In contrast to grains, beans have a good quantity of protein.

Of all the varieties of these beans, soy is at the top of the list in terms of protein quality, requiring only small amounts of complementary protein foods to be ideal. As a matter of fact, in terms of actual amounts of most amino acids, soy rates higher than meat, fish, poultry, eggs, and cheese, which means that when it is employed to its full potential it provides better value than animal protein. Soy is somewhat lower in carbohydrate than other beans and also has more fat, but largely in unsaturated form. At present, use of soy is limited in the Western diet, but it is time we began exploring the use of such varied products as soybean cheese (tofu), soy milk, soy flour, soy grits, soy nuts, soybean paste (miso), and fermented soy cakes (tempeh), in addition to the bean itself.

Food*	Calories	Protein (grams)
1 ounce common beans, dried	100	6.7
1 cup common beans, cooked	225–50	14–16
1 cup sprouted beans	35	4
1 ounce soybeans, dried	115	10
1 cup soybeans, cooked	235	20
4-ounce piece soybean cheese (tofu)	85	9
½ cup soybean flour	150	15
1 cup soybean sprouts	45	6

* All figures are approximate, derived from "Nutritive Value of American Foods," Agriculture Handbook No. 456, USDA and *The Dieter's Companion*, Signet, 1975.

that has migrated from the Middle East into Western kitchens.

Seasoned in a variety of ways, beans also provide a sauce for grains, a filling for tacos or pastry shells, a gravy for biscuits, toast, or hamburger buns, or a side dish to round out the rest of the meal.

Then too, there are bean soups, bean stews, and bean-based casseroles. Some of these may be familiar to you; for example, minestrone soup, split pea soup, Cuban black bean soup, chili, and baked beans.

In addition to being served whole, beans can be pureed to provide wonderful dips (hummus, the garlic-laden chick-pea puree from the Middle East, is now a Western favorite) as well as ground to chopped meat consistency and used in just about the same way to make bean balls, bean burgers, and bean loaves.

Beans bought dry and cooked are the least expensive and allow you to control the amount of salt, but canned beans are certainly good pinch-hitters. Be sure to cook extra-large potfuls of dried beans; they can be refrigerated for a week or two or frozen for the future.

To add to the bean specialties, uncooked dried beans can also be sprouted for a surprisingly vibrant vegetable.

Nuts and Seeds

While nuts and seeds are a versatile and valuable source of protein, they can add up in both cost and amount of fat if they are over-used. If the main dish includes nuts or seeds, do not use them elsewhere. If, however, beans or grains are featured, nuts and seeds can be used to enrich this protein. Added to salads, vegetables, sandwich fillings, crumb toppings, or even as a garnish to cooked grain, nuts and seeds can really brighten these dishes. Ground into meal, they can be used to thicken soups and stews, in combination with bread crumbs in toppings and coatings, or to replace part of the flour in baking. Nut and seed butters can add a protein-enriching spread to serve with soups, stews, and salads. Nuts and seeds are also excellent in desserts, which may be treated as an integral part of your menu, or can provide an after-dinner snack.

THE VALUE OF NUTS AND SEEDS

Pine nuts, peanuts, black walnuts, and unroasted cashews have the highest protein value per calorie. Peanuts, although used like other nuts, have an amino acid arrangement that is similar to certain beans. Thus, their protein quality is enhanced by mixing them with other foods in the nuts and seeds group. Of course, the grain foods and animal proteins also make ideal complements.

Too often when peanut butter is served, the principle of protein combining is ignored. Remember, peanut butter alone, or even on white bread with a glass of juice, is far less nourishing than when complemented by whole grain bread and a glass of milk.

Spreads or "butters" of cashews, almonds, walnuts, etc., should also be complemented to be of best value; serve on whole grain crackers or bread, make crunchy with a layer of wheat germ, mix with peanut butter, thin with yogurt, or serve along with a milk-, cheese-, egg-, or bean-rich dish.

Seeds, such as sunflower, pumpkin, and sesame, can be used in much the same manner as nuts and are generally lower in fat and calories and higher in protein. The most common seed butter is called tahini. Derived from sesame seeds, it is a staple ingredient in Mideast cooking. It too is improved by any of the preceding combinations. In addition, tahini provides substantial calcium, making it especially valuable in a diet that lacks milk and other dairy products. Unlike the saturated fat in dairy foods, the fat in tahini is largely polyunsaturated, another point in its favor.

The table below provides protein comparisons for you to use when adding these foods to the menu.

Food	Calories	Protein (grams)
½ cup almonds	425	13
½ cup Brazil nuts	460	10
½ cup cashews	375	12
½ cup filberts (hazelnuts)	425	8.5
½ cup peanuts	420	19
2 tablespoons peanut butter	190	8
½ cup pecans	370	5
½ cup pine nuts	430	24
½ cup pistachios	370	12
½ cup pumpkin seeds	350	18
½ cup sesame seeds	435	14
2 tablespoons sesame butter (tahini)	190	6
½ cup sunflower seeds	360	15
½ cup black walnuts	380	13
½ cup English walnuts	325	7

Eggs and Dairy Foods

While both eggs and dairy foods are a convenient source of protein for the nonmeat meal, they should not be given undue emphasis. If eggs, cheese, or milk are supplied in abundance at breakfast or lunch, their use should be minimized at dinner. Often a generous garnish of eggs, cheese, or yogurt will be enough to insure adequate protein. A heavy cheese or egg dish in a meal that already contains good protein from vegetable sources is wasteful.

At a meal where the protein quantity or quality is questionable, eggs and milk products can be used to great advantage. A vegetable salad, for instance, can be enhanced with a yogurt or cottage cheese dressing or a cheese plate on the side. A cooked vegetable platter can be a nutritious dinner with a milk-, yogurt-, or cheese-based gravy. A savory cottage cheese or yogurt dip, a "cream" soup, a fried cheese appetizer, or a milk-pudding dessert can all be used in this manner. But none of these choices should appear on the menu with an egg-rich soufflé, a savory cheese pastry, or such amply endowed main dishes as eggplant Parmesan, ricotta-stuffed pasta, macaroni and cheese, vegetables baked with cottage cheese, etc.

Adding Meat, Fish and Poultry

When Thomas Jefferson, who according to legend could be found working in his famous garden until his death at age eighty-three, was asked to what he attributed his good health, he replied, "Eating little animal foods, and that, not as an aliment so much as a *condiment* for the vegetables, which constitute my principal diet." As this Jeffersonian viewpoint was not widely heeded, we now lack the experience for adding meat to other dishes, and recognize only how to approach meals from the opposite perspective tacking other foods onto the meat dish.

Probably the most familiar model we have to draw on today is found in Oriental cooking, in which small amounts of meat, fish, and poultry are cooked into the soup, vegetables, or rice. In this way, meat lends its flavor and enhances nourishment but does not overload the meal with protein and saturated fat. We see this principle again in the Latin American *cocina* where chili beans are merely "seasoned" with beef and the traditional stews incorporate pork primarily for flavor but rely on the beans for real nourishment.

Generally, one to two ounces of meat, fish, or poultry, when combined with beans or grains in a soup, casserole, stew, or stir-fry, add up to half the estimated adult daily protein requirement. Even without the complementary value of the vegetable protein foods, consider that one-half cup of tuna salad on the lunch platter gives a sensible one third of the day's protein; finishing off the whole can of fish, however, furnishes

THE VALUE OF THE ANIMAL PROTEINS

Wholefoods cuisine does not necessarily exclude animal foods but aims at keeping them in their proper and historic proportions. The previous pages furnished the approximate protein values of the vegetable protein foods. Following is a list of what you receive from small amounts of eggs, dairy, meat, fish, and poultry. Use these foods in moderation to enhance the other proteins in your diet or when vegetable proteins are missing from the meal. Do not, however, make the mistake of using large amounts of animal foods *and* the principles of protein complementation at the same time. As our dietary goals state, most people need between 35 and 55 grams of protein daily. By learning the basic value range of all protein foods you will not waste this valuable nutrient.

Food	Calories	Protein (grams)
1 cup milk, whole	160	8.5
1 cup milk, skim	88	8.8
1 cup yogurt	120–150	8–13
1 ounce natural cheese	80–110	6–8
½ cup creamed cottage cheese	120	13
½ cup part-skim ricotta cheese	170	14
½ cup sour cream	245	3.5
1 large egg	88	7
1 ounce boneless beef, lamb, pork, veal	70–100	4–6
1 ounce processed meats (frankfurters, bologna, sausage, liverwurst, etc.)	90	3.5–4.5
1 ounce boneless chicken	50–55	7–8
1 ounce boneless fish	25–40	6–7

45 grams, or for most people a full day's ration. A few slices of lean meat on a sandwich may be fine, but the more typical, 4-ounce, deli-style version supplies about 40 grams of protein in a single sitting. A chef's salad, with just a couple of slices of ham, turkey, cheese, and a hard-cooked egg, quickly adds up to 50 grams of protein, again more than the majority of people need to eat in an entire day.

Keep the protein values in mind when you plan meals that include meat, fish, and poultry so that you will not squander this expensive nutrient needlessly.

The Course Approach

The Main Dish

The most logical place to begin menu planning is with the main dish since this is still the focal point of the meal. Your choice of a main dish recipe will be narrowed down by many factors—the time you have available for cooking; the number of people you are feeding (some dishes are more appropriate to small service, some to large); the cost; the weather; the available help, and naturally, what you feel like eating.

The main dish you select can either be a complemented source of protein (denoted in our recipes as Major Protein or Minor Protein), something you can complement (denoted as Protein Complement), or something innately complete (such as eggs, cheese, or animal flesh).

If you already have some food on hand, see how you can use what you have, rather than choose a recipe that ignores your well-planned pantry.

Once the main dish choice is made, you can start filling in around it. Depending on your selection, you may only need to add a whole grain breadstuff and fruit or vegetable. For more variety, you may want to add several other items to the menu.

Making Use of the Appetizer Course

The brief first course can do more than tantalize and excite the taste buds. For those accustomed to big meals the inclusion of an appetizer may make the menu more satisfying. This is especially true when serving a one-dish main course like a stew or salad that does not lend itself to an accompaniment of vegetables, beans, or grain, but might very well be preceded by a cold marinated vegetable, a light soup, a cheese spread or dip, a simple juice, melon or grapefruit opener, or something else from the "Appetizers and Hors d'Oeuvres" section.

Small portions remaining from a previous meal are ideal as a first course. You'd be surprised how different yesterday's bean or vegetable dish seems served cold with a seasoned dressing, or how far a wedge of bean loaf or a few crepes will go when meant to stimulate rather than satisfy the appetite.

The beginning of the meal when hunger is at its peak is the time to take into account nutritional needs. Later on, when hunger is not so acute and the appetite less eager, the nutritional potential of food frequently goes to waste.

Viewed in this way, the American restaurant tradition of serving salad before the main course, considered uncivilized by Europeans, does make some sense. (Conversely, the offering of sherbet before the main course, common in many stylish restaurants, is counterproductive as it satisfies caloric needs and little else.)

While there is no hard-and-fast rule as to what foods meet the qualifications of an appetizer, it goes without saying that the appetizer should suit the meal to follow rather than detract from it.

• The appetizer should not repeat basic ingredients of other dishes on the menu; thus an eggplant salad is not a suitable appetizer when eggplant Parmesan is the featured dish.

• The appetizer should compensate for aesthetic or nutritional elements missing from the rest of the meal. Fruit- and vegetable-based appetizers are an excellent introduction to a meal that is primarily protein and starch: for example, marinated vegetables preceding pizza or baked macaroni. A protein-rich appetizer is one way to complement or boost the quality of a protein-deficient main dish: for example, cottage cheese-stuffed celery or fried cheese presented before a primarily vegetable casserole.

• The appetizer should not be so heavy as to depress hunger with the result that the main course is ignored. A pasta first course is not a recommended prelude to a hearty casserole but may be suited to a lighter vegetable dinner.

• Unless an appetizer has concentrated food value, it should not be offered to those with small appetites, who will then be unable to enjoy the most important dishes on the menu. A glass of apple juice (of minimal nutritional content) can help suppress hearty appetites but may be too filling for reluctant eaters.

• The appetizer should not be so sweet or spicy as to dull the taste buds for the meal to come.

While we have devoted an entire chapter to appetizers, many salads, vegetable dishes, beverages, and main dishes offered in small-size portions can serve just as well. Soup, crackers and cheese, and pantry condiments are standbys that may also fit the occasion.

Add-a-Salad

There are many ways to incorporate fresh produce at mealtime, but the easiest by far is to add a salad—anything from cut-up pieces of favorite vegetables, to a mound of sprouts, to a multi-vegetable–fruit assemblage.

If you have incorporated fruits and vegetables into other parts of the meal, it is possible to skip this course. On the other hand, if you are at all concerned about the general sufficiency of the meal itself, your daily nutrition, or your overall diet, you can't go wrong adding something from our salad section.

Of course, "salad" can be much more than a few fresh fruits and vegetables. Enhance it with condiments from the pantry and its appeal will be that much greater; add beans, grains, nuts, eggs or cheese, and valuable protein will be derived. A yogurt, cottage cheese, or tofu dressing can extend the nourishment value of any salad.

Like every other item on the menu, the salad must be weighed in terms of its potential overall contribution. If the meal has a low-fat content, an oil and vinegar dressing is perfectly acceptable. However, if large amounts of cheese, eggs, nuts, or meat are being served, a low-fat dressing is more appropriate.

Making Dessert an Essential Part of the Meal

When it is chosen to complement the rest of the menu, even dessert can make a very substantial contribution. Please forgive us for saying it, but in the American Wholefoods kitchen you *can* "have your cake and eat it" too.

Dessert can add protein directly to the meal, as in a milk-based pudding, a cheese or yogurt pastry, or an egg-y custard. Or, it can help augment protein by incorporating nut butter or ground nuts, rolled oats, cornmeal, rice and other grains to complement beans or other vegetable proteins elsewhere on the menu. In using the protein-boosting qualities of dessert, it is important to balance out your choice with the rest of the menu. For example, nut cutlets can be enhanced by a rice pudding dessert, bean soup by oatmeal cookies, and pasta by a peanut butter confection. Do not, however, try to balance a grain-rich entrée with a grain dessert, or use a nutted dessert to raise the quality of a primarily nut-based main course.

Whole grain cakes and cookies at dessert time can take the place of whole grain bread, while the fruit and vegetable requirement can be satisfied by a fresh fruit salad, fresh fruit pudding or sherbet, or one of the baked fruit desserts offered herein.

Liquid Refreshment

Most people like to have something to drink with their meal. All too often, however, the beverage merely serves to wash down the food rather than add to it.

When fruits and vegetables have been underplayed, a fruit or vegetable juice can help to make up for it. For example, a glass of tomato juice can add some of the missing elements to a cheese sandwich, just as can orange juice to a simple egg dish.

When the protein content is in question, a dairy drink can be added. A baked potato or vegetable plate benefits from a yogurt shake. However, cheese quiche, milk-based soups, cheese-based cutlets, or pasta with cheese do not require this sort of beverage.

A meal that is already well balanced in every way is probably best served with plain or sparkling water. If you wish to add interest with a beverage but minimize calories, mix carbonated water into a Seltzer Fizz with a favorite juice (see page 417). In addition, hot or cold herb teas can be served at mealtime, but only if they are taken with little or no added sweetening. (Oversweetened tea is no more sound nutritionally than soda pop or commercial juice drinks.)

For some people alcoholic beverages are a traditional part of the meal. According to *Healthy People,* the Surgeon General's report on health promotion and disease prevention, consumption of "small amounts" of alcohol is considered by some investigators to have a positive influence in controlling heart disease. We emphasize, however, that this applies only to *limited* use, and if you enjoy beer or wine (which can be diluted with seltzer), you might want to make an attempt to discover which brands are manufactured without chemical adulterants.

Take a pitcher of water to dinner. The addition of water to any meal can have an important health benefit. Not only do our bodies need the liquid, but according to dental authorities, rinsing the mouth out within a few minutes of eating can dramatically curtail the cavity-causing action of many foods— particularly important when sweet or "sticky" foods are served.

Meals for One

Many individuals, even those who enjoy eating and cooking, often do not take the time to feed themselves properly when they are alone. They may claim they lack time; indeed, in some circles it is "chic" to have an almost barren kitchen.

More likely, people do not cook for themselves because it seems like too much effort for a single meal, particularly when most recipes are written for four or more; somehow, making a good meal for yourself is thought to be self indulgent—it's all right to treat others well but not yourself.

Any sensible person recognizes that a good diet is not a sign of indulgence but of self-respect. The reality is, we all make time to eat each day, so even if you have no intention of cooking, simply keeping some basic wholefoods on hand can mean improved nourishment. It is no more difficult to grab a meal of whole grain crackers, chunks of cheddar, and a fresh pear or can of fruit packed in water or juice, than to end up with processed cheese spread on a saltine-type cracker and a can of fruit packed in heavy syrup.

Our opening recipe section, "Short-Order Cooking," was created to demonstrate what can be done when there are limitations on time and energy.

Here are some ways you can improve your dining choices in a household of one:

• Make use of the wholefoods pantry. You will be surprised by what you can create in just a few minutes from the condiments you've been collecting; olives, pickled vegetables, artichoke hearts, or eggplant caponata can dress up the simplest salad, soup, or sandwich. A can of beans on the shelf becomes taco filling or beans in Quick Barbecue Sauce in 10 minutes. With an assortment of whole grain crackers and a nut or seed butter, "bread and spread" is always available.

• Use yogurt and cottage cheese for instant dips. Even a raw vegetable and cheese plate, followed by a selection of nuts, dried fruit, and fresh fruit in season can provide leisurely snacking and excellent nourishment without any cooking.

• Take the opportunity to experiment

with new dishes before you try them on friends. Also, think of all the delicacies that are too costly or bothersome to prepare in quantity and treat yourself.

• Prepare full-service recipes for four or more and wrap them in individual portions for freezer storage.

• If you have more time available for cooking late at night or at other nonmeal hours, think about cultivating cooking as a hobby and form of relaxation. Try kneading bread to release the tensions of the day, or cooking a rich homey soup or stew. The results can be savored the next day or, again, stored in the freezer for the future.

• Eating alone "lacks the condiment of companions." If you resist cooking for yourself because you do not enjoy eating alone, the obvious remedy is to begin inviting others to share meals with you—not only friends but co-workers and neighbors as well. Do it often enough and they'll have to return the favor; pretty soon you'll be eating better and enjoying an active social life. As someone once said: "Every problem is an opportunity in disguise."

COOKING
IN THE
WHOLEFOODS
STYLE

Recipe Notes

Those of you who read this book straight through will learn a great deal about the fundamental principles underlying most of the recipes. We realize, however, that many of you may prefer to just get on with the cooking and eating of some good food. For this reason, we set forth here some of the basic information necessary for the successful execution of these dishes as well as some suggestions as to how to include them in a well-thought-out meal.

PROTEIN CONTENT

RECIPE RATINGS

"Major Protein" signifies that a particular dish is of good-quality protein, offering 15 grams or more per serving, or *what you would expect from any nourishing main dish.*

A "Minor Protein" is a dish that supplies good-quality protein, *but a single serving does not contain enough of this nutrient* to serve as the only protein-giving food at a meal. That is, in normal amounts, it provides fewer than 15 grams. To make a meal adequate in protein a Minor Protein should be served with another Minor Protein or a Protein Complement.

"Protein Complement" is reserved for dishes that contain some but not all of the protein-building elements the body requires for optimal nourishment. In other words, the quality of the protein is lacking. Such foods can be raised to Major Protein status by combining them with a Minor Protein or the appropriate complement, as indicated by the diagram on page 8.

If you are eager to incorporate these recipes into your daily routine, you will want to know their relative usefulness. This is why we have included the terms "Major Protein," "Minor Protein," and "Protein Complement" on the recipes where pertinent.

Menu suggestions are provided with the main dish recipes that need such assistance, and there are sample menus beginning on page 451. Do not feel restricted by these suggestions; rather, let them be your guide in adding similar dishes. Once you have a bit of experience, this will all become much easier than it may now appear.

Those recipes that have none of these terms offer good nutritional value but simply do not offer protein. We have chosen to emphasize only protein in this manner to put those who are unsure about vegetable proteins at ease. We recognize, of course, that carbohydrates, fat, sodium, and a host of other nutrients are just as important, and we have tried to keep these at optimal levels. If you utilize the Food Spectrums on pages 4–5, you will be able to make evaluations about foods on your own.

If using vegetable proteins is new to you or the term "complementary protein" unfamiliar, you should read the detailed discussion in "The Protein Principle" section (page 5).

PREPARATION AND COOKING TIME

Preparation times vary depending on the proficiency of the cook, and cooking times may be affected by differences in burners and ovens, by the degree to which utensils conduct heat, and by the ratio of contents to capacity. Check five minutes ahead of schedule to make sure the food isn't already cooked and be prepared to wait five to ten minutes beyond the expected cooking time. Having a store of cooked beans, grains, hard-cooked eggs, and other similar versatile foods on hand will be useful for expediting the preparation of many recipes.

SEASONING

The most difficult place to be precise when writing a recipe is in the seasoning. Place of origin and growing, drying and storing conditions all alter the potency of flavoring ingredients. Even more difficult to contend with is personal sensitivity which leaves each one of us with highly sensitive taste buds.

Thus it is possible you will want to adjust the seasoning in some recipes "to taste." Most professional chefs and experienced home cooks can rarely tell you how much of any herb or spice they use; they just taste and add, taste and add. The more home cooking you do, the easier seasoning will become. Until you feel comfortable about your own judgment, however, the recipe measurements will act as a good guideline.

The taste for salt, in particular, is largely adaptive. The main reason we give a salt measurement in recipes is that it is difficult to "salt to taste" a raw batter, uncooked soup or stew, and similar preparations that bear little relation to the final dish. Those accustomed to cooking with little or no salt may revise our guidelines. For those with a taste for more salty foods, we suggest following the recipe and then making salt and other flavor enhancers available at the table for whose who need them. This will give your palate a chance to begin the process of savoring tastes other than salty.

Instead of adding salt, you can give foods a lift in cooking or at the table with fresh garlic, a dash of vinegar or fresh lemon juice, hot pepper sauce or fresh ground pepper, additional herbs and spices, ground kelp (a seaweed) or sesame salt (also called Gomasio, see recipe page 306).

Unlike salt, we rarely give a measure for pepper. This is because we do all our "peppering" with a grinder, and it is a nuisance to grind and measure. Since pepper is best added at the last minute (it can turn bitter during cooking), it is no problem to add this seasoning "to taste."

FAT

The best oils for cooking are corn, peanut, soy, and in some special instances olive, since these oils withstand heat better than the lighter varieties such as sunflower and safflower. We use butter in cooking primarily for its taste. Where the choice of fat is subject to personal preference, it is listed in the ingredients as "oil/butter," which means either one or any combination.

For those who are insistent on eliminating fats in cooking, an equal amount of vegetable broth or water can generally replace the fat meant for sautéing, so that the food is braised instead. However, dishes prepared this way will lack some of their intended richness.

MILK

In the recipes, "milk" means you may use raw or pasteurized, whole or fat-reduced, or the equivalent in dry milk powder. Even soy milk may be used if preferred. Any exceptions to this will be specifically indicated.

Buttermilk, sour milk (not a common item since pasteurization), and yogurt thinned with milk to buttermilk consistency may be used interchangeably in cooking. If you have only regular milk, it can be "soured" by adding 1 tablespoon of vinegar or lemon juice to 1 cup, minus 1 tablespoon of milk. Let this stand in a warm spot for 10 minutes to "clabber."

EGGS

Unless otherwise directed, use large eggs (average two ounces each). Use of smaller or larger eggs will slightly alter results, especially if the recipe calls for more than two eggs.

RECIPE REFERENCES

The names of all recipes that appear in *American Wholefoods Cuisine* are designated by initial capital letters. When one recipe is an essential ingredient in another, page references are always provided. In the text where page references are not provided, the recipe can easily be located by using the index.

As our final advice before you go into the kitchen, here is the Master Rule for kitchen success:

MASTER RULE

Begin each recipe by reading it through completely. Gather all the ingredients and appropriate utensils at your work space. *Do as much measuring, peeling, chopping, etc., as is practical before beginning to combine ingredients.* Prepare pans and oven if necessary. You are now ready to assemble, mix, cook, and concentrate on any unfamiliar techniques—*mastering* the recipe.

Short-Order Cooking

David is our short-order chef. Having spent many of his formative years behind a counter and waiting on tables, he grew up with a great affection for this style of cooking.

For many obvious reasons, though, traditional short-order cooking does not enjoy a particularly good reputation. Too often the quality of ingredients is marginal and knowledge of cooking techniques minimal; deep-frying and overcooking are part of the tradition, as are highly processed foods. But the idea of cooking good luncheonette-diner-drugstore meals appeals to all at one time or another. Most people enjoy, at least occasionally, fulfilling their kitchen fantasies by turning out omelets, grilled and over-stuffed sandwiches, or bowls of chili.

Short-order cooking implies meals made with a minimum of effort, and, for this reason, a short-order dish must have only a few ingredients and be simple to assemble. Happily, such convenience translates easily to wholefoods cooking.

This chapter is devoted to promoting the best of this institution and demonstrating how even straightforward recipes can be served with style. We believe the shortcomings that do exist in short-order cooking can be corrected. Thus, even fried foods, properly prepared, are included in our short-order kitchen, and utilization of a steamer or wok cooking, an Oriental fast-food technique, guarantees that vegetables are not overcooked.

In addition to bringing out the short-order chef in you, this section is designed to assist the restaurateur. Maybe someday soon we will actually see American Wholefoods luncheonettes that provide wholesome, reasonably priced food, like the dishes served up here.

THE SHORT-ORDER KITCHEN

The short-order storeroom is not extensive and the Minimal Pantry presented in "The Wholefoods Pantry" can serve as the shopping list.

Equipment, like effort, can be abbreviated. A toaster oven or broiler is particularly useful; we have ours on a shelf over the stove, duplicating the professionals' system for defrosting, holding cooked food, turning out stacks of toast, etc. Here is a rundown of appropriate utensils:

vegetable scrub brush
vegetable peeler
strainer/colander
box or drum grater
tongs
long-handled fork
metal spatula
ladle
citrus squeezer
tea strainer
sharp knives
vegetable steamer
scissors
egg slicer
cheese slicer
pot holders
small casserole or oven trays
several saucepans (1- to 5-quart capacity)
6- to 8-inch omelet pan
10- to 12-inch omelet pan
12- to 15-inch skillet
tea kettle

Other useful items include:

wok
pan with nonstick finish
griddle
electric skillet
food processor
salad spinner
muffin tin
baking sheet
loaf pan
chef's apron

COLD SANDWICHES AND SALAD PLATTERS

Overstuffed sandwiches and copious salad platters provide filling meals that are enjoyable and easy to assemble. Many are based on traditional luncheonette fare; others make clever use of vegetable proteins to create familiar textures and tastes. While the term "chicken salad" conjures up a definite image for most people, Chopped Bean Liver or Chick-Pea Salad may suffer from a lack of gustatory associations. However, despite their unglamorous names and basic ingredients, the sandwich fillings in this section make surprisingly good eating and are particularly valuable for the interest they can add to packed lunches. Moreover, many of them can be piled onto a bed of lettuce for salad platter entrées.

Additional ideas along these lines, including more cheese-based spreads and sandwich fillings, are presented in "Appetizers and Hors d'Oeuvres."

Note: Those recipes classified as "Minor Protein" or "Protein Complement" will achieve main dish status when served on whole grain bread.

CHEESON

Fried provolone cheese, which we call "Cheeson," resembles bacon to a remarkable degree. It even releases its own natural fat as it cooks, making the similarity more striking. In addition to being used in sandwiches, Cheeson can be crumbled onto salads or served with pancakes, eggs, or whenever you would welcome its salty-smoky taste and crisp texture. For best results, use high-quality aged provolone.

Place sliced provolone cheese in a well-seasoned skillet or pan with a nonstick finish over medium-high heat. Cook until bubbles appear and break on the surface and cheese begins to show color through the holes. (Keep in mind that cheese will continue to cook until removed from pan. After a few times, you will recognize the proper degree of doneness.) For crisp rather than silky Cheeson, you can turn the cheese and cook the other side.

Remove from heat and let Cheeson sit in the pan a few minutes to harden. Lift from pan. When cool, tear into strips about 1½ inches wide, or 3 per slice.

CLT

Combine Cheeson with the traditional ingredients for the American Wholefoods version of the classic BLT.

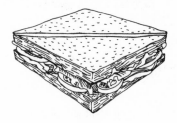

1½ slices (1½ ounces) Cheeson per sandwich
2 slices whole wheat toast
mayonnaise
lettuce
sliced tomato

Serves 1
Major Protein

C & C

The best of two worlds—the smoothness of cream cheese and the nourishment of cottage cheese.

2 slices whole grain bread, plain or toasted
2 tablespoons cream cheese
¼ cup cottage cheese

Spread cream cheese to cover one slice of bread. Top with cottage cheese, add a garnish from the list below, if desired, and close sandwich.

Serves 1

Major Protein

Garnishes: Filling can be enhanced with sliced tomato, chopped olives, finely chopped nuts, sliced cucumber, sprouts, or other chopped or shredded vegetable. Can also be made sweet with sliced banana, crushed pineapple, fruit butter, a thin coating of honey, or honey-sweetened preserves.

ANTIPASTO HEROES

Once you have the good Italian bread essential to an antipasto hero, your pantry and imagination are your only limitations. Here we pay tribute to New York's Trinacria, which became a legend with their salad on a sandwich.

For each serving:

1 6- to 8-inch hero roll or ¼ large Italian bread (page 340)
about ½ tablespoon olive oil
about 1 teaspoon vinegar
1 clove garlic, split (optional)
¼ cup finely shredded greens
1½ to 2 ounces sliced provolone cheese
several slices steamed potato
3 half-slices tomato
several Marinated Artichoke Hearts (page 65)
pimientos
capers
hot pickled peppers (or other pickled vegetable)
sliced olives
grated Parmesan cheese
about ½ teaspoon mustard
oregano
crushed red pepper

Split the roll or bread. (If very bready, remove some of the soft interior and save for crumbs or the birds.) Spread bottom half with oil and vinegar. If desired, rub with cut edge of garlic.

Layer greens on bread. Top with cheese, a layer of potato, tomato, and artichoke; add pimiento strips, capers, pickled vegetables, olives, and grated Parmesan, as desired. (This list of condiments is governed by personal tastes, and all can be used or any omitted.)

Spread inside top half of roll or bread with mustard. Sprinkle with a little oregano and crushed red pepper. When you close the sandwich, press both halves together firmly to help keep the ingredients from falling out as you eat (this is really inevitable and part of the fun) and to improve the chances that it will fit in your mouth.

Serves 1

Major Protein

Note: If you are going to prepare heroes for 4, you will need to steam a large 6- to 8-ounce potato and prepare a full recipe of Marinated Artichoke Hearts. In addition, you will need 1 large tomato, 1 cup shredded greens, and 6 ounces provolone.

LIMA BEAN–EGG SALAD

Serve on a bed of greens, on crackers, or a crusty roll. As part of a salad platter, this can be joined with Tofu "Chicken" Salad or garnished with cheese wedges.

2 cups cooked dried lima beans, drained
2 hard-cooked eggs
2 carrots
½ teaspoon prepared mustard
2 tablespoons yogurt
3 tablespoons mayonnaise

If large limas are used, chop coarsely with a knife; small limas can be left whole. Chop egg. Grate carrot finely. Combine all ingredients and mix well.

Makes 2¼ cups; serves 4 to 6

Minor Protein

KIDNEY BEAN LUNCHEON SALAD

2 cups cooked kidney or pink beans, drained
½ cup chopped celery
¼ cup chopped green pepper
2 diced hard-cooked eggs
2 tablespoons mayonnaise

2 tablespoons yogurt
salt (omit if beans are salted)
pepper

Combine all ingredients, adding mayonnaise and yogurt to moisten; season to taste.
Serves 4
Minor Protein
Note: If you have any homemade pickle relish or similar high-quality relish, add ¼ cup to bean mixture.

CHICK-PEA SALAD

Use this as you would tuna salad.

1 cup cooked chick-peas, drained
1 stalk celery, chopped
up to ¼ cup chopped raw onion
1 hard-cooked egg, chopped (optional)
1 generous tablespoon mayonnaise
dash prepared mustard
lemon wedge
salt
pepper

Grind chick-peas in a processor or food mill, or mince fine by hand. Combine with celery, onion, and egg, if desired; add mayonnaise and mustard. Squeeze in lemon juice (which will reduce the need for salt) and season to taste with salt and pepper.
Makes about ⅔ cup; serves 2
Minor Protein; Protein Complement without egg

OLIVE–BEAN SALAD

1 cup cooked soybeans, drained
¼ cup chopped green olives
1 generous tablespoon mayonnaise
1 teaspoon nutritional yeast

Grind beans in a processor or food mill or mince fine by hand. Combine with remaining ingredients and mix well.
Makes about ⅔ cup; serves 2
Minor Protein
Variation: Chopped sweet pickle or relish can also be added or used in place of the olives.

CHOPPED BEAN LIVER

A savory sandwich spread on the order of chopped liver.

1 cup cooked white beans or soy-beans, drained
1 medium onion, chopped
1 tablespoon oil
1 teaspoon nutritional yeast
salt
pepper
soy sauce (optional)

Grind beans in a processor or food mill or mince until fine. Sauté onion in oil until well browned. Mix beans, onion, and yeast, and season to taste. If desired, add soy sauce to darken to a liverlike color. Serve on bread or crackers, or mound onto a salad plate.
Makes about ⅔ cup; serves 2
Minor Protein
Note: A mashed hard-cooked egg can be added for improved protein value. If recipe is doubled, use only 1 egg per 4 servings.

TOMATO–BEAN PÂTÉ

1 cup cooked red or pink beans (pinto, kidney, etc.), drained
2 to 3 tablespoons peanut butter
2 to 3 tablespoons tomato paste

Mash cooked beans with a fork. Add remaining ingredients to taste and mix until smooth.
Makes 1 cup (enough for crackers for 6, or 4 sandwiches)
Minor Protein

SESAME–BEAN PÂTÉ

1 cup cooked beans, drained
¼ cup tahini
about 2 teaspoons soy sauce
1 to 2 tablespoons any combination minced celery, green pepper, onion, scallion, parsley
1 clove garlic, minced

Grind beans, or mash with a fork if they are soft. Mix in tahini to form a thick, smooth paste and season with soy sauce, adjusting according to saltiness of beans. Add any combination of the remaining ingredients you wish.

Makes about 1 cup (enough for 4 sandwiches)
Minor Protein

TOFU "EGG" SALAD

The mild flavor of tofu is easily enhanced by a well-seasoned dressing. Since fresh tofu has the texture of hard-cooked eggs and doesn't require cooking, it's even more convenient to prepare.

4 ounces tofu
1 to 2 tablespoons any combination chopped celery, chopped green pepper, chopped onion
mayonnaise
mustard, dill, curry powder to taste

Dice tofu as you would hard-cooked eggs for salad. Add chopped celery, green pepper, and/or onion to taste. Add enough mayonnaise to make mixture creamy and season with any or all of the above seasonings or others of your own choosing.

Makes ½ cup; serves 1
Protein Complement

DEVILED TOFU

Mustard dominates this pungent spread.

8 ounces tofu
2 teaspoons prepared mustard
½ teaspoon soy sauce
⅛ teaspoon turmeric (for color)
¼ cup minced green pepper
¼ cup minced onion (optional)
salt
⅛ teaspoon paprika

Mash tofu with fork until crumbly. Add remaining ingredients, except paprika, and mix well. Sprinkle paprika on top.

Makes 1½ cups (3 sandwiches or hors d'oeuvres for 4 to 6)
Protein Complement

TOFU "CHICKEN" SALAD

Even more convenient than chicken salad since you don't have to cook the tofu first.

8 ounces frozen tofu (see page 166)
1 large stalk celery, chopped
about 3 tablespoons yogurt
about 2 tablespoons sour cream or mayonnaise
2 tablespoons minced parsley
dash soy sauce
salt

Unwrap tofu, place in deep bowl, and cover with boiling water. Let stand 10 minutes to defrost, then press out moisture between palms. If still frozen, repeat process. Shred tofu with your fingers and combine with remaining ingredients, moistening and seasoning to taste.

Makes about 1⅓ cups (serves 2 on a platter or fills 4 sandwiches)
Minor Protein
Variations: Adaptable to any chicken salad recipe; for example, replace parsley with 1 tablespoon fresh dill weed or add diced pineapple or walnuts to the mixture.

MILD CHEESE AND TOMATO SPREAD

1 cup (4 ounces) shredded cheddar cheese
6 tablespoons ricotta cheese
1½ tablespoons tomato paste
¼ to ½ teaspoon hot pepper sauce

Mash first 3 ingredients together until smooth; add hot pepper sauce to taste.

Makes 1 cup (enough for 4 sandwiches)
Minor Protein

CELERY CHEDDAR SPREAD

1 cup (4 ounces) shredded cheddar cheese
¼ cup finely chopped celery
2 tablespoons mayonnaise

Combine all ingredients, mashing with a fork to form a uniform paste.

Makes 1 cup (enough for 4 sandwiches)
Minor Protein

PEANUT BUTTER COMPLEMENTS

These peanut butter combinations offer the best taste and greatly elevate the protein quality.

Peanut–Sesame Butter
4 parts peanut butter:
1 part tahini (sesame butter)

Peanut–Sunflower Crunch
2 parts peanut butter:
1 part chopped sunflower seeds

Creamy Peanut Butter
Add 1 tablespoon yogurt to each 4 tablespoons plain peanut butter or any of the complemented spreads above

Minor Protein
Note: To save time in sandwich preparation, peanut butter can be premixed with tahini or sunflower seeds and stored in the refrigerator.

AMERICAN WHOLEFOODS DELI PLATTER

A delicatessen-type platter composed of salads and condiments.

assorted greens
Mushroom Pâté (page 67)
Tofu "Egg" Salad (page 30) or Tofu "Chicken" Salad (page 30) or Tempeh Sandwich Salad (page 175)
shredded carrots
shredded raw beets
alfalfa sprouts
green pepper rings
Quick Pickles (page 310)

Cover a flat serving plate with greens. Mound Mushroom Pâté at one end of plate, tofu or tempeh at the other. Surround one of these salads with carrots, the other with beets.

Place green pepper rings between the two salads and fill them with sprouts. Place Quick Pickles along the side.

Major Protein
Menu Suggestions: Serve with a basket of whole grain crackers or rolls.

Instead of celery tonic, have a Seltzer Fizz.

CHEF'S SPECIAL SALAD OR SALAD BAR

This meal is dependent on the whims of the salad maker. The more you add, the better the salad will be—the list of ingredients below is just a start. Assemble the salad in the kitchen or serve the ingredients buffet style for individual assembly.

mixed greens
raw vegetables cut in bite-size pieces, including:

> **broccoli**
> **cauliflower**
> **green beans**
> **cucumber**
> **zucchini**
> **avocado**
> **radish**
> **scallions or red onion**
> **tomato**
> **mushrooms**
> **jicima**
> **grated raw carrots**
> **grated raw beets**
> **sprouts**

cooked beans or sliced cooked potatoes
2 tablespoons toasted pumpkin seeds per serving
1 4-ounce square tofu, diced, per serving
½ cup shredded or crumbled cheese per serving, including:

> **feta**
> **blue**
> **cottage**
> **Swiss**
> **Jack**
> **cheddar**
> **Cheeson (page 27)**

sliced hard-cooked egg
dressing of choice

Tear greens into bite-size pieces. Combine all ingredients as desired in a salad bowl. Dress to taste.

Major Protein

GREEK COUNTRY SALAD

Prepare on one large platter or divide ingredients among 4 bowls.

6 cups bite-size pieces romaine lettuce
2 tomatoes, cut in wedges
2 cups cooked chick-peas, drained
1 small cucumber, peeled and thinly sliced
1 cup (6 ounces) feta cheese, cut in small pieces
black olives
red onion, cut in thin slices
capers
pickled hot peppers (optional)
stuffed grape leaves, canned or home-made (page 82, optional)
anchovies (optional)
salt
pepper
dried oregano
about 3 tablespoons lemon juice
about ⅓ cup olive oil

Toss lettuce with tomatoes, chick-peas, and cucumber. Top evenly with feta, olives, onion rings, and capers.

Garnish as desired with hot peppers, grape leaves, and anchovies.

Season lightly with salt (if feta is mild and anchovies excluded), and generously with pepper and oregano. Dress to taste with lemon juice and oil. Toss before serving.

Serves 4
Major Protein
Note: As an accompaniment to a meal, this will provide a Minor Protein for 6 to 8.

STUFFED AVOCADO SALAD

mixed greens
½ avocado, cut lengthwise through stem end
lemon wedge
½ cup cottage cheese
shredded carrots
shredded beets
chopped scallions
alfalfa sprouts
tomato wedges or orange sections
cooked chick-peas or toasted pumpkin seeds
olives

celery sticks
Dressing: Lemon-Tahini (page 290), Light French Tomato (page 57), or Creamy Blue Cheese (page 57) (optional)

Cover serving plate generously with greens. Remove pit from avocado half and sprinkle exposed surface with lemon juice. Avocado can be left in the shell, or skin can be removed with a sharp paring knife.

Mound cottage cheese in the cavity left by the pit and place the stuffed avocado on the greens. Top the cottage cheese with shredded carrots, beets, scallions, and the sprouts, letting the excess flow over onto the greens. Surround with any of the remaining ingredients you desire and dress to taste. (You may not even need dressing, as the cottage cheese makes the vegetables moist.)

Serves 1
Major Protein
Variations: For *Hot Stuffed Avocado Salad,* fill the avocado hollow with ½ cup cottage cheese mixed with ¼ cup shredded cheese and bake in a 375°F. oven or toaster oven for 15 minutes.

For *Stuffed Tomato Salad,* substitute 1 medium tomato for avocado half, remove a slice from the top and the meat from inside to make a hollow shell. Stuff with cottage cheese, or prepare as for Hot Stuffed Avocado. (The inside of the tomato can be added to the other vegetables or reserved for seasoning soup, sauces, or stews.)

MEXICAN STUFFED AVOCADO SALAD

mixed greens
½ avocado, cut lengthwise through stem end
lemon wedge
½ cup cooked kidney or pinto beans, drained
chopped canned chilies
¼ cup shredded Jack or cheddar cheese
yogurt, or yogurt seasoned lightly with sour cream

tomato wedges
olives
pickled hot peppers
sweet green and red pepper wedges
Dressing: Light Mexican Tomato
Dressing (page 57) or Mexican
Tomato Vinaigrette (page 288)
2 taco shells

Cover serving plate generously with greens.

Remove pit from avocado half and sprinkle exposed surface with lemon juice. Avocado can either be left in the shell and scooped out with the filling as you eat, or the skin can be removed with a small, sharp paring knife.

Place avocado half on greens and fill cavity with beans mixed to taste with canned chilies. Let any excess beans flow onto greens. Top with shredded cheese and a dollop of plain or seasoned yogurt.

Surround with the remaining ingredients as desired and dress to taste. Use the tacos to shovel the salad onto the fork, or pile the salad onto the tacos and eat out of hand.

Serves 1
Major Protein
Variation: If desired, the bean-stuffed, cheese-topped avocado can be placed in a 350°F. oven or under the broiler to melt cheese.

HOT SANDWICHES AND ENTRÉES

Many recipes in this section that call for broiling or baking are most efficiently done for one or two in a toaster oven.

FRESH TOMATO PITA PIZZA

A variation on the now classic English muffin pizza.

1 whole wheat pita bread
4 tomato slices or ¼ cup of Italian-style tomato sauce (15-Minute Italian Tomato Sauce, page 58, or other sauce of choice)

½ cup shredded mozzarella cheese
mixed with Parmesan to taste
sliced fresh mushrooms, olives, sweet
peppers, onion (optional)
pinch of oregano
oil

Preheat oven or toaster oven to 375°F. Separate pita bread into 2 rounds by piercing around circumference with the tines of a fork and gently prying apart. Place on baking sheet. Cover each round of bread with tomato slices or spread with sauce, cheese, and any of the optional ingredients you want; season with oregano; drizzle with a little oil. Bake for 10 minutes.
Serves 1
Major Protein

QUICK CALZONE

A creamy ricotta filling warmed inside of pita bread pockets makes a quick substitute for the classic version of Calzone presented on page 221.

¾ cup ricotta cheese
½ cup shredded mozzarella cheese
¼ cup shredded provolone cheese
¼ teaspoon oregano
salt
pepper
½ medium tomato, chopped and drained
2 whole wheat pita breads
pickled peppers or canned chilies (optional)

Preheat oven or toaster oven to 375°F. Mix cheeses and oregano thoroughly. Add salt and pepper to taste. Gently fold in tomato.

Cut each bread in half to form two pockets. Open carefully and stuff each with about ⅓ cup filling. Insert a few thin slices of pepper or chilies into each, if desired.

Place in a baking dish with cut side tilted up so filling doesn't ooze out. Bake for 10 to 15 minutes until filling is melted and very hot. Eat as a sandwich.
Serves 2
Major Protein

INDIVIDUAL BEAN PIZZAS

1 cup cooked chick-peas or kidney beans, drained
1 small onion, minced
¼ cup minced green pepper
1 small clove garlic, minced
½ teaspoon oregano
¼ teaspoon dried basil
¼ cup tomato juice
salt (omit if beans are salted)
2 whole wheat pita breads
½ cup shredded mozzarella or provolone cheese
1 tablespoon oil
crushed red pepper (optional)

Preheat oven or toaster oven to 450°F. Grind beans in a food mill or processor, mince fine by hand, or mash with a fork if very soft. Mix with onion, green pepper, garlic, herbs, and tomato juice until nicely moistened. Add salt only if necessary.

Cut each pita bread in two flat circles by punching with tines of fork around circumference and gently prying apart. Spread bean mixture to cover surface of rounds, using about ¼ cup for each. Cover with cheese and drizzle with oil. Top with crushed red pepper, if desired, or reserve for the table for individual seasoning.

Place on a baking sheet and bake for 10 minutes until very hot and cheese is lightly colored.

Serves 2
Major Protein
Note: Serves 4 as an accompaniment to light pasta dishes.

FRENCH-TOASTED CHEESE SANDWICH

1 to 2 ounces sliced cheese
2 slices whole grain bread
1 egg
2 tablespoons milk
¼ teaspoon dry mustard
pinch salt
butter/oil

Sandwich cheese between slices of bread. Beat egg with milk, mustard, and salt. Soak sandwich in egg mixture on each side until all egg is absorbed.

Add butter alone or with oil to cover surface of skillet; heat. Sauté sandwich 3 to 5 minutes on each side until browned.

Serves 1
Major Protein

SOUFFLÉED CHEESE SANDWICH

An embellished open-face cheese sandwich that is tasty, easy, light, novel, and a perfect example of how to make something fancy out of simple, everyday ingredients.

1 egg, separated
pinch dry mustard
dash hot pepper sauce
⅓ cup shredded cheese
salt
2 slices whole grain bread
butter

Preheat oven or toaster oven to 350°F. Beat egg yolk with mustard and hot pepper sauce until light. Mix in cheese. Beat egg white until stiff, adding a pinch of salt when foamy. Fold into yolk mixture.

Toast bread on one side in broiler or toaster oven. Lightly butter untoasted side and cover with cheese mixture. Place on baking sheet and bake for 10 to 12 minutes until puffed and set.

Serves 1
Major Protein
Note: A half serving, or one slice of bread with soufflé topping, is an excellent Minor Protein accompaniment for soups, salads, bean casseroles, vegetable dishes, and other light meals.

AVOCADO–CHEESE MELT

Dedicated to the spirit of the Joyous Lake.

1 slice whole grain bread per sandwich
ricotta or cottage cheese
avocado
salt
lemon juice
1 to 2 ounces sliced Jack, cheddar, or Swiss cheese
sesame or sunflower seeds

Cover bread with a thin layer of ricotta or cottage cheese. Top with avocado that has been mashed and lightly seasoned with salt and lemon juice. Add sliced cheese, sprinkle with seeds, and melt cheese under broiler or in toaster oven.
Serves 1
Major Protein

VEGGIE REUBEN

An open-face melted cheese sandwich that gets a lift from the crunchy, flavorful coleslaw beneath the cheese.

1 oversize or 2 average slices whole grain bread
Revisionist Dressing (page 57)
⅓ to ½ cup Tangy Coleslaw (page 46) or your favorite recipe
2 tomato slices, cut in half
1½ to 2 ounces sliced Swiss, Muenster, cheddar, or colby cheese

Preheat oven or toaster oven to 350°F. Spread bread with dressing. Arrange coleslaw on top to cover, then add tomato slices and cheese. Bake about 10 minutes until cheese melts.
Serves 1
Major Protein
Note: If desired, add sliced raw onion, pickle relish, or bread and butter pickles. Recipes for homemade pickles appear on pages 437–440.

PEPPER AND EGG HERO

Like its cold counterpart, the hot Hero (known also as a Sub, Grinder, Poor Boy, Hoagie, and Torpedo) knows no limits except a good bread and some inventiveness. Herewith, a favorite filling.

1 tablespoon butter/oil
½ large green pepper, cut in strips
3 eggs
salt
pepper
2 individual hero rolls or half a large Italian bread

Heat fat in a 10- to 12-inch skillet; sauté pepper 5 minutes or longer, until tender. Beat eggs and season with salt and pepper. Pour over softened pepper and when eggs begin to set, stir gently to break up the omelet. Cook to taste. Cut bread as for a sandwich, fill with pepper and eggs, and eat.
Serves 2
Major Protein
Note: Grated Parmesan makes a nice seasoning for the egg mixture.

GRILLED OPEN-FACE TOFU SANDWICH

1 small cake tofu (4 ounces)
2 slices whole grain bread
butter
prepared mustard
soy sauce
sliced tomato (optional)
mayonnaise (optional)

Slice tofu into 4 thin pieces and press with absorbent paper to remove excess moisture. Toast bread lightly and spread with butter and a thin layer of mustard. Top with tofu and season lightly with soy sauce; add a slice of tomato, if desired, and broil until tofu is lightly browned. Serve hot with a dollop of mayonnaise on top, if desired, for extra flavor.
Serves 1
Major Protein

TOFU PITA

1 whole wheat pita bread
tahini
soy sauce
4 ounces tofu, thinly sliced
2 to 3 thin tomato slices
alfalfa sprouts
mayonnaise

Preheat oven or toaster oven to 350°F. Separate pita bread into two rounds by piercing around the circumference with a fork and gently prying apart. Season tahini with soy sauce to taste and spread generously on one pita round. Layer sliced tofu on tahini. Cover with tomato and bake about 10 minutes until hot. Arrange sprouts over tofu and tomato. Spread remaining pita round lightly with mayonnaise and close sandwich.

Serves 1
Major Protein
Variation: For *Tempeh Pita,* replace tofu with thinly sliced tempeh that has been pan-fried. Baking is not needed in this version; however, you may wish to warm the pita bread before filling it.

RYEBURGERS

Bread is the basis of this burger and it is more tasty than you might imagine from the description of ingredients. Two ryeburgers and a salad make a very nice meal.

catsup
1 slice thin whole grain rye bread
relish
sliced onion (optional)
1½ to 2 ounces sliced cheese
butter/oil

Spread a thin layer of catsup on bread, top with relish and onion, if desired, and cover completely with cheese. Heat enough butter alone or with oil to cover surface of a skillet. Add bread and cook until bottom browns. Cover pan and cook over low heat about a minute until cheese melts.

Makes 1 burger
Major Protein

MEXICAN PIZZA

Italian fast food with Mexican ingredients.

2 corn tortillas
¼ cup Emergency Mexican Tomato Sauce (page 58) or similar sauce
¼ cup combined shredded cheddar and Jack cheeses
several canned chili strips
a scant teaspoon oil

Preheat oven or toaster oven to 375°F. Place tortillas on a baking sheet and spread with sauce, cheese, and chili strips; drizzle lightly with oil. Bake for 10 minutes.

Serves 1
Major Protein

BEAN TACOS

Bean tacos are valued for their simplicity and festive qualities.

3 taco shells
¾ cup Refried Beans (page 54)
chopped tomato
chopped raw onion
chopped green pepper
chopped cucumber
shredded lettuce
¼ cup or more shredded Jack or cheddar cheese
¼ cup or more Emergency Mexican Tomato Sauce at room temperature (page 58) or Enchilada Sauce (page 317)
Quick Mexican Hot Sauce (optional, page 58)

Stuff each taco with ¼ cup beans, garnish to taste with vegetables, sprinkle with a generous spoonful of cheese, and smother with tomato sauce. Season with Hot Sauce to taste.

Serves 1
Major Protein
Note: For quantity service, bring all ingredients to the table and have everyone assemble their own tacos.
Variation: For *Chalupas* replace tacos with cornmeal tortillas, allowing 2 per person and fry one at a time in oil heated to generously cover a skillet. Top each flat, crisp tortilla with above ingredients, adding a layer of guacamole and a topping of yogurt flavored with sour cream to taste.
Menu Suggestions: Serve as a complete meal with Guacamole or raw vegetables and a favorite dip, or combine on the menu with Cheese Enchi-

ladas or Chili Rellenos as a double entrée.

TORTILLA PYRAMID

A stack of tortillas layered with cheese and topped with an egg is a more filling dish than you might expect, and as easy to make for many as for one.

3 cornmeal tortillas
½ cup shredded Jack or cheddar cheese
1 tablespoon chopped olives
1 egg
oil
about ¼ cup Salsa Cruda (page 308) or Quick Mexican Hot Sauce (page 58) or chopped raw onions and tomatoes flavored with hot pepper sauce

Toast each tortilla lightly in toaster oven, toaster, broiler, or by toasting over an open flame (using long-handled tongs). Stack on a baking pan with grated cheese and chopped olives between each layer.

Preheat oven or toaster oven to 375°F. Fry egg in oil until white is set but yolk is still soft. Place on top of tortillas, drizzle with a little oil, and bake for 5 to 10 minutes, just to melt cheese.

Season at the table with one of the recommended sauces.

Serves 1
Major Protein

BROCCOLI TOSTADOS

Vegetable-topped tortillas in a bean-cheese sauce.

½ pound broccoli, chopped (about 2 cups)
4 cornmeal tortillas
Bean–Cheese Sauce (recipe follows)

Steam broccoli about 10 minutes until barely tender. Toast tortillas lightly in toaster or toaster oven set on "light," in broiler, or in an ungreased skillet. Pile broccoli on top of tortillas and cover with a generous amount of sauce.

Bean–Cheese Sauce
¾ cup cooked pinto or kidney beans, drained
⅓ cup milk
¾ cup diced cheddar or Jack cheese
¼ teaspoon salt (adjust if beans are salted)
¼ teaspoon hot pepper sauce

Combine all ingredients in blender or processor fitted with steel blade and puree until smooth. Transfer to a pot and heat gently until cheese melts and sauce is warm.

Serves 2
Major Protein

CHEESE RAREBIT

Rich cheese sauce over bread makes a delicious and warming meal. Serve pickles on the side for proper contrast.

4 slices whole grain bread
¾ cup Double Cheese Sauce (page 58)

Toast bread (do not butter it) and let sit at room temperature until sauce is made. (Day-old bread, rather than fresh, is actually better for this dish, and leftover toast from early in the day can be used as long as it is unbuttered.) Place 2 slices of bread on each serving plate and drown in sauce.

Serves 2
Major Protein

POTATO PANCAKES

As easy to make as an omelet.

about 1 pound raw unpeeled potatoes (to make 2 cups shredded)
1 small onion, grated
1 egg, lightly beaten
½ teaspoon salt
1 tablespoon wheat germ
about 1 tablespoon whole wheat flour
oil
Whipped Cottage Cream (page 56)

Shred potatoes coarsely using the shredding disk of a food processor, or a box grater. If desired, grate a portion more finely to make centers of pancakes chewy. Drain all liquid from potatoes by pressing in a strainer. Mix remaining ingredients into drained potatoes. If liquid or very loose, add more flour or some whole wheat cracker crumbs.

Cover surface of large, heavy skillet with oil. When oil is hot, drop potato mixture by soupspoonfuls into the pan. Cook until brown underneath and easily turned, 5 to 8 minutes. Turn and brown the other side. Serve with Whipped Cottage Cream.

Makes about 10 pancakes; serves 2
Major Protein (with topping)

Note: If you are cooking potato pancakes for a family or a crowd, keep the first batches warm in a 300°F. oven while you are cooking the rest.

Menu Suggestion: Potato pancakes are traditionally served with applesauce and sour cream. However, to make them an appropriate main dish, Whipped Cottage Cream is the topping of choice.

CRISP CHEESE PANCAKES

Serve these savory pancakes as a hot entrée or cold sandwich filling.

1 cup shredded cheese
2 tablespoons whole wheat flour
¼ teaspoon salt (less with a salted cheese)
1 teaspoon prepared mustard
2 eggs, lightly beaten
¼ cup yogurt
oil

Combine all ingredients except oil to make a uniform batter. Cover the surface of a griddle or skillet with oil and heat. When hot, drop batter by tablespoonfuls into the pan. Cook until brown underneath and easily moved with a spatula, 5 to 8 minutes. Turn and brown about 3 minutes on the other side.

Serves 2 generously as an entrée (4 as a sandwich filling)
Major Protein

Note: If you are making a number of pancakes, keep the ones that have been cooked warm in a 250° to 300°F. oven or toaster oven.

COTTAGE CHEESE CUTLETS

A quick and especially satisfying cutlet. Serve plain, Italian style with tomato sauce and grated Parmesan cheese, or Russian style with a topping of yogurt and fresh dill.

1 egg
1 slice whole grain bread
1 cup dry-curd pot cheese, or well-drained cottage cheese
¼ teaspoon salt
1 tablespoon minced parsley
¼ cup whole wheat flour
oil

Beat egg, then shred bread into beaten egg and let stand a few minutes to absorb. Add cottage cheese, salt, parsley, and 2 tablespoons of flour to the egg mixture. Stir until smooth.

Put remaining flour on a plate; taking ¼ cup of the cottage cheese mixture at a time, shape into 2-inch rounds and dredge with flour. Batter will be fairly soft but should hold together nicely.

Cover surface of a 15-inch skillet with oil and heat. When hot, fry cheese cutlets on each side until brown, or about 5 minutes per side. Serve plain or with any of the sauces described above.

Makes 4 cutlets; serves 2
Major Protein

Note: To drain cottage cheese, place in strainer lined with a linen napkin or cheesecloth and let stand while assembling ingredients. Gather cloth around cheese like a bag and squeeze to extract as much liquid as possible.

RICE PANCAKES

Although we originally designed this dish for breakfast, most people find these pancakes best for a quick lunch or dinner entrée. Crisp on the surface and tender inside, they need no embellishments although catsup or a light yogurt–mayonnaise mixture can be used for seasoning.

1 cup cooked brown rice
1 egg
½ cup milk
½ cup diced Muenster or Jack cheese
oil

Combine rice, egg, and milk in a blender or a processor fitted with a steel blade and process to combine. Add cheese and puree until evenly blended but still lumpy.

Heat enough oil to just cover the surface of a heavy skillet or griddle. Pour on batter, allowing ¼ cup per pancake. When edges become crisp and a spatula can easily be slid underneath, flip and cook until the bottom sets.

Makes 10 pancakes; serves 2

Major Protein

Note: Unless you have a very large griddle, you may need two pans. If you cook pancakes in separate batches, keep them warm in a 300°F. oven.

CAMELLIA GRILL OMELET

A treasured eating spot in New Orleans is the Camellia Grill, and it is there we first had the omelet that inspired this hybrid of tender pancake with egg.

1 egg
¼ cup milk
⅛ teaspoon salt
2 tablespoons whole wheat flour
butter

Beat all ingredients together using an egg beater, wire whisk, or blender. (At the Camellia they use a malted mixer.) Place a 15-inch skillet over medium heat. Rub the surface with a little butter to just coat.

When pan is hot, pour egg mixture in and let it spread as thin as possible. Cook until top is set but not dry and egg can be lifted with ease from the pan. (Lift the edge and check the color; it should be golden.) Fold omelet by bringing two sides to the middle, then folding in the other two sides to form a neat package. Serve hot from the pan.

Serves 1

Minor Protein

Variations: Camellia Grill Omelets filled ¼ to ½ cup shredded cheddar cheese or ½ cup chili, as is popular at the Louisiana diner, are especially recommended and will be a *Major Protein* dish. Set the filling in the center of the large "pancake" just before folding and enclose in the bundle.

MANICOTTI OMELET

If you like manicotti but think it's a bother to prepare just for yourself, try this delicious omelet.

1 egg
1 tablespoon whole wheat flour
1 tablespoon milk
salt
pepper
¼ cup ricotta cheese
¼ cup shredded mozzarella and provolone cheeses, combined in any proportion
pinch oregano
1 tablespoon minced parsley
oil/butter
about ½ tablespoon grated Parmesan cheese
¼ cup tomato sauce (optional)

Beat together egg, flour, and milk. Season lightly with salt and pepper. Combine ricotta, mozzarella and provolone, oregano, parsley, and a generous amount of pepper.

Heat enough oil and/or butter to cover a 6- to 8-inch omelet pan. (A well-seasoned pan will only need about ¼ tablespoon fat.) When hot, pour in egg and cook, lifting as edges set to let egg run underneath. When top is soft but no longer runny, loosen entire omelet so it is free of pan.

Place ricotta mixture on half the omelet and fold to enclose filling. Cover pan and let cook for 3 to 5 minutes to heat through. Sprinkle with Parmesan and slide onto plate. Serve with sauce if desired.

Serves 1

Major Protein

Note: To serve 2, double all ingredients, but increase the number of eggs to 3. Prepare in a 10- to 12-inch skillet and cut in half to serve.

ONE-POT BAKED MACARONI AND CHEESE

2¼ cups uncooked whole wheat elbows, spirals, or small shells
1 cup shredded cheddar or cheese of choice
1½ cups milk

2 tablespoons whole grain cracker or dried bread crumbs
1 tablespoon wheat germ
½ tablespoon butter

Preheat oven to 350°F. Combine pasta and shredded cheese in a greased, shallow 1-quart casserole. Add milk. Cover and bake for 30 minutes. Mix halfway through to submerge pasta in milk.

After 30 minutes, remove cover from casserole. Combine crumbs and wheat germ and sprinkle mixture over casserole; dot top with butter and return to oven uncovered for 10 minutes.
Serves 2
Major Protein
Note: Since most natural cheeses are not colored, this dish will be creamy white rather than yellow.

CREAMY PASTA WITH CHEESE

This rich Parmesan cheese sauce is reminiscent of Fettuccine Alfredo with less fat and far fewer calories.

½ pound whole wheat or spinach linguini
2 tablespoons butter
1 cup ricotta cheese
½ cup yogurt
1 cup grated Parmesan cheese
pepper

Bring a pot of water to a boil, salt lightly, and cook pasta for 10 to 12 minutes, or until cooked to taste. Drain. Return pasta to the pot, add butter, and toss over low heat until butter melts and coats pasta. If pasta seems a bit dry, add a little oil to coat completely.

Stir ricotta and yogurt into pasta and gradually add Parmesan cheese, stirring continuously until sauce is warm and creamy and cheese melts. Season liberally with pepper and serve.
Serves 4
Major Protein
Note: The success of this dish depends on using freshly grated cheese of good quality. Parmesan, romano, loca-

telli, pecorino, or a similar hard grating cheese can be used.
Variation: For *Creamy Pasta with Cheese and Herbs* add ⅓ cup chopped scallion, ⅓ cup minced parsley, and 2 tablespoons minced fresh basil with the butter, and proceed as above.

ZITI WITH CHEESE

½ pound whole wheat ziti or spirals
1½ cups diced mozzarella and provolone cheese, combined in any proportion
¼ cup grated Parmesan cheese
½ cup minced parsley
1 teaspoon dried basil
2 cloves garlic, split
2 tablespoons oil (at least part olive preferred)
pepper

Bring a pot of water to a boil, salt lightly, and cook pasta until just tender, about 12 minutes. Combine cheeses, parsley and basil.

Put split cloves of garlic in a small saucepan or heatproof measuring cup with oil and cook slowly over low heat until garlic is just brown. Discard garlic.

Drain pasta. Return to pot and toss with cheeses, herbs, and hot garlic oil. Warm gently until cheese softens but still holds its shape. Season liberally with pepper.
Serves 4
Major Protein

TOMATO SHELLS

Homemade "canned" spaghetti.

¼ cup oil
3 cups uncooked small whole wheat shells or elbows
¼ cup chopped onion
½ cup chopped celery
½ cup chopped green pepper
1 clove garlic, minced
4 cups tomato juice
½ teaspoon salt
¼ teaspoon hot pepper sauce

Heat oil in a 3-quart saucepan and sauté pasta and vegetables over moderate heat for about 10 minutes until pasta begins to color slightly. Stir occasionally. Add tomato juice and seasonings; bring to a boil. Cover and simmer over low heat for about 20 minutes until pasta is tender.

Serves 4
Protein Complement
Menu Suggestion: Complete with a generous amount of grated cheese or add beans or cheese somewhere else on the menu.

STEAMED VEGETABLES WITH CHEESE

A platter of steamed vegetables topped with a rich cheese sauce can be a substantial main dish.

1 pound vegetables (individually or in combination):
    broccoli
    cauliflower
    green beans
    potatoes
¾ cup Double Cheese Sauce (page 58)

Prepare vegetables (dividing broccoli into trees and peeling the outer layer of stems if tough, dividing cauliflower into large buds, trimming ends of beans, and cutting unpeeled potatoes into halves or quarters).

Place vegetables in a steamer. If cooking more than one vegetable, add successively, to allow for varying cooking times. (Potatoes will need about 20 minutes, broccoli 12 to 15 minutes, green beans 10 minutes, and cauliflower 8 to 10 minutes, so they should be cooked in this order.) Steam until fork-tender.

Prepare sauce while vegetables steam. Place hot vegetables on serving plates and smother with sauce.

Serves 2
Major Protein

AIOLI WITH VEGETABLES

This dish, which originated in the south of France, is a simple platter of cooked vegetables and beans topped with a garlic-laden sauce. We have refined the traditional Provençal recipe to provide a less fatty, more nourishing main dish. It is easy to prepare for any number of people.

¾ cup yogurt
¼ cup mayonnaise
1 clove garlic, minced
½ pound potatoes
about 1 pound assorted vegetables: carrots, cauliflower, broccoli, leeks, parsnips, zucchini, green beans, bean sprouts, etc.
1 onion, cut in crescents
1 cup cooked beans, drained

Prepare sauce by mixing yogurt, mayonnaise, and garlic; allow this sauce to develop flavor at room temperature while vegetables cook.

Cut potatoes into chunks and begin steaming. They will take about 20 minutes to become tender. Meanwhile, cut other vegetables into chunks and add to steamer at appropriate intervals so that they will all be done at the same time. (Allow 12 to 15 minutes for broccoli, carrots, and leeks, 10 minutes for parsnips and green beans, 8 to 10 minutes for cauliflower, zucchini, and bean sprouts.) During the last 10 minutes, place onion over the other vegetables. Heat beans in a separate pot.

Arrange vegetables and beans on a serving platter or spoon some of each onto individual plates. Top with generous amounts of sauce.

Serves 2
Major Protein

VEGETABLES WITH CURRY CREAM

This platter of cooked vegetables in a flavorful protein-rich sauce may be served either warm or cold.

about 1 pound assorted steamed vegetables
1 cup cooked beans, drained
1 stalk celery, chopped
2 scallions, thinly sliced
¾ cup yogurt
¼ cup mayonnaise
1 tablespoon curry powder (commercial or Goldbecks' Masala, page 445)
1 tablespoon lemon juice

Arrange vegetables with beans and celery on a serving platter in individual piles or combined. Serve scallions in a separate bowl. Mix remaining ingredients for sauce, which should also be served separately. To serve, let everyone help themselves to some of the vegetables, adding sauce and scallions as they wish.

Serves 2

Major Protein

Note: For a *Curried Vegetable Sandwich,* stuff some cooked vegetables and beans into pockets of pita bread. Top each half with ¼ cup of sauce plus some raw celery and scallion.

Menu Suggestions: If beans are not among the vegetables chosen, serve with a lentil dish. Accompany entrée with pita bread or chapatis, or a base of cooked grain.

MAIN DISH STIR-FRY

A plate of wok-cooked tofu and vegetables makes an Oriental short order meal. Serve over brown rice or crumbled rice crackers.

2 tablespoons oil
1 clove garlic, cut in half
4 scallions, cut in 1-inch sections
1 pound fresh or frozen tofu or tempeh, cut in strips
8 cups mixed vegetables in any proportion, cut attractively in bite-size pieces:

> **carrots**
> **broccoli**
> **cauliflower**
> **green pepper**
> **zucchini**
> **Chinese greens**
> **celery**
> **bean sprouts**
> **asparagus**
> **snow peas**
> **green beans**
> **mushrooms**
> (or cook's choice)

½ cup water
2 tablespoons soy sauce
2 tablespoons cooking sherry or vinegar
2 teaspoons sesame oil or hot oil

Heat oil in a wok and stir-fry garlic, scallions, and tofu or tempeh over medium high heat until lightly colored. Add vegetables and stir-fry 5 to 8 minutes longer until vegetables are crisp-tender. Add water, soy sauce, and sherry or vinegar; cover and cook over low heat for 5 minutes. Stir in oil and serve at once.

Serves 4

Major Protein served over grain

Note: For additional seasoning at the table, offer Chinese Mustard and soy sauce.

SKILLET STEW

Fresh vegetables under a blanket of cheese.

1 tablespoon oil
1 small onion, chopped
1 small clove garlic, chopped
¼ cup chopped green pepper
3 cups sliced summer squash (about ¾ pound)
1 tomato, diced
salt
pepper
1 cup shredded cheddar cheese

Heat oil in a 10- to 12-inch skillet and sauté onion, garlic, and green pepper for 3 minutes. Add squash and tomato; cover and cook over low heat for 10 to 15 minutes until tender. Season vegetables lightly with salt and pepper. Cover with cheese. Remove from heat, cover, and let stand for 5 minutes to melt.

Serves 2

Major Protein

Variations: Substitute green beans, broccoli, or corn for squash, or use a combination of vegetables.

Menu Suggestions: Can be served on a grain or pasta, or accompanied by a muffin (see Quick Mixes in "The Food Factory"). Complete the meal with a tossed salad.

SKILLET CORN, CHILIES, AND CHEESE

A quick and easy vegetable entrée to serve on rice or crisp tacos.

1 tablespoon oil
1 clove garlic, chopped
1 small onion, chopped
4-ounce can chilies, drained
2 cups fresh corn kernels
½ teaspoon salt
4 ounces mild cheddar, Jack, or mozzarella cheese, cut in cubes
yogurt

Heat oil in a skillet and sauté garlic and onion until soft but not brown, about 3 minutes. Cut chilies into 1-inch strips and add to pan along with corn and salt. Cover and cook over low heat until corn is tender. This will take from 5 to 10 minutes, depending on the age of the corn.

Add cheese cubes, cover, and cook without stirring until cheese runs. Be sure to wait until just before serving to add the cheese, as it toughens on re-heating. Serve on a base of your choice (rice, tacos, or even toast) and top with spoonfuls of yogurt.

Serves 2
Major Protein
Note: Although this is best when made with fresh corn, frozen corn can be used. For reduced calories, spoon the mixture over crisp lettuce leaves.

Variations: Substitute cooked kidney, pinto, lima, or soybeans for one third of the corn.

B.O.B. (BEANS ON BOARD)

Beans in a barbecue-style sauce served on toast.

1 small onion, chopped
1 small clove garlic, chopped
1 scant tablespoon oil
1 teaspoon chili powder
1½ cups cooked kidney or pinto beans, lightly drained
2 tablespoons catsup
½ teaspoon molasses
dash soy sauce
tomato juice (optional)
2 tablespoons wheat germ
4 slices whole grain toast
shredded cheddar cheese

Sauté onion and garlic in oil for about 5 minutes until they begin to color. Add chili powder and cook for 30 seconds. Stir in beans, catsup, molasses, and a little soy. If dry, add enough tomato juice to moisten. Heat through.

Stir in wheat germ to make thick (if too dry add more tomato juice). When hot, spoon over toast and top with cheese.

Serves 2
Major Protein

CHILI

A bowl of chili garnished at the table is as satisfying and nourishing as the most expensive restaurant meal.

2 tablespoons oil
2 cloves garlic, chopped
2 large onions, chopped
¼ teaspoon cayenne
2 tablespoons chili powder
1 teaspoon cumin
1 teaspoon oregano
1 medium green pepper, chopped
2 cups tomatoes, either drained canned or fresh chopped
4 cups cooked kidney or pinto beans, drained
1 teaspoon salt (less if beans are presalted)
1 tablespoon nutritional yeast (optional)

Heat oil in a 3-quart pot and sauté garlic for 1 minute until it begins to color. Add onion and cook for 3 minutes until softened. Add seasonings and green pepper and cook for 1 minute longer.

Add remaining ingredients, adjusting salt as needed. Bring to a boil, cover, and simmer over low heat for 20 to 30 minutes until thickened. For a hearty taste, we recommend stirring in nutritional yeast just before serving; this will add good flavor and thicken the chili slightly.

Serves 4 generously; 6 if served in taco shells rather than bowls

Protein Complement (Major Protein when served as directed in Menu Suggestions below)

Note: This recipe produces a hot but not fiery chili; increase or decrease cayenne according to your own tastes.

Menu Suggestions: To make the most of the beans, serve them with chopped raw onion, shredded greens doused with fresh lemon juice, shredded cheddar cheese, or pumpkin seeds toasted in a skillet and lightly crushed, and one or more of the following:

crisp corn tacos, 2 per person
brown rice, ½ cup per person
corn bread or muffins
crushed whole wheat crackers

If you are considering another item on the menu, add an avocado salad.

SLOPPY BEANS

A creamy version of Sloppy Joes for a quick, nourishing, hot open-face sandwich.

1 tablespoon oil
¼ cup chopped onion
¼ cup chopped green pepper
2 cups cooked black, brown, or red beans, drained
2 tablespoons catsup
½ teaspoon prepared mustard
¾ cup creamed cottage cheese
¼ cup sour cream
2 to 3 whole wheat hamburger rolls, biscuits, or 6 slices whole grain toast

Heat oil in a large skillet and sauté onion and pepper for 5 to 10 minutes until browned. Add beans and cook, mashing gently, for 2 to 3 minutes. Add remaining ingredients and stir over low heat for 5 to 10 minutes. (Depending on cottage cheese, sauce will turn completely smooth or some curds will remain.) Serve hot over bread base.

Serves 2 to 3
Major Protein

BOSTON ROAST

This American bean roast was popularized in the meat-saving era of World War II. It is tender and flavorful, good plain or with tomato sauce, and the cold leftovers can be used for sandwiches.

1 cup soft whole wheat bread crumbs or 2 slices bread
1½ cups grated cheese
2 cups cooked kidney beans or other red beans, drained and ground or chopped fine
¼ cup wheat germ
1 teaspoon grated onion
1 teaspoon to 1 tablespoon chili powder (depending on personal preferences)
1 teaspoon salt (omit if beans are salted)
pepper

Preheat oven to 350°F. Prepare bread crumbs, grated cheese, and ground beans (in that order if using the same utensil to avoid washing). Combine all ingredients and shape into a single loaf or 4 individual mounds on an oiled baking sheet. Bake for about 30 minutes until crusty, basting once or twice with oil during cooking.

Serves 4
Major Protein

PEANUT BUTTER LOAF

One of the easiest nut-grain loaves to assemble and very good eating served plain or with catsup or mustard.

1 cup peanut butter
1 cup soft whole wheat bread crumbs
1 cup cooked brown rice
1 stalk celery, chopped
1 egg, beaten
1 cup milk
1 teaspoon soy sauce

Preheat oven to 350°F. Combine all ingredients in a mixing bowl and stir until evenly blended. Place in a well-oiled 8-inch loaf pan and bake for 45 minutes until top is firm and brown. Cool for at least 10 minutes in pan before turning out. Serve warm, at room temperature, or chilled.

Serves 4 to 6

Major Protein

Menu Suggestions: Serve with any fresh vegetables and a fruit or vegetable salad. For a more substantial meal, begin with a light vegetable soup.

LAYERED TOMATO CASSEROLE

1 pound tomatoes (3 medium)
1 cup fresh whole wheat bread crumbs
¼ cup wheat germ
1 cup grated cheese
½ teaspoon salt
¼ cup chopped onion
2 tablespoons minced parsley
1 teaspoon dried basil
2 tablespoons butter

Preheat oven to 350°F. Slice tomatoes thin. Combine bread crumbs, wheat germ, cheese, and salt.

Butter a shallow 1-quart baking dish and layer one third crumbs, one half tomato slices, one half chopped onion, 1 tablespoon parsley, and ½ teaspoon basil. Repeat the layers and top with remaining crumbs. Dot with butter. Bake for about 30 minutes until browned.

Serves 2 to 3

Major Protein

Note: To serve 4 to 6, double the recipe and bake in a shallow 9 x 13-inch pan.

MATZO LASAGNE

Elements from two different worlds form a happy liaison that is easy to make with basic pantry ingredients.

2 medium onions, thinly sliced
6 whole wheat matzos
3 cups cottage cheese
1 cup shredded mozzarella cheese
½ cup shredded cheddar cheese
4 medium tomatoes, sliced, or 2 cups canned, drained tomatoes
½ teaspoon salt
pepper
1½ cups tomato juice

Preheat oven to 350°F. Place half the onion slices in a shallow 2-quart baking dish generously greased with oil. Cover with 2 of the matzos, broken into pieces if necessary. Top with 1½ cups cottage cheese, ½ cup mozzarella, ¼ cup cheddar, and half the tomatoes. Season with half the salt and pepper. Top with 2 more matzos, remaining onion, cottage cheese, shredded cheese, tomato, and seasonings. Cover with last 2 matzos. Pour juice evenly over top; cover and bake for 20 minutes.

Uncover, sprinkle with additional cheese if desired, and bake 10 minutes longer. Let sit at room temperature for 10 minutes before serving.

Serves 4 to 6

Major Protein

Note: Transfer any leftovers to a pan that holds them comfortably and refrigerate. To restore, add a little tomato juice, cover and bake in a 350° to 375°F. oven for about 10 minutes until hot and bubbly. Uncover, top with some shredded cheese, and return to the oven to melt.

QUICK, CREAMY ONION PIE

The richness of the filling is surprising in view of the modest ingredients. This is an extremely easy pie to make.

1 9-inch Caraway Cracker Crumb Crust (recipe follows)
3 large onions, thinly sliced
1 tablespoon oil
1 tablespoon butter
2 cups creamed cottage cheese
¼ teaspoon salt
pepper
⅛ teaspoon cayenne
1 teaspoon paprika

Preheat oven to 400°F. Bake crust for about 10 minutes until lightly colored. While crust bakes, combine onions, oil, and butter in a 1-quart pot. Cover and stew over low heat for 10 minutes until onion is softened.

Mix cottage cheese with salt and pepper. Place in baked crust. Top with onions and distribute cayenne and paprika evenly over surface.

Return to oven for 15 minutes. Let sit for at least 10 minutes before serving; serve while still warm or at room temperature. Chill leftovers and serve cold.

Serves 4

Major Protein

Menu Suggestions: Serve with a large salad or a cooked vegetable plate.

SAVORY CRACKER CRUMB CRUST

¾ cup rye, corn, or whole wheat cracker crumbs or a combination
½ cup wheat germ
¼ teaspoon salt
2 tablespoons oil

Combine crumbs, wheat germ, and salt. Stir in oil until completely moistened. Press over bottom and sides of a 9-inch pie pan. Chill for at least 15 minutes or prebake in a 400°F. oven, depending on recipe directions.

Makes a 9-inch pie crust

Variation: For *Caraway Cracker Crumb Crust,* add ½ tablespoon caraway seeds.

SIDE DISHES

TANGY COLESLAW

This coleslaw with its light tomato flavor is especially good in Veggie Reubens.

3 to 4 cups finely or coarsely shredded cabbage
¼ teaspoon dry mustard
1 tablespoon lemon juice
2 tablespoons tomato juice
2 tablespoons oil
2 tablespoons mayonnaise

Place cabbage in a bowl. Combine remaining ingredients and mix well with cabbage. If made in advance, chill before serving.

Serves 4

AMERICAN-STYLE POTATO SALAD

1 pound potatoes, steamed and sliced (about 3 cups)
¼ cup mayonnaise
¼ cup yogurt
1½ tablespoons wine vinegar
¼ teaspoon salt
pepper
¼ cup chopped scallions
¼ cup chopped sweet green or red pepper
paprika

Cooked potatoes should be at room temperature or chilled. Combine mayonnaise, yogurt, vinegar, salt, and pepper to make a smooth dressing. Add scallion, sweet pepper, and potatoes; stir gently to coat well without breaking up potatoes.

Chill if not for immediate use, but remove about 15 minutes before serving. Sprinkle liberally with paprika.

Serves 4

RICOTTA–CUCUMBER SALAD

This is similar to potato salad in consistency and flavor.

1 cup ricotta cheese
1 medium cucumber, peeled and cubed
2 scallions, thinly sliced
½ teaspoon dried basil
salt
pepper

Combine all ingredients, adding salt if desired and pepper for a little bite. Serve on a bed of lettuce. Garnish with olives and pimientos.

Serves 4

Minor Protein

GUACAMOLE

The standard Mexican avocado "salad." Serve with tacos or mound on lettuce leaves on individual serving plates.

1 clove garlic
1 large or 2 small very ripe avocados
1 tablespoon lemon juice

1 small tomato, finely chopped
½ teaspoon salt
¼ teaspoon hot pepper sauce

Cut garlic in half and rub bowl well with cut surface. Discard. Cut avocado meat from peel and mash in serving bowl with fork. Add remaining ingredients. Serve immediately or place avocado pit in center, cover, and refrigerate until serving. (This will keep the avocado from turning brown.)
Serves 4

PIMIENTO–CHEESE DIP

½ cup yogurt
2 whole pimientos, or 4-ounce jar, drained
1 teaspoon Dijon mustard
2 teaspoons soy sauce
1 cup (about 4 ounces) cheddar cheese, cut in small pieces

Puree yogurt, pimientos, mustard, and soy sauce in a blender or a processor with a steel chopping blade. With machine running, gradually feed in cheese. Puree until smooth. Stop machine and scrape dip from sides with rubber spatula as necessary.
Makes 1¼ cups
Minor Protein
Note: See "Appetizers and Hors d'Oeuvres" for similar dips.

COLD STUFFED TOMATO

Use this dish to add a little protein to a pasta or bean entrée.

2 medium tomatoes
1 slice whole grain bread
1 tablespoon wine vinegar
⅛ teaspoon salt
pepper
1 tablespoon minced parsley
1 teaspoon minced fresh basil or ½ teaspoon dried
2 tablespoons cottage cheese

Cut a thin slice from top of tomatoes and scoop out pulp, leaving a shell. Invert to drain. Save liquid for stock and dice pulp.
Dice bread and mix with tomato pulp, vinegar, salt, a generous amount of fresh pepper, and herbs. Let stand until well moistened (10 minutes is long enough but this can also be prepared hours in advance). Before serving, mix cottage cheese with bread filling and pack into tomato shells.
Serves 2
Minor Protein

PIZZA SALAD

An excellent booster for pasta and bean-based entrées.

4 cups shredded greens
1 medium tomato, cut in thin wedges
½ cup shredded mozzarella cheese
¼ cup shredded provolone cheese
½ green pepper cut in thin slivers
¼ cup sliced olives (optional)
¼ cup sliced mushrooms (optional)
3 tablespoons grated Parmesan cheese
½ cup Light Italian Tomato Dressing (page 57) or Italian Tomato Vinaigrette (page 288)

Spread greens out in individual bowls or a single shallow dish. Top with tomato. Cover with shredded cheeses. Decorate with green pepper, olives, and mushrooms. Coat with grated Parmesan. Add dressing at serving time.
Serves 4
Minor Protein

VEGETABLE COTTAGE CHEESE

This high-protein salad can be served on a bed of greens, in avocado shells, on a baked potato, on sliced tomatoes, or on crackers.

1 cup cottage cheese
1 cup mixed vegetables from the following, chopped as fine or coarse as you wish:

carrot	scallion
green pepper	cucumber
celery	tomato
radish	parsley

1 tablespoon cider vinegar or lemon juice
2 tablespoons yogurt, sour cream, or mayonnaise
½ teaspoon of one of the following:

paprika	dill
soy sauce	oregano
cumin	celery seed
caraway seeds	

2 dashes hot pepper sauce (optional)

Combine all ingredients to taste.
Serves 4
Minor Protein
Note: If portion sizes are doubled, this can serve as a Major Protein main course dish for lunch or a light supper.

COLD TAHINI BEANS

¼ to ⅓ cup water or cooking liquid from beans
2 tablespoons tahini
⅛ teaspoon cayenne
lemon juice
salt (omit if beans are salted)
3 cups cooked chick-peas, white beans, or fava beans, drained

Stir liquid gradually into tahini until smooth and of thin gravy consistency. Add cayenne, a little lemon juice to taste, and salt (if beans are unsalted). Stir in beans and serve.
Serves 4
Minor Protein
Note: This recipe can be used to improve the flavor of canned beans.

MACARONI SALAD

A new version of a common buffet salad that is rich in flavor and protein.

1 cup ricotta cheese
½ cup yogurt
1 teaspoon prepared mustard
4 cups cooked small whole wheat pasta (elbows, small shells, spirals)
2 tablespoons chopped green olives
2 tablespoons chopped sweet red or green pepper
2 minced scallions
1 tablespoon minced parsley
salt
pepper

Mix ricotta, yogurt, and mustard until it has a smooth, mayonnaise-like consistency. If too stiff, add 1 to 2 tablespoons water. Stir pasta and remaining ingredients into dressing, seasoning to taste with salt and pepper.
Serves 4 to 6
Minor Protein
Note: Cottage cheese can be used instead of ricotta for a chunky rather than a smooth dressing.

MACARONI AND CHEESE SALAD

Wholesome enough to serve as an entrée at lunchtime or for a light dinner.

½ cup yogurt
¼ cup mayonnaise
4 cups cooked small whole wheat pasta (elbows, spirals, shells, or broad noodles)
¼ cup chopped scallion
¼ cup chopped green pepper or relish (see recipes pages 437–440)
1 cup tiny cubes cheddar or colby cheese
1 cup cooked beans, corn, or raw peas

Mix yogurt and mayonnaise until smooth. Add remaining ingredients and stir to coat.
Serves 4 to 6
Minor Protein; Major Protein with large portions

COLD PASTA WITH TOMATO DRESSING

Prepare with fresh cooked or leftover pasta.

2 large tomatoes, cut in wedges
2 thin slices red onion, cut in quarters
6 sliced olives
2 tablespoons oil
1 tablespoon wine vinegar
½ teaspoon salt
pepper
5 to 6 fresh basil leaves, minced, or 2 tablespoons minced parsley
1 cup slivered provolone and/or mozzarella cheese
2 cups cooked whole wheat pasta

Combine tomato, onion, olives, oil, vinegar, and seasonings, and mix well. Let stand for a few minutes. Add cheese and pasta to tomato dressing. Serve at room temperature.
Serves 4
Minor Protein

CRACKED WHEAT PILAF

A fast cooking whole grain.

1 cup cracked wheat (sometimes called bulgur)
1 small onion, chopped

1½ tablespoons oil
½ teaspoon salt
2 cups water or vegetable broth

Sauté cracked wheat and onion in oil until onion is transparent and wheat glazed. Add salt and liquid and bring to a boil. Cover and cook over low heat for 15 minutes until liquid is absorbed and grain tender. Lift cover partially to let steam escape.

Serves 4
Protein Complement
Note: This recipe allows for ½-cup servings and is meant as a side dish. To serve as a base under a main dish, double the portions.
Variation: For *Mushroom Pilaf,* sauté ¼ pound (1 heavy cup) diced mushrooms along with cracked wheat and onion.

BROWN "RICE-A-RONI"

Rice and pasta cooked together are more than twice as good as each cooked alone.

2 tablespoons butter
½ cup whole wheat spaghetti, broken into 1-inch pieces
1 cup uncooked brown rice
2 cups boiling water
1 tablespoon soy sauce
¼ teaspoon salt

Melt butter in a 2-quart pot, add spaghetti and rice, and sauté for 3 to 5 minutes until golden. Stir frequently and avoid overcooking. Add remaining ingredients, cover, and simmer over low heat until liquid is completely absorbed and grain is tender, about 45 minutes.

Serves 4
Protein Complement

BUTTER NUT GRAINS

To cheer up leftover grains.

1 cup mixed nuts including cashews, peanuts, sunflower and pumpkin seeds
3 cups cooked grains (one or more: brown rice, cracked wheat, kasha, millet)
2 tablespoons butter

In large ungreased skillet brown nuts over medium heat for 5 to 10 minutes, watching carefully so they do not burn. Add grains; stir briefly, breaking up any clumps with a fork. Dot top with butter, turn heat as low as you can, cover and cook 5 minutes until heated through.

Serves 4 to 6
Minor Protein

PARMESAN TOAST

Good with Italian food and vegetable meals in need of a little boost.

2 thin slices rye or whole wheat bread
butter
2 tablespoons grated Parmesan cheese (or romano, locatelli, sardo, etc.)

Toast bread lightly and spread with a thin layer of butter. Top each slice with 1 tablespoon grated cheese. Broil or top brown in toaster oven until bubbly.

Serves 1 to 2
Minor Protein

GARLIC-SESAME BREAD

A good accompaniment to Italian meals when a whole wheat Italian loaf is not available.

4 slices whole wheat bread
1½ tablespoons tahini
1½ tablespoons olive oil
1 small clove garlic, minced
pinch salt
sesame seeds

Toast bread lightly. Beat together tahini, oil, garlic, and salt. Spread liberally on toast. Sprinkle lightly with sesame seeds.

Broil or top brown in toaster oven just before serving so that spread bubbles a bit; watch carefully so that seeds don't burn, and serve while hot.

Serves 2 to 4
Variation: For *Parsley–Sesame Bread,* replace garlic with 1 tablespoon dried parsley.

BREAD & SPREAD

This delicious, nourishing spread for bread replaces butter in many health-conscious kitchens.

½ cup tahini
1 tablespoon soy sauce
2 tablespoons lemon juice
about 1 tablespoon water
1 clove garlic, crushed
dill, cumin, parsley

Using a fork, beat together tahini, soy sauce, and lemon juice to make a thick paste. Beat in a little water to make a thick spread. Flavor with garlic and other herbs from those suggested here or use your favorites.

Makes ½ cup
Protein Complement
Note: Stored in the refrigerator, this will keep one week.

VEGETABLE COOKERY

The wholefoods short-order chef discards the boiling of vegetables in favor of simple steaming, baking, or stir-frying techniques, described fully in "On Cooking."

STIR-STEAMED VEGETABLES

Steaming vegetables by adding a little liquid to the pan after stir-frying gives them a more tender texture. The use of butter makes a rich sauce that needs no seasoning, allowing you to appreciate the taste of the vegetable.

2 tablespoons butter, or half butter, half oil
1 medium onion, sliced
4 cups thinly sliced vegetables of choice (see Variations)
½ cup water

Heat fat in a wok or skillet, add vegetables, and stir-fry over medium-high heat for 5 to 10 minutes until edges begin to brown. Add water, cover, reduce heat, and cook 5 to 10 minutes longer until tender.
Serves 4

Variations: This recipe can be prepared with one vegetable or a combination. For *Winter Stir-Steamed Vegetables,* prepare a mixture of peeled parsnips, peeled turnips, carrots, cauliflower, and leeks.

For *Summer Stir-Steamed Vegetables,* combine young carrots, zucchini, green beans, fresh corn, and peas. If desired, add some tomato to the steaming step. If you prepare vegetables in chunks rather than thin slices, increase the steaming time to about 20 minutes for "summer" vegetables, 30 for "winter" recommendations.

STEAMED BROCCOLI

All parts of the broccoli are edible, including the leaves and stems. The stems are often difficult to chew because of the tough, fibrous layer on the surface. Underneath this, however, is a tender, succulent layer, which is why you should peel the stalks thinly if you haven't enjoyed them up to now.

Clean broccoli, peel if desired, and separate into trees. If stalks are thick, slit to shorten cooking time. For more information, see the Table of Specific Vegetable Preparation in "On Cooking," page 497.

Place on vegetable steamer and steam for 10 minutes. If not tender, cook 5 minutes longer. Serve with fresh lemon wedges.
1 pound serves 4 to 6

CORN ON THE COB

Contrary to popular practice, corn needs only a few minutes to cook to perfection.

unshucked corn

Bring water to a boil in a large covered pot. Do not add salt or sugar. When water is boiling, remove husks and silky strands from corn and plunge into hot water. When boiling resumes, cook for 3 minutes, then drain and serve.
Note: If you do not wish to butter your corn, try seasoning it with soy sauce.

PAN-FRIED ASPARAGUS

When asparagus is quickly stir-fried it becomes sweet and crunchy and is as much fun to eat as candy.

1½ to 2 pounds asparagus
2 tablespoons butter/oil
salt
pepper

Trim asparagus by snapping the ends (see Table of Specific Vegetable Preparation, page 497) and slice into 1½-inch lengths. Heat fat in a skillet or wok and stir-fry asparagus over high heat for 5 minutes until crisp-tender. Season to taste with salt and pepper.
Serves 4

PAN-FRIED CABBAGE

A universally overcooked vegetable gets proper treatment here.

2 tablespoons oil/butter
3 tablespoons sesame seeds
6 cups cabbage, sliced into strips (about ¾ pound)

Heat fat in a large skillet and toast sesame seeds lightly for 1 minute. Add cabbage, stir to coat with fat and seeds, cover, and cook over medium heat for about 10 minutes until wilted. Stir once again just before serving.
Serves 4

ORANGE-GLAZED CARROTS

Carrots glazed by a delicate, sweet sauce.

1 tablespoon butter
1 pound carrots, cut into coins
½ cup orange juice
1 tablespoon honey

Melt butter in a 1-quart saucepan or skillet. Add carrots and stir to coat. Add orange juice, cover and simmer for 10 minutes until just tender. Stir in honey, raise heat and boil rapidly, uncovered, until liquid is reduced.
Serves 4
Variation: For *Orange-Glazed Parsnips,* replace carrots with peeled, sliced parsnips.

HOT DRESSED VEGETABLES

Fresh cooked vegetables in a hot salad dressing.

¾ pound vegetable of choice (broccoli, cauliflower, green beans, beets, potato), cut in manageable pieces
2 tablespoons wine or cider vinegar
¼ cup oil
dash prepared mustard
¼ teaspoon salt
½ teaspoon soy sauce
½ teaspoon dried chervil or 1 tablespoon fresh parsley
1 hard-cooked egg, chopped

Steam vegetables. Combine vinegar, oil, mustard, and salt in a small saucepan and bring to a boil. Remove from heat and beat in soy sauce, herbs, and the egg. Pour warm dressing over hot vegetable in serving dish.
Serves 4
Variation: Use ½ cup prepared oil and vinegar dressing as the base, heating and seasoning as above.

VEGETABLES WITH RICH CRUMB TOPPING

A savory crumb topping can add richness to your favorite vegetables and interest to less favored ones. Try it out on those who shun vegetables.

1 pound vegetables
1½ cups mixed fresh or dried whole grain bread crumbs, wheat germ, and nut meal
¼ teaspoon salt (optional)
3 tablespoons oil/butter
1 clove garlic, minced (optional)

Steam vegetables until just tender. Make a mixture of crumbs, wheat germ, and nuts, including at least some ground sunflower seeds, soy nuts, or peanuts. Ingredients can be used in any proportion but about half bread crumbs is a good measure. Season with salt if desired.

Heat fat in a 10-inch skillet and cook garlic briefly (if included). Add crumbs and sauté quickly, stirring until crisp and golden. Place vegetables on a serving plate and top with crumbs.

Serves 4

Minor Protein

Note: Vegetables that are especially good this way include leeks, cauliflower, green beans, carrots, sweet potatoes. Many seasonings can be added to the bread crumbs including thyme and sage for a "stuffing" flavor, oregano and basil for Italian vegetables, cinnamon, nutmeg, and ginger for those suited to sweet tastes, and nutritional yeast for just about everything.

CHEESE-STUFFED MUSHROOMS

16 medium to large mushrooms
½ cup creamed cottage cheese or ricotta cheese
¼ cup wheat germ
½ teaspoon salt
1 teaspoon oregano
pepper
paprika

Preheat oven or toaster oven to 400°F. Remove stems from mushrooms, clean and chop. Mix chopped mushroom stems with cottage cheese, wheat germ, salt, oregano, and pepper.

Clean caps and stuff with cheese filling. Place, filling up, in a well-oiled baking dish; sprinkle liberally with paprika and bake for 10 minutes until hot and tender. Serve at once.

Serves 4

Minor Protein

Note: Mushrooms can be stuffed in advance and refrigerated until baking time.

MOZZARELLA-STUFFED TOMATO

Use this stuffed tomato as an accompaniment to pasta or grain entrées, or double the serving sizes and use on any plain pasta or grain dish instead of sauce.

4 medium tomatoes
salt
1 cup finely diced mozzarella cheese (about 4 ounces)
1 tablespoon chopped fresh basil or 1 teaspoon dried
pepper
olive oil

Cut tops from tomatoes and scoop out seeds and liquid with a small spoon. Leave pulp intact. Salt lightly and invert for 10 to 15 minutes to drain. Preheat oven or toaster oven to 350°F. Mix diced cheese with basil and pack into tomatoes. Season generously with pepper.

Place tomatoes close together in a baking dish well coated with olive oil. Drizzle a little oil on each tomato. Bake for about 15 minutes until tomato is hot and cheese melted.

Serves 4

Minor Protein; Major Protein when doubled

Note: This can be prepared in advance and baked just before serving.

TOASTED NOODLES

This is a simple way to make a great snack, sandwich accompaniment or crunchy noodles for Chinese food. It is easily made in the toaster oven or broiler with leftover spaghetti.

whole wheat spaghetti, broken into 1-inch pieces
oil

Cook spaghetti in boiling salted water as usual until just tender, about 10 minutes. Drain well, cool under cold running water, and pat dry. When pasta is dry, coat lightly with oil, using 1 tablespoon per 2 cups spaghetti. Place on broiler tray and brown, tossing a few times so it cooks evenly. It is best when served soon after cooking.

Makes 2 cups; serves 4

Protein Complement

BROILER POTATO CRISPS

Crisp broiled potato slices can be served hot from the broiler or munched like potato chips with dips.

raw potatoes (allow 1 medium potato per serving)
oil
salt (optional)

Scrub potatoes and, if time permits, chill them. Slice into ⅛-inch-thick rounds using a knife or the slicing blade of a food processor. Place on an oiled baking sheet and brush with oil.

Broil about 3½ inches beneath heat for about 10 minutes until golden. Turn and broil 5 to 10 minutes longer. Check frequently to avoid overcooking. Some pieces will cook more quickly than others and should be removed when done. (Alternately, potatoes can be "crisped" in a 450°F. oven for about 10 minutes.) Sprinkle lightly with salt, if desired, before serving.

Note: For individual servings, prepare in toaster oven. Potato Crisps can be seasoned at the table with a light sprinkling of vinegar instead of salt.

DAVID'S PAN FRIES

If you want to brown potatoes on the outside and get them tender on the inside without deep-frying or preboiling them, keep the heat low under the pan and be patient. These are exceptional with eggs.

1 to 1½ pounds potatoes
oil
salt
pepper

Scrub potatoes and slice ¼ inch thick. Heat enough oil to cover the surface of a heavy skillet. Add as many potato slices as will fit without piling. If you need more room, use another pan.

Cook over low heat, shaking the pan and loosening with a spatula every so often. Check progress by lifting with tongs or a spatula (do not pierce with a fork). Keep close watch once browning begins. When potatoes are a deep bronze, turn and cook the other side. It will brown faster than the first side. Cooking time is highly variable but plan on about 45 minutes. Season to taste with salt and pepper and serve.

Serves 4

THE STANDARD BAKED POTATO

By now most people know that it's not the potato but what we generally put on it that has given it a "fattening" reputation. The average potato furnishes no more calories than the average orange or a slice of bread—but even so, what a delightful indulgence it is. Soft and steamy inside, brown and crunchy on the surface, the baked potato really doesn't need anything at all to improve it. In case you don't agree, try any of the suggested toppings that follow the directions for baking. If you select one of the Minor Protein toppings, the baked potato will practically serve as a complete entrée.

Before we go on to tell you the right way to bake potatoes, we'd like to suggest "a potato party" for your next group function. There is no easier way to entertain than to pack your oven full of potatoes and then serve them on a platter with a broad array of toppings. It adds up to very little work for the cook, minimal clean-up, and a good time for everyone.

medium-size potatoes (about 3 per pound)

Preheat oven to 400°F. Scrub potato clean and cut out any sprouts or eyes. Dry well with paper towels. Pierce in several places with the prongs of a fork to prevent bursting in the oven. *Do not wrap in foil.*

Place on a baking sheet or directly on the rack of the oven and bake for about 45 minutes. When done, potato will yield readily to gentle pressure with a mitted hand, or a skewer will easily pierce through to the center. Naturally, larger potatoes require longer baking, small ones less.

Note: Potatoes can actually bake in oven heats ranging from 325° to 450°F. in case you want to cook them with other foods at the same time. Adjust the timing up or down according to the temperature.

When you bake potatoes directly in hot coals, wrapping in foil *is* recommended, but to prevent steaming the foil should have several punctures. Before serving, unwrap them and let the skin char a few minutes.

Baked Potato Toppings
  Chopped pimiento
  Melted lemon butter, plain or with chives
  Prepared mustard
  Mushrooms marinated in oil and vinegar
  Spiced Spinach (page 250)

Minor Protein Toppings
  Cottage cheese and chives or scallions
  Vegetable Cottage Cheese (page 47)
  Whipped Cottage Cream (page 56)
  Shredded cheese
  Shredded cheese and a spoonful of stewed tomatoes
  Melted mozzarella cheese and tomato sauce for Potato Pizzaiola
  Feta cheese or blue cheese mashed with yogurt and coarse black pepper
  Poached eggs
  Peanut butter
  Spinach–Yogurt Salad (page 299)
  Curry Dip (page 64)

BAKED SWEET POTATOES AND YAMS

  Sweet potatoes or yams

Preheat oven to 350° to 375°F. Scrub potatoes and dry them. Prick in several places with a fork to prevent them from bursting in the oven. Bake for 40 to 50 minutes until potato yields when pressed gently with a mitted hand.

REFRIED BEANS

Refried beans, which are a Mexican staple, are really nothing more complicated than precooked beans mashed in hot oil.

  2 tablespoons oil
  1 small onion, chopped
  ½ to 1 tablespoon chili powder (optional)
  3 cups cooked pinto or kidney beans, drained

Heat oil in a 10- to 12-inch skillet and brown onion lightly. Add chili powder, if desired, and cook for 30 seconds. Add beans and mash with a potato masher or fork until beans are a thick mush. If necessary add a little bean cooking liquid to help soften the mixture. When completely mashed, raise the heat and cook until quite dry.
Serves 4
Protein Complement
Variation: For *Refried Beans with Cheese,* scatter some Jack or cheddar cheese over the beans after mashing, cover pan, and remove from heat to melt.

VERY QUICK CURRIED CHICK-PEAS

A lightly spiced bean accompaniment.

  1 clove garlic, chopped
  1 small onion, chopped
  1 tablespoon oil
  2 teaspoons curry powder
  1 cup chopped tomato
  3 cups cooked chick-peas, drained

Sauté garlic and onion in oil for 2 to 3 minutes until tender and transparent. Add curry powder and sauté 1 minute longer. Add tomatoes and chick-peas, cover and cook for about 10 minutes until tomato is soft and beans are hot.
Serves 4
Protein Complement
Note: For a spicier taste, increase curry powder to 1 tablespoon.

SOUPS

INSTANT SOUP

This is a basic recipe that can vary depending on your pantry. Only the base itself is constant.

Base
  2 cups water
  ¼ to ½ cup tomato juice, or 1 tablespoon tomato paste diluted in ¼ cup warm water, or a few Tomato Cubes (see page 430)
  1 to 2 tablespoons soy sauce
  1 scallion, thinly sliced

Vegetable Enrichment
  Shredded lettuce or spinach
  Grated carrot
  Grated zucchini
  Corn kernels
  Any cooked vegetable or bean
  Any cooked grain
  Couscous
  Tofu

Seasoning Ingredients
  Vegetable bouillon (add initially)
  Split clove garlic (add initially)
  Pinch turmeric (add just before serving)
  ½ tablespoon nutritional yeast (add just before serving to thicken)
  ½ tablespoon oil (add just before serving for richness)
  Sesame salt (add at table)

Combine all Base ingredients, varying the amount of tomato and soy sauce to taste. Bring to a boil and add any of the items listed under Vegetable Enrichment. Cook for 5 minutes. If uncooked pasta is added, increase cooking to 10 to 15 minutes. Season with any of the Seasoning Ingredients, as directed in that list. If no grain is added, crumble whole grain crackers into the soup before eating.
Serves 2

TAMARI BROTH

A basic broth that you can use to create any one or a combination of variations.

  8 scallions, minced
  1 tablespoon oil
  4 cups water
  ¼ cup soy sauce
  ½ teaspoon salt

Cook scallions in oil for 1 minute to soften. Add water, bring to a boil, and simmer for 10 minutes. Add soy sauce and salt and return to a boil.
Serves 4
Variations: For *Tamari Broth with Greens,* shred 4 outer leaves of romaine lettuce and add when water comes to a boil.

For *Tamari Broth with Tofu,* add 8 ounces sliced fresh or frozen tofu after water has simmered for 5 minutes.

Add soy sauce and salt and simmer 10 minutes longer.

For *Tamari Broth with Grain,* divide ½ pound cooked noodles or 2 cups cooked rice into 4 serving bowls. Pour basic broth or a variation over the grain. Consume the grain with chopsticks and drink the broth left at the end.

EGG DROP SOUP

Add interest and substance to any broth with this simple technique.

  3½ cups vegetable broth, tomato broth, or Tamari Broth
  2 teaspoons soy sauce (omit with Tamari Broth)
  2 scallions, thinly sliced
  1 egg, slightly beaten

Bring broth to a boil. Add soy sauce and scallions and simmer for 5 minutes. Just before serving, drizzle egg into simmering soup in a slow, steady stream. When egg "sets" or coagulates, give the soup a stir and serve.
Serves 4
Variation: For a slightly tart soup, add 1 tablespoon lemon juice to the broth initially.

PORTUGUESE BREAD AND GARLIC SOUP

This very substantial soup, made from the most modest ingredients, can be prepared in 10 minutes.

  4½ cups water
  4 cloves garlic, cut in pieces
  1 teaspoon salt
  4 to 6 slices (6 ounces) whole grain bread
  pepper
  parsley

Bring water to a boil. Add garlic, salt, and bread torn into tiny pieces; simmer for 5 minutes, or until very soft. Mash soup with a spoon or fork. Return briefly to a boil. Season generously with fresh ground pepper, adjust salt if necessary to taste, and sprinkle with parsley.
Serves 4
Menu Suggestions: To make this into

a Minor Protein, put ¼ cup or more of diced mozzarella, provolone, Swiss, or other stringy melting cheese in each bowl before adding hot soup; or top each bowl with ¼ cup of grated cheese.

CREAMED CORN SOUP

2 cups corn kernels
4 cups milk
¼ cup nonfat dry milk powder
1 thin slice onion
2 teaspoons salt
2 slices whole grain bread

Combine all ingredients in a blender or a processor fitted with a steel chopping blade. Process at high speed for about 30 seconds, or until corn is coarsely pureed. Pour into a saucepan and warm over moderate heat without boiling.
Serves 4 to 6
Major Protein
Note: This soup can be prepared with whole, skim, or buttermilk, or the milk can be replaced with water and a total of 1¼ cups of nonfat dry milk powder.

RAW ONION MILK SOUP

Quick, delicate, and as soothing as "milk toast."

1½ cups milk
¼ teaspoon salt
1 cup thinly sliced onion
about 1 teaspoon butter
paprika or nutmeg
crackers or croutons

Bring milk just to the boiling point and remove from heat. Add salt and onion and mash with a wooden spoon to extract onion flavor. Cover and let sit for a few minutes.

If soup has cooled, warm through, then strain liquid into serving bowls, add a little butter to each, and sprinkle surface with paprika or nutmeg. Serve with crushed crackers or croutons.
Serves 2
Minor Protein
Note: The remaining onions will be quite sweet and mild. Refrigerate and use on salads and sandwiches.

BLENDER SALAD SOUP

Similar to a classic gazpacho but with all the vegetables chopped right along with the tomato, making it much quicker to prepare.

4 medium-size ripe tomatoes
½ large green pepper
½ small onion
1 small cucumber
1 clove garlic
¼ teaspoon hot pepper sauce
1 teaspoon salt
2 tablespoons olive oil
3 tablespoons wine vinegar
½ cup ice water
6 ice cubes

Quarter tomatoes; seed and slice green pepper; peel and slice onion and cucumber; peel garlic.

Place vegetables and remaining ingredients except ice in a blender or a processor fitted with a steel blade and blend for about 3 seconds, until vegetables are finely chopped but not reduced to puree. Spoon soup into bowls and place an ice cube in each so it becomes very cold.
Serves 6
Note: If blender or processor cannot handle this quantity, process in batches.

DRESSINGS AND SAUCES

WHIPPED COTTAGE CREAM

Use as a dressing on potato pancakes, baked potatoes, tacos, enchiladas, and anything else you might use sour cream on. This dressing is low in fat and calories and high in protein.

1 cup cottage cheese
1 tablespoon yogurt or milk, as needed
dash lemon juice

Puree cottage cheese until smooth in a processor fitted with a plastic blade or in a blender. Add yogurt or milk, if needed, to get the blender moving. If you have neither machine, cottage cheese can be pureed in a food mill or pressed through a sieve, then thinned by beating in the yogurt or milk with a fork or wire whisk. Season to taste with a little lemon juice for a "sour" effect.

Makes 1 cup
Minor Protein

BOTTOM-OF-THE-BOWL DRESSING

If you don't care about having extra dressing to store, the easiest approach to salad making is to prepare the dressing in the bottom of the bowl. The greens and vegetables are placed on top, and the salad is tossed just before eating to bring up the dressing and coat the vegetables.

For a salad for one:
Squeeze juice of ½ small lemon in the bottom of a bowl. Dip the tip of a clean fork into your favorite prepared mustard and beat lemon juice around the bowl with this fork.

Gradually beat in about 1 tablespoon oil so that dressing becomes creamy and spreads around bottom and slightly up sides of the bowl. Taste and adjust with salt, pepper, and more oil or lemon to taste. If desired, add some chervil, parsley, basil, or other favorite seasoning. When dressing is to your taste, prepare the salad.

For a salad for two:
Use ½ medium to large lemon, dip deeper into the mustard, and increase the oil proportionately. Double this recipe to serve up to 4. After this number, the dressing is best made in a separate container.

REVISIONIST DRESSING

This is the American Wholefoods version of Russian Dressing.

⅓ **cup mayonnaise**
⅔ **cup yogurt**
½ **cup tomato juice**
1 **teaspoon soy sauce**
¼ **teaspoon hot pepper sauce**

Combine all ingredients and mix until smooth.

Makes 1½ cups
Minor Protein

LIGHT FRENCH TOMATO DRESSING

This is a very pleasing dressing with only one third the calories of standard salad dressings.

½ **cup tomato juice**
2 **tablespoons wine vinegar**
¼ **cup olive oil**
1 **clove garlic, split**
¼ **teaspoon salt**
1 **tablespoon minced fresh parsley or**
  1 **teaspoon dried chervil**
pepper
½ **teaspoon honey**

Combine all ingredients in a jar and shake to mix.

Makes 1 cup
Variations: For *Light Italian Tomato Dressing,* add ½ teaspoon dried oregano, ½ teaspoon dried basil, and a dash of hot pepper sauce.

For *Light Mexican Tomato Dressing,* replace some or all of the vinegar with fresh lemon or lime juice. Add 1 teaspoon chili powder and ¼ teaspoon hot pepper sauce.

THICK CREAMY BLUE CHEESE DRESSING

½ **cup yogurt**
2 **tablespoons mayonnaise**
¼ **cup crumbled blue or Roquefort cheese**

Combine all ingredients and mix well.

Makes ¾ cup
Minor Protein

BROWNED ONION RELISH

Use this as a garnish for burgers, egg dishes, or even a baked potato.

2 **medium onions cut in ¼-inch dice**
½ **tablespoon paprika**
1 **tablespoon oil**
1 **tablespoon soy sauce**

Toss onions with paprika in a large skillet until evenly colored. Pour oil over onions and stir to coat. Add soy sauce, place over low heat, cover, and cook for 15 minutes until tender. Stir occasionally. Serve warm or at room temperature.

Serves 2 to 3
Note: Refrigerate leftovers.

DOUBLE CHEESE SAUCE

Excellent on rarebits and vegetables, this cheese sauce has no starch thickener, less milk, about twice the cheese, and is much quicker to prepare than the traditional sauce.

1 tablespoon butter
2 cups shredded cheese, mostly cheddar mixed with some Edam, Muenster, or Jack for a mellow flavor
½ cup milk
¾ teaspoon prepared mustard
1½ teaspoons soy sauce
⅛ teaspoon cayenne

Melt butter in a small saucepan set on a heatproof pad or in top of a double boiler. Add cheese and stir with a wire whisk until it begins to melt. Gradually stir in milk and seasonings and cook, continuing to stir, until creamy and heated through. Be sure to keep heat extremely low and do not boil.

Makes 1½ cups; serves 4
Major Protein

15-MINUTE ITALIAN TOMATO SAUCE

A quick topping, using tomato juice or puree, for bean balls, pasta, eggplant, and hot hero sandwiches.

1 clove garlic, minced
1 medium green pepper, cut in thin 1-inch pieces
1 tablespoon oil (olive preferred)
1½ cups tomato juice or puree
1 tablespoon tomato paste
½ teaspoon oregano
½ teaspoon dried basil

Sauté garlic and pepper in oil for about 3 minutes until garlic begins to color. Stir in remaining ingredients, bring to a boil, and simmer uncovered for 10 minutes.

Makes 1½ cups; serves 2

Variations: Add ½ to 1 cup sliced mushrooms with peppers. For *Chunky Pasta Sauce,* add a chopped onion with the green pepper and 1 cup coarsely chopped cooked kidney beans to the remaining ingredients.

Note: Leftover tomato paste can be stored in ice cube trays in the freezer. Measure out 2 tablespoons per cube. Use without defrosting.

EMERGENCY MEXICAN TOMATO SAUCE

A last-minute sauce for diverse use on enchiladas, tacos, bean balls, etc.

½ small onion, chopped
1 clove garlic, chopped
2 teaspoons minced hot chili pepper or ¼ teaspoon cayenne
1 tablespoon oil
1 tablespoon chili powder
3 cups tomato juice or puree

Sauté onion, garlic, and hot pepper in oil for about 3 minutes until they just begin to color. Add chili powder (and cayenne, if you are using that instead of chili pepper) and cook briefly. Stir in tomato juice and simmer, uncovered, for 5 to 10 minutes until sauce is slightly thickened.

Makes 3 cups

QUICK MEXICAN HOT SAUCE

To be used in small amounts to add flavor and heat to beans, enchiladas, eggs, tacos, chili rellenos, etc., which may already have a milder sauce.

1 tablespoon minced onion
½ small clove garlic, minced
1 tablespoon oil
1-inch piece hot chili pepper, minced, or ⅛ teaspoon or more cayenne
½ tablespoon chili powder
¾ cup tomato juice
1 tablespoon lemon juice

Sauté onion, garlic, and hot pepper in oil for about 3 minutes until just beginning to color. Add chili powder (and cayenne if you are using that instead of chili pepper) and cook 1 minute longer. Add tomato juice and lemon juice and simmer, uncovered, for 5 to 10 minutes until slightly thickened. Use warm or cold.

Makes ⅔ cup (enough for 6 as a seasoning)

Note: Can be stored in a covered container in the refrigerator for up to 2 weeks.

QUICK BARBECUE SAUCE

A sauce for burgers, bean balls, plain beans, grains, or tofu.

1 small onion, chopped
1 small clove garlic, chopped
2 tablespoons oil
1 tablespoon chili powder
2 teaspoons honey
2 teaspoons prepared mustard
1½ cups tomato juice
2 tablespoons lemon juice

Sauté onion and garlic in oil for about 3 minutes until softened. Add chili powder and cook briefly. Add remaining ingredients, bring to a boil, and simmer, uncovered, for 5 to 10 minutes until slightly thickened.

Makes 1½ cups; serves 4

DESSERTS

BANANA SOFT-SERVE

It takes nothing more than a banana from the freezer to produce one of the creamiest, smoothest-textured frozen desserts around. It's hard to believe there is neither cream nor sweetening in this confection.

Place bananas, 1 per serving, directly in the freezer. They do not need to be peeled, but if you wish to, they must be wrapped airtight for freezing. Otherwise, the skin itself will serve as protection.

Just before serving, remove skin with a small paring knife, cut frozen banana in chunks, and place in a processor fitted with a steel blade or in the blender. Process until banana breaks up, passes the icy stage, and becomes creamy and

whipped with air. The consistency will be that of frozen custard. Spoon into a bowl, a paper cup, or a cone, and dig in.

Note: If peeling more than 1 or 2 frozen bananas at a time, protect fingers with gloves or a soft kitchen cloth.

Variations: You can add frozen berries or peaches and whip these with the banana, but for best texture at least half the mixture should be banana.

TORTONI

This simple yet luxurious Italian dessert is frozen in paper cups.

1 cup ricotta cheese
2 tablespoons honey
½ teaspoon almond extract
4 teaspoons finely ground almonds

Whip ricotta, honey, and almond extract with a rotary or electric beater until light and fluffy. Line a muffin tin with 4 paper liners and fill with mixture. Sprinkle each with 1 teaspoon ground almonds. Freeze. When solid, remove from tin and wrap in freezer bags or foil. Let stand for 10 to 15 minutes at room temperature to soften slightly before serving.

Serves 4
Minor Protein
Note: These are a mere 130 calories each when made with part-skim milk ricotta.

PINEAPPLE SHERBET

You can turn canned pineapple into a light, refreshing dessert in minutes with some advance planning. You should allow at least 3 hours to freeze pineapple and can keep the can in the freezer for as long as 3 months.

20-ounce can crushed pineapple in unsweetened juice, frozen in can until solid

Just before serving, remove both ends of the can and push the frozen mass into the blender or a food processor fitted with a steel blade. Process until fruit is of sherbet consistency, stopping and stirring with a rubber spatula as needed until mixture is smooth. Serve immediately.

Serves 6

Note: A mere 60 calories per serving, this sherbet is not very sweet; although a little honey can be added, it is best unsweetened so that its delicate pineapple flavor can be appreciated. Leftovers can be refrozen and served with or without reprocessing.

QUICK-COOKING CUSTARD

For custard lovers who won't take the time to bake it just for themselves, this quick top-of-the-stove version is quite acceptable. Although it does not have the fine, smooth texture of the baked, it is nonetheless tender and just as flavorful.

1 egg
¾ cup milk (whole preferred)
2 tablespoons honey or a combination of honey and maple syrup or molasses
¼ teaspoon vanilla extract
nutmeg

Beat egg with milk, sweetening, and vanilla, using a fork or wire whisk. Pour into two custard cups. Sprinkle with nutmeg.

Place a wire rack in the bottom of a pot deep enough to hold custard cups when covered. Place filled cups on rack. Add enough hot water to reach about halfway up the cups. Bring water to a boil; cover pot and cook over fairly low heat, keeping water just at a boil for about 15 minutes until custard is set and knife inserted comes out clean. Transfer to a rack to cool to room temperature, then chill.

Serves 2
Minor Protein

FAVORITE FRUIT SALAD

Almost any combination of fruit can serve you well in fruit salad, but to make the mixture extra special we have two recommendations: walnuts and dates.

2 apples, peeled and diced
2 bananas, peeled and diced
other fruits in season as desired
juice of 3 oranges
8 to 12 dates
generous amount walnut pieces

Combine apples and bananas with other fruits in season in a bowl. Add orange juice to the fruit to preserve the color and furnish a syrup. Cut dates into small pieces and add to fruit. Top with an impressive amount of nuts.

Serves 4

DRIED FRUIT COMPOTE

Stewed dried fruit keeps for weeks in the refrigerator and can be a great asset for a quick dessert or even a breakfast combined with yogurt.

2 cups dried fruit (prunes, raisins, peaches, apricots, figs, and apples in any proportion)
2 cups water
1 cinnamon stick
2 thin slices unpeeled orange
2 thin slices unpeeled lemon

Combine all ingredients in a saucepan and bring to a boil. Cover, remove from heat, and let cool to room temperature. Transfer to storage container and chill several hours before using.

Makes about 1 quart

STEAMED APPLES

For any less than 6 servings, steaming rather than baking apples has many advantages: it takes less time, uses less energy, and allows partial cooking in advance with easy reheating just before serving without inconvenience to the cook.

1 to 5 apples
½ to 2½ tablespoons honey or maple syrup
raisins and nuts (optional)

Wash apples, peel upper third, and remove core. Place bottom-up on steamer and steam for 10 minutes.

Invert and drizzle a little honey or maple syrup over exposed peeled flesh and into hollow. If desired, raisins and nuts can be inserted into the core space. Continue steaming until apples are fork-tender, about 10 minutes for medium apples. Serve warm, garnished, if desired, with a little yogurt, sour cream, plain cream, or ice cream, and a sprinkling of cinnamon, nutmeg, and grated nutmeats.

Serves 1 to 5

Note: If prepared in advance, under-cook slightly and warm just before serving by steaming for 2 minutes. Since only 5 apples fit comfortably in the steaming basket at one time, baking is a more efficient method for 6 or more servings.

BROILED ORANGE

Broiling brings out the sweetness of an orange and makes an excellent low-calorie, fat- and sugar-free dessert. It is especially welcome in winter when cold desserts seem less appealing. How-ever, the heating of citrus fruit on a regular basis is not recommended as it destroys vitamin C.

1 good-size eating orange
¼ teaspoon cinnamon
⅛ teaspoon nutmeg

Cut orange in half crosswise and re-move any seeds. Using a serrated grapefruit knife, cut around each sec-tion. Sprinkle some cinnamon and nut-meg over each half. Broil for 5 minutes, or until juice begins to bubble and orange is heated throughout. Serve at once.

Serves 2

BUTTERED PEARS

A delicate yet very comforting winter dessert.

2 tablespoons butter
1 tablespoon lemon juice
2 tablespoons honey
4 medium pears
nutmeg

Melt butter in a large skillet. Stir in lemon and honey. While butter melts, peel pears and cut lengthwise into eighths, cutting away the pits.

Place pear wedges in hot honey-butter and sauté, turning carefully and cooking until pears are tender but not mushy, about 5 to 8 minutes. Transfer pears with some of the butter sauce to individual serving plates. Sprinkle with nutmeg and serve while still warm.

Serves 4

Variation: Substitute apples for the pears.

MONKEYS IN A BLANKET

Banana baked in bread is a quick and easy dessert that can be made for one or for a crowd.

1 slice whole grain bread
honey or honey-sweetened preserves
½ banana
½ tablespoon melted butter
cinnamon

Preheat oven or toaster oven to 400°F. Roll bread flat with a rolling pin and trim crust. Spread with a thin layer of honey or preserves. Place banana half on bread and wrap jelly-roll fashion.

Melt butter in a shallow baking dish in preheating oven or toaster oven tray. Allow 1 tablespoon for each whole banana. Roll bread-covered banana in melted butter, sprinkle with cinnamon, and bake for 15 minutes until crust is crisp and banana hot and creamy.

Serves 1

Note: Bananas should be served shortly after baking but can be wrapped in bread and refrigerated for advance preparation.

QUICK FRUIT TARTS

A good spur-of-the-moment dessert.

whole grain bread
softened butter
plums, pears, peaches, nectarines,
**   bananas, strawberries**
honey
slivered almonds

Preheat oven or toaster oven to 375°F. Cut bread thin and spread with a layer of butter. Cover with fruit of choice cut in slices. Press into butter. Drizzle with honey and top with some slivered almonds. Bake for about 30 minutes until fruit is tender and bread crisp. Serve warm.

DATE-NUT BREAD PUDDING

This dessert requires no cooking, no added sweetening, and is very rich.

1¾ cups fresh whole grain bread crumbs
¼ cup wheat germ
1 cup chopped dates
½ cup mixed chopped almonds, cashews, and sunflower seeds
⅔ cup orange juice or a combination of orange and apple juice

Combine bread crumbs, wheat germ, dates, and nuts. Add juice until mixture is moist but not soggy. Line a 9-inch pie pan with waxed paper and press mixture into pan. Cover loosely with waxed paper, foil, or plastic wrap. Chill for several hours.

To serve, lift waxed paper with pudding from pan and slice into thin wedges. Serve with Whipped Ricotta Topping, Yogurt Cream, Whipped Soy Cream, or honey-sweetened yogurt or sour cream.

Serves 8
Minor Protein

Appetizers and Hors d'Oeuvres

An appetizer introduces the meal and whets the appetite for the food to come, although many consider it more as a means of forestalling hunger. The classification of a dish as an appetizer is quite arbitrary, as anyone knows who has made a main course of "appetizers" in a restaurant or, conversely, expanded a traditional appetizer into an entrée. The recipes that follow have been grouped as appetizers and hors d'oeuvres primarily by tradition or because we have found these dishes to be most suited to first-course service. If you are looking for more ideas, check through the recipes for salads, condiments, vegetables, savory pastries, and bean, grain, and pasta accompaniments; some main dishes may also qualify—allow two to three appetizer servings from every main dish serving.

If you are uncertain as to how to select a first course that is appropriate to the rest of the meal, use "The New American Menu: Making Use of the Appetizer Course" (p. 16) as your guide. Ideally, the appetizer will complement the other dishes you serve in taste, texture, appearance, and nourishment.

Lastly, even if you have no plans to serve a first course, don't miss out on the recipes in this section. You might enjoy them combined as a main course or singly as a side dish.

DIPS

Dips are no longer reserved just for chips; now they come to the table with all sorts of raw vegetables: sticks of summer squash, green beans, broccoli trees, clusters of cauliflower, asparagus, mushrooms, cucumbers, green pepper wedges, and, of course, celery and carrots. This presentation of vegetables with a dip is referred to as *crudités*. For those still wedded to tradition, unsalted potato chips are available; tacos, divided into wedges, offer another vehicle for dips and are generally of better quality than the commercial taco chips sold for this purpose. Triangles of pita bread and whole grain crackers are also suitable.

In addition to its role as appetizer, a dip with vegetables can serve in place of a salad as an accompaniment. While a full recipe of dip will generally serve four, when consumed by just one as a snack or at mealtime, many dips can actually supply enough protein to replace the main course. Dips can also be thinned slightly with milk and used as salad dressings. All recipes are easily multiplied or divided.

Because its speed can be varied, the blender is a better tool for preparing dips than the single high-speed food processor. If you use a low setting, dips will be thick and creamy. If you use a processor, work quickly and be careful not to overprocess, as this will thin many dips to a souplike consistency. To minimize this risk, add only part of the yogurt, sour cream, or mayonnaise called for and stir the remainder into the processed ingredients after they are smooth.

In addition to the dips that follow, salad dressing recipes, most notably Green Goddess, Avocado, Creamy Tomato, and Creamy Tofu Garlic, as well as the Revisionist Dressing in the "Short-Order" section, are thick and flavorful enough to serve as dips.

ONION DIP

This is a dip everyone is familiar with, but few realize it can be made a lot better—and for a lot less money—if you don't employ a packaged soup mix.

> 1½ tablespoons instant minced onion
> ⅓ cup sour cream
> ⅔ cup yogurt
> 2 teaspoons dried parsley
> good dash soy sauce

Combine all ingredients and let stand at least 20 minutes to develop flavor.
Makes 1 cup
Minor Protein

GREEN DIP

> ½ cup cottage cheese
> ½ cup yogurt
> 2 scallions, cut up
> ½ cup parsley, tightly packed
> ¼ teaspoon dry mustard
> dash hot pepper sauce

Combine all ingredients in a blender and process until mixture is smooth and parsley is finely chopped.
Makes 1 cup
Minor Protein
Note: To prepare in a food processor, use the steel chopping blade and add only 2 tablespoons yogurt initially. Stir in remaining yogurt after processing.
Variations: Add 1 teaspoon fresh dill or 1 tablespoon fresh basil leaves.

HERB DIP

> 1 cup cottage cheese
> ½ cup yogurt
> ¼ cup mayonnaise
> 1 tablespoon lemon juice
> 1 tablespoon dried herbs: parsley, basil, chervil

Puree smooth in a blender or processor using the plastic mixing blade.
Makes 1½ cups
Minor Protein
Variations: Replace dried herbs with 2 tablespoons chopped scallion and a dash of hot pepper sauce, *or* replace dried herbs with 1 tablespoon home-made or commercial curry powder, *or* add 2 tablespoons crumbled blue cheese.

BLUE CHEESE DIP

> 2 cups cottage cheese
> ¼ cup milk
> 1 teaspoon salt
> 1 tomato, chopped
> 1 tablespoon chopped chives
> ½ cup crumbled blue cheese

Puree cottage cheese, milk, and salt in a blender or food processor until creamy. Stir in remaining ingredients until smooth.
Makes 2 cups
Minor Protein

CURRY DIP

> 1 cup cottage cheese
> ½ cup watercress leaves and tender stems
> 1 scallion, cut up
> 1 tomato, cut up
> ¼ teaspoon salt
> 1½ teaspoons curry powder

Combine all ingredients in a blender or processor fitted with a steel blade. Puree until smooth.
Makes 2 cups
Minor Protein

RELISH TRAY

The lazy susan relish tray offered in many restaurants can easily be duplicated at home. Selections can start with plain or herb-seasoned cottage cheese, a bean salad, or a ready-made condiment such as canned eggplant caponata. Fill in with the sampling of fresh condiments that follows, or with one of the homemade pickles or relishes featured in "The Food Factory."

SWEET AND SOUR SPROUTS

You can serve these sprouts as a salad or use them as a garnish.

> 1½ cups (½ pound) mung bean sprouts
> 1 cup water

½ teaspoon salt
2 tablespoons oil
3 tablespoons wine or cider vinegar
1 tablespoon honey

In a small saucepan combine sprouts, water, and ¼ teaspoon salt. Bring to a boil for 1 minute, drain, and rinse with cold water. Drain well. Combine remaining salt, oil, vinegar, and honey. Pour over sprouts and marinate for a few hours at least.

Makes 1½ cups; serves 6
Protein Complement
Note: These sprouts will keep for several days with refrigeration.

MARINATED CUCUMBER SALAD

2 medium cucumbers, peeled if necessary, and sliced thin
¼ cup cider vinegar
2 tablespoons water
1½ teaspoons honey
4 thin slices onion
¼ teaspoon prepared mustard or 1½ teaspoons caraway seeds or 1 tablespoon fresh dill or 1 teaspoon celery seed

Toss cucumber with vinegar, water, honey, onion, and seasoning of choice.
Serves 4 to 6

GREEK OLIVES

Here is a simple but effective way to improve on bland canned black olives.

1 can (7¼ to 8 ounces drained weight) unpitted black olives
2 tablespoons wine vinegar
2 tablespoons olive oil
¼ teaspoon crushed dried oregano
1 clove garlic, sliced

Drain liquid from canned olives, reserving ½ cup. Combine canning liquid with remaining ingredients and pour over olives in a bowl or jar. Cover and marinate in the refrigerator for 12 hours before use.
Note: These can be stored in the refrigerator for about 2 weeks.

THREE-BEAN SALAD

Make this early in the day or when you begin preparing the meal so the beans have time to marinate.

1 cup green beans cut into 2-inch pieces
1 cup cooked kidney or pinto beans, drained
1 cup cooked soybeans, chick-peas, or white beans, drained
¼ cup sliced Spanish or Bermuda onion
4 tablespoons wine or cider vinegar
4 tablespoons oil
2 teaspoons honey
¼ teaspoon salt (omit if beans are salted)
pepper

Steam green beans for 5 minutes until barely tender. Mix all beans and onion in a serving bowl.

Prepare dressing by beating vinegar, oil, honey, and seasonings together until honey "melts." Pour dressing over beans. Let marinate at room temperature for 30 minutes to 2 hours, or longer in the refrigerator.
Serves 6
Protein Complement

MARINATED ARTICHOKE HEARTS

Brighten up canned artichokes with your own marinade.

15-ounce can artichoke hearts packed in water
2 tablespoons lemon juice
3 tablespoons oil (at least part olive preferred)
¾ teaspoon oregano
¼ teaspoon salt
pepper

Drain artichokes, rinse, and cut in quarters. Pour lemon juice and oil over artichokes. Add seasonings and mix well. Taste and adjust salt if necessary. Let stand at room temperature for use within several hours, or refrigerate. Stir occasionally for even marination.
Serves 4

PICKLED MUSHROOMS

1 pound mushrooms
1 cup red wine vinegar
½ cup water
8 peppercorns
1 bay leaf
1 teaspoon salt
2 cloves garlic, crushed with the flat
blade of a knife
1 to 2 tablespoons oil

Clean mushrooms. Combine all ingredients except mushrooms and oil in a saucepan and bring to a boil. Add mushrooms and simmer for 2 minutes. Remove from heat and cool to room temperature.

Remove garlic and transfer mushrooms and broth to a jar. Slowly pour oil on top. Cover jar and chill for 24 hours before using.

Note: Can be stored for several weeks in refrigerator.

RAW CRANBERRY RELISH

2 cups cranberries
1 thin-skinned orange (seedless if possible), cut in eighths
½ cup honey

Combine cranberries and unpeeled, seeded orange in a processor fitted with a steel blade or in a food grinder. Process until minced. Stir honey into minced fruit and let stand for several hours in the refrigerator to mellow.

Makes 2 cups

Note: Relish should be prepared in advance. It can be stored in the refrigerator for several weeks.

Variations: Add ½ cup chopped walnuts or pecans, ½ cup chopped tart apple, and/or ¼ cup drained crushed pineapple.

PÂTÉS AND SPREADS

MARINATED ZUCCHINI STICKS

These flavorful zucchini sticks can be served as a salad or as a salad garnish.

2 medium zucchini (about 1 pound)
4 tablespoons wine vinegar
2 tablespoons oil
1 clove garlic, split
¼ teaspoon salt
pepper
1 teaspoon dried basil
1 tablespoon minced parsley

Trim ends of zucchini and cut into sticks 1½ inches long and ½ inch wide. Combine remaining ingredients in a small saucepan and bring to a boil. Pour over zucchini and mix well.

Chill zucchini several hours, stirring occasionally so all pieces are marinated. To store, transfer to a covered jar.

Serves 4 to 6

Note: This dish should be prepared in advance. It keeps in the refrigerator about 5 days.

WHITE BEAN PÂTÉ

A lusty pâté for crackers or a crusty bread.

1 tablespoon oil
1 small clove garlic, minced
⅛ teaspoon cayenne
2 cups cooked white beans, well
drained
1 teaspoon soy sauce
2 tablespoons cooking sherry
1 tablespoon melted butter
minced parsley or paprika

Heat oil in a small skillet and sauté garlic quickly until it begins to color. Add cayenne and cook for 30 seconds. Add beans and mash with a fork as they cook until you have a puree. Stir in soy sauce and sherry and cook 1 to 2 minutes longer until dry.

Pack into an oiled crock or bowl. Pour melted butter over the surface and poke holes with a toothpick to allow most of the butter to penetrate the interior. Cover and chill. To serve, unmold onto a plate and decorate generously with parsley or paprika. Serve with crackers.

Makes 1½ cups; serves 8
Protein Complement

NANETTE'S VEGETABLE PÂTÉ

A first-class first course for a sophisticated sitdown dinner. Serve with a crusty French bread or thin whole grain crackers.

¼ **cup butter/oil**
1½ **cups grated carrot**
1½ **cups minced celery**
1 **cup minced onion**
3 **cloves garlic, minced**
3½ **cups chick-peas, well drained**
3 **scallions, cut up**
4 **eggs, beaten**
½ **cup yogurt**
¾ **cup fresh whole grain bread crumbs**
¼ **cup minced parsley**
1½ **teaspoons salt (reduce if beans are salted)**
1 **teaspoon thyme**
1 **tablespoon tarragon**
3 **tablespoons apple juice**

Preheat oven to 350°F. Heat fat in a large skillet and sauté carrots, celery, onion, and garlic over medium-high heat for about 8 minutes until soft.

Grind chick-peas and scallions using the steel blade of a food processor or a food mill. Combine all ingredients in a large bowl and mix well. Transfer to a well-oiled 9½ x 5½-inch loaf pan. Tap on the counter to remove any air bubbles. Cover with foil and bake for 1 hour.

Cool in the pan before removing. Serve warm or chilled in individual slices on a bed of greens. Decorate with strips of sweet pepper or other garnish of choice.

Serves 8 to 12
Minor Protein
Variation: Apple juice can be replaced with brandy for added elegance.

MUSHROOM PÂTÉ

Serve as a spread for crackers or place small mounds on a bed of greens for individual appetizers. Mushroom pâté can also be used as a sandwich filling or as part of a main dish salad platter.

3 **cups diced mushrooms**
2 **tablespoons oil**
1½ **cups chopped onion**
½ **cup sunflower seeds or soy nuts, ground into meal**
½ **teaspoon salt**
1½ **teaspoons nutritional yeast**
1 **hard-cooked egg, mashed (optional)**

Prepare mushrooms and set aside. Heat oil in a skillet and sauté onion until lightly browned. Add mushrooms and sauté, stirring frequently for 3 to 5 minutes until just tender.

Transfer cooked mushroom mixture to a blender or processor and puree to a coarse grind. Or chop fine by hand with a heavy knife.

Stir ground nuts, salt, yeast, and egg, if desired, into mushroom paste until evenly blended. Mixture should resemble chopped liver. Chill before serving.

Makes 1½ cups
Minor Protein

PEA PÂTÉ

Serve as a spread for crackers, or make canapés by spreading pâté on cucumber or zucchini rounds or stuffing into raw mushroom caps.

2 **cups fresh or frozen peas**
1 **large scallion, sliced**
1 **tablespoon butter or oil**
4 **tablespoons water**
2 **tablespoons soy flour**
1 **teaspoon nutritional yeast**

Combine peas, scallion, butter, and 2 tablespoons water in a small saucepan. Cover and cook over medium heat until peas are tender, about 8 minutes. Puree smooth in food mill, blender, or processor.

Mix soy flour with remaining 2 tablespoons water to form a smooth paste. Stir into pea paste and return to saucepan over medium heat, stirring until mixture thickens and begins to boil, about 3 minutes.

Remove from heat, stir in yeast, and cool to room temperature. Then chill thoroughly until serving time.

Makes 1⅓ cups; serves 8

Variations: Replace peas with carrots, green beans, or cooked beans.

The following spreads are to be served on crackers, sliced vegetable rounds, or used to stuff celery, raw mushrooms, or green pepper wedges. They can also be used as sandwich fillings. All should be stored in the refrigerator.

BABA GHANOUJ

This eggplant dip laced with garlic is a specialty from the Mideast. There it is served in a common bowl into which everyone dips pieces of warmed pita bread.

1 medium eggplant (about 1½ pounds)
1 teaspoon salt
2 cloves garlic, finely minced
¼ cup lemon juice
3 tablespoons tahini
1 to 2 tablespoons olive oil
¼ teaspoon ground cumin

Place eggplant on a baking sheet and bake in a 375°F. oven for about 45 minutes until quite tender. Or spear with a long fork or skewer and hold eggplant directly over a flame, turning frequently until charred outside and soft inside. When eggplant is cool enough to handle, remove peel and chop pulp very fine.

In a shallow bowl, combine eggplant pulp, salt, garlic, and lemon juice. Beat in tahini with a fork to form a smooth paste. Let stand at room temperature, allowing at least 30 minutes for flavor to develop. Drizzle oil over surface and sprinkle with cumin just before serving.

Serves 4

Note: Charring the eggplant over an open flame is quicker and imparts a better flavor than baking.

ISRAELI EGGPLANT SPREAD

This variant of Baba Ghanouj utilizes hard-cooked egg instead of tahini.

1 small eggplant (1 pound)
2 hard-cooked eggs
1 tablespoon lemon juice
2 tablespoons mayonnaise
2 minced scallions
¼ teaspoon salt

Roast eggplant over a flame, turning to cook evenly until charred outside and soft inside. This will take 10 to 15 minutes. Remove from heat and when cool enough to handle, remove skin and mash interior smooth with a fork, in the food processor, or by mincing fine with a knife.

Mash in egg. Add lemon juice, mayonnaise, and scallion, and mix well. Season with salt, adjusting the amount to taste. Chill and serve cold as a dip or spread for crackers, bread, and raw vegetables.

Makes about 1½ cups; serves 6 to 8

Note: Instead of roasting, eggplant can be peeled, cut in chunks, and steamed for 15 minutes until tender. The charring, however, lends a distinct, robust flavor to the spread, a flavor that is even more pronounced when charring is done over a wood fire.

HUMMUS

This is similar to Baba Ghanouj except that the base is pureed chick-peas. Provide raw carrots, green pepper wedges, and cauliflowerets for dipping as well as the traditional pita bread.

2 cups cooked chick-peas
¼ cup bean liquid
¼ cup lemon juice
2 cloves garlic, finely minced
1 teaspoon salt (reduce if beans are well salted)
3 tablespoons tahini
2 tablespoons chopped parsley
2 tablespoons olive oil (optional)

Puree chick-peas in a processor or blender, adding the liquid for a smooth, creamy puree. Transfer to a shallow serving bowl and beat in lemon juice, garlic, and salt; then gradually add tahini to form a thick, light paste.

Let stand for about 30 minutes so flavor has a chance to develop. Sprinkle with parsley and, if desired, drizzle oil over surface just before serving.

Serves 4
Minor Protein

OLIVE AND PIMIENTO CHEESE SPREAD

1 cup (4 ounces) shredded cheddar or Jack cheese
2 tablespoons chopped pimientos and green olives (or use pimiento-stuffed olives)
½ teaspoon prepared mustard
¼ cup ricotta or small-curd cottage cheese

Combine all ingredients, mashing with a fork to a smooth, spreadable consistency.

Makes 1 cup
Minor Protein
Variation: Shape into a brick 3 x 2 x 2 inches. Chill. Served cut into 8 slices on a bed of lettuce. Top with a dollop of mayonnaise.

SHARP CHEESE AND TOMATO SPREAD

1 cup (4 ounces) shredded cheddar cheese
¼ cup blue cheese
2 tablespoons yogurt
1½ tablespoons tomato paste
½ teaspoon hot pepper sauce

Mash all ingredients to a smooth paste.

Makes 1 cup
Minor Protein

CHEESE–NUT SPREAD

¼ cup peanuts
2 tablespoons sunflower seeds
4 ounces cheese cubed
½ cup cottage cheese

1 to 2 tablespoons milk
hot pepper sauce

In a blender or processor fitted with a steel blade, grind peanuts and sunflower seeds to a fine meal. With machine running, add cheese cubes and process until grated. Add cottage cheese and process to a smooth paste. If necessary, add milk. Season with a dash of pepper sauce.

Makes 1¼ cups
Minor Protein
Variation: For a dip, blend in additional milk to desired consistency.

CURRY CASHEW SPREAD

A novel hors d'oeuvre can be made by serving Curry Cashew Spread on fresh apple rings.

½ cup cream cheese
½ cup cottage cheese
½ to 1 teaspoon curry powder
½ cup chopped cashews

Mash cheeses together. Add curry powder (use 1 teaspoon for a spicy spread). Mix in nuts.

Makes 1 cup
Minor Protein

PROTEIN SPREAD

This simple spread is a good base for a variety of flavors. Be sure to try it.

1 cup cottage cheese
½ cup tahini
seasoning of choice: dill, cumin, caraway seeds, or other herbs
salt

Mash cottage cheese and tahini together until evenly blended. Flavor to taste with herbs of choice and salt.

Makes about 1¼ cups
Minor Protein

TOFU CREAM CHEESE AND VEGETABLES

8 ounces tofu
1 tablespoon lemon juice
¼ teaspoon salt
¼ cup minced green pepper, scallion, celery, and radish in any proportion

Place tofu in a saucepan with water to cover and bring to a boil for 1 minute. Drain, place in a clean linen napkin and draw the ends together to form a sack. Twist gently, squeezing out all the moisture.

Transfer tofu to blender or processor fitted with plastic blade and blend with lemon juice and salt. Add water as needed to make a smooth, thick paste. Mix in vegetables. Spread on bread or crackers as you would cream cheese.

Makes about ⅔ cup
Protein Complement

CHEESE AND EGG APPETIZERS

OIL-CURED MOZZARELLA

Inspired by the Café des Artistes in New York City.

8 ounces mozzarella, cut in ¾-inch cubes
2 tablespoons olive oil
2 tablespoons light vegetable oil (sunflower or safflower)
2 teaspoons lemon juice
½ teaspoon dried crushed oregano
2 tablespoons chopped fresh parsley

Mix all ingredients and let stand for several hours to marinate. Serve at room temperature with a garnish of olives, tomato wedges, and capers.

Serves 6 to 8
Minor Protein
Note: Refrigerate in covered container for use within 2 weeks.
Menu Suggestions: This is a good choice as a first course preceding a pasta entrée.

BAKED BRIE WITH ALMONDS

A specialty of Mr. B's of New Orleans as reproduced in our kitchen.

8-ounce wheel Brie
2 tablespoons sliced almonds
½ tablespoon butter

Preheat oven or toaster oven to 325°F. Remove top layer of rind from cheese. Place in small oven-to-table baking dish. Spread almonds over exposed cheese. Dot with butter. Bake about 15 minutes until soft and runny. Serve at once.

Serves 4
Minor Protein
Note: To serve, scoop cheese out of rind onto serving plates with a spoon. Eat on crisp whole grain crackers. As the cheese cools, it will become firm and the rind and remaining cheese can be cut into wedges and eaten with a fork.

Variation: For *Baked Camembert with Almonds*, replace Brie with Camembert. The wheels packed in tins available at supermarkets are perfectly adequate for this dish.

FRIED CAMEMBERT

Butterfield's of Los Angeles stimulated this idea.

8-ounce wheel Camembert
1 egg, beaten
¼ cup dried whole wheat bread or cracker crumbs
2 tablespoons wheat germ
oil

Cut cheese into 8 wedges. Place beaten egg in a shallow bowl and combine crumbs and wheat germ in another bowl.

Coat each cheese wedge with egg, then roll in crumb mixture so that all surfaces are well covered. Add additional crumbs if necessary. Chill to help dry coating.

Heat enough oil to generously cover surface of a skillet large enough to hold all the cheese wedges. When hot, add cheese and brown on top and bottom. Drain on absorbent paper and serve hot.

Serves 4
Minor Protein
Note: This can be assembled several hours in advance and chilled until just before cooking. Cooking takes only about 5 minutes and should be done immediately before serving.

CORN-CRUSTED CHEESE

Batter-fried cheese on a stick.

8 to 12 ounces firm cheese (Swiss, cheddar or Gouda) in a single block
toothpicks
¼ cup whole wheat flour
¼ cup cornmeal
1 tablespoon nonfat dry milk powder
¼ teaspoon salt
½ teaspoon dry mustard
½ teaspoon baking powder
1 egg, beaten
½ teaspoon honey
½ tablespoon oil
⅓ cup water

Cut cheese into sticks about 2 inches long and ¾ inch thick. Insert a toothpick into the end of each so that it holds securely.

Prepare batter by mixing dry ingredients, adding wet ingredients, and stirring until smooth.

Heat enough oil to generously cover the surface of a large, heavy skillet. When oil is hot, dip each cheese stick into the batter, holding on to the toothpick. Coat generously and then let excess batter run off.

Place cheese sticks, with toothpicks still inserted, in hot oil. Sauté until well browned, then slip spatula underneath and flip to brown the other side. Coating should be brown and crusty. Allow about 2 to 3 minutes per side. Drain on absorbent paper and serve hot.

Serves 4 to 6
Minor Protein
Variation: For *Corn-Crusted Mushrooms* replace cheese with 16 to 20 medium mushrooms.

STUFFED SQUASH BLOSSOMS

We don't usually eat flowers, but we gladly make an exception for this dish. If you are a gardener, be sure to plant zucchini, if not for the squash itself, at least for the blossoms, which are a true delicacy when prepared in this manner.

12 squash blossoms
3 ounces mild cheese (Jack, mozzarella, or Muenster)
1 egg
pinch salt
1 tablespoon cornmeal
oil/butter

Wash squash blossoms carefully. Make a tiny slit along one side and remove the pistil or stamen, keeping the stem end intact. (This is a bit tedious but the dish is well worth the time). Cut cheese in small pieces and insert in flower. Wrap petals around cheese to completely enclose.

Separate egg and beat white until stiff peaks form. Beat in salt and yolk and fold in cornmeal.

Heat enough oil mixed with butter to coat a 12- to 15-inch skillet. When fat is hot, dip each flower into batter, holding with a tongs or your fingers, and transfer at once to frying pan. Sauté until set and golden on each side, about 5 minutes in all.

Serves 3 to 4
Major Protein
Note: If you can't get enough blossoms to make full-size servings, prepare a mixed grill, combining them with Chili Rellenos (page 158) so they can at least be sampled; the single-egg batter will coat 4 to 8 stuffed squash blossoms and 2 to 4 chilies.

SPIEDINI

These miniature cheese sandwiches are fried in batter and topped with a thick cold dressing lavishly seasoned with capers and olives.

6 slices whole wheat bread
6 ounces unsliced mozzarella cheese
3 eggs, separated
pinch salt
butter/oil
⅓ cup Caper Sauce (recipe follows)

Slice cheese and place evenly on 3 slices of bread. Top with remaining bread to form sandwiches. Cut each in quarters.

Beat egg whites to stiff peaks. Beat in salt and yolks, one at a time, until smooth.

Heat enough butter and/or oil to generously cover the surface of a large skillet. When fat is hot, dip each sandwich square into egg batter, holding with tongs or your fingers. Coat generously, then place immediately in hot pan.

Brown sandwiches on each side. Total cooking time will be only 5 to 8 minutes. Serve at once with Caper Sauce spooned on top.

Serves 4
Major Protein
Menu Suggestions: Serve with a light main course that does not emphasize cheese or eggs, such as pasta with tomato sauce or Italian Beans and Greens.

CAPER SAUCE

1 slice whole grain bread, crumbled
1 tablespoon wine vinegar
¼ cup parsley
1 tablespoon onion or 1 small clove garlic
⅛ teaspoon hot pepper sauce
4 tablespoons olive oil
1 tablespoon chopped capers
1 tablespoon chopped black olives

Crumble bread into container of blender or processor fitted with steel blade; pour in vinegar and mash with a fork. Let stand while preparing remaining ingredients.

Add parsley, onion or garlic, pepper sauce, and oil to the bread and process until smooth. If necessary, add water to obtain a thick puree. Transfer puree to serving bowl and stir in capers and olives. Do not keep more than a day.

Makes ⅓ cup; serves 4

SPICY CHEESE ROLLS AND CHEESE TRUFFLES

These two cheese novelties are made from the same base and are especially suited to entertaining.

Base Ingredients
2 cups (8 ounces) grated cheddar, Gouda, or Edam cheese
½ cup ricotta cheese
1 teaspoon soy sauce

For Spicy Cheese Rolls
1 tablespoon paprika
½ teaspoon chili powder
⅛ teaspoon cayenne

For Cheese Truffles
6 tablespoons grated or finely chopped pecans or walnuts
3 tablespoons wheat germ
⅛ teaspoon paprika or 2 tablespoons minced fresh parsley

Mash Base Ingredients together until smooth and evenly combined, adding as much ricotta as necessary to form a stiff "dough" that can be molded.

For *Spicy Cheese Roll,* shape into 2 logs, each 1½ inches across and about 5 inches long. Mix spices together on wax paper and roll logs to coat all surfaces generously.

For *Cheese Truffles,* form mixture into about 24 1-inch balls. Combine nuts, wheat germ, and paprika or parsley, and roll each ball to coat completely. Cover with plastic wrap and chill until needed.

Makes 2 logs, or 24 truffles
Minor Protein
Note: To serve roll, slice thin and place on crackers. Truffles can be eaten out of hand or on picks.

STUFFED LEMON EGGS

Cold eggs with a light lemony filling.

6 hard-cooked eggs
¼ teaspoon finely minced lemon rind
1 tablespoon lemon juice
3 tablespoons yogurt
½ teaspoon salt
dash hot pepper sauce
12 capers

Peel eggs and halve lengthwise. Remove yolks and mash with lemon rind, juice, yogurt, salt, and hot pepper sauce. Adjust seasoning to taste.

Fill whites with yolk mixture. Top each half with a caper. If not served promptly, cover and chill.

12 halves; serves 6
Minor Protein

ROLLED OMELET SLICES

Segments of seasoned omelet make an important contribution when eggs are not already a part of the meal.

1 egg
⅛ teaspoon salt
½ teaspoon soy sauce
1 tablespoon shredded carrot or minced onion

Beat egg with remaining ingredients. Heat a small 6- to 8-inch omelet pan and rub surface evenly with oil. Pour in egg and cook quickly until bottom is set and top is no longer runny. Lift edges and tilt pan so egg can run underneath if necessary.

Gently loosen omelet and slide onto a plate. Flip back into pan and cook briefly to set under side. Remove omelet to plate, cool slightly, then roll, pressing lightly to keep shape. Serve warm or at room temperature, slicing on the diagonal into 1-inch pieces.

Serves 2

Minor Protein

Note: A 2-egg omelet to serve 4 can be prepared in a 10- to 12-inch pan.

Menu Suggestions: Serve with vegetable stews, and rice and vegetable entrées, as well as with Oriental meals.

STEAMED EGG ROLLS

Shredded vegetables enclosed in simple paper-thin omelets make a very easy first course at an Oriental meal. Eat out of hand and use the remaining marinating sauce or additional Chinese Mustard for seasoning at the table.

2½ cups slivered vegetables including scallions, celery, green pepper, carrot, mushrooms, green beans, cabbage, even cold cooked rice
salt
dash hot pepper sauce
2 tablespoons soy sauce
2 tablespoons sherry
2 eggs
1 teaspoon Chinese Mustard (page 307)

Combine the vegetables in a bowl and season lightly with salt and hot pepper sauce. Mix in soy sauce and sherry and let marinate for 15 minutes to several hours.

Beat eggs until well combined. Add a pinch of salt. Heat a 6- to 8-inch omelet or crepe pan. Wipe with oil. When very hot, pour in 2 tablespoons of beaten egg and quickly tilt the pan, as for crepes, so batter spreads over bottom. As soon as set (in about 30 seconds), lift gently and transfer, cooked side down, to a plate. Continue using all but a bit of the egg, which should be saved to seal the egg rolls shut. The pan will probably not need any additional oiling, but if the omelet is difficult to lift, wipe with oil between each preparation.

To assemble, drain liquid from marinating vegetables; reserve as a dipping sauce or keep as seasoning for rice or soup. Lightly coat uncooked side of each omelet with some Chinese mustard. Put a small mound of vegetables in the center and fold in ends and sides to enclose. Use a little remaining egg to seal the edges.

Place egg rolls in a single layer on a vegetable steamer and steam for 10 minutes. Carefully remove to serving platter.

Makes 6 rolls; serves 3 to 6

Minor Protein

Note: Steamed Egg Rolls can be served hot or at room temperature. The component parts can be prepared well in advance, or the egg rolls can be assembled prior to cooking or even reheated if necessary.

ZUCCHINI ROULADE

This is the kind of appetizer you would expect to find in a high class restaurant, yet it is quick and easy to prepare at home. To serve, slice filled egg rolls into segments and garnish with thin tomato slices, carrot curls, and whole black olives.

Zucchini Filling
2 cups shredded zucchini
½ teaspoon salt
¼ cup chopped black olives
1 teaspoon prepared mustard
1 teaspoon chopped chives
generous amount pepper
⅓ to ½ cup cottage cheese, drained of moisture

Egg Rolls
   4 eggs
   salt
   pepper

To make filling, sprinkle zucchini with salt and let stand for 10 minutes to draw out moisture. (Egg rolls can be made while you wait.) Squeeze and drain all moisture from zucchini and pat dry. Mix zucchini with remaining ingredients, adding cottage cheese to bind.

To make egg rolls, beat eggs and season lightly with salt and pepper. Heat a 10- to 12-inch omelet pan and wipe generously with a paper towel impregnated with oil.

Pour half the eggs into the pan and cook, lifting the edges as they set and letting soft egg run underneath. When bottom is firm but not brown, and top is still slightly soft, slide omelet onto plate and flip back into pan. Cook briefly to set. Transfer omelet to plate and cool to room temperature. Repeat with remaining egg.

Place half the filling in a strip down the center of each cooled omelet. Roll omelets around filling. Serve at once, or chill.
   Serves 4 to 6
   Minor Protein

QUICHE

Quiche is the French name given to a custard-filled appetizer pie that may also serve as a main course by doubling the portion sizes. Ideally, the pastry on this pie is rolled extremely thin so that when the quiche is served the creamy filling is held in a scant but crisp crust. While the crust can be prepared well in advance and even frozen for convenience, the pie itself is most delicate and flavorful when assembled and baked just prior to service. It should be offered still warm rather than reheated. Nevertheless, quiche often is reheated and, although this renders the crust a bit soggy and the filling a bit tough, most people don't seem to mind.

Prebaking the shell, as recommended in the recipes which follow, is not mandatory but does enhance the crispness and produces a more tender filling since it is not exposed to high temperatures. If you prefer to add the filling to the unbaked shell, place the filled pie in a 425°F. oven for 10 minutes, reduce the heat to 350°F., and continue to bake for 30 to 40 minutes, or until just set.

CLASSIC CHEESE QUICHE

   1 unbaked 9-inch pie crust, as Standard Pastry (page 399) or Plus Pastry (page 399)
   ½ cup chopped onion
   1¼ cups shredded Swiss cheese
   ¼ cup grated Parmesan cheese
   3 eggs
   1½ cups whole milk
   ½ teaspoon salt
   ¼ teaspoon nutmeg

Preheat oven to 400°F. Prick surface of crust liberally with a fork and bake for 10 minutes. Remove and lower heat to 350°F.

Place chopped onion in shell, then cheese. Beat eggs lightly, beat in milk and salt, and pour over cheese in crust. Sprinkle nutmeg evenly over surface.

Bake until just set and lightly colored on top, or about 40 minutes. Let stand at least 10 minutes before slicing to set filling.
   Makes a 9-inch pie; serves 8
   Minor Protein
   Variations: Vary cheese as desired with cheddar, Gouda, provolone, etc. For *Mushroom Quiche,* sauté onion and ¾ cup sliced raw mushroom in 1 tablespoon butter until soft. Drain moisture and spread in partially baked shell. Proceed as above. For *Vegetable Quiche,* add ½ cup cooked asparagus, broccoli, zucchini, sautéed sliced sweet red or green pepper, and combine with raw onion.

SPINACH QUICHE

   1 unbaked 9-inch pie crust
   1 tablespoon butter
   2 large scallions, thinly sliced
   5 cups finely chopped raw spinach (about 6 ounces)

1½ teaspoons prepared mustard
¾ cup shredded cheese (Gouda, Swiss, provolone, or your choice)
3 eggs
1 cup yogurt
½ cup whole milk
½ teaspoon salt
paprika

Preheat oven to 400°F. Prick surface of crust liberally with a fork and bake for 10 minutes. Remove and lower heat to 350°F.

Meanwhile melt butter in a large skillet and sauté scallion and spinach until soft and dry, 5 to 8 minutes. Drain if necessary.

Spread mustard over bottom of crust; cover evenly with spinach mixture, then cheese. Beat eggs lightly, then beat in yogurt, milk, and salt; pour over cheese in crust. Sprinkle surface generously with paprika.

Bake until just set, or about 45 minutes. Let stand at least 10 minutes before slicing to set filling.

Makes a 9-inch pie; serves 8
Minor Protein

ONION PIE

1 unbaked 9-inch pie crust
1 tablespoon oil
1 tablespoon butter
1 pound onions, thinly sliced (3½ to 4 cups)
2½ teaspoons paprika
1½ cups yogurt
2 eggs
2 tablespoons whole wheat flour
1½ teaspoons salt

Preheat oven to 400°F. Prick surface of crust liberally with a fork and bake for 10 minutes. Remove and lower heat to 350°F.

Meanwhile melt butter with oil in a 10-inch skillet, add onion, cover, and stew for 10 to 15 minutes until onions are tender. Stir in 2 teaspoons paprika.

Beat yogurt smooth with a fork and beat in eggs, one at a time. Beat in flour and salt.

Fill partially baked shell with the onions, pour in yogurt mixture, and sprinkle with remaining ½ teaspoon paprika.

Bake about 25 minutes, or until filling is just set. Let stand at least 10 minutes before slicing, or serve at room temperature.

Serves 6 to 8
Minor Protein

CARROT TART

This carrot-custard pie is an excellent first course for a bean or bean–grain entrée.

1 unbaked 9-inch pie crust
1½ cups cut-up carrots
2 cups water
1 tablespoon butter
1 tablespoon honey
½ cup nonfat dry milk powder
½ teaspoon ground ginger
2 eggs

Preheat oven to 400°F. Prick crust liberally with a fork and bake for 10 minutes. Remove and lower heat to 350°F.

Meanwhile, bring the water to a boil in a pot that can accommodate a vegetable steamer. Place carrots in steamer, insert over boiling water, cover, and cook for 10 minutes.

Puree cooked carrots in food mill, blender, or processor, gradually adding 1 cup of the cooking liquid. Beat remaining ingredients into carrot puree and pour this mixture into partially baked crust.

Bake about 35 minutes, or until set. Let stand for 10 minutes before slicing. Serve warm or at room temperature.

Serves 6 to 8
Minor Protein

RICOTTA TORTE

A creamy ricotta filling inside a wheat–rice crust.

Crust
¾ cup whole wheat flour
¾ cup cooked brown rice
1½ teaspoons baking powder
¼ teaspoon salt
3 tablespoons oil
3 tablespoons water

Filling
1 cup ricotta cheese
1 cup shredded mozzarella cheese (4 ounces)
¼ teaspoon salt
¼ teaspoon dried basil
¼ teaspoon dried oregano
1 large canned pimiento, cut in strips
4 pitted black olives, sliced into 4 rounds each

Preheat oven to 350°F. Combine dry ingredients for crust. Stir in oil and water until evenly moistened. Knead dough lightly on a floured surface until uniformly blended. Press into an oiled, floured 9-inch pie plate.

Prick surface of crust liberally with a fork and bake for 10 to 12 minutes, or until just beginning to color.

Mix cheese and seasonings and spread over partially baked crust. Make a lattice over the surface with the pimiento strips. Garnish the open spaces with olive rounds.

Return to oven for 20 minutes. Let stand for 10 minutes before slicing.
Serves 6
Minor Protein
Note: To increase service, double recipe and bake in a jelly-roll pan or 9 x 13-inch oblong.

VEGETABLE APPETIZERS

AVOCADO COCKTAIL

2 small to medium avocados
1 cup Spicy Tomato Dressing and Cocktail Marinade (recipe follows)
shredded lettuce or alfalfa sprouts

Peel avocado and cut in cubes. Mix with dressing and marinate at least 30 minutes. Serve on individual plates on bed of shredded lettuce or mound of alfalfa sprouts.
Serves 4

MUSHROOM COCKTAIL

½ pound mushrooms
1 cup Spicy Tomato Dressing and Cocktail Marinade (recipe follows)
shredded lettuce or alfalfa sprouts

Clean mushrooms. If small, leave whole; cut into halves or quarters if large. Pieces should be of substantial size. Mix with dressing and marinate at least 30 minutes. Serve on individual plates on bed of shredded lettuce or mound of alfalfa sprouts.
Serves 4

SPICY TOMATO DRESSING AND COCKTAIL MARINADE

½ cup tomato juice
¼ teaspoon hot pepper sauce
2 tablespoons minced onion
½ clove garlic
¼ teaspoon salt
2 tablespoons wine vinegar
¼ cup oil (at least part olive preferred)

Combine all ingredients. Use for appetizer service (as in recipes above) or as a salad dressing.
Makes 1 cup

OVERSTUFFED MUSHROOMS

¾ pound large to medium mushrooms (24 to 32)
2 tablespoons oil
1 large clove garlic, minced
¼ cup chopped onion
½ cup soft bread crumbs
¼ cup sunflower seeds, ground to meal
1 tablespoon wheat germ
1 tablespoon chopped parsley
½ teaspoon oregano
¼ teaspoon salt
pepper
¼ cup grated Swiss cheese or cheese of choice

Preheat oven to 400°F. Clean mushrooms. Remove stems and chop. Reserve caps. Heat 1 tablespoon oil in a skillet and sauté chopped mushroom stems, garlic, and onion about 5 minutes until dry and lightly colored. Add crumbs, seedmeal, wheat germ, seasonings, and cheese.

Select a baking dish that will hold mushroom caps in a single layer, rub with oil, and arrange mushrooms hollow side up. Spoon filling into and around mushroom caps. Drizzle remaining 1 tablespoon oil over all.

Bake about 10 minutes until mushrooms cook and filling is hot. Serve at once.

Serves 4

Minor Protein

Note: To prepare in advance, spoon filling into mushrooms as directed above, cover, and refrigerate. Drizzle with oil and bake just before serving.

BAKED MUSHROOMS

Mushrooms in a delicate "cream" sauce.

1 cup yogurt
½ teaspoon salt
¼ teaspoon hot pepper sauce
1½ teaspoons cornstarch or arrowroot
24 medium mushrooms (about 10 ounces)
1 tablespoon butter
paprika

Preheat oven to 375°F. Combine yogurt, salt, pepper sauce, and starch in a shallow baking dish large enough to hold all the mushrooms in a single layer.

Remove mushroom stems and reserve for another use. Clean caps and place hollow side down in yogurt sauce. Dot with butter and sprinkle liberally with paprika. Bake for 10 minutes.

Serves 4

Minor Protein

Note: This can be assembled ahead of time and baked just before serving. If waiting time is more than one hour, refrigerate.

MUSHROOMS IN GARLIC BUTTER

16 large to 24 medium mushrooms (8 to 10 ounces)
4 tablespoons butter
2 tablespoons oil
1 cup parsley, loosely packed
2 cloves garlic, sliced
¼ medium onion, cut up
1½ teaspoons lemon juice
¼ teaspoon salt

Preheat oven to 350° to 375°F. Remove mushroom stems and reserve for another use. Clean caps and place hollow side up in a shallow baking dish.

Melt butter and puree with remaining ingredients in blender or processor. Spoon butter puree into caps and place any extra in pan around them.

Bake about 15 minutes until hot and bubbly. Serve hot with plenty of bread to sop up the garlic butter.

Serves 4

MARINATED EGGPLANT APPETIZER

Serve by itself or as part of an antipasto.

1 medium eggplant (1 to 1¼ pounds), cut in 1-inch cubes
½ cup white vinegar
1 teaspoon salt
1 clove garlic, split
1 teaspoon oregano
1 teaspoon dried basil
¼ teaspoon pepper
about 2 tablespoons olive oil

Steam eggplant cubes until just tender, 10 to 15 minutes.

Combine vinegar and seasonings and bring to a boil. Pour hot vinegar mixture over steamed eggplant and let marinate at room temperature for several hours. Refrigerate.

Drizzle oil over eggplant mixture just before serving.

Serves 4 to 6

Note: Keeps several weeks with refrigeration.

EGGPLANT CAPONATA

Caponata can be served as part of an antipasto spread on crackers or crusty bread, or used to garnish salads, omelets or sandwiches.

¼ cup oil (at least part olive preferred)
2 onions, chopped
1 pound eggplant, peeled and diced small
1 cup tomato juice
2 tablespoons tomato paste
2 stalks celery, minced (about ¾ cup)
2 tablespoons chopped capers
½ cup chopped green olives
2 tablespoons wine vinegar
2 tablespoons lemon juice
2 teaspoons honey

Heat oil in a large skillet and cook onion for 3 to 5 minutes until softened but not brown. Add eggplant, tomato juice, and tomato paste. Stir until evenly blended, cover, and simmer for 30 minutes. Add remaining ingredients, cover and cook for 10 minutes. Chill overnight and serve very cold.

Makes 1 quart; serves 8 to 10

Note: This must be prepared in advance so that the sweet-sour sauce can permeate the vegetables. It will keep several weeks under refrigeration.

EGGPLANT CAVIAR

As Russian as the real thing. Serve very cold accompanied by crackers or dark bread and spoon plain yogurt or sour cream on top to taste.

1 pound eggplant
½ cup finely chopped onion
½ cup finely chopped tomato
1 teaspoon salt
pepper
2 tablespoons lemon juice
2 tablespoons oil (olive preferred)

Make an inch-long slit in eggplant to release steam and cook by baking in a 350°F. oven. Or, cut into cubes and steam until tender. When cool enough to handle, peel and chop very fine. (You should have about 1½ cups.) Combine eggplant with remaining ingredients and chill.

Serves 8

Note: This keeps up to 2 weeks with refrigeration.

VEGETABLES À LA GRECQUE

This delicate vegetable marinade will serve you by itself or as a salad garnish.

2½ cups (about ¾ pound) mixed vegetables (green beans, artichoke hearts, cauliflower, leeks, radishes, celery, carrot, zucchini, mushrooms)
2 tablespoons olive oil
2 tablespoons lemon juice
¾ cup water
1 bay leaf

½ teaspoon salt
3 peppercorns crushed with the flat of a knife blade
2 medium tomatoes, peeled and diced (optional)

Scrub and peel vegetables, if necessary, and cut into cubes, sticks, or other manageable size pieces.

Combine remaining ingredients in a pot and bring to a boil. Add vegetables and simmer, uncovered, for 20 minutes. (If you are using zucchini or mushrooms they should be added during the last 10 minutes.)

Remove from heat and let cool to room temperature before serving.

Serves 4

Note: Keeps well for 1 to 2 weeks in the refrigerator. If chilled, remove about 1 hour before serving for best flavor.

THOUSAND ISLAND SALAD

Vegetables can be varied depending on your pantry.

3 cups cooked cauliflower
1½ cups cooked, sliced potato
3 carrots, cooked and sliced on the diagonal
12 raw or lightly steamed green beans, cut in 2-inch lengths
⅔ cup Thousand Island Dressing (page 289)

Arrange some of each vegetable on individual serving plates. Top with dressing.

Serves 6

BROCCOLI TROPICANA

The light orange dressing wakes up vegetables and appetites.

½ pound broccoli
3 tablespoons mayonnaise
3 tablespoons yogurt
3 tablespoons orange juice
grated orange rind

Cut broccoli into thin stalks. If stems are especially thick or tough, peel outer layer. Steam until tender, 10 to 15 minutes. Cool to room temperature or chill if prepared well in advance.

Mix mayonnaise, yogurt, and orange juice. Spoon dressing over broccoli at serving time and garnish with a little grated orange rind.

Serves 4

Variations: Replace broccoli with steamed asparagus spears (about 3 per serving) or cooked, sliced beets.

CELERY RÉMOULADE

This is modeled after one of the most famous French hors d'oeuvres. Ideally it is made with celeriac (celery root or knob), but since this vegetable is difficult to obtain in the States, we use celery or one of the other variations described below. This is a very popular appetizer, so you should have plenty of opportunity to try out all these versions.

2 cups celery cut in 1-inch matchsticks
¼ cup mayonnaise
2 tablespoons yogurt
2 teaspoons Dijon or sweet mustard
1 tablespoon lemon juice

Combine celery in a saucepan with water to just cover, bring to a boil, simmer 2 minutes; drain and rinse with cold water to cool quickly.

Combine remaining ingredients to make dressing. Pat vegetable dry and mix with dressing. Chill until serving time.

Serves 4

Variations: For *Spaghetti Squash Rémoulade,* cut spaghetti squash in half and steam about 15 minutes, until cooked enough to scrape from shell, but not quite soft. When cool enough to handle, separate from skin using a fork, divide into strands, drain well, and mix with dressing. This preparation can be done well in advance and the strands of squash can be refrigerated in a brine of 1 cup water plus 2 tablespoons vinegar for several days. Rinse and drain well before dressing. For *Sprouts Rémoulade,* blanch 2 cups soy or mung bean sprouts in boiling water to cover for 2 minutes. Drain, cool under cold water, pat dry, and dress as for celery.

CAULIFLOWER RÉMOULADE

2 to 2½ cups cauliflower (¾ pound), separated into small buds
¼ cup mayonnaise
2 tablespoons yogurt
2 tablespoons Green Tomato Relish (page 440) or Zucchini Relish (page 440)
1 teaspoon Dijon mustard
1 tablespoon capers
1 teaspoon dried chervil

Steam cauliflower buds for 5 to 8 minutes until barely tender. Cool quickly under running water. Drain.

Combine remaining ingredients to make dressing. Stir vegetables into dressing until well coated. Chill until ready to serve.

Serves 4

Variation: If relish is unavailable, substitute chopped pickle.

SCHOOLHOUSE SALAD

This is a perfect vehicle for leftover vegetables, but if you don't have any, go out of your way to prepare them fresh, for the combination is winning.

2 cups cooked vegetables, cut into ½-inch cubes
½ cup Tartar Sauce (page 308)
1 teaspoon prepared mustard
2 tablespoons chopped parsley

Combine all ingredients and chill until serving time. If vegetables are prepared especially for this, add dressing when warm but not hot.

Serves 4

Note: This should be made with a mixture of vegetables. Those that work well together include carrots, potatoes, celery, zucchini, green peas, green beans, corn, cauliflower, sweet potatoes, and even some cooked beans. If no leftovers are available, dice vegetables of choice and steam until just tender. Fibrous vegetables like carrots and potatoes will cook sufficiently in 10 minutes, while more delicate peas or zucchini require only 5 minutes steaming.

FILLED CROUSTADES WITH SALPICON

Croustade is French for an individual tart shell made from bread, which is used to encase a variety of fillings. To reduce sogginess, fill just before serving.

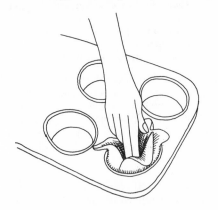

Preheat oven to 400°F. For each shell trim crust from a slice of whole grain bread and flatten gently with a rolling pin. Ease bread into a well-oiled muffin tin. If bread cracks, simply press together at the seam. Brush surface liberally with melted butter. Bake for 10 to 15 minutes, until golden. Remove from tin carefully and cool.

Salpicon

A salpicon is a preparation of "sauced vegetables" made from one or several ingredients diced small and bound together with a thick sauce. This is an excellent way to transform leftover cooked vegetables. Some of our favorite combinations follow. Use a salpicon to fill Croustades or in pastry tarts, cream puffs, or even hollowed-out tomatoes.

1. Steam your favorite vegetable about 5 minutes until barely tender, or use any leftover. Asparagus, green beans, broccoli, carrots, green peas, and sweet potatoes are all excellent choices. Cut in ¼-inch dice. Add a sauce of equal parts mayonnaise and thick plain yogurt to just coat.

2. Stew eggplant, peeled and cut in ½-inch dice, in oil or butter until tender. Moisten with thick plain yogurt and season to taste with cumin.

3. Dice cooked beets and season with salt, pepper, lemon, and oil. Stir in ricotta cheese to bind.

4. Combine diced cooked potatoes, blue cheese, cottage cheese, and a little yogurt to moisten.

5. Peel and dice a cucumber, sprinkle with salt, and let stand to extract moisture. Drain. Bind with cottage cheese, a dash of vinegar, and season with chopped chives.

6. Dice cooked carrots, broccoli, winter squash, zucchini, or cooked beans and mix with thick white sauce. Spoon into shell and serve at once.

7. Other suitable Croustade fillings include Ratatouille, Schoolhouse Salad, Vegetable Cottage Cheese, egg salad, bean casserole leftovers, and Creamy Mushrooms and Onions.

ASPARAGUS IN A BLANKET

fresh asparagus
whole grain bread
thinly sliced Swiss cheese (optional)
oil/butter

Preheat oven to 375°F. Trim ends of asparagus where they snap; wash and dry. For every 2 asparagus flatten 1 slice of bread gently with a rolling pin. Cut in half.

Put Swiss cheese, if desired, over each piece of bread. Top with asparagus spear and roll to completely encase.

Take a pan large enough to hold asparagus in a single layer and add enough oil alone or mixed with butter to cover. Warm in preheating oven.

Roll each blanketed asparagus in the hot fat and leave seam side down in the pan. Bake for 20 minutes, or until bread is crisp. Serve warm as an appetizer or party hors d'oeuvres.

Minor Protein with cheese

VEGETABLE DERMA

Stuffed derma is a traditional Jewish dish made by packing a savory bread crumb mixture into commercial beef casings not unlike the skins used to make frankfurters and sausages. Our flavorful stuffing mixture is baked without the casing, so the name we have chosen is something of a misnomer. A platter of sliced vegetable derma is an excellent party hors d'oeuvre.

4 ounces whole wheat crackers
2 tablespoons wheat germ
1 teaspoon salt
1 large carrot
1 medium onion
1½ stalks celery
3 to 4 tablespoons combination oil and melted butter (the butter is for flavor)

Preheat oven to 350°F. Grind crackers into fine crumbs. You should have a scant 1¼ cups. Transfer to a mixing bowl and add wheat germ and salt.

Chop vegetables as fine as you can. A food processor with the steel chopping blade is the fastest way to accomplish this. You should have ½ cup each packed carrot and onion and ⅔ cup celery.

Mix vegetables with cracker crumbs and add enough fat to make a moldable mixture. Shape into 2 logs, each about 1½ inches in diameter and 6½ inches long. Place on an oiled baking sheet and bake about 45 minutes until browned. Serve hot from the oven, making slices ½ to ¾ inches thick.

Makes 16 slices; serves 4 to 8

Note: Derma can be frozen for cooking at a later date. Wrap the shaped log in plastic or foil. Bake unwrapped but still frozen on an oiled baking sheet for 50 minutes to 1 hour. Cooked derma can be reheated if necessary. To prevent drying, baste with melted butter or oil while reheating.

STEAMED ARTICHOKES WITH DIPPING SAUCE

Artichoke is not a vegetable to serve when you're in a hurry. It takes time to eat your way to the succulent heart in the center, but we believe it is well worth the effort. As a matter of fact, this time-consuming food is actually an asset, for it promotes leisurely dining, relaxed conversation, and sets a nice pace for the rest of the meal.

Newcomers may need some instruction: Remove leaves one by one. Hold at narrow upper portion and dip wide bottom in accompanying sauce; pull sauced portion through teeth, scraping off the meaty part at the base; discard remaining leaf (bowls should be provided for this purpose). The small leaves in the center are not for eating, but don't neglect the solid center "heart" they cling to. Scrape off these tiny leaves and remove all of the hairy portion in the middle. Smother the remaining heart in sauce and savor it.

The Artichoke
1 per serving

Trim as directed in the Table of Vegetable Preparation on page 497, leaving stem and choke intact.

Place on a steamer or directly in a pot with 1 to 2 inches of boiling water. Cover and cook until fork penetrates base easily and leaves can be removed without effort. This will take 30 to 45 minutes, depending on the size.

Remove from pot and invert vegetable to drain. Serve warm or cold.

The Sauce
¼ cup per artichoke

Try a French or Italian oil-and-vinegar dressing, a creamy yogurt–mayonnaise dressing seasoned generously with mustard, melted butter with lemon, or for a most elegant and extravagant dish, the Creamy Lemon Butter below.

CREAMY LEMON BUTTER

¼ cup lemon juice
1 cup sweet butter, divided into tablespoons
¼ teaspoon salt (optional)

Boil lemon juice in a small saucepan until 2 tablespoons remain. Remove from heat and beat in 1 tablespoon butter with wire whip until melted. Repeat with second tablespoon butter.

Return to a very low burner, covered with a heat-resistant pad if possible, and continue to add butter, one tablespoon at a time, beating well after each addition until butter is melted and mixture thick and creamy. Season with salt if desired. Serve while still warm.

Makes 1 cup; serves 4

FRIED ARTICHOKE HEARTS

12 cooked fresh or canned artichoke hearts (2 14-ounce cans)
2 eggs, beaten
about ½ cup whole grain cracker crumbs
2 tablespoons wheat germ
2 tablespoons grated Parmesan cheese
¼ teaspoon salt
½ teaspoon oregano
pepper
oil
lemon

Drain artichokes and pat dry. If large, cut in half through stem. Have beaten egg in one bowl. Combine crumbs, wheat germ, cheese, and seasonings in another.

Dip each artichoke heart in egg, then roll in crumbs to completely cover. Place on wire rack and if there is time, chill to give coating a chance to dry.

Heat enough oil to cover surface of a large skillet. When hot, add hearts and brown on all sides. This will only take about 5 minutes. Serve warm with a wedge of fresh lemon.

Serves 4 to 6
Minor Protein

STUFFED ARTICHOKES

4 artichokes
½ cup dry whole grain bread crumbs
¼ cup wheat germ
¼ cup combined ground sunflower seeds and almonds
2 tablespoons grated Parmesan cheese
2 tablespoons chopped fresh parsley
1 clove garlic, minced
½ teaspoon salt
pepper
½ teaspoon oregano
2 tablespoons olive oil

To prepare artichokes, remove stem and bottom leaves and cut tips of remaining leaves about one third the way down. Spread leaves and, using a small paring knife, remove pale small leaves in center and hairy choke. As you finish

working with each artichoke, place it in a bowl of cold water with lemon juice to keep it from darkening. Drain and pat dry before filling.

Mix remaining ingredients to make filling. Spoon into center of artichoke, placing a little between the leaves as well.

Place artichokes side by side in a deep pot and add water to a depth of 1 inch. Bring to a boil, cover, and steam until tender, 30 to 45 minutes depending on age and size of artichokes. They will be ready to serve although you can transfer them to a 375°F. oven for about 10 minutes to crisp if you wish.

Serves 4
Minor Protein
Note: Artichokes can be stuffed and steamed in advance, then chilled and baked, as described, just before serving. Wrap cooked leftovers in foil and freeze. To use, unwrap and place in a pot with 1 inch boiling water; cover and steam as above until just heated through.

GREEK STUFFED CABBAGE OR GRAPE LEAVES

10 to 12 cabbage leaves or 20 to 24 grape leaves
3 tablespoons olive oil
1 cup chopped onion
½ cup raw brown rice
¼ cup chopped parsley
½ teaspoon salt
2 tablespoons sunflower seeds
¾ cup water
1 cup liquid from canned tomatoes or water
¼ cup lemon juice

See directions for preparing cabbage for stuffing, page 164. (If using grape leaves preserved in brine, rinse under cold water, separate, and pat dry.)

To prepare filling, heat 2 tablespoons oil in a small saucepan, add onion, cover and cook over moderate heat for 5 minutes. Add rice and stir to coat with oil, cooking for a minute or so. Add parsley, salt, sunflower seeds, the ¾ cup water, and bring to a boil; cover and simmer over low heat for 25 to 30 minutes until liquid is absorbed.

To fill cabbage leaves, place a tablespoon of filling between center and stem end, following the natural curve. (Lay grape leaves dull side up and place a rounded teaspoon of filling between center and stem end.)

Turn stem end over filling, fold each side over filling, then roll toward top, making a compact cylinder. To secure, tuck the tip into the pocket made where the two sides cross.

Place leaves close together in a large skillet. Add tomato liquid or water, lemon juice, and remaining tablespoon oil. Bring to a boil, cover tightly, and simmer until tender, about 45 minutes. Remove cover and cool to room temperature before serving.

Serves 6

Note: Stuffed leaves can be refrigerated and kept several hours or overnight before cooking.

Variation: Substitute 1½ cups cooked brown rice for uncooked rice and mix with cooked onion, seeds, and seasonings. Omit the ¾ cup water and the initial cooking of the filling.

SWEET STUFFED PEPPERS, ITALIAN STYLE

These are very rich and although a little unusual, very well received as a part of a hot antipasto or even as a side dish in an Italian dinner. Half a pepper is a fair-size appetizer portion, but it's a good idea to have extras for enthusiastic eaters.

4 medium green peppers
¾ cup fresh whole wheat bread crumbs
4 ounces provolone cheese, shredded (1 cup)
¼ cup capers
¼ cup chopped raisins or currants
¼ cup toasted pumpkin seeds
¼ cup chopped parsley
¼ cup chopped olives
1 large clove garlic, minced
½ teaspoon salt
pepper
¼ cup olive oil

Preheat oven to 350°F. Roast peppers over a flame until charred on all surfaces; when cool enough to handle, peel. Cut peppers in half lengthwise, pat dry and place close together in a well-oiled baking dish.

Combine remaining ingredients and pack into pepper halves. Bake for 25 to 30 minutes until tender. Serve hot or at room temperature.

Makes 8 halves; serves 4 to 8
Minor Protein
Variation: Sunflower seeds can be substituted for pumpkin seeds.

SPRING LETTUCE ROLLS

This Chinese appetizer is very simple to fix and can be prepared well in advance of the meal. It is eaten like an egg roll, with lettuce leaves forming the wrapper. Spoon Sweet Chinese Dipping Sauce onto filling as you eat.

1 tablespoon oil
2 teaspoons minced fresh ginger
1 small clove garlic, minced
2 large dried Chinese mushrooms, soaked and cut in thin strips
1 cup slivered carrots
1 cup bean sprouts
½ cup celery matchsticks
½ cup thin strips scallion
½ cup (4 ounces) tofu, fresh or frozen
2 tablespoons soy sauce
2 teaspoons sherry
2 teaspoons Oriental sesame oil
8 Romaine or Boston lettuce leaves

Heat oil in a wok. Add ginger and garlic, and cook briefly. Add vegetables and tofu, and stir-fry for 3 minutes. Add soy sauce, sherry, and sesame oil, and cook 1 minute longer. Transfer to a bowl to cool.

Serve filling on lettuce leaves and fold sides toward center and roll to form a bundle to eat.

Makes 8 rolls; serves 4 to 6
Minor Protein

STEAMED CHINESE DUMPLINGS

The Chinese fill pasta dough with a shredded vegetable mixture similar to egg-roll filling, shape it into compact bundles, and steam them to make a very tasty hors d'oeuvre. For added flavor, each dumpling is doused with soy sauce or Chinese Dipping Sauce to taste at the table. This is something you might want to try the next time you give an Oriental dinner.

For the Dough
1 cup whole wheat flour or a combination of whole wheat and soy flour
¼ teaspoon salt
1 tablespoon oil
¼ cup water

For the Filling
¾ cup cooked brown rice
1 to 2 scallions, chopped
½ cup shredded tofu
½ cup shredded raw or cooked vegetables
2 teaspoons soy sauce

To make dough:
Mix flour and salt in a bowl. With your fingers, work in oil, then water to form a dough that holds together.

Knead dough on an oiled work surface for 10 minutes until smooth and elastic. Divide into 7 balls, cover with a damp cloth, and let rest 30 minutes before rolling and filling. While dough rests, prepare filling by combining all filling ingredients.

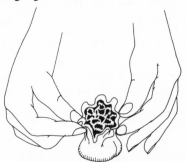

To assemble:
Take one ball of dough at a time, divide it in half and roll into 2 thin 4- to 5-inch rounds. Place 1 tablespoon filling in center, bring dough up around filling like a sack so it pleats naturally, and pinch around the neck to hold together. The top will resemble a flower. Repeat with all dough to make 14 dumplings. Drape a cloth over finished dumplings

to keep them from drying out. If they are not to be cooked right away, refrigerate them.

To cook, line vegetable steamer with leafy greens or damp cheesecloth. Place dumplings on steamer, leaving a little space between to prevent sticking. Insert steamer over boiling water, cover and steam for 15 to 20 minutes until tender. Serve very hot.

Makes 14 dumplings; serves 4
Minor Protein

GREEN BANANA ESCABECHE

This pickled banana salad of Puerto Rican extraction makes a very nice prelude to Paella or Puerto Rican Rice and Beans. As green bananas taste very much like potatoes, this dish is not as strange as it sounds.

3 unripe bananas
salt
½ cup cider vinegar
⅓ cup water
¼ teaspoon salt
1 bay leaf
1 small onion, thinly sliced
5 peppercorns
1 teaspoon honey
¼ cup sliced green olives

Peel bananas and cut into 1-inch chunks. Place in saucepan with cold water to cover and salt lightly. Bring to a boil and simmer for 10 to 15 minutes until tender. Drain and transfer to a bowl.

Combine remaining ingredients except for olives and boil for 3 minutes. Pour over bananas and let stand at room temperature for several hours to marinate. When it has cooled add the olives. Refrigerate for storage.

Serves 4 to 6

BITE-SIZE KNISH

This caterers' cocktail party favorite is designed for elaborate affairs. You can make two varieties from this one recipe.

The Dough
3 cups whole wheat flour
1 teaspoon baking powder

½ teaspoon salt
1 tablespoon oil
1 egg, lightly beaten
½ cup water

Mix dry ingredients. Add oil, egg, and enough water to make a stiff dough. Knead on a lightly floured surface about 5 minutes until dough is elastic. Cover dough and let stand for 30 minutes while preparing the filling.

Makes dough for 8 rolls or 96 bite-size knishes

Potato Filling
1½ pounds potatoes
salt
pepper
1½ cups chopped onion
2 tablespoons oil

Steam potatoes until tender; press through a sieve or mash with a fork until light and fluffy. Season to taste with salt and pepper. For a more nourishing filling, prepare according to directions for Mashed Potatoes on page 248.

Sauté onion in oil until nicely browned. Mix into potato. Use at once or chill until needed.

Makes 3 cups filling (enough for 4 rolls or 48 bite-size knishes)

Note: Can be prepared a day or two in advance.

Kasha Filling
1½ cups chopped onion
2 tablespoons oil
¾ cup kasha
2 cups boiling water
1 teaspoon salt

Sauté onion in oil in 1- to 2-quart pot until golden. Add kasha and brown lightly. Pour on boiling water and salt, cover and cook over low heat until liquid is completely absorbed, 15 to 20 minutes. Remove cover to dry slightly. Use at once or chill until needed.

Makes 3 cups (enough for 4 rolls or 48 bite-size knishes)

Note: Can be prepared a day or two in advance.

To Assemble
Dough
oil
Potato Filling
  and/or
Kasha Filling
beaten egg

Preheat oven to 375° F. Divide dough into 4 pieces. Roll one at a time into a very thin 12-inch square. Divide each square in half.

Brush surface of dough lightly with oil. Place about ¾ cup filling in a long strip down the center. Fold one side of dough completely over filling, then roll to enclose filling completely. Pinch ends to seal.

Place filled dough seam side down on oiled baking sheet. Brush surface with a little beaten egg or oil. Bake for 20 to 25 minutes until surface is brown and firm. Transfer to rack to cool slightly. Cut into 1-inch pieces and serve warm.

Makes 8 rolls; 96 bite-size pieces

Note: Can either be assembled well in advance and cooked just before serving or conveniently reheated or kept warm on a hot tray; also may be frozen and cooked as needed.

POACHED SPINACH–POTATO PÂTÉ

The idea for this dinner party appetizer came from the Market Bar and Dining Room in the World Trade Center in New York. It is composed of a delicate potato dough stuffed with chopped seasoned spinach, which is poached, sliced, and served with melted butter and freshly grated cheese.

½ recipe (1 pound) Potato Dough (page 206)
½ pound spinach, finely chopped
1 tablespoon oil
1 small clove garlic, minced
2 scallions, minced
¼ teaspoon salt
hot pepper sauce
1 egg, lightly beaten
½ cup fresh whole grain bread crumbs
2 tablespoons wheat germ
4 tablespoons grated Parmesan cheese
whole wheat flour
additional grated Parmesan cheese
about ½ cup melted butter

Prepare Potato Dough; cover and chill until needed.

To prepare filling, sauté spinach in oil with garlic and scallion until wilted and dry, about 5 minutes. Remove from heat and stir in seasoning, egg, bread crumbs, wheat germ, and grated cheese. Use at once or refrigerate until needed.

Divide dough in half on a well-floured surface and pat into a rectangle 5 x 10 inches. Turn over in flour so both sides are dredged. Repeat with remaining dough.

Place ½ cup spinach filling in a long row down the center of each rectangle of dough. Fold both sides of dough over filling and roll gently so filling is completely ensconced in a sausage about 12 inches long.

Slide each roll onto a separate double layer of cheesecloth large enough to fold over the roll; secure at each end with string. Cook at once or chill.

To cook, bring water to a boil in a large, wide pot; add salt and lower dough wrapped in cheesecloth gently into boiling water. Cover and poach for 20 minutes, keeping water at a gentle boil. Lift from water, drain, remove cheesecloth, and slice in 1-inch sections. Place 3 sections flat on each serving plate. Top with a scant tablespoon grated cheese and drizzle with melted butter. Serve warm.

Makes 2 rolls; serves 8 to 10

Minor Protein

Note: Try to serve within 15 minutes of poaching. If necessary, keep warm in poaching liquid, off the heat, until ready to slice. If already sliced, place on heatproof platter in a low (200° to 250°F.) oven to keep warm. Do not add cheese or melted butter until just before serving. If your dinner party is small, freeze one roll, wrapped in cheesecloth, then overwrapped for freezing. Remove outer freezer wrapping and cook as above without defrosting, adding 5 minutes to the cooking time. Use within 3 months.

BEAN APPETIZERS

TOFU ANTIPASTO SALAD

In our experience, one of the best ways to serve tofu.

1⅓ cups sliced mushrooms
1 cup sliced celery
1½ cups tomato chunks
½ cup small strips green pepper
1½ cups diced tofu
¼ cup lemon juice
6 tablespoons oil (part olive preferred)
1½ teaspoons oregano
½ teaspoon salt
pepper

Combine all vegetables and tofu. Pour on lemon juice, oil, and seasonings. Mix gently to combine. Marinate at room temperature for 30 minutes, or longer in the refrigerator. Adjust salt and pepper to taste before serving.

Serves 6

Minor Protein

STUFFED CLAM SHELLS AREGANATA

This dish uses the shell, not the clam.

2 tablespoons butter
¼ cup minced onion
1 clove garlic, minced
1 cup minced tofu (fresh or defrosted frozen)
¾ cup fresh whole wheat bread crumbs
¼ cup wheat germ
¼ cup minced celery
2 tablespoons minced parsley
½ teaspoon dried basil
1 teaspoon oregano
½ teaspoon salt
pepper
2 tablespoons dry white wine
1 tablespoon oil

Preheat oven to 350° to 375°F. Melt butter in skillet and sauté onion and garlic until tender but not brown. Remove from heat and add remaining ingredients. Stuff mixture into clam shells or small ceramic ramekins. If you have neither, fashion your own with foil as described below.

Bake for 10 minutes until crispy. Serve hot.

Serves 4; 8 shells
Minor Protein
Note: Sterilized, reusable clam shells are available commercially. Lacking a suitable container you can fashion small shallow cups by molding foil around the bottom of a custard cup or glass. Leave a small lip about ¼ inch high to contain the filling. Stuffed shells can be assembled in advance and chilled until ready to bake.

PARTY MOUSSE

See if your inquisitive friends can guess how you made this.

4 cups cooked soybeans, drained
1 cup yogurt
½ cup mayonnaise
1 envelope unflavored gelatin
½ cup cooking liquid
3 tablespoons chopped parsley
1 tablespoon chopped chives
2 teaspoons chopped fresh dill
2 tablespoons lemon juice
2 teaspoons Dijon mustard

Grind beans in a processor or blender, adding yogurt and mayonnaise as needed to obtain a smooth puree. Depending on the machine capacity, you may have to do this in two or three batches. Eventually the beans should form a smooth paste with all the yogurt and mayonnaise.

Sprinkle gelatin over reserved cooking liquid and let soften a few minutes. Then place over low heat and cook, stirring for about 3 minutes until gelatin is dissolved.

Add dissolved gelatin and seasonings to soybean puree. Turn into a 6-cup mold (a fish shape or ring mold is nice for appearance) and chill for several hours until firm.

Serves 12 or more

Minor Protein
Note: Prepare several hours ahead to allow for chilling. Unmold and decorate with parsley, olives, capers, and scallion. Mousse may be eaten with a fork or spread on crackers.

NIKKI'S SPECIAL KIBBI

Arab tartar "steak" with no meat in the mix. A little unusual and extremely good eating, especially if you like onions.

1 cup cracked wheat
2 cups hot water
1½ cups cooked chick-peas, drained
¼ teaspoon nutmeg
⅛ teaspoon cayenne
½ teaspoon salt (adjust if beans are salted)
lots of fresh ground pepper
¼ cup oil (all or part olive preferred)
1 cup chopped onion

Place cracked wheat in a bowl, cover with hot water, and let soak for 10 minutes or longer. Grind chick-peas in processor or drum grater.

Squeeze all moisture from soaked wheat. Mix with ground beans and seasonings, kneading with hands until mixture is even. Shape into 8 patties, 2 inches around, using about ⅓ cup mixture for each. Place on serving plate and use fingers to mold a depression in the center of each patty.

Heat oil in a skillet, add onion, cover and stew over low heat for 3 to 5 minutes to lightly cook. Spoon some oil and onion into each depression just before serving.

Serves 8
Minor Protein
Note: Patties can be made well in advance and chilled, but onions should not be added until just before serving.

Menu Suggestions: Kibbi should open a Mideastern meal along with Baba Ghanouj; follow with Greek Artichokes and Dill or Atlantic Avenue Green Beans, Greek Coleslaw, feta cheese, olives, and lots of pita bread.

DAHI VADDI

These lentil balls in spicy yogurt sauce make a superb addition to an Indian dinner.

For the Balls
½ cup dried lentils
1 cup warm water
½ teaspoon salt
1 teaspoon cumin
pinch cayenne
oil

For the Sauce
1 cup yogurt
2 tablespoons minced parsley
¼ teaspoon salt
¼ teaspoon cayenne
½ teaspoon cumin
2 tablespoons shredded unsweetened coconut (optional)

Several hours in advance of the meal combine lentils and warm water and let soak for 2 hours or more.

Combine soaked lentils and any unabsorbed water with salt, cumin, and cayenne in a blender or processor fitted with a steel blade. Process to a thick, fairly smooth puree. Cook at once or let stand at room temperature until needed, up to several hours.

To cook, heat about 1 cup oil in a wok to 375°F. Drop lentil batter by tablespoons into hot oil. Cook only 3 or 4 at a time to avoid crowding. Cook about 3 minutes until brown, then turn to brown other side. Remove and drain on absorbent paper. Continue until puree is used up.

For sauce, combine yogurt, parsley, salt, and cayenne. Just before serving put lentil balls in sauce and stir gently to coat. Sprinkle with cumin. If desired, sprinkle coconut on top as well.

Serves 4; 12 to 16 balls
Minor Protein
Note: For fresh-ground cumin, toast cumin seeds in a dry skillet until aromatic, then crush in a mortar and pestle. Although pre-ground cumin can be used, the fresh-ground is far more flavorful.

Soups

The delight of soup is that it offers so much and requires so little. For this reason, soups are a favorite of casual cooks, providing inexpensive nourishment and the freedom to play around with the recipe. For most of us there is also an emotional aspect to soup; as one letter writer, commenting on his need to retreat with soup and crackers when feeling low, put it: "Soup makes me feel tender toward my delicate self."

A soup can take on myriad forms, flavors, textures, temperatures, and aromas. And, although there is vast choice, you really only need to master one or two specialties for each season to take advantage of what is fresh. Moreover, while the soup pot has been a traditional recipient of leftovers, it shouldn't be a kitchen dumping ground or the soup will end up a muddle of tastes. "Keep it simple" is the basic rule in making soup, but within this guideline there are a number of attractive ways to enhance the end result.

• For robust flavor, add soy sauce or nutritional yeast. The use of yeast will improve the food value of soups and is highly recommended.

• To add protein, place 1 to 2 ounces diced cheese or tofu in the bottom of each serving bowl before adding the hot soup. The cheese will melt into creamy filaments.

• For a meat soup, add shreds of leftover cooked poultry, fish, or meat to the pot or add meat bones or raw scraps and cook for at least one hour.

• For substance and texture, grains and vegetables may be added.

• To wake up the flavor, add a dash of vinegar or lemon juice or a pinch of cayenne.

• For enrichment, add a little oil, butter, or cream to the pot, or add yogurt at the table.

• To make a bulkier soup, thicken as described on this page.

You will find examples of all of these ideas in the soup recipes that follow.

Note that although we have used water as the principal liquid ingredient in most recipes (due to the poor quality of commercial broths and bouillons and the fact that few people take the time to make fresh stock these days), the substitution of more flavorful liquid will always benefit the soup. The best way to accumulate vegetable stock is to use ice cube trays to freeze the liquid left from all your vegetable cookery, from canned tomatoes, and from previously prepared soups. Use these cubes to replace some or all of the water whenever the opportunity arises.

Soup Thickeners

For a lightly thickened soup, proceed as follows:

• Stir ½ cup dried bread crumbs or 1 scant cup fresh bread crumbs into 1 quart of simmering soup. It will thicken in just a few minutes.

• Mix 2 tablespoons flour or 1 tablespoon cornstarch or arrowroot with a little cold water to form a paste. Stir into 1 quart of simmering soup and cook, continuing to stir, until soup thickens. Simmer 2 minutes longer if flour is used; otherwise serve at once.

• Slice small pieces of Instant Sauce Balls (page 315) into simmering soup, allowing 2 balls per quart of liquid. Stir gently as nuggets soften and thicken the soup. Simmer for 1 minute longer.

• Beat 1 egg or 2 egg yolks lightly for each 4 to 6 cups of soup to be thickened. Gradually beat a little of the hot soup into the egg, then stir gently into the hot soup without letting it boil. Serve at once.

• Grate ½ pound raw potato into the

pot for each 4 to 6 cups of liquid soup. Simmer at least 15 minutes before serving.

• Before serving, stir in up to 1 tablespoon nutritional yeast per quart of soup. Avoid boiling again if possible, as this will harm some of the B vitamins gained from the yeast.

CONVENIENCE SOUPS

Although nothing can equal the flavor of a slow-simmered soup, there are many excellent homemade soups that can be prepared in a matter of minutes. This chapter begins with these soups of convenience, welcome when time is an important ingredient.

QUICK MIXED VEGETABLE SOUP

A real "soup 'n' sandwich" soup

2 medium carrots, cut-up
2 stalks celery with leaves, cut-up
½ cup onion pieces
several leafy greens or parsley sprigs
2 cups water
2 cups tomato juice
½ teaspoon salt
¼ teaspoon dried basil
1 teaspoon soy sauce
1 tablespoon butter or oil
pepper
1 tablespoon nutritional yeast (optional)

In a blender or processor fitted with a steel chopping blade combine vegetables and 1 cup water. Process to a thick puree.

Combine vegetable puree, remaining water, and tomato juice in a pot and bring to a boil. Add salt, basil, and soy sauce, and simmer for 5 minutes.

Remove from heat and stir in oil or butter to melt, pepper to taste, and, if desired, the nutritional yeast, which will thicken the soup slightly.

Serves 4

Variations: For a more substantial soup, add ½ cup uncooked pasta, cracked wheat, or kasha along with the seasonings and simmer for 15 minutes,

or until tender. Leftover cooked grain, beans, or vegetables can also be added.

QUICK TOMATO–ONION SOUP

A good appetizer or lunch soup that can be prepared in less than half an hour.

2 tablespoons oil
2 cups chopped onion
3 cups vegetable broth or water
2 cups tomato juice
salt
pepper
1 teaspoon butter
2 to 3 cups Cheese Croutons (recipe follows)

Put oil and onions in a saucepan and cook over low heat until onions begin to color lightly, about 10 minutes.

Add broth, cover, and simmer for 10 minutes. Stir in tomato juice and salt and pepper to taste. Bring to a boil. Stir in butter and, when melted, serve with Cheese Croutons (allow ½ cup per person).

Variation: Replace vegetable broth and tomato juice with 5 cups liquid drained from canned tomatoes or frozen Tomato Broth (see "The Food Factory," page 420).

CHEESE CROUTONS

whole grain bread
finely grated Parmesan cheese
oil (optional)

Preheat oven to 350°F. Cut bread into ¼-inch cubes. Mix with one fourth their volume finely grated Parmesan cheese (¼ cup cheese for each cup bread cubes).

Place in a well-buttered baking dish and bake for about 10 minutes, or until golden. Stir a few times during baking and drizzle with a little oil if desired.

Serve straight from the oven, or let cool to room temperature. Any cheese that adheres to the pan should be loosened and mixed with the croutons or sprinkled into the soup.

Minor Protein

Note: These can be used to garnish salads as well as soups.

CHINESE GREENS IN BROTH

A nice light soup to precede a Chinese meal.

2 tablespoons dried Chinese mushrooms
4 cups vegetable broth or water
2 tablespoons dehydrated soup greens or vegetable flakes
2 tablespoons soy sauce
¾ teaspoon salt (less if broth is salted)
1 clove garlic, split
2 cups shredded greens (spinach, romaine, Chinese cabbage, etc.)
1 tablespoon chopped scallion
1 teaspoon Oriental sesame oil

Break mushrooms into pieces and soak in hot water to cover for about 20 minutes until tender. Drain, using liquid as part of the vegetable broth.

Combine the broth or water, soup greens, soy sauce, salt, garlic, and drained mushrooms. Bring to a boil and simmer for 5 minutes. Add greens and simmer 3 to 5 minutes longer.

Remove from heat; add scallions and oil and serve at once.
Serves 4
Variation: To turn this into a Major Protein *Oriental Soup Dinner* for 2, add 8 ounces diced tofu or tempeh and 3 ounces uncooked pasta initially. If desired, diced broccoli, cauliflower, zucchini, or other fresh vegetables of choice may be added. Reduce greens to 1 cup. Cook for a total of 10 to 15 minutes, or until pasta is tender.

STRACCIATELLA

This is really an Italian egg-drop soup.

1 clove garlic, split
6 cups vegetable broth, or stock made by combining water and tomato juice, Tomato Cubes (page 430), a little tomato paste, or the liquid from canned beans or canned tomatoes
salt
6 cups shredded escarole or romaine
2 eggs
¼ cup grated Parmesan cheese
¼ cup fresh whole grain bread crumbs

Add garlic to stock and salt to taste. Bring to a boil, add greens, and simmer for 5 minutes.

Beat egg with cheese and bread crumbs. Just before serving, add egg mixture gradually to simmering soup and when it "sets," stir gently and serve.
Serves 6
Minor Protein

SPANISH GARLIC SOUP

This garlic soup is like a consommé and should be used as a light first course. Without the bread it makes a good basic stock.

12 cloves garlic, peeled and chopped
1 teaspoon salt
½ teaspoon black pepper or a generous pinch of cayenne
1 teaspoon mixed dried herbs (basil, oregano, sage, thyme)
1 bay leaf
5 cups water
2 tablespoons oil
2 slices (2 ounces) whole grain bread
grated Parmesan cheese (optional)

Combine garlic, seasoning, water, and oil and bring to a boil. Cover and simmer for 30 minutes. Crumble bread into soup and return to a boil. Serve plain or with grated cheese.
Serves 4

INSTANT ASOPA

This soup-stew based on leftovers is a hearty main course when served with a Minor Protein.

1½ cups leftover cooked vegetable-grain or vegetable-potato stew, such as Greek Spinach Rice, Marseilles Spinach Stew, Paella, or Couscous
1½ cups vegetable broth, tomato broth, or water diluted with tomato juice
salt
pepper
1 tablespoon olive oil or butter
1 slice whole grain bread
grated cheese (optional)

Combine vegetable leftovers and liquid and bring to a boil. Taste for seasoning. Add oil or butter, tear bread into the simmering soup, cover, remove from heat, and serve within the next few minutes. Add grated cheese at the table, if desired.

Serves 2 as a main dish (3 as a first course)

QUICK CREAMY BEAN SOUP

An excellent use for cooked beans, either plain or in a seasoned sauce, this basic recipe can be varied as desired for a thick or thinner soup.

Combine cooked beans with an equal amount of milk, allowing 1 cup each for 2 small servings, 1½ cups each for a generous bowlful. Puree smooth in a blender or processor fitted with the steel chopping blade.

If beans are unseasoned, flavor as desired with salt, pepper, cumin, cayenne, or hot pepper sauce. Warm through and serve.

Major Protein

Note: Soup can be varied by using leftover cheese sauce instead of plain milk, or by adding grated cheese at the end and letting it melt in.

EVERYDAY SOUPS

From the many soups we have dined on, the following are the ones we could eat with great frequency. Some are earthy, others extravagant, but for the most part they are a composite of family favorites from the world's kitchens, and thus there should be soups to suit everyone's style.

VEGETABLE SOUP

3 carrots
2 stalks celery with leaves
1 medium onion
2 leeks
2 tablespoons oil
6 cups broth (vegetable stock, water

and soy sauce, or water and tomato juice or broth in any proportions)
¼ cup chopped fresh parsley or 2 tablespoons dried
1½ teaspoons salt (reduce if broth is salted)
¼ teaspoon pepper
1 to 2 cups chopped greens

Clean vegetables and cut into small dice. Combine with oil in soup pot, cover, and stew for 5 minutes.

Add broth, parsley, salt, and pepper, bring to a boil, cover, and simmer for 45 minutes, or until vegetables are tender.

Add greens, cover, and cook for 5 minutes longer.

Makes 2 quarts; serves 6 to 8

Note: If desired, each bowl of soup can be garnished with grated cheese, or thin slices of buttered toast can be floated on top.

Variations: Add additional diced vegetables to taste (potato, parsnip, turnip, zucchini, corn, green beans, okra, cooked beans).

Add diced tofu during the last 10 minutes.

Add ½ cup uncooked whole wheat pasta during last 20 minutes.

Add ½ cup raw brown rice with the broth. Cook soup 1 hour, or until rice is tender.

For a hearty *Vegetable Barley Soup,* replace leeks with 2 scallions, add 1 small turnip and ½ pound diced potato. Use 4½ cups water and 1½ cups tomato juice for the liquid. When soup is boiling, stir in ½ cup barley. Cook 1 to 1½ hours, or until barley is tender.

POTAGE BONNE FEMME

A French country soup that takes the place of chicken soup in a nonmeat kitchen.

2 tablespoons butter
1 tablespoon oil
1½ cups sliced leeks

2½ cups diced carrots
3 cups diced potatoes
6 cups water
2 teaspoons salt
1 teaspoon honey
pepper
chopped parsley

Heat oil and butter in a 5-quart soup pot. When melted, add leeks and carrot, stir to coat, and cook over gentle heat until hot and impregnated with fat.

Potatoes can be scrubbed and diced while the other vegetables are cooking. Add to the pot along with water, salt, and honey. Bring to a boil, cover, and simmer gently for 30 minutes.

Puree soup through a coarse sieve. This is preferred to electric pureeing in the blender or processor as the vegetable is reduced to fine light shreds rather than a mash; however, these appliances can be used.

Adjust salt and pepper to taste and garnish with parsley. Reheat if necessary.

Makes 2 quarts; serves 6 to 8

HOT BORSCHT

This Russian vegetable soup contains no fat. Serve it with plenty of yogurt to spoon into the soup bowls.

3 cups water
1 cup tomato pulp or puree
1 onion, diced
1 cup shredded or finely chopped carrot
1 cup peeled and shredded or finely chopped beets
1 cup shredded or slivered potato
2 cups thinly shredded cabbage
2 teaspoons salt
1 tablespoon lemon juice

Combine water and tomato and bring to a boil. Add vegetables, season with salt, cover and simmer about 30 minutes until vegetables are tender. When cooking is completed, add lemon juice.

Makes 1½ quarts; serves 4 to 6

FRESH TOMATO SOUP

2 tablespoons butter
1 medium onion, chopped
1 clove garlic, chopped
1 carrot, chopped
1 stalk celery with leaves, chopped
3 to 4 cups chopped tomatoes (1½ pounds)
1 tablespoon whole wheat flour
3 cups water
1 tablespoon fresh basil or 1 teaspoon dried
1 teaspoon salt
1 teaspoon tomato paste (if soup is made from winter tomatoes)

Melt 1 tablespoon of butter in a 2- to 3-quart pot. Add onion, garlic, carrot, and celery, and sauté for 5 minutes until onion is transparent.

Add tomatoes and simmer for 10 minutes, mashing occasionally with a wooden spoon until soft and pulpy. Sprinkle flour over tomatoes and stir smooth.

Add water and seasonings, bring to a boil, and simmer uncovered for 20 minutes if soup is to be pureed, 30 if not.

Puree if desired in food mill (discarding peel) or in the blender or processor. Reheat before serving and add the remaining tablespoon of butter.

Makes 1½ quarts; serves 4 to 6

Note: This soup can be pureed or left chunky. If pureeing is to be done in the processor or blender, or if soup is left chunky, you may wish to peel tomatoes for appearance sake only. If soup is pureed in a food mill, the skins can be separated later.

This soup can be frozen, but do not add last tablespoon of butter until serving.

Variations: For a refreshing lift, omit last tablespoon of butter and add a scant tablespoon of lemon juice just before serving instead.

For *Thick Tomato-Rice Soup,* add ¾ cup uncooked brown rice when tomato–water combination comes to a boil. Cover and simmer about 50 minutes, until grain is tender. Do not puree. Add remaining butter and ladle soup into serving bowls containing ¼ cup shredded Swiss cheese in each. Stir to melt. *Minor Protein.*

CAULIFLOWER–CHEESE CHOWDER

4 cups diced cauliflower, including tender parts of core
1 cup chopped onion
½ cup chopped celery
1 cup chopped fresh or canned tomatoes, or tomato juice
2½ cups water
1½ teaspoons salt
2 tablespoons chopped parsley
¼ cup whole wheat flour
2 tablespoons butter
1½ cups milk
½ teaspoon dry mustard
½ teaspoon soy sauce
2 cups shredded cheddar cheese

Combine vegetables, water, salt, and parsley in soup pot. Bring to a boil, cover, and simmer until cauliflower is tender, 15 to 20 minutes.

Knead flour into butter to form a smooth mass. Drop by bits into simmering soup and stir until smooth and slightly thickened.

Gradually stir milk into soup, then add mustard and soy sauce. Heat through. Add cheese in stages, stirring to melt.

Makes 2 quarts; serves 6
Minor Protein
Note: Butter and flour can be replaced by 4 Instant Sauce Balls (see page 315). Not recommended for freezing, but leftovers reheat nicely.

OKRA CHOWDER

2 tablespoons oil or butter
2 cups sliced okra
2 cups diced celery
1 small onion, chopped
1 green pepper, chopped
4 cups water
1 cup diced tomatoes or tomato puree
1 teaspoon salt
pepper
1 tablespoon nutritional yeast (optional)

Heat oil in soup pot and sauté okra, celery, onion, and green pepper for 5 minutes. Add water, tomato, and salt, bring to a boil, cover, and simmer for 30 minutes, or until vegetables are tender. Adjust salt and pepper to taste and, if desired, add yeast to thicken slightly.

Makes 1½ quarts; serves 4 to 6
Variation: After soup has simmered for 20 minutes, add a cup of leftover cooked grains.

POTATO AND GREENS

This is a simple country soup from Italy, the product of times when both money and fresh vegetables were scarce. Not only cheap and easy to make, but very tasty. It is particularly good served before a cheese or egg entrée.

3 cups diced potatoes (about 1 pound)
1 clove garlic, cut in half
4 cups water
2 cups sliced dark leafy greens (escarole, chard, kale, chickory, or wild greens)
1 teaspoon salt
1 cup diced stale whole grain bread
2 tablespoons olive oil
pepper

Combine potatoes, garlic, and water in a soup pot and bring to a boil. Cover and simmer until potatoes are not quite tender, 10 to 15 minutes. Add greens and salt to pot, cover, and cook 10 to 15 minutes longer, or until tender.

Remove from heat, add bread, cover, and let stand off the heat, for 10 minutes. Stir in oil, season with lots of fresh ground pepper, and serve.

Serves 4
Note: Soup should not be reheated once bread is added or it will become a thick porridge rather than a broth with floating bread cubes. Oil other than olive can be used, but the results will be less satisfying.

MASHED POTATO SOUP

Easily prepared and appealing despite the strange combination of ingredients.

2 cups mashed potatoes, or 1 pound potatoes, peeled and cut up, plus 1½ to 2 cups water
3½ cups milk
2 teaspoons grated onion
¼ cup peanut butter
1 tablespoon butter
¼ cup catsup
salt
pepper

If you are starting with fresh potatoes, combine them in a pot with 1½ cups water, bring to a boil, cover, and cook for 15 to 20 minutes until soft enough to puree. (Add remaining water during cooking if needed to keep potatoes from burning.) When potatoes are cooked, most of the liquid should be gone. Puree potatoes until completely smooth.

Add milk, onion, peanut butter, and butter to potatoes, and cook, stirring occasionally, over moderate heat until mixture thickens and comes to boiling point. Cook a bit longer, continuing to stir until soup is thickened and creamy. Stir in catsup. Season with salt and pepper if needed.

Makes 5 cups; serves 4
Minor Protein

BROCCOLI AND MACARONI SOUP

1 tablespoon oil
1 small clove garlic, chopped
4 cups tomato broth, or water plus 2 tablespoons tomato paste
1 teaspoon salt
pepper
4 cups chopped broccoli
1 cup small whole wheat shells or macaroni
¼ cup grated Parmesan cheese

Heat oil in a 3-quart pot and sauté garlic until lightly colored. Add tomato broth, salt, a generous turn of pepper, and bring to a boil.

Add broccoli; cover and simmer for 10 minutes. Add pasta, cover, and simmer 10 minutes longer, or until tender. Sprinkle with cheese and serve.

Serves 4
Minor Protein

BROCCOLI, BREAD, AND CHEESE SOUP

A satisfying main dish soup that can be prepared in the simple manner presented in the recipe or given a dramatic touch (and crusty topping) by baking it in the oven. The baking option is extremely useful if eating is done in shifts—simply prepare the soup in individual casseroles and heat each as it is needed.

6 onions, thinly sliced
2 cloves garlic, minced
2 tablespoons oil
1 pound broccoli
2 tablespoons soy sauce
2 teaspoons salt
6 cups water
6 thin slices whole grain bread, cut in half
1½ cups grated Swiss cheese
1 cup grated Parmesan cheese

Sauté onion and garlic in oil until softened, 3 to 5 minutes. Meanwhile chop broccoli quite small, including buds, stems, and leaves.

Add broccoli and soy sauce to onion, cover, and let stew over moderate heat for 10 minutes. Add salt and water and bring to a boil; cover and cook over low heat for 20 minutes, or until broccoli is tender.

For simplest service, put 1½ slices bread in each serving bowl, top with ½ cup of the combined cheeses, and pour in the hot soup. Sprinkle some of the remaining cheese on top of each bowl.

Serves 4
Major Protein
Note: For soup for 6, increase water to 8 cups, bread to 8 slices, and each of the cheeses by ½ cup. Leftover soup can be poured through a strainer to clear and saved as stock for other soups or cooking grains.

Variation: For *Baked Broccoli, Bread, and Cheese Soup,* line bottom of a 4-quart casserole or 4 individual oven-proof dishes with bread. Cover with cheese, reserving ½ cup. Pour in hot soup, sprinkle with remaining cheese, and bake in a 375°F. oven for 15 to 20 minutes until crusty.

FRENCH ONION SOUP

This delicious onion soup can be prepared without the lengthy cooking that is required by most recipes.

- **2 tablespoons oil**
- **4 cups thinly sliced onion (1½ pounds)**
- **3 tablespoons soy sauce**
- **6 cups water**
- **1½ teaspoons salt**
- **4 slices whole grain bread, lightly ·toasted**
- **1 cup shredded Swiss cheese**

Heat oil in a soup pot; add onion and soy sauce, cover, and stew over low heat until soft and pulpy, about 20 minutes. Add water and salt, bring to a boil and simmer, uncovered, for 10 minutes.

Place 1 slice of toast in each serving plate and pour on boiling soup. Sprinkle with cheese.

Serves 4

Minor Protein

Variation: For *Baked Onion Soup,* ladle soup into individual ovenproof ramekins. Top with toast slices and a generous layer of cheese. Bake in a 325°F. oven until top is crusty.

Menu Suggestions: This filling soup can serve as a meal when accompanied by a whole grain bread and a Minor Protein salad.

FRENCH ONION SOUP COUNTRY-STYLE

Less filling than the cheese-topped version, this soup is designed for appetizer service.

- **French Onion Soup (recipe above), without cheese**
- **2 egg yolks**
- **½ teaspoon lemon juice or a few drops vinegar**
- **4 slices whole grain bread, lightly toasted**

Prepare onion soup as directed in preceding recipe. Beat egg yolks with lemon or vinegar. Slowly beat in some of the hot soup. Return to soup pot and cook over low heat to warm through and thicken without boiling.

Cut toast in quarters and divide into serving bowls. Pour in hot soup.

Serves 6

Note: If prepared for 4 or less, use only 1 egg yolk and a few drops vinegar or lemon.

MINESTRONE

- **1 clove garlic, chopped**
- **1 tablespoon oil**
- **½ cup chopped onion**
- **6 cups tomato broth (liquid from drained canned tomatoes, an equal dilution of tomato juice and water, or water flavored with tomato paste or Tomato Cubes, page 430)**
- **2 carrots, diced**
- **1 stalk celery, diced**
- **½ pound potatoes, diced**
- **1 teaspoon salt**
- **1 tablespoon chopped parsley**
- **1 tablespoon fresh or 1 teaspoon dried basil**
- **1 small (6- to 8-ounce) zucchini, diced**
- **½ cup whole wheat elbow macaroni, small shells, or broken spaghetti**
- **1 cup cooked beans**
- **2½ cups shredded greens (spinach, romaine, chard, chicory, etc.)**
- **grated Parmesan cheese**

Sauté garlic briefly in oil. Add onion and cook until softened. Add tomato broth, carrots, celery, potatoes, salt, and remaining seasonings. Bring to a boil, cover, and simmer for 20 minutes.

Add remaining ingredients, cover, and simmer 20 to 30 minutes longer, or until vegetables are quite tender. Serve with grated Parmesan cheese.

Makes 1½ quarts; serves 6 to 8

Minor Protein

Variations: Add up to 1 cup cut-up green beans with first group of vegetables and/or ½ cup fresh peas with second group of vegetables. For *Minestrone Genovese,* omit oil, garlic, parsley, and basil. Combine onions with tomato broth and continue as directed. When soup is ready, stir in 2 tablespoons fresh-made or frozen Pesto (page 318).

For *Pistou,* make a paste of 2 tablespoons fresh basil leaves, 1 clove garlic, 2 tablespoons grated Parmesan, 1 tablespoon olive oil, and a pinch of salt. Mash smooth. Use to season soup at the table.

Menu Suggestions: A suitable first course if the meal to follow is not a heavy one, or a meal in itself with the addition of cheese to the soup and a Minor Protein savory pastry accompaniment.

ITALIAN CABBAGE AND RICE SOUP

A good first-course choice when the main dish features beans, or as a main dish in itself, accompanied by crusty bread and a bean salad.

1 tablespoon oil
1 tablespoon butter
1 clove garlic, split in half
1 large onion, chopped
4 cups sliced cabbage (about ¾ pound)
6 cups water or vegetable stock
2 tablespoons soy sauce
¾ cup raw brown rice
1½ teaspoons salt (reduce if stock contains salt)
¾ cup grated cheese, preferably a mixture of provolone and Parmesan, but Parmesan plus mozzarella or Swiss will do

Heat oil and butter in a 3- to 5-quart pot to melt. Add split clove garlic and brown. Remove garlic, add onion, and sauté until limp, 3 to 5 minutes. (Cabbage can be cut up during this time.)

Add cabbage to pot and stir to coat with fat. Cook until it begins to soften, about 5 minutes.

Add water or stock and soy sauce and bring to a boil. Add rice, cover, and simmer for 30 minutes. At this time add salt and cook until rice is tender, another 30 minutes. Serve, adding grated cheese at the table.

Makes 1½ to 2 quarts; serves 4 as main dish, 6 as appetizer
Minor Protein

DELUXE MUSHROOM–BARLEY SOUP

This thick hearty soup makes an excellent winter meal with biscuits and cheese or Cheese Crackers and cottage cheese salad. It freezes well and leftovers can easily be varied as described below.

6 cups water
1 onion, diced
1 potato, diced
2 stalks celery with tops, diced
2 carrots, chopped
½ cup chopped parsnip, rutabaga, or turnip (optional)
½ cup tomato pieces, puree, or juice, or 1½ teaspoons tomato paste diluted with ½ cup water
¼ cup dried lima beans
¼ cup dried split peas (yellow preferred)
¼ cup barley
¼ cup brown rice
¼ cup dried mushrooms
1 tablespoon oil
1 teaspoon salt
1 tablespoon fresh snipped dill or parsley
yogurt (optional)

Combine all ingredients in a 5-quart pot. Bring to a boil, cover, and simmer over low heat until very tender, about 1½ hours. Adjust salt and pepper to taste. Serve plain or with yogurt.

Makes 2 quarts; serves 4 to 6
Minor Protein
Variations: For extending leftovers into a soupier soup, thin to desired consistency with tomato juice and heat. To make a casserole with leftovers, top with cheese and bake.

ANABELLA'S OATMEAL SOUP

The inspiration for the recipe on the following page comes from San Miguel, Mexico, where Anabella ran what was reputed to be a fine vegetarian restaurant. This particular recipe certainly meets those expectations. It is particularly popular with children.

¼ cup chopped onion
1 to 2 cloves garlic, minced
2 tablespoons oil
1 tomato, diced, or ⅓ cup canned tomato pulp, puree, juice, or 3 Tomato Cubes (page 430)
3 cups vegetable broth or water
1 large carrot, diced
1 medium zucchini, diced (about 1½ cups)
½ cup raw peas
1 bay leaf
1 teaspoon salt (reduce if broth is salted)
¾ cup oats
½ cup milk

Sauté onion and garlic in oil in a 2- to 3-quart pot until soft, 3 to 5 minutes. Add liquid, remaining vegetables, and seasoning. Bring to a boil, cover, and simmer for 15 minutes.

While soup simmers, brown oats in ungreased skillet set over moderate heat. This will take approximately 15 minutes. Stir occasionally or shake to promote even toasting. Once oats begin to color, keep an eye on them to prevent over-cooking. Remove from heat when lightly colored.

Add oats to soup and simmer, uncovered, for 10 minutes. Just before serving, stir milk into hot soup. Season to taste at the table with salt and pepper.

Makes 1 quart; serves 4
Minor Protein
Note: The addition of 1 tablespoon of nutritional yeast along with the milk improves the flavor and food value.

MEXICAN CORN SOUP

An ideal opener for a taco dinner.

½ pound tomatoes (1 large or 2 small)
¼ cup onion pieces
4-ounce can whole or chopped green chilies
2 tablespoons butter
5 to 6 ears corn or 3½ to 4 cups corn kernels
2 cups milk
½ teaspoon salt
1 cup diced Jack, Muenster, or mozzarella cheese

Roast tomatoes by placing on a long-handled fork over a flame until skin is charred and easily removed. This gives soup a special flavor, but if necessary peel can be removed in another manner or left intact.

Combine peeled tomato and onion in a blender or processor fitted with steel blade and puree smooth. Set aside.

Drain chilies and, if whole, cut in thin strips. Melt butter in a 2- to 3-quart pot and sauté chilies for 2 to 3 minutes. Do not brown. Add tomato puree to pot and cook for 5 minutes until slightly thickened. Remove from heat to cool a little.

Cut kernels from corn and put 3 cups of kernels in the blender or processor along with the milk. Puree until smooth. Add corn puree to cooled tomato puree a little at a time to prevent curdling. (Should the milk curdle anyway, only the appearance will be harmed.)

Add salt and the remaining corn kernels and cook over low heat for 15 to 20 minutes until soup is quite hot. Pour over cheese cubes in soup bowls.

Serves 6
Minor Protein
Note: This soup does not freeze well. Leftovers can be kept a day or two and reheated over low heat or in a double boiler. Avoid vigorous boiling.

CHEDDAR SOUP

This soup is easily executed but does demand attention.

¼ cup chopped onion or scallion
2 tablespoons butter, oil, or preferably a mixture
¼ cup whole wheat flour
3 cups milk
2 cups vegetable broth
1 teaspoon salt (reduce if broth is salted)
½ teaspoon dry mustard
2 cups shredded cheddar cheese
cayenne
paprika
chopped green pepper

Sauté onion or scallion in fat until soft but not brown (about 5 minutes). Remove from heat and stir in flour. Return to heat and stir for 1 minute without browning.

Gradually stir in milk and broth and bring to a boil. Add salt, mustard, and cheese in stages, stirring to melt.

Sprinkle soup sparingly with cayenne, generously with paprika, and serve. Garnish each bowl with green pepper.

Serves 4
Major Protein
Note: If you like your soup on the thick side, reduce milk to 2 cups.

LEEK AND CHEDDAR SOUP

This has a more pronounced flavor than plain Cheddar Soup. We suspect it will be preferred by adults, but perhaps not by all children.

2 tablespoons butter, oil, or preferably a mixture
1½ cups sliced leeks
3 cups milk
2 cups vegetable broth
½ pound potatoes (2 small or 1 large)
1 teaspoon salt
½ teaspoon dry mustard
2 cups shredded cheddar cheese
⅛ to ¼ teaspoon cayenne
paprika

Melt fat and sauté leeks for 3 to 5 minutes until softened. Add milk and broth and heat to boiling. As mixture heats, grate potato finely into pot. Simmer, uncovered, for 15 minutes until potato is cooked and soup thickens.

Add salt, mustard, and gradually the cheese, stirring to melt. Adjust salt, if necessary; sprinkle with enough cayenne to give soup a bite and enough paprika to enhance the color.

Serves 4
Major Protein

CREAM OF MUSHROOM SOUP

1 tablespoon butter
1 tablespoon oil
¼ cup minced onion
1 pound mushrooms, finely chopped (about 5 cups)
5 tablespoons whole wheat flour

4 cups whole milk, or skim milk with an added ¼ cup dry milk
½ teaspoon salt
2 teaspoons soy sauce
¼ teaspoon nutmeg
pepper
1 teaspoon nutritional yeast (optional)

Heat butter and oil in a 3-quart saucepan to melt. Add onion and mushrooms and cook over low heat, stirring occasionally, about 5 minutes, or until liquid runs freely.

Stir in flour until thick and smooth. Cook for 1 minute. Gradually add milk, salt, soy sauce, and nutmeg. Cook, stirring frequently, until soup is very hot and creamy. This will take about 10 minutes over low heat. Add a little pepper, and for additional flavor stir in yeast and mix smooth just before serving.

Makes 1½ quarts; serves 4 to 6
Minor Protein

CREAM OF SPINACH SOUP

1 tablespoon butter
1 tablespoon oil
¼ cup minced onion
¾ pound spinach, chopped very fine
3 tablespoons cornstarch or arrowroot
2 cups water or vegetable broth
1 to 1½ teaspoons salt (less if broth is salted)
2 cups whole milk, or skim milk with an added ¼ cup dry milk
2 tablespoons sherry
¼ teaspoon nutmeg

Melt butter with oil in a 3-quart pot, then add onion and cook for 1 minute. Add spinach and cook, stirring, until spinach softens, 3 to 5 minutes.

Remove from heat and stir in starch until no longer visible. Return to heat and gradually stir in water or broth. Add salt and bring soup to a gentle boil, stirring occasionally.

Add milk and heat through. Stir in sherry, nutmeg, adjust salt if needed, and cook 1 minute longer.

Makes 5 cups; serves 4
Minor Protein

GOLDEN CARROT SOUP

¾ pound carrots, diced (about 2 cups)
1 medium potato, peeled and diced (about 1 cup)
2 tablespoons oil, butter, or a mixture
1 teaspoon salt
1 teaspoon honey
3 cups water
½ cup nonfat dry milk powder
¼ teaspoon ground ginger

Combine vegetables, fat, salt, and honey in a 3-quart soup pot. Cover and stew over moderate heat for 15 minutes. Add 2½ cups water, bring to a boil, cover, and simmer for 15 minutes until vegetables are tender.

Puree in a food mill, blender, or processor. Dissolve milk powder in remaining ½ cup water and add to carrot puree along with ginger. Heat through without boiling.

Makes about 1 quart; serves 4
Minor Protein

NEW ENGLAND BEAN CHOWDER

This soup has the appeal of the famed New England clam chowder.

1 cup dried pea, navy, or lima beans
5 cups water
1 onion, chopped
1 cup celery, cut in small dice
1 cup carrot, cut in small dice
1½ cups potato, cut in ½-inch cubes
1 cup fresh or canned drained tomatoes
1½ teaspoons salt
⅛ teaspoon cayenne pepper
1½ cups milk
1 tablespoon nutritional yeast

Soak beans in water as for cooking dried beans, then bring to a boil, cover, and cook over low heat for 30 minutes or until partially tender.

Add vegetables, salt, and cayenne, and cook 30 to 45 minutes longer, or until beans and vegetables are tender. Remove 1 cup soup and puree.

Stir the milk and yeast gradually into the puree, then slowly stir this back into the soup pot. Cook over low heat, uncovered, stirring until soup thickens slightly and is heated through. Adjust seasoning to taste.

Makes 2 quarts; serves 6
Minor Protein

SENATE BEAN SOUP

The soup that gained its fame in the U.S. Senate cafeteria.

1 pound dried white beans (pea, navy, great northern, or marrow)
6 cups water
1 bay leaf
⅛ teaspoon powdered thyme or ¼ teaspoon crushed leaves
½ pound potatoes
¼ cup milk
½ cup chopped celery
½ cup chopped onion
¼ cup chopped parsley
1 small clove garlic, chopped
1½ teaspoons salt

Soak beans in water as for cooking dried beans, then bring to a boil, add bay leaf and thyme, cover, and cook over low heat until tender, 45 minutes to 1 hour.

Meanwhile scrub potatoes, cut in halves or quarters, and steam until tender. Put through ricer or mash well with a fork. Beat in milk to make fluffy.

Add potatoes and remaining ingredients to cooked beans, cover and cook gently for 1 hour, stirring occasionally and lightly mashing beans to a pulpy consistency with the back of a spoon. Adjust seasoning and serve.

Makes 1½ quarts; serves 4 to 6
Minor Protein
Menu Suggestions: When served with fresh bread and a protein containing salad, this soup makes a substantial meal.

MOM'S THICK SPLIT-PEA SOUP

This is the soup that Nikki grew up with; it is presented in such a generous amount here since the more it is reheated, the thicker and better it gets.

2 cups dried split peas
8 cups water
2 onions, chopped
4 carrots, chopped
4 to 6 leafy celery tops, chopped
1 large bay leaf
2 teaspoons salt
pepper

Combine peas and water in a large soup pot. Bring to a boil. While you are waiting, the vegetables can be prepared and added to the pot along with seasonings.

Once it is boiling, cover and cook over low heat for 1 to 1½ hours until peas are very soft. Mash with a fork or puree in a food mill. Cook several minutes uncovered to thicken if necessary.

Makes about 2 quarts; serves 8
Protein Complement
Note: For a thinner soup, puree in blender or processor.

Variations: For *Puree Mongole,* a tomato-flavored pea soup, combine this soup with an equal amount of tomato juice, tomato puree, stewed tomatoes, or a combination of one of these and fresh chopped tomatoes. Simmer for 5 minutes. This is an excellent way to stretch split-pea soup leftovers; about 1½ cups soup, plus the same amount of tomato, will make 2 generous servings.

For *Cold Dilled Pea Soup,* puree 2 cups cold split-pea soup with 2 cups milk and 1 tablespoon fresh dill. Stir in 1 cup yogurt, adjust salt and pepper to taste and, if bland, add a little fresh lemon juice. Serve very cold with a garnish of chopped tomatoes and additional yogurt.

Menu Suggestions: Split-pea soup is nicely complemented with cheese cubes in the bowl or a topping of yogurt and a whole grain breadstuff, especially corn bread or rice crackers.

GREEK LENTIL SOUP

From the women of Asini, a small Greek farming town in the Peloponnese.

2 tablespoons oil
2 medium to large onions, chopped

2 stalks celery, chopped
2 cups dried lentils
8 cups water
1 cup tomato broth, or 8 Tomato Cubes (page 430), or 1 tablespoon tomato paste diluted with water, or equal parts tomato juice and water
1 bay leaf
2 teaspoons salt
4 cups shredded spinach or other dark leafy green
1 cup small whole wheat shells, macaroni, or broken spaghetti, or 2 cups cooked brown rice
2 to 3 tablespoons lemon juice or vinegar
yogurt

Heat oil in a 5-quart pot and sauté onion about 3 minutes until limp. Add celery, lentils, liquid, and bay leaf. Bring to a boil, cover, and simmer over low heat about 45 minutes until lentils are just tender.

Add salt, greens, and grain, cover, and cook for 15 minutes, or until grains and beans are tender. If soup appears to be too dry at this time, add more liquid. (This should be a thick stewlike soup, but if heat is too high there may be too much evaporation.)

When fully cooked, stir in lemon juice or vinegar to taste. Garnish each bowl with generous spoonfuls of yogurt.

Makes 2½ quarts; serves 8 as first course, 6 as a main dish
Minor Protein for 8 or more; *Major Protein* for 6 or less

Variations: If desired, add some peeled, diced carrots along with the celery. Some like to add hot pepper sauce. This can be done in the pot or to taste at the table. For *Italian Lentil Soup,* add 1 large clove chopped garlic to the sautéing onion. Add 2 teaspoons oregano with the bay leaf. Serve with grated Parmesan cheese. For a thinner, less filling soup, pasta or grain can be omitted, but the bean in the soup should be complemented by something else on the menu.

Menu Suggestions: Add whole grain crackers or pita bread, a tahini dip or spread, and a salad with feta cheese for a complete dinner.

MULLIGATAWNY SOUP

This thin broth is delicately spiced but has a definite bite; the lentils lend a bit of texture. Indian in origin, it is welcome at all Indian meals that are not heavily weighted with beans.

> 1 tablespoon oil
> 1 tablespoon butter
> 1 medium onion, chopped
> 1 large clove garlic, chopped
> ¼ teaspoon crushed red pepper
> 1 teaspoon cumin
> 1 teaspoon turmeric
> ½ teaspoon coriander
> 6 cups water
> ⅔ cup dry lentils
> 1 teaspoon salt
> 1½ teaspoons lemon juice

Heat oil and butter in a 3-quart pot and sauté onion and garlic about 3 minutes to soften. Add spices and cook for 1 minute.

Add water and lentils and bring to a boil. Cover and simmer over low heat for 50 to 60 minutes until lentils are quite tender. Salt sometime after the first 30 minutes. When cooking is completed, stir in lemon juice.

Makes 1½ quarts; serves 6
Protein Complement
Variation: Split peas can be used instead of lentils.

PASTA FAGIOLI SOUP

This well-known Italian macaroni and bean soup, made with precooked beans, can serve as a first course or as the entrée.

> 2 tablespoons oil
> 2 cloves garlic, minced
> 1 large onion, chopped
> 2 stalks celery, chopped
> 6 cups tomato broth or equal parts tomato juice and water
> 3 cups cooked beans
> 1½ teaspoons salt (reduce if broth or beans are salty)
> 1 cup small whole wheat shells or macaroni
> 5 cups shredded spinach or lettuce
> grated Parmesan cheese

Heat oil in a 5-quart pot and sauté garlic, onion, and celery for 5 minutes, or until onion is softened. Add broth and beans, bring to a boil, cover and simmer for 10 minutes. If beans are not tender, cook until they are. Add salt as needed.

Add pasta, cover and simmer until tender, 10 to 15 minutes. Add greens, cover and cook for 5 minutes. Serve, adding cheese to taste at the table.

Makes 2 quarts; serves 8 as a soup course, 4 as a main course
Minor Protein for 8; *Major Protein* for 4
Variation: For *Mexican Macaroni and Bean Soup,* add 2 tablespoons chili powder to sautéed vegetables and cook for 1 minute before adding broth. Replace pasta with 2 cups corn kernels and 2 corn tortillas cut in thin strips. Cook 5 minutes, then add greens. Replace Parmesan with shredded cheddar or Jack cheese.

BLACK BEAN SOUP

The accompaniments to this soup are its natural complements, rice and yogurt, along with chopped raw onion; just fill the serving bowls with soup and then spoon in these condiments at the table. Add a crusty bread and salad and dinner is complete.

> 1 cup black beans
> 3½ cups water
> 1 bay leaf
> 1 clove garlic, minced
> 1 small onion, chopped
> ½ green pepper, chopped
> 1 teaspoon oregano
> 2 teaspoons salt
> 2 tablespoons wine vinegar
> ½ teaspoon hot pepper sauce

Combine beans and water in a soup pot and let soak for 8 hours, or bring to a boil for 1 minute, remove from heat, cover, and let soak for 1 to 2 hours.

Add bay leaf, garlic, onion, green pepper, and oregano to soaked beans, bring to a boil, cover, and simmer over low heat for 1 hour, or until beans are tender.

Add salt, vinegar, and pepper sauce and cook 5 minutes longer. Taste for seasoning, adjust if necessary, and remove about half the beans from the pot. Puree these beans, then stir them back into the soup and cook for a few minutes until slightly thickened. If soup is too thick, add up to ½ cup water.

Serves 4

Protein Complement; Major Protein with rice and yogurt garnish

Note: This soup freezes well so you may want to double or triple the recipe and put the excess in the freezer.

MEXICAN BEAN SOUP

Serve as a prelude to a meal or as a meal in itself. This bean puree is both filling and enticing with cubes of melting cheese throughout and a garnish of tortillas and peppers.

> **2 medium tomatoes (about ¾ pound)**
> **¼ small onion**
> **1 clove garlic**
> **1 canned green chili**
> **1 tablespoon oil**
> **3 cups cooked pinto or other red bean, lightly drained**
> **2 cups bean broth or water**
> **salt (optional)**
> **hot pepper sauce or crushed red pepper (optional)**
> **3 tortillas**
> **½ cup yogurt**
> **¼ cup sour cream**
> **1½ cups cubed Muenster or Jack cheese (about 6 ounces)**
> **1 canned green chili, cut in strips**

Roast tomatoes over a flame until charred all over. This is not essential to the recipe but adds robust flavor. Combine tomato, onion, garlic, and chili in a blender or processor fitted with a steel blade. Blend to a puree.

Heat oil in a 3-quart pot, add tomato puree, and cook over high heat for 5 minutes. Place beans in a blender or processor and puree smooth. Add to tomato mixture and stir over medium-low heat for 5 minutes.

Add bean broth or water and cook, stirring occasionally, for 10 minutes.

Add salt, if necessary, and for a spicy soup a little hot pepper sauce or crushed red pepper to taste.

While soup simmers, toast tortillas and cut in strips. Combine yogurt with sour cream. Place some cheese cubes in each bowl. Ladle soup over cheese. Garnish with tortilla and chili strips and dollops of the cold yogurt–sour cream mixture.

Makes 1½ quarts; serves 6

Major Protein

Note: Beans can be prepared from ½ pound dry or you can use two 1-pound cans.

AFRICAN BEAN SOUP

A flavorful soup, chock full of beans, that ranges from spicy to fiery, depending on the amount of hot pepper that is included.

> **½ cup dried limas**
> **½ cup dried white beans (pea, navy, great northern, etc.)**
> **½ cup pink or red beans**
> **4½ cups water**
> **2 tablespoons oil**
> **1 cup chopped onion**
> **½ cup chopped green pepper**
> **½ to 1 inch fresh or frozen hot red pepper, chopped, or ¼ to ⅓ teaspoon crushed dried red pepper**
> **2 stalks celery with tops, chopped**
> **¼ cup chopped parsley**
> **1 tablespoon fresh or frozen basil or 1 teaspoon dried**
> **½ teaspoon cumin**
> **1½ teaspoons salt**
> **⅓ cup peanuts, ground to meal (or ½ cup meal)**

Combine beans and water, bring to a boil for 2 minutes, cover, remove from heat, and let soak for 1 to 2 hours. Then return to a boil and cook over low heat for 1 hour.

While beans cook, heat oil in a skillet and add onion and pepper and sauté until soft but not brown, about 5 minutes. Add celery and parsley and cook 3 minutes longer.

Add sautéed vegetables to beans along with seasonings. Continue to cook, covered, until very tender, or 1 to 1½ hours longer. When just about cooked, stir in ground peanuts and cook for 15 minutes.

Serves 4

Protein Complement

Note: If you wish to make this soup from precooked beans, begin by sautée-ing vegetables in a 3-quart pot. Add 4 cups cooked beans and 1½ to 2 cups cooking liquid or water. Add season-ings, omitting salt if beans are presalted, bring to a boil, cover, and cook over low heat for 30 to 45 minutes, depend-ing on the beans. Add peanut meal during last 15 minutes.

Menu Suggestions: This soup is in-tended for main dish service and can be complemented by any good whole grain bread. We prefer corn and recommend cheese-rich Harvest Corncake; for something quicker, roll corn tortillas around cheese and warm to melt. Com-plete menu with sliced tomato or green salad.

CREAMY LIMA BEAN SOUP

   3 cups cooked dried lima beans, drained
   2 cups cooking liquid or water
   2 tablespoons oil, butter, or a mixture
   ½ cup chopped onion
   1 cup finely chopped carrot
   1 tablespoon whole wheat flour
   1 teaspoon salt (reduce if beans are salted)
   1 teaspoon thyme, sage, or dill
   pinch cayenne
   1 cup milk

Puree beans with liquid until smooth. In a 2- to 3-quart pot mix fat with onion and carrot and cook, covered, over medium heat for 10 minutes, or until carrot is just tender.

Stir in flour and seasonings and gradually add milk, cooking and stirring until mixture is thick and comes to a gentle boil. Simmer for 1 minute. Stir in bean puree, heat to boiling, and ad-just seasoning to taste.

Makes 1½ quarts; serves 4

Major Protein

Note: To prepare beans from scratch, cook ½ pound dried lima beans in 5 cups water for 1 hour, or until tender.

Variation: Replace limas with a cooked white bean (cannellini, great northern or pea).

PUREED BEAN SOUP

Here we describe the basic recipe which you can adapt to personal taste and the ingredients on hand.

   ½ **pound dried beans**
   6 **cups water**
   1 **teaspoon salt**
   vegetables of choice:
      1 **onion, diced**
      2 **leeks, sliced**
      2 **carrots or celery stalks, diced**
      4 **cups shredded lettuce or spinach or 2 cups cabbage**
   1 **clove garlic, split**
   1 **tablespoon butter or oil (optional)**

Soak beans in water as for general bean cookery. Then bring to a boil, cover, and cook over low heat until tender. If you wish to cook extra beans for another occasion at the same time, increase as desired and when done, re-move 3 cups cooked beans and about 4 cups cooking liquid to make the soup.

To cooked beans, add salt and de-sired vegetables. Cover and simmer un-til tender, about 10 minutes for greens alone, 15 with onion or leek, and 20 if carrot or celery is added. You may also choose to add some tomato pulp or replace some of the cooking liquid with tomato broth or juice.

When vegetable is tender, puree the soup, then return to the pot, adjust salt and pepper to taste, and cook until slightly thickened. If desired, add fat at the end for extra richness.

Makes 1½ quarts; serves 4 to 6

Protein Complement

Menu Suggestions: All pureed bean soups benefit from a topping of plain yogurt or yogurt mixed with sour cream, and a handful of croutons or crumbled crackers.

SPECIALTY SOUPS

Here are a few soups from our collection that are set apart from the others because of their extreme delicacy or unusual flavor, which we feel merits special consideration. They are by no means any more complicated to produce, and by calling attention to them in this manner we don't mean to imply that they are not suited to family dinners.

ITALIAN MUSHROOM SOUP

This has a very elegant appearance despite the fact that it is quick and easy to prepare.

1 tablespoon oil (olive preferred for flavor)
1 clove garlic, chopped
½ pound mushrooms, sliced (2½ to 2¾ cups)
2 cups fresh tomatoes, peeled and chopped, or 1½ cups canned
½ teaspoon salt
½ teaspoon dried oregano
pepper
2½ cups water
1 egg
¼ cup grated Parmesan cheese

Heat oil in a 2-quart pot and cook garlic briefly. Add mushrooms and cook for 5 minutes until liquid runs freely. Add tomatoes and seasonings, cover, and cook over low heat for 15 minutes. Add water, bring to a boil, cover, and cook 15 minutes longer.

Just before serving, beat egg with cheese and slowly beat in some of the hot soup until egg mixture is warm. Add this back to the remaining soup without reheating. Serve at once.
Serves 4
Minor Protein
Note: This is designed to be a light appetizer. For more generous servings you may want to double the recipe. If necessary, cooking time can be reduced, but the time recommended here maximizes the flavor. This soup does not reheat well, so if it is prepared in advance the last step should be put off until serving time. Then return to a boil and proceed as directed. If it must be reheated, do so in a double boiler or place pot on a heat-resistant pad.

FRENCH MUSHROOM SOUP

This is another delicate mushroom soup that is only slightly less aristocratic than the previous version and can be ready for service in less than half an hour. It does, however, depend on prepared vegetable broth for some of its flavor.

3 tablespoons butter
¾ pound mushrooms, quartered (about 4 cups)
1 small clove garlic
¼ teaspoon nutmeg
2 tablespoons chopped parsley
generous grind of pepper
½ teaspoon salt (omit if broth is salted)
4 cups vegetable broth
2 slices whole wheat bread
½ cup yogurt

Melt butter in a 2-quart pot and sauté mushrooms about 5 minutes until liquid runs freely. Add garlic, nutmeg, parsley, pepper, and salt. Cook 1 minute longer.

Add broth and bread, bring to a boil, cover, and simmer over low heat for 10 minutes.

Transfer to a blender or processor fitted with steel chopping blade and coarse-chop. Soup should be chunky, with tiny pieces of mushroom, rather than smooth.

Just before serving, reheat soup if need be, then cool slightly and slowly stir in yogurt until smooth.
Serves 4
Minor Protein
Note: Do not reheat once yogurt has been added.

MIDEAST CARROT AND CHICK-PEA PUREE

These flavors meld beautifully, offering a hint of garlic and a hint of mint. A garnish of fresh mint leaves, if available, adds to the flavor and appearance, and the yogurt topping enhances both the flavor and food value of the soup.

1½ cups cooked chick-peas, drained
1 pound carrots, diced (about 3 cups)
2 cloves garlic, split
½ cup chopped onion
4 cups bean cooking liquid or water
1½ teaspoons dried mint
1 tablespoon lemon juice
salt
pepper
fresh mint leaves, chopped (optional)
yogurt

Combine chick-peas, vegetables, and liquid and bring to a boil. Cover and simmer until carrot is tender enough to puree, about 20 minutes.

Puree through the fine sieve of a food mill or, lacking this, in the blender. Return puree to the pot and add dried mint, lemon juice, ½ teaspoon salt (if liquid and beans were not previously salted), and a generous amount of pepper.

Simmer for 5 minutes. Sprinkle fresh chopped mint leaves on top if desired and add yogurt to each dish at the table.

Makes 1½ quarts; serves 4
Minor Protein
Menu Suggestions: This soup should precede a grain-based main course or be served at a meal offering a grain accompaniment.

PUMPKIN SOUP

The use of pumpkin in soup may seem unusual, but the outcome is a pleasing broth that can be used as a first course for almost any meal.

1 tablespoon oil or butter
1 medium onion, chopped
1 tablespoon peeled, chopped ginger
4 cups vegetable broth or water
1 teaspoon salt (omit if broth is salted)
1 tablespoon soy sauce
2 cups pumpkin puree (1-pound can)
½ cup milk
¼ cup nonfat dry milk powder

Heat fat in a 3-quart pot and sauté onion and ginger for 3 to 5 minutes to soften. Add liquid, salt, and soy sauce and bring to a boil.

Stir pumpkin into boiling soup and cook until smooth and heated through. Before serving, combine milk and milk powder to dissolve, stir into soup, and warm without boiling.

Makes 1½ quarts; serves 6
Minor Protein
Menu Suggestions: Pumpkin Soup is especially good preceding bean, grain, and nut burgers and loaves, as well as most Mexican meals.

CELERY SOUP WITH CREAMY CHEESE

When the hot soup is poured over the cheese cubes in the serving plates they turn into lush, creamy filaments.

1 tablespoon butter
2 cups diced celery
½ cup thinly sliced carrot
¼ cup sliced leeks or scallion
3 cups water
½ teaspoon salt
pepper
½ cup yogurt
1 egg yolk
¼ cup grated Parmesan, cheddar, or Swiss cheese
4 ounces stringy melting cheese, as mozzarella, Muenster, Jack, or provolone, cut in small cubes
1 celery heart, thinly sliced

Melt butter in a 2-quart pot. Add vegetables, cover, and stew for 5 minutes. Add 1 cup water, bring to a boil, cover, and cook gently for 10 minutes, or until vegetables are soft enough to puree.

Puree in blender, processor, or food mill. Add remaining water and salt and pepper, bring to a boil, and simmer, uncovered, for 5 minutes until very hot.

Just before serving, beat together yogurt, egg yolk, and grated cheese. Stir a little hot soup into this mixture, continuing until it is warm. Then add to hot soup in pot and serve at once.

For proper effect, the soup should be very hot when ladled into the soup bowls containing the cubes of cheese.

The thinly sliced celery heart should be floated on top as a garnish.

Makes 1 quart; serves 4
Minor Protein

Note: The amount of salt needed depends largely on the cheese, so do not oversalt initially. Salt can always be added at the table. If you wish to increase the recipe and freeze some, you will have surprisingly good results, despite the "unsuitable" ingredients. The soup, however, must be defrosted fully at room temperature, then heated gently in the top of a double boiler; or you can place it in a heatproof jar in a pot of boiling water and allow it to remain in this continually boiling water bath until it is quite hot, about 10 minutes.

Variation: If you have leftovers, chill thoroughly and serve cold with croutons and a chopped tomato garnish.

CREOLE TOMATO AND PEANUT SOUP

Despite the unusual mixture, this lightly spiced blend of tomato and peanut is acceptable even to unadventurous palates.

2 tablespoons oil
1 cup chopped onion
¼ cup chopped green pepper
¼ teaspoon cayenne
1 tablespoon whole wheat flour
1 cup milk
½ cup smooth or chunky peanut butter
1 cup fresh or canned tomato pulp
2 cups tomato juice

Heat oil in a 2-quart pot and sauté onion and green pepper about 5 minutes until softened. Add cayenne and cook for 1 minute longer.

Stir in flour and, when smooth, add milk and peanut butter. Continue to cook over moderate heat, stirring all the while until the soup is smooth, hot, and thickened. This will take 5 to 10 minutes. Slowly stir in tomato and tomato juice and warm through.

Makes 1 quart; serves 4
Minor Protein

Note: Tomato pulp can be replaced by an additional cup of tomato juice, but soup will not be as delicate.

Menu Suggestions: The perfect prelude to Hoppin' John or any other traditional Southern meal. A wedge of corn bread on the side is also a recommended accompaniment.

CHINESE HOT AND SOUR SOUP

Like many Chinese dishes the preparation exceeds the cooking time, but the advantage of this is that most of the work can be done and set aside, freeing you to concentrate on the rest of the meal. Don't be put off by the lengthy directions—they are intended to help you organize and time yourself properly.

6 dried Chinese mushrooms
1 cup hot water
20 dried lily buds (optional)
4 cups vegetable broth
2 scallions, sliced
2 tablespoons soy sauce
½ teaspoon salt (omit if broth is salted)
1½ cups corn kernels or green peas
½ pound tofu, cut in thin strips
½ teaspoon fine-ground pepper
3 tablespoons white or wine vinegar
2 tablespoons cornstarch or arrowroot
2 tablespoons cold water
1 egg
1 teaspoon Oriental sesame oil

Pour very hot water over mushrooms in a bowl and let soak for 30 minutes. Do the same with lily buds, if used, in a separate container.

Bring broth to a boil and drain mushroom soaking liquid into this. Slice the mushrooms and add them to the pot along with the drained lily buds (discard their liquid), scallions, soy sauce, salt, and corn.

Cover and simmer over low heat for 5 minutes. Add tofu, pepper, and vinegar. Simmer for 1 to 2 minutes and taste. If not sour enough, add ½ to 1 tablespoon vinegar. If not spicy enough, add another ½ teaspoon pepper or hot pepper sauce to taste. If soup is being prepared in advance, stop here, then reheat a few minutes before serving and continue as directed.

Mix starch and water to a paste and add to hot soup. Cook, stirring, until slightly thickened. Beat egg; remove soup from heat and slowly pour in egg, stirring soup continuously with a chopstick or fork until egg "strings." Stir in sesame oil and serve.

Serves 6
Minor Protein

COLD SOUPS

The soup season needn't end with the coming of warm weather. One of the great advantages of cold soups is that they can be prepared in advance, so that even those that require some cooking can be gotten out of the way in the cool morning or late evening hours when you may feel more like spending time in the kitchen. When time is short, these soups can be placed in the freezer for about 30 minutes to chill.

GAZPACHO

For those who have never encountered gazpacho, it is a spicy, chilled, raw tomato soup of Spanish origin that is an unsurpassed delight when made with fresh, ripe tomatoes. The traditional accoutrements include bowls of chopped green pepper, diced cucumber, chopped onion or scallion, and croutons to be added as desired. Although not part of this tradition, yogurt makes a nice garnish too.

2 slices whole grain bread
1½ cups cold water
1 large clove garlic, chopped
1 teaspoon salt
3 tablespoons olive oil
3 tablespoons wine vinegar
1½ pounds tomatoes, cut up (about 4 cups)
2 tablespoons minced onion
¼ teaspoon hot pepper sauce

Tear bread into small pieces and place in a blender container or processor fitted with a steel blade. Pour in ½ cup water. Add garlic, salt, oil, vinegar, tomatoes, onion, and pepper sauce. Let marinate about 30 minutes.

After marinating, process until tomato has been completely pureed. Then stir in remaining 1 cup water. If too thick, add additional water to make a thick but not mushy soup.

Chill before serving, and serve very cold with the accompaniments suggested above.

Serves 4 generously (6 more modestly)

Variation: For *Italian Chilled Tomato Soup,* use a small clove of garlic and stir in 1 cup of cooked white beans along with the remaining cup of water. If too thick, add additional water to thin. Serve very cold with a garnish of grated cheese.

WHITE GAZPACHO

This soup offers the alluring flavor of garlic that characterizes traditional gazpacho, but in a cucumber base. For those who object to garlic, it can be omitted and replaced with 2 tablespoons fresh dill. Serve this soup very cold with a choice of garnishes including croutons, diced tomato, chopped scallion, and chopped sweet red or green pepper.

2 cups peeled, diced cucumber
1 small clove garlic
½ cup parsley
2 tablespoons white vinegar
½ teaspoon salt
2 cups yogurt
½ cup sour cream

Combine cucumber, garlic, parsley, salt, and vinegar in a blender or processor fitted with a steel blade and blend smooth. Stir in yogurt and sour cream until evenly mixed. Chill before serving.

Makes 1 quart; serves 4
Minor Protein
Note: To make this soup without a blender or processor, grate cucumber fine on a cheese grater, mash garlic, chop parsley very fine, and mix all ingredients together.

MOROCCAN YOGURT SOUP

In this mellow soup the fresh mint works to counteract the aftereffects of the garlic.

2 cups yogurt
¼ cup coarsely chopped walnuts
1 cup peeled, shredded cucumber
1 small clove garlic, crushed
¼ cup chopped fresh mint
½ teaspoon salt
4 ice cubes

Beat yogurt with a wire whisk or fork until smooth. Stir in remaining ingredients except for the ice. Chill. Serve with an ice cube in each bowl.
Serves 4
Minor Protein
Variation: Some finely chopped pistachios sprinkled on top of each serving adds a glamorous touch.
Menu Suggestions: Serve at a meal that emphasizes grain. It is particularly pleasing with Couscous.

VICHYSSOISE

Despite its French-sounding name, the icy-cold leek and potato soup known as vichyssoise is an American invention.

2 tablespoons butter
2 tablespoons oil
1 cup chopped onion
1 cup sliced leeks
4 to 6 cups diced potatoes (1 to 1½ pounds)
2 quarts water or vegetable broth
1 tablespoon salt (reduce if broth is salted)
pepper
1 cup nonfat dry milk powder
1 cup half-and-half or whole milk
parsley

Heat butter and oil to melt in a 5-quart pot. Sauté onion and leek in fat until limp, 3 to 4 minutes. Add potatoes, liquid, and salt and bring to a boil; cover and simmer over low heat about 20 minutes until potatoes are soft enough to puree.

Puree smooth in blender, processor, or food mill. Add pepper and nonfat dry milk powder.

Chill and serve icy cold, adding half and half or whole milk and a sprinkling of fresh parsley just before serving.
Makes 2 quarts; serves 6 to 8
Minor Protein
Variations: For *Hot Leek and Potato Soup,* puree as directed, add pepper and milk powder, and warm through without boiling. Garnish with parsley and serve. For *Watercress Soup,* add 1½ cups watercress leaves and tender stems to soup after it has simmered for 15 minutes. Cook 10 minutes longer, then puree and proceed as above. Serve hot or chilled, garnishing with an additional ½ cup chopped watercress. For *Wild Green Soup,* replace watercress with purslane, sorrel, dandelion greens, or other wild edibles.

BORSCHT WITH CUCUMBER

There are many ways to make this soup, which is one of the classics of Jewish dairy cooking.

4 medium beets (about 2 pounds)
1 cup chopped onion
1½ teaspoons salt
4 cups water
1 tablespoon honey
1 tablespoon lemon juice
thin cucumber rounds

Peel beets and chop. You should have 3½ to 4 cups. Combine beets with onion, salt, and water in a pot and bring to a boil. Cover and simmer over low heat for 35 minutes.

Add honey and lemon juice and chill thoroughly. Float cucumber rounds in each bowl when serving and offer a choice of the condiments described below.
Serves 4 to 6
Note: If soup is not thoroughly chilled at serving time, add 1 ice cube to each bowl. Soup will keep several weeks under refrigeration.
Menu Suggestions: Garnish with sliced hard-cooked egg, boiled potato, minced scallion, and fresh chopped dill. It is customary to offer sour cream at the table, which, when stirred in, turns the clear scarlet broth into a bright pink cream; we prefer to use yogurt or a mixture of yogurt and sour cream for its improved food value.

COLD CREAMY BORSCHT

In this version the soup is already in the creamy state before it comes to the table. A little bit of powdered ascorbic acid served at the table allows everyone to adjust the tartness of this soup to their own taste.

1 pound beets
2 cups water
½ teaspoon honey
2 cups buttermilk
1 tablespoon lemon juice
1 tablespoon chopped fresh dill
½ cup diced fresh cucumber
2 tablespoons chopped scallion
1 large potato, steamed and cubed
salt
pepper

Scrub beets and cook, without cutting or peeling, in water until tender. This will vary from 30 to 45 minutes, depending on size and age.

Remove from cooking liquid, reserving 1 cup, and when cool enough to handle, peel and grate. You should have about 1¾ cups beets.

Combine grated beets with the reserved cup cooking liquid and honey; chill. When cold, combine with buttermilk, lemon juice, and dill. Season with salt and pepper to taste. Stir in vegetables, or offer them on separate plates at the table for each to add as desired.

Serves 4
Minor Protein

COLD CURRY-APPLE SOUP

Sometimes called Senegalese Soup, this is very appealing if you are at all fond of curry.

2 tablespoons oil
2½ cups diced zucchini
2 cups peeled, diced apple
1 stalk celery, diced
1 tablespoon curry powder (Goldbecks' Masala, page 445, preferred)
3 cups vegetable broth with some tomato added
1 tablespoon chopped parsley
1 teaspoon salt (reduce if broth is salted)
1 cup yogurt

Heat oil in a 2- or 3-quart pot and sauté zucchini, apple, and celery, stirring occasionally for 5 to 10 minutes. Add curry and cook 1 minute longer.

Add broth, parsley and salt and bring to a boil; cover and simmer for 20 to 30 minutes, or until vegetables are soft enough to puree.

Puree smooth in blender, processor, or food mill. Chill. When cold, stir in yogurt and adjust salt to taste.

Makes 1½ quarts; serves 4 to 6

Note: Soup can be stored in the refrigerator for a week or more, or even frozen if the yogurt has not been added; thus, it is best to wait until just before serving to do the final mixing.

Menu Suggestions: Serve with a rice pilaf or a cold rice salad.

The Main Course

The main course, or entrée, is determined primarily by its designation as the focal point of the meal. It is generally the dish consumed in greatest quantity. We tend to think of the main course as the principal source of protein, but this need not be the case if this nutrient is adequately provided by other components of the meal, such as the appetizer, soup, salad, or some accompaniment.

You may find that your meals occasionally lack a main dish, being composed instead of several smaller dishes that add up to good nourishment. Or, you may prepare small servings of more than one main dish in order to have a well-endowed meal of greater variety.

For your convenience, all the main-dish recipes have been given a designation indicating their potential as the protein portion of the meal.

"Major Protein" means that a particular dish supplies 15 grams or more of protein per average serving (or what you would expect from any nourishing main dish).

"Minor Protein" signifies a dish that supplies less protein per average serving than is needed to make a complete meal. To make the meal adequate, serve it with either another Minor Protein dish or a Protein Complement.

"Protein Complement" describes those dishes that must be coupled with another protein dish to bring them to the level of a Major Protein. This is accomplished by combining them with an appropriate Protein Complement, as indicated in the diagram on page 8, or by coupling them with any Minor Protein. To help orient you, we have often provided complementary menu suggestions. Do not feel restricted by them, however; rather, use them as a guide for adding similar dishes to design menus of your own.

PASTA ENTRÉES

Pasta is one food that pleases just about everyone. Although plain pasta lacks the protein necessary for a complete entrée, with the addition of cheese, beans, or nuts it can be as nourishing as steak.

In the recipes that follow, whole grain pasta is always implied although we have chosen not to repeat this in each ingredient listing. You may be greatly surprised by the variety offered in wholefoods stores. One form can easily be substituted for another, if necessary: that is, spirals for small shells, elbows for bow ties, etc. If you find one kind of whole grain pasta too heavy initially, try another brand or shape, as there can be quite a difference. In general, we have found the greatest preference is for spirals and shells. If you cannot make the switch to whole grain pasta exclusively, try one of the pastas that are protein-fortified with wheat germ, nutritional yeast, soy flour, or the amino acid, lysine. Use it alone or mix it with some of the whole grain variety for a two-tone effect.

As an additional choice, "artichoke noodles," made of a combination of flour derived from the Jerusalem artichoke, wheat, and soy, are also available. These noodles are quite tender and are lower in carbohydrate than other pasta. Of course, if you want to make your pasta dishes extra special, homemade pasta, following the recipes beginning on page 274, is the best of all.

Despite the fact that pasta itself is rich in carbohydrate, most people welcome bread on the same menu. If you do not have a whole grain Italian bread, both Parmesan Toast (page 49) and Garlic Sesame Bread (page 49) make good choices. Pita bread, despite its Mideast origins, goes well with pasta and is good for soaking up the sauce.

A green salad is a nice contrast to pasta, as are tomatoes if they are not an ingredient in the pasta dish itself. And, even with a Major Protein dish, beans usually fit comfortably into the meal either as a salad or an appetizer. For a larger meal, add a cooked vegetable accompaniment or begin with a light soup or antipasto plate.

STOVE-TOP MACARONI AND CHEESE

If you are willing to dirty two pots, this is very quick and extremely tasty.

> 3 to 4 cups uncooked spirals, elbows, or small shells (or 4 to 6 cups cooked)
> 1 tablespoon butter
> 2 cups shredded cheddar cheese mixed with a little Gouda, Edam, or Jack
> ⅓ cup milk
> ¼ teaspoon prepared mustard
> 1½ teaspoons soy sauce
> ⅛ teaspoon cayenne

Cook pasta in boiling salted water until tender, about 12 minutes, and drain.

Meanwhile, melt butter in a small saucepan; add cheese and stir with a wire whisk over low heat until it begins to melt. Add milk and seasoning and continue to cook and stir until smooth.

Add pasta to sauce, mix well, and serve.

Serves 4

Major Protein

Variations: For *Superb Macaroni and Cheese,* turn into a shallow baking dish and place in a 350°F. oven for about 10 minutes. For *Sensational Macaroni and Cheese,* top the casserole with bread crumbs and dot with butter before baking.

BAKED MACARONI AND CHEESE WITH EGG

> ½ pound elbows, spirals, small shells, or egg noodles (or 4 to 6 cups cooked)

> 2¼ cups shredded cheese
> 2 eggs
> 1 cup milk
> 1 teaspoon salt
> pepper
> 2 tablespoons butter

Preheat oven to 375°F.

Cook pasta in boiling salted water until not quite tender, about 10 minutes. Drain. Layer pasta and 2 cups cheese alternately in a greased, shallow 2-quart casserole.

Beat eggs with milk and seasoning. Pour over pasta. Sprinkle with remaining ¼ cup cheese and dot with butter. Bake for 25 minutes, or until set.

Let stand for 5 minutes at room temperature before serving.

Serves 4

Major Protein

Note: For added interest, use spinach noodles and a combination of Swiss and Parmesan cheeses.

Variation: Layer 1 to 2 cups cooked chopped broccoli along with pasta and cheese.

ITALIAN MACARONI AND CHEESE

> 1 quart undrained canned tomatoes
> 2 cups uncooked small pasta
> 1 tablespoon nutritional yeast
> ½ cup shredded provolone cheese
> 1 cup shredded mozzarella cheese
> 1 teaspoon crushed oregano
> ½ teaspoon dried basil
> ¼ cup yogurt
> 2 tablespoons grated Parmesan cheese

Preheat oven to 350°F.

Bring tomatoes to a boil, add pasta, and cook for 10 to 12 minutes until pasta is al dente. Stir in yeast to thicken. Remove from heat and add cheese and seasonings.

Pour into 1-quart casserole, top with yogurt and grated cheese, and bake for about 10 minutes until bubbly.

Serves 2 generously or 3 modestly

Major Protein

Variation: For a one-pot, fast-food meal just stir cheese and seasonings into pasta over low heat to melt. Remove from heat and add yogurt.

BAKED ZITI

½ pound ziti, spirals, or small shells (or 4 to 5 cups cooked)
2 cups Italian Tomato Sauce (page 317)
1 cup ricotta cheese
4 ounces thinly sliced mozzarella cheese or a combination of mozzarella and provolone cheeses

Preheat oven to 350°F. Cook pasta in boiling salted water until barely tender, about 10 minutes. Drain.

Combine pasta, tomato sauce, and ricotta in a 2-quart baking dish. Top with cheese slices. Bake for about 15 minutes until very hot and cheese is melted.

Serves 4
Major Protein

ITALIAN SPAGHETTI STEW

A rich stew that includes chunks of corn on the cob for a taste and textural change; eating with fingers is definitely permitted.

1 tablespoon oil
1 large clove garlic, chopped
2 quarts canned, undrained tomatoes
1 teaspoon dried basil
1 teaspoon crushed oregano
½ pound spaghetti
2 cups cooked chick-peas
4 ears corn on the cob, cut in 2-inch segments
2 cups shredded romaine or other leafy greens
grated Parmesan cheese

Heat oil in a 3- to 5-quart pot and sauté garlic briefly. Before it begins to color, add tomato and seasonings; bring to a boil and simmer for 10 minutes.

Add spaghetti, chick-peas, and corn, and simmer for 15 to 20 minutes, or until spaghetti is tender. Add greens and cook 2 minutes longer, just to wilt.

Taste for seasoning, adding salt if necessary. Serve with generous amount of Parmesan.

Serves 4 to 6
Major Protein

PASTA WITH CREAMY SPINACH

¾ pound spaghetti or linguine
¾ pound spinach
2 tablespoons butter
1½ cups ricotta cheese
⅓ cup grated Parmesan cheese
3 tablespoons yogurt
¼ teaspoon nutmeg
salt
pepper

Cook pasta in boiling salted water until just tender, about 12 minutes, while preparing remaining ingredients.

Wash spinach, drain well, and chop fine. (You should have about 4 cups.) Melt butter in a saucepan, add spinach, and cook, stirring occasionally, until soft and moisture is evaporated, about 5 minutes.

Turn heat very low and stir in cheeses, yogurt, and seasonings. Warm through, stirring, without letting mixture boil, for 3 to 5 minutes. Drain pasta and top with sauce.

Serves 4 to 6
Major Protein

GREEN LINGUINE WITH WHITE MUSHROOM SAUCE

½ pound spinach linguine
2 cups Mushroom Sauce (page 314)
1½ cups ricotta cheese
pepper
grated Parmesan cheese

Bring salted water to a boil for pasta while you assemble remaining ingredients. Add pasta and cook until just tender, about 12 minutes. Meanwhile prepare Mushroom Sauce.

Drain pasta and place in a shallow serving dish. Top pasta with ricotta and pour Mushroom Sauce over all. Season liberally with coarsely ground pepper and Parmesan.

Serves 4
Major Protein
Variation: Prepare 2 cups sauce from Mushroom Sauce Mix (page 444). Quarter 1 cup fresh mushrooms and add to pasta during last 5 minutes of cooking.

GREEN LINGUINE WITH RED MUSHROOM SAUCE

½ pound spinach linguine
2 cups mushroom pieces
2 cups Italian Tomato Sauce (page 317)
nutritional yeast or tomato paste (optional)
1½ cups ricotta cheese
grated Parmesan cheese

Bring salted water to a boil for pasta while you assemble remaining ingredients. Add pasta and cook until just tender, about 12 minutes.

Meanwhile, add mushrooms to Italian Tomato Sauce and simmer for 10 minutes. If sauce seems thin, add a little nutritional yeast or tomato paste.

Drain pasta and place in a shallow serving dish. Top pasta with ricotta and pour sauce over all. Serve with grated Parmesan.

Serves 4
Major Protein

PASTA WITH PESTO AND SLIVERED CHEESE

Traditionally Italian, pesto is a rich basil-and-parsley sauce heavily spiked with garlic and served as a dressing on pasta or sometimes on vegetables. It is used here to adorn a platter of pasta and cheese.

½ pound spaghetti or linguine
1 cup Pesto (plain or tomato, pages 318, 319)
4 ounces combined provolone and mozzarella cheeses
2 tomatoes

Cook pasta in boiling salted water until tender, about 12 minutes. Meanwhile prepare Pesto, cut cheese in slivers, and tomato in wedges.

Drain pasta and pile, still hot, on a serving platter. Spoon half of Pesto on top. Scatter cheese over all and garnish with tomato. Serve remaining sauce on the side to be added to taste.

Serves 4
Major Protein
Note: If desired, Pesto and cheese

can be prepared well in advance, leaving you free to do other things while the pasta cooks.

Variations: Steamed broccoli buds can be used with tomato wedges as a garnish. For a light, low-calorie meal, replace pasta with 6 cups cooked spaghetti squash spooned out of the shell and broken into strands. This dish will not have the protein value of the pasta version and should be boosted with a bean salad. Of course, the original recipe can be accompanied by a bean dish too.

PASTA WITH ONION SAUCE

A very gentle sauce, despite the pound and a half of onion.

2 tablespoons butter
2 tablespoons oil (olive preferred)
1½ pounds Spanish onions, sliced thin (about 6 cups)
2 tablespoons tomato paste
1 cup hot water
salt
pepper
¾ pound pasta
2 eggs
⅔ cup grated Parmesan cheese

Melt butter and oil in a 2- to 3-quart saucepan, add onions, cover, and stew until onions "melt," about 30 minutes. Stir occasionally.

After about 20 minutes, put a pot of water on to boil for pasta.

Dissolve tomato paste in 1 cup hot water and add to cooked onions along with a generous pinch of salt and pepper. Simmer, uncovered for 10 minutes, then cover and remove from heat until needed. While onion sauce simmers, cook pasta.

Beat eggs and stir in a little hot onion sauce. When warmed, stir back into pot of hot sauce.

Drain pasta and place in a serving bowl. Top with onion sauce. Sprinkle with cheese.

Serves 4 to 6
Major Protein
Note: If sauce needs to be reheated

after egg is added, do so over very low heat and do not boil.

Menu Suggestions: This is an ample meal when preceded by an antipasto platter or mixed salad enhanced with beans or cheese slivers. Garlic Sesame Bread is nice with this, as it is with most pasta dishes. By adding cooked zucchini, eggplant, or some Italian-style vegetable dish you will have a full menu for 6.

LINGUINE COUNTRY-STYLE

Pasta, cheese, and a light, crisp vegetable sauce.

½ **pound linguine**
4 **cups mixed leeks, onions, carrot, celery, and zucchini, cut in thin strips 1 to 2 inches long**
2 **tablespoons butter**
1 **cup shredded Swiss cheese**
½ **cup grated Parmesan cheese**
½ **teaspoon nutmeg**
salt
pepper

Bring salted water to a boil for cooking pasta. Meanwhile assemble remaining ingredients.

Cook pasta until tender, about 12 minutes. At the same time, place vegetables in a saucepan with butter, cover, and stew over low heat for 10 minutes until just tender.

Drain pasta and toss with cheeses, nutmeg, and salt and pepper to taste. Mix until cheese melts, returning to low heat if necessary. Stir vegetables into pasta and serve.

Serves 4
Major Protein

PASTA WITH GREEN BEANS

2 **tablespoons oil (olive preferred)**
2 **teaspoons chopped garlic (about 4 cloves)**
1½ **pounds green beans, trimmed of ends and either left whole or "Frenched"**
2 **cups fresh or canned tomato pulp**

½ **teaspoon salt**
pepper
½ **pound spaghetti or linguine**
⅓ **cup pumpkin seeds**
¼ **cup raisins**
2 **tablespoons lemon juice**
2 **tablespoons butter**
¾ **cup grated Parmesan cheese or a mixture of Parmesan and provolone cheeses**

Heat oil in a large, heavy skillet or wok and sauté garlic for 1 to 2 minutes until just barely colored. Add beans and stir-fry for 3 minutes. Add tomato, salt, and pepper; cover and stew for 15 to 20 minutes, or until beans are just tender.

Bring salted water to a boil and cook pasta until tender.

Meanwhile toast pumpkin seeds in a dry frying pan until they begin to pop. Be careful not to burn them. Add toasted seeds, raisins, and lemon juice to beans; cover and cook 5 minutes longer.

Drain pasta and toss with butter and cheese in a serving dish. Top with vegetable sauce. Toss once more at the table to mix in the sauce before serving.

Serves 4 quite generously
Major Protein
Note: If you wish to serve this as only part of a larger Italian dinner, just add another 4 ounces of pasta to the pot and it will feed 6.

Variations: For *Pasta with Broccoli,* substitute 1½ pounds broccoli for green beans. Peel tough outer layer of stalks and cut in sticks ¼ inch around and 2 to 3 inches long. Leave buds in big pieces. For *Pasta with Zucchini,* replace beans with 1½ pounds zucchini cut into thin sticks. Reduce initial cooking to 10 minutes.

For *Pasta with Green Beans Alfredo-Style,* place the pasta mixed with butter and cheese in a casserole, spread 2 cups ricotta cheese on top, arrange the vegetable mixture over this and sprinkle some additional grated cheese over all. Bake in a 350°F. oven for about 15 minutes until cheese is creamy. Casserole can be assembled in advance or the dish can be made from leftovers.

SPAGHETTI WITH ZUCCHINI SAUCE

A thick, delicate vegetable sauce laced with cheese. This dish is very pleasing to the palate and the sauce can be prepared in the time it takes the pasta to cook.

½ pound spaghetti
2 tablespoons oil
1 large clove garlic, minced
4 scallions, cut in 1-inch slivers
½ cup slivered sweet red or green pepper (optional)
1 pound zucchini, shredded (about 3 cups)
2 medium tomatoes, diced
1 tablespoon minced fresh basil or 1 teaspoon dried
¼ cup minced parsley
2 eggs
½ teaspoon nutmeg
pepper
½ cup grated provolone cheese
½ cup grated Parmesan cheese

Bring water to a boil for pasta while preparing the ingredients for the sauce. Cook pasta at the same time as the sauce.

Heat oil in a 10- to 12-inch skillet and sauté garlic, scallion, and pepper for 2 to 3 minutes until lightly colored. Add zucchini, tomatoes, basil, and parsley. Cook, uncovered, about 5 minutes until softened.

Beat eggs. Remove vegetables from heat and stir in eggs, nutmeg, pepper, and cheeses. Stir to melt. Return to low heat for a few minutes and stir until sauce is soft and creamy.

When pasta is cooked to taste (about 10 minutes), drain and transfer to a serving bowl. Spoon sauce over pasta and serve.

Serves 4
Major Protein

SPAGHETTI WITH EGGPLANT SAUCE

1 medium eggplant (about 1½ pounds)
3 tablespoons oil (part olive preferred)
1 clove garlic, split
1 large green pepper, cut in strips
½ teaspoon salt
pepper
2 cups chopped fresh tomatoes or 1 cup canned, lightly drained
1 teaspoon oregano
2 cups cottage cheese
½ pound spaghetti

Cut unpeeled eggplant into large cubes. Heat oil in a large, heavy skillet and cook garlic until lightly colored. Add eggplant, pepper strips, salt, and pepper, and cook over low heat until surface colors, about 15 minutes. Stir as needed to prevent sticking. Add tomato and oregano, cover, and cook over low heat about 15 minutes longer until eggplant is quite soft.

About 15 minutes before serving time, bring water to a boil and cook pasta. Drain when tender.

About 5 minutes before serving, stir cottage cheese into eggplant sauce and cook until it "melts" into sauce. Some varieties of cottage cheese will string like pizza cheese, while others will retain tiny curds. Spoon sauce over pasta to serve.

Serves 4
Major Protein

CREOLE NOODLES

A spicy creole tomato sauce chock full of pasta and beans.

1 medium onion, chopped
1 green pepper, cut in 1-inch strips
2 tablespoons oil
2 cups chopped tomatoes, lightly drained (fresh, canned, or a combination)
2 cups sliced okra or green beans cut in 1-inch segments
4 sprigs parsley
2 teaspoons minced hot pepper or ¼ teaspoon hot pepper sauce
½ teaspoon dried basil or a few fresh leaves
½ teaspoon salt (reduce if tomatoes are salted)
3 cups cooked noodles or whole wheat spirals or shells
2 cups cooked kidney or pinto beans, drained

Sauté onion and pepper in oil in a 3-quart pot for 5 minutes to soften. Add tomato, okra or green beans, parsley, and seasonings. Cover and simmer for 15 minutes until vegetables are just tender. Add pasta and beans and simmer uncovered for 10 minutes.

Serves 4

Minor Protein

Note: For 3 cups noodles, cook 2½ cups (5 ounces) pasta in boiling salted water for 10 minutes until barely tender. This can be done either in advance or while the sauce simmers.

Menu Suggestions: Boost with a cheese appetizer or with American Wholefoods Broccoli Hollandaise; serve with a green salad. Use fresh fruit for dessert.

PASTA WITH LENTIL SAUCE

1 tablespoon oil
1 large clove garlic, chopped
1 large onion, chopped
about 1¼ cups (½ pound) lentils
3 cups water
1 teaspoon salt (reduce if you use salted canned tomatoes)
½ teaspoon oregano
several basil leaves or ¼ teaspoon dried basil
1- to 2-inch segment hot red pepper, sliced, or ¼ to ½ teaspoon crushed dried red pepper
2 cups chopped, drained tomato (fresh, frozen, or canned)
4 to 6 tablespoons tomato paste
¾ pound pasta
grated cheese (optional)

Heat oil in a 2- to 3-quart pot and sauté garlic and onion about 3 minutes until tender. Add lentils and water. Bring to a boil, cover, and simmer over low heat for 30 minutes.

Add seasonings and tomato to lentils and cook about 20 minutes longer, or until beans are tender. Add tomato paste and simmer gently, uncovered, for about 5 minutes until thickened. Adjust the amount of tomato paste to produce a rich, thick sauce.

About 15 minutes before serving, bring water to a boil for pasta and cook until tender. Drain. Pour lentil sauce over pasta. Top with grated cheese at the table if desired.

Serves 6

Major Protein

Note: This sauce is quite spicy; if you do not like hot food, you may wish to cut back on the red pepper.

Menu Suggestions: This recipe serves 6 quite generously, so a salad on the side may be all that's needed to complete the meal. To serve 8, you might consider adding another 4 ounces of pasta and offering smaller portions with another course. For example, White Broccoli Mozzarella complements this quite nicely.

FETTUCCINE WITH SPRING VEGETABLES

Pasta with a heavy cheese sauce and crisp vegetables.

½ pound linguine
2 cups medium White Sauce (page 313)
½ cup grated Parmesan cheese
salt
pepper
2 tablespoons butter (or half olive oil, half butter)
1 clove garlic, split in half
6 scallions, cut in thin strips 2 inches long
2 cups fresh snow peas
1 medium zucchini, cut in sticks ¼ inch in diameter and 2 inches long
½ medium green pepper, cut in thin strips
¼ cup chopped parsley

Bring salted water to a boil for cooking pasta. Meanwhile prepare White Sauce. Add cheese and season to taste with salt and pepper. Cover and remove from heat until needed.

Cook pasta until just tender, about 12 minutes. While pasta cooks, melt butter in a large skillet; cook garlic briefly, add remaining vegetables, stir to coat with fat, cover, and cook for 5 to 7 minutes until just tender but still crisp.

Drain pasta. Reheat cheese sauce if necessary and mix with pasta. Top with vegetables and serve at once. If desired, additional cheese can be added at the table.

Serves 4

Major Protein

Variations: If desired, substitute 2 cups peeled broccoli stalks cut in thin sticks and some broccoli buds for the snow peas or the zucchini.

COLD PASTA AND BROCCOLI

A pasta salad to serve as the main course.

4 to 5 cups cooked spirals or shells (½ pound uncooked pasta)
2 cups cooked kidney beans, drained
4 cups diced, lightly steamed broccoli (about 1 pound)
6 tablespoons oil (part olive preferred)
3 tablespoons wine vinegar
1 teaspoon soy sauce
1 split clove garlic (optional)
¾ cup grated Parmesan cheese

Prepare pasta and beans if you do not have them already on hand. Steam broccoli for 8 to 10 minutes until barely tender. Combine oil, vinegar, soy sauce, and garlic, if desired, in a large, shallow serving bowl. Add pasta, beans, and broccoli, and mix well to serve. Add cheese at the table.

Serves 6

Major Protein

Note: Refrigeration is recommended if this is made more than an hour in advance, but let stand at room temperature for at least 15 minutes to remove chill before serving.

Menu Suggestions: For a hot weather meal, serve with Italian Chilled Tomato Soup and a good crusty bread. If cheese is not added to the pasta, it should appear elsewhere on the menu, perhaps as a savory pastry accompaniment such as Fresh Tomato Pita Pizza or Quick Calzone, or just as a good eating cheese served on the side.

CONFETTI PASTA

As pleasant to look at as it is to eat. Don't overlook the tofu variation, as it is a good way to introduce this somewhat foreign food.

½ pound pasta
2 tablespoons oil
6 scallions, sliced
1 large clove garlic, chopped
½ cup diced sweet red or green pepper
2 cups sliced mushrooms
2 cups corn kernels
1½ cups ricotta cheese
salt
pepper

Cook pasta in boiling salted water until tender, about 12 minutes.

While pasta is cooking, heat oil in a skillet or wok, add vegetables, and stir-fry for 5 to 7 minutes until just tender.

Stir cheese into vegetables and cook over low heat, continuing to stir, for 2 to 3 minutes until heated through. Season to taste with salt and pepper. Drain pasta and serve with vegetable sauce.

Serves 4

Major Protein

Variation: Replace ricotta with 1 pound of tofu that has been pureed smooth in a blender or processor fitted with a plastic mixing blade. Add a little water to the tofu, if necessary, to process.

SPAGHETTI FANTASY

Spaghetti studded with herbs, nuts, and olives.

½ pound spaghetti
3 tablespoons oil (at least part olive)
2 to 3 cloves garlic, chopped
1 cup sliced almonds, peanuts, or sunflower seeds (preferably a combination)
½ cup chopped olives
½ cup chopped sweet red or green pepper
½ cup minced parsley
2 tablespoons minced fresh basil or 1 teaspoon dried
grated Parmesan cheese

Cook pasta in boiling salted water until tender, about 12 minutes.

Drain spaghetti and combine oil and garlic in the spaghetti cooking pot. Cook about 1 minute, or until garlic just begins to color.

Add spaghetti, nuts, olives, sweet pepper, and herbs to garlic oil and heat through, mixing until pasta is well coated. Serve, adding cheese to taste at the table.

Serves 4

Minor Protein

Menu Suggestions: This crunchy pasta dish could use a slight protein boost, although if served with a generous amount of grated cheese on top, it can stand alone. Otherwise, a cheese-based appetizer or protein-rich salad is suggested.

VEGETABLE CHOP SUEY

2 tablespoons oil
1 cup onion crescents
2 large celery stalks, sliced on the diagonal
1 sweet red or green pepper, cut in strips 1 inch long
2 good-size carrots, cut in matchsticks
2 cups fresh or canned tomato pieces, or tomato puree
2 cups bean sprouts
½ pound mushrooms, sliced
up to 1 cup vegetables of choice (see Note)
1 teaspoon salt
2 tablespoons soy sauce
½ teaspoon honey
½ pound spaghetti, cooked until tender (can be cooked any time before or during preparation of this recipe)

Heat oil in a wok and sauté onion, celery, and pepper about 5 minutes. Add remaining ingredients except for the spaghetti, cover and simmer for 20 minutes until vegetables are just tender. Stir in cooked spaghetti and heat through.

Serves 4

Minor Protein

Major Protein if ¾ to 1 pound tofu, sliced in strips, is added along with the vegetables.

Note: For vegetables of choice you may add any of the following: zucchini sticks, water chestnuts, snow peas, sliced Chinese cabbage, sliced Jerusalem artichoke, cauliflower, sliced cabbage, asparagus sections, broccoli florets.

If you make your own sprouts, sprouted dried whole peas are especially recommended for this recipe.

Menu Suggestions: Good choices to help complete the menu include Steamed Egg Roll, Rolled Omelet Slices, or a tofu accompaniment. Add Chinese Radish Salad, Cucumber Salad with Spicy Dressing, or Spinach–Bean Sprout Salad for textural contrast, and a light dessert of plain or poached fruit to finish the meal.

HUNGARIAN CABBAGE NOODLES

A platter of noodles topped with cottage cheese and caraway-flavored cabbage.

2 tablespoons butter, oil, or a combination
1½ pounds cabbage, cut in thin strips (about 10 cups)
2 tablespoons caraway seeds
1 pound noodles
3 cups (1½ pounds) cottage cheese at room temperature

Heat butter or oil in a large skillet or wok, add cabbage, and stir to coat well. Sprinkle with caraway, cover, and cook about 10 minutes; cabbage should still be a little crisp when done rather than soft or soggy.

While cabbage cooks, cook noodles until tender. Drain noodles, place on a serving platter, top with cottage cheese, and cover with cabbage.

Serves 6

Note: If you wish to make homemade noodles for this dish, Yogurt Noodles are especially good.

Menu Suggestions: A fresh fruit appetizer, a salad featuring tomatoes, carrots, or beets, plus pickles and a dense whole grain bread will round out this menu.

LO MEIN— CHINESE FRIED NOODLES

The assembly of the ingredients is the most time-consuming part of this recipe, but fortunately much of the preparation can be done in advance.

½ pound spaghetti
4 tablespoons oil
2 medium carrots, cut in thin sticks
1 medium zucchini or peeled cucumber, cut in thin sticks
2 cups thin slices sweet red or green pepper
½ cup thin onion crescents
1 cup sliced mushrooms
4 scallions, sliced
1 cup bean sprouts
½ pound tofu, diced
2 tablespoons soy sauce
2 eggs, beaten

Cook pasta in boiling salted water until just tender, 10 to 12 minutes. Drain and cool quickly under cold running water. Drain and toss with 1 tablespoon oil in a bowl; cover and refrigerate. This should be done at least an hour in advance but can be done as much as a day ahead; or, if you have 4 cups of spaghetti left over from a previous meal, toss with oil and chill.

Mix all vegetables together with tofu. If prepared in advance, cover and chill.

Heat 2 tablespoons oil in a wok and add chilled spaghetti; mix evenly to coat. Stir-fry over medium heat to brown the outside lightly, keeping the interior soft. This will take about 8 to 10 minutes.

Push pasta up the sides of the wok, add remaining tablespoon of oil, and stir-fry the vegetable mixture for 5 minutes, gradually mixing the pasta in with the vegetables.

Stir in soy sauce, cover and steam over low heat for 5 minutes. Remove cover, raise heat, pour on the eggs, and stir until just set. Serve at once.

Serves 4

Major Protein

Variations: Vegetables can be varied in kind and amount; you may substitute green beans, peas, asparagus, celery, shredded greens, cauliflower, etc., as available, for any of the vegetables listed in the recipe. For *Chinese-Style Fried Rice,* replace spaghetti with 4 cups cooked brown rice.

BAMI GORENG— INDONESIAN FRIED NOODLES

The Indonesian version of fried noodles is more highly seasoned than the Chinese and does not contain tofu; here the eggs are poached and served on top of the dish.

½ pound spaghetti
4 tablespoons oil
½ teaspoon crushed red pepper
½ teaspoon cumin
1 teaspoon turmeric
2 medium carrots, cut in thin sticks
1 medium zucchini or peeled cucumber, cut in thin sticks
2 cups thin slices sweet red or green pepper
½ cup thin onion crescents
1 cup sliced mushrooms
4 scallions, sliced
1 cup bean sprouts
2 tablespoons soy sauce
4 eggs
⅓ cup chopped peanuts

Cook pasta in boiling salted water until just tender, 10 to 12 minutes. Drain and cool quickly under cold running water. Drain and toss with 1 tablespoon oil in a bowl; cover and refrigerate for at least 1 hour.

Heat 2 tablespoons oil in a wok. Add crushed pepper, cumin, and turmeric and cook for 1 minute. Add pasta and mix evenly to coat. Stir-fry over medium-high heat, browning the outside lightly but keeping the interior soft. This will take about 8 to 10 minutes.

Push pasta up the sides of the wok, add remaining tablespoon oil, and stir-fry the vegetables for 5 minutes, gradually mixing in the pasta.

Season with soy sauce, then break eggs carefully on top, keeping the yolks intact. Cover, lower heat, and cook until eggs are just set, about 10 minutes. Serve immediately, placing one poached egg on a bed of noodles and vegetables on each plate. Top with chopped peanuts.

Serves 4

Major Protein

Note: To serve 6, add 2 eggs and increase peanuts to ½ cup.

Variations: Vary vegetables as suggested for Lo Mein in preceding recipe. For *Nasi Goreng,* replace spaghetti with 4 cups cooked brown rice.

RED OR WHITE CHEESE RAVIOLI

1 recipe Ricotta Noodles (page 276)
1½ cups ricotta cheese
2 tablespoons grated Parmesan cheese
2 tablespoons minced parsley
¼ teaspoon salt
1 egg yolk
additional grated Parmesan cheese
3 to 4 cups Italian Tomato Sauce (page 317) or 2 to 3 cups White Sauce (page 313)

Prepare pasta dough and roll out two sheets, each about ⅛ inch thick.

Mix ricotta, Parmesan, parsley, salt, and egg yolk to form a smooth mixture. Use 1 tablespoon cheese mixture to fill each ravioli square, placing mounds of filling at intervals along a sheet of dough, covering with a second sheet of dough, then pressing around each mound with fingers to seal. (For miniature ravioli, use 1 teaspoon per square.)

Cut into 2- to 2½-inch squares and pinch around each to secure edges. A ravioli mold or a 2-inch tartmaker, which cuts and seals dough in one operation, can simplify this job.

Let ravioli rest for 15 to 30 minutes if possible, in order to dry surface.

Drop into boiling salted water and cook until just tender, 10 to 12 minutes. Drain thoroughly and serve with grated cheese and either Tomato or White Sauce.

Serves 3 to 4

Major Protein

Note: This recipe makes about 20 large 2½-inch ravioli, or about 1½ pounds. It should be enough to feed 4, but if served with just a salad or to very hungry people it may only be sufficient for 3. As it is not really much more time-consuming to double this recipe, you may want to do so in order to make sure you have enough. Any extra uncooked ravioli can be frozen for about 3 months.

SPINACH–NOODLE CASSEROLE

½ pound broad noodles or small shells or spirals
2 tablespoons oil
1 cup chopped onion
1½ pounds fresh spinach, coarsely chopped (about 15 cups)
¾ teaspoon salt
pepper
1 cup cottage cheese
1¼ cups grated cheese of choice
2 tablespoons butter, melted
½ cup dry whole grain bread crumbs
2 tablespoons wheat germ

Preheat oven to 350°F. Cook pasta in boiling salted water until barely tender, about 10 minutes.

Meanwhile, heat oil in a large skillet or pot and sauté onion until limp, 3 to 5 minutes. Add spinach and cook, uncovered, stirring occasionally, for 5 to 10 minutes until cooked down. Season with ½ teaspoon salt.

Drain pasta and mix with remaining ¼ teaspoon salt, a generous amount pepper, cottage cheese, and 1 cup of grated cheese.

In a greased, shallow 2-quart baking dish, layer half the pasta mixture, half the spinach, the remaining pasta, and top with remaining spinach.

Combine melted butter, bread crumbs, wheat germ, and remaining ¼ cup grated cheese. Sprinkle on top of casserole.

Bake about 20 minutes until top is golden.

Serves 4 quite generously
Major Protein
Menu Suggestions: A fresh fruit or a

simple vegetable appetizer based on tomato, mushroom, artichoke, or avocado will precede this nicely. As an accompaniment, carrots, summer or winter squash, cucumber, or one of the previously suggested vegetables can be added. Steer clear of other grain dishes or heavy dairy foods at this meal. A green salad is somewhat redundant because of the spinach in this entrée.

SAVORY NOODLE PUDDING

6 ounces broad noodles or spirals (about 3½ cups cooked)
1 cup cottage cheese
½ cup yogurt
1 egg
½ cup shredded Gouda or similar cheese
¼ cup chopped sweet Spanish or Bermuda onion
¼ cup chopped green pepper
½ teaspoon dry mustard
¼ teaspoon salt
1 teaspoon soy sauce
1 tablespoon wheat germ
¼ teaspoon paprika
about ½ tablespoon butter

Preheat oven to 350°F. Cook noodles in boiling salted water until just tender, about 10 minutes. Drain.

Meanwhile prepare remaining ingredients and combine all but last 3. Stir in cooked noodles.

Place mixture in a greased, deep 1½- to 2-quart baking dish. Sprinkle with wheat germ and paprika, and dot lightly with butter.

Bake for 30 minutes. Let sit at room temperature for 5 to 10 minutes before serving.

Serves 3 to 4
Major Protein
Note: Recipe can be doubled using a 3- to 4-quart casserole. Increase baking time by 5 to 10 minutes. Leftovers store well in the refrigerator and are tasty cold or reheated in a 325°F. oven.

FRUIT NOODLE PUDDING

This is not a sweet dessert pudding but a delicate main dish.

6 ounces broad noodles or spirals (about 3½ cups cooked)
1 cup cottage cheese
½ cup yogurt
1 egg
½ cup shredded Jack or Gouda-type cheese
¼ cup raisins
1 cup chopped, peeled apple
¼ teaspoon salt
3 tablespoons slivered almonds
¼ teaspoon cinnamon
about ½ tablespoon butter

Preheat oven to 350°F. Cook noodles in boiling salted water until just tender, about 10 minutes. Drain.

Meanwhile combine all but last 3 ingredients. Stir in cooked noodles.

Place mixture in a greased, deep 1½- to 2-quart baking dish. Top with slivered almonds and cinnamon, and dot lightly with butter.

Bake for 30 minutes. Let sit at room temperature for 5 to 10 minutes before serving.

Serves 3 to 4
Major Protein
Note: This dish, which is easily multiplied, can be kept warm, reheated, or served at room temperature, making it suitable for parties and buffets. Leftovers make an excellent dessert with a drizzle of maple syrup and some half-and-half poured on top.

Menu Suggestions: Serve with a big green salad and bread for a light meal; add a vegetable appetizer for a larger dinner.

About Lasagne

Lasagne is composed of layers of broad noodles and cheese that are covered with sauce and baked. While the most familiar form of lasagne is the Italian restaurant version with tomato or meat sauce, in classic Italian cuisine there is actually much more variety to the sauce. The most important part of the lasagne, however, is the pasta. Because of the multiple layers, it is essential that a light, flavorful pasta is used. Unfortunately, many of the commercial whole grain lasagne noodles are thick and doughy, ruining the delicate flavor of this dish. If you wish to make a really superb lasagne, this is the time to make your own noodles. Because the sheets of dough are large, this also happens to be the easiest of all the homemade pastas to prepare. (Directions are given in "Pasta Accompaniments," page 274.)

Two ricotta fillings are presented in the following recipes, one plain and one with spinach. If desired, they can be interchanged.

A pan of lasagne to serve 6 takes about 4 cups of sauce.

It is important to let baked lasagne sit for 10 to 20 minutes before cutting so that the cheese can set. In fact, many prefer reheated lasagne because of its firmer texture. If lasagne is to be reheated or must wait after cooking for more than the 20 minutes, it should be covered to prevent drying out. When reheating chilled lasagne, top with more grated Parmesan cheese and a little sauce if available to give it a new freshness. The heaviness of reheated lasagne can be lightened with dollops of plain ricotta spread over the casserole before it is returned to the oven.

LASAGNE WITH BEAN SAUCE

In this version, the noodles cook in the oven, greatly reducing the work.

For the Bean Sauce
    1 clove garlic, split
    1 tablespoon oil
    1 small onion, chopped
    2 cups cooked red or brown beans, drained and coarsely chopped
    4 cups tomato puree
    1 teaspoon oregano
    ½ teaspoon dried basil
    ½ teaspoon salt

For the Lasagne
    Bean Sauce
    ¾ pound lasagne noodles

    2 cups ricotta cheese
    8 ounces mozzarella cheese, thinly sliced
    ¼ cup grated Parmesan cheese

To prepare sauce, brown garlic in oil in saucepan and discard. Add onion and beans and sauté about 5 minutes, until beans are slightly softened and break up easily with a fork. Add tomato puree and seasonings, bring to a boil, and simmer for 5 minutes.

Preheat oven to 350°F.

To assemble, spread a little sauce in a 9 x 13-inch or shallow 2-quart baking dish. Cover with one third of the noodles, 1 cup ricotta, half the mozzarella, and top with some sauce. Repeat these layers. Top with remaining noodles, sauce, and Parmesan cheese.

Cover pan and bake for about 1 hour. Remove cover and bake 15 to 30 minutes longer, until liquid is absorbed and pasta tender. Let sit for 10 minutes before serving.

Serves 6

Major Protein

Note: For a moist lasagne, serve extra sauce on the side. For a softer, cheesier lasagne, double the amount of ricotta. If desired, replace some or all of the ricotta with farmer or cottage cheese or mashed tofu. Tomato puree can be replaced with 2 quarts of canned tomatoes and a 6-ounce can of tomato paste; or, replace with 4 cups well-seasoned tomato sauce and simmer chopped beans in the sauce for 5 minutes.

You may want to use a plain tomato sauce rather than the chunky bean–tomato sauce given here. Or, you may replace the beans with mushrooms or diced eggplant. If you do not use any of these ingredients to lend texture to the sauce, canned artichoke hearts or small pieces of walnut added to the cheese layers can create an interesting contrast.

If lasagne noodles are precooked, reduce baking to 25 minutes and bake uncovered. Leftovers can be frozen; bake without defrosting in foil wrapping or covered casserole in a 350°F. oven for about 40 minutes until heated through.

WHITE LASAGNE

The filling for this lasagne is flavored with spinach; the sauce is creamy mushrooms.

For the Filling
½ pound spinach
½ teaspoon salt
2 cups ricotta cheese
8 ounces mozzarella cheese, thinly sliced or shredded (about 2 cups)

For the Sauce
1 tablespoon butter
½ pound mushrooms, chopped (about 2¼ cups)
2 scallions, minced
⅛ teaspoon cayenne
¼ teaspoon nutmeg
3 tablespoons arrowroot or cornstarch
2½ cups milk
1 teaspoon salt

For the Lasagne
¾ pound lasagne noodles
Filling
Sauce
⅓ cup grated Parmesan cheese

Chop spinach fine by hand or in a food processor to make 3 cups minced spinach. Place in a colander, sprinkle with salt, and let stand for about 30 minutes while preparing the sauce and the noodles.

For the sauce, melt butter in a saucepan, add mushrooms and scallions, cover and cook for 5 minutes until liquid runs freely. Stir in cayenne, nutmeg, and starch, and cook until smooth. Gradually add milk. Stir over low heat until sauce thickens, 5 to 10 minutes. Remove from heat before it boils. Add salt.

While preparing the sauce, bring water to a boil for pasta. Cook noodles until barely tender, 3 to 5 minutes if fresh, 10 if dried. Drain, rinse with cold water, and lay flat on a kitchen towel without piling.

Squeeze spinach to extract all moisture. Mix with ricotta.

Preheat oven to 350°F. To assemble, spread a thin layer of sauce, using about ½ cup, over a 9 x 13-inch baking dish. Cover with one third the noodles, half

the spinach–ricotta mixture, and half the mozzarella. Cover with 1 cup sauce. Repeat these layers. Cover with the remaining noodles and sauce, and sprinkle with Parmesan.

Bake for 25 minutes until top is lightly browned. Let stand for 15 to 20 minutes before serving.

Serves 6
Major Protein
Note: Lasagne can be assembled and refrigerated until time to bake. Whenever a starch-thickened sauce is served with pasta it must be delicate or it will weigh down the noodles. For this reason arrowroot or cornstarch is the thickener of choice in this recipe.

CHEESE ENTRÉES

Cheese is a common ingredient in many wholefoods recipes. What distinguishes the dishes in this section is that they are predominantly cheese, and without this essential ingredient they would have no substance.

Because cheese is such a concentrated form of protein, cheese entrées generally suffice as the protein-giving portion of the meal. Thus, the accompanying foods should stress the nutrients that cheese lacks. Beans, grains, fresh fruit, and vegetables in almost any form are appropriate to meals featuring cheese. Nuts should be used sparingly with entrées that are based on high-fat cheeses so that the meal does not become weighted with fat and calories.

CROQUE MADAME

Baked French toast with a mushroom–cheese topping makes a nice light supper or hot lunch entrée. This is a two-step operation; the sauce can be made while the bread bakes.

For the Base
1 egg
¼ cup milk
¼ teaspoon dry mustard
pinch salt
4 slices whole grain bread

Preheat oven to 450°F. Beat together egg, milk, and seasonings. Dip bread so both sides are coated and all egg mixture is absorbed.

Place on a buttered baking sheet and bake for about 8 minutes, or until bottom is golden. Turn and bake 3 to 5 minutes longer.

Prepare sauce while bread bakes.

For the Sauce
1 tablespoon butter
1 cup sliced mushrooms
pinch salt
2 tablespoons milk
1 cup shredded Swiss cheese
pinch cayenne

Melt butter in a small saucepan and sauté mushrooms for 5 minutes until lightly cooked. Add salt and milk and, with heat turned very low, gradually add cheese, stirring until it melts and forms a thick paste.

Spread cheese paste on baked bread slices. Sprinkle a few grains cayenne on each.

Return to oven, turn off heat, and let sit for 1 minute, just to warm through. Serve at once.
Serves 2
Major Protein

CHEESE STEAK

Dense and chewy like a piece of meat, yet light and easily digested. While it is delicious plain, the addition of mushroom or onion gravy, especially on a cold day, makes this extra satisfying.

4 eggs, separated
2 tablespoons butter, cut in small pieces
2½ cups shredded cheddar cheese (about 10 ounces)
¼ cup finely ground almonds or sunflower seeds
½ cup milk
½ cup whole wheat flour
½ teaspoon salt

Preheat oven to 375°F. Using a fork, beat egg yolks in a roomy bowl until thick; beat in butter and cheese to form a uniform mixture.

Add ground nuts or seeds and milk and flour alternately, beating until smooth. Mixture will be quite thick.

Beat egg whites until stiff, adding salt at the end. Fold into cheese mixture.

Spread to cover a greased, floured 9 x 13-inch baking pan or two 8-inch pie plates.

Bake for 30 to 35 minutes until browned.
Serves 4 generously; 6 modestly
Major Protein
Note: Leftovers can be wrapped in foil and frozen. To reheat, place wrapped in a 375°F. oven for 15 minutes, then unwrap and continue to bake until hot.

BAKED CHEESE–NUT CUTLETS

An excellent "meaty" cutlet. Unlike other cutlets of this sort, all the chopping can be done by hand, so if you don't own a blender or a food processor this is an ideal recipe.

1½ cups chopped onion
2 tablespoons oil
½ cup walnuts, chopped fine by hand so small pieces remain
½ cup sunflower seeds, chopped like the walnuts
2 cups shredded cheddar or combination cheddar and provolone, Edam, Gouda, or similar cheese (about 8 ounces)
4 eggs, beaten
½ teaspoon salt
2 tablespoons lemon juice
flour or wheat germ
½ teaspoon paprika

Preheat oven to 350°F. Sauté onion in oil until golden. Combine with nuts, seeds, cheese, eggs, salt, and lemon juice.

Oil two 9-inch pans or a 9 x 13-inch baking dish and coat with flour or wheat germ. Spread nut mixture evenly in pan. Sprinkle top with paprika.

Bake for 20 to 25 minutes until firm and golden. Cut into large squares.
Serves 6
Major Protein
Note: This recipe is lower in carbo-

hydrate than most other "cutlets"; each serving (⅙ of the recipe) contains only 9 grams.

Menu Suggestions: These cutlets need no condiments but are especially nice with a thin layer of yogurt on top. If you complete the meal with baked potato and a salad, it will resemble the typical steak and potato dinner.

CHEESE–NUT ROAST

Good plain, but best with Brown Gravy.

1 tablespoon oil
½ cup chopped onion
1 cup soft whole wheat bread crumbs
¼ cup wheat germ
¾ cup nuts, ground fine (any combination—almonds, peanuts, sunflower, sesame and pumpkin seeds —will do)
1 cup grated cheddar cheese
1 tablespoon lemon juice
½ teaspoon salt
½ cup milk, or ½ cup water plus 2 tablespoons nonfat dry milk powder

Preheat oven to 375°F. Heat oil in a small skillet, add onion, cover and stew about 3 minutes until tender but uncolored.

Meanwhile, combine remaining ingredients and shape into a slightly mounded oval in a well-oiled, shallow baking pan. Top loaf with stewed onions and any oil that remains in the pan.

Bake until onions are well browned and bottom of loaf is crisp, about 30 minutes. If a deeper color is desired, baste with oil during cooking.

Serves 4
Major Protein
Menu Suggestions: Serve with a vegetable soup or fruit appetizer, a cooked vegetable accompaniment and a raw salad. Present the leftovers on a cold platter with a garnish of mayonnaise, catsup, or Revisionist Dressing.

ITALIAN CHEESE STUFFING BALLS

Succulent, flavorful bread and cheese balls stewed in tomato sauce.

2 eggs
½ teaspoon dried basil
1 teaspoon dried oregano
½ teaspoon salt
1 clove garlic, minced
pepper
1 cup ricotta cheese
1 cup shredded mozzarella or a combination mozzarella and provolone cheeses
½ cup minced onion
3 cups dried bread cubes (from 6 slices whole wheat bread cut in ½-inch dice)
3 cups tomato sauce

Beat eggs with seasonings. Stir in cheeses and onion and mix smooth. Add bread cubes and let stand for about 10 minutes to soften.

Spoon 2 cups sauce into a large skillet and heat.

Form cheese mixture into balls, using a scant ¼ cup for each. Place in a single layer in sauce as they are shaped.

Cover and simmer over very low heat for 15 minutes. Serve with additional sauce spooned on top.

Makes 16 balls; serves 4
Major Protein
Variation: For *Italian Tofu Balls*, replace ricotta with 1 cup mashed tofu.

Menu Suggestions: Because these balls are quite bready, they are best served with a cooked vegetable or salad, and perhaps a bean dish; avoid bread or pasta.

RICOTTA–SPINACH DUMPLINGS

These can be made fairly large, as described here, or into miniatures if you prefer. A variety of serving ideas follow the recipe.

½ pound lightly trimmed spinach (about 7 cups, tightly packed)
1½ cups ricotta cheese
2 eggs, lightly beaten
6 tablespoons whole wheat flour
½ cup cornmeal
½ cup grated Parmesan cheese
¼ teaspoon salt
pepper

Wash and drain spinach well. Chop fine. This can be done quickly in a food processor. Sprinkle chopped spinach with a little salt and let stand for 10 minutes or longer to extract moisture. Squeeze very dry; 1 cup spinach should remain.

Combine remaining ingredients and fold in spinach. Chill, if at all possible, for 30 minutes or longer.

To cook, bring a large broad pot half filled with water to a boil. Salt. Taking one spoonful of ricotta mixture at a time, form into 1½-inch balls, molding lightly with your hands, and drop into boiling water. Do not crowd. If pot is broad enough, you will be able to cook about half the batter at a time.

Cover and simmer for 5 minutes until dumplings puff up and float. Remove with a slotted spoon and drain.

Serve in any one of the following ways: (1) with a generous covering of tomato sauce; (2) as a topping for pasta; (3) baked with cheese (arrange cooked dumplings in a shallow baking dish, cover with ½ cup grated Parmesan cheese, drizzle with 2 tablespoons melted butter, and bake in a 400°F. oven for 5 to 10 minutes until hot and melted); (4) cold on bread with a little tomato sauce (recommended for leftovers).

Makes about 20 large dumplings (many more small ones); *serves 4*
Major Protein

CHEESE CROQUETTES

Each sphere contains about 6 grams of protein, making this an excellent snack or a main dish when accompanied by a simple soup or salad. Although they are delicious plain, you may wish to serve the croquettes with tomato sauce, mustard, or other condiments of choice.

1½ cups shredded Swiss cheese (about 6 ounces)
1½ cups shredded cheddar cheese (about 6 ounces)
2 teaspoons prepared mustard
¼ teaspoon salt
2 tablespoons minced parsley, scallion, or chives

3 tablespoons softened butter
1 cup whole grain cracker crumbs
¼ cup wheat germ
¼ cup sunflower seeds, ground fine (or ⅓ cup meal)
oil for frying

Combine all ingredients except the oil and shape into small balls, using about 2 tablespoons for each. Flatten slightly. Chill for at least 1 hour, or as long as 24, so that balls harden.

Heat oil to a depth of ½ inch in a heavy skillet or, for deep-frying in a wok.

When hot, fry croquettes, browning on both sides. Each batch should cook within 5 minutes. Do not cook more than will fit comfortably in the pan at one time. Drain on absorbent paper.

Makes about 20 croquettes; serves 4 generously
Major Protein

BAKED VEGETABLE CHEESE

Soft cheese and vegetables baked together for a light entrée or a sandwich filling.

2 cups (1 pound) ricotta or farmer cheese
2 eggs, separated
½ teaspoon salt
1 small carrot, chopped
1 rib celery, chopped
¼ cup green pepper, chopped
1 scallion, thinly sliced
3 small mushrooms, chopped

Preheat oven to 350°F. Combine cheese and egg yolks and beat until smooth. Add salt and chopped vegetables and mix well.

Beat egg whites until stiff. Fold into the cheese-vegetable mixture.

Spread mixture in a 9-inch pie plate or shallow 1-quart casserole. Bake for 35 minutes until browned on top.

Let cool for 5 to 10 minutes before cutting, or serve at room temperature.
Serves 4
Major Protein
Note: Leftovers are delicious chilled

and served plain or on crackers, bagels, or toast.

Variations: Vegetables can be varied, using chopped cauliflower, broccoli, sweet red pepper, squash, or others of choice. Any shredded cheese can also be added. For *Baked Vegetable Tofu,* replace cheese with 1 pound tofu pureed smooth in a blender or processor. Add 1½ teaspoons soy sauce in seasoning.

MUSHROOM CUSTARD

A delicate quiche filling without the crust.

1 tablespoon oil
6 ounces mushrooms, sliced (about 2 cups)
1 cup ricotta cheese
1 cup milk
2 eggs
1 cup shredded mozzarella cheese
¼ cup grated Parmesan cheese
½ teaspoon salt
¼ teaspoon nutmeg

Preheat oven to 325°F. Heat oil and sauté mushrooms until tender and moisture is evaporated, 5 to 8 minutes.

Spread mushrooms over bottom of a buttered, shallow 1-quart baking dish or glass pie plate.

In a blender or processor puree ricotta and gradually add milk to make a smooth "cream." Add eggs and process briefly until smooth. Stir in cheeses and salt.

Pour cheese batter over mushrooms in baking dish. Sprinkle with nutmeg. Place in a pan slightly larger than the baking dish and surround with hot water to a depth of about 1 inch.

Bake until set, about 50 minutes. Remove from water bath and let stand for at least 10 minutes before serving. Can be served at room temperature if desired.

Serves 4 generously; 6 modestly
Major Protein
Menu Suggestion: Intended for 4, this can be extended for 6 when accompanied by pasta, a cooked vegetable, salad, and bread.

MEXICAN QUICHE

This must be made in 4 individual baking dishes; if you have this equipment the rest is quite simple.

1 tablespoon oil
1 cup chopped onion
4 cornmeal tortillas
1 cup shredded cheddar, Jack, or Muenster cheese
2 tablespoons chopped canned chilies
4 eggs
2 cups milk
½ teaspoon salt
½ teaspoon chili powder
¼ teaspoon cumin

Preheat oven to 350°F.

Heat oil in a small skillet and sauté onion until browned.

Gently ease each tortilla into an individual baking dish. Put one fourth the cheese, chilies, and browned onion in each tortilla.

Beat eggs with milk and seasonings and pour into each baking dish, using about ¾ cup mixture in each.

Bake about 25 minutes until set and lightly browned.

Let stand at least 5 minutes before serving; it is best if allowed to cool for 15 minutes to set filling and enhance flavor.

Serves 4
Major Protein
Menu Suggestions: Serve with a bean dish such as Refried Beans or Baked Mexican Lima Beans and a salad.

MEXICAN CHEESE MELT WITH CORN

A creamy blend of tomato, corn, and cheese to be served over plain tacos, bean tacos, or on a tortilla with poached egg on top; over rice or rice crackers; on toast, or as a sauce over steamed vegetables, particularly cauliflower, broccoli, green beans, or potatoes.

1 tablespoon oil
¾ cup chopped green pepper
1 inch hot chili pepper (optional)

1½ cups drained tomato pulp or juice
½ teaspoon salt
¾ teaspoon cumin
¼ teaspoon cayenne (omit if hot pepper is used)
1½ cups corn kernels
1½ tablespoons whole wheat flour
¼ cup milk
2 cups shredded Jack, cheddar, or preferably a combination of these cheeses

Heat oil in a saucepan. Add green peppers and chili and sauté until wilted, about 5 minutes.

Add tomato, seasonings, and corn, bring to a boil, and simmer for 5 minutes.

Make a paste of flour and milk and stir into hot tomato mixture. Simmer, stirring, about 5 minutes until thickened. Just before serving stir in cheese to melt.

Serves 4
Major Protein

ITALIAN CHEESE MELT WITH CECI

A creamy blend of tomato, beans, and cheese served over pasta, rice, or toasted whole grain Italian bread to create a hot open-faced Italian cheese sandwich.

2 tablespoons oil
1 cup chopped green pepper
2 cups drained tomato pulp or tomato juice
3 cups cooked chick-peas, drained
2 teaspoons oregano
½ teaspoon salt (omit if beans are salted)
¼ teaspoon cayenne, or to taste (optional)
2 tablespoons whole wheat flour
½ cup milk
1½ cups shredded mozzarella cheese
1 cup shredded provolone cheese
½ cup grated Parmesan cheese
crushed red pepper (optional)

Heat oil in a saucepan. Add pepper and sauté until wilted, about 5 minutes.

Add tomato, beans, and seasonings, and bring to a boil. Simmer for 5 minutes.

Make a paste of flour and milk and stir into hot tomato mixture. Cook, stirring, about 5 minutes until thickened. Just before serving stir in cheeses, cooking until they melt.

Spoon over a base of pasta, rice, or bread. Sprinkle crushed pepper on top to taste at the table.

Serves 6
Major Protein

RACLETTE

Raclette is a Swiss specialty of cheese melted by an open fire, scraped onto serving plates, and eaten with potatoes and pickled vegetables. The combined textural qualities of these three ingredients are delightful. As with fondue, another Swiss entrée, the eating of raclette is as much an event as it is a meal, with cooking and serving traditionally done right at the fireplace. This insures that the cheese will be piping hot when it is served, and that is the one essential—you wait for raclette, it never waits for you; if it does, it becomes quite stringy and is nowhere near as luscious as the liquid cheese that comes from the initial melting.

1 pound Raclette, Bagnes, or Belalp cheese in one chunk
4 medium potatoes or 8 small new potatoes
tiny pickled onions and/or pickled vegetables (commercial or homemade as presented on page 439)

Steam potatoes and have them hot and ready to serve as soon as the cheese is done.

For open-fire cookery, place cheese on a shallow baking dish before the fireplace or similar open flame. Place heatproof dishes by the fire so they become quite warm. As cheese melts, scrape with a knife onto serving plates. Eat at once with potatoes, pickled vegetables, and a good crusty bread.

For oven cooking, preheat oven to 450°F. Cut cheese into 12 slices. Place 3 slices on each ovenproof plate and place on bottom rack of a very hot oven for about 5 minutes until cheese is very creamy but not at all colored. Set plates at once on hot pads, heatproof service plates, or some other appropriate surface, surround with potatoes and pickled vegetables, and eat.

Serves 4

Major Protein

Note: To serve Raclette, you must have heatproof plates, hot pads, or other suitable heatproof material to set the plates on and, if cooked by the fire, a blunt knife with which to scrape the cheese.

The cheeses intended for Raclette include Raclette, Bagnes, and Belalp. Ask for them specifically in your cheese shop. You may experiment with others if you like.

If you do not have pickled vegetables and know in advance you will be preparing Raclette, Quick Pickles will do very well in their place.

EGG ENTRÉES

When eggs are downplayed at breakfast and lunch they can be featured at dinner. While any egg dish makes a suitable entrée, those presented here are more appropriate to the evening than the morning meal.

Surprisingly, many egg entrées need additional protein, for a single large egg only furnishes about 7 grams of protein. Beans and grain, both low in fat, are recommended for raising the protein value of the meal. A whole grain breadstuff, a salad with beans, a pasta dish, or a potato accompaniment are all possible additions.

To round out the menu, add a fresh fruit or vegetable appetizer or salad and, if desired, a cooked vegetable on the side.

EGGS AND POTATOES

Eggs and potatoes are a classic combination in almost every culture. In the following version, with its various cooking adaptations, the potatoes can be the cold leftovers of a previous meal or they can either be parboiled separately or cooked in the egg pan.

Warning: This is not a refined dish and you may not want to use your best omelet pan as the frying and stirring may mar its surface. In any pan, however, cleaning will be easy if the pan is set to soak in hot water immediately after the eggs are removed.

2 tablespoons oil
¼ cup thinly sliced onion
½ cup thinly sliced sweet red or green pepper
½ pound raw potatoes, sliced very thin, or 1 to 1½ cups sliced cooked potato
¼ teaspoon salt
pepper
4 eggs

Heat oil in a 10-inch skillet and sauté onion, pepper, and potatoes, stirring to prevent sticking, for about 5 minutes. If raw potatoes are used, cover and cook over low heat for about 15 minutes, or until potatoes are tender. If cooked potatoes are used, continue to sauté, stirring occasionally, until potatoes are browned on both sides, 10 to 15 minutes. When potatoes are cooked to taste, season with salt and pepper.

Beat eggs and pour over potatoes. Cook over medium heat until set on the bottom. Then proceed according to one of the following methods:

Farmer's Eggs: This is the simplest approach. When eggs are set on the bottom, turn by large spoonfuls and continue to cook until completely set. The outcome of this scrambling will be much like a well-cooked, broken-up omelet.

Tortilla de Patatas: This is the Spanish version and would be known as Potato Frittata in Italy. Finish by placing the partially set omelet under the broiler for 3 to 4 minutes to brown the top, or by covering the pan and continuing to cook on the stove until the top is firm, 3 to 5 minutes. This omelet should be cut in wedges and may even be served at room temperature.

Omelet Parmentier: When the French make eggs and potatoes they lift the partially set omelet around the edges and tilt the pan so the uncooked egg runs underneath. When there is nothing left to run off on top but the surface is still creamy, the omelet is folded in half or thirds and served very hot with a light sprinkling of grated Swiss or Parmesan cheese.

American Potato Omelet: When eggs are set on the bottom, loosen around the edges and let unset portions run underneath as for the Omelet Parmentier. Then sprinkle 1 to 2 tablespoons shredded cheddar or similar cheese *per egg* over top. Brown briefly under broiler, or cover and cook until eggs are set and cheese melts, 2 to 3 minutes.

Serves 2

Major Protein

Note: For a single serving prepare 2 eggs in a small 6- to 8-inch pan. For 6 to 8 eggs choose a 12- to 15-inch skillet. You can actually prepare this with as many as 12 eggs, for 6 servings, using a large 15-inch pan, but if so, it is best to use the "scrambling" technique described in Farmer's Eggs to insure thorough cooking.

SCRAMBLED EGGS WITH TOMATOES

1 tablespoon butter
2 scallions, thinly sliced
1 medium tomato, diced
½ tablespoon chopped fresh basil
4 eggs
salt
pepper
6 sliced olives (optional)
grated Swiss cheese

Melt butter in a 10- to 12-inch skillet and sauté scallions until softened, about 2 minutes.

Drain any liquid that has accumulated around the tomato and add the pulp to the skillet along with basil. Cook until most of the moisture evaporates, about 5 minutes.

Beat eggs with a pinch of salt and generous turn of the pepper mill. Pour into pan and cook as for scrambled eggs, stirring as they begin to set, until they reach desired degree of doneness.

Just before serving, stir in olives, if desired. Top with grated cheese.

Serves 2

Major Protein

Note: If recipe is multiplied by two or three, it can be prepared in a 12- to 15-inch skillet.

HUEVOS RANCHEROS

Eggs poached in a spicy Spanish tomato sauce.

1 tablespoon oil
1 small clove garlic, minced
¼ cup chopped onion
¼ cup chopped green pepper
½ teaspoon chopped Jalapeño pepper or 1/16 to ⅛ teaspoon cayenne pepper
¼ teaspoon salt
½ teaspoon oregano
1 cup fresh or canned diced tomato
4 eggs

Heat oil in a 10-inch skillet and sauté garlic, onion, and green pepper for 3 to 5 minutes until softened.

Add hot pepper as desired and cook briefly. Then add remaining ingredients and simmer uncovered for 8 to 10 minutes until tomato softens and liquid runs freely.

Break eggs and place at intervals in sauce. Continue to cook until bottom of egg is set and white is almost cooked, about 8 minutes. Cover and cook briefly until white is firm and yolk lightly cooked but still runny.

Transfer eggs carefully to serving plates and top with sauce.

Serves 2

Major Protein

Note: If you double the recipe to serve 4, use a 15-inch pan. For more than 8 eggs, use two pans.

Menu Suggestions: The eggs may be served on a bed of rice or accompanied by corn bread or tortillas warmed in the oven or toasted over an open flame. If divided among 4 people to provide Minor Protein, combine with bean or cheese enchiladas, tostadas, or another Minor Protein along these lines.

GREEK BEANS, EGGS, AND CHEESE

1 tablespoon oil
2 tablespoons chopped scallion
¾ cup cooked chick-peas or white beans, drained
4 eggs
¼ teaspoon oregano
2 tablespoons minced fresh parsley
⅓ cup feta cheese
pepper

Heat oil in a 10- to 12-inch skillet and sauté scallions until they soften slightly. Stir in beans.

Beat eggs with oregano and parsley and pour over beans. As eggs begin to set, stir as for scrambled eggs. When set but still soft, add feta cheese in small cubes. Cook to desired consistency (loose or tight).

Season generously with pepper; reserve salt for seasoning at the table as needed.

Serves 2
Major Protein
Variations: For *Italian Beans, Eggs, and Cheese,* replace feta with ½ cup diced mozzarella, provolone, or a combination of these two cheeses. Serve with tomato sauce and grated Parmesan cheese.

For *Mexican Beans, Eggs, and Cheese,* replace chick-peas with cooked kidney or pinto beans. Use ½ cup diced Jack cheese instead of feta and season scallions in skillet with ⅛ teaspoon cayenne pepper and up to 1 tablespoon chili powder before adding beans.

Menu Suggestions: For a Greek meal, add pita bread, sliced fresh tomato, olives, and plain yogurt or yogurt seasoned with cucumber and mint. For a more ample dinner, you could add stuffed grape leaves, Greek Spinach Rice, or Atlantic Avenue Green Beans. The Italian counterpart will include Italian bread, olives, a salad of tomatoes and mixed greens, and for big eaters, a side dish of pasta. For a Mexican meal, serve with raw or cooked Mexican Tomato Sauce (for seasoning eggs), corn tortillas or crisp tacos, and shredded greens.

OMELET FINES HERBES

Egg chefs recommend making additional omelets for more than two servings rather than increasing the size of the omelet.

4 eggs
2 tablespoons chopped parsley
1 tablespoon chopped chives
½ teaspoon dried chervil or 2 teaspoons minced fresh, if available
pinch salt
1 tablespoon butter
grated Swiss and/or Parmesan cheese (optional)

Beat eggs with seasonings.

Melt butter in a 10-inch omelet pan. Pour in eggs and cook until bottom is set. Loosen at edges and lift egg away from pan while you tilt it to allow unset egg on top to run down sides and underneath.

When set but still slightly soft on top, fold omelet in half, or roll in thirds and transfer to a serving plate. Sprinkle cheese on top if desired.

Serves 2
Major Protein

FRENCH CHEESE OMELET

4 eggs
¼ teaspoon salt
½ cup shredded Emmentaler or Gruyère, or a mixture of one of these Swiss cheeses and grated Parmesan cheese
1 tablespoon butter
pepper
grated Parmesan cheese (optional)

Beat eggs with salt and add cheese.

Melt butter in a 10-inch omelet pan. When hot, add eggs and cook until bottom is set. Loosen at edges and lift egg away from sides of pan while you tilt it to allow unset egg on top to run underneath.

When fully cooked, roll and season generously with pepper and additional grated cheese if desired.

Serves 2
Major Protein

Variation: For *French Tomato Omelet,* cut one small tomato into thin slices; cut each slice in half. Arrange tomato slices down center of omelet just before rolling and cook a minute longer to heat tomatoes slightly.

FLUFFY OMELET

This light, airy omelet is designed to be folded around a rich sauce, then bedded down under more of the same sauce. First we give you the omelet, then two suggested modes of service.

3 to 4 eggs
pinch salt
½ tablespoon butter

Preheat oven to 300°F.

Separate eggs, combining all the whites in a mixing bowl and leaving the yolks in half of each shell.

Beat whites to the soft peak stage. Beat in salt and then yolks, one at a time, until just blended.

Melt butter in a 10- to 12-inch omelet pan. Pour in egg batter and cook until bottom is set.

Transfer pan to oven and cook until top sets, about 10 minutes. Bottom should be nicely colored by this time, although top will still be pale.

To serve, place filling of choice on half the omelet, fold to cover filling, then spoon remaining sauce on top.

Serves 2
Major or *Minor Protein*

FLUFFY MUSHROOM OMELET

1 Fluffy Omelet prepared according
to preceding recipe
1 tablespoon butter
¼ cup chopped onion
pinch cayenne pepper
1 cup sliced mushrooms
¼ cup sour cream
¾ cup yogurt
¼ teaspoon salt

While omelet is in oven, or even before you begin omelet preparation, melt butter in skillet and sauté onion until just softened, about 3 minutes.

Add cayenne and sliced mushrooms and sauté until barely cooked, 3 to 5 minutes.

Remove from heeat and gradually stir in sour cream, then yogurt. Season with salt to taste.

Avoid reheating sauce, as it is easily curdled. If necessary, place in double boiler over hot water and stir until just warmed through.

When omelet is ready, spoon on some of sauce, fold in half, and top with remaining sauce.

Serves 2
Major Protein

SPANISH OMELET

Most impressive as a Fluffy Omelet, but a standard omelet could be prepared to hold the sauce if preferred.

1 3- to 4-egg plain or Fluffy Omelet
(prepared according to preceding
recipe)
1 tablespoon oil
¼ cup chopped onion
¼ cup chopped green pepper
1/16 teaspoon cayenne pepper
1 cup sliced mushrooms
1 cup diced canned tomato
¼ teaspoon salt (omit if tomato is
salted)
¼ teaspoon honey
shredded cheddar cheese (optional)

Heat oil in a small skillet or saucepan and sauté onion and green peppers for 3 to 5 minutes until softened. Add cayenne and cook briefly. Add mushrooms and stir over heat for 1 minute.

Add tomato, salt, and honey. Simmer, uncovered, for 10 to 15 minutes until sauce thickens.

While sauce simmers, prepare omelet. When omelet is done, spoon on some of sauce, fold, and top with remaining sauce.

Sprinkle with cheese before serving if desired.

Serves 2
Major Protein
Menu Suggestions: If cheese is not added, include some additional protein on the menu, either in the form of

bread, beans in the salad, or a more elaborate bean and/or grain accompaniment.

Frittatas

The frittata, or Italian omelet, is designed to be firm and dense, unlike the French omelet, which is soft and delicate. It is a traditional vehicle for leftovers, including vegetables, beans, and even pasta. To add to its appeal, the frittata can be served hot, cold, or at room temperature and thus does not have to be as intricately timed as other egg entrées.

No more than 6 eggs should go into the pan at a time; this will produce an omelet adequate for 4. If it is served as an appetizer rather than a main dish, it will be enough for 6. Those trying to cut down on costs or egg consumption might try replacing one to two of the eggs in a 6-egg frittata with 2 tablespoons whole wheat flour mixed to a smooth paste with 2 tablespoons water or milk. This omelet will be heavy, but not unpleasantly so.

If you are not skilled at turning omelets, you may prefer to brown the top of the frittata under the boiler; the partially cooked omelet can also be transferred to a moderate (325° to 350°F.) oven until set, about 10 minutes.

The following examples of frittata will serve as models for adaptations of your own; the beauty of this Italian specialty is that it takes advantage of your pantry and your imagination.

ITALIAN SPINACH FRITTATA

2 tablespoons olive oil
¾ cup thinly sliced small white onions
6 eggs
1½ cups coarsely chopped spinach
½ teaspoon salt
pepper
¼ teaspoon dried basil
2 tablespoons minced parsley
⅓ cup grated Parmesan cheese
2 firm tomatoes, thinly sliced
8 black olives, pitted and sliced

Heat oil in a 12-inch omelet pan and cook onion until soft and transparent.

Beat eggs and add spinach, seasonings, and cheese. Pour over onions in pan and cook over low heat, gently lifting edges as egg sets and tilting to allow soft egg to run underneath.

When still slightly soft on top, arrange tomato slices and olives in a decorative manner.

Place omelet under broiler, about 3 inches from heat, and cook until set and lightly browned on top, about 5 minutes.

Cut into wedges and serve directly from pan.

Serves 4
Minor Protein
Menu Suggestions: Toss some beans into a green salad and add a crusty bread for ample service.

SPAGHETTI FRITTATA

A Neapolitan specialty that can be made with leftover pasta.

4 eggs
⅓ cup grated Parmesan cheese
pepper
2 cups cooked spaghetti or other pasta, plain or in any sauce
1 tablespoon butter or olive oil

Beat eggs with cheese and pepper. Fold in pasta.

Heat fat in a 12-inch skillet. Pour in eggs and cook over very low heat for about 5 minutes, then move skillet around on burner so edges are at the heat spot. Continue to cook and move in this manner so that egg cooks slowly and evenly and browns on bottom, about 10 minutes in all.

Loosen omelet from pan. Slide onto a plate and flip back into pan. If omelet was difficult to remove, add a little fat to the pan before cooking the second side.

Continue to cook for another 10 minutes in the same manner. When done, transfer to a serving plate and cut in wedges. Serve hot or at room temperature.

Serves 2 as a single entrée, 4 as part of a larger meal

Major Protein for 2; *Minor Protein* for more

Note: The long, slow cooking makes the frittata firm, but tender. If leftover pasta is already mixed with cheese, the Parmesan can be reduced or omitted.

Menu Suggestions: For a single entrée, serve with an antipasto and bread. For a more generous meal, add a vegetable dish such as White Broccoli Mozzarella or a bean dish such as Italian Beans and Greens.

ZUCCHINI FRITTATA

For zucchini lovers.

2 tablespoons oil (at least part olive preferred)
1 pound zucchini, sliced (about 4 cups)
6 eggs
¼ cup minced parsley
1 teaspoon oregano
½ teaspoon salt
pepper

Heat oil in a 12-inch omelet pan. Sauté zucchini over moderately high heat, turning occasionally, until vegetable softens and begins to color.

Beat eggs with herbs and seasonings, lower heat, and pour over zucchini.

As omelet sets, lift edges and tilt to let uncooked egg filter down sides. When almost set, slip spatula underneath, slide omelet onto a plate, invert back into pan, and brown underside.

Cut into wedges and serve hot or at room temperature.

Serves 4

Minor Protein

Menu Suggestions: Additional protein can come from either a bean or pasta accompaniment, or both.

MEXICAN OMELET (TORTILLA)

Serve the tortilla plain or put a bowl of a spicy Mexican tomato sauce on the table for individual seasoning. This can be offered as a main course, or half-sized portions can be served as part of a more ambitious Mexican meal.

1 tablespoon oil
¼ cup chopped green pepper
½ teaspoon chili powder
4 eggs
3 tablespoons cornmeal
salt
¾ cup shredded mixed Jack and cheddar cheeses
½ cup chopped fresh tomato, drained
½ cup cooked kidney or other red beans, drained
pepper

Heat oil in a 10-inch omelet pan and sauté green pepper for 5 minutes. Add chili powder and cook ½ minute longer. Spread pepper evenly in pan.

Beat eggs with cornmeal and a pinch of salt. Pour over green pepper. Cook, lifting edges, tilting so unset egg runs underneath. Top will still be soft in spots.

Loosen edges and run spatula underneath omelet so it is free of pan and will not stick when ready to serve.

Cover omelet with cheese, then distribute tomato and kidney beans evenly on top. Sprinkle with pepper. Cover and cook for 1 to 2 minutes over low heat until cheese melts.

Transfer to a serving platter or serve directly from the pan, cutting into wedges.

Serves 2 as main dish, 4 as one part of the entrée

Major Protein when serving 2; a little extra protein should be added if recipe is stretched to serve 4

Note: As with most 4-egg omelets, this can be halved and prepared in an 8-inch pan; while it could conceivably be doubled and prepared in a 15-inch skillet, it is advisable to make two separate omelets instead. While the second cooks, the first can be kept warm in a low oven.

EGG FU YUNG

Miniature omelets in a brown gravy.

Fu Yung Sauce
1 cup water
1 tablespoon cornstarch or arrowroot
2 tablespoons soy sauce
1 teaspoon molasses or honey

Stir water gradually into starch in a small saucepan to form a smooth mixture. Add remaining ingredients.

Place over low heat and cook, stirring constantly, until mixture reaches the boiling point.

Cook just below boiling for 1 minute. Remove from heat or keep in a double boiler or set on a flame tamer while preparing eggs.

Omelets
6 eggs
2 teaspoons soy sauce
2 tablespoons whole wheat flour
1½ cups mung or soybean sprouts
½ cup thinly sliced scallions
oil

Preheat oven to 300°F. Beat eggs with soy sauce and flour. Add vegetables.

Place an 8-inch omelet pan over moderate heat for about 30 seconds. Pour in 1 teaspoon oil and, using a paper towel, rub pan to coat. Return to heat for 30 seconds longer.

Keeping the heat moderate, add ¼ cup egg mixture to pan, forming a thin omelet. When top is almost set, slide omelet onto a plate, invert back into pan, and cook until set. It will take less than a minute to cook each omelet; the time will be reduced as you proceed and pan becomes hotter.

If the pan is well seasoned and hot, it should not need additional oil. If need be, however, wipe with an oiled paper towel between omelets.

Make 8 omelets, keeping finished ones warm in the oven.

To serve, pile 2 omelets on each plate and top with Fu Yung Sauce.

Serves 4

Minor Protein

Menu Suggestions: For a simple meal just add rice and a Chinese salad like Chinese Radish Salad or Cucumbers with Spicy Dressing. A more ambitious cook might want to add a wok-cooked vegetable, like Broccoli with Peanuts in Sweet and Sour Sauce, or Simple Vegetable Stir-Fry.

BAKED VEGETABLE OMELET

3 medium carrots (about ½ pound)
1 medium zucchini (10 to 12 ounces)
4 eggs
1 cup shredded cheddar cheese
¼ cup minced parsley
2 tablespoons chopped scallion
¼ cup whole wheat flour
2 tablespoons wheat germ
¼ teaspoon salt
pepper
1 tablespoon butter

Preheat oven to 375°F. Shred vegetables on a coarse grater or in a processor. Pack gently into a measuring cup; you should have 1½ cups each. Squeeze as much moisture as possible from zucchini.

In a large bowl beat eggs, then mix in vegetables and remaining ingredients except for butter.

Grease a 9- or 10-inch casserole or deep glass pie pan. Fill with egg mixture, dot with butter, and bake about 30 minutes until firm.

Let cool at least 5 minutes before cutting; best served warm, not hot.

Serves 4

Major Protein

BAKED EGGS FLORENTINE

Eggs baked to perfection on a bed of spinach, then generously covered with cheese sauce.

The Spinach Bed
2 pounds fresh spinach
1 tablespoon butter
2 small or 1 large clove garlic, minced
½ teaspoon salt

Wash, drain, and chop spinach coarsely. You should have about 20 cups, loosely packed.

Melt butter in a large skillet; add garlic, sauté briefly to soften, then add spinach, stirring and sautéeing until wilted. (It should cook down to 4 cups.)

The Cheese Sauce
4 tablespoons butter
4 tablespoons whole wheat flour
2 cups milk
¼ teaspoon salt
¼ teaspoon nutmeg
1 cup combined shredded Swiss and Parmesan cheeses or cheeses of choice

Prepare a white sauce by melting butter, stirring in flour, then gradually adding milk over moderate heat. Cook, stirring, until sauce thickens and comes to a boil. Boil gently for 1 minute. Season with salt and nutmeg and stir in cheese to melt.

The Assembly
Spinach Bed
6 to 12 eggs
Cheese Sauce

Preheat oven to 375°F.
Spread spinach in a shallow casserole large enough to hold all the eggs, or divide into 6 individual casseroles.
Break eggs carefully over spinach at intervals, allowing one or two per serving as desired. Spoon sauce over all.
Bake until white is set but yolk is still runny, about 15 minutes. Season with lots of fresh ground pepper before serving.
Serves 6
Major Protein
Note: If desired, 2 cups medium white sauce made from White Sauce Mix (page 443) can be used, seasoned with nutmeg and cheese as above. The elements of this casserole (that is, the spinach and the sauce) can be prepared several hours in advance and refrigerated, to be assembled just before baking if this is more convenient.
The eggs are easiest to serve and eat when prepared in individual baking dishes, but a single casserole may be preferred by the dish washer.

FRESH CORN PUDDING

4 good-sized ears corn
4 eggs
2 cups milk
2 tablespoons melted butter
1 teaspoon salt
1 tablespoon honey
paprika

Preheat oven to 350°F.
Scrape corn from cob, retaining both the kernels and the milk. Break up kernels gently with a fork to release more milk. You should have at least 2 cups corn mixture.
Beat in eggs, then milk and seasonings. Pour into a greased, shallow 1½-quart baking dish or four 1½-cup casseroles. Place in a larger baking pan and surround with ½ inch hot water.
Bake until set, 45 minutes for single baking dish, 30 minutes for individual casseroles. Remove from the water bath and let stand for 10 minutes before serving.
Serves 4
Major Protein
Variation: For *Cheese–Corn Pudding,* pour half of the mixture into a baking dish. Top with 2 to 3 ounces thinly sliced or shredded cheese. Pour on remaining corn mixture, top with another layer of cheese, sprinkle with paprika, and bake as above.

Soufflés

If you have never made a soufflé, here are a few pointers that will insure success. Despite the French name and elegant reputation, a soufflé is very simple to prepare. Broken down into its components, it is no more than a thick white sauce combined with flavoring ingredients such as cheese and/or vegetables and eggs.
The outcome of your soufflé depends on several factors:
1. Separate the eggs before you begin making the sauce. This will give the whites a chance to come to room temperature and whip to maximum volume.
2. While flour can be used to thicken the sauce, it will make the soufflé a bit "bready." Thus, for a delicate dish, arrowroot or cornstarch is preferred.
3. Allow the sauce to cool slightly

before adding egg yolks. If it is too hot, the eggs will "cook." Use the waiting time to prepare the baking dish.

4. The proper beating of the egg whites creates the height and lightness. Beat until stiff peaks form, but do not overbeat so that the whites deflate in the oven. For directions on beating egg whites, see On Cooking: Egg Handling.

5. Fold whites gently into yolk mixture until evenly dispersed, but not necessarily smooth. To make this step easier, fold just a bit of the whites in first to loosen the mixture. Avoid overmixing and rough handling, as this too will reduce the volume.

6. Choose a deep, straight-sided baking dish. The depth and a straight rather than curved contour are essential for proper rising. A soufflé for 4 to 6, using 6 eggs, is baked in a 1½- to 1¾- quart dish; half the recipe, or a soufflé for 2, can be baked in a 1-quart dish; or soufflés can be baked in individual dishes or even in scooped-out tomato shells. If you double the recipe to feed 8 to 12, bake the soufflé in two dishes or in individual dishes.

A pan that is too large will dwarf the soufflé. A pan that is too small can be compensated for by adding a foil collar at the top.

7. A range of baking time is provided, depending on how you like your eggs cooked. The shorter time produces a soft creamy center which acts as a sauce for the firmer egg at the edges— this is the French way. The full baking time results in a firm, omelet-like soufflé. Most people choose something in the middle.

Recommended baking times are as follows:

6-egg soufflé in a 1½- to 1¾-dish— 30 to 40 minutes

3-egg soufflé in a 1-quart dish—20 to 30 minutes

Individual soufflés—12 to 18 minutes

8. You wait for the soufflé, it does not wait for you. To be impressive, your soufflé must be served within minutes of baking. Otherwise it will sink and you will miss out on all the pre-dinner exclamations. It is best to put the soufflé into the oven only when you are certain of the dining schedule. This is not as difficult as it may seem, for everything can be pre-made up to the point of whipping and folding in the egg whites. If the sauce–egg yolk mixture is prepared well in advance it should be refrigerated, then brought to room temperature while the oven is preheating. If the sauce is very cold it will be difficult to incorporate the whites. To take off the chill and thin the sauce slightly, set the container with sauce in a bowl of warm water, double-boiler style, for 5 to 10 minutes.

9. A final admonition for the soufflé maker: do not open the oven until the soufflé is almost done. The rush of cool air is likely to cause the soufflé to fall if the outside structure is not set. To test for doneness, shake lightly. If the soufflé shakes all over, it is not done. If it shakes in the middle, it is French style; if it does not move, it is firm. Do not overbake.

CHEESE SOUFFLÉ

The standard cheese for a classic soufflé is equal parts of Swiss and Parmesan. If you wish, you can vary the proportion of the cheeses, experimenting with your personal favorites.

3 tablespoons butter
3 tablespoons arrowroot, cornstarch, or potato starch, or 6 tablespoons whole wheat flour
1½ cups milk

½ teaspoon salt
pepper
¼ teaspoon nutmeg
½ teaspoon dry mustard
2 cups plus 1½ tablespoons grated
  cheese
6 eggs, separated

Preheat oven to 375°F.
Melt butter in small saucepan. Remove from heat and stir in starch to make a smooth paste.
Return to low heat and gradually stir in milk. Cook, stirring gently, until sauce thickens and comes to the boiling point.
Remove from heat and stir in seasonings and the 2 cups of cheese, adding cheese gradually and stirring after each addition to melt.
Cool sauce slightly, then beat in egg yolks, one at a time.
Prepare baking dish (either a single 1¾-quart dish or individual dishes) by rubbing bottom and sides with butter and shaking the remaining 1½ tablespoons cheese over the inside to coat.
Beat egg whites until stiff. Fold into cheese sauce. Pour into prepared pan and bake for 30 to 40 minutes, depending on desired texture (instructions on pages 137–138), or 12 to 18 minutes for individual soufflés.
Serve at once, spooning from baking dish.
Serves 4; 6 as part of a large meal
Major Protein

MUSHROOM SOUFFLÉ

While any cheese can be used in preparing this soufflé, we recommend a mixture of mozzarella, provolone, and Parmesan, or the classic Swiss–Parmesan mix.

3 tablespoons butter
¾ pound mushrooms, thinly sliced
3 tablespoons arrowroot, cornstarch,
  or potato starch, or 6 tablespoons
  whole wheat flour
1 cup milk
½ teaspoon salt
pepper
¼ teaspoon nutmeg

1 tablespoon lemon juice
1 cup shredded cheese
6 eggs, separated
wheat germ

Preheat oven to 375°F.
Melt butter in a small saucepan and cook mushrooms, stirring occasionally, until softened and liquid runs freely, about 5 minutes.
Mix starch with enough milk to form a smooth paste and stir into hot mushroom mixture. Gradually stir in remaining milk and cook over low heat, stirring frequently, until mixture thickens and reaches the boiling point.
Remove from heat and add seasonings and cheese, stirring to melt.
Cool sauce slightly, then beat in egg yolks, one at a time.
Prepare baking dish by rubbing bottom and sides with butter, then coating with wheat germ. Shake out any wheat germ that does not adhere.
Beat whites until stiff. Fold into mushroom sauce. Pour into prepared dish and bake for 30 to 40 minutes, depending on desired texture (see pages 137–138), or 12 to 18 minutes for individual soufflés.
Serve at once, spooning soufflé from baking dish.
Serves 4; 6 as part of large meal
Major Protein

STOVE-TOP VEGETABLES

As there is very little protein in vegetables themselves, they are generally coupled with cheese, eggs, or grains either in the recipe or on the menu. Since many of the following recipes already contain a dairy product, a complete meal is best composed by adding a grain accompaniment, dumpling, or breadstuff, a salad, and, if desired, a second cooked vegetable dish. Bean salads and spreads also go well with Stove-Top Vegetable entrées. In addition to these general recommendations, you will find that most recipes have specific menu suggestions.

VEGETABLES MOZZARELLA

The vegetable can be varied with the season, choosing from broccoli, zucchini, eggplant, or even green beans or asparagus.

1 tablespoon oil
1 clove garlic, minced
2 cups chopped fresh tomato or 1½ cups lightly drained canned tomato pulp
½ tablespoon chopped fresh basil or ½ teaspoon dried
½ teaspoon oregano
¼ teaspoon salt
dash honey (optional)
¾ pound vegetable of choice, cut in individual spears or half-inch rounds, depending on your selection
1 tablespoon nutritional yeast or ½ tablespoon tomato paste (optional)
3 ounces sliced or shredded mozzarella cheese (about ¾ cup)

Heat oil in a skillet and sauté garlic until it just begins to color. Add tomatoes and seasonings and simmer until soft and slightly reduced, about 10 minutes. If tomatoes are very acid, add honey.

Place vegetables in sauce, cover and simmer until just fork-tender, 15 to 20 minutes.

Remove cover and, if sauce is watery, stir in yeast or tomato paste to thicken. Top with cheese, cover and cook briefly to melt.

Serves 2
Minor Protein
Menu Suggestions: There will be adequate protein at this meal if you serve the vegetables on a bed of pasta or, if you like, polenta. A marinated bean salad provides excellent contrast in flavor and texture.

SKILLET VEGETABLES WITH YOGURT AND CHEESE

Simple and flavorful.

2 tablespoons oil
1 large green pepper, chopped
½ cup sliced scallions, including the green tops
3 to 4 medium carrots, shredded (about 1½ cups)
½ cup minced parsley
1 pound green or yellow squash, cut into small sticks (about 3 cups)
16 small to medium mushrooms, cut in half or into bite-size pieces
several sprigs fresh dill
¾ teaspoon salt
1 cup yogurt
1 cup grated cheese of choice

Heat oil in a large skillet and sauté pepper and scallions about 3 minutes until softened. Add carrots and parsley and cook 3 minutes longer. Add squash, mushrooms, dill, and salt; cover and cook gently for about 8 minutes until vegetables are barely tender.

Combine yogurt and grated cheese and, when vegetables are cooked, remove from heat, stir in cheese mixture, cover, and let stand off heat about a minute to melt.

Serve hot. If service is delayed, put off adding cheese mixture until the last minute, as it is best not heated. Vegetables can stand off the heat, covered, and if they cool down, can be reheated briefly *before* adding cheese.

Serves 4
Minor Protein
Menu Suggestions: The little bit of protein needed to fill out this meal is best provided by a base of grain or potato, or wedges of bread to sop up the sauce.

EGGPLANT CUTLETS

Crumb-coating and shallow-frying anything, whether it is chicken, veal, or eggplant, requires space and organization. But eggplant cutlets prepared in this manner are worth the effort, for beneath the crusty coating is a soft, creamy center that has shown us where the "egg" in eggplant comes from.

1 medium eggplant (1 to 1½ pounds)
¼ cup whole wheat flour
2 eggs, beaten
½ cup fine dry whole wheat bread or cracker crumbs
2 tablespoons wheat germ
½ teaspoon salt

pepper
½ teaspoon oregano
½ teaspoon dried basil
oil

Cut eggplant crosswise into ½-inch thick rounds. You should get 8 to 12, depending on the shape.

Place flour on one plate, eggs in a bowl; combine crumbs, wheat germ, and seasonings and put some of this mixture on a plate.

If you plan to cook cutlets immediately, generously cover surface of a heavy 15-inch skillet with oil and allow it to heat up while you prepare eggplant. If more convenient, eggplant can be coated and chilled to set coating.

Dredge each eggplant slice with flour, dip in egg to coat both sides, and cover completely with crumb mixture. If crumbs become soggy, replace them with fresh ones. Set each coated slice on a wire rack and continue until you have at least a pan full.

When oil is hot, place eggplant slices in the pan; in a 15-inch skillet you will be able to accommodate 4 to 6 slices at a time. Sauté until well browned, 3 to 5 minutes per side. Turn only once and cook until center is soft, which can be determined by piercing the cutlet with a fork.

If you are preparing more than one batch, transfer the cooked cutlets to a baking sheet and keep warm in a 325°F. oven.

Serve plain or enhance cutlets as directed in Variations.

Serves 4
Minor Protein
Variations: For *Eggplant Cutlets Parmesan,* top each Eggplant Cutlet with 2 tablespoons Italian Tomato Sauce, sprinkle with some grated Parmesan cheese, cover with thinly sliced mozzarella and melt cheese on top of the stove by covering the skillet, or while keeping cutlets warm in the oven.

For *Eggplant Cutlets Provolone,* place a thin slice of tomato and some alfalfa sprouts on each cutlet. Cover with thinly sliced provolone cheese. Melt cheese as directed above.

For *Eggplant Cheeseburgers,* top each cutlet with 2 tablespoons Quick Barbecue Sauce or Tomato–Mushroom Burger Sauce and thinly sliced cheddar cheese. Melt cheese as directed above.

All variations supply *Major Protein.*

Menu Suggestions: A side dish of rice or pasta, a hot or cold bean accompaniment, or the leftovers of any bean–grain entrée can appear on the menu with the cutlets. Add salad for a complete meal.

CARROT STEW

This sweet and flavorful carrot sauce depends on a base of grains, a side dish of yogurt, and a bean accompaniment to supply all the elements of a meal.

2 tablespoons oil
1 large onion, sliced
2 medium green peppers, cut in strips
2 teaspoons minced, fresh hot chili pepper, or ¼ teaspoon cayenne (optional)
4 cups canned tomato pulp or drained stewed tomatoes
1 pound carrots, cut into thick coins
½ teaspoon salt
3 to 5 cups cooked grain (or at least ¾ cup per person)

Heat oil in a 3-quart pot and sauté onion and peppers until limp, about 5 minutes.

Add tomato, carrots and salt, bring to a boil, cover, and simmer over low heat until carrots are tender, 30 to 40 minutes.

If sauce is too liquid, remove cover and boil gently to thicken; or remove from heat and stir in 2 to 3 teaspoons nutritional yeast, as needed, to thicken. Serve over grain.

Serves 4 to 6
Protein Complement
Variations: Rather than serving a bean accompaniment you can make *Bean–Carrot Stew* by adding 2 cups cooked white beans, lima beans, or chick-peas to stew during the last 10 minutes of cooking. To turn leftovers into *Carrot Gravy,* puree smooth in a blender or processor with an equal amount of tomato juice. Heat until thick and bubbling. To make *Carrot Soup* from

leftovers, puree in a blender or processor with twice as much tomato juice as leftover stew. Heat and serve with croutons or crushed crackers.

MUSHROOM PAPRIKASH

Meaty mushrooms in a creamy paprika sauce. Serve over noodles, brown rice, or on a base of biscuits or toast.

¾ pound mushrooms
1 tablespoon oil
1 medium onion, cut in thin crescents
¼ cup tomato juice
1 teaspoon cornstarch or arrowroot
1 tablespoon paprika
½ teaspoon salt
2 cups creamed cottage cheese

Clean mushrooms; cut stems in small sticks, large caps in halves or quarters, but leave small caps whole.

Heat oil in a saucepan and cook onion until limp and transparent, about 5 minutes. Add mushrooms, cover, and cook over medium heat for 5 minutes.

Stir tomato juice into starch to form a smooth paste. Stir along with seasonings into cooked mushrooms, cover and cook over low heat for 3 minutes.

Add cottage cheese and cook, stirring constantly, for about 5 minutes, until cheese melts. Sauce may become completely smooth or tiny curds may remain, depending on the cottage cheese. Serve over a grain base.

Serves 4
Major Protein
Menu Suggestions: Broccoli, asparagus, or another green vegetable in season, lightly steamed and seasoned with fresh lemon wedges, makes a suitable vegetable accompaniment.

ILSE'S VEGETABLES IN CREAM SAUCE

A cold and tangy sauce of yogurt, sour cream, and vegetables generously ladled over warm steamed potatoes. The perfect hot-weather entrée, for which David's mother is owed the credit.

4 medium potatoes
2 medium onions, sliced
2 cups sour cream
2 cups yogurt
½ cup vinegar or pickling juice
½ teaspoon salt (omit with pickling juice)
2 small tomatoes, cut in bite-size pieces
6 radishes, sliced
1 cucumber, peeled and cubed
1 sour pickle cut in quarter-inch cubes

Cut potatoes into quarters and steam for about 15 minutes, or until tender.

Place onion slices over potatoes in steamer initially and steam for 2 minutes. Remove and run under cold water to cool.

In a large serving bowl combine sour cream, yogurt, and vinegar or pickling juice. The amount of vinegar and/or pickling juice can be adjusted to taste.

Add salt, onion, tomatoes, radishes, cucumber, and pickle, and mix gently.

Serve at once over warm potatoes, or chill if prepared in advance.

Serves 6
Minor Protein
Menu Suggestions: Be sure to include whole grain bread to eat with any extra sauce. Vegetable Derma makes an ideal appetizer if you're willing to take the time. Homemade cookies or cake make the best dessert.

POTATOES PIZZAIOLA

1 pound potatoes
1 tablespoon olive oil
1 clove garlic, chopped
1 sweet Italian pepper or ½ medium green pepper, cut in thin strips
½ teaspoon salt
½ teaspoon oregano
pepper
1 cup tomato juice
½ cup diced fresh tomato
4 ounces sliced or 1 cup shredded mozzarella cheese

Cut unpeeled potatoes into thin slices, barely ⅛ inch thick. Use a food processor fitted with a slicing blade if you have one.

Heat oil in a 10-inch skillet and sauté garlic, pepper, and potatoes, stirring occasionally, until potato begins to turn transparent, about 5 minutes.

Add seasonings, juice, and tomato, cover and simmer over low heat until tender, 30 to 40 minutes. Stir once or twice during cooking to bring potatoes on bottom to top for even cooking.

Top with cheese, remove from heat, cover and let stand for 1 to 2 minutes to melt.

Serves 2 as a generous main dish, or 4 as an accompaniment

Major Protein

Note: For a single serving, halve recipe and prepare in an 8-inch skillet; for double the recipe, use a 15-inch skillet.

Variation: Sliced eggplant can be substituted for half the potato.

POTATOES NIÇOISE

Potatoes stewed in a garlicky broth, then sprinkled with cheese, are typical of southern French cuisine.

4 tablespoons oil (at least half olive)
1 large clove garlic, chopped
1½ pounds potatoes, thinly sliced
1 teaspoon thyme
½ teaspoon dried basil
4 tablespoons minced fresh parsley
2 teaspoons salt
3 medium red Bermuda onions, thinly sliced
1½ pounds tomatoes, thinly sliced
½ teaspoon nutmeg
1 cup shredded Swiss cheese
8 or more pitted black olives

Heat 2 tablespoons oil in a heavy 15-inch skillet and sauté garlic briefly to extract flavor.

Remove pan from heat and cover with half the potatoes and half the thyme, basil, parsley, and salt. Top with half the onions and half the tomatoes. Repeat these layers.

Sprinkle nutmeg over top layer of tomato and drizzle with remaining 2 tablespoons oil.

Place over low to moderate heat, cover, and cook until potatoes are quite tender, 40 to 50 minutes.

Remove from heat, sprinkle cheese evenly over top, decorate with olives, and cover to melt cheese.

Serves 4 to 6 as single main dish, 8 to 10 as a combined entrée

Minor Protein

Note: Leftovers make a delicious cold side dish or appetizer.

Menu Suggestions: For a full meal, begin with a substantial appetizer like Steamed Artichokes with a Dipping Sauce, Overstuffed Mushrooms, Celery or Cauliflower Rémoulade, or a generous crudité. Follow the main course with a green salad, then a cheese plate. Of course, no French meal would be complete without plenty of bread. For a really elaborate meal serve a double entrée of Potatoes Niçoise plus an omelet or quiche; if either of these is quite cheesy, leave the cheese out of the potatoes.

MARSEILLES SPINACH STEW

This is the type of dish you would be likely to eat in the home of a French family in this port city.

2 pounds spinach, chard, kale, or a combination of these greens
¼ cup oil (at least part olive preferred)
1 large onion, chopped
2 pounds potatoes, sliced thin
1 tablespoon chopped garlic
1 teaspoon salt
¼ teaspoon pepper
good pinch saffron, if available
2 sprigs fresh dill
2 sprigs fresh parsley
4 cups water
6 eggs
6 slices whole grain bread

Chop greens coarsely. (You should have about 24 cups.)

Heat oil in a large, broad pot. Add onion and cook until soft but still pale, 3 to 5 minutes. Add greens, cover, and cook until limp, 5 minutes. If the pot is not very deep you may have to cook down some of the greens before the rest will fit.

Add potatoes to greens along with garlic, salt, pepper, saffron, dill, and parsley. Pour in water and bring to a boil. Cover and simmer over low heat until potatoes are just tender, 30 to 40 minutes depending on their thickness. When done there should still be liquid in the pot. If not, add some water and heat to the boiling point.

Shortly before serving, carefully break eggs and slip at intervals into simmering stew. Cover and cook gently until white is just set and yolk is still runny, about 8 minutes.

To serve, spoon egg onto a slice of bread on each plate. Surround with vegetables. Season with additional salt and pepper to taste.

Serves 6
Major Protein
Note: If you are serving only 4, use the same recipe but reduce the eggs and bread and save the remaining vegetables; the leftovers can be diluted with tomato juice for a delicious soup (see Instant Asopa).

GERMAN-STYLE NEW POTATOES

Potatoes mixed with seasoned cottage cheese; a relative of noodles and cheese.

2 pounds (16 to 24) new or small potatoes
2 cups cottage cheese
4 chopped scallions
1 tablespoon caraway seeds
yogurt
salt
pepper

Steam whole unpeeled potatoes until fork-tender, about 30 minutes. Mean-

while, combine cottage cheese, scallions, and caraway seeds in a serving bowl and let stand at room temperature. Add hot, cooked potatoes, leaving them whole or cut in halves. Mix and serve at once, letting each person add yogurt individually at the table, as well as salt and pepper to taste.

Serves 4
Major Protein

COLOMBIAN POTATOES

From South America, a steamed vegetable plate with a spicy fresh tomato–cheese sauce spooned on top.

4 medium or 10 small new potatoes (about 1½ pounds)
1 pound green beans, cut in 2-inch lengths

For the Sauce
1 tablespoon butter
4 scallions, sliced
¼ cup chopped green pepper
2 teaspoons minced hot pepper
2 cups diced tomatoes
2 tablespoons minced parsley
2 cups diced mild cheese such as mozzarella, Jack, or in combination with provolone
1 egg, beaten

Scrub potatoes and cut in quarters if large, halves if "new." Place on vegetable steamer and steam for 10 minutes. Meanwhile prepare green beans. After 10 minutes, place beans over potatoes in steamer and continue cooking for 10 minutes until vegetables are tender.

While vegetables steam, melt butter in a 10- to 12-inch skillet or a 1-quart saucepan and sauté scallions and peppers for 3 minutes to soften. Add tomato and parsley and simmer, uncovered, for 10 minutes.

With heat very low, add cheese. When melted, remove pan from heat and stir in the beaten egg. Return to low heat briefly to warm through, but do not boil.

To serve, place steamed vegetables on a plate and smother with sauce.

Serves 4
Major Protein
Variations: This delicious and nour-

ishing sauce can also be served over brown rice, baked potato, steamed spaghetti squash, or any other favorite vegetables, or even over whole grain biscuits or toast. If desired, hot pepper can be omitted. In that case, season sauce before serving with a pinch of salt, some fresh ground pepper, and a little paprika.

PERUVIAN MOUNTAIN POTATOES

This is an adaptation of a traditional dish that comes from the Indians of Peru. Supposedly the poorer the family, the less cheese and the more chilies the mixture contained. For convenience the recipe is divided into three easy parts.

For the Spiced Onions
1 large onion, cut in rings
2 tablespoons lemon juice
¾ teaspoon crushed dried red pepper
¼ teaspoon salt

Mix and marinate at room temperature while potatoes cook.

For the Steamed Potatoes
6 medium potatoes (2 pounds)

Quarter potatoes and steam until tender, but not mushy, about 20 minutes. Cut into bite-size pieces.

For the Cheese Sauce
1 cup shredded mild cheese such as mozzarella, Muenster, or Jack
½ cup milk
1 teaspoon turmeric
¼ teaspoon salt
2 tablespoons olive oil
2 teaspoons chopped fresh or canned hot chili pepper

Combine cheese, milk, turmeric, and salt by beating with a fork or pureeing in a blender or processor.
Heat oil in a small saucepan and sauté hot pepper for 1 minute. Stir in cheese mixture and cook over low heat until smooth and creamy, about 5 minutes.

For the Finished Dish
Steamed Potatoes
Cheese Sauce
Spiced Onions
canned mild chili pepper
16 to 20 olives, halved
2 hard-cooked eggs, sliced

Mix potatoes with Cheese Sauce. Drain onions and stir in.
Place in a serving dish and garnish with strips of chili pepper, olive halves, and egg slices.
Serves 4
Major Protein
Note: Egg garnish can be omitted, but if so, a little additional protein should be added to the menu.
Menu Suggestions: Serve this with a crusty bread and two vegetable dishes from the following list: squash, pan-fried cabbage or other greens, fresh sliced tomato, avocado wedges, or pickles.

COLCANNON

A typical Irish potato-and-cabbage dish.

1 recipe Basic Mashed Potatoes (page 248)
4 cups shredded cabbage
2 tablespoons butter
6 scallions, chopped
salt
pepper
paprika

While potatoes steam for the mashed potatoes, sauté cabbage in melted butter in a skillet until limp, about 10 minutes. Add scallions.
Stir cabbage into mashed potatoes until thoroughly blended. Adjust salt and pepper to taste and sprinkle generously with paprika.
Serves 4
Minor Protein
Menu Suggestions: Serve in the traditional manner with Oatcakes and butter, hunks of cheddar cheese, pickles or a cucumber salad, and apple cider.

HUNGARIAN VEGETABLES GULYAS

In Hungary, thick stews and dumplings are constant companions. Bread Meat, which can be prepared ahead or while the vegetables cook, is our companion of choice.

2 large onions
1 large green pepper
1 pound potatoes, or half potatoes, half turnips
1 pound carrots, or half carrots, half parsnips
¾ pound cabbage
1½ tablespoons oil
2 tablespoons paprika
generous pinch cayenne (optional)
2 cups water
1½ teaspoons salt
⅔ cup yogurt
⅓ cup sour cream
1 recipe Bread Meat (pages 205–206)

Peel vegetables only where necessary and cut into 1-inch chunks.

Heat oil in a 3- to 5-quart pot and sauté onion and green pepper for a few minutes to soften. Add paprika and, if it is not a fine fresh Hungarian or comparable variety, add cayenne as well.

Add remaining vegetables, water, and salt. Bring to a boil, cover, and simmer over low heat until vegetables are quite tender, about 40 minutes.

Meanwhile mix yogurt with sour cream and let stand at room temperature; prepare Bread Meat.

To serve, place stew in shallow bowls. Cut up Bread Meat and add some to each plate. Stir in some of the yogurt for a creamy sauce.

Serves 4
Major Protein
Menu Suggestions: Begin with a fresh fruit appetizer, or a mushroom dish if serving really big appetites. Pickles are as traditional as the dumplings with these stews.

VEGETABLES WITH APRICOT SAUCE

Delicate with gentle sweetness. Serve over cracked wheat, barley, millet, or whole wheat noodles.

½ cup quartered dried apricots
2 tablespoons raisins
2 tablespoons oil
1 large onion, coarsely chopped
1 pound eggplant, patty pan, zucchini, or winter squash
1 cup cooked chick-peas
1 teaspoon salt (adjust if beans are salted)
½ teaspoon cinnamon
1 cup water from soaking fruit combined witth bean cooking liquid or plain water
cooked pasta or grain

Soak dried fruit in hot water to cover while preparing remaining ingredients.

Heat oil in a 2- to 3-quart pot and cook onion over medium heat until lightly colored, about 10 minutes.

While onion cooks, peel vegetables if necessary and cut in bite-size cubes. Add to onion and stir to coat.

Drain fruit, reserving liquid, and add to pot along with chick-peas and seasoning.

Measure reserved liquid and, if necessary, add water or bean liquid to make 1 cup. Add to pot, bring to a boil, cover, and simmer over low heat about 30 minutes until vegetable is just tender. Serve over grain.

Serves 4
Minor Protein (including grain)
Menu Suggestions: Add additional protein with a salad or appetizer containing cheese, yogurt, or egg.

GREEN BEAN CHOW MEIN

2 tablespoons oil
2 medium onions, cut in crescents (about 1 cup)
4 stalks celery, cut on the diagonal (about 2 cups)
1 pound green beans, cut in 1-inch segments (about 3 cups)
1½ cups water
2 tablespoons soy sauce
2 teaspoons molasses
1 teaspoon salt
3 cups bean sprouts
⅔ cup coarsely chopped almonds
2 teaspoons cornstarch or arrowroot
1 tablespoon water
2 teaspoons sherry

Heat oil in a wok and stir-fry onion and celery for 5 minutes. Add beans and stir-fry for 1 minute longer.

Add water, soy sauce, molasses, and salt; turn heat low, cover, and simmer for 15 minutes. Add sprouts and almonds, replace cover and cook 5 minutes more.

Combine starch and water to make a smooth paste and add to vegetables along with sherry. Cook until mixture thickens and reaches the boiling point.

Serves 4

Minor Protein

Note: If you use unblanched almonds, the skins are likely to slip off and become mixed in with the vegetables during cooking. This does not disturb us, but if it bothers you, blanch the almonds before chopping.

Menu Suggestions: Traditional service is over rice or Chinese Fried Noodles; for real quick service try crumbled rice crackers from the pantry. Accompany with a light soup, Rolled Omelet Slices for additional protein, and Cucumber Salad with Spicy Dressing or Chinese Radish Salad for added zip.

BROCCOLI WITH PEANUTS IN SWEET AND SOUR SAUCE

1½ pounds broccoli
1 green pepper
2 tablespoons oil
⅔ cup unsalted peanuts
¼ cup broth or water
2 medium tomatoes, cut in thin wedges
¼ cup soy sauce
3 tablespoons honey
¼ cup cider vinegar
½ cup apple juice
2 tablespoons cornstarch or arrowroot

Peel broccoli stalks thinly if thick and tough and slice broccoli into small trees. Slice pepper into strips.

Heat oil in a wok and stir-fry nuts until they begin to color, about 1 minute. Do not overcook. Add broccoli and pepper and stir to coat with oil. Add broth and tomatoes, cover, and cook over moderate heat until vegetables are barely tender, about 15 minutes.

While vegetables cook, combine remaining ingredients for sauce.

When vegetables are cooked, and a few minutes before serving, stir sauce mixture to recombine, pour over vegetables in wok, and cook, stirring, until thickened and at boiling point. This will take 3 to 5 minutes. Serve at once.

Serves 4 or 6 as one of several entrées

Protein Complement

Variation: For *Cauliflower with Peanuts in Sweet and Sour Sauce,* replace broccoli with 1½ pounds cauliflower. Divide into florets and slice central core into strips. Test for tenderness after 15 minutes (cauliflower may require 5 additional minutes of cooking); cook until just tender, not soft or mushy.

Menu Suggestions: When served on 1 cup of rice or pasta per person, this Protein Complement is completed. If grain is omitted, be sure to include another protein dish, such as one containing tofu or egg. Of course, instead of plain rice or noodles, Chinese-Style Fried Rice or Lo Mein is welcome on the menu. If several such dishes are included, the broccoli should suffice for an additional two servings.

MEXICAN VEGETABLES

A thick, flavorful vegetable sauce. Serve over corn bread or tacos and top with cheese.

2 tablespoons oil
1 clove garlic, minced
1 onion, chopped
1 hot fresh chili pepper, chopped, or ¼ cup chopped green pepper plus ¼ teaspoon cayenne and 1 to 2 tablespoons chili powder
2 cups fresh chopped or drained canned tomatoes
½ teaspoon salt
4 cups diced vegetables including 1 cup cooked soy or lima beans, 2 ears corn on the cob cut in 1-inch segments or 1 cup corn kernels, and any amount of green beans, squash, and/or cauliflower
corn bread or grain of choice
1 cup or more shredded cheddar cheese

Heat oil in a 2- to 3-quart saucepan and sauté garlic, onion, chili pepper or green pepper until soft and transparent, about 5 minutes. If chili pepper is omitted, add spices and cook 30 seconds longer.

Add tomatoes and salt and bring to a boil.

Add vegetables, cover, and cook gently over low heat until tender, or about 30 minutes depending on the vegetables chosen.

Serve over corn bread, sprinkling on cheese to taste at the table.

Serves 4

Major Protein including corn bread or grain

Note: A range is given for the chili powder so you may vary it, depending on the strength of your blend and the resistance of your palate.

PAKISTANI CURRY

A mild but flavorful and very aromatic blend of spices, mushrooms, potatoes, peas, and egg. A good first introduction to the world of curry.

 2 tablespoons oil
 1 clove garlic, chopped
 1 teaspoon grated or finely chopped fresh ginger
 1 teaspoon chili powder
 1 teaspoon turmeric
 ½ teaspoon cumin
 1 pound mushrooms, sliced
 1½ pounds potatoes, cut in ½-inch cubes
 1 teaspoon salt
 1½ cups fresh or frozen green peas
 2 medium tomatoes, chopped
 4 eggs
 ¼ cup minced scallion

Heat oil in a 15-inch skillet and cook garlic and ginger about 1 minute until lightly colored. Add chili, turmeric, and cumin and cook 1 minute longer. Add mushrooms, potato, salt, and peas, if fresh. Cover and cook for 15 minutes until potatoes are beginning to soften.

If frozen peas are used, add with tomatoes, cover, and cook 10 minutes longer, or until potatoes are tender. Mixture can be held at this point if

necessary; do not proceed with the final step until shortly before serving.

Carefully break eggs and slip onto hot vegetables, keeping yolks intact. Cover and cook until white is set and yolk lightly cooked but still runny, or about 10 minutes.

Sprinkle with scallion and serve.

Serves 4

Minor Protein

Menu Suggestions: Serve with a flat bread like Chapati or Dhal Pouree Roti or pita and any raita or shredded vegetable salad. If the raita does not contain yogurt, a side dish of plain yogurt makes a soothing contrast and a nourishing meal.

VEGETABLE–CHEESE CURRY

In traditional Indian fashion the list of spices is long. Don't let this dissuade you, for the preparation is simple and the result quite pleasing (and spicy).

 2 tablespoons oil
 ½ pound farmer cheese, cut in ½-inch cubes
 4 cloves
 1 tablespoon cinnamon
 ¼ teaspoon ground or ½ teaspoon crushed cardamom seeds
 ¼ teaspoon crushed red pepper
 2½ teaspoons ground ginger
 2 teaspoons turmeric
 ½ teaspoon chili powder
 1 teaspoon cumin
 2 tomatoes, diced
 1 cauliflower, separated into florets
 1½ teaspoons salt
 1 teaspoon honey
 1 cup water
 1 lemon, cut in wedges
 yogurt

Heat oil in a 2- to 3-quart pot. Add cheese and sauté for 2 to 3 minutes until cubes are creamy. Remove from pot and reserve.

Add cloves, cinnamon, cardamom, and red pepper to pot and fry for ½ minute. Add ginger, turmeric, chili powder, and cumin and fry for ½ minute more.

Add tomato, cauliflower, salt, honey, and water. Bring to a boil, cover, and simmer until cauliflower is just tender, 10 to 15 minutes.

To serve, place some cheese cubes in each dish, spoon vegetable mixture on cheese, and garnish with lemon wedge. Let each person squeeze in some lemon juice to taste and add yogurt for cooling contrast.

Serves 4

Minor Protein

Note: If you wish to make *Home-made Farmer Cheese* for this recipe, combine 6 cups milk (any type) with 4 tablespoons lemon juice and let stand for 10 minutes at room temperature to sour. Cook over moderate heat until milk comes to a boil and separates into curds and whey. Pour through a strainer lined with several layers of cheesecloth or a linen napkin. When liquid has run through, gather cloth around the solids like a bag and tie. Hang several hours to drain. When firm, shape into cubes. Use at once or cover and refrigerate.

Variation: For *Vegetable–Tofu Curry,* replace cheese with 1 pound of tofu cut into cubes and cooked as for cheese.

Menu Suggestions: Rice can be served with the curry but is not essential. A cooling raita is. A bean dish is recommended and so is bread, either in the form of Chapatis (plain or stuffed) or Pita Bread. Another curried dish could be served simultaneously, such as Fried Cabbage and Potatoes, Indian Style, or perhaps Spiced Green Beans.

GADO GADO

This dish is typical of Indonesian cuisine. The spicy peanut butter sauce is spooned over a mixture of steamed tofu and vegetables.

2 carrots, cut in thin 2-inch sticks

6 to 8 ounces tofu (1 large cake or 2 small), cut in thick strips

4 ounces spinach or cabbage, cut in strips

4 ounces broccoli, cut in thin trees, or string beans or snow peas

½ medium zucchini, cut in thin 2-inch sticks

¾ cup bean sprouts

2 scallions, cut in slivers 1 to 2 inches long

¼ medium green pepper, cut in slivers 1 inch long

½ cup warm water

¼ cup unsalted, unsweetened peanut butter

1 clove garlic, minced

¼ teaspoon crushed red pepper

1 tablespoon lemon juice

2 teaspoons molasses

2 to 3 teaspoons soy sauce

Steam vegetables so that all are done at the same time. Carrots, tofu, broccoli, and string beans require about 10 minutes to be just tender. Snow peas, the greens, zucchini, and sprouts need only 5 minutes steaming and can be added to the first batch of vegetables when they are half tender. Leave scallions and green pepper raw.

While vegetables cook, stir water into peanut butter in a small saucepan, add garlic, crushed pepper, lemon juice, and molasses, and heat through, stirring, until sauce becomes thick and creamy. Add soy sauce a teaspoon at a time to taste. If not "hot," add additional crushed pepper. If too thick, add water.

To serve, arrange vegetables on a serving platter, either in separate piles, which is the traditional way, or mixed together and topped with raw scallions and green pepper slivers.

Let each person take some of each vegetable and cover with sauce to taste.

Serves 2

Major Protein

Note: If peanut butter is presalted, reduce soy sauce to 1 teaspoon. If presweetened, reduce molasses to ½ to 1 teaspoon so sauce is slightly sweet.

BAKED VEGETABLE ENTRÉES

The entrées that follow also emphasize vegetables but are dependent on the oven for part or all of their cooking. Like their Stove-Top cousins, these dishes often rely on added protein from other foods to make them of main dish quality. The inclusion of cheese in

Baked Vegetable Entrées makes beans (as soup or salad), grains (including pasta and breadstuffs), and fruit or vegetable appetizers and/or salads suitable accompaniments.

Since the oven will be in use, this is a good time to make fresh rolls, biscuits, or muffins. If different temperatures are required, the bread can be baked first and allowed to cool, or cooked after, permitting the vegetable casserole to sit at room temperature, as many recipes require.

Appetizers and accompaniments can also take advantage of the lighted oven. Some appropriate choices include Mushrooms in Garlic Butter, Stuffed Clam Shells Areganata, Baked Asparagus, Sliced Baked Beets, Nutted Baked Onions, Baked Parsley Tomatoes, baked winter squash, Pan-Roasted Potatoes, or a baked plain or sweet potato. Baked desserts can complete these oven-cooked meals.

CAULIFLOWER PUFF

Cauliflower with a puffed-up omelet baked on top.

1 large or 2 small heads cauliflower (5 to 6 cups florets)
4 eggs, separated
1 cup yogurt
1 cup shredded cheese of choice
1 teaspoon salt
pepper
1 tablespoon minced chives

Preheat oven to 350° to 375°F.
Break cauliflower into florets and steam for 5 to 7 minutes until barely tender.
Place steamed vegetable close together in a greased 9-inch baking dish.
Beat egg yolks with yogurt, cheese, and seasonings. Beat whites until stiff and fold into yolks until evenly combined. Spread over vegetable in casserole.
Bake for 15 to 20 minutes until puffed and brown. Serve hot.
Serves 4
Major Protein

Variation: Replace cauliflower with 1½ pounds broccoli, cut in buds with diced stems; steam for 10 minutes.

VEGETABLES WITH SOUFFLÉ SAUCE

The puffed, airy topping on these vegetables is lighter than the one on Cauliflower Puff, due to the absence of egg yolks.

1½ pounds broccoli and/or cauliflower (6 to 8 cups pieces)
¾ cup yogurt
¼ cup mayonnaise
2 teaspoons prepared mustard
¼ teaspoon cayenne
1 cup shredded cheese of choice
2 egg whites

Preheat oven to 350° to 375°F.
Divide vegetables into florets and cut broccoli stems into bite-size pieces. Steam until just tender, about 10 minutes for broccoli, 7 for cauliflower.
Meanwhile combine yogurt, mayonnaise, seasonings, and cheese. Beat egg whites stiff and fold in.
Place vegetables close together in a greased 9-inch baking dish. Cover with cheese mixture and bake for 15 to 20 minutes until nicely browned.
Serves 4; 6 as a joint entrée
Minor Protein
Menu Suggestions: This dish can be the main attraction with a grain or baked potato and salad, or joined by Bread-Stuffed Peppers or Apple-Bean Bake for a double entrée meal.

EGGPLANT RATATOUILLE PIE

Good for family meals and entertaining.

about ⅓ cup olive oil
2 medium eggplants (about 3 pounds), sliced paper-thin
4 sliced fresh tomatoes or 2 cups drained canned pulp
1 cup sliced onion
2 medium green peppers, sliced
½ teaspoon salt

2 teaspoons each dried basil and oregano
8 ounces sliced provolone cheese
2 cloves garlic, minced
2 tablespoons wine vinegar
1 cup grated Parmesan cheese

Preheat oven to 375°F.

Pour about ¼ cup oil into a 9 x 13-inch baking dish or a shallow 3- to 4-quart casserole.

Make layers of half the eggplant, half the tomato, half the onion, half the pepper; season with half the salt, basil, and oregano. Top with all of the sliced provolone, then repeat vegetable layers and seasoning. Distribute garlic evenly on top; drizzle with remaining oil and vinegar. Cover with lid or foil.

Bake for 30 minutes. Eggplant should be fork-tender. If not, return to oven to complete baking.

Remove lid and sprinkle grated Parmesan on top. Bake uncovered for 10 minutes to melt.

Serves 6
Major Protein
Menu Suggestions: Serve with rice or pasta and a bean salad.

EGGPLANT PARMESAN

There are endless versions of this favored dish. We prefer this one, as it is not greasy or over-breaded like most, and gets its substance instead from the creamy melted cheese throughout.

1 large eggplant (about 2 pounds)
oil
½ pound mozzarella cheese, thinly sliced
2 cups Italian Tomato Sauce (page 317) or sauce of choice
¾ cup grated Parmesan cheese

Trim ends from eggplant and cut into unpeeled rounds ¼ inch thick. Place in a single layer on a baking sheet or broiler pan and brush surface with oil. Broil 3 inches from the heat for about 5 minutes until lightly browned. Turn, brush uncooked side with oil, and broil for 3 minutes.

Preheat oven to 350°F.

Place single layer of cooked eggplant slices on the bottom of a 2-quart or 9 x 13-inch pan. Top with a single layer of mozzarella, sauce to cover, and some grated Parmesan. Repeat layers until all eggplant is used, adding the Parmesan every few layers rather than each time. End with tomato sauce and a generous sprinkling of Parmesan.

Bake for 15 to 20 minutes until sauce bubbles and cheese melts.

Serves 4
Major Protein
Note: Casserole can be assembled in advance and refrigerated until it is to be baked. Let stand at room temperature while oven heats to remove chill, or increase baking time by about 5 minutes.

Recipe can easily be increased by adding 1 small eggplant (about 1 pound), ¼ pound mozzarella, 1 cup sauce, and about ⅓ cup Parmesan for each 2 servings.

EGGPLANT LASAGNE

Lasagne made with layers of eggplant instead of pasta.

1 large eggplant (about 2 pounds)
oil
2 cups Italian Tomato Sauce (page 317) or sauce of choice
1 cup ricotta cheese
¼ cup minced parsley
4 ounces mozzarella cheese, thinly sliced
¼ cup grated Parmesan cheese

Trim ends of eggplant and slice into unpeeled rounds ¼ inch thick. Place on baking sheet or broiler pan in a single layer, brush surface with oil, and broil about 5 minutes until lightly browned. Turn, brush with oil, and brown other side for 3 to 5 minutes.

Preheat oven to 350°F.

Layer ingredients in a 9 x 13-inch or a 2-quart casserole, beginning with a little sauce, eggplant, ricotta mixed with parsley, and alternating layers of mozzarella and Parmesan. Continue until all ingredients are used up, ending with sauce, a layer of mozzarella, and a sprinkling of Parmesan.

Bake about 20 minutes until cheese is melted and sauce is bubbling.

Serves 4

Major Protein

Note: Casserole can be assembled in advance and refrigerated until it is to be baked. Bring to room temperature while oven preheats and increase baking time by about 5 to 10 minutes if necessary.

For each 2 additional servings add 1 small (1 pound) eggplant, ½ cup ricotta, 2 tablespoons parsley, 2 ounces mozzarella, 2 tablespoons Parmesan, and 1 cup sauce.

BAKED SUMMER VEGETABLES WITH CHEESE

Easy and pleasing and even better lukewarm than right from the oven. If the dish seems a little moist just drain the excess liquid back into the pan as you serve it.

3 cups sliced zucchini (about 1 pound)
¾ teaspoon salt
4 ears corn
3 medium tomatoes, sliced
1½ cups cottage cheese (pot style or low fat preferred)
¾ cup dry whole grain bread cumbs
¼ cup wheat germ
2 tablespoons minced parsley
1 tablespoon chopped fresh basil
1½ tablespoons butter
3 ounces cheese, cut in thin strips

Place zucchini in a colander. Toss with ¼ teaspoon salt and let stand for about 15 minutes, or at least while preparing rest of casserole, to extract liquid.

Preheat oven to 350°F.

Cut corn from cobs.

Mix together cottage cheese, bread crumbs, wheat germ, parsley, basil, and remaining ½ teaspoon salt.

To assemble, press zucchini to extract moisture and pat dry with a paper towel. Grease a shallow 2-quart baking dish and cover bottom with zucchini. Top with half of cottage cheese mixture. Cover with corn, remaining cottage cheese, then tomatoes. Dot with butter. Arrange cheese strips lattice-fashion over top.

Bake for 30 minutes until vegetables are tender and casserole quite hot.

Cool at room temperature for 10 minutes before serving.

Serves 6

Major Protein

BAKED BROCCOLI AND CHEESE CASSEROLE

1 pound broccoli
2 eggs
1 cup cottage cheese (preferably pot style or low fat)
¼ cup chopped scallion
1 cup shredded cheese
¼ to ½ teaspoon salt
½ cup crumb mix made from whole wheat bread or cracker crumbs, wheat germ, and ground nuts in any proportion
scant 2 tablespoons oil

Chop broccoli, including stems and leaves, into small pieces (about 5 cups). Steam for 10 minutes.

Preheat oven to 350°F.

Combine eggs, cottage cheese, scallion, and shredded cheese. Season to taste with salt according to saltiness of cheese.

Grease a shallow 2-quart baking dish and cover with half the broccoli, half the cheese mixture, the remaining broccoli and remaining cheese.

Combine crumbs with enough oil to moisten and sprinkle on top of casserole.

Bake for 25 to 30 minutes until set and brown on top.

Cool for 10 minutes at room temperature before serving.

Serves 4

Major Protein

Note: For a crowd, double the recipe, using a shallow 4-quart casserole or 9 x 13-inch baking dish.

BAKED SPINACH AND RICOTTA

The closer this gets to room temperature the better it tastes. This is very much like spinach pie without the crust, and if you wish you can even bake it in a 10-inch crust that has been partially baked beforehand.

1½ pounds spinach
1 teaspoon salt
2 cups ricotta cheese
4 eggs, separated
½ cup chopped or shredded provolone cheese
¼ cup grated Parmesan cheese
pepper
pinch nutmeg
butter
wheat germ

Chop spinach quite fine. You can use a processor to do this, but do not over-process or you will have a puree.

Stir salt into spinach and let stand for 10 to 20 minutes while preparing the rest of the ingredients. Just before using, stir again, turn into a strainer, and press out all the moisture until very dry. (You should have about 3 cups.)

Preheat oven to 350°F.

Beat together ricotta, egg yolks, cheeses, and seasonings. Stir in spinach.

Beat egg whites until stiff and fold into spinach mixture.

Grease a 2-quart casserole or soufflé dish with butter. Add wheat germ and shake to coat. Discard what doesn't stick. Turn spinach mixture into prepared dish. Bake for 30 to 40 minutes until firm.

Let cool for at least 10 minutes before serving.

Serves 4 to 6

Major Protein

Note: While this is excellent as is, you could serve it with tomato sauce. Leftovers are delicious cold in sandwiches. If you replace provolone with a less salty cheese like mozzarella, Jack, or Swiss, taste for seasoning. You may have to add up to ½ teaspoon salt.

Menu Suggestions: If you do not use a crust, a plain pasta or grain dish makes a nice accompaniment.

BAKED SPINACH AND FETA

As is, this can be classified as a crustless pie; if you want a crustier version, try one of the variations below.

¾ pound spinach
½ teaspoon salt
2 eggs
¼ cup chopped scallion
¼ cup minced parsley
2 tablespoons fresh dill weed
¾ cup crumbled feta cheese
1 cup cottage cheese (pot style or low fat preferred), drained of all moisture
salt
pepper
1 tablespoon olive oil

Chop spinach fine and sprinkle with salt. Let stand for 20 minutes or longer to extract moisture. Drain off liquid and press dry before using. You should have about 1 cup spinach.

Preheat oven to 350°F.

Beat eggs and add spinach, scallion, parsley, dill, crumbled feta, well-drained cottage cheese, and seasoning. If feta is salty, you may not need any salt; if it is bland, add salt to taste.

Oil a shallow 1½-quart casserole or 9-inch baking pan. Fill with spinach mixture. Drizzle with oil.

Bake for 30 minutes. Let stand at room temperature at least 10 minutes; it should be served lukewarm.

Serves 4; 6 if part of a large Mideastern meal

Major Protein

Note: This casserole can be assembled ahead of time and refrigerated until it is to be baked, or it can be baked, chilled, then brought back to room temperature on the counter while the rest of the meal is prepared.

Variation: For a *Greek Spinach–Feta Pie,* you will need the mixture above plus about 12 sheets of filo dough and additional olive oil. To assemble, oil a 9- or 10-inch square pan and line with 4 to 6 sheets of filo in several layers; brush each layer with some olive oil and let some of the pastry come up the sides of the pan. Spread the spinach-cheese mixture over the filo. Cover with

4 to 6 more sheets of pastry, again brushing each with oil. Brush top with oil, sprinkle lightly with water, and bake in a 350°F. oven until crisp and golden, or about 30 minutes.

For an *American Spinach–Feta Pie,* line a 9-inch pie pan or spring form with whole wheat pastry, rolled very thin. Chill. Fill with spinach-cheese mixture, drizzle with oil, and bake in a 450°F. oven for 10 minutes. Reduce temperature to 350°F. and continue baking for 20 to 30 minutes until set. Be sure to let stand at least 10 minutes before serving.

For a *Top-Crusted Spinach–Feta Casserole,* mix ½ cup whole grain cracker or dry bread crumbs with 2 tablespoons of olive oil and sprinkle on top of spinach mixture in the baking dish. Do not drizzle with oil as previously directed. Bake and handle as for the original recipe.

Menu Suggestions: The complete menu might include Hummus or a chick-pea salad, yogurt and cucumbers, tomatoes and olives, and pita or a crusty bread. For a more elaborate meal, add a second entrée of Kitchree or Greek Artichokes and Dill.

CHEESE–VEGETABLE–BARLEY BAKE

- 2 tablespoons oil
- 2 cloves garlic, minced
- 1½ cups chopped onion
- 2 average carrots, sliced
- 2 medium zucchini, sliced
- 2 medium potatoes, sliced
- ½ pound eggplant, cut in ½- to 1-inch dice
- ¾ cup barley
- 1½ cups tomato broth (from drained tomatoes, or diluted juice or puree)
- 1 teaspoon salt
- 1 teaspoon oregano
- pepper
- 2 cups shredded Jack cheese

Heat oil in a large, heavy skillet and sauté garlic and onion until softened, 3 to 5 minutes. Add remaining vegetables and sauté, stirring a few times, for 5 minutes.

Add barley, tomato broth, and seasonings; bring to a boil, cover, and simmer for about 10 minutes.

Preheat oven to 350°F.

Transfer contents of the skillet to a shallow 4-quart casserole; stir in 1 cup of the cheese. Cover and bake for 45 minutes. Vegetables and barley should be tender. If not, replace cover and cook longer.

Top casserole with remaining cheese and return to oven, uncovered, for about 10 minutes to melt.

Serves 6

Major Protein

Note: Vegetables can be varied in proportion or kind, using cauliflower, green beans, spaghetti squash, or any other vegetable; total should be about 10 cups cut up.

Menu Suggestions: Complete the meal with a fresh fruit appetizer, a green salad, and bread.

ITALIAN VEGETABLE CASSEROLE

This casserole, which consists of a bread base and vegetable topping, can be conveniently assembled if you follow directions carefully. The reward awaits you at the table.

For the Base

- 6 slices whole grain bread
- 4 eggs, lightly beaten
- ¼ teaspoon salt
- 1 large clove garlic, minced
- 4 tablespoons wheat germ

For the Filling

- 2 tablespoons oil
- 2 cups chopped onion
- 1 large clove garlic, minced
- ½ cup chopped green pepper
- about 8 cups mixed diced vegetables, including green beans, sliced mushrooms, zucchini, carrot, celery, and at least 1 cup cooked beans
- 2 medium tomatoes, diced
- 2 teaspoons oregano
- 2 tablespoons fresh or 1 teaspoon dried basil

¼ cup tomato paste
½ teaspoon salt
¼ teaspoon hot pepper sauce
1 cup grated Parmesan cheese
6 ounces thinly sliced combined mozzarella and provolone cheeses

Preheat oven to 375°F.

First prepare the base by tearing bread into pieces and adding them to the eggs together with salt, garlic, and wheat germ. Let stand until well moistened, then press into the bottom of a greased 9 x 13-inch baking pan. About 10 minutes before you are ready to fill it, place base in the oven for partial baking.

To prepare the filling, heat oil in a 15-inch skillet and sauté onion, garlic, and green pepper until lightly colored, about 5 minutes. Add remaining vegetables, including the tomato, oregano, and basil, and cook for 5 minutes.

Stir in tomato paste and cook, stirring, until hot and well blended. Season with salt and pepper sauce and remove from heat. Stir in grated Parmesan.

Arrange vegetable mixture on top of partially baked base. Return to the oven for 15 minutes.

Place sliced cheese over vegetables and bake for 5 minutes longer to melt. Let stand for 5 to 10 minutes before serving.

Serves 6
Major Protein
Note: Filling can be prepared in advance and refrigerated, but assemble and bake just before serving for best results.

POTATO PUDDING

This adaptation of the Jewish specialty can be baked in a variety of forms depending on its intended use and how soon you want to serve it.

4 ounces cheese of choice
1½ pounds potatoes, diced (4 to 5 cups)
2 eggs
1 medium onion, cut up
1 teaspoon salt

½ cup wheat germ
paprika

Preheat oven to 375°F.

Grate cheese in a blender or processor fitted with a steel chopping blade. Add potatoes, eggs, and onion, and puree until mixture is like thick applesauce. You may have to start and stop machine and push mixture around at first to get it going.

Stir in salt and wheat germ.

Pour into a well-greased, shallow 2-quart baking dish or a deep 9- to 10-inch glass pie plate. Sprinkle with paprika and bake for 45 minutes, or until firm and golden on top.

Let stand at room temperature for 10 minutes before cutting.

Serves 4; 6 as an accompaniment
Major Protein
Note: Potato Pudding can be baked in 4 individual baking dishes, which will require only 30 to 35 minutes, or in a muffin pan, where 12 individual "muffins" can be baked in 20 minutes. Double the recipe, using a 9 x 13-inch pan, will take close to an hour to bake. Cut in small squares for a hot party hors d'oeuvre.

COTTAGE PIE

Also known as Shepherd's Pie, this dish, inspired by English country cooking, makes a real stick-to-the-ribs winter meal. Because there are two main tasks involved, using quite a few utensils and up to 30 minutes of your time, this is not a dish to make when you are rushed. It is good enough to be worth the effort, however, and, if more convenient, can be assembled, refrigerated, and baked later on.

For the Filling
1 tablespoon oil
½ cup chopped onion
½ pound mushrooms, sliced
1½ cups cottage cheese (dry curd or uncreamed preferred)
1 egg, lightly beaten
¼ teaspoon pepper sauce
1 teaspoon poultry seasoning
1½ teaspoons soy sauce

For the Potato Topping
1 pound potatoes
¼ cup nonfat dry milk powder
⅓ cup yogurt
½ teaspoon salt
pepper
1 tablespoon butter
paprika

Begin by cutting potatoes in quarters and steaming until tender, about 15 to 20 minutes.

Preheat oven to 350°F.

Meanwhile to prepare filling, heat oil in a 10-inch skillet and sauté onion until softened, about 3 minutes. Add sliced mushrooms and sauté until just tender, or 5 minutes. Remove from heat and mix with cottage cheese, egg, pepper sauce, poultry seasoning, and soy sauce.

Place filling in a greased, deep 9- to 10-inch glass pie pan or shallow 2-quart baking dish. Do not use metal.

When potatoes are tender, puree as for mashed potatoes. Beat in dry milk powder, yogurt, salt, and pepper. Spread evenly over filling in pan to completely cover. Dot surface with butter and sprinkle with paprika.

Bake for 30 minutes until potato topping is lightly colored.

Let stand for 5 to 10 minutes before spooning onto serving plates.

Serves 4

Major Protein

Note: Potato topping can be replaced with 2½ cups leftover mashed potatoes.

Variation: If you want to get really elaborate, make 4 depressions in the potato topping with the back of a soup spoon. After 15 minutes of baking, break an egg carefully into each depression and continue to bake for 15 to 20 minutes until yolk just sets. Leftovers can be rejuvenated in this manner, or served with a poached or fried egg on top.

Menu Suggestions: Serve with anything green or orange (soup, cooked vegetable, salad) and fresh bread, if desired.

STUFFED VEGETABLE ENTRÉES

Stuffing Peppers

Because they provide such a simple shell, peppers lend themselves to myriad stuffings. On occasion, especially when leftovers are used for the filling, the pepper shell is cooked separately or may even be served crisp and uncooked. More often, the filling is cooked inside the shell until it is tender. When cooking time is short, however, the pepper may be precooked for about 5 minutes to soften it. Traditionally this is done by plunging the peppers into a boiling water bath, but it can be accomplished just as well in a vegetable steamer. Be sure to drain the peppers thoroughly before filling or they will be watery.

To form a shell, the pepper may either be cut in half or left whole with just the top removed and the seeds scooped out. The whole shells give a more impressive appearance, but the halves are easier to manage when eating.

RICOTTA-STUFFED PEPPERS

Cooked entirely on top of the stove.

4 medium green peppers
2 cups ricotta cheese
1 cup shredded mozzarella cheese
2 tablespoons grated Parmesan cheese
1 egg
½ teaspoon oregano
2 cups Italian-style tomato sauce well flavored with garlic, basil, and oregano

Cut peppers in half through the stem. Remove seeds and any thick inside ribs.

Mix cheeses with egg and oregano. Stuff into pepper halves.

Heat sauce in a skillet large enough to hold peppers in a single layer. When simmering, arrange peppers, stuffing side up, in sauce; cover and simmer over low heat for about 20 minutes until pepper is tender, but still crisp. Spoon sauce on top to serve.

Serves 4

Major Protein

PEPPERS STUFFED WITH CORN AND BEANS

The corn, beans, and cheese inside the peppers complement each other nicely but must be given a little protein boost, which we provide with a generous yogurt topping.

4 medium to large green peppers
2 cups corn kernels
1 cup cooked beans
½ cup shredded cheddar or Jack cheese
½ teaspoon salt (omit if beans are salted)
1 tablespoon butter
paprika
1½ cups yogurt, plain or tempered with sour cream

Preheat oven to 375°F.

Cut peppers in half through the stem, or leave whole and remove top. Remove seeds and any tough ribs. Plunge into a pot of boiling water and cook for 5 minutes. Remove immediately and drain.

Combine corn, beans, cheese, and, if necessary, salt. Stuff into peppers. Dot with butter and sprinkle generously with paprika.

Place peppers in a baking dish and surround with a little water to keep them moist. Bake for 20 minutes. Serve topped with a generous mound of yogurt.

Serves 4
Major Protein
Variation: For a Mideast version, replace cheddar with feta cheese, butter with olive oil, and paprika with cumin. Omit salt.

BREAD-STUFFED PEPPERS

If you are wondering what to do with the stuffing without the turkey come Thanksgiving, you might try serving it this way. On top, of course, goes gravy —choose from our plain Brown Gravy, Mushroom Gravy, Tahini Gravy, or Cashew Gravy.

4 large green peppers
1 recipe Bread Stuffing (page 262)

Preheat oven to 350° to 375°F. Cut tops from peppers and remove seeds and any tough inner ribs. Steam the peppers for 5 minutes to soften slightly. Stuff with bread mixture and place upright in a baking dish. Surround peppers with hot water to a depth of 1 inch. Bake, uncovered, for 30 minutes.

Serves 4
Minor Protein
Menu Suggestions: To go with this, serve Vegetables with Soufflé Sauce, or Cauliflower Puff, or simply a steamed vegetable topped with cheese, plus a bean salad and Raw or Cooked Cranberry Sauce.

TAMALE PEPPERS

The soft, spicy cornmeal filling is studded with complementary corn and beans. The best way to eat this is to cut the pepper in half on your plate and let the filling ooze over the pepper "bowls."

1 tablespoon oil
½ cup chopped onion
1 clove garlic, chopped
1 tablespoon chili powder
½ teaspoon ground cumin
2 cups drained, canned tomatoes
½ cup cornmeal
½ teaspoon salt
1 cup cooked pink or black beans, drained
1 cup corn kernels
1 cup shredded cheddar cheese
4 large green peppers

Heat oil in a 1- to 2-quart saucepan and sauté onion and garlic until softened, 3 to 5 minutes. Add chili and cumin, cook briefly, then stir in tomatoes, cornmeal, and salt. Cook, stirring occasionally, until mixture is thick and bubbling, about 10 minutes. When thick, stir in beans, corn, and ½ cup cheese.

Preheat oven to 350°F.

While cornmeal cooks, slice tops from peppers, remove seeds and tough inner ribs, and blanch in boiling water or in a steamer for 5 minutes. Drain.

Spoon cornmeal mixture into peppers. Top thickly with remaining cheese. Place peppers upright in a baking dish and surround with hot water to a depth of ½ inch.

Bake for about 40 minutes until peppers are tender.

Serves 4

Major Protein

Note: If this is to be served as part of a dinner with other cheese-containing dishes, you can omit cheese from this recipe or use just the cheese sprinkled on top. This reduces the protein content, turning the peppers into a Minor Protein.

Menu Suggestions: For a Mexican dinner, serve with Guacamole and either a fruit or vegetable salad. For entertaining you might want to couple the stuffed peppers with tacos, enchiladas, or Tortilla Pyramids for a double entrée.

CHILI RELLENOS

Mexican batter-fried, cheese-stuffed peppers.

6 fresh Italian cooking peppers or two 4-ounce cans whole green chilies
3 to 4 ounces Jack cheese
1 egg, separated
pinch salt
1 tablespoon cornmeal
oil/butter

If fresh peppers are selected, hold over a high flame or place under the broiler, turning so skin blisters and chars all around. Wrap in a damp cloth or plastic bag and let sit for about 15 minutes, allowing the flesh to soften in the steam created. Peel off skin. Make a slit up the side and remove seeds. Pat dry. If using canned chilies, gently remove from can and pat dry.

Cut cheese into thin sticks and slide into peppers until well stuffed.

Beat egg white until stiff peaks form. Beat in salt and yolk until evenly mixed. Fold in cornmeal.

Heat enough oil and/or butter to generously cover a large, heavy skillet. When hot, dip chilies, one at a time,

into egg batter to coat (use tongs or your hands to hold them) and slip into hot fat. Cook until just set and golden on both sides, about 5 minutes. Serve plain or with any raw or cooked Mexican tomato sauce.

Serves 2 generously; 3 as one of several entrées in a Mexican dinner

Major Protein (When served for 3, at least one of the other dishes should include some protein.)

Note: This particular version, which is pan-fried, is most appropriate for 2 to 3 servings. You could double the recipe for cooking in two pans or two shifts; however, the baked version that follows is a lot simpler for quantity cooking.

CHILI RELLENOS FOR A CROWD

Cooking of these batter-coated, cheese-stuffed peppers takes place in the oven, freeing the cook to attend to something else. Serve with your favorite spicy Mexican tomato sauce.

12 fresh Italian cooking peppers or four 4-ounce cans whole green chilies
2 cups shredded Jack cheese (8 ounces)
3 eggs, separated
¼ teaspoon salt
2 tablespoons cornmeal

Preheat oven to 375°F. To prepare fresh peppers see directions in the preceding recipe for Chili Rellenos. Pat peppers dry and make a slit up the side, removing any seeds. Stuff each with about 2 rounded tablespoons shredded cheese and press closed.

Beat egg yolks with salt until creamy. Beat egg whites until stiff peaks form. Gently fold egg yolks and cornmeal into whites making a uniform mixture.

Oil a 9 x 13-inch baking pan generously and spread half of the egg batter evenly into the pan. Arrange stuffed chilies at even intervals in egg batter and spread remaining batter on top to cover. Bake for 15 minutes, or until puffed and brown.

Serves 4 to 6

Major Protein (When served for 6, at least one of the other dishes should include some protein.)

Note: Although fresh peppers can be roasted well in advance, actual stuffing, assembly, and baking should take place just before service.

ITALIAN STUFFED SPAGHETTI SQUASH

Spaghetti squash is fairly new on the market and worth getting to know. The cooked squash breaks up into thin strands, making it much like spaghetti in both shape and use.

2 small to medium spaghetti squash (about 2 to 2½ pounds each)
2 cups ricotta cheese
1 cup shredded mozzarella cheese
¼ cup grated Parmesan cheese
½ teaspoon oregano
pepper
2 cups tomato sauce
a few thin slices mozzarella or provolone cheese

Cut squash in half lengthwise and steam for 15 minutes until barely tender. Scoop out seeds. Using the prongs of a fork, gently loosen squash pulp from skin. Pour off any liquid that accumulates and pat surface dry.

Preheat oven to 350° to 375°F.

Combine ricotta with shredded mozzarella, Parmesan, and seasonings.

Fill cavity of squash with cheese mixture. Top with a little of the tomato sauce and some cheese slices. Bake for 15 minutes until cheese is hot and gooey.

Serve with remaining sauce. As you eat, pull squash strands loose with a fork and mix with the cheesy topping.

Serves 4

Major Protein

Menu Suggestions: Just add bread and a big salad to this dish to make a complete dinner.

TURKISH SQUASH

With the aid of a grapefruit knife, yellow crookneck squash can be fashioned into "boats," then stuffed with its own meat in a flavorful yogurt sauce. Don't forget, the shell itself is meant to be eaten.

4 medium yellow squash (about 2 pounds)
2 tablespoons oil or part oil/part butter
1 cup chopped onion
1½ tablespoons whole wheat flour
2 teaspoons coriander
1 teaspoon cumin
½ teaspoon salt
1½ cups yogurt
2 tablespoons lemon juice
paprika

Preheat oven to 350° to 375°F.

Split squash in half lengthwise and steam for 5 to 8 minutes. Using a small curved grapefruit knife, scoop out centers, leaving shell intact. Dice pulp and drain off excess moisture in colander, pressing gently. Pat shells dry with paper towels and arrange closely in a shallow baking dish.

Heat fat in a 10-inch skillet or small saucepan and sauté onion until it just begins to color, 5 to 10 minutes. Add squash pulp and cook until moisture evaporates, about 5 minutes. Remove from heat.

Stir flour, coriander, cumin, and salt into yogurt and mix smooth. Add lemon juice. Combine ½ cup of this mixture with squash and stuff into squash shells.

Pour remaining yogurt over squash. Sprinkle with paprika. Bake for about 20 minutes until hot and fork-tender.

Serves 4

Minor Protein

Menu Suggestions: Serve with a simple cracked wheat or millet accompaniment or a more elaborate pilaf, plus salad and perhaps a savory pastry accompaniment. Our choice would be Armenian Bean Pies, which can go into the oven for brief cooking as soon as the squash is removed.

STUFFED ZUCCHINI WITH CHEESE AND RAISINS

Cracked wheat, feta cheese, and raisins team up to give this filling a Mideastern flavor.

¾ cup uncooked cracked wheat
½ cup crumbled feta cheese
½ cup shredded mild cheese, such as Jack, Muenster, or mozzarella
¼ cup chopped onions
2 tablespoons raisins
2 tablespoons chopped sweet red or green pepper
1 tablespoon minced parsley
4 tablespoons tomato paste
½ teaspoon salt
2½ cups boiling water
2 large or 4 medium zucchini (about 2½ pounds in all)

Combine grain, cheeses, onion, raisins, pepper, parsley, 1 tablespoon tomato paste, and ¼ teaspoon salt in a mixing bowl. Pour on ½ cup boiling water and let sit while you prepare squash.

Cut zucchini in half lengthwise. Scoop out pulp, using a curved grapefruit knife. Save the pulp for soup or salad, or sauté in oil with garlic as a side dish.

Place zucchini shells in a skillet and fill lightly with grain mixture.

Dilute remaining 3 tablespoons tomato paste with remaining 2 cups boiling water and season with ¼ teaspoon salt. Pour gently over and around squash in skillet. Cover and simmer over low heat for 30 to 35 minutes until tender.

When squash is done, spoon any sauce remaining in the pan on top.

Serves 4

Minor Protein

Note: If recipe is increased and does not fit comfortably on top of the stove, prepare in one or more baking dishes, cover, and bake in a 350°F. oven for 45 minutes to 1 hour until squash is tender.

Menu Suggestions: Beans are especially compatible with this entrée and may be presented as a cup of lentil soup or Hummus for appetizers, or as an accompaniment of Chick-Peas with Gravy, Cold Tahini Beans, or Mideast Chick-Pea Salad.

STUFFED ZUCCHINI ROUNDS

The hollowed-out zucchini is stuffed with a flavorful nut and bread crumb filling, and once cooked, inch-thick slices are laid on a plate and covered with a cooked or raw tomato sauce.

4 medium or 2 large zucchini (about 2½ pounds in all)
1 cup fresh whole grain bread crumbs
1 large clove garlic, chopped
½ cup finely chopped onion
¼ cup finely chopped walnuts
2 tablespoons tomato paste
½ cup wheat germ
1 tablespoon nutritional yeast
2 eggs, lightly beaten
¾ teaspoon salt
tomato sauce of choice

Remove one end of each zucchini or, if large, cut in half crosswise. Using a small thin-bladed knife scoop out pulp, leaving a ¼- to ⅜-inch rim all around. Let stand while preparing filling.

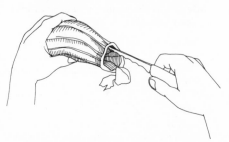

Chop pulp finely to make 1 cup and squeeze out as much moisture as possible. Reserve any remaining pulp for soup or salad. Combine chopped zucchini with remaining ingredients, except tomato sauce. Mix until evenly blended.

Pat inside of hollowed-out zucchini dry with paper towels, and pack with stuffing mixture. If you have any extra, shape into small sausages, using 2 tablespoons for each.

Place zucchini and any extra "sausages" on steamer and steam for 15 minutes until vegetable is fork-tender and filling is firm. Slice into rounds 1 inch thick, lay flat on a plate, and top with your favorite tomato sauce.

Serves 4

Major Protein

CHICK-PEAS ON THE HALF SHELL

Lightly spiced beans and garlic croutons top a shell of baked acorn squash.

2 acorn squash
1 tablespoon butter
1 clove garlic, cut in half
2 slices whole grain bread, diced into small cubes
1 tablespoon oil
1 medium onion, chopped
½ cup chopped green pepper
⅛ teaspoon cayenne
¼ teaspoon cumin
2 tablespoons minced fresh parsley
1½ cups cooked chick-peas, drained

Preheat oven to 375°F.

Cut squash in half lengthwise through stem, scoop out seeds, and set, cavity up, in a baking dish. Surround with ½ inch hot water, cover pan, and bake for about 30 minutes until just tender.

While squash bakes, melt butter in a skillet, add garlic, and cook for 1 minute. Add bread cubes and cook, stirring several times, until browned. Transfer bread to a plate and discard garlic.

Add oil to the skillet and sauté onion and green pepper for 3 to 5 minutes until tender. Add cayenne and cumin and mix well, heating for about 30 seconds longer. Remove from heat and add parsley and chick-peas.

Drain any liquid that has accumulated in the squash. Fill hollow with bean mixture. Cover with croutons, pressing them gently into the surface so they hold.

Return pan, uncovered, to the oven and bake for about 15 minutes, or until filling is hot and squash is tender.

Serves 4

Minor Protein

Note: Partial baking and stuffing can be done in advance for convenience and the squash can be refrigerated if it is being held for more than an hour.

For best flavor and a moist squash, reserve final baking until just before serving. Be sure to mix the squash meat with the filling as you eat from the shell.

Menu Suggestion: This versatile vegetable dish can be accompanied by pasta, cheese, or eggs.

STUFFED EGGPLANT

There are many ways to stuff an eggplant. Here is the basic pattern which you can adapt to the ingredients in your pantry.

1 medium eggplant (about 1 to 1½ pounds)

For the Filling

2 tablespoons oil
1 medium onion, chopped
1 clove garlic, chopped (optional)
1 cup chopped celery and/or green pepper
1 cup diced tomato or ¼ cup tomato juice or sauce
as desired:
   up to 1 cup cooked grain
   up to ½ cup shredded cheese
   ½ cup ricotta cheese
   up to ½ cup chopped nuts
½ teaspoon oregano
¼ teaspoon dried basil
salt
pepper

For the Top

¼ cup grated cheese or whole grain bread crumbs or a combination
½ tablespoon oil or butter
¼ cup tomato sauce

To prepare eggplant, cut in half lengthwise. Using a curved grapefruit knife, scoop out pulp, leaving a shell about ½ inch thick. Salt shell lightly. Dice pulp.

For filling, heat oil in a large skillet and add onion and garlic, if desired. Sauté until just tender, 3 to 5 minutes. Add eggplant pulp, celery, pepper, and the tomato pulp or liquid. Cook, stirring occasionally, for about 10 minutes until eggplant is softened. Add grain, cheese, and nuts as desired. Season.

Preheat oven to 350°F.

Stuff filling into eggplant shells. Top

with cheese or cheese-bread crumb mixture. If plain bread crumbs are used, drizzle with oil or dot top with butter. If no crumbs are used, top with tomato sauce.

Place in a baking dish and surround with about ½ inch hot water. Cover and bake for 20 to 30 minutes until shell is almost soft. Uncover and bake 10 minutes longer.

Serve plain or with tomato sauce.

Serves 2

Protein value depends on the amount of grains, nuts, or cheese used.

EGGPLANT ROLLATINI

Eggplant is delicious sliced, steamed, and rolled around a filling, much the same way as the pasta in canneloni. Despite the lengthy directions, the preparation of this rollatini is easy and the results are excellent.

2 medium eggplants (2 to 2½ pounds)

For the Filling
3 cups cooked beans, drained
1 cup shredded cheese
¼ cup minced onion
1 teaspoon salt (omit if beans are salted)
1 tablespoon chili powder
¼ cup wheat germ
¼ cup bran

For the Sauce
2 cups tomato sauce
or
2 cups tomato juice seasoned with:
½ teaspoon salt
½ teaspoon pepper
1 teaspoon paprika
2 teaspoons lemon juice

Cut eggplants lengthwise into a total of 16 slices, each about ¼ inch thick. Pile on vegetable steamer and steam for 10 minutes, or until pliable.

While eggplant cooks, prepare filling. Grind beans in a processor or food mill, or chop fine with a knife. If very soft, they can even be mashed with a fork. Combine with remaining filling ingredients to form a stiff, well-mixed paste.

Preheat oven to 350°F.

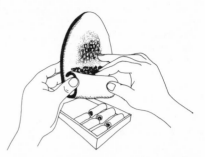

Place a sausage-like strip of bean mixture across the center of each eggplant slice, using about 2 tablespoons on each. Roll eggplant over filling.

Place filled eggplant rolls side by side in a 9 x 13-inch baking pan. Pour on sauce, cover, and bake for 20 minutes. Remove cover and bake for 10 minutes longer, or until easily pierced with a fork.

Makes 16 rolls; serves 4

Major Protein

Note: This can be assembled in advance and refrigerated for later baking and, in addition, reheats quite well. Freezing, however, is not recommended.

Menu Suggestions: Serve with a grain dish and salad.

EGGPLANT MANICOTTI

A traditional manicotti filling of ricotta and cheese encased in eggplant, rather than pasta, makes this a low-calorie, low-carbohydrate entrée.

2 medium eggplants (2 to 2½ pounds)
2 cups ricotta cheese
1 cup shredded or diced mozzarella cheese
½ cup shredded or diced provolone cheese
½ cup grated Parmesan cheese
1 egg, lightly beaten
½ teaspoon nutmeg
½ teaspoon salt
pepper
2 cups Italian Tomato Sauce or Marinara Sauce (pages 317 and 316)

Cut eggplants lengthwise into a total of 16 slices, each about ¼ inch thick. Pile on vegetable steamer and steam for 10 minutes until pliable.

While eggplant cooks, combine cheeses, egg, and seasonings for filling. Salt will have to be adjusted to the saltiness of the cheeses and may be unnecessary.

Preheat oven to 350°F.

Place about 2 tablespoons of filling in a strip across the center of each slice of eggplant and roll to enclose.

Spoon some of the sauce to cover the bottom of a 9 x 13-inch baking dish. Place eggplant rolls close together in sauce. Top with remaining sauce.

Cover baking dish and bake for 20 minutes. Remove cover and bake 10 minutes longer, or until easily pierced with a fork.

Makes 16 rolls; serves 4

Major Protein

Note: This dish can be assembled in advance and refrigerated until ready to bake. Leftovers can be successfully frozen, then reheated in the oven, removing the cover from the baking dish after 20 to 30 minutes, or as soon as filling softens. Continue to bake until sauce bubbles.

Menu Suggestions: If you feel the need for pasta, serve it on the side, along with salad and a crusty bread.

FLUFFY STUFFED BAKED POTATOES

A simple baked potato can become a substantial main dish when its insides are scooped out, whipped and seasoned, and stuffed back into the skin. This should be especially good news to those who routinely pass up potatoes in favor of what they believe to be more nutritious, less fattening dishes on the menu. The fact is, in each of the following variations you get main-dish quality protein with fewer than 300 calories.

4 baked potatoes, freshly made or prepared in advance (see page 53)
½ teaspoon salt
pepper
½ cup yogurt
¼ cup nonfat dry milk powder
1 egg, lightly beaten (desirable but optional)
1 cup cottage cheese
¼ cup minced scallions
2 tablespoons minced green pepper

Preheat oven to 350° to 375°F.

If potato is hot, hold it in a kitchen towel. Cut in half lengthwise and let the steam escape. Holding the potato halves in a towel, carefully scoop out the pulp, leaving the shell intact.

Mash potato thoroughly by hand, wire whip, rotary or electric beater, or by pureeing in a food mill. If using a food processor, be very cautious not to over-process, turning the potatoes into a soft, gluey paste.

Beat remaining ingredients into potato puree and mound back into shells.

Return to the oven and bake for 15 to 20 minutes until hot and lightly crusted on top.

Makes 8 halves; serves 4 as an entrée, 8 as an accompaniment

Major Protein

Note: If the idea of a potato as the focal point of the meal does not appeal to you, you can use half the baked stuffed potato as a Minor Protein. If you like the idea but can't justify keeping the oven hot for the time it takes to bake the potatoes initially, steam them instead, then mash and season as for stuffing. Turn the recipe into *Potato Mountains* by shaping the mixture into mounds on an oiled baking sheet; dot sparingly with butter, generously with paprika, and bake as for the stuffed version.

Fluffy Stuffed Baked Potatoes can be frozen for future use. Wrap in heavy-duty foil for freezing. To use, place still wrapped and frozen in a 400°F. oven and bake for about 40 minutes until softened. Remove foil and bake for 5 to 10 minutes longer until hot and crusty.

Variations: For *Creamy Stuffed Baked Potatoes,* fold 1½ cups diced gooey, melting cheese like mozzarella, provolone, Swiss, or Jack into mashed potato mixture. Mound back into skins and sprinkle liberally with paprika. Bake as above.

For *Stuffed Blue Cheese Potatoes,*

reduce salt to ¼ teaspoon and cottage cheese to ½ cup. Omit scallion and green pepper. Add ½ cup crumbled blue cheese. Mound back into skins, sprinkle with paprika, and bake as directed.

Menu Suggestions: For main dish service, accompany with salad, another cooked vegetable, and bread.

Stuffing Cabbage

Before a cabbage leaf is stuffed, it must be made soft enough to roll without breaking. This is most easily accomplished by plunging the leaves into a bath of boiling water. For more explicit directions on both separating the leaves from the head and preparing them for stuffing, consult "On Cooking: Table of Specific Vegetable Preparation."

To make a neat little bundle with the cabbage leaf, place on the work surface, following the natural curve of the leaf,

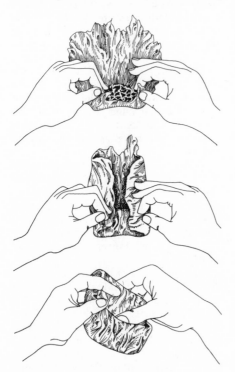

and mound a small amount of filling between the center and stem end. Turn stem end over filling, next fold in the sides, and finally roll toward the top to make a compact cylinder. To hold it together, tuck the tip into the pocket, created where the sides cross, and place fold-side down.

The entire procedure is really quite simple, and once you have seen it done or gained a little firsthand experience, you will approach stuffing cabbage with confidence and ease.

As with stuffed peppers, leftovers, especially those that are primarily grain, lend themselves nicely to bundling inside cabbage leaves. The recipes that follow should give you enough of an idea of the procedure so that you can design some additional stuffed cabbage recipes around what your pantry has to offer.

Stuffed cabbage reheats well and also can be frozen. If packaged in sauce, it can be revived in a covered dish in the oven by baking at a moderate temperature until the liquid is bubbling and the inside warmed through. This takes about 45 minutes from the hard-frozen state. If packaged dry, the stuffed cabbage rolls can be steamed, which takes only 20 to 30 minutes, depending on how thickly they are filled.

SWEET AND SOUR STUFFED CABBAGE

12 large cabbage leaves, prepared for stuffing

For the Filling
¾ cup cracked wheat
1 cup boiling water
1½ cups minced or ground cooked beans
⅓ cup minced onion
½ cup shredded carrot
2 teaspoons soy sauce
½ teaspoon salt

For the Sauce
2½ cups tomato juice
3 tablespoons lemon juice
2 tablespoons molasses
2 tablespoons raisins
1-inch stick cinnamon

To prepare filling, pour boiling water over cracked wheat in a bowl and let stand about 10 minutes to absorb liquid. Meanwhile, prepare the remaining filling ingredients. Stir these into the swollen grain.

Combine all the sauce ingredients in a heavy 15-inch skillet.

Stuff each cabbage leaf with 2 rounded tablespoons of filling and roll into a neat bundle. Place in sauce.

Bring sauce and cabbage to a boil; cover and simmer over low heat for 30 minutes. Spoon some sauce over cabbage rolls occasionally. If sauce becomes too thick, which may happen if it cooks too vigorously, stir in a little water to thin it.

Makes 12 rolls; serves 4
Minor Protein
Variations: If you are particularly fond of raisins, increase the amount to ¼ cup. For *Sweet and Sour Stuffed Lettuce,* replace cabbage with about 20 Boston lettuce leaves. While these are a bit harder to handle and must be secured with a toothpick to keep them intact, their flavor is extremely delicate.

Menu Suggestions: Top generously with plain yogurt or yogurt–sour cream mixture for adequate protein.

CHEESE-STUFFED CABBAGE

12 large cabbage leaves, prepared for stuffing

For the Filling
2 cups cooked millet or brown rice, tightly packed
¾ cup shredded mild cheese, such as Muenster, Jack, mozzarella, or mild cheddar
1 cup cottage cheese
1 egg, lightly beaten
2 teaspoons nutritional yeast
½ teaspoon salt
¼ teaspoon cayenne

For the Sauce
2 cups tomato broth (liquid from canned tomatoes or diluted tomato juice)
4 slices onion
1 stalk celery, sliced
½ cup green pepper strips

½ teaspoon salt (only if liquid is unsalted)

Optional Sauce Ingredients
1 tablespoon tomato paste or ⅓ cup tomato juice
hot pepper sauce
1 teaspoon nutritional yeast

To prepare filling, mix grain, cheeses, egg, and seasonings until evenly blended.

Place a small mound of filling, about 3 tablespoons, on each cabbage leaf and roll into bundles as directed on page 164.

To prepare sauce, combine broth, onion, celery, green pepper, and salt in a heavy 15-inch skillet. Bring to a boil.

Place cabbage rolls in sauce, cover, and, with heat very low, simmer for 30 minutes. Spoon sauce over cabbage once or twice during cooking.

To thicken sauce for serving—and this is optional—remove cabbage rolls to a plate and cover to keep warm. Add tomato paste or juice to liquid in skillet and boil for 3 to 5 minutes until slightly thickened. Add a dash of pepper sauce, remove from heat, and stir in the yeast to dissolve. Spoon over cabbage on serving plate.

Makes 12 rolls; serves 4
Major Protein

STUFFED CABBAGE STROGANOFF

The Basil Pot restaurant, in Columbia, South Carolina, provided the inspiration for this dish. Rather than forming the cabbage into tight little rolls, the leaves are shaped into bowls to contain the rich savory filling and the creamy sauce that goes on top.

6 large or 8 medium cabbage leaves, prepared for stuffing

For the Filling
3 cups cooked brown rice
¾ cup chopped scallion
1½ cups chopped mushrooms
½ cup almond halves
2 tablespoons minced parsley
1 tablespoon soy sauce
¼ teaspoon pepper
1 cup yogurt
½ cup sour cream

For the Sauce
1½ tablespoons oil or butter
⅓ cup chopped onion
1½ cups thinly sliced mushrooms
¼ teaspoon cayenne
2 tablespoons arrowroot or cornstarch
2 tablespoons soy sauce
1¼ cups water
3 tablespoons nonfat dry milk powder

Preheat oven to 350°F. Mix together all filling ingredients; adjust seasoning to taste. Place a large mound of filling, using ½ to ¾ cup, in the center of each cabbage leaf. Fold sides over filling to form a loose bowl. Place close together in single layer in a baking dish.

To prepare sauce, melt fat in a small saucepan. Sauté onion until softened, about 3 minutes. Add mushrooms and cayenne and cook for 5 minutes. Stir in starch, then gradually add remaining ingredients, continuing to stir over moderate heat until thickened. Spoon ½ cup of sauce over the cabbage. Cover and bake for 20 to 25 minutes until very hot. Serve with remaining sauce.

Makes 6 large or 8 medium rolls; serves 4 to 8

Major Protein for 4; *Minor Protein* for 8

Note: The cayenne in the sauce makes this dish quite spicy. If desired, cut the amount in half for just a hint of its potential.

Menu Suggestions: Beans are recommended elsewhere on the menu, either as pâté on crackers to begin the meal, as an accompanying salad, or as ingredients in a tossed salad.

TOFU DISHES

In the Orient tofu is known as the "meat of the fields" since its high protein content provides nourishment similar to that of animal flesh. In consistency, however, tofu more closely resembles cheese and actually is even similarly produced from soybeans that have been soaked, cooked, ground, and treated with a precipitating salt, much in the same manner that cottage cheese is made from milk. Because of its remarkable versatility and high protein, low fat content, tofu will become of increasing importance in the Western diet.

Tofu is rather bland in taste. While it can be eaten plain, uncooked and unseasoned, it is generally given some further culinary attention.

There are several different types on the market, but most are found pressed into cakes that weigh about four ounces each for the standard small 2½ x 2½ x 1-inch size, and eight to ten ounces each for the large ones. There is a firm tofu, the most commonly available, which is best for stir-frying and simmering, a soft tofu preferred for pureeing and dessert recipes, and a smoked tofu that is quite dense and brown on the surface rather than milk white. This tofu can be sliced for sandwiches and snacking without further preparation.

Tofu is low in saturated fat and low in sodium; an average four-ounce cake provides about 80 calories and eight grams of protein, contains no cholesterol, and is extremely rich in choline, the vitamin involved in proper breakdown of fats in the body. It is easily digested, making it especially suited for infants and people with delicate systems.

Because tofu is relatively new to the Western diet, we have kept our main dishes familiar. If you are intrigued by this valuable and adaptable food, you can gain enough experience from these recipes to be able to venture forth on your own.

In using tofu, don't overlook the versatility of frozen tofu. Freezing causes dramatic changes in texture, and it is hard to distinguish frozen tofu from chicken or veal in many dishes. Freezing also makes it possible to have this matchless resource on hand at all times. Freezing takes little effort and directions are given in "On Cooking: Cooking with Tofu," as are the terms used in tofu preparation.

A basic pattern for stir-frying tofu with vegetables is outlined in the Main Dish Stir-Fry recipe on page 42.

TOFU WITH ONIONS AND CHEESE

Adapted from the wonderful *Book of Tofu*, this recipe for stewed onions with a tofu and cheese topping affords a good introduction to tofu.

2 tablespoons oil
4 medium to large onions, thinly sliced
¼ cup soy sauce
1 pound tofu
1 tablespoon sherry
4 ounces Muenster cheese, thinly sliced or shredded (about 1 cup)

Combine oil, onions, and 2 tablespoons soy sauce in a 15-inch skillet. Cover and cook over low heat for 10 minutes until softened.

While onions cook, slice tofu ¼ inch thick and press to expel moisture. (See "On Cooking," page 502.) When onions have softened, remove tofu from pressing cloth and cut into cubes.

Add remaining soy sauce, sherry, and tofu to onions, cover, and cook for 10 minutes. Top tofu with cheese, remove pan from heat, cover and let stand for a few minutes to melt.

Serves 4
Major Protein
Menu Suggestions: Serve on rice, rice crackers, or toast if desired, with any vegetable and salad on the side. For an Oriental touch, accompany with Simple Vegetable Stir-Fry or Broccoli with Peanuts in Sweet and Sour Sauce.

OVEN-FRIED TOFU

At first glance you might mistake these for fish sticks, and, when served with lemon wedges and Tartar Sauce, or topped with tomato sauce, the effect on the palate is very much the same.

2 pounds tofu
¼ cup whole wheat flour
2 eggs, lightly beaten
1¼ cups fine dried whole wheat bread or cracker crumbs
¼ cup wheat germ
1 teaspoon salt
1 teaspoon paprika
¼ teaspoon pepper

Preheat oven to 350°F.

For "sticks," cut into pieces about ¾ inch wide and 1 inch thick; for "filets," cut into 1-inch-thick slices. Press between paper towels for a few minutes to expel moisture.

Place flour on one plate, eggs in a bowl, and combine remaining ingredients in a third container. Dredge each piece of tofu with flour, dip in egg, and coat generously with crumb mixture. Transfer to a wire rack while preparing remaining pieces. If there is time before baking, chill to set coating.

Place coated tofu on a well-oiled baking sheet. Bake for 15 to 20 minutes until outside is crisp.

Serve with Tartar Sauce, tomato sauce, catsup, or mayonnaise blended with yogurt.

Serves 4 to 6
Major Protein
Note: Although baking is preferred, coated tofu pieces can be shallow-fried in hot oil.

Menu Suggestions: Complete the meal with potatoes, rice, or pasta, a cooked vegetable, if desired, and coleslaw or tossed salad.

SOUTHERN-FRIED TOFU

Batter-coated tofu for a "Kentucky Fried" meal.

1 pound frozen tofu
1 cup cold water
2 tablespoons soy sauce

For the Batter
1 egg
½ cup milk
1 tablespoon oil
1 teaspoon baking powder
½ teaspoon salt
½ cup whole wheat flour
½ cup cornmeal
2 tablespoons water
oil for frying

Unwrap tofu, place in a deep bowl, cover with boiling water, and let stand for 10 minutes or longer to defrost. Squeeze gently to expel moisture. Combine water and soy sauce and marinate tofu for a few minutes. Squeeze again and pat surface dry.

Beat egg with milk, then stir in remaining ingredients for a smooth, thick batter.

Cut each 2-ounce piece of tofu into 3 strips (24 in all). Dip in batter, one at a time, transfer to a wire rack set over a plate to catch drippings, and continue until all pieces are coated. Refrigerate for at least 15 minutes.

Pour oil in a heavy 15-inch skillet to a depth of ¼ inch and heat.

Brown batter-coated tofu in hot oil, about 8 pieces at a time. If oil is sufficiently heated, each batch should be cooked in 5 minutes. Drain on absorbent paper and serve.

Serves 4

Major Protein

Menu Suggestions: Chicken Style Gravy is excellent on the crunchy fried tofu pieces served over a bed of rice. For simpler service, catsup will do. Be sure to include a salad.

TOFU À LA KING

A new slant on the old-fashioned à la king sauce and it's hard to notice the change. Serve in the customary way on biscuits or on a base of toast or whole grain muffins.

¾ **pound frozen tofu**
1 cup cold water
2 tablespoons soy sauce
2 tablespoons butter
1 medium onion, chopped
¼ cup chopped green pepper
2 cups diced mushrooms
¼ cup whole wheat flour
1½ cups milk
½ cup chopped pimiento
3 tablespoons sherry
½ teaspoon salt
dash hot pepper sauce
2 small biscuits, 2 slices unbuttered toast, or 1 large muffin per serving

Unwrap tofu and place in a bowl. Cover with boiling water and let stand while preparing remaining ingredients. When defrosted, drain and squeeze each piece dry between your palms. Combine cold water and soy sauce and marinate tofu while cooking sauce.

Melt butter in a 1- to 1½-quart saucepan. Sauté onion, green pepper, and mushrooms for about 5 minutes until soft and moist. Stir in flour, then gradually add milk.

Cook over medium heat, stirring frequently, until thick and bubbling, about 5 minutes.

Drain tofu and press once again between palms to expel moisture. Tear into bite-size pieces.

Add tofu, pimiento, and seasonings to sauce and cook, stirring, for about 5 minutes to heat through. Adjust seasonings to taste.

Spoon over bread base to serve.

Serves 4

Major Protein

Variation: For a more colorful sauce, ½ cup frozen peas can be added with the tofu.

Menu Suggestions: While almost any breadstuff can be used for the base, if you are making some specially, Cheese Bread makes excellent toast, and if you want muffins, Wheat Germ Muffins are the top choice. Any biscuit will serve well, including those from our Multi-Purpose Flour Mixes. A green salad is a must, and cooked carrots are a fitting accompaniment if you want another vegetable.

HOT OPEN-FACED TOFU "TURKEY" SANDWICHES

The tofu is pressed, simmered in seasoned broth, then layered over stuffing or sliced bread and topped with gravy for a hot open-faced sandwich.

4 ounces tofu (½ large or 1 small cake)
½ cup vegetable broth
1 teaspoon soy sauce
1 cup Bread Stuffing (page 262) or 2 slices whole grain bread
¼ cup Brown Gravy (page 313) or Tahini Gravy (page 314)

Slice tofu so that each square is ¼ inch thick. Press tofu for 20 minutes following directions in "On Cooking," pages 502–503.

Select a skillet that will hold the tofu in a single layer and in it heat the broth and soy sauce to boiling. Add the pressed tofu, cover and simmer for 10 minutes.

Drain tofu and place over stuffing or bread. Top with gravy.

Serves 1

Major Protein

Note: If Bread Stuffing is made fresh, prepare tofu while stuffing bakes. Prepare gravy while tofu is "pressing."

Variation: Prepare with frozen tofu that has been defrosted.

SAVORY SMOKY TOFU

This is quick and easy to prepare and can boost the food value of many Chinese vegetable dishes.

1 pound frozen tofu
2 tablespoons oil
4 scallions, sliced
2 tablespoons soy sauce

Reconstitute tofu in hot water as described on page 503. Press gently to expel water. Cut each piece into 4 squares.

Heat oil in a wok or skillet. Add scallion and cook for 1 minute. Add tofu and cook for 5 minutes, turning pieces as they begin to color.

Sprinkle tofu with soy sauce, stir quickly but gently and, when dry, remove from heat.

Serves 4

Minor Protein

Menu Suggestions: Especially good with Mu Shu Vegetables with Mandarin Pancakes or Spring Lettuce Rolls. For a change from rice, serve Noodles with Sesame Paste.

SPICY BEAN CURD

Well-seasoned tofu in a thick, dark sauce. In addition to being quick and easy to prepare, this dish is best made in a skillet, freeing the wok for other components of the meal.

2 large or 4 small dried Chinese mushrooms
¼ cup hot water
¼ teaspoon peppercorns, crushed with the flat of a knife blade
2 tablespoons soy sauce
1 tablespoon sherry

½ teaspoon honey
¼ teaspoon cayenne
1 tablespoon chopped fresh ginger
2 scallions, minced
¼ cup vegetable broth or water
1 pound tofu
½ cup bean sprouts
1 teaspoon arrowroot or cornstarch
1 tablespoon water
2 teaspoons Chinese sesame oil

Soak mushrooms in hot water. In a small bowl combine crushed peppercorns, soy sauce, sherry, honey, cayenne, ginger, scallions and broth. When mushrooms have softened, chop and add them along with any remaining water.

Slice tofu into 20 strips, 1 inch wide and ½ inch thick.

Bring the seasoned broth to a boil in a large skillet. Add tofu and sprouts, cover and simmer over low heat for 3 to 5 minutes.

Mix starch with water to form a paste and stir into pan. Cook, stirring, until thick. Add sesame oil and serve.

Serves 4

Minor Protein

Menu Suggestions: A good second entrée with Green Bean Chow Mein, Broccoli with Peanuts in Sweet and Sour Sauce, or Mu Shu Vegetables with Mandarin Pancakes.

PORTUGUESE STEW

A tomato sauce like this one is the base for a popular fish and potato stew in Portugal. We have replaced the fish with tofu and are quite pleased with the results.

1 pound potatoes
2 tablespoons oil
2 cloves garlic
1 large onion, thinly sliced
2 small to medium green peppers, cut in strips
4 cups diced fresh or canned undrained tomatoes
½ teaspoon salt
1 bay leaf
1 tablespoon paprika
1 teaspoon wine vinegar
1 pound tofu, cut into cubes or small strips

Cut potatoes in half and steam for 20 to 25 minutes until tender.

While potatoes steam, heat oil in a large skillet, crush garlic with the flat blade of a knife, and sauté in the oil until colored. Remove.

Add onion and green pepper to oil and sauté for 5 minutes until onion is transparent. Add tomatoes, salt, bay leaf, and paprika, and simmer, uncovered, for 15 minutes, or until potato has finished steaming.

Add wine vinegar to tomato sauce, slice in the steamed potatoes, add tofu, cover, and cook for 10 minutes. Adjust salt to taste and serve.

Serves 4

Minor Protein

Note: For a delicious side dish, chill leftovers and serve cold.

Menu Suggestions: Serve with bread to sop up the gravy and Spinach Salad.

TOFU STROGANOFF

2 tablespoons oil or part oil, part butter
1 onion, cut in thin crescents
generous ⅛ teaspoon cayenne
½ pound mushrooms, cut in halves or quarters (about 3 cups)
2 tablespoons sherry
1 pound tofu, cut in ½- to 1-inch cubes
½ teaspoon salt
½ tablespoon arrowroot or cornstarch
¾ cup yogurt
¼ cup sour cream
½ cup minced parsley
¾ pound noodles

Let yogurt and sour cream stand at room temperature to remove chill. Bring water to a boil for noodles and cook at the same time as the stroganoff.

Heat fat in a 3-quart pot and sauté onion until limp, 3 to 5 minutes. Add cayenne and cook briefly. Add mushrooms and 1 tablespoon sherry, cover and cook for 5 minutes until quite liquid.

Add tofu and salt, mix gently, cover, and cook a few minutes to heat through.

If dinner will not be served within the next 10 minutes, remove from heat at this point and wait to proceed with the rest of the recipe until just before serving.

Make a paste of the starch and remaining 1 tablespoon sherry. Stir into the hot tofu mixture and cook over low heat until it becomes quite thick.

Remove from heat and stir in the yogurt and sour cream. Place back on very low heat and stir to warm through. Do not boil.

Garnish with parsley and serve over hot noodles.

Serves 4

Major Protein

Note: Fresh chopped parsley is essential as a garnish, for without it this dish is very white. If smoked tofu is available, use it for a stroganoff with a rich, meaty taste.

Menu Suggestions: The mild flavor of the stroganoff is best set off by a well-seasoned salad or vegetable accompaniment.

BARBECUED TOFU AND VEGETABLES

Tofu and vegetables cooked in a flavorful barbecue sauce. Serve over rice or with plenty of bread to soak up the sauce and complement the tofu.

Quick Barbecue Sauce (page 59)
½ cup tomato juice
1 pound tofu, cut in 1- to 1½-inch cubes
16 medium mushrooms
1 large green pepper, cut in strips
1 medium onion, cut in crescents
1 pound vegetables of choice (eggplant, zucchini, green beans, carrots, cauliflower), cut in 1-inch cubes or segments

Prepare Barbecue Sauce as directed in a heavy 15-inch skillet. Add the additional ½ cup tomato juice and bring just to a boil.

Add tofu and vegetables, cover, and simmer over low heat for about 30 minutes until vegetables are fork-tender but not mushy. Spoon some of the sauce over the tofu and vegetables several times during cooking.

Serves 4
Minor Protein

SWEET AND SOUR POLYNESIAN TOFU

A delicious sauce that is neither very sweet nor very sour, but a fine balance that brings out the best of the tofu.

1½ cups pineapple or peach chunks, fresh or canned in unsweetened juice
apple juice
2½ tablespoons arrowroot or cornstarch
⅓ cup cider vinegar
¼ cup honey
2 tablespoons oil
½ tablespoon grated fresh ginger
1 medium onion, cut in crescents
1 large green pepper, cut in thick strips
2 carrots, cut in 2-inch matchsticks
1 medium zucchini, cut in 2-inch matchsticks
1 pound tofu, cut in cubes
2 cups bean sprouts
¼ cup water
3 tablespoons soy sauce

If canned fruit is used, drain liquid and mix with some apple juice to make 1 cup. If fresh fruit is used, measure 1 cup apple juice. To the juice add starch, vinegar, and honey. Set aside.

Heat oil in a wok. Stir-fry ginger, onion, and green pepper for 3 minutes. Add carrots and zucchini and stir-fry for 5 minutes. Add tofu, sprouts, water, soy sauce, and fruit if fresh. Cover and cook over low heat for 10 minutes, or until vegetables are barely tender.

Stir apple juice mixture to recombine and add to wok. Canned fruit, if used, should be added at this point. Cook, stirring gently, until sauce thickens and reaches the boiling point, 3 to 5 minutes. Remove from heat at once and serve.

Serves 4 to 6
Major Protein when served over grain
Menu Suggestions: Cook up a pot of rice or millet for a base. Add at least one other vegetable dish to the menu, perhaps a side of Stir-Fried Greens, Chinese-Style, or for an elaborate menu Spring Lettuce Rolls. A spicy salad is always nice for nibbling—Chinese Radish Salad is a quick addition that gets consistently good reviews.

TOFU–VEGETABLE TEMPURA

Crisp batter-fried tofu and vegetables can be made with an egg or no-egg batter. Serve with Oriental Dipping Sauce for individual seasoning at the table.

The Tofu and Vegetables
8 ounces tofu
¾ pound assorted vegetables:
cauliflorets
thin broccoli trees
carrots sliced on the diagonal
parsnips sliced on the diagonal
sliced sweet potato
winter squash cut in half-circles
cucumber or zucchini sticks
onion rings
green tomato wedges
whole mushrooms
parsley sprigs

Pat tofu so surface is dry. Cut into fingers the full thickness of the small cakes or half thickness of large 8-ounce cakes.

Select several vegetables from the list and prepare as directed. Have enough of each for each person. (Other vegetables can be used, but we have found these work the best. Celery and green pepper, for example, do not hold the batter well.)

Chill vegetables and tofu while preparing batter.

Batter #1: Japanese Tempura Batter
1 cup whole wheat flour
½ teaspoon salt
1 cup water
1 egg, separated

Mix flour, salt, water, and egg yolk into a smooth batter.

Beat egg white until stiff. Fold into batter gently but thoroughly.

Batter #2: No-Egg Batter
¾ cup whole wheat flour
2 tablespoons soy flour
1 teaspoon baking powder
½ teaspoon salt
¾ cup cold water

Combine all ingredients into a smooth batter. If too thick, or if batter thickens on standing, thin with up to ¼ cup additional water.

Cooking the Tempura
prepared tofu and vegetables
Batter #1 or #2
oil (about 1 cup)

Preheat oven to 250° to 300°F.

Heat oil in a wok for deep frying to a temperature of 375°F.

Dip a few pieces of vegetable or tofu into batter, holding with tongs or chopsticks. Raise over bowl and let any excess batter fall back in.

Slip pieces into hot fat without crowding (about 4 pieces at a time). Fry until golden, turning to cook evenly.

Drain on absorbent paper, then transfer to a wire rack set on a baking sheet or shallow baking pan and keep warm in the oven as remaining tofu and vegetables are fried. Serve immediately when frying is completed.

Serves 2

Major Protein

Note: Be sure to let fat heat up again after frying each batch. This will keep the crust crisp and the tempura greaseless.

Variations: For *Cheese–Vegetable Tempura,* replace tofu with 4 to 6 ounces of cheese cut into cubes or sticks. For *All-Vegetable Tempura,* use 1 pound of vegetables. Serve as a side dish for 4.

Preparing tempura as a main dish for 4 or more can be quite tedious and the first pieces are likely to become limp by the time frying is over. To get around this, you may want to consider *Tempura Fondue:* Prepare tofu and vegetables as described, adjusting proportionately to the number of servings. Prepare batter of choice, multiplying the recipe as needed. Heat oil to half-fill fondue pot or heavy metal saucepan. Even the wok can be used if it will fit comfortably on the sterno or warming stand you use at the table. Bring platter of chilled food to the table and position bowls of batter within easy reach of each person. When oil reaches 375°F., set it over the table flame, as for any fondue. Now each person can spear his or her own food and dip and fry it for fresh, crisp tempura. This makes for a long but leisurely meal.

Menu Suggestions: In addition to the Oriental Dipping Sauce (or at least some soy sauce on the table), rice or noodles with Tahini or Cashew Gravy, and a mixed green, spinach, or cabbage salad should be served with tempura. Keep the dessert light, and end the meal with herb tea.

VEGETABLE KEBABS

Skewers of marinated tofu and vegetables can be grilled over a fire or in the broiler. An excellent choice for barbecues.

1 pound tofu (2 large firm cakes, preferably, or 4 small squares)
1 large onion
1 orange
2 small to medium, firm tomatoes
1 green pepper
12 large mushrooms

Marinade
¼ cup lemon juice
¼ cup oil
¼ cup soy sauce
1 teaspoon grated fresh ginger (peeling not necessary)
1 clove garlic, crushed

Cut each piece of tofu into 6 cubes; cut onion and unpeeled orange into 6 wedges; cut each tomato into 4 wedges; cut green pepper into 3 wedges and each wedge across to make 6 broad pieces; leave mushrooms whole.

For the marinade, combine lemon juice, oil, soy sauce, ginger, and garlic in a large, shallow bowl or heavy-duty plastic bag.

Add tofu, onion, orange, and mushrooms to this marinade and let sit for 1 hour or longer. Turn vegetables a few times so that the marinade penetrates all surfaces.

Arrange on 6 skewers allowing 2 mushrooms, 2 to 4 pieces tofu (depending on what size cakes were used), 1 wedge tomato, onion, and orange (insert skewer through orange peel), and 1 piece green pepper per skewer. (There will be 2 tomato wedges left, which can be added to a skewer or saved for the salad.)

Cook over hot coals until all surfaces are lightly charred; cooking time will vary with the heat of the fire and the distance of the grill, but should be fairly rapid, probably less than 5 minutes per side. Serve hot. (If you prefer, kebabs can be placed on a broiler pan and cooked in the broiler.)

Serves 3 to 6 (depending on the rest of the meal)

Minor Protein

Note: If possible, use flat rather than round skewers so food does not rotate when turned. Although pieces should be alternated on each skewer, if thin tofu cubes are used it is better to place two together for support. To secure mushroom without splitting, insert skewer on an angle through side of stem emerging through the cap.

Variations: The proportion of vegetables on the skewers can be varied to suit tastes, with the exception of the tofu, which can be increased but certainly not decreased. Other possible ingredients include fresh peach wedges, fresh pineapple chunks, or 1½ - to 2-inch cubes of unpeeled eggplant. These should be marinated first.

Menu Suggestions: Serve with rice and several cold salads.

OUTDOOR MIXED GRILL

Eggplant and tofu steaks cooked on the grill can be eaten from a plate, served on bread, or inserted into buns. The fruit, added here as a garnish, is a pleasing accompaniment.

Marinade from Vegetable Kebabs (page 172)

1 eggplant

6 4-ounce squares or 3 large 8-ounce pieces tofu (firm rather than soft style)

2 to 3 peaches or nectarines, quartered

Cut eggplant lengthwise, from stem to blossom end, into at least 6 slices, ¼ to ½ inch thick. If large tofu is used, slice into two flat squares; otherwise leave whole.

Marinate eggplant, tofu, and fruit for 1 hour or longer, turning several times.

Place on a grill over hot coals and cook until tofu and eggplant are well browned on each side and fruit is hot and lightly colored. (Time varies, depending on heat and distance from coals; tofu will need about 5 minutes per side, eggplant slightly longer, and fruit 5 to 8 minutes with no turning needed.

Serves 4 to 6

Minor Protein

Menu Suggestions: A cold grain salad and a vegetable salad complete the menu.

TEMPEH

Tempeh, like tofu, is a soybean product that is new to the West although it has been eaten for centuries in Indonesia. Tempeh is made by a process of fermentation, as are other products we eat, such as soy sauce, miso, wine, cheese, and yogurt.

In making tempeh, the split soybean is bound together by a fragrant mold to form compact cakes or patties. As Americans are not accustomed to eating mold, except perhaps in blue cheese, many people feel insecure about tempeh. But once you let go of your instinctive rejection and give tempeh a try, you will have found a very versatile ingredient that can be broiled, fried, or simmered for use in soups, sandwiches, casseroles, taco fillings, or any other place your creative instincts suggest. Tempeh is more flavorful than tofu, but still mild tasting, and has a pleasant, chewy, texture.

In addition to its aesthetic qualities, it has exceptional nutritional value. Four ounces of tempeh provide 22 grams of easily digested protein and it is thought to be one of the rare non-animal resources of vitamin B_{12}.

Because tempeh is a perishable food, it must be kept chilled. It should be frozen for long-term storage and used within six to nine months.

Following are a few simple, satisfying tempeh dishes. A basic pattern for stir-frying tempeh with vegetables is outlined in the Main Dish Stir-Fry recipe on page 42.

TEMPEH BURGERS

An easy way to begin with this intriguing food.

4 ounces tempeh
oil

Cut tempeh into burger-size squares. Heat oil to cover surface of skillet and, when hot, add tempeh squares. Cook about 5 minutes, or until bottom is golden.

Carefully add a few tablespoons of water to the pan, standing back so the spattering of water as it turns to steam does not burn you. Cover pan and steam tempeh a minute. Repeat process.

Turn tempeh, add a little oil to pan if necessary, and brown. Repeat steaming process two more times to soften.

Makes 2 burgers; serves 1
Major Protein
Menu Suggestions: Serve on a plate or bun with Browned Onion Relish, catsup, lettuce, and tomato. Try Broiler Potato Crisps on the side.

HOT OPEN-FACE
TEMPEH SANDWICH

3 tablespoons butter or oil
1 medium onion, chopped
¼ cup whole wheat flour
2 cups water or broth
2 tablespoons soy sauce
¼ teaspoon salt (omit if broth is salted)
1 tablespoon nutritional yeast

½ teaspoon thyme, sage, poultry seasoning, or other herb of choice
1 pound tempeh
8 to 12 pieces whole grain toast
few sprigs parsley (optional)

Preheat oven to 350°F. Heat fat in a small saucepan and sauté onion over moderate heat until softened and translucent. Remove from heat and stir in flour. Return to heat and gradually stir in water. Continue to cook and stir over gentle heat until gravy thickens and comes to a boil. Add soy sauce, salt, yeast, and herbs of choice and remove from heat.

Cut tempeh into pieces measuring about 2 inches by 2½ inches and then cut each piece so it is ⅛ to ¼ inch thick. This will be half to one-fourth the original thickness, depending on the brand. Place tempeh in a shallow baking dish and cover with the gravy. Bake for 20 minutes.

Cover toast with baked tempeh and gravy, garnish with parsley if desired.
Serves 4 to 6
Major Protein
Note: The tempeh and gravy may be served over grain or pasta instead of bread. Tempeh may also be baked in tomato sauce and other gravies.

TEMPEH PARMESAN

Breaded tempeh is well suited to preparation "Parmesan style" and is easily accepted, even by newcomers.

1½ pounds tempeh
⅓ cup whole wheat flour
2 eggs
pinch salt
pepper
¾ to 1 cup dried whole wheat bread crumbs
½ teaspoon oregano
½ teaspoon dried basil
2 cups tomato sauce
oil
6 ounces mozzarella cheese, thinly sliced

Cut tempeh into 12 pieces. Place flour on a plate. Beat eggs in a shallow bowl, into which a piece of tempeh will comfortably fit, and season with salt and pepper. Combine bread crumbs with oregano and basil and place some of this mixture in a third dish.

Working with one piece of tempeh at a time, dredge with flour, coat with egg, then cover liberally with bread crumbs. Replenish bread crumbs every few pieces as needed; this keeps them from becoming soggy. As each piece of tempeh is coated, place it on a wire rack and let it set.

Preheat oven to 325°F. Warm tomato sauce. Heat enough oil to coat the surface of a large heavy skillet and brown breaded tempeh on each side. This amount of tempeh will have to be cooked in several batches. Transfer tempeh to a baking dish and spoon tomato sauce on top. Cover with a thin layer of cheese. Place in the oven 5 to 10 minutes to melt cheese.

Serves 6 to 8

Major Protein

Note: For convenience, tempeh can be breaded in advance and chilled, giving the coating time to set. Or, the breaded tempeh can be browned and the entire dish assembled and chilled; bake in a 350°F. oven for 15 to 20 minutes just before serving, until sauce is hot and cheese melts.

TEMPEH KEBABS WITH PINEAPPLE BARBECUE SAUCE

Tempeh is quite firm and dense, making it easy to skewer and cook on the grill for a charcoal flavor.

1 pound tempeh
2 cups water
¼ cup soy sauce
2 green peppers
1 large onion
16 plum or egg tomatoes or other small variety

For the Sauce

2 cups pineapple juice
¼ cup catsup
2 tablespoons molasses
2 tablespoons cider vinegar
1 tablespoon soy sauce
2 teaspoons prepared mustard
dash hot pepper sauce
1 teaspoon nutritional yeast

Cut tempeh into 1-inch cubes. (You should have 48 pieces.)

Combine water and soy sauce and marinate tempeh for 10 to 15 minutes.

Cut each green pepper into quarters and each quarter into halves. Cut onion into four crescents through "core" and separate the layers to make 16 pieces.

Drain tempeh and alternate with the vegetables on 8 skewers, allowing 6 pieces of tempeh and 2 of each vegetable per skewer.

Place on a grill over hot coals and cook about 20 minutes until well charred on all sides.

Meanwhile combine all sauce ingredients and heat through. Remove the grilled tempeh and vegetables from the skewers and serve on a bed of rice; spoon sauce over all.

Serves 4

Major Protein

Variations: For *Tempeh Kebabs with Tomato Barbecue Sauce,* replace sauce with 3 cups Quick Barbecue Sauce from the "Short Order" section. Other foods that can be used on the skewers include mushrooms, eggplant or zucchini cut in 1½-inch cubes, chunks of fresh pineapple, and wedges of firm peaches or nectarines.

Menu Suggestion: In addition to rice, serve with a mixed green salad.

TEMPEH SANDWICH SALAD

For salad platters or sandwiches.

¾ pound tempeh
about ⅓ cup mayonnaise
about ¼ cup yogurt
2 stalks celery, chopped
2 teaspoons prepared mustard
salt
pepper

Steam tempeh in a vegetable steamer for 15 minutes, then cool to room temperature. Dice small. Mix with remaining ingredients, seasoning to taste.

Serves 4

Major Protein

Variation: Add onion, green pepper, chopped pickles or relish, walnuts, apple, parsley, or herbs.

MAINLY BEANS

Until recently if you asked most Americans how they ate beans they would probably answer, "Baked, with franks." While most other countries emphasize bean dishes in their native cuisine, the legume family has been put on a back shelf in the American kitchen.

The value of beans as a high protein food is viewed in detail in "The Protein Principle." When beans are properly prepared, the only quality more praiseworthy than their food value is their taste, and this is our primary consideration in selecting the Mainly Beans dishes that follow, all of them to be used as the featured item in the meal. Still, their nourishing role should not be forgotten, and to make the most of it, keep in mind that if grains, nuts, seeds, eggs, dairy, or a bit of meat or fish are not part of the bean dish itself, they should be somewhere else on the menu.

In preparing these recipes, one bean can often be substituted for another. If you have your mind set on a particular dish and do not have the beans that are called for, feel free to replace them with your choice. If you have any questions concerning a particular procedure, see "On Cooking: Basic Bean Preparation," in which the techniques for preparing dried beans and substituting canned beans for the dried are explained.

Unless otherwise noted, all the following recipes can easily be multiplied or divided with no adjustments.

KIDNEY BEANS IN CHEDDAR SAUCE

Cheese sauce studded with beans blanketing crisp bread. If you have pre-cooked beans on hand, dinner can be ready in minutes.

1 cup medium White Sauce (page 313) or made from White Sauce Mix (page 443)
1 teaspoon Dijon mustard
1 tablespoon sherry
½ cup shredded cheddar cheese
2½ to 3 cups cooked kidney beans, drained
4 whole wheat English muffins, hamburger buns, biscuits, or 8 slices whole grain bread

Add mustard, sherry, and cheese to prepared White Sauce, stirring over low heat until melted. Add beans and heat through.

Toast muffins or bread. Spoon beans on top and serve.

Serves 4
Major Protein
Menu Suggestions: Complete the menu with a fresh fruit appetizer and any vegetables in cooked form and in salad.

PIZZA-TOPPED BEANS

A crisp bean base topped with familiar pizza ingredients; prepare to eat this pizza with a knife and fork.

2 cups cooked pink beans, drained and patted dry
1 slice whole grain bread ✕
1 clove garlic, minced
½ teaspoon oregano
½ teaspoon salt (omit if beans are salted)
¾ cup tomato sauce seasoned with oregano and basil
1 cup shredded mozzarella cheese
2 tablespoons grated Parmesan cheese
olive oil

Preheat oven to 400°F.

Using a fork, mash beans with bread, garlic, oregano, and salt if needed. When well softened and evenly blended, shape into one big circle, or 2 to 4 individual circles, on a well-oiled baking sheet. Press gently to make bottom flat and create slightly raised edges.

Bake bean shell (or shells) for 15 minutes. Remove from oven and reduce heat to 350°F.

Top bean shell with most of tomato sauce, distribute mozzarella evenly on top, cover with the remaining sauce and grated Parmesan, and drizzle surface lightly with oil.

Return to oven for 10 minutes until hot and bubbly. Serve with crushed red pepper for individual seasoning.

Serves 2 generously (4 as part of a larger meal)

Major Protein

Variation: For *Mexican-Style Bean Pizza*, use Enchilada Sauce and replace mozzarella cheese with Jack cheese and Parmesan with cheddar. Decorate top with strips of canned chili peppers.

Menu Suggestions: Serve with a big antipasto platter or vegetable salad. Pizza-topped Beans also go well with pasta or eggs for a double entrée for large dinners.

Serve Mexican-Style Bean Pizza as a single entrée or combine with Chili Rellenos, Cheese Enchiladas, Broccoli Tostados, etc.

CHICK-PEA GUMBO

Beans and okra in a tomato base make a flavorful main dish that is meant to be served over plain cooked rice or Rice Patties with a garnish of chopped peanuts.

3 tablespoons oil
1 large onion, chopped
1 medium clove garlic, chopped
½ cup green pepper pieces
1-inch segment hot chili pepper, sliced thin (optional)
¾ pound okra, sliced into wheels (2½ to 3 cups)
2 cups canned or fresh diced tomatoes
4 sprigs parsley
1 bay leaf
½ teaspoon dried basil or 4 fresh leaves
2 cups cooked chick-peas, drained
about 1 cup bean cooking liquid
½ teaspoon salt (omit if beans are salted)
about ¼ teaspoon hot pepper sauce (optional)
1 tablespoon lemon juice
cooked rice or Rice Patties (page 268)
½ cup chopped peanuts

Heat oil and sauté onion and garlic until transparent, 3 to 5 minutes. Add peppers and okra and sauté 5 minutes longer.

Add tomatoes and seasonings, cover and simmer for 15 to 20 minutes over low heat, until okra is tender.

Add beans and enough bean liquid to make a generous amount of thick gravy. Add salt if necessary and, if you haven't already added hot pepper, the hot pepper sauce to taste. Heat through. Stir in lemon juice and adjust salt to taste.

Serve over rice or Rice Patties and garnish with chopped peanuts.

Serves 4

Protein Complement completed with rice and peanuts

Menu Suggestions: Accompany with a cabbage salad and corn bread or crackers.

SPANISH-STYLE CHICK-PEAS

There are three separate parts to this recipe: the cooking of the beans, the preparation of the sauce, and the cooking of the grains, all of which can be done anytime in advance of the meal.

1 pound dried chick-peas, cooked (about 6 cups cooked)
¾ cup raw brown rice, cooked (about 2 cups cooked)
1 cup raw cracked wheat or buckwheat, cooked (about 3 cups cooked)
2 tablespoons oil
1 medium green pepper, chopped
1 medium sweet red pepper, chopped
1 hot chili pepper, chopped
1 large onion, chopped
1 large clove garlic, chopped
4 cups chopped tomatoes
1 tablespoon minced parsley
1 teaspoon salt (omit if beans are salted)
1 tablespoon nutritional yeast

As chick-peas take about 2½ hours to cook (plus time to soak) and rice takes 45 minutes to 1 hour, their preparation should be scheduled accordingly. The cracked wheat or buckwheat can either be cooked well in advance or while the sauce is being made.

For the sauce, heat oil in a 15-inch skillet and sauté peppers, onion, and garlic for about 5 minutes until onion is tender but uncolored. Add tomatoes, parsley, and salt, if needed, and simmer, uncovered, over low heat for about 30 minutes until reduced to a thick, pulpy sauce.

Stir cooked beans into sauce and cook until heated through and beans are completely tender. Stir in yeast to thicken sauce slightly.

Mix grains together and use as a bed for the beans in their gravy.

Serves 6 generously

Major Protein with grain

Menu Suggestions: You might want to serve this with two salads, one primarily greens and the other based on cucumber or squash. A yogurt or tahini dressing on either one adds to the meal.

HOPPIN' JOHN

Rice and black-eyed peas with a bit of a "bite" were common eating in the Old South, but today, when our everyday diets are not dictated by where we reside, it is less of a regional specialty. It is traditional to have hot pepper sauce on the table for individual seasoning.

½ pound (about 1½ cups) dried black-eyed peas
3 cups water
1 teaspoon crushed red pepper or ½ fresh chili pepper, chopped
¾ teaspoon salt
1 good-sized onion, coarsely chopped
1 cup raw brown rice (3 cups cooked)

Combine black-eyed peas and water, bring to a boil for a minute; cover, remove from heat, and let soak for one hour or longer.

Return beans to a boil, add hot pepper and cook, covered, over low heat for 30 to 45 minutes until partially done. Add salt and onion and continue

to cook for another 45 minutes until tender.

While the beans cook, and at least 45 minutes to 1 hour before dining, cook the rice.

Serve hot beans in their gravy on top of the grain, and don't forget the hot pepper sauce for seasoning at the table.

Serves 4

Protein Complement (provided by the rice)

Note: The beans in their gravy freeze well, so make double the recipe for a future meal.

Menu Suggestions: Coleslaw or Orange Section Salad provides a cooling contrast. Corn bread or biscuits would be in keeping with tradition if you plan to call this a "Southern" meal. For a real feast, begin with Creole Tomato and Peanut Soup and add a vegetable accompaniment.

SPINACH AND CHICK-PEAS WITH FETA

This dish is toothsome as well as quick and easy if precooked chick-peas are on hand.

3 cups cooked chick-peas, drained
½ cup bean liquid
1 tablespoon oil (olive preferred)
1 pound spinach, chopped (about 10 cups)
1 teaspoon cumin
1 tablespoon lemon juice
8 ounces (about 1⅓ cups) crumbled feta cheese
pepper

Combine beans, bean liquid, oil, spinach, and cumin in a large pot, cover and cook over low heat until spinach is tender and everything else is quite hot. This will take 5 to 10 minutes.

Stir in lemon juice, crumble in feta, add a generous amount of pepper, and remove from heat. Serve hot or at room temperature.

Serves 6

Major Protein

Menu Suggestions: Include a side dish of Peanut Buttered Grain, String Bean and Tomato Salad, pita bread, and some plain yogurt.

PASTA E FAGIOLI

Italian for macaroni and beans. In this version a rich, savory bean stew is topped with a mound of tiny spaghetti strands. Grated Parmesan adds a finishing touch.

> 1 pound (2½ to 3 cups) dried beans (great northern, white cannellini, cranberry, pink, or black-eyed peas)
> 4 carrots, sliced in rounds
> 1 cup celery tops, plus stalks if needed
> 2 tablespoons tomato paste or 6 tablespoons tomato puree (3 Tomato Cubes, page 430)
> ¼ cup oil (part olive preferred)
> 1½ teaspoons salt
> 2 cups uncooked whole wheat spaghetti, broken into 1-inch pieces
> grated Parmesan cheese (optional)

Combine beans in a 3-quart pot with twice their volume of water, bring to a boil for 1 minute, cover, remove from heat, and let stand for 1 to 2 hours to swell. Or, prepare according to standard long-soaking or quick-freezer soaking directions.

After soaking, return beans to a boil, cover, and cook over low heat for 1 hour, or until almost tender.

Add carrots, celery, tomato paste, oil, and salt, replace cover, and continue to cook until tender, 45 minutes to 1½ hours, depending on bean. Beans should be very soft and surrounded by thick, rich gravy. If they dry out during cooking, add additional water.

Shortly before serving, cook spaghetti in boiling salted water until tender, about 12 minutes. Drain. Mound on top of beans to serve.

Add grated cheese at the table.

Serves 6

Major Protein

Note: The amount of oil can be reduced or even omitted, but this will affect the richness of the gravy. You can use 6 cups cooked beans instead of 1 pound dried. Add vegetables and seasoning as directed and cook for 45 minutes to 1 hour until quite tender. Be sure to adjust the salt if beans are presalted.

BARBECUED EGGPLANT AND LENTILS

Eggplant prepared this way is thick and meaty and the surrounding sauce is equally as rich.

> 1 cup dried lentils
> 2 cups water
> 1 medium eggplant (about 1½ pounds)
> ½ cup whole wheat flour
> ½ teaspoon salt
> ¼ cup oil
> 2 onions, thinly sliced
> 2 cups tomato puree, mashed tomato pulp, tomato juice, or a combination
> 2 tablespoons wine or cider vinegar
> 2 tablespoons soy sauce
> 1½ tablespoons honey
> 2 teaspoons chili powder
> ¼ to ½ teaspoon hot pepper sauce, or to taste

Combine lentils and water in a 2-quart pot, bring to a boil, cover, and simmer over low heat for 30 minutes.

Meanwhile, cut eggplant into 1-inch cubes, combine flour and salt in a paper bag, and shake eggplant in this mixture to coat.

Heat oil in a large, heavy skillet, add eggplant, and cook about 10 minutes, turning to brown all sides. Add all the other ingredients except the lentils, bring to a gentle boil, cover, and cook over low heat for 15 to 20 minutes, while waiting for the lentils.

Taste sauce for seasoning and adjust if necessary. Stir in lentils, replace cover, and continue to cook until lentils are quite tender, about 30 minutes. If sauce becomes too thick or dry, add more tomato liquid as needed. Cooking too vigorously will cause liquid to evaporate, so try to keep sauce just at a simmer.

Serves 4 to 6

Protein Complement

Menu Suggestions: Serve over rice,

pasta, or toasted buns. Raw vegetables with a yogurt or tahini dip are welcome beforehand or on the side, as is a tossed salad in a light dressing.

BASQUE COUNTRY STEW

Whether it is called cholent, cassoulet, tzimmis, or just plain stew, and regardless of how it is cooked (sometimes on top of the stove, sometimes in the oven), the combination of beans, grain, potatoes, winter squash, cabbage, and other closely related vegetables, sometimes with added meat or bones, is common in almost every peasant culture because it is both economical and filling. This version comes from the highlands that lie between France and Spain.

    2 tablespoons oil
    1 large onion, chopped
    2 cloves garlic, minced
    3 cups pumpkin or winter squash, peeled and cubed (about 1 pound)
    3 cups cabbage, coarsely chopped (about ½ pound)
    1 cup dried lima beans
    ¼ cup dried yellow split peas
    1 cup uncooked cracked wheat
    2 teaspoons salt
    1 fresh hot pepper (optional)
    6 cups water

Heat oil in a 3- to 5-quart pot and sauté onion and garlic for about 5 minutes until tender but uncolored. Add remaining ingredients, bring to a boil, cover and set over low heat until beans are tender, about 1¼ hours.

The result will be a thick soupy stew that is soft to the point of mushiness. If allowed to stand, or if chilled and reheated, it will thicken substantially; many people prefer it this way.

Serves 6

Minor Protein

Note: This dish freezes well. For a substantial soup, thin leftovers as desired with tomato broth or juice.

Menu Suggestions: Serve with a crunchy raw vegetable salad for textural variety. A baked custard, pudding, or other dairy-rich dessert can furnish the additional protein.

BEANS FROM BRITTANY

Brittany is a very beautiful and romantic part of France. Cider and savory crepes made from buckwheat flour are among the regional specialties and would be welcome accompaniments to this dish.

    ½ pound (about 1¼ cups) dried brown, white, or speckled beans
    2½ cups water
    1 large onion, cut in crescents
    1 large carrot, diced
    1 stalk celery, diced
    3 cloves
    1 bay leaf
    2 fresh tomatoes, chopped, or ¾ cup pulp, puree, or juice
    1 teaspoon salt
    1 stick cinnamon, broken in two
    1 pound cabbage, sliced
    2 tablespoons oil or butter
    ¼ cup apple juice or hard cider

Soak beans in water, using the most convenient method. Bring beans to a boil, add onion, carrot, celery, cloves, and bay leaf, cover and cook for about 1½ hours, or until just tender.

Add remaining ingredients, replace cover, and continue cooking for about 30 minutes, until sauce is thick and beans are tender.

Serves 4

Protein Complement

Note: This dish reheats well and freezes successfully. If you wish to experiment or vary the leftovers, some diced fresh apple, curry powder, and a little mustard can be cooked with the beans for an interesting taste.

Menu Suggestions: If you are not making crepes, consider Apple–Oat Muffins or any dense, crusty homemade or store-bought whole grain bread. This dish is also nicely presented on a bed of rice. As a first course, serve steamed broccoli or artichokes with American Wholefoods Hollandaise, or try Celery Rémoulade. And don't forget the salad.

LIMA BEAN TZIMMIS

A lightly sweetened bean, grain, dried fruit, and vegetable stew typical of those commonly eaten in the Balkans, Romania, and other parts of eastern Europe.

1 cup dried lima beans
5 cups water
¾ cup uncooked brown rice
1¼ cups halved prunes
1 large onion, coarsely chopped
4 good-sized carrots, cut in 1-inch segments
½ teaspoon cinnamon
1 teaspoon salt
2 tablespoons honey
1 tablespoon lemon juice

Cook lima beans in water in a covered pot for about 30 minutes until partially tender. Add rice, prunes, onion, carrots, and cinnamon; replace cover and cook gently for 30 minutes. Add salt and honey, cover and cook 30 to 60 minutes longer, or until stew is thick and all the ingredients are tender. Stir in lemon juice before serving.

Serves 4 to 6
Minor Protein
Variation: Prunes can be replaced in part by dried peaches or apricots.
Menu Suggestions: Serve with a yogurt salad or tossed salad with yogurt dressing and take advantage of the long, slow cooking of the stew to make Wheat Germ Muffins or All-Soy Muffins to serve with it.

GERMAN BEAN TZIMMIS

A sweet bean dish. The traditional way to serve this tzimmis is with sliced bread dumplings and our Bread Meat is perfect for this. If this does not suit you, serve the beans with any plain or seasoned rice dish.

3 cups cooked lima beans, white beans, or pink beans (singly or in combination), drained
¼ cup bean cooking liquid
1 pound pears, peeled and sliced (about 3 cups)
1 large onion, sliced
1 strip lemon peel
2 tablespoons honey
2 tablespoons lemon juice
2 tablespoons cider vinegar

Combine beans, bean liquid, pears, onion, and lemon rind in a 1½- to 2-quart pot, cover and simmer for about 30 minutes until both beans and pears are quite tender. Check during cooking that they do not become dry, and add additional bean liquid if necessary.

Add remaining ingredients, uncover, and cook 10 minutes longer.

Serves 4 to 6
Protein Complement (*Major Protein* with dumpling or rice)

ALGERIAN CHICK-PEAS WITH CHEESE CROQUETTES

This three-step operation includes preparing the beans, their sauce, and the croquettes, and each is essential to the end product, which consists of chick-peas in a light lemon sauce topped by very flavorful cheese balls. This is a truly delicious dish and a good choice for entertaining.

For the Beans
½ pound (about 1⅓ cups) dried chick-peas
3 cups water
1 small onion, chopped
1 teaspoon salt
½ teaspoon cinnamon

For the Cheese Croquettes
6 slices whole grain bread
1 cup milk
1 egg, lightly beaten
1½ cups shredded Swiss cheese
¼ teaspoon cinnamon
¼ teaspoon salt

For the Sauce
1 egg, separated
2 tablespoons lemon juice
½ cup hot broth from beans
2 tablespoons minced parsley

Begin by combining the beans and water in a 3-quart pot; boil for 1 minute, cover, remove from heat, and let soak for 1 hour. Bring back to a boil, simmer for 1 hour until partially cooked, add onion, salt, and cinnamon, and continue to cook until tender, 1 to 1½ hours longer.

Anytime during this step, prepare the mixture for the croquettes. Tear bread into small pieces in a mixing bowl. Pour milk over bread, mix well, and let stand for about 10 minutes to soften. Squeeze out and discard as much moisture as possible, then mix in egg, cheese, cinnamon, and salt. If done in advance, chill; this will enhance the cooking.

When you are ready to assemble the meal, preheat oven to 375°F. and form croquette mixture into 1-inch balls with a light hand, using about 1 tablespoonful for each; you should have about 20 balls. Generously oil a shallow baking dish large enough to hold the balls in a single layer and place them in the pan without touching one another. Bake for 15 to 20 minutes until firm and crisp on the bottom.

While croquettes bake, reheat beans if they were prepared ahead of time.

A few minutes before serving, assemble sauce ingredients. Beat egg white until foamy. Beat in yolk. Slowly beat in lemon juice, then the hot broth. Stir sauce into beans set over very low heat. Do not let this boil.

To serve, transfer beans in sauce to a shallow bowl. Arrange Cheese Croquettes on top. Sprinkle with parsley.

Serves 4

Major Protein

Note: If preferred, croquettes can be shallow-fried in about ¼ inch hot oil in a skillet or wok, but this requires more of the cook's attention and is of no advantage unless an oven is unavailable.

Menu Suggestions: Serve with any cooked vegetable accompaniment, one spicy salad, greens with Lemon–Tahini Dressing, and bread if desired.

PUERTO RICAN RICE AND BEANS

This "national dish" has a special sweet-savory flavor.

½ pound (about 1⅓ cups) dried white beans
4 cups water
2 tablespoons oil
1 medium onion, chopped
2 tomatoes, chopped

1 green pepper, chopped
1 Italian cooking pepper or sweet red pepper, chopped
1 large clove garlic, chopped
1 small acorn squash, peeled and cut in cubes
1 cup uncooked brown rice
2 sprigs fresh coriander or parsley
2 teaspoons salt
1 tablespoon capers
¼ teaspoon hot pepper sauce

Place beans and water in a 3- to 5-quart pot, bring to a boil for 1 minute, cover, remove from heat, and let stand for at least 1 hour. After soaking, cook over low heat for 1 hour until almost tender.

While beans cook, heat oil in a skillet and sauté onion, tomato, peppers, and garlic for about 5 minutes until tender.

Measure liquid in cooked beans and add water if necessary to obtain 3 cups. Return to bean pot along with sautéed vegetables, squash, rice, and seasonings. Cover and cook over low heat until rice is tender, about 1 hour.

Remove from heat and let sit, covered, until serving time. The longer this sits, the thicker it will get (it goes from a soup–stew consistency to an almost dry rice–bean dish after 30 minutes).

Serves 6

Minor Protein

Menu Suggestions: Serve with Fried Plantains and a crusty whole grain bread or Apple Corn Sticks, or combine the vegetable and bread course in Plantain Cake. For the salad choose Puerto Rican Cabbage Salad and for dessert serve a baked custard, Mango Jam with white cheese, or fresh fruit.

SOPONES

This generous stew is an example of a traditional Puerto Rican one-pot bean-vegetable dinner. Serve hot pepper sauce along with it at the table.

½ pound (about 1¼ cups) dried kidney beans
4 cups water
1 medium onion, chopped

1 small green pepper, chopped
1 large tomato, chopped
½ pound yam or winter squash, peeled and cut in chunks
½ pound potato, cut in chunks
1 medium plantain (about 8 ounces), peeled and cut in 1-inch segments
1 large ear corn, cut in 1-inch sections, or ¼ pound green beans, cut in 1-inch pieces (about 1 cup)
1 cup whole wheat spaghetti (about 2 ounces), broken into 2-inch pieces
2 cups cabbage cut in 1-inch pieces (about ¼ pound)
1½ teaspoons salt

Soak beans in water in a 3-quart pot using the quick or long soak method. Then bring to a boil, cover, and simmer until partially tender, about 45 minutes.

Add remaining ingredients to beans, cover and cook over low heat until tender, 45 minutes to 1 hour. If stew is cooking dry, add additional water. Stew will be quite thick when done, and the longer it stands after cooking the thicker it will get.

Serves 4
Major Protein
Note: If plantains are not available, green bananas can be substituted. Freezing of stew is not recommended.
Menu Suggestions: Serve with a good crusty bread and a refreshing green salad. If there is plantain left, prepare Fried Plantains to serve with the stew. Fresh fruit or light Egg White Almond Custard is pleasing after this hearty dish.

POROTOS GRANADOS WITH HOT SAUCE

This is the national bean dish of Chile, a rather innocent soup-stew of beans and vegetables that is given a jolt with the Hot Sauce that accompanies it.

For the Stew
½ pound (about 1¼ cups) dried small white or pink beans
4 cups water
2 tablespoons oil
1½ cups diced onion
1 large clove garlic, minced

1½ cups chopped fresh or drained canned tomatoes
1 teaspoon dried basil
1 teaspoon oregano
1½ teaspoons salt
1 pound winter squash, peeled and cut into 1-inch cubes (about 2½ cups)
1½ cups corn kernels

For the Hot Sauce
2 tablespoons oil
1 small clove garlic, minced
1 teaspoon minced hot fresh chili pepper
½ cup minced onion
½ cup minced parsley or fresh coriander if available
1 tablespoon wine vinegar
½ cup water
¼ teaspoon salt
crushed dried red pepper (optional)

Combine beans and water in a 3-quart pot, boil for 1 minute and soak for 1 hour or longer. Return to a boil, cover, and simmer until beans are partially tender, about 45 minutes.

While beans cook, heat oil in a small saucepan and sauté onion and garlic for 3 to 5 minutes until limp but not colored. Add tomato and seasonings and simmer for about 10 minutes until slightly thickened.

Add tomato mixture to beans along with squash; cover and simmer until beans and squash are quite soft, 45 minutes to 1 hour. Add corn 10 minutes before cooking is completed.

Prepare sauce while beans cook. Heat oil in a small skillet and sauté garlic, hot pepper, and onion for about 3 minutes until soft and transparent but not brown. Transfer to a bowl and add remaining ingredients. Let stand for one hour or longer to develop flavor. If not hot enough, add crushed pepper to taste.

Serve stew in shallow bowls and spoon sauce on to taste at the table.

Serves 6
Minor Protein
Note: Can be frozen successfully.
Menu Suggestions: Nachos, soft corn tortillas with cheese melted inside, or a similar bread–cheese combination can

be used to increase the protein value of the meal. A green salad rounds out the menu.

FEJOIDA

Brazil claims this rice and bean assemblage as the national dish. While the version presented here contains five separate components, the work is surprisingly easy if properly coordinated. Finally, the meal is presented as a platter of spicy (but not alarmingly hot) black beans garnished with fresh orange, on a base of rice cooked in a light tomato broth, with spicy onions for individual seasoning, and a side dish of cooked greens.

For the Beans
   1 pound (about 2½ cups) dried black beans
   5 cups water
   1 tablespoon oil
   ¾ cup chopped onion
   ½ tablespoon minced garlic
   2 tablespoons chopped hot pepper
   2 medium tomatoes, diced, or 1 cup canned drained tomato
   1 teaspoon salt

For the Rice
   3½ cups combined water and liquid from canned tomatoes, or equal parts water and tomato juice or water seasoned with 1 to 2 tablespoons tomato paste
   2 cups uncooked brown rice
   ½ teaspoon salt

For the Onions
   1½ cups thinly sliced onion
   3 tablespoons lime juice
   ¾ teaspoon hot pepper sauce

For the Greens
   2 tablespoons oil
   ½ cup chopped onion
   12 cups shredded greens, including kale, collards, chicory, romaine, or any combination (about 1½ pounds)

For the Garnish
   3 oranges

Begin by soaking the beans in water, using the short or long soaking method; then simmer in a covered pot until soft, 1½ to 2 hours. When tender, heat the oil in a skillet and sauté the onion and garlic until softened, 3 to 5 minutes. Add the hot pepper and cook 1 minute longer, then add the tomatoes and salt and simmer for about 5 minutes to make a sauce. Add 1 cup of cooked beans and mash well into the tomato mixture, cooking gently until thick. Return this to the bean pot and simmer, uncovered, for 30 minutes to thicken.

While the beans are cooking, bring the liquid for cooking the rice to a boil, sprinkle in the grain, cover, and simmer over low heat until tender, about 50 minutes. Add salt halfway through the cooking.

Prepare the onions at least 30 minutes before dinner so they have a chance to marinate. This is best done while the rice and beans are cooking, but they can be prepared well in advance if preferred. Place onions in a bowl and cover with boiling water. Let stand for 5 minutes, drain, rinse with cold water, and pat dry. Return to bowl and add lime juice and hot pepper sauce.

The greens can be cut up at any time, but cooking should be reserved until shortly before dinner. Heat oil in a large skillet and sauté onion until lightly colored. Add greens, and cook, stirring, until wilted. Cover pot and continue to cook until greens are tender but still crunchy, about 5 minutes for romaine, up to 15 for collards.

Shortly before serving, peel the oranges and cut in slices or chunks.

When you are ready to serve, transfer beans to a serving bowl and top with oranges; spoon on top of rice on individual serving plates. Serve greens on the side and pass the bowl of spicy onions for individual seasoning.

Serves 6
Major Protein
Menu Suggestions: A simple crusty bread will complete the menu, but for entertaining we find Plantain Cake better than any bread. Finish with tropical fruit or Egg White Almond Custard.

LIMA BEAN-CHEESE BAKE

Limas in a colorful, flavorful cheese sauce that is mixed right in the baking pan.

3 cups cooked dried lima beans, drained
¼ cup chopped sweet red pepper
1 medium onion, chopped
3 tablespoons catsup
3 tablespoons whole wheat flour
1½ cups shredded cheddar cheese
1½ cups milk
¼ cup slivered almonds
1 tablespoon butter (optional)

Preheat oven to 350°F.
Combine beans, pepper, onion, catsup, and flour in a greased shallow 2-quart casserole. Add 1 cup cheese.
Pour milk over beans, top with remaining cheese, and sprinkle with almonds. Dot with butter if desired.
Bake uncovered for 30 minutes until sauce is thickened and bubbling. As it cools, the sauce will thicken further.
Serves 4 to 6
Major Protein
Note: 1½ cups pre-made medium White Sauce can replace flour and milk. Reduce baking time to 20 minutes. Almost any cooked bean can replace the limas.
Menu Suggestions: Begin with melon or grapefruit halves, then accompany the casserole with muffins and any simple vegetable salad. You can bake the muffins while you assemble the casserole, then reduce the oven temperature and bake the casserole while the muffins cool.

MEXICAN BEANS AND PASTA BAKE

A casserole of beans, macaroni, and corn with a cheese/taco topping. A family and entertaining favorite. Yogurt, lightly flavored with sour cream, makes a nice topping that can be spooned on at the table.

1 tablespoon oil
1 medium onion, chopped
1 large clove garlic, chopped
2-inch segment hot chili pepper, minced, or ¼ teaspoon cayenne
1 tablespoon chili powder
1 quart undrained canned tomatoes
1 teaspoon oregano
½ teaspoon cumin
1 cup uncooked whole wheat elbow macaroni or other pasta broken into pieces
1½ cups corn kernels
3 cups cooked pink or black beans
⅓ cup sliced olives
1 cup broken corn tacos
1 cup shredded Jack cheese

Heat oil in a 2-quart pot and sauté onion, garlic, and hot pepper for 3 minutes to soften. Add cayenne (if included) and chili powder and cook briefly. Add tomatoes, oregano, and cumin, and bring to a boil.
Add pasta and corn and simmer, uncovered, for 15 minutes until pasta is just tender. Stir in beans and olives.
Preheat oven to 325°F.
Transfer bean mixture to a shallow 2-quart casserole. Top with tacos and cheese.
Bake for 10 minutes to melt cheese. If casserole is assembled in advance of baking and chilled, increase baking time to approximately 20 minutes, or until heated through.
Serves 6
Major Protein
Menu Suggestions: Serve with a refreshing salad of Lemon Greens.

BEAN MOUSSAKA

Moussaka, a typical Greek casserole of layered eggplant with a delicate cheese topping, is a somewhat complicated dish to prepare but one that many people choose for entertaining. It suits this purpose for several reasons: the component parts can be prepared well in advance; the cooked casserole can be kept warm in a low oven for up to 30 minutes without damage; and, like most Greek dishes it is not meant to be served piping hot and therefore can easily wait if dinner is delayed.

1 large or 2 small eggplants (2 to 2½ pounds), sliced paper-thin

For the Filling

2 cups cooked lentils, chick-peas, fava or small white beans
2 tablespoons olive oil
1 large onion, chopped
1 clove garlic, chopped
2 cups fresh or canned tomato pulp
2 to 4 tablespoons dry red wine (optional)
½ teaspoon salt (omit if beans are salted)
pepper
½ teaspoon cinnamon

For the Sauce

2 tablespoons butter
¼ cup whole wheat flour
2 cups milk
½ teaspoon salt
¼ teaspoon nutmeg
1 cup grated Parmesan cheese
2 eggs

Sprinkle sliced eggplant with salt and let sit for about 30 minutes to draw out moisture.

Drain beans thoroughly and chop coarsely. To prepare filling, heat oil in a 1- to 2-quart pot and cook onion and garlic over moderate heat until just beginning to color. Add tomato, wine, salt, pepper, cinnamon, and chopped beans, and simmer uncovered until thick, 15 to 20 minutes.

To prepare sauce, melt butter in a small saucepan. Stir in flour and, when smooth, gradually add milk. Stir over moderate heat until mixture thickens and comes to a boil. This will take 5 to 10 minutes. When thick, add salt and nutmeg, remove from heat, and stir in ⅔ cup of the cheese. Let sauce cool a bit while you assemble the casserole. Then beat eggs lightly, beat in a little of the cheese sauce to temper, and slowly beat back into the remaining sauce with a fork.

Preheat oven to 350°F. To assemble the casserole, pour oil over the bottom of a 9 x 13-inch or 2½-quart casserole to cover generously. Layer one third the eggplant in overlapping slices. Spread half the bean filling over egg-plant; cover with another layer of egg-plant, beans, and remaining eggplant.

Pour sauce over all and sprinkle with remaining ⅓ cup cheese. Bake for about 1 hour until top is browned and eggplant is tender. Let sit at room temperature for at least 10 minutes before cutting.

Serves 6

Major Protein

Note: For advance preparation, bean filling can be made up to several days ahead; beans and eggplant can be layered in the casserole several hours in advance and refrigerated; sauce *minus the eggs* can be made several hours before it is needed but should be warmed gently before the eggs are added. It is best to add the sauce just prior to baking.

KEDGEREE

A simple rice and bean curry of British-Indian persuasion.

2 tablespoons oil
¼ cup chopped scallion or onion
1 tablespoon curry powder (commercial or Goldbecks' Masala, page 445)
3 cups cooked brown rice
2 cups cooked beans, drained
1 tablespoon lemon juice
2 tablespoons chopped pimiento
dash soy sauce
salt (only if rice and beans are unsalted)
2 hard-cooked eggs, separated

Heat oil in a 15-inch skillet or wok. Sauté scallion for 3 minutes to soften, add curry powder, and cook for 1 minute.

Add rice and beans to pan and heat through, stirring to prevent sticking.

Stir in lemon juice, pimiento, a dash of soy, and salt if needed. Chop and mix in the egg whites. When hot, top with crumbled egg yolk, remove from heat and serve.

Serves 4

Major Protein
Menu Suggestions: Serve with a yogurt-vegetable salad or raw vegetables with Curry Dip.

KITCHREE

Rice and lentils are traditional staples in almost every bean/grain culture. This dish, made with varying amounts of the bean and/or grain and with several different spices and adornments depending on the country of origin, appears often on the family table. Kitchree, also known as *khichadi* and *kedegeree,* is rooted in India; in Lebanon it is called *megadarrah* or *majaddarah,* and in Egypt a similar combination, called *kosheri* (for which we include a recipe following this one), is based on the same principles. While in its native lands this dish is reserved for family feeding, its novelty in the West makes it suitable even for entertaining, especially when accompanied by other ethnic specialties.

2 tablespoons oil
1 large onion, chopped
1 cup brown rice, short or medium grain preferred
1 cup dried lentils
3 cups boiling water
1 bay leaf, crushed
1-inch stick cinnamon
¼ teaspoon peppercorns
6 cardamom pods, crushed, or 6 cloves, or 1 teaspoon cumin seed
1 teaspoon salt

Heat oil in a 3-quart pot and sauté onions until golden.

Rinse rice and lentils in a colander and drain. Add to onions and sauté for 2 to 3 minutes to dry.

Add boiling water and seasonings. Cover and simmer over low heat until quite tender, about 1 hour. Check after about 45 minutes and, if dry but not yet tender, add additional water.

Adjust salt to taste and serve while still very hot.

Serves 4; 6 as part of a large dinner

Major Protein for 4; *Minor Protein* for 6
Menu Suggestions: If you are serving this as family fare, include a yogurt dish and vegetable salad plus pita bread or chapatis to maneuver the components on the plate. For entertaining, serve smaller portions of Kitchree and, in addition to the preceding side dishes, an appetizer (anything from fried cheese to quiche to crepes to a marinated vegetable is appropriate) and a cooked vegetable.

KOSHERI

In Egypt there are special restaurants that serve nothing but kosheri, and this seemingly simple dish of rice, lentils, and macaroni topped with crisp onions and a spicy sauce draws huge crowds of diners nightly. By the way, the only other item served in these establishments, and consumed as copiously as the kosheri, is water to put out the fire.

4 cups cooked brown rice
4 cups cooked lentils
2 cups cooked whole wheat elbow macaroni
2 to 4 cups Light Fresh Tomato Sauce (page 316)
Crisp Fried Onions (page 246) made with 2 onions
1⅓ cups Spicy Tunisian Sauce, regular or fiery (page 309)

Cook rice, lentils, and pasta separately according to basic cooking instructions in "On Cooking."

To serve, mound rice on serving plates, top with lentils and macaroni, and pour about ½ cup Light Fresh Tomato Sauce on each serving to moisten. Garnish with Crisp Fried Onions and season to taste with the Spicy Tunisian Sauce, or for those who prefer milder food, with additional Light Fresh Tomato Sauce as desired.

Serves 4
Major Protein
Note: This dish is as easy to prepare for many as for only a few, making it well suited to feeding groups.

GRAIN MAINS

Although pasta is readily accepted as the focal point of a meal, it is less common to see other primarily grain dishes. Cornmeal, rice, millet, cracked wheat, and barley are well suited to main-dish recipes because they can be mixed with a wide variety of ingredients and flavors to offset their own rather unprepossessing tastes. At the same time they are quite filling.

It is important to remember, however, that if grains are to provide nourishment equal to their enjoyability, they must be coupled with beans, nuts, seeds, eggs, dairy, or animal flesh. When they are not complemented in this manner within a recipe, include another item in the meal that provides at least one of these ingredients.

WOODSTOCK RICE AND VEGETABLES

One of the longest-lasting effects of the '60s was an awakening to basic foods and their many possibilities. There is probably no dish more symbolic of the "Woodstock Generation" than this one.

> 2 cups uncooked brown rice or 6 cups cooked
> 4 cups mixed vegetables from the following list (make sure to include the first three):
>> scallions
>> carrots
>> tofu or cooked beans
>> zucchini
>> mushrooms
>> green beans
>> celery
>> corn
>> sprouts
>> shredded lettuce or spinach
> ½ cup pumpkin seeds
> 1 tablespoon oil
> soy sauce

If rice is uncooked, prepare as for basic brown rice in 4 cups water, cooking 45 to 50 minutes, until tender. Clean vegetables and cut into small sticks, rounds, or dice, as desired.

Shortly before serving, sauté pumpkin seeds in a dry wok or skillet until they pop. Add the oil and about one fourth the rice and vegetables. Sprinkle well with soy sauce and stir-fry for 3 to 5 minutes until vegetables are crisp-tender. Push food up the sides of the wok, or to the edges of the skillet. Add more rice, vegetables, and soy sauce, and cook in the same manner. Continue until all the rice and vegetables have been added. Stir together and serve.

Serves 4

Minor Protein

Note: To prepare for more (or less), allow ½ cup uncooked rice or 1½ cups cooked rice, 2 tablespoons pumpkin seeds, and 1 cup vegetables per person. Leftovers reheat well and also provide a good base for Rice Salad. Woodstock Rice and Vegetables is best eaten with chopsticks.

Menu Suggestions: Serve with chopped mixed greens and Creamy Carrot Dressing or Creamy Tofu–Garlic Dressing. Add a dense whole grain bread or crackers with a peanut butter or tahini-based spread and apple juice and herb tea to drink.

GREEN RICE WITH STUFFED CHILIS

> 2 tablespoons oil
> 1 small onion, chopped
> 1 clove garlic, chopped
> 1½ cups uncooked brown rice
> ¼ cup minced parsley
> 3½ cups milk
> 1 teaspoon salt
> 6 canned whole green chilies (8 ounces)
> 4 ounces cheddar cheese, cut in sticks

Heat oil in a 3-quart pot and sauté onion, garlic, and rice, stirring, for about 5 minutes. Add parsley, milk, and salt, bring just to a boil, cover, and cook over low heat until rice is tender, 45 to 60 minutes. This can be done at any time in advance of the meal.

Stuff chilies with cheese, trying not to damage them. Set into rice and, if you have made a tear or slit in the peppers, place them facing up so cheese doesn't seep out.

Set over low heat for 10 to 15 minutes to melt cheese.

Serves 6

Major Protein

Menu Suggestions: Add a cooked vegetable or bean accompaniment and any cold salad or appetizer featuring tomato, avocado, or mushrooms. For bread, try corn tortillas or tacos. For a more elaborate dinner you might serve this as a double entrée with Bean Tacos or Chalupas.

ARROZ CON QUESO

This version of rice, chilies, and cheese is based on precooked rice and cooks in the oven.

4 cups cooked brown rice
½ teaspoon salt (if rice is unseasoned)
½ cup chopped scallions
1 4-ounce can whole green chilies, drained and cut in wide strips
1 cup farmer or dry curd (pot style) cottage cheese
1½ cups shredded or 6 ounces sliced Jack or Muenster cheese
½ cup shredded cheddar cheese

Preheat oven to 350°F.

Season rice with salt if needed; add scallions.

Place half the rice in a greased 2-quart casserole. Top with half the chilies.

If Jack or Muenster cheese has been shredded, combine it with the cottage cheese and spread over the rice and chilies. If cheese is sliced, top rice and chilies with the cottage cheese, then layer cheese on top.

Cover with remaining rice, sprinkle with shredded cheddar, and arrange remaining chili strips over all.

Bake for 30 minutes.

Serves 4 to 6

Major Protein

Note: This can be made with plain brown rice or rice cooked in a seasoned or light tomato broth.

BAKED RICE AND BLUE CHEESE

A casserole for blue cheese lovers made with precooked rice.

4 cups cooked brown rice
¼ cup lemon juice
1 teaspoon dry mustard
4 scallions, sliced
1 cup yogurt
½ cup sliced olives
4 ounces blue cheese, cut in small cubes (about ½ cup)

Preheat oven to 350°F.

Combine all ingredients, tossing gently so that the cheese remains in chunks.

Place in an oiled 9-inch or 1½-quart baking dish; cover and bake for 20 minutes.

Serves 4

Minor Protein

Menu Suggestions: A crisp cooked vegetable with nuts, such as Asparagus with Cashews or Carrots with Walnuts or Sunflower Seeds, and a salad with beans and lots of crunchy sprouts would be one approach to a menu with this entrée. Dessert can complement the meal nicely when nuts are a featured ingredient as in Peanut Kisses, Almond Drops, Lemon-Nut Cookies, or something more elaborate, like Viennese Plum Tart or Pecan Pie.

RICE WITH CABBAGE AND CHEESE

From the archives of classic home-cooked Italian food.

1½ cups raw brown rice or 5 cups cooked
salt
¼ cup oil (at least part olive preferred)
2 large cloves garlic, minced
1½ pounds cabbage, coarsely chopped (7 to 8 cups)
pepper
1½ cups shredded combined mozzarella and provolone cheeses (equal amounts of each or as desired)
½ cup grated Parmesan cheese

If rice is uncooked, prepare as for basic brown rice in 3 cups water, cooking until tender. Salt lightly.

Heat oil in a large skillet and sauté garlic until lightly colored, about 3 minutes. Add cabbage, stir to coat with oil, cover and cook for 10 minutes until tender. Season generously with pepper.

Place hot rice in a serving bowl. Top with cheeses; add hot cabbage with any remaining oil from the pan. Mix thoroughly and serve.

Serves 6

Major Protein

Note: Leftovers make a good stuffing for mushrooms (fill and bake), artichokes (steam, remove choke, stuff mixture into center and between leaves, top with buttered crumbs, bake in a 350°F. oven for 15 minutes, and serve at once), or winter squash (bake, fill cavity with stuffing, cover and return to 350°F. oven for about 15 minutes, or until hot and creamy).

Menu Suggestions: Precede with fruit, juice, or a light soup; accompany with any vegetable as long as it does not contain cheese (baked winter squash, zucchini, Smothered Jerusalem Artichokes, mushrooms) plus a salad composed mainly of tomatoes, mushrooms, or fruit, such as Pear Salad.

PAELLA

Paella is a specialty of Puerto Rico and southern Spain, where restaurants feature large pans of this seasoned rice adorned with chicken and sausage. Our version succeeds without the meat components.

3 tablespoons oil (olive preferred)
1 large onion, chopped
½ tablespoon chopped garlic
1 medium green or sweet red pepper, chopped
1½ cups uncooked long grain brown rice
3 cups tomato broth (liquid from canned tomatoes or tomato juice diluted with an equal amount of water)
1 teaspoon salt
1 teaspoon saffron
2 large fresh artichokes or 1 14-ounce can
1 cup green peas (about ¾ pound in the shell)
2 cups cooked kidney beans, black beans, or chick-peas, well drained
1 pimiento, cut in strips

If you do not have a special paella pan, a wok will do beautifully. Heat oil in the pan and sauté onion, garlic, sweet pepper, and rice for about 5 minutes until grain begins to color. Add the broth, salt, and saffron, bring to a boil, cover, and cook over low heat for 15 minutes.

Meanwhile, trim artichokes as explained in "On Cooking: Table of Specific Vegetable Preparation" (page 497) and cut in sixths. (Canned artichokes should be rinsed, drained, and halved.)

If using fresh artichokes and fresh peas, add after cooking rice for 15 minutes; replace cover and continue to cook for 30 minutes.

Stir beans into pan along with artichokes, if canned, and peas, if frozen. Cover and cook 15 minutes longer, or until rice is tender. Garnish with pimiento strips.

Serves 4

Major Protein

Menu Suggestions: If you are open to an eating adventure, try Green Banana Escabeche as the appetizer for a touch of real native cuisine; Pimiento-Cheese Dip served with corn tacos and raw green beans can also be used to begin the meal. The main course can be accompanied by bread or plantains, a green salad, and for dessert, Coconut Custard Pie.

SOYFOOD PAELLA

Three different forms of soy food stand in for the usual seafood in this classic Spanish dish.

3 tablespoons oil
1 pound tempeh, cut in ½ x 2-inch strips
1 tablespoon chopped garlic
1 tablespoon vinegar
1 large onion, cut in thin crescents

1 large sweet red or green pepper, cut
in thin strips
2 cups brown rice
½ cup whole wheat spaghetti, broken
into 1-inch pieces
3½ cups water
2 large tomatoes, chopped
4 tablespoons soy sauce
2 teaspoons oregano
2 tablespoons capers
¾ teaspoon salt
8 ounces frozen tofu
8 ounces fresh tofu, diced small
1½ cups green peas
1 large pimiento, cut in strips
1 hard-cooked egg, chopped

Heat 1 tablespoon oil in a wok or
paella pan. Brown tempeh along with 1
teaspoon garlic over high heat. Add
vinegar, cover, and steam for 1 minute.
Remove from the pan and reserve.

Add the remaining 2 tablespoons oil
to the pan. Stir-fry remaining garlic,
onion, pepper, rice, and spaghetti about
5 minutes, until grain just begins to
color. Add water, tomato, 2 tablespoons
soy sauce, oregano, and capers. Bring
to a boil, cover, and cook over low heat
for about 50 minutes, until grain is
tender and liquid is absorbed. Add salt
about halfway through the cooking.

While grain is cooking, defrost frozen
tofu in boiling water and press dry (see
directions in "Cooking with Tofu").
Combine remaining 2 tablespoons soy
sauce with 1 cup cold water and marinate defrosted tofu. Just before adding
to paella, cut into thin strips.

When grain is tender, add marinated
tofu strips, diced fresh tofu, peas, and
reserved tempeh. Cover and cook for
10 minutes.

Garnish with pimiento and chopped
egg before serving.
Serves 6
Major Protein

TUCHMAN'S WHEAT BERRY BAKE

A layer of crunchy grain topped with
creamy vegetables.

2½ cups wheat berries
4 cups water

2 tablespoons oil
2 cloves garlic, chopped
2 medium onions, cut in thin crescents
8 cups bite-size pieces of broccoli, or
broccoli combined with cauliflower
and/or carrots
3 tablespoons soy sauce
4 eggs
⅔ cup yogurt
3 cups shredded cheese
¼ cup whole grain bread crumbs

Combine wheat berries with water in
a pot, bring to a boil, cover, and simmer
over low heat for about 50 minutes until
water is absorbed and wheat berries are
tender but chewy.

Heat oil in a large skillet and sauté
garlic and onions over moderate heat
for about 8 minutes until softened and
lightly colored. Add remaining vegetables, cover, and stew for 10 to 15
minutes until tender but still crisp.

Preheat oven to 350°F. When wheat
berries are cooked, season with 2 tablespoons of soy sauce, or to taste, and
mix with 2 beaten eggs. Cover a well-
oiled lasagne pan or a shallow 4-quart
casserole with the wheat berry mixture;
raise the grain slightly along the edges
to contain the topping.

Beat the remaining 2 eggs with yogurt,
cheese, and remaining soy sauce. Fold
in cooked vegetables and bread crumbs.
Spread over grain.

Bake for 20 minutes. Remove from
oven and let rest for 10 minutes before
serving.
Serves 8
Major Protein
Note: Leftovers can be successfully
frozen.
Variation: For *Rye Berry Casserole*,
replace wheat berries with an equal
amount of rye berries. If grain is precooked you will need 6 cups.

COUSCOUS

Couscous is another one of those dishes
that has many variations around the
world. Essentially it is a base of grain
topped with vegetables and a spicy

sauce, traditionally eaten without any utensils, using bread instead as a scoop. Although there is a refined semolina marketed as couscous, more traditional Old World grains were used in the original dish. We revert to tradition in all but the first version, which follows.

Couscous is best served freshly made, but it can be resteamed if you have leftovers. It is also delicious for nibbling cold, but is not recommended for freezing.

FRENCH-STYLE COUSCOUS

Made with commercial couscous, this is the dish as the French have adapted it from its Algerian homeland.

For the Grain
    1 cup couscous
    1 cup boiling water
    1 teaspoon salt
    2 tablespoons butter

For the Vegetable Sauce
    1 tablespoon oil or butter
    1 large onion, chopped
    3 medium tomatoes, diced
    1 green pepper, sliced
    2 carrots, cut in rounds
    1 zucchini, cubed
    1 cup peas
    1 diced fennel root (optional)
    2 cups cooked beans, drained
    1 teaspoon salt (reduce by half if
       beans are salted)
    ¼ teaspoon hot pepper sauce
    8 small to medium mushrooms
    ¼ cup raisins

Place couscous in a bowl and stir in water and salt. Let soak for about 20 minutes until liquid is absorbed. Rub grain between your fingers until there are no lumps. Then place in a vegetable steamer lined with cheesecloth and steam for 30 minutes.

Heat fat for sauce in a 1-quart pot and sauté onion for 3 to 5 minutes to soften. Add tomato, green pepper, carrots, zucchini, peas, fennel, beans, and salt; cover and cook over low heat for 15 minutes. Add pepper sauce, mushrooms, and raisins; cover and continue cooking for 5 to 10 minutes until all vegetables are tender.

When ready to serve, place couscous in a bowl, stir in the remaining 2 tablespoons butter to melt, and top with the vegetable sauce either in the serving dish or on individual plates.
Serves 4
Minor Protein
Note: A less authentic but actually quite satisfactory method of preparing the grain is to place it in a pot with two times its volume of water, bring to a boil, remove from heat, and let sit for 10 minutes. The grain is swollen and tender enough to eat and only slightly less fluffy than in the steamer.
Menu Suggestions: Moroccan Yogurt Soup can precede the couscous, and pita pockets heated in the oven with cheese inside make a more substantial accompaniment than bread alone.

ARMENIAN COUSCOUS

Typically served with pita bread, olives, pickled vegetables, and yogurt or feta cheese.

For the Grain
    4 cups water
    1 teaspoon salt
    1½ cups cracked wheat (bulgur)
    2 tablespoons butter
    1 tablespoon slivered hot pepper

For the Vegetables
    1 small winter squash, peeled and cut
       in large chunks (about 4 cups)
    ½ pound parsnips, peeled and cut in
       1-inch chunks (about 2 cups)
    ¾ pound cabbage, cut in chunks
       (about 3 cups)
    2 cups cooked white beans, drained
    6 dried apricots or peach halves,
       halved

For Seasoning
    2½ cups Fiery Red Pepper Sauce
       (page 318)

Bring water to a boil, add salt, and sprinkle in the bulgur. Simmer for 10 minutes. Line a vegetable steamer with cheesecloth and pour partially cooked grain through it to drain. Mix in the butter and hot pepper.

Arrange vegetables and dried fruit over grain in steamer, place over boiling water, and steam until vegetables are quite tender, about 30 minutes.

While bulgur and vegetables steam, prepare the hot sauce. Serve at the table for individual seasoning.

Serves 4 to 5
Major Protein

MOROCCAN COUSCOUS

This is the most elaborate couscous and the one we reserve for entertaining.

For the Grain
 4 cups water
 1 teaspoon salt
 1 cup millet or barley
 2 tablespoons butter
 1 tablespoon slivered hot pepper

For the Vegetables
 1 large onion, cut in crescents
 2 large carrots, cut in sticks or chunks
 1 pound summer or winter squash, peeled if necessary and cut in chunks (about 4 cups)
 ½ medium cauliflower (about ¾ pound), divided into florets (about 3 cups)
 2 cups cooked chick-peas, drained

For Seasoning
 4 cups diced tomato (about 1½ pounds)
 1 teaspoon salt
 Spicy Tunisian Sauce (page 309)

Bring water to a boil. Add salt and sprinkle in the grain. Simmer for 20 minutes, then pour through vegetable steamer lined with cheesecloth to drain. Mix in butter and hot pepper.

Arrange vegetables over grain in steamer and steam until vegetables are quite tender, 20 to 30 minutes.

While grain and vegetables steam, cook tomatoes with salt in a small uncovered saucepan for about 10 minutes until liquid runs freely and tomatoes soften.

To serve, transfer grain-vegetable mixture to a large serving platter and pour on the tomatoes. Serve Spicy Tunisian Sauce on the side for seasoning.

Serves 4 to 5
Minor Protein

Note: As there is a lot to do for this meal, the Spicy Tunisian Sauce is best prepared first, allowing time for the flavors to blend. If prepared far enough in advance to be refrigerated, let stand at room temperature to remove chill while couscous cooks.

Menu Suggestions: For a sumptuous meal, serve with a grated vegetable salad (Sweet Carrot Raita or Cucumber Cuchumber), a yogurt-vegetable combination (Mideast Relish, Cabbage Raita, Carrot Raita, or Yogurt Squash), Bread Turnovers with Cheese or cheese-stuffed pita, and a sweet honeydew, or cold Poached Peaches and Cream, or Pears in Vanilla Syrup for dessert.

CORNMEAL-CHEESE PUDDING

Delicate, moist, and creamy, like a cheese soufflé, but more sturdy, so it does not collapse if the meal is delayed.

 1 cup cornmeal
 3 cups milk
 1 teaspoon salt
 ½ teaspoon dry mustard
 1 cup shredded cheddar cheese
 3 eggs, separated

Combine cornmeal with 1 cup milk. Heat remaining 2 cups milk in saucepan and stir in cornmeal mixture. Stir over low heat for 3 to 5 minutes until thickened.

Remove cornmeal from heat and stir in salt, mustard, and cheese to melt.

Beat egg yolks; beat in a little of the cornmeal mixture to temper, then gradually stir this back into the cornmeal. Let cool for a few minutes.

Preheat oven to 350°F.

Beat egg whites until stiff. Fold into cornmeal gently but thoroughly.

Pour mixture into a greased, deep 2-quart casserole or soufflé dish. Bake for about 40 minutes until puffed and brown. Turn off heat and leave pudding in oven 10 minutes longer before serving.

Serves 4

Major Protein

Menu Suggestions: Serve with any cooked vegetables and/or cold marinated vegetables and a green salad. Bread is not needed with this meal.

POLENTA

Cornmeal cooked to a thick porridge, then garnished with sauce (and in good times, cheese), is another international peasant staple. In Italian homes it is known as polenta, and when grandma still lived with the family it might have been her job to tend the polenta while it cooked, sometimes for hours. When it came to the table, it was often stiff enough to slice (with a string, not a knife) and ready to be topped with tomato sauce. In Rumania, mammaliga, the same cornmeal base prepared to thick cereal consistency, serves as a vehicle for a blend of pot cheese, yogurt, and sometimes feta cheese, all garnished with fresh dill and olives. Following is the basic recipe and some of our serving variations.

Basic Polenta

1 cup cornmeal

½ teaspoon salt

1 cup nonfat dry milk powder

¼ cup wheat germ

4 cups water

In a 2-quart pot, mix cornmeal with salt, dry milk, and wheat germ. Stir in 1 cup water to make a smooth paste.

Bring remaining water to a boil over medium heat and add cornmeal paste, stirring constantly. Turn heat low and simmer, stirring occasionally, for 30 to 45 minutes until cornmeal is very thick and leaves the sides of the pan easily. Serve in one of the ways suggested in Variations, below.

Serves 4

Minor Protein plain, *Major Protein* for all variations

Note: Dry milk powder and wheat germ are not traditional in polenta, but they provide an essential nutritional balance. Following tradition, polenta is stirred only with a wooden stick or spoon.

Variations: For *Italian-Style Polenta,* stir 1 tablespoon butter and 1 cup grated Parmesan cheese into the polenta to melt. Spoon into four serving dishes, top each with ½ cup tomato sauce, and add additional cheese to taste.

For *Polenta with Three Cheeses,* stir a mixture of ½ cup each diced provolone or Italian fontina and mozzarella cheeses into the polenta during the last few minutes of cooking. Keep stirring until cheese strings. Turn into four serving bowls, sprinkle each with 1 tablespoon grated Parmesan cheese, and pour on ½ tablespoon melted butter.

For *Rumanian Mammaliga,* spoon polenta into four individual bowls. Make a depression in the center and dot each serving with about ½ tablespoon butter. Top each with ½ cup cottage cheese, 1 tablespoon feta or blue cheese, if desired, and garnish with olives and snipped fresh dill.

For *Baked Polenta,* spread cooked polenta into an oiled 9 x 13-inch baking dish or two 9-inch pans. It should be about ½ inch thick. Chill. Sprinkle 1 cup grated Parmesan cheese over chilled, firm polenta, dot with 2 tablespoons butter, and bake in a 400°F. oven for about 15 minutes until crisp and brown on top. Scoop out onto serving plates and top each serving with ½ cup tomato sauce. This is an especially good way to use leftover polenta and can be made with a version to which cheese has been previously added, as Italian-Style Polenta or Polenta with Three Cheeses.

PATTIES, BALLS, AND LOAVES

In this section the emphasis is on form rather than substance: patties, balls, roasts, and loaves, are all familiar whether the predominant ingredient is beans, grains, nuts, or vegetables. These dishes are meant to be eaten plain or with sauce, some on a base of rice or pasta, others on bread, and all with your choice of cooked vegetable and salad on the side.

All recipes are easy to multiply or divide. If you wish to double a recipe made in a loaf pan in order to serve a crowd, it can be baked in a 9- by 13-inch casserole rather than in 2 loaves. To serve, cut into squares instead of slicing.

CHOPPED EGGPLANT STEAK

This recipe produces eight quarter-pound steaks that make an excellent "chopped steak dinner" served with mashed potatoes and gravy, or a "supreme steakless dinner" accompanied by french fries or baked potato and salad. Top with Tomato-Mushroom Burger Sauce, Brown Gravy, Mushroom Gravy or Tahini Gravy, or just plain catsup.

2 pounds eggplant
2 tablespoons oil
2 cloves garlic, minced
1 large onion, minced
1½ cups cooked soybeans, ground (2 cups), or 2 cups soy grits
1 cup rolled oats
1 cup wheat germ
1½ teaspoon salt
¼ teaspoon pepper

Peel eggplant and chop very fine as for chopped meat. You should have about 8 cups pulp. This can be done in batches using the food processor fitted with a steel blade, or by hand.

Heat oil in a large skillet and sauté garlic and onion for about 3 minutes to soften. Add eggplant, stir well, cover, and cook over medium heat for 10 minutes until tender. Stir once or twice while cooking.

Remove eggplant from heat and stir in remaining ingredients. Recipe can be made up to this point and then held at room temperature for about 30 minutes or can be refrigerated for later use. Do not freeze.

When cool enough to handle, shape mixture into 8 flat 3½-inch patties, using about ½ cup mixture for each.

Steaks can be cooked by pan-frying or broiling, the first method producing slightly better results, the second probably easier for mass cooking.

To pan-fry, heat enough oil to cover a large, heavy skillet or griddle. When just warm, add eggplant steaks. Cook over moderate heat so that steak browns slowly on each side and becomes crisp. Allow about 10 minutes per side.

To broil, oil pan, arrange steaks, and set about 5 inches from heat. Broil until crisp and brown, turning once. Broiling will take 5 to 8 minutes per side and varies with the distance from the heat. Do not put too close or inside will not cook properly and will become dry rather than remaining soft and moist.

Serves 4
Major Protein
Note: Leftover cooked steaks can be wrapped in foil and frozen. Cook without thawing or unwrapping in a 350°F. oven for 30 minutes until hot and steamy inside.

ZUCCHINI PANCAKES

An unusual and delicious vegetable pancake that is an addition to any Greek meal.

1 pound zucchini
1 teaspoon salt
2 eggs
1 cup crumbled feta cheese
1 teaspoon dried mint or 1 table-spoon minced fresh mint
¼ cup whole wheat flour
pepper
oil

Shred zucchini, mix with salt, and let drain in a colander for about 30 minutes. Press to extract moisture. (You should have about 1½ cups.)

Beat eggs, add zucchini and remaining ingredients, except oil, and stir to a thick batter.

Heat enough oil or a combination of oil and butter to cover the surface of a large, heavy skillet or griddle. When hot, add batter by tablespoonfuls. Cook over medium heat until brown on the bottom and spatula easily slips underneath, 5 to 10 minutes. Turn and brown the other side. Keep warm in a 300° to 325°F. oven while remainder cooks. Serve with lots of freshly ground pepper on top.

Makes 16 pancakes; serves 4

Minor Protein

Menu Suggestions: Couple with Greek Spinach Rice or Greek Artichokes and Dill, add some pita bread, olives, and a bowl of plain yogurt, and the meal is ready.

BEAN BURGERS

Cook indoors or out and serve as you would any other burger on a bun with a choice of fixings. Top with cheese for a cheeseburger. Loaded up, a burger is a burger.

1⅓ cups sunflower seeds, or 2 cups meal

4 cups cooked red or pink beans, drained

½ cup chopped onion

1 teaspoon chili powder

about 1 teaspoon salt (omit with well-salted beans)

3 to 4 tablespoons catsup

wheat germ

Using a processor fitted with a steel cutting blade grind seeds to a fine meal and transfer to a large mixing bowl. Grind beans.

Mix ground beans, onion, chili powder, and salt to taste with the seed meal. Add sufficient catsup to make the mixture damp enough to mold, without being soft. If too soft, add wheat germ as needed.

Shape into patties, using about ⅓ cup for each.

To cook, sauté in oil, or bake in a 350°F. oven about 20 minutes until brown and crusty on the surface, or broil 3 inches from the heat, about 5 to 8 minutes on each side, or cook over coals until charred on each side. Cooking time on the grill will vary with the heat of the coals and the distance of the grate; as the inside is already completely cooked, you can gauge by the color on the surface.

Makes 12 burgers; serves 6

Major Protein

Note: For a juicier, crustier burger, surface can be basted with a little oil during baking or broiling.

SOYBURGERS

A tender, juicy burger.

1⅓ cups sunflower seeds or a combination of seeds and peanuts

4 cups cooked soybeans, drained

1 large onion, chopped

3 tablespoons soy sauce

wheat germ or dry bread or cracker crumbs

Grind seeds and nuts to a fine meal. Grind beans to a dry pulp.

Combine ground mixtures, onion, and soy sauce. If mixture is too soft to hold shape, add some wheat germ or crumbs. Form into patties using ½ cup mixture for each.

To cook, bake in a 350°F. oven for 20 minutes, or broil about 3 inches from heat for 5 to 8 minutes per side until browned, or cook on a grill over coals.

Makes 8 burgers; serves 4

Major Protein

Variation: For *Onion Soyburgers,* sauté a little chopped onion and garlic in some oil, then add patties and pan-fry.

Menu Suggestions: Serve on toast or buns with catsup, tomato sauce, Quick Barbecue Sauce, or Mushroom Gravy.

GRAIN BURGERS

Burgers made with leftover cooked grain are very tasty but are not meant to be served on bread.

4 cups cold, cooked grain (millet, kasha, cracked wheat, etc.)

2 eggs, lightly beaten

⅓ cup sunflower seeds, ground (or ½ cup meal)

½ cup wheat germ

1 medium onion, minced

2 tablespoons nutritional yeast

2 tablespoons soy sauce

2 tablespoons catsup
whole wheat flour
oil

Combine all ingredients except the flour and oil and, with moist hands, shape into patties. For adult-size servings, use about ⅓ cup; for children, ¼ cup.

Spread flour on flat surface and dredge each burger. Chill if possible, even if only while pan heats.

Generously cover surface of a large skillet with oil and heat. Place burgers in hot oil and sauté for about 5 minutes on each side until golden.

Makes 8 large or 12 small burgers; serves 4 to 6

Minor Protein

Note: To broil, place on a well-oiled tray, drizzle top lightly with oil, and cook 3½ to 4 inches from heat for 3 to 5 minutes per side until golden. Broiling is more convenient, but burgers will be less juicy. Cooked leftovers can be wrapped in foil and frozen. To use, bake still wrapped and frozen in a 350°F. oven for about 15 minutes, or until very hot inside.

Menu Suggestions: If you do not add protein in the form of soup, salad, or perhaps dessert, top each burger with a slice of cheese for ample main dish nourishment.

RICE CHEESEBURGERS

This burger mixture is especially useful for those who like to prepare food in advance. The longer the burgers are chilled, the better they taste, and they can be refrigerated for as long as 24 hours, or even frozen without cooking.

2 packed cups cooked brown rice
1 cup cottage cheese
½ cup shredded mild cheese (mozzarella, Muenster, or Jack)
½ teaspoon salt
pepper
½ teaspoon paprika
1 egg, lightly beaten
½ cup cornmeal
¼ packed cup grated Parmesan cheese
oil

Combine rice, cottage cheese, shredded cheese, and seasonings to form a stiff paste. Shape into eight 3-inch patties using moist hands.

Beat egg in a shallow bowl. Combine cornmeal and Parmesan cheese on a flat plate. Dip each patty into egg, holding with tongs or your hands, then coat completely with dry mixture, shaking off any excess. Place on a wire rack and refrigerate to dry. They should be allowed to chill for at least 30 minutes.

Heat enough oil to cover surface of a large skillet. When hot, sauté patties quickly over medium heat for about 3 to 5 minutes on each side, until well browned.

Makes 8 burgers; serves 4

Major Protein

Note: Wrap leftover uncooked burgers separately and freeze. To use, brown in hot oil for about 5 minutes per side without defrosting, then cover pan, turn heat very low, and cook for 5 to 8 minutes until heated through.

Menu Suggestions: Good with any number of toppings including Sweet Red Pepper Sauce, Creamy Pimiento Sauce, a garnish of sautéed sweet peppers and onions, or nothing more elaborate than catsup. Serve leftovers cold with catsup or mayonnaise.

CASHEW BURGERS

These excellent burgers can be accompanied by any gravy or eaten plain. While they are well suited to a variety of cooking methods, for the cook's convenience they are best broiled (indoors or out).

1 cup milk
4 slices whole grain bread
2 cups mixed nuts (mostly cashews and the remainder sunflower and sesame seeds)
¼ teaspoon chili powder
1 teaspoon salt (omit if nuts are salted or soy-roasted)
2 tablespoons minced parsley
2 eggs, lightly beaten

Pour milk over bread in a bowl and let soften while preparing remaining ingredients. Squeeze out all liquid, saving it for gravy (or the cat).

Grind nuts and seeds to a fine meal. Add with seasonings to softened bread. Stir in eggs and mix well.

Form mixture into 8 small burgers, using ¼ cup for each.

Place on well-oiled broiler pan and cook about 5 inches from heat until golden, about 5 minutes per side. To cook outdoors, place on grill over hot coals and brown.

Makes 8 small burgers; serves 4
Major Protein
Note: For economy, ¼ cup wheat germ can replace ¼ cup ground nuts. For a meatier flavor, add 1 tablespoon nutritional yeast. If the oven is already in use, you may prefer to bake the burgers for 20 to 25 minutes in a 375°F. oven. Broiling, however, is faster and better. Burgers may also be browned in oil in a hot frying pan.

BEAN SAUSAGES

As with other sausages, these are good with fried eggs, or in a sauce with peppers and onions over spaghetti.

    3 cups cooked beans, drained and
        ground
    1 cup soft whole wheat bread
        crumbs
    1 teaspoon dried sage
    1 teaspoon salt (omit if beans are
        well salted)
    ¼ teaspoon pepper
    1 large clove garlic, minced
    2 eggs
    2 tablespoons water
    about ¼ cup whole wheat flour
    oil

Combine ground beans, bread crumbs, seasonings, and 1 egg.

Form into sausages about 3 inches long and ½ inch thick.

Beat remaining egg with water. Place flour on a plate. Dip each sausage into egg, then roll in flour to coat.

To cook, heat enough oil to generously cover a large skillet and sauté the sausages, shaking to brown all sides. Or place in a flat pan, drizzle lightly with oil, and broil for about 5 minutes on each side until nicely browned.

Makes 20 sausages; serves 4 (or 6 when accompanied by eggs)
Major Protein
Variations: For *Sausages, Onions, and Pepper,* sauté some sliced onions and sweet peppers in a skillet to soften, then add sausages and cook as directed. Add tomato sauce to cover and heat through; serve over spaghetti. For a spicy version, add hot peppers or a good pinch of cayenne.

MEXICAN BEAN BALLS

Tiny bean balls in spicy sauce to serve on rice or bread, or to roll into tortillas. Spoon yogurt flavored lightly with sour cream on top for a nice touch.

    3 cups cooked black or brown beans,
        drained and ground
    1 small onion, minced
    1 clove garlic, minced
    ½ teaspoon salt (omit if beans are
        salted)
    ½ teaspoon oregano
    ¼ cup cornmeal
    1 egg, lightly beaten
    3 cups Emergency Mexican Tomato
        Sauce (page 58) or Enchilada Sauce
        (page 317)

Mix ground beans with seasonings, cornmeal, and egg to form a soft patty mixture.

Heat sauce in a wide pot or heavy skillet and simmer for 5 to 10 minutes.

Scoop up a teaspoon of bean mixture at a time and form into small balls ½ to 1 inch in diameter. As they are formed, drop them into the simmering sauce. Cover and simmer over low heat for 5 to 10 minutes. Cooking too long or too vigorously may cause the tender bean balls to fall apart. Should this occur, you will have a delicious, rich bean sauce that can be used in the same manner as the bean balls.

Makes 50 to 60 small balls; serves 6
Protein Complement (completed by grain base or tortillas and/or yogurt garnish)

Menu Suggestions: Serve with Guacamole or Avocado Cocktail and a green salad, or as a double entrée with Stuffed Squash Blossoms, Chili Rellenos, or Cheese Enchiladas.

SWEDISH BEAN BALLS

These juicy bean balls are cooked in a vegetable steamer and served on rice with Mushroom or Onion Sauce.

1 cup soft whole wheat bread crumbs
¾ cup wheat germ
1 cup milk
3 cups cooked white beans, drained
1 teaspoon salt (omit if beans are salted)
¼ cup minced onion
½ teaspoon nutmeg
pepper
9 cups cooked brown rice
2 cups Mushroom Sauce (page 314) or Onion Sauce (page 314)

Combine bread crumbs, ½ cup wheat germ, and milk, and let stand to absorb liquid while preparing remaining ingredients.

Grind beans. Squeeze soaked bread crumb mixture dry, reserving any liquid for the sauce. Add beans, seasonings, and the remaining ¼ cup wheat germ to the softened crumbs.

Shape into 1-inch balls, using about 1 tablespoon per ball (making about 36 in all). Chill if desired until cooking time.

To cook, place in a vegetable steamer and steam for 10 minutes. Let sit a minute or two before removing from tray to firm. Serve on rice and cover with gravy.

Serves 6
Major Protein
Note: The rice takes the most time to cook, so prepare it first. The sauce takes only about 15 minutes and can be cooking while bean balls steam. Leftover bean balls can be frozen after cooking. To restore, place unwrapped, but still frozen in a steamer and heat through for about 10 minutes.

Menu Suggestions: Complete the meal with a cooked vegetable and salad.

SOYBALLS

Serve on pasta, grain, or bread with any sauce you choose. Cold leftovers are good on sandwiches or with cocktail sauce as hors d'oeuvres.

3 cups cooked soybeans, drained and ground
1 teaspoon salt (omit if beans are salted)
1 large clove garlic, minced
2 tablespoons minced onion
1 teaspoon oregano
½ teaspoon dried basil
¼ teaspoon pepper
1 tablespoon nutritional yeast (optional)
1 egg, lightly beaten
½ cup wheat germ
oil

Combine all ingredients except the oil to form a soft, moldable patty mixture.

Heat enough oil to generously cover surface of a large, heavy skillet. Shape mixture into 1-inch balls and, as they are formed, drop them into the hot pan. Brown on all sides, turning as necessary.

To keep balls warm while others cook, place in a covered pan in a low (300° to 325°F.) oven or transfer them to a sauce and warm through over low heat for 5 minutes. Do not cook vigorously.

Makes about 32 balls; serves 4 to 6
Major Protein
Note: Mixture can be prepared in advance and refrigerated for use as needed over several days. Leftover cooked soyballs can be frozen and reheated by cooking them in a simmering sauce for 10 to 15 minutes. Prepare about 4 cups sauce to accommodate all the soyballs.

FALAFEL-I

Falafel is a popular Middle Eastern street food, akin to our hotdog. It is composed of chick-pea fritters stuffed into pita bread, topped with shredded salad and bathed in a tangy sesame seed sauce. As such, it is an ideal one-dish meal for kids.

For the Falafel
3 cups cooked chick-peas, drained and ground
1 teaspoon salt (omit if beans are well salted)
⅛ teaspoon cayenne
1 tablespoon minced parsley
1 teaspoon minced garlic
2 tablespoons wheat germ
2 eggs, lightly beaten
oil

Combine all ingredients except the oil and mix thoroughly. Shape into 24 balls, about 1 inch in diameter, and flatten slightly.

Heat oil in a wok or fill a heavy skillet to a depth of ½ inch with oil. When oil temperature is 365° to 375°F., fry balls 4 at a time, or as many as will comfortably fit in the pan, until crisp. Drain on absorbent paper. Keep warm in a 300°F. oven, if desired.

Serve with Tahini Sauce (recipe follows) on a plate or stuffed into pita bread, as described above.

Makes 24 balls; serves 4 to 6

Major Protein when served with Tahini Sauce

Variations: 1 cup cooked soybeans can replace 1 cup chick-peas. If preferred, Falafel can be baked in an oiled baking pan in a 375°F. oven for 20 minutes until browned. For a crisp surface, loosen from pan and shake during baking.

Tahini Sauce
¾ cup tahini
½ teaspoon minced garlic (optional)
¾ teaspoon salt
⅓ cup lemon juice
½ to ⅔ cup water

Mix tahini, garlic, salt, and lemon juice to form a smooth, thick paste. Gradually beat in water with a fork or wire whisk until sauce is well blended and the consistency of heavy cream.

Menu Suggestions: Both Tabouli and Israeli Salad are excellent choices for this menu and sometimes both are served with Falafel at the same time. For entertaining, we recommend adding Baba Ghanouj for an appetizer, and an array of condiments including olives, hot pickled peppers, and other marinated vegetables. We call this offering Mideast Smorgasbord.

FALAFEL-II

This recipe offers the convenience of not having to precook the chick-peas, but does require a processor, grinder, or blender to grind them.

½ pound dried chick-peas (about 1⅓ cups)
2 cloves garlic, minced
2 tablespoons minced parsley
1 teaspoon salt
1 tablespoon nutritional yeast
¼ cup wheat germ
¼ cup whole wheat flour
1 teaspoon paprika
oil

Place beans in a pot with water to cover, bring to a boil for 2 minutes, cover, remove from heat and let soak for at least 6 hours or as long as 24 (if over 12 hours, refrigerate).

Drain beans thoroughly, add garlic and parsley, and grind to a pulp in several batches, using a blender, meat grinder, or processor fitted with a steel blade.

Mix remaining ingredients except the oil into the bean pulp. (This is best done by transferring the mixture to a bowl.) Shape into small balls, using a rounded teaspoonful for each. Chill until ready to cook, or cook at once.

Heat oil in a wok for deep-frying. When temperature reaches 365°F., fry balls, 4 to 6 at a time, until browned. Turn to cook on both sides. Each batch should take about 5 minutes. Drain on absorbent paper while cooking the next batch. They can be kept warm in a 300°F. oven, but this is not really necessary as they retain heat fairly well and do not have to be served very hot.

Serve in pita bread with salad and Tahini Sauce, as in the preceding recipe.

Makes 24 balls; serves 4 to 6

Major Protein when served with Tahini Sauce

BAKED RICE BALLS

These are chewy, but not heavy, and taste delicious blanketed by Mushroom or Onion Sauce, Tomato Cashew Gravy, or your favorite. Chilled leftovers make a delicious lunch or snack dipped in mustard, catsup, or mayonnaise.

 1 cup cooked brown rice
 1 egg, lightly beaten
 ½ teaspoon salt (omit if grain is salted)
 ½ cup peanuts and/or almonds, ground
 ½ cup grated cheese
 1 teaspoon lemon juice
к about ⅓ cup wheat germ

Preheat oven to 375°F.

Combine all ingredients except the wheat germ and shape into balls using 1 rounded tablespoonful for each. Roll in wheat germ and place in well-oiled baking dish.

Bake for 30 minutes, or until bottom is nicely browned. Serve brown side up for most attractive appearance.

Makes 15 balls; serves 2 (with leftovers for snacking the next day)

Major Protein

Note: Allow ½ to ¾ cup sauce per serving.

Menu Suggestions: Add a salad and a simple steamed vegetable for a quick, hearty meal.

ITALIAN RICE CROQUETTES

Inside each is a surprise creamy filling.

 2 cups cooked brown rice
 ½ cup grated Parmesan cheese
 1 egg, lightly beaten
 ½ teaspoon salt (omit if rice is well seasoned)
 pepper
 2 ounces unsliced mozzarella cheese, cut in 9 ¾-inch cubes
 about ¼ cup wheat germ
 oil

Combine rice, Parmesan, egg, and seasoning. Shape into nine 2-inch balls. Push a cube of mozzarella inside each and reshape, making sure cheese is completely covered with rice. Roll balls in wheat germ to coat. Chill until ready to cook.

Heat oil to a depth of ½ inch in a wok or heavy skillet. When hot, fry rice balls until brown on all sides, about 5 minutes. Drain on absorbent paper. Continue until all are cooked. As these are good at room temperature, those that have cooked need not be kept warm.

Makes 9 croquettes; serves 3

Major Protein

Note: Alternately, Italian Rice Croquettes can be baked in a well-oiled pan in a 375°F. oven for 30 minutes, which may be more convenient if recipe is increased. Leftovers store well in the refrigerator or freezer and can be cooked in the oven, as above, without defrosting.

Menu Suggestions: Serve plain or with tomato sauce, hot or at room temperature. Croquettes may be joined on the menu with one or more cooked vegetable dishes and one or more salads, as just about everything goes well with them.

MIXED GRAIN BALLS

A rich savory that is reminiscent of the Jewish specialty, stuffed derma, and has as many uses as meat balls.

 ¾ cup cornmeal
 ¼ cup rye flour
 ½ cup whole wheat flour
 6 tablespoons nonfat dry milk powder
 1 small onion, minced
 1 clove garlic, minced
 ½ teaspoon salt
 1 teaspoon soy sauce
 1 tablespoon oil
 ½ to ¾ cup water

Preheat oven to 375°F.

Combine grains, dry milk powder, onion, garlic, and salt. Stir in soy sauce, oil, and ½ cup water, mixing well until dough is moist and slightly sticky. If dry, add additional water by the tablespoonful.

Form into balls, using a generous tablespoonful for each. Keep hands moist while working, using cold water to prevent sticking.

Place balls in a generously oiled, shallow baking dish. Roll them around in the oil, then bake for 20 to 25 minutes until firm and golden.

Makes 12 balls; serves 2 to 3
Major Protein
Note: For a nondairy product, replace dry milk powder with ¼ cup soy flour. Make balls half-size for party hors d'oeuvres.

Menu Suggestions: If you don't wish to eat these plain, add them to vegetable stews, or serve on Cabbage Noodles in Tomato Broth, cloak them in any gravy, or accompany them with any yogurt-mayonnaise or soy sauce-based dipping sauce.

MUSHROOM RISSOLES

Individual pyramid-shaped mushroom roasts to serve with Cashew or Brown Gravy. A good choice for those who like to plan ahead, as the mixture should be chilled before shaping.

3 tablespoons oil
½ pound mushrooms, chopped (about 3 cups)
1 medium onion, chopped
2 stalks celery, minced
2 teaspoons poultry seasoning
½ cup milk
2 tablespoons soy flour
2 eggs, lightly beaten
1 teaspoon salt
2 slices whole grain bread, crumbled, or 1 cup soft bread crumbs
½ cup combined walnuts and sunflower seeds, ground
about ¾ cup wheat germ

Heat 2 tablespoons oil in a skillet or small saucepan and sauté mushrooms, onion, celery, and poultry seasoning for 10 minutes.

Gradually stir milk into soy flour and stir this mixture into mushrooms. Cook, stirring for 3 to 5 minutes until thickened. Remove from heat and cool slightly.

Add eggs, salt, bread crumbs, nut meal, and ½ cup wheat germ. Chill for several hours for easier shaping.

Preheat oven to 375°F.

Form mixture into 6 to 8 mounds. Dredge with remaining wheat germ. Place on an oiled baking sheet and drizzle with remaining tablespoon oil. Bake for 30 minutes.

Prepare a gravy while rissoles bake and spoon on top to serve.

Serves 4
Major Protein
Variation: For an egg-free version, increase milk to 1 cup and soy flour to ¼ cup.

LIVERISH

A nut steak with a flavor and aroma that is astonishingly liver-ish. One of our favorite recipes.

1 small onion, diced
1 tablespoon oil
2 eggs
½ cup milk
½ teaspoon sage
¼ teaspoon thyme
¼ teaspoon celery seed
¼ teaspoon salt
1½ teaspoons soy sauce
dash hot pepper sauce
2 tablespoons wheat germ
2 tablespoons soy flour
1 cup fresh whole wheat bread crumbs (2 slices bread)
½ cup combined sesame seeds, sunflower seeds, peanuts, and almonds, ground to meal

Preheat oven to 350°F.

Sauté onion in oil for 3 to 5 minutes until tender.

Beat eggs with milk and seasonings. Add remaining ingredients, including the sautéed onion.

Spread mixture in an oiled 8- or 9-inch square pan.

Bake for 20 to 25 minutes until firm and golden. Cut in large pieces to serve.

Serves 3
Major Protein
Note: Excellent served warm or at

room temperature. Leftovers can be chilled and used for hors d'oeuvres cut in bite-size squares, skewered on a pick, and dunked in Quick Cocktail Sauce.

To serve 6, double the recipe and bake in two 8- or 9-inch pans or a single 9 x 13-inch baking dish. If desired, 3 eggs can be used instead of 4.

Menu Suggestions: Liverish can be served plain or with Brown or Mushroom Gravy or, of course, catsup. A salad is a must, and almost any vegetable dish makes a suitable accompaniment. Those containing carrots, winter squash, or tomatoes provide a nice visual contrast.

VEGETABLE ROAST

This is the kind of entrée made popular by Jewish dairy restaurants.

2 cups oats
2 cups boiling water
1 large onion
4 stalks celery
2 carrots
2 tablespoons oil
½ cup green peas
1 teaspoon poultry seasoning
1½ tablespoons nutritional yeast
1½ teaspoons salt
pepper
¾ cup nonfat dry milk powder
½ cup wheat germ
1½ cups soft whole wheat bread crumbs or 3 slices bread, crumbled

Preheat oven to 350°F.

Place oats in a large mixing bowl and pour on boiling water. Let stand for 10 minutes to soften while preparing remaining ingredients.

Chop onion, celery, and carrots and sauté in oil for about 10 minutes.

Add cooked vegetables, raw peas, and remaining ingredients to softened oats. Mix well.

Pack into an oiled 9-inch loaf pan or a deep 9- to 10-inch pie plate and bake for about 1 hour until firm and lightly crusted on top.

Serves 6

Major Protein when served with gravy

Note: For reduced cooking time, shape mixture into 6 individual roasts on an oiled baking sheet and bake in a 375°F. oven for about 30 minutes until brown and crusty.

Menu Suggestions: Vegetable Roast is customarily served with Mushroom or Brown Gravy, mashed potatoes, and cooked string beans or creamed spinach.

BEAN BIRDS

Mini roasts that make a warming winter meal with gravy, cranberry sauce, cooked vegetable, and salad. Cold leftovers make delicious sandwiches seasoned with cranberry sauce or catsup.

½ cup soft whole wheat bread crumbs or 1 slice whole grain bread
3 cups cooked soybeans, lima beans, chick-peas, or white beans, drained
¼ cup wheat germ
¾ cup chopped onion
½ cup chopped celery
1 teaspoon salt (reduce by half if beans are salted)
1½ teaspoons poultry seasoning
1 egg, lightly beaten
½ cup tomato juice

Preheat oven to 350°F.

If you do not have crumbs made, first process bread into crumbs in a processor. Remove to mixing bowl and grind beans.

Combine all ingredients and shape into 6 or 8 mounds on a well-oiled baking sheet. Brush surface lightly with oil and bake for about 30 minutes, or until firm and crusty. For best crust, baste with additional oil midway through cooking.

Serves 4 to 6

Major Protein

Note: If used to serve 6 and not topped with protein-rich gravy, an additional protein dish should be included in the menu.

Variation: For *Vegan Bean Birds,* replace egg with 2 tablespoons peanut butter.

HAWAIIAN BEAN LOAF

1 cup soft whole grain bread crumbs
½ cup sunflower seeds, ground (⅔ cup meal)
3 cups cooked, drained white beans, ground
1-pound can sliced or crushed pineapple in juice
1 teaspoon salt (omit if beans are salted)
1 cup chopped green pepper
2 eggs, lightly beaten
1 tablespoon molasses
2 teaspoons prepared mustard
1 tablespoon oil

Preheat oven to 350° to 375°F.

Prepare bread crumbs, sunflower seed meal, and ground beans (in that order, if using the same utensils, to avoid washing).

Drain pineapple well and reserve ¼ cup of the juice.

Combine ¼ cup pineapple juice with bread crumbs, seed meal, ground beans, and remaining ingredients except pineapple and oil. If dry, add additional juice to moisten.

Pack into a deep, oiled 9- to 10-inch pie plate. Drizzle with oil and arrange pineapple to cover as much surface as possible.

Bake for about 45 minutes until firm and edges are brown.

Serves 4 to 6
Major Protein
Note: Serve leftovers cold with mustard; makes a nice sandwich.

COTTAGE CHEESE AND BEAN LOAF

The texture and seasonings give this a fishlike quality.

3 cups cooked, drained lima beans, soybeans, or white beans, ground
1 cup cottage cheese
2 eggs, lightly beaten
2 cups cooked brown rice or soft whole grain bread crumbs, or a combination
½ cup sliced pitted green olives
2 teaspoons prepared mustard
¼ cup minced fresh parsley or 1 tablespoon dried

¾ teaspoon salt (omit if beans are salted)
¼ cup lemon juice

Preheat oven to 350°F.

Combine all ingredients. Pack into a 9-inch loaf pan or a deep 9- to 10-inch pie plate that has been oiled and coated with wheat germ.

Bake until firm and lightly colored, about 45 minutes for pie, 1 hour for loaf. Let cool for 10 minutes in the pan before slicing. If desired, entire loaf can be unmolded before cutting.

Serves 4 to 6
Major Protein
Note: Beans can be chopped by hand rather than ground if necessary.

Menu Suggestions: Serve with a dressing of Tartar Sauce or Sweet Red Pepper Sauce. Excellent cold, too.

COLD COTTAGE CHEESE AND BEAN LOAF

A gelatin mold that provides a no-cook warm-weather entrée. Allow several hours to chill when planning your schedule. Unmold to serve and garnish with greens, olives, and cucumber slices.

1 envelope unflavored gelatin
1 cup milk
1½ cups cottage cheese
1 tablespoon finely chopped onion
2 tablespoons lemon juice
2 tablespoons mayonnaise
1 teaspoon paprika
¼ teaspoon salt (omit if beans are salted)
1½ cups cooked beans, well drained
1 cup shredded or chopped cabbage

Sprinkle gelatin over ½ cup milk in a saucepan and let stand for 5 minutes to soften. Place over low heat and cook, stirring, until dissolved, about 3 minutes.

In a large bowl, mix cottage cheese, onion, lemon juice, mayonnaise, paprika, salt if needed, and remaining ½ cup milk. Stir in dissolved gelatin. Chill until slightly thickened.

Fold beans and cabbage into thickened mixture, pour into a 4-cup mold or 8-inch loaf pan, and chill until firm, 1 hour or longer.

To serve, unmold and slice.
Serves 6 to 8
Minor Protein

SPAGHETTI ROAST

A good use for leftover spaghetti. Serve with tomato sauce or Brown Gravy. Serve cold leftovers with mayonnaise or catsup.

2 cups cooked spaghetti
1 medium onion, chopped
¾ cup soft whole wheat bread crumbs
¾ cup coarsely chopped nuts (a combination of cashews, sunflower seeds, and a few walnuts preferred)
1 teaspoon salt
1 tablespoon minced parsley
½ teaspoon poultry seasoning
1 tablespoon nutritional yeast (optional)
2 eggs, lightly beaten

Preheat oven to 350°F.
Cut spaghetti into small strands. Combine with remaining ingredients.
Shape into a mound on oiled baking sheet or shallow pan. Drizzle some oil over the top.
Bake until firm and browned, about 35 minutes.
Serves 4
Major Protein

RICE–NUT LOAF

Serve with Brown Gravy or any tomato or mushroom sauce. This is very popular among our friends.

1½ cups cooked brown rice
½ cup wheat germ
¾ cup chopped walnuts
¼ cup chopped sunflower seeds
1 large onion, chopped
½ pound sharp cheddar cheese, shredded (about 2 cups)
½ teaspoon salt
pepper
1 tablespoon nutritional yeast (optional)
4 eggs, lightly beaten

Preheat oven to 350°F.
Combine all ingredients and pack into an oiled 9-inch loaf pan.

Bake for about 50 minutes until firm. Let cool in pan for 10 minutes; unmold and slice.
Serves 6
Major Protein

LUNCHEON WHEAT GERM LOAF

This loaf turns out soft, moist, and a little bit sweet. Serve plain or with catsup or tomato sauce. Use chilled as a sandwich filling.

1 cup wheat germ
about 1 cup milk
1 cup ground nuts (combination of cashews, sunflower seeds, peanuts, and almonds)
1 medium onion, minced
1 green pepper, minced
½ teaspoon salt
2 tablespoons lemon juice
1 tablespoon oil
1 egg, lightly beaten

Preheat oven to 350°F.
Put wheat germ in a bowl and gradually stir in milk until no more can be absorbed. Let sit a few minutes, then drain off any excess milk. Stir in remaining ingredients.
Turn mixture into an oiled 8-inch loaf pan. Bake for about 45 minutes until top is firm and lightly browned. Let set for 10 minutes before slicing.
Serves 4 to 6
Major Protein
Note: Leftovers can be frozen sliced or unsliced. Bake frozen unsliced loaf, wrapped in foil, in a 350°F. oven for about 30 to 40 minutes until heated through. Bake slices in the same manner for 20 minutes, then open packet and bake for 10 minutes until hot but not dry.

BREAD MEAT

An oversized dumpling with a dense but tender, chewy texture that provides valuable protein in a familiar meaty form. This is an important recipe that can be used in many ways, as outlined on the following page.

6 slices whole grain bread, diced (about 3½ cups)
¼ cup wheat germ
¼ cup nonfat dry milk powder
½ teaspoon salt
½ teaspoon nutmeg
1 tablespoon nutritional yeast (optional)
2 eggs
⅔ cup water
1 tablespoon melted butter

Combine bread cubes, wheat germ, dry milk powder, and seasonings in a bowl. Beat eggs with water and pour over bread mixture. Let stand until well absorbed, then stir in melted butter.

While bread mixture is softening, bring a deep, wide-mouthed pot half filled with water to a boil.

Divide bread mixture in half and shape each into an 8-inch cylinder in the center of clean cloth napkins. Roll napkins loosely around the cylinders and tie ends to secure.

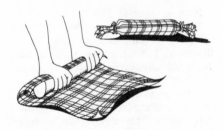

Lower into boiling water, cover and simmer for 20 minutes until firm.

Lift from pot, drain off liquid, open cloth, and remove Bread Meat. Slice and serve as directed or desired.

Serves 4
Minor Protein
Note: Bread mixture can also be placed in one lump in the center of a cloth napkin with the ends gathered together at the top to form a loose bag. Tie to secure and cook in boiling water for 30 minutes until firm.

Bread Meat can be cooked and stored in the refrigerator up to one week for use as needed. Bread Meat can be eaten cold or can be reheated by steaming or by simmering in sauce.

Variations: For *Spicy Bread Meat,* omit nutmeg and add 1 tablespoon chili powder. Replace water with tomato juice.

Uses:

• Slice and serve as dumplings in bean or vegetable stew.

• Slice and simmer in 3 cups of your favorite tomato sauce for about 5 minutes just to heat through; tastes like meat loaf.

• Slice and serve warm with Brown or Mushroom Gravy.

• Cut into small cubes and serve warm or cold with catsup as an hors d'oeuvre.

POTATO DOUGH

A dough made from potatoes is common in both Italian and eastern European cooking. As a main dish it is the basis for Gnocchi (potato dumplings) and Semel Bresel (potato noodles). As an accompaniment to the meal, it can be shaped into a potato Knish or rolled around cheese for a fried Hot Potato Turnover.

1½ pounds potatoes
2 eggs
1 teaspoon salt
pepper
1½ tablespoons oil, butter, or a mixture
6 tablespoons nonfat dry milk powder
✗ 1 to 1½ cups whole wheat flour

Quarter potatoes and steam about 20 minutes until tender. Press through a food mill or mash by hand. Do not puree in a blender or processor. When mashed, you should have about 3 cups.

Beat in remaining ingredients in the order listed, adding flour as needed to form a dough than is soft but can be handled without sticking.

Use as directed in specific recipes.

Makes 3 cups or about 2 pounds dough; enough for 6 servings of Gnocchi (page 207) or Semel Bresel (page 207), or 18 Knishes (page 283) or Hot Potato Turnovers (page 283).

Note: Dough can be refrigerated up to 24 hours before use. You may wish to divide the dough so you can prepare two dishes at one time. While Gnocchi and Semel Bresel are best freshly prepared, Potato Knish can be baked and frozen and Turnovers can be frozen even before cooking.

ITALIAN GNOCCHI

Gnocchi is an Italian specialty made by poaching potato dough in water; the tiny tender dumplings are then served in tomato sauce.

Potato Dough (page 206)
whole wheat flour
butter
about ¾ cup grated Parmesan cheese
4 cups seasoned tomato sauce (such as Italian Tomato Sauce, page 317)

Prepare dough and pat ¼ inch thick on a well-floured surface. Flour top as well so dough is easy to handle.

Heat water to half-fill a large, broad-mouthed pot. When it reaches a slow boil, add a spoonful of salt.

Pinch off 1-inch fingers of dough, roll lightly in flour, and drop into gently boiling water. This part is somewhat tedious, but the cooking is fast. Only add as much to the pot as will fit comfortably, or about half the dough in a broad 5-quart pot.

When dumplings rise to the surface, cover and simmer for 5 to 8 minutes until light. Taste one, and if tender, remove gnocchi from pot with a slotted spoon.

If more are to be cooked, transfer cooked gnocchi to a shallow baking dish, dot with butter, sprinkle with some of the cheese, and keep warm in a 300° to 325°F. oven.

When all are cooked, place on a bed of sauce in each serving bowl, blanket with grated cheese, and pass additional cheese and sauce at the table for those who want more.

Serves 6
Minor Protein
Note: This dish actually only needs a slight increase in protein, easily obtained by adding more than the specified amount of cheese; it can also be supplied by serving a varied antipasto platter along with the gnocchi.

SEMEL BRESEL

Fried potato noodles which taste like tender potato puffs and are made from the same basic potato dough that is used in Gnocchi, Potato Knish, and Hot Potato Turnovers.

Potato Dough (page 206)
whole wheat flour
oil
3 large onions, coarsely chopped
yogurt or Whipped Cottage Cream (page 56)

Prepare dough and pat into a rectangle ¼ inch thick on a well-floured surface. Flour top of dough so it is easy to handle. Cut into fingers 2 inches long and ¼ inch wide and roll in flour.

Heat enough oil to cover a large, heavy skillet. Sauté onions until they begin to color, about 5 minutes.

Add potato "noodles" and sauté until well browned on all sides, shaking and turning in the pan to do so.

Serve hot topped with yogurt or Whipped Cottage Cream.

Serves 6
Major Protein
Menu Suggestions: A nice meal with a steamed green vegetable and a tomato salad. If you omit the topping, serve with Vegetable Cottage Cheese, Cucumbers with Creamy Cottage Cheese, or a similar accompaniment for added protein.

POLISH PIEROGI

Buckwheat dumplings mixed with cottage cheese and browned onions is one of the easiest dumpling dishes to prepare and makes for very hearty eating.

For the Dumplings
1½ cups boiling water
1 cup buckwheat flour
1½ cups whole wheat flour
¾ teaspoon salt
3 quarts boiling salted water

Pour 1½ cups boiling water over buckwheat flour in a mixing bowl. Mix thoroughly. Add whole wheat flour and salt and mix until smooth. This will form a thick, slightly gluey dough.

Turn out onto a floured surface and divide dough into four equal pieces. Roll each into a rope about 12 inches long and 1 inch in diameter. Cut into segments barely ½ inch wide.

Have water boiling in a wide 5-quart pot or two 3-quart pots. Add about 2 teaspoons salt. Ease dumplings into boiling water and when boiling resumes, cover, turn heat so water just simmers, and cook dumplings for 20 minutes.

Remove dumplings from water with a slotted spoon and drain in a colander. Toss with the dumpling garnish, prepared as directed below, and serve.

Dumpling Garnish
   2 tablespoons oil/butter
   2 cups chopped onion
   2 to 3 cups cottage cheese
   ¼ cup chopped parsley

Heat oil and/or butter in a skillet and sauté onion until golden. This can be done while dumplings cook.

Place cooked onions in the bottom of a serving bowl. Top with ½ cup cottage cheese for each main-dish serving. Place dumplings on top, scatter parsley over all, and mix gently but thoroughly.
   Serves 4 to 6
   Major Protein
   Note: Dumplings may also be served as an accompaniment, in which case they become a Minor Protein for 8.

FILLED PANCAKES

While in America pancakes are best known as a breakfast dish, to be served with sweet syrup, the same basic ingredients combine to create many savory specialties throughout the world. In England, wholefoods restaurants excel in the production of tender, whole grain pancakes to serve beneath thick creamy vegetable-bean-grain gravies. Blini, yeast-raised buckwheat pancakes, are a great Russian favorite folded over sour cream and red caviar. Of course, thin egg-lightened pancakes, known by their French name "crepes," are already popular in American kitchens where they appear as appetizers and entrées with any number of fillings and sauces. The crepe is also the classic encasement for ricotta cheese in the original version of Italian manicotti, and fried it becomes a blintz or an egg roll.

The recipes that follow are based on ordinary pancakes. You may be surprised at the variety of forms a simple batter can take merely by altering the filling.

Raised Pancakes

A pancake batter may be leavened with yeast, baking powder, or baking soda, all of which contribute to the lightness of the final product. No matter what recipe you use for preparing these leavened pancakes, the same basic cooking principles always apply:
• Mix batter gently but thoroughly so that all ingredients are moistened. A few small lumps left in the batter will not be in the way, but large clumps of flour will remain as hard dry lumps after cooking.
• Preheat the pan over moderate heat before introducing the batter. Once a few drops of water "dance" when sprinkled on the surface, the pan is ready to receive the pancakes. (If water does not bounce immediately, the pan is still too cold; if it sputters and turns to steam, it is too hot.) Rub the surface with a paper towel impregnated with oil and begin cooking.
• Turn pancakes only once. When the bottom is firm enough for turning, the spatula will slip underneath easily. This cannot be rushed by increasing the heat, or the bottom will burn before the center has a chance to cook. The second side will generally cook in half the time, and as cooking continues, later batches will cook more rapidly than the first.
• To keep pancakes warm, place on a heatproof platter or baking pan, cover with a linen napkin to retain the steam

and prevent drying, and set in a low (250° to 300°F.) oven.

• Although pancakes are best freshly made, leftovers can be frozen successfully. Separate with foil, plastic wrap, or wax paper so they can be removed one at a time if necessary. When only a couple of pancakes are needed, restore by light toasting. For reheating an entire packet, remove any plastic or other unsuitable wrapping used to separate them, wrap in foil, and bake in a moderate (350° to 375°F.) oven for 10 to 15 minutes, or until heated through. Or place the foil packet in a vegetable steamer and steam for 10 minutes to revive.

To serve pancakes as a dinner entrée, allow 3 to 5 per person. Top with cooked vegetables or beans in a creamy cheese or tomato sauce (allow about ¼ cup vegetables in sauce per pancake), or with yogurt and syrup, or strips of Cheeson and syrup. The topping you select should provide additional protein, especially for those pancakes labeled Minor Protein.

Savory pancakes can be accompanied on the menu by almost any soup, salad, bean or vegetable accompaniment. Those served sweet are better suited to a fruit salad accompaniment.

Note: Additional recipes for pancakes are found with the homemade mixes on pages 447 and 449.

CORN–CHEESE PANCAKES

These cheese-flavored cornmeal pancakes can be used as a base for any cooked bean dish in a thick sauce, then topped with yogurt or additional grated cheese; or top with Guacamole and a spoonful of yogurt, or any well-flavored vegetable in a thick, creamy gravy. They can even be used like tortillas or chapatis by rolling the filling inside and eating out of hand.

1 cup cornmeal
½ teaspoon baking soda
½ teaspoon salt
⅓ cup grated cheddar cheese (about 1½ ounces)
1 egg, lightly beaten

1¼ cups buttermilk
1 tablespoon oil

Mix together cornmeal, baking soda, salt, and cheese.

Make a well in the center and add egg, buttermilk, and oil. Stir gently until thoroughly moistened.

Heat a large, heavy skillet or griddle. When a few drops of water dance on the surface, rub with a paper towel impregnated with oil.

Pour batter onto the hot pan and cook as for any pancakes, turning as they set and spatula slips underneath easily. (If necessary, cooked pancakes can be covered and kept warm in the oven until all the batter is used up.) Fill as desired and serve hot.

Makes 8 to 9 pancakes; serves 2 to 3
Major Protein

FILLED ENGLISH PANCAKES

A vegetable stew inside a cheese-flavored pancake topped with a creamy sauce.

¼ cup chopped green pepper
1 large onion, chopped
2 tablespoons oil
2 cups cooked beans or raw potatoes cut in ½-inch dice
2 cups mixed diced vegetables of choice (mushrooms, carrots, parsnips, green beans, peas, corn, zucchini)
1 tablespoon water
1 tablespoon soy sauce
16 Corn-Cheese Pancakes (see preceding recipe) or Quick Corn-Cheese Pancakes (page 449)

Sauté green pepper and onion in oil in a 2- to 3-quart pot, cooking for 3 to 5 minutes, or until just softened.

Add remaining ingredients except pancakes; cover and stew for 15 to 20 minutes or until vegetables are fork-tender.

While filling cooks, prepare pancakes. Roll pancakes around filling. Top with Mushroom or Tomato Gravy or a cold sauce of yogurt lightly flavored with sour cream.

Serves 4
Major Protein

BEAN-STUDDED PANCAKES

Pancakes with chunks of beans throughout.

½ cup cornmeal
½ cup whole wheat flour
1 teaspoon baking powder
½ teaspoon salt
¼ teaspoon cayenne
½ cup milk
1 tablespoon oil
1 tablespoon molasses
1 egg, lightly beaten
1½ cups cooked kidney beans, well drained
yogurt

Mix the cornmeal, flour, baking powder, salt, and cayenne.

Make a well in the center of the dry ingredients and add milk, oil, molasses, and egg. Stir gently until the batter is smooth. Stir in beans, mashing gently against the sides of the bowl.

Heat a heavy skillet or griddle and, when hot, rub surface generously with an oil-impregnated paper towel. Drop in batter by rounded tablespoonfuls and cook until brown and set on the bottom and spatula slips underneath easily, about 5 minutes. Turn and cook until set, about 3 minutes.

Serve hot with a generous topping of yogurt and desired sauce.

Makes 12 pancakes; serves 4
Major Protein
Menu Suggestions: Delicious topped with yogurt and Chili Sauce or, if sweet is preferred to spicy, yogurt and warm maple syrup or a mixture of maple syrup and molasses.

BEAN BLINI

These very delicate pancakes make an excellent base for many vegetables, or they can be eaten plain with a little catsup or tomato sauce. Unlike most pancakes, they do not get heavy or soggy when kept in a warm oven.

2 cups cooked beans, well drained
2 eggs, separated
½ cup whole wheat flour
1 cup milk
1 teaspoon salt (omit if beans are salted)
¼ teaspoon cayenne
1 teaspoon baking powder
2 tablespoons oil

Puree beans in a blender or processor fitted with a steel cutting blade. Gradually add egg yolks, flour, milk, salt, cayenne, baking powder, and oil, and process until smooth.

Beat egg whites to stiff peaks. Pour bean mixture evenly over the whites and fold gently until blended and whites disappear.

Heat a heavy skillet or griddle and rub with oil. When hot, pour in batter by ¼ cupfuls. When bottom is set and brown and spatula slips underneath easily, turn and cook the other side.

Keep warm if necessary in a low oven as directed in the introductory notes on pancakes.

Makes 24 small pancakes; serves 4
Major Protein
Menu Suggestions: Suggested toppings include Mushroom Sauce, any cooked vegetable in yogurt or White Sauce, or a mixture of yogurt and sour cream stirred into chopped tomato or avocado.

Crepes

A crepe is a thin, delicate pancake that is designed to enclose a filling, even if that filling is nothing more than jam or sugar. Crepes appear on the menu in the form of appetizer, main course, or dessert, depending on the filling and the mode of service; they have been described as "an inspired way to use leftovers," for small portions of food extended in a sauce can be stretched to many more feedings when rolled inside a crepe.

Some people adore crepe making and routinely make such dishes for company dinners. Part of their allure is the fact that they are made from ingredients almost always found in the kitchen (eggs, milk, and flour) and that the preparation of the batter takes only seconds. However, until you've actually had a little practice, crepe cooking can be a slow, tedious process. The following information will help explain the activity to you, but until you have had the experience, make sure you leave yourself plenty of time (each crepe is cooked individually) and try to set up a relaxed atmosphere in which to do the job. After the first few crepes are completed, you should gain confidence; once mastered, crepe making is a skill you will retain.

Preparing the Batter

It is difficult to give an exact liquid measurement for a crepe batter since flours differ in their ability to absorb moisture. The objective is to produce a mixture that can be poured quickly in a thin, even film. Too thick a batter will not spread fast enough or thin enough; a batter that is too diluted does not adhere to the pan or set when cooking.

Blend crepe batter quickly and thoroughly so that no lumps remain, but do not handle it more than necessary. Overmixing can toughen crepes.

It is generally advised to let the batter rest for 30 minutes or longer before cooking. This is not imperative but does improve the texture of the finished crepe. You will find that as the batter stands it increases in viscosity; if it seems too thick as you work with it, more liquid can be added. When it seems too thin, add a little more flour.

Cooking

The real challenge in crepe making comes with the cooking. The trick is to coat the hot pan completely with a thin film of batter before it has a chance to cook. At the same time, you want the pancake to cook rapidly, otherwise it will stick to the pan or be unattractively gummy.

Essential to this skill is a *well-seasoned, hot* pan. An omelet pan with gently sloping sides is well suited for this purpose, although if you are a dedicated crepe maker with a large kitchen space you may prefer to get yourself a special crepe pan. No matter which pan you choose, it must be wiped evenly with oil and set over the heat until a few drops of water quickly bounce on the surface and disappear. Remember, "bounce" not "sizzle," or the pan will be too hot and the crepes may burn.

When you feel the pan is ready, lift it from the heat, pour a few tablespoons of batter into the center, and as you pour, quickly rotate your wrist so the batter forms a thin covering over the entire surface. (Any batter that does not adhere can be poured back into the bowl.) Now return the pan to the heat, and as soon as the pancake is set on the bottom, flip it over.

Flipping

You do not need a spatula for this step and, as a matter of fact, once your fingers are sufficiently conditioned, you won't require any utensils at all. In the beginning, however, you can loosen the crepe around the edges of the pan with the tip of a knife. Then quickly peel it from the pan with your fingers and turn it over. Don't be alarmed if the first crepe does not lift off smoothly. This frequently happens if the pan was not sufficiently heated and can be remedied by wiping the pan clean, rubbing it again with an oil-impregnated paper towel, and returning it to the stove to heat properly.

The second side of the crepe is cooked only until no longer damp, not long enough to become crisp. Thirty seconds should be adequate.

As each crepe is finished, it is transferred to a flat surface by flipping the pan over. A doubled tablecloth or towel placed on the counter makes an excellent surface to flip onto. Cover crepe loosely with a cloth to keep warm and soft for immediate filling, or leave uncovered to cool for storage. Do not stack crepes directly on top of one another as they will stick together and be impossible to separate.

Advance Preparation

Once you get going, making crepes develops a rhythm of its own, and somehow you are encouraged to prepare a lot at one time. When David worked as a waiter he observed chefs making hundreds of crepes in only a few hours, using the basic procedures we have outlined here.

Precooked crepes can be frozen for future use and defrosted and filled as needed. Cool crepes completely before wrapping and cover each one with a piece of foil, plastic wrap, or wax paper so it can be separated with ease later on. Before use crepes must be defrosted enough so that they can be rolled around the filling; this takes only about 15 minutes at room temperature.

Prefilled crepes can be frozen, but the degree of success varies with the filling. Blintzes and egg rolls, for example, do very well when stuffed and frozen for cooking later. However, crepes with a creamy filling have a tendency to become soggy if they are prefilled. If you insist on advance filling, wrap the package for baking in an aluminum freezer tray or foil-lined casserole and cover the crepes with a compatible sauce so that they do not dry out when they are cooked. When the time comes, pop the entire package directly from the freezer into a preheated oven.

The Value of Crepes

The crepe itself supplies a limited amount of protein, but in most cases the predominant nutritive value of the dish will come from the filling.

We will begin by giving some basic crepe recipes and then some suggested fillings and assembled crepe dishes. If you use a filling of your own, allow about 3 tablespoons per crepe, or 3 cups for 16 crepes, plus some extra for a sauce on top if desired. The filling should be quite thick so it does not run out or make the crepes soggy. What's left can be thinned to make a lighter sauce.

DINNER CREPES

This is a good all-around crepe.

1½ cups whole wheat flour
½ teaspoon salt
2 tablespoons oil
2 eggs
1 cup milk
½ to 1 cup water

Combine all ingredients, using ½ cup water, to make a smooth batter by hand, blender, or processor fitted with a plastic mixing blade. Let rest for 1 hour. Batter should be the consistency of heavy cream. Thin with additional water if necessary.

Heat crepe pan, wipe with oil, and cook crepes as directed in introductory notes, using about 3 tablespoons batter for each.

Makes 24 to 28 crepes; serves 6
Minor Protein
Variation: Replace ½ cup whole-wheat flour with rye or buckwheat. For *Spinach Crepes,* chop ½ pound spinach very fine; the processor is ideal for this purpose. Sprinkle with ¼ teaspoon salt and let rest about 30 minutes. Squeeze out all moisture. You should have ⅔ to ¾ cup dry spinach. Stir this into the batter after it has rested the specified amount of time. (Spinach can be prepared during the resting period.)

EGG CREPES

The most delicate crepe of all, this can be made for one person or many. It is highly recommended for homemade manicotti.

1 egg
2 tablespoons milk
salt
pepper

Beat egg with milk, using a fork or wire whisk. Season lightly.

Heat a 6-inch crepe or omelet pan as for all crepe making. When hot, wipe generously with oil.

Pour in about 2 tablespoons egg, tilt quickly to cover entire surface thinly, and cook until set on the bottom and lightly colored. Loosen edges with a knife, lift from pan with fingers, and place cooked-side down on kitchen cloth. Continue using all the egg.

Makes 4 crepes; serves 1
Minor Protein
Note: Obviously this can be made in any amount simply by adding more eggs and milk. When making a batch, don't worry if one or two stick at first. Save them to patch up any holes in later crepes, and if you run short at the end, you can always beat another egg and make four more.

HI-PROTEIN CREPES

A tender crepe that needs only 15 minutes resting time and is so nourishing it can be filled with almost anything and still provide a substantial dish.

⅔ cup cottage cheese
4 eggs
¼ cup whole wheat flour
1 tablespoon oil
¼ teaspoon salt
1 teaspoon honey, for sweet fillings (optional)

Combine all ingredients in a blender or processor and puree until smooth. Let rest for 15 minutes, then cook in a hot, oiled pan as for other crepes, using about 2 tablespoons batter for each.

Makes about 20 crepes; serves 4
Minor Protein
Menu Suggestions: For simple savory service, fill with Vegetable Cottage Cheese, roll, and eat as a snack or accompaniment to soup or salad. For sweet service, spread with a little honey or jam, top with sliced fruit and a dollop of yogurt, roll and eat as a light meal or dessert.

MANICOTTI

In its original form, manicotti was made with thin crepes, not commercial noodles. This version is particularly delicate and flavorful and worth the trouble of making the pancakes from scratch.

2 cups ricotta cheese
2 cups shredded mozzarella and provolone cheeses, combined in any proportion
¾ cup grated Parmesan cheese
⅓ cup minced parsley
¼ teaspoon nutmeg
pepper
16 Hi Protein or Egg Crepes (page 212)
2 cups Italian Tomato Sauce (page 317) or any well-seasoned tomato sauce

Preheat oven to 350° to 375°F.
Combine ricotta, mozzarella, provolone, ½ cup Parmesan, parsley, and seasonings.
Place about 3 tablespoons of mixture in a sausage shape in the center of each crepe and roll.
Place crepes close together in a single layer in a 9 x 13-inch baking dish. Spoon tomato sauce over all, and sprinkle with remaining ¼ cup Parmesan.
Bake until hot and creamy, about 15 minutes.

Serves 4
Major Protein
Note: Crepes can be made well in advance, or the entire dish can be assembled and refrigerated or frozen. If baked from the frozen state, keep covered during baking for about 30 minutes until defrosted throughout; remove cover and bake 10 minutes longer until cheese melts and sauce is bubbly.

MUSHROOM–SPINACH CREPES

1 tablespoon oil or butter
½ pound mushrooms, chopped
2 cups chopped spinach
½ cup chopped walnuts
16 to 20 thin slices provolone cheese
16 to 20 Dinner Crepes (page 212)

Preheat oven to 350°F.
Heat fat in a skillet and sauté mushrooms until tender, about 5 minutes. Add spinach; cover and cook for 5 minutes until wilted. Remove from heat and stir in walnuts.
Place 1 slice provolone to cover the

pale side of each crepe. Drain moisture from mushroom filling and place 1 tablespoon on each crepe. Roll.

Place crepes side by side in an oiled baking dish. More than one layer of crepes can be made if necessary.

Tear any remaining cheese into small pieces and place over crepes. Spoon any remaining filling on top.

Bake for 10 minutes until cheese melts.

Serves 4

Major Protein

Note: If crepes are assembled ahead and refrigerated, increase baking time to 15 minutes.

FRESH TOMATO-FILLED CREPES

Especially good in Spinach Crepes, but suitable to any crepe you choose.

2 pounds tomatoes, coarsely chopped (about 5 cups)
2 tablespoons butter
2 tablespoons chopped fresh basil
¼ teaspoon salt
pepper
½ to ¾ cup yogurt
½ to ¾ cup sour cream
16 crepes of choice

Cook chopped tomatoes in butter along with basil for 5 to 10 minutes until softened. Season with salt and pepper and remove from heat. Let cool for 10 minutes or longer until lukewarm.

Stir ½ cup each yogurt and sour cream into tomato mixture.

Preheat oven to 350°F.

Roll crepes around filling and place side by side in a baking dish. Mix any leftover filling with additional yogurt and sour cream to make a little sauce for the top. Spoon over crepes.

Bake for about 10 minutes to warm through.

Serves 4

Major Protein

Note: Entire dish can be pre-made and refrigerated. Increase baking time by about 5 minutes, or until well heated.

CREAMED CARROT AND ZUCCHINI CREPES

2 tablespoons butter
4 cups diced zucchini
4 cups diced carrot
½ cup chopped green pepper
1 teaspoon Dijon mustard
½ teaspoon salt
1½ cups yogurt
1½ tablespoons arrowroot or corn-starch
sour cream
16 to 18 crepes of choice

Melt butter in a large skillet. Add vegetables, cover, and stew for 10 minutes to soften. Stir in mustard and salt.

Combine yogurt and starch; stir in a little hot vegetable mixture to temper, then gradually stir yogurt back into skillet. Cook over low heat, stirring until thick.

Preheat oven to 350°F.

Roll filling inside crepes, place side by side in an oiled baking pan, top with dollops of sour cream, and bake for 10 minutes, or until heated through.

Serves 4

Major Protein

Note: Filling and crepes can be made in advance, but assembly is best done shortly before baking.

BLINTZES

Blintzes are another specialty rooted in kosher dairy cuisine. Each individual blintz is composed of a thin crepe totally enclosing a filling of pot cheese, potato, kasha, or fruit. This neat little bundle is pan-fried so that it is crisp outside and hot and tender within. In form it is actually much like an egg roll, but of course the latter is filled with vegetables and cooked to a much crunchier texture by deep-frying.

Blintz Crepes
2 eggs
½ cup whole wheat flour
¾ cup milk
⅛ teaspoon salt
1 tablespoon oil

Combine all ingredients to a smooth batter in a blender, processor, or with a hand beater.

Heat pan until water dances on the surface; rub with oil and cook as for crepes, using about 1 tablespoon batter for a 6-inch crepe, 2 tablespoons for an 8-inch crepe. Cook on one side only and turn cooked-side up onto a clean kitchen towel or doubled tablecloth.

When all crepes are cooked, fill as directed below.

Makes 16 small or 8 large crepes; serves 4

Note: Don't forget that the first crepe in the batch is often a throwaway.

Blintz Fillings

(Fills 16 small or 8 large crepes.)

Cheese

> **2 pounds (4 cups) farmer or pot-style cottage cheese**
> **2 egg yolks or 1 egg yolk plus 2 tablespoons whole wheat flour**
> **¼ cup honey**
> **pinch salt**
> **cinnamon**

Mash all ingredients with a fork until evenly mixed.

Note: Do not use regular cottage cheese as the filling will be too wet.

Kasha

> **2 tablespoons oil**
> **1½ cups chopped onion**
> **1 cup uncooked kasha**
> **3 cups boiling water**
> **1 teaspoon salt**

Heat oil in a 1½- to 2-quart pot and sauté onion over medium heat for about 10 minutes until golden. Stir in grain and sauté for a minute or two. Add the boiling water and salt. Cover pot, reduce heat to low, and cook until liquid is absorbed, 15 to 20 minutes. Remove cover to dry slightly.

Note: Filling can be cooking while crepes are being made, or it can be made in advance and used even after it has chilled.

Potato

> **about 2 pounds potatoes**
> **1½ cups chopped onions**
> **2 tablespoons oil**
> **¼ cup nonfat dry milk powder**
> **1 teaspoon salt**
> **pepper**

Cut potatoes into quarters and steam until tender, 15 to 20 minutes. Press through a food mill or sieve to form a smooth, thick puree.

While potatoes steam, sauté onions in oil until golden, about 10 minutes over moderate heat.

Combine sieved potatoes, sautéed onions, and remaining ingredients.

Note: As this filling demands a little attention, it is best prepared before the crepes. For an unconventional potato filling, add ½ cup shredded cheddar cheese.

Assembly and Cooking

> **crepes**
> **filling of choice**
> **oil/butter**

For each large crepe, spread about ½ cup filling in a line about 2 inches from the edge. For small crepes, follow same procedure, using ¼ cup filling and positioning it about 1½ inches from the edge.

Fold sides over filling, as illustrated below, then roll, starting with the end the filling is on.

To cook, heat butter alone or combined with oil to cover the surface of the skillet. Place blintzes seam-side down in hot fat and brown on the bottom, 3 to 5 minutes over moderate heat. Turn and brown the other side.

Serve hot, topping as suggested below.

Serves 4

Major Protein when topping is included

Note: Blintzes are often made with two different fillings for variety. (Either double the batter recipe or divide the filling recipes in half.)

Blintzes can be cooked in the oven, where they will become firm but not crisp. Place in a single layer in a greased, shallow baking pan and bake in a 400°F. oven for 10 minutes. Baked blintzes are good but cannot rival the pan-fried.

If blintzes are not cooked immediately after filling, they should be refrigerated or, if they are to be held longer than a day, frozen. To cook frozen blintzes, sauté in hot fat as for regular cooking, but keep the heat medium low and cover until bottom is brown, 5 to 8 minutes. Turn, replace cover, and cook for 5 minutes longer, or until brown on the other side.

Toppings

Serve Kasha Blintzes and Potato Blintzes with Whipped Cottage Cream.

Serve Cheese Blintzes with yogurt and either diced fresh fruit, honey, or preserves. If desired, a little sour cream can be combined with either of these toppings, but sour cream alone is not recommended.

MU SHU VEGETABLES WITH MANDARIN PANCAKES

If you wish to entertain with a Chinese meal, these chapati-like pancakes, filled with vegetables and rolled at the table, are a first-rate dish. Although preparation of the pancakes is time-consuming, it can be done in advance. This recipe even allows for extra pancakes to be frozen for another time. The filling can be assembled at any time but should not be cooked until just before service.

For Mandarin Pancakes

1¾ cups whole wheat flour
¼ cup soy flour
¾ cup boiling water
about 2 tablespoons Chinese sesame oil or plain oil

Combine flours in a mixing bowl. Make a well in the center and add boiling water. Stir to make a soft dough.

Knead dough on a lightly oiled surface for about 10 minutes until smooth and elastic. Cover with a damp cloth and let rest for 15 minutes.

Divide dough in half and roll ¼ inch thick. Cut into 2½-inch rounds with a cookie cutter or a glass. Reroll outtakes. Yield should be at least 24 rounds.

Wipe surface of half the rounds with sesame or plain oil. Top with the remaining rounds to form small sandwiches.

Roll one at a time with a rolling pin, pressing gently from the center out in all directions to keep shape uniform and turning to work on both sides until you have a pancake 6 inches in diameter. Pancakes can be rolled all at once and covered with a cloth until time to cook, or can be rolled one at a time while the previous one cooks.

To cook, heat an 8- to 10-inch omelet pan over medium-high heat. When quite hot, turn heat low and cook one pancake at a time until each side is set but not browned. This will require ½ to 1 minute per side. As they are finished, remove from pan and gently peel apart. Transfer to a flat surface and keep covered with a cloth so they remain pliable. Continue until all are cooked.

When completed, there will be about 24 pancakes; 3 pancakes make a good-size serving. Divide into stacks, based on how many you will use at a sitting (a stack of 12 serves 4), and wrap in a packet with foil. Reserve until 15 minutes before the meal. If preparation is done well in advance, refrigerate or, for long-term use, freeze.

Shortly before serving, place foil-wrapped pancakes over boiling water in a vegetable steamer. Steam for 15 minutes. Bring pancakes to the table in the foil wrapper and remove as needed.

Makes 24 pancakes

Note: Recipe may make more than 24 pancakes, which can come in handy because pancakes are sometimes hard to peel apart.

Since the filling is for 12 pancakes, the pancake recipe can be halved, or the extras frozen for future use. Restore by steaming (still frozen in foil wrapper) for 20 minutes.

For Vegetable Filling

6 cups assorted vegetables cut in very thin strips (carrots, celery, green

beans, zucchini, mushrooms, green pepper, broccoli stalks, shredded greens, sprouts, and reconstituted dried Chinese vegetables, such as tiger lily buds and bean thread)
4 scallions, cut in slivers
3 eggs, beaten
3 tablespoons soy sauce
1½ tablespoons sherry
½ teaspoon salt
½ teaspoon honey
1 teaspoon cornstarch or arrowroot
2 tablespoons oil
1 teaspoon Chinese sesame oil

Combine all vegetables. Beat eggs and set aside. Combine soy sauce, sherry, salt, honey, and starch.

About 10 minutes before the meal, while pancakes are steaming, heat oil in a wok or large skillet and stir-fry vegetables for 5 minutes. Add eggs, cook until set, and then scramble into vegetables.

Stir soy sauce mixture into vegetables and cook until thickened.

Turn off heat, stir in sesame oil, cover, and serve as soon as possible.

Makes enough filling for 12 pancakes

Assembly
12 Mandarin Pancakes
Vegetable Filling

Place hot steamed pancake flat on a plate; spoon some of the filling in the center. Fold opposite sides over filling, then fold in remaining ends to form a neat bundle. Pick up with hands and take a bite. As you eat, filling will fall out here and there, and the pancake will begin to leak juice; never mind, it will taste delicious and you will have an enjoyable if messy time. Do not serve to anyone inhibited about handling their food.

Serves 4
Minor Protein

CHEESE ENCHILADAS

The Mexican crepe.

3 cups shredded Jack cheese alone or combined with cheddar
⅓ cup yogurt
½ cup chopped onion
2 cups Enchilada Sauce (page 317)
12 cornmeal tortillas

Preheat oven to 350°F.

Mix cheese, yogurt, and onion until evenly combined.

Heat Enchilada Sauce to boiling and, holding a tortilla with tongs, dip into hot sauce briefly until pliable. Place 2 rounded tablespoons cheese filling in a strip along the center and roll tortilla to completely cover. Place seam-side down in a large, shallow, oiled baking pan.

Continue with each tortilla, placing them side by side in the pan, but not on top of one another. If desired, casserole can be refrigerated at this time for cooking later.

When ready to cook, spoon remaining sauce over filled tortillas and bake for about 10 minutes, or until cheese melts and sauce is bubbly. If chilled, increase cooking time to 15 or 20 minutes.

Serves 4 (or 6 at a larger meal as one of several entrées)
Major Protein
Note: Leftovers can be refrigerated or frozen. Frozen enchiladas should be reheated covered in a 375°F. oven for about 30 minutes, or until cheese melts and sauce bubbles.

FRIED TACOS

Soft tortillas, folded over your choice of filling and pan-fried until they are just chewy. As with many such dishes, the filling ingredients are variable and so are the serving sizes, depending largely on what else is offered with them. Thus, we provide the general pattern and leave you to adapt it to your needs. We generally allow 2 tacos per serving.

shredded lettuce
radishes
olives
2 cups filling (see suggestions below)
8 cornmeal tortillas
oil
any Mexican tomato sauce
6 tablespoons yogurt mixed with 2 tablespoons sour cream

After you have assembled all the ingredients, prepare the serving platter by covering it with shredded greens and garnishing it with radishes and olives and any other condiments you choose.

Place about ¼ cup filling on half of each tortilla without going right to the edge. Fold in half to cover filling. Don't worry if it doesn't hold; this can be remedied during cooking.

Heat enough oil to generously cover the surface of a large skillet. Place tortillas in hot oil without crowding and cook quickly until lightly colored but not crisp (this is the preferred way in South America). Press gently with a spatula to keep tortilla folded over filling, then turn and cook the other side.

Tacos should not be greasy, but if they are, blot with absorbent paper and place on the prepared platter. Serve while still hot; garnish to taste at the table with tomato sauce and yogurt mixed with sour cream.

Makes 8 tacos; serves 4 to 8
Minor Protein
Suggested Fillings: Refried beans with or without added cheese; pot-style cottage cheese mixed with green chilies; any thick bean stew; Mexican Vegetables (page 147); Sunflower Squash (page 252) combined with sliced cheddar or Jack cheese; mashed potatoes combined with sliced cheddar or Jack cheese. Or use your imagination.

TACOS WITH SPECIAL BEAN FILLING

This is an especially festive variation of the Fried Taco. As in the previous recipe, present on a platter of shredded greens garnished with olives, radishes, tomato wedges, chili peppers, and any other decorative condiments. Offer Chili Sauce or a similar sauce at the table for individual spicing.

> 2½ cups cooked white or pink beans, drained
> ½ cup chopped olives
> ½ cup chopped raisins
> ¾ cup toasted pumpkin seeds, chopped (see directions for toasting, page 298)
> 1 teaspoon cumin
> 2 eggs, lightly beaten
> 12 cornmeal tortillas
> oil

Mash beans lightly with a fork and add olives, raisins, pumpkin seeds, and cumin.

Dip tortillas one by one into egg to moisten both sides and place about 2 tablespoons filling down the center. Fold and secure with a toothpick.

Heat enough oil to cover the surface of a heavy skillet. When hot, sauté the tacos about 3 to 5 minutes on each side until lightly colored but not crisp enough to break.

Serve while still hot on the garnished platter.

Serves 4 (6 if only one of several entrées)
Major Protein
Note: Toasting pumpkin seeds in a dry skillet greatly enhances their flavor and makes them easier to chop or crush; untoasted pumpkin seeds can be used if preferred.

SAVORY PASTRIES

Savory pastries can take the familiar form of pies and tarts, or may be composed of a filling entirely encased in dough, as in turnovers. Probably the most famous example of a savory pastry is pizza. Other well-known favorites include the French-inspired quiche, Greek cheese-and-spinach pies, knishes, and Russian piroshki.

Many people seem to be in awe of working with any kind of dough. We have simplified the dough-making procedure as much as possible with some crust recipes that can tolerate an inordinate amount of handling and abuse. These are clearly marked, and if you have any fear of pastry-making, try one and see if you don't change your mind. We hope you will not be put off by the mystique often associated with some of these dishes, for actually they are among the easiest and most rewarding. For some reason, even a rather mundane filling placed inside a pastry shell makes a very impressive dish.

There are a number of different crusts that can be used for savory pastries, with the simplest molded from bread and rolls. A little more effort extends the range to common pie crusts, quick-leavened biscuit-type doughs, cream puff shells, and breadlike yeast doughs. Within each of these categories there are endless modifications in terms of both ingredients and final shaping.

Most of the doughs used for savory pastries freeze well but lose quality after one to three months. It is preferable to shape them first; they are easier to handle before freezing and will be ready to use immediately. Pies and tarts are best frozen unfilled and unbaked. Pastries in which the filling is completely sealed, including knishes, turnovers, and piroshki, can be frozen filled, either unbaked or prebaked as directed in the recipe.

To prevent sogginess, fill shells just prior to serving or baking. Often the pastry can be partially baked to insure crispness, then filled and baked completely.

Savory pastries may come to the table hot or cold and the fillings can be even more varied and imaginative than the vessel in which they are contained.

Cooked, chilled vegetables bound with mayonnaise, yogurt, or a cheese paste may show up in pastry shells as a first course or warm weather entrée, as can a cold, marinated rice or bean salad. Vegetables, beans, or grains may also be bound together with a thick white sauce or gravy and served piping hot inside a crust. These are most commonly presented in individual shells or as sealed turnovers.

Custard fillings (as in quiche) are generally baked directly in an unbaked or partially baked crust. They taste best when allowed to sit for 10 to 15 minutes after baking but should be served while still warm and fresh. For convenience, however, they are often served at room temperature or reheated, although both these practices may render the crust somewhat soggy.

In the recipes that follow, you will find savory pastries that are designed to be the featured item on the menu. Additional recipes can be found in "Appetizers and Hors d'Oeuvres" and "Side Dishes: Savory Pastry Accompaniments." You can enjoy these recipes as they are presented, or use them to spark your imagination for similar creations of your own.

PIZZA

Pizza is probably the most widely consumed savory pastry in America, and while it needs no introduction, it is worth pointing out that it is as nourishing as it is enjoyable to eat, especially when the crust is a whole grain variety.

You will find several variations of pizza in these pages. This is the classic one, made with a yeast-leavened crust, and thus it requires enough advance planning so that the dough can rise (a minimum of two hours). Directions for preparing the dough well ahead of time are contained in the recipe notes.

Pizza Dough
1 tablespoon yeast
1 cup plus 2 tablespoons warm water
1 teaspoon salt
1 teaspoon honey
1 tablespoon oil
2½ to 3 cups whole wheat flour
cornmeal

Soften yeast in 2 tablespoons warm water in a large mixing bowl.

In about 5 minutes, when yeast is dissolved, add remaining 1 cup water, salt, honey, oil, and 2 cups flour, beating with a wooden spoon until dough becomes too hard to manipulate.

Turn dough out onto a well-floured surface and knead in remaining flour as necessary to make a smooth dough. Knead for 5 to 10 minutes.

Place dough in an oiled bowl. Turn so that entire surface is greased, cover with a cloth, and let rise in a warm spot a minimum of 2 hours or as long as 10 hours.

When you are ready to assemble the pizza, punch down the dough, let rest for 5 to 10 minutes to make handling easier, then divide in half, and shape.

For two large pizzas, roll each half of dough into a 12- to 14-inch circle. For two-person pizzas, roll each half of dough into two 8-inch circles. The crust should be about ¼ inch thick. As you roll the dough, turn it over several times to make shaping easier. When proper size and thickness are obtained, place on a baking sheet or pizza pan dusted with cornmeal and, with your fingers, push dough from the center toward the edge to thin the bottom crust and provide a thick rim around the circle. Pizza is now ready to fill as directed below.

Makes 2 large or 4 small pizza crusts
Note: As pizza is something you will probably want to make again, the dough recipe is enough for 2 large pies; if you don't consume both of them at once, you have something to put in the freezer for the future. Wrap extra dough in a ball in freezer paper after it has risen. To use, unwrap frozen dough, place in a bowl in a warm spot, cover, and let return to room temperature for several hours. If you have enough room in the freezer, the crust can be frozen pre-shaped, in which case thawing before use will not be necessary. The prepared dough can also be refrigerated after rising if you will not be using it the same day. Remove from the refrigerator for 30 minutes before shaping so it is at room temperature.

If desired, ¼ cup soy flour can be added and the amount of whole wheat flour adjusted as necessary.

Fresh Tomato Pizza
   ½ **Pizza Dough recipe (or one 14-inch or two 8-inch crusts)**
   1½ cups shredded mozzarella cheese
   2 medium tomatoes, sliced
   1 teaspoon oregano
   ½ teaspoon dried basil
   salt
   pepper
   1 tablespoon grated Parmesan cheese
   1 tablespoon olive oil

Preheat oven to 425°F.
Scatter mozzarella over crust to just inside the edge. Cover with sliced tomatoes. Sprinkle with oregano, basil, a few pinches of salt, and a few turns of the pepper mill. Top evenly with Parmesan and oil.

Bake for 15 to 20 minutes until crust is crisp and golden around the edges and cheese is gooey.
Makes 1 large or 2 small pizzas; serves 4
   Major Protein
   Variations: For *Regular Tomato Pizza,* replace fresh tomatoes with 1½ cups drained, mashed, canned tomatoes or 1 to 1½ cups tomato sauce. Spread tomatoes directly on crust, top with shredded mozzarella, season, and proceed as for Fresh Tomato Pizza. It is best not to assemble this pizza until just before baking to prevent sogginess.

If desired, top pizza with fresh sliced mushrooms, green pepper slices, sliced olives, pickled hot pepper strips, or other flavoring of choice before sprinkling with Parmesan cheese and oil.
   Menu Suggestions: When coupled with an antipasto platter of various vegetables, beans, and condiments, pizza can be built into an elaborate meal.

BISCUIT-CRUST PIZZA

A very good spur-of-the-moment pizza can be made by using biscuit dough rather than a yeast-leavened crust. This makes a thicker, cakier base, more like the Sicilian-style pie.

Biscuit Crust
   2¼ cups whole wheat flour
   ¼ cup wheat germ
   3 teaspoons baking powder
   ½ teaspoon salt
   ¼ cup oil
   1 teaspoon honey
   ⅔ cup water
   Cornmeal

Topping
   2 cups drained canned or stewed tomatoes, or 1½ cups tomato sauce
   1½ cups shredded mozzarella cheese
   ¼ cup grated Parmesan cheese
   salt
   pepper
   oregano
   oil

Preheat oven to 425°F.

Combine the flour, wheat germ, baking powder, and salt in a large mixing bowl.

Pour in the oil and mix with a fork until it is evenly dispersed.

Add the honey and water all at once and mix dough gently and thoroughly until it holds together. If it is too crumbly, add a few more tablespoons water as needed.

Oil a jellyroll pan, 14-inch pizza pan, or baking sheet and dust with cornmeal. Moisten hands and press dough gently into pan to form a *thin* crust over the entire surface. Keep dough uniform in thickness and do not raise the crust at the edges. Bake for about 8 minutes.

Spread the tomatoes over the entire crust area. Top with the cheeses. Season lightly with salt and generously with pepper and oregano. Drizzle a little oil over all.

Return to the oven for 12 to 15 minutes.

Serves 3 to 4
Major Protein

CALZONE

A turnover of Italian descent in which a pizza dough crust encloses a savory ricotta cheese filling.

½ Pizza Dough recipe (page 219)
1½ cups ricotta cheese
1 cup shredded mozzarella cheese
½ cup shredded provolone cheese
½ teaspoon oregano
pepper
salt
cornmeal

Preheat oven to 425°F.

Roll pizza dough into 4 circles, each 7 to 8 inches round and ⅛ inch thick.

Combine remaining ingredients except cornmeal for filling.

Place about ¾ cup filling to cover half of each round, leaving ½ inch dough uncovered at edge. Fold dough over filling, stretching gently and carefully so dough does not tear. Pinch edges together and roll bottom edge over top; pinch with fingers as for pie crust edge.

Place on a baking sheet that has been lightly floured or dusted with cornmeal. Dampen surface of each calzone with wet hands or a pastry brush dipped in water.

Bake for 15 minutes until crust is firm, crisp, and golden.

Serves 4
Major Protein
Note: Best freshly made but can be reheated if necessary.

BEAN-STUFFED PITA POCKETS

These bread pockets can be stuffed with a variety of bean mixtures for a delicious and filling sandwich. Use the suggestions below to trigger your imagination for similar sandwiches using other hot bean dishes and salads from these pages.

When cutting pita bread for sandwiches there are two possibilities. The bread can be cut across the middle into half moons, or sliced along the top for one large, filled sandwich. Either way you will need from ⅔ to 1 cup filling per bread and one bread per person.

Indian Bean Pita
2 whole wheat pita breads
½ cup yogurt
1 cup Quick Curried Beans (page 258)
¾ cup alfalfa or bean sprouts
½ cup chopped tomato

Warm pita breads and cut as desired. Open gently and spread with a little yogurt.

Stuff with beans and some of each vegetable and top with more yogurt.

Serves 2
Major Protein

Mexican Bean Pita
2 whole wheat pita breads
½ cup Enchilada Sauce (page 317)
1 cup Chili (page 43)
¾ cup shredded lettuce
½ cup chopped tomato
½ cup shredded cheddar cheese

Warm pita breads and cut as desired. Open gently and spread with a little sauce.

Stuff with chili, some of each vegetable, and top with more sauce. Sprinkle cheese on top.

Serves 2
Major Protein

Mideast Bean Pita

¼ cup boiling water
2 tablespoons cracked wheat
2 cups cooked white beans or chick-peas, drained
2 tablespoons minced parsley
2 tablespoons minced scallion
1 teaspoon crushed dried mint
2 tablespoons lemon juice
4 whole wheat pita breads
1 cup Yogurt–Tahini Sauce (page 319)

Pour boiling water over cracked wheat in a bowl and let stand while preparing remaining ingredients. Drain and squeeze dry.

Combine beans, parsley, scallion, mint, lemon juice, and soaked cracked wheat.

Warm breads and cut as desired. Open gently and spread with a little Yogurt–Tahini Sauce.

Fill with bean mixture and top with remaining sauce.

Serves 4
Major Protein

Bean Salad Pita

2 cups cooked drained beans
2 tablespoons lemon juice
2 tablespoons oil
1 teaspoon oregano
½ teaspoon cumin
½ teaspoon salt (omit if beans are salted)
pepper
2 tablespoons minced parsley
1 clove garlic, minced (optional)
¼ cup chopped onion (optional)
¼ cup chopped sweet pepper (optional)
2 medium tomatoes, diced
½ medium cucumber, peeled and diced
¾ cup (3 ounces) diced feta, mozzarella, cheddar, Jack, provolone, or Muenster cheese
4 whole wheat pita breads

Combine all ingredients except bread (including optional ingredients of choice). Let marinate for 30 minutes or longer. Mixture can be made a day or two in advance for use as needed.

Cut pita breads as desired and stuff with bean salad.

Serves 4
Major Protein

PAN BAGNIA

A main-dish sandwich from the South of France, best described as a salad on bread.

3 tablespoons wine vinegar
6 tablespoons oil (at least half olive preferred)
1 clove garlic, split
¼ teaspoon dried basil or a few fresh leaves
¼ teaspoon salt
pepper
1 cup shredded lettuce
1 cup cooked chick-peas, drained
2 hard-cooked eggs, sliced
1 tomato, cut in thin half-slices
2 tablespoons capers
1 small red onion, thinly sliced
8 pimiento-stuffed or plain green olives, cut up
4 Hero Rolls (page 345) or Crusty Sandwich Rolls (page 343)

Make a dressing with vinegar, oil, and seasonings.

Combine lettuce, chick-peas, eggs, tomato, capers, onion, and olives and mix with dressing.

Slice rolls for sandwiches. Pull out some of the soft center and save for bread crumbs or the birds.

Brush cut bread surfaces with a little of the dressing. Fill with salad mixture and press closed.

Serves 4
Major Protein
Menu Suggestions: Ricotta–Cucumber Salad or Ricotta–Potato Salad provides an excellent accompaniment.

TUNISIAN SANDWICHES

Sandwiches such as these, served on crusty rolls with a variety of vegetables and a spicy sauce inside, are very popular on the Parisian Left Bank. Even the tradition-oriented French are willing to accept new influences on their cuisine, especially one as tantalizing as this.

> 3 tablespoons wine vinegar
> 6 tablespoons oil (at least half olive preferred)
> ¼ teaspoon salt
> pepper
> 1 cup shredded lettuce
> 1½ cups sliced cooked potato (1 large or 2 medium)
> 4 Crusty Sandwich Rolls (page 343)
> 1 cup cooked chick-peas, drained
> 8 pickled hot peppers
> 4 slices tomato
> 8 olives, sliced
> ½ cup or more Fiery Tunisian Sauce (page 309)

Make a dressing with vinegar, oil, salt, and pepper. Combine ¼ cup with the lettuce in one bowl and 3 tablespoons with potatoes in another.

Slice rolls for sandwiches. Brush a little remaining dressing on the bottom half. Then layer ingredients as follows: lettuce, beans, potato, peppers, tomato, and olives.

Spread about 2 tablespoons of Tunisian Sauce on the top half of the roll, cover, and serve. More sauce can be added to taste while eating.

Serves 4

Minor Protein

Menu Suggestions: While this is adequate for a "walk-away" meal, if you serve it at the table, add a yogurt-cucumber salad to cool the palate and add to the protein.

SEALED SANDWICHES

A sandwich with the filling baked right inside.

For the Bread
> 1 tablespoon yeast
> ¾ cup warm water
> 1 tablespoon honey
> 1 teaspoon salt
> ¼ cup nonfat dry milk powder
> 1¾ to 2 cups whole wheat flour
> 1 cup shredded cheddar cheese

Sprinkle yeast over ¼ cup warm water in a large mixing bowl and let stand about 5 minutes to soften. Stir to combine.

Add remaining water, honey, salt, and dry milk to yeast. Vigorously beat in 1 cup of flour and the cheese. Add additional flour to form a dough you can turn out of the bowl and knead.

Flour work surface and knead dough, adding remaining flour as necessary. Knead for 3 to 5 minutes.

Cover dough and let stand for 15 minutes. Meanwhile prepare filling.

For the Filling
> 2 cups cooked beans, coarsely chopped or ground
> ½ teaspoon salt (omit if beans are salted)
> pepper
> ¼ cup chopped pickle or relish (for homemade varieties, see recipes on pages 437–440)
> 2 tablespoons minced onion
> 2 tablespoons catsup
> soy sauce

Combine all ingredients, adding a little soy sauce to taste.

Assembly

Divide dough in half and roll each half into a thin square 10 x 10 inches. Cut each square in half and each half into thirds to make 6 rectangles, 3 inches x 5 inches, from each half of dough.

Place 2 tablespoons filling on each piece of dough and fold dough over filling. Pinch all around edges to seal and press with tines of fork for decorative trim. Cut three small slits in top to allow steam to escape during baking.

Place on a greased baking sheet, cover, and let rise in a warm place for 45 minutes to 1½ hours.

If you wish to bake sandwiches later than this, refrigerate immediately after filling and let rise before baking.

Preheat oven to 400°F. Bake for 12 to 15 minutes until nicely browned.

Cool a few minutes before serving, or serve at room temperature.

Makes 12 sandwiches; serves 6 as an entrée

Major Protein (one sandwich as an accompaniment provides a Minor Protein)

Note: Freeze any extras after baking. For a portable lunch, take directly from the freezer in the morning. By lunch time sandwiches will be ready to eat.

Menu Suggestions: Serve with soup or salad for a complete meal.

CORNISH PASTIES

This substantial vegetable turnover originated in Cornwall, England, where the tradition was to carve the initials of each family member into their pastie crust. Pasties are filling enough to be a main dish with a generous soup or salad, and they also make a nice portable lunch.

1 medium onion, coarsely chopped
1 large carrot, finely chopped
½ cup coarsely chopped turnip
½ pound potatoes, finely chopped (about 1¼ cups)
1½ cups cooked beans, drained
1 tablespoon oil
pepper
about ½ teaspoon salt
Cheddar Pastry (page 229), chilled

Measure vegetables, but do not combine. You should have about 4 cups; add more if you do not, since filling cooks down.

Heat oil in a small saucepan and sauté onion for 3 to 5 minutes until tender. Add carrot, turnip, and potato; cover and cook for 5 minutes. Remove from heat and stir in beans. Add a generous amount of pepper and salt to taste.

Preheat oven to 400°F.

Roll pastry ⅛ inch thick and cut into eight 6-inch rounds. Place ¼ cup filling on each round and fold into half circles. With moistened fingers, pinch edges together and roll gently to seal. Cut two 1-inch slits on top of each pastie.

Place pasties on an oiled baking sheet. (If not baked at once, cover and chill.) Bake for 15 minutes; reduce heat to 350°F. and bake for about 20 minutes longer, or until nicely browned. Serve warm or at room temperature.

Makes 8 turnovers; serves 8

Minor Protein

Note: If you do not need 8 at once, unbaked pasties may be stored in the freezer for up to 6 months. Bake as directed for unfrozen pasties, reducing the heat after 15 minutes, and continuing to bake until brown.

VEGETABLE STRUDEL

A savory vegetable filling encased in dough is an attractive dish for entertaining. The filling need not follow strict rules but can be varied to suit your pantry and your taste buds.

For the Strudel Dough
1½ cups whole wheat flour
½ teaspoon baking powder
¼ teaspoon salt
½ tablespoon oil
1 egg, separated
¼ cup water

Combine dry ingredients in a mixing bowl. Stir in oil, egg yolk, and water. (Save egg white for later.) Mix with your hands until dough holds together.

Turn dough onto a work surface wiped with oil and knead for a full 10 minutes until as stiff and smooth as modeling clay.

Drape a cloth over the dough or cover with an inverted mixing bowl and let rest for 30 minutes.

For the Strudel Filling
4 cups shredded mixed vegetables including onion, leek, or scallion, carrot, some leafy greens, green pepper, zucchini, celery, green beans, etc.
2 tablespoons oil
¼ cup soy flour
2 tablespoons water
2 tablespoons soy sauce

¼ cup chopped parsley
1 cup cooked grain
1 cup crumbled farmer cheese, tofu,
   or shredded cheese
salt
pepper

Stew shredded vegetables in oil in a covered pot for 10 minutes. Make a paste of soy flour, water, and soy sauce. Stir into vegetables and cook for 2 to 3 minutes until very thick. Remove from heat and cool slightly. (Roll dough during this time.)

Add parsley, grain, and cheese or tofu to vegetables and season with salt and pepper to taste.

Assembly
Strudel Dough
Strudel Filling
oil
egg white
sesame seeds

Preheat oven to 375°F. Divide dough in half and roll each into a 12-inch square as thin as possible. Brush surface with oil.

Put half of filling in a thick strip down the center of each square of dough. Fold one side of dough over filling, then roll gently to completely encase. Pinch ends to seal and place seam-side down on an oiled baking sheet. Beat reserved egg white and brush over the surface of each roll, (crust can be rubbed with oil instead). Sprinkle with sesame seeds.

Bake for 20 to 25 minutes until crust is crisp and golden. Serve warm but not hot, letting strudel cool for at least 10 minutes before cutting.

Makes 2 rolls; serves 6 to 8
Minor Protein
Note: If desired, dough can be prepared as much as a day in advance, refrigerated immediately after kneading, then allowed to sit at room temperature for 30 minutes before being rolled. Baked strudel can be reheated and, if you only need one roll at a time, the extra roll can be frozen after baking. To use, bake, still wrapped, in a 350°F. oven for 20 minutes, then uncover and bake about 10 minutes longer, until crisp.

ONION SHORTCAKE

An easy-to-assemble onion "cake."

   2 tablespoons butter/oil
   3 cups thinly sliced onions
   3 tablespoons soy sauce
   1 pound tofu
   2 eggs
   ¼ teaspoon salt
   4 to 6 slices whole grain bread
   ½ cup grated cheese (optional)

Heat fat in a skillet, add onions and soy sauce, cover and stew over low heat for 10 minutes.

Preheat oven to 350°F.

Puree tofu in a blender or processor fitted with a plastic mixing blade. Quickly mix in eggs and salt.

Butter the bottom of a 9 x 13-inch casserole and cover with bread, cutting slices as necessary to cover pan completely. Spread stewed onions on bread. Spread tofu mixture evenly over onions. Sprinkle with cheese if desired.

Bake for about 25 minutes until top is firm. Let rest for 5 to 10 minutes before cutting. Cut into squares to serve.

Serves 4 to 6
Major Protein
Note: This recipe is easily divided to serve 2; bake in a shallow 1-quart pan. To serve 8 to 12, double the recipe, but use only 3 eggs and 5 tablespoons soy sauce. Bake in two 9 x 13-inch pans.
Variation: Tofu can be replaced with 1½ cups yogurt. Beat in eggs by hand; do not use a blender or processor.

Menu Suggestions: Serve with a cooked green or orange vegetable accompaniment and a salad.

BROCCOLI CUSTARD PIE

   1 unbaked 9-inch crust (Cornmeal
      Crust, Rye-Oat Pastry, or Savory
      Soy Crust, pages 228–229)
   2 cups broccoli buds, finely chopped
   3 eggs
   1 cup yogurt
   ¼ cup mayonnaise
   ½ teaspoon prepared mustard
   ¼ teaspoon hot pepper sauce (omit if
      mustard is spicy)
   1 tablespoon dill
   ¾ cup shredded cheddar cheese

Preheat oven to 400°F.

Prebake crust for 10 minutes, or as directed in crust recipe. Remove from oven and reduce heat to 325°F.

Place broccoli in shell.

Beat eggs with fork or wire whisk; beat in yogurt, mayonnaise, seasonings, then cheese. Pour over broccoli in crust.

Bake for 25 to 30 minutes until set. Let rest for 10 minutes before cutting.

Serves 4

Major Protein

Menu Suggestions: Serve with a fresh fruit appetizer and a vegetable salad accompaniment. A cooked grain or vegetable can be included if desired.

Deep-Dish Pies

Deep-dish pies, often known as "pot pies," are a form of savory pastry with only a top crust. This crust may be made from any pie dough, as well as from biscuit, muffin, or bread batter.

For simplest presentation, almost any muffin batter can be spooned onto a casserole or creamed vegetable mixture, then baked. This tender topping adds texture and interest to the dish and acts as a "sponge" for the liquid in the casserole.

With only slightly more effort, a rolled pie crust or biscuit dough can be laid directly over a filling, making a few slits so that steam can escape. Or, if you prefer, decorative pastry cutouts can be arranged on the surface; they are somewhat easier to transfer and require less pastry. These crusts can be used on top of a specially prepared filling or may be used to enliven leftovers.

Pot pies can be assembled in aluminum baking pans and frozen unbaked. Bake without thawing according to the temperature cited in the recipe, but increase the baking time by about 10 minutes.

DECORATIVE PASTRY CUTOUTS

These can be used for topping pies in the same way you would use lattice strips.

any rolled pie dough

Roll dough as for crust but make slightly thicker than usual, about ⅜ inch.

Using a cookie cutter, glass, or knife for a free-form design, cut into desired shapes.

Lay gently over pie filling so that tips of pieces just touch. There will be spaces left through which steam can escape during baking.

MUFFIN-TOPPED DEEP-DISH VEGETABLE PIE

This vegetable pie with a cakey topping can be prepared in individual baking dishes or a single casserole. Makes good use of leftovers.

8 cups any bean or vegetable mixture in sauce, or 8 cups cooked, mixed vegetables and beans of choice combined with 2 cups medium White Sauce (page 313) or Cheese Sauce (page 313)

½ any muffin recipe using 1 whole egg or omitting egg and adding an extra ¼ teaspoon baking powder (especially recommended are Whole Wheat Muffins (page 327), Sweet Corn Muffins (page 329), Wheat Germ Muffins (page 328, or any "Quick Mix" Muffins, pages 446–449)

Preheat oven to 400°F. Place filling in 4 greased, individual 2-cup baking dishes or a shallow 2-quart baking dish. Prepare muffin batter and drop by spoonfuls to cover filling. Bake for 15 to 20 minutes until top is firm and lightly browned.

Serves 4

Major Protein with bean filling or cheese sauce; *Minor Protein* with all-vegetable filling

Note: To serve 6, increase filling by 2 cups. (Batter will still be adequate.) It is most practical to prepare the full muffin recipe and use the remaining half to bake muffins along with the casserole, to be enjoyed later.

AMBASSADOR POT PIE WITH BISCUIT CRUST

One way to construct a pot pie using biscuit dough for the crust.

½ any biscuit recipe, including Basic Biscuits and variations (page 326), or any "Quick Mix" Biscuits (pages 446–449)
6 cups diced cooked vegetables
1 small onion, chopped
1 tablespoon minced fresh parsley or 1 teaspoon fresh dill or a pinch of dried thyme
2 cups shredded cheese
cottage cheese or gravy
salt
pepper

Preheat oven to 425°.

Prepare biscuit dough and roll ⅛ to ¼ inch thick.

Combine remaining ingredients in a greased 1-quart casserole, 8- or 9-inch pie pan, or 4 individual baking dishes. Add cottage cheese or gravy as needed to moisten, and if cheese is bland, salt lightly.

Place crust to completely cover filling. Cut a few slits in the top to allow steam to escape.

Bake for about 20 minutes until top is brown.

Serves 4

Major Protein

Note: Double recipe for 8, using a 9 x 13-inch pan; half recipe can be made in individual casseroles.

BEAN POT PIE

Bean filling and biscuit topping are meant to go together.

½ any biscuit recipe, including Basic Biscuits and variations (page 326), or any "Quick Mix" Biscuits (pages 446–449)
4 cups cooked beans, drained
2 tablespoons chopped green pepper
1 small onion, chopped
1 medium tomato, chopped
1 clove garlic, chopped
2 tablespoons catsup
1 tablespoon nutritional yeast (optional)
4 to 8 ounces sliced or 1 to 2 cups shredded cheddar or similar cheese

Preheat oven to 425°F.

Prepare biscuit dough and roll ⅛ to ¼ inch thick.

Combine beans, vegetables, and seasonings in a 1-quart or 8- or 9-inch casserole or pie pan, or 4 individual baking dishes. Top with cheese.

Place crust to completely cover filling. Cut a few slits in the top to allow steam to escape.

Bake for about 20 minutes until top is brown.

Serves 4

Major Protein

Note: Double recipe for 8, using a 9 x 13-inch pan; half recipe can be made in individual casseroles.

TAMALE PIE

Cheese and a cornmeal crust make a moist, dense cover for leftover beans. Any thick bean stew can provide the base.

3 to 4 cups leftover bean dish
1 cup shredded cheddar or Jack cheese
1 cup cornmeal
1 teaspoon salt
1 tablespoon oil
1 teaspoon honey
1 cup boiling water

Preheat oven to 400°F.

Place beans in an oiled, shallow

1-quart baking dish or 8- or 9-inch pan. Cover with cheese.

Mix cornmeal with salt, stir in oil and honey, and beat in boiling water until mixture is smooth. Drop by spoonfuls over beans and cheese, then spread gently so surface is covered.

Bake for 25 to 30 minutes, or until crusty.

Serves 4

Major Protein

Note: If the leftover beans seem liquid, stir in a few spoonfuls of bran to thicken; if dry, moisten with tomato juice. To prepare Tamale Pie when you have no leftovers, for every 4 servings, season 3 to 4 cups cooked kidney or pinto beans with 1 large chopped onion, 1 chopped clove garlic, 2 teaspoons chili powder, and about ½ cup tomato juice, or enough to moisten. Use as directed for leftover beans. Tamale Pie can also be baked in individual baking dishes, in a deep 10-inch pie plate for 6, in a 9 x 13-inch pan for 8, or for a crowd in a lasagne pan.

BAKED RICE CRUST

This rice crust is the perfect edible container for leftovers. Fill with any creamed vegetable or bean mixture.

3 cups cooked brown rice
1 egg, lightly beaten
⅓ cup grated Parmesan cheese
pepper

Preheat oven to 350°F.

Combine all ingredients and press over bottom and sides of oiled, deep 9- or 10-inch pie pan.

Bake crust for 15 minutes if filling will later be cooked in the shell. Bake for 20 to 25 minutes until just lightly colored if filling with a completely cooked mixture.

Serves 4

Serving Suggestions: Fill partially baked crust with any lightly cooked vegetables or bean–vegetable mixture and cover with any cheese sauce or sliced cheese and some tomato sauce. Return pie to oven for 10 to 15 minutes, until piping hot. Crust will hold 3 to 4 cups filling.

CORNMEAL CRUST

A flavorful crust with a crunchy texture. Simple to prepare and excellent for custard and creamy cheese fillings, as in quiche.

1 cup whole wheat flour
½ cup cornmeal
¼ teaspoon salt
⅓ cup oil

Preheat oven to 400°F.

Combine dry ingredients. Add oil and stir to form a crumbly dough.

Press evenly over bottom and up sides of a 9-inch pie pan. Chill.

Prick liberally with a fork and, before filling, partially bake for 10 to 12 minutes until firm and barely colored. Fill with custard-type filling and return to oven following recipe directions.

Makes one 9-inch crust

Note: Freezing is not recommended.

SAVORY SOY CRUST

A crisp crust that is low in fat and easy to transfer to the pie tin, as it is only partially rolled before fitting.

1½ cups whole wheat flour
½ cup soy flour
½ teaspoon salt
1 tablespoon poppy, caraway, or dill
** seed (optional)**
¼ cup oil
2 to 3 tablespoons cold water

Combine dry ingredients, including seeds if desired. Cut in oil with fork or pastry blender. Stir in enough water to hold dough together.

Divide dough in half and form into two balls. Place each ball on waxed paper and roll to the size of the bottom of pie pan. Invert into pan, remove paper, and, using tips of fingers, work from center out, pushing dough up sides of the pan to form a thin bottom crust. Use as recipe directs.

Makes two 9-inch pie shells

Note: Freezes well; for directions, see "Desserts: Pies and Individual Pastries." For prebaked crust, prick liberally with a fork and bake in a 425°F., oven for about 15 minutes.

CHEDDAR PASTRY

An excellent pastry for vegetable pies, tarts, and turnovers and one that is easy to handle. /

2 cups whole wheat flour
1 cup shredded cheddar cheese
¼ teaspoon salt
5 tablespoons butter
3 tablespoons oil
⅓ to ½ cup cold water

Mix flour, cheese, and salt. Cut in butter and oil with a pastry blender or wire whisk. Add enough water to form dough into a ball.

Chill pastry if possible. Roll as needed for tarts, turnovers, or pies.

Makes pastry for three 9-inch pies (or about 24 tarts or 8 large turnovers)

Note: To prepare in a food processor, grate cheese, then insert plastic mixing blade and combine cheese with dry ingredients. Process in fat, then add water gradually, with machine running, until dough forms a ball. Dough freezes well. For directions, see "Desserts: Pies and Individual Pastries." For prebaked crust, prick liberally with a fork and bake in a 400°F. oven for 10 to 12 minutes until golden.

RYE–OAT PASTRY

A very flaky crust with less fat than most. It must be prebaked before filling and can withstand a lot of handling.

¾ cup rye flour
½ cup oats
½ teaspoon salt
¼ cup oil
2 tablespoons cold water

Preheat oven to 425°F.
Combine dry ingredients. Stir in oil and then water until mixture just holds together.

Press over bottom and sides of an 8-inch pie pan or divide into 4 parts, form into balls, and press into individual tart pans or a deep muffin tin.

Prick bottom liberally with a fork and bake for about 12 minutes until browned.

Makes one 8-inch shell or 4 tarts

Note: Not recommended for freezing.

BEAN PATTY SHELLS

Tart shells made from ground beans.

1½ cups cooked beans, well drained
1 cup whole wheat flour
1 teaspoon baking powder
½ teaspoon salt (omit if beans are salted)
2 tablespoons oil
about ¼ cup milk

Preheat oven to 400°F.

Grind beans to a pulp as for Chopped Beat (see directions, page 502).

Add remaining ingredients to bean pulp, adding enough milk to make a soft dough. Knead gently on a floured surface to make uniform. If too soft to handle, add flour; if too dry, add milk.

Divide dough into 8 pieces and shape into 8 shells over the back of a large muffin tin.

Prick surface liberally and bake on the inverted tin for 15 minutes for prebaked shells.

Makes 8 large shells

Note: Will form as many as 12 shells in small, individual tart pans or if shaped inside a muffin tin (⅓ cup filling needed for each large shell; ¼ cup filling needed for small tarts). Dough is not recommended for freezing.

Serving Suggestion: Fill prebaked shells with any creamed vegetable, or fill partially baked tarts with the ricotta filling for Eggplant Manicotti or the rice mixture for Rice Cheeseburgers and return to the oven until filling is hot and creamy and crust is brown.

Side Dishes

The recipes in this section will most often be chosen as accompaniments to the main course. We point out, however, that when selected with an eye to their protein value, side dishes can be assembled to replace the entrée entirely. House favorites include a vegetable accompaniment like White Broccoli Mozzarella with a side dish of Pasta, Artichokes, and Chick-Peas with Lemon Dressing; Quick Creamed Green Beans, Sliced Baked Beets, and Bread Stuffing; or a combination of Indian Lentils, Aromatic Rice with Green Beans, and Tomato Pachadi (a salad of tomatoes and yogurt). Many similar menu suggestions will be found among the recipes.

VEGETABLE ACCOMPANIMENTS

Fresh vegetables are seasonal guests, bringing fresh new tastes to the table. There is no limit to the number of vegetables you can serve in a meal or a day; vegetable dishes play a major role in menu planning not only because of their excellent food value but also for the variety they offer.

When selecting vegetables, consider quality, since no vegetable is improved by cooking. Vegetables that are limp, discolored, overgrown, of poor color, or have other visible defects should not be purchased. If their quality depreciates at home, use them in the soup pot.

Unfortunately, poor cooking methods have done much to ruin the reputation of many vegetables. Before you go on to try some of these recipes you may want to read "On Cooking: Preparing Vegetables" for basic instructions on washing, trimming, cutting, and cooking. Remember, for plain vegetable accompaniments, steaming, baking, and stir-frying are the best cooking techniques to use. Cook vegetables only long enough to make them tender but still crisp; soft, mushy vegetables are very unappealing. For anyone on a restricted fat regime, oil or butter can be omitted from any recipe and replaced with an equal amount of unsalted broth or water. To enhance flavor, a splash of vinegar or lemon juice can then be added to the finished dish.

As there are many uses for precooked vegetables, you can save yourself time by preparing extra amounts to be used the following day in casseroles, savory fillings, and salads.

The vegetable accompaniments that follow are organized in alphabetical order; the predominant vegetable dictates the placement of the recipe. At the end of this section are a group of recipes that are appropriate for many vegetables. All of these accompaniments involve some cooking; uncooked vegetable dishes appear in the salad section.

STEWED ARTICHOKES, ITALIAN STYLE

An excellent accompaniment to pasta or rice entrées. You can also turn this into a main course by serving the vegetables over grain with a generous topping of grated Parmesan cheese.

1 large red onion, thinly sliced
1 clove garlic, quartered
¼ cup olive oil
2 large artichokes
1 teaspoon oregano
2 sprigs parsley
2 cups cooked chick-peas, drained
½ teaspoon salt (omit if beans are salted)
pepper

Cook onion and garlic in oil slowly over low heat for about 10 minutes until soft but not brown. This can be done in a skillet or a 1½- to 2-quart pot.

While onion cooks, trim artichokes as directed in the Table of Specific Vegetable Preparation (page 497). Cut each artichoke in half and each half into 4 to 8 wedges. Keep prepared pieces in a water bath.

Drain artichokes and add to onion with oregano and parsley. Cover and cook over low heat until just tender. Young artichokes cook in about 10 minutes; old or tough specimens take longer.

Add chick-peas, salt, and pepper to taste, cover and cook 5 to 10 minutes longer until well heated and quite tender.

Serves 4
Protein Complement

GREEK ARTICHOKES AND DILL

During the springtime artichoke harvest in Greece, a dozen artichokes may sell for the price of a single one in the American market. Because this is such an appealing dish, the cost differential is easy to overlook.

4 large or 16 baby artichokes
¼ cup olive oil
1 small onion, chopped, or 3 scallions, sliced
1 large bunch dill
4 medium potatoes, cut in thin slices
1 rounded tablespoon tomato paste diluted in 3 cups water, or 3 cups liquid from drained canned tomatoes, or water mixed with a few Tomato Cubes (page 430), or some combination of water and tomato juice
1 teaspoon salt
pepper
2 tablespoons lemon juice

Trim artichokes as described in the Table of Specific Vegetable Preparation (page 497). Cut small artichokes in half, large ones in sixths. Peel stems lightly and slice into sticks.

Heat oil in a 3-quart pot, add onion and artichokes, cover and stew over low heat for 10 minutes. Add sprigs of dill to the pot, along with potatoes, liquid, salt, pepper, and lemon, and bring to a boil. Cover the pot and cook gently until tender, 45 minutes to 1 hour. Remove cover to let heat escape and serve lukewarm rather than piping hot.

Serves 4 to 6

Variations: For a lighter accompaniment, replace potatoes with 2 carrots cut in 1-inch sticks. Reduce liquid to 1 cup. For *Artichokes Avgolemono*, prepare recipe with plain water and omit lemon. Just before serving, separate 2 eggs, beat whites until foamy, beat in yolks until light, and then add the juice of a fresh lemon. Gradually beat in some of the warm artichoke broth, return this sauce to the pot and heat through, without boiling. If carrots and only 1 cup liquid are used, prepare the same sauce with 1 egg and ½ lemon.

Menu Suggestions: We often serve this as a main dish for 4, providing protein elsewhere on the menu as the Greeks do, by serving feta cheese and yogurt at the same meal. An essential component is a good bread for sopping up the rich sauce.

BAKED JERUSALEM ARTICHOKES

Jerusalem artichokes, which are prepared and cooked like potatoes, are sweeter in taste and less starchy in texture, with their own distinctive, earthy flavor. This recipe is a good introduction, for the artichokes are served like a baked potato with salt, pepper, and butter, if desired.

1 pound Jerusalem artichokes

Preheat oven to 400°F. Scrub artichokes but do not peel. Dry with a cloth or paper towel. Bake for 20 to 40 minutes, depending on size. If you are baking something else at 350°F., the artichokes can be baked simultaneously, but allow about 45 minutes for a medium-size artichoke to cook. If it is not quite tender at the end of this time, raise the heat to 400°F. and bake 5 to 15 minutes longer. Jerusalem artichokes will be obviously soft when they are done.

Serves 4

Note: To bake in hot coals, wrap in foil and place directly in coals for 20 to 30 minutes, depending on size. When tender, open foil and bake 5 minutes longer to crisp skin.

SMOTHERED JERUSALEM ARTICHOKES

Jerusalem artichokes, smothered in onions and tomato, make a very tasty side dish.

1 pound Jerusalem artichokes
1 large onion
2 tablespoons oil
1 clove garlic, chopped
1 cup diced fresh or canned tomatoes
2 tablespoons minced fresh parsley or 2 teaspoons dried
¼ teaspoon salt
pepper

Scrub and peel artichokes. Cut in rounds about 1 inch thick. You should have about 3 cups. Cut onion in half, then slice thin.

Heat oil in a skillet or a 1½- to 2-quart pot and cook onion over medium-high heat, stirring to prevent sticking, for about 5 minutes until lightly colored. Add garlic and cook briefly. Add tomatoes and parsley, turn heat low, and simmer for 2 to 3 minutes.

Add artichoke pieces, salt, and plenty of pepper. Cover and cook over very low heat for about 25 minutes until quite tender.

Serves 4

Variations: If the meal needs more protein, sprinkle the vegetables with grated Parmesan cheese. For *Smothered Cauliflower,* replace artichokes with cauliflower pieces.

Menu Suggestions: An excellent accompaniment to rice or pasta dishes that do not emphasize tomato, such as Rice with Cabbage and Cheese, Zita with Cheese, Pasta with Creamy Spinach, Rice with Egg and Lemon, or with frittatas, Eggplant Cutlets, or Baked Spinach and Ricotta.

BAKED ASPARAGUS

Fresh asparagus is crisp and in no way resembles the canned variety. Cooking fresh asparagus in the oven retains its color, flavor, and texture, and keeps it from becoming stringy.

asparagus
butter
foil

Preheat oven to 350°F. Wash asparagus and trim the tough ends. As the cooking time varies with their size, separate asparagus if of vastly different thicknesses and place each bunch on a double layer of foil. Dot lightly with butter and wrap to enclose in a foil packet. Place in the oven for about 20 minutes. This will be long enough for medium-size asparagus to become tender yet still be crunchy. Alternately, the foil-wrapped asparagus can be cooked over hot coals. Serve hot; if serving is delayed, keep wrapped.

Allow 1½ pounds to serve 4

ASPARAGUS WITH CASHEWS

1½ pounds asparagus
2 tablespoons butter or half butter half oil
¼ cup raw cashew halves or pieces
1 tablespoon lemon juice
¼ teaspoon salt
½ teaspoon dried chervil or parsley

Trim asparagus and break into 1- to 1½-inch lengths.

Heat fat in a wok or skillet over medium-high heat and sauté cashews quickly until they just begin to color. Do not overcook.

Add asparagus and stir-fry for 5 minutes; asparagus should remain crisp. Stir in remaining ingredients and serve.

Serves 4

SPICED GREEN BEANS

1 pound green beans, broken into 1-inch pieces
2 tablespoons oil
1 small onion, chopped
1 teaspoon chili powder
pinch turmeric
½ teaspoon salt

Steam beans for 10 minutes.

Heat oil in a 10-inch skillet and brown onion. Add chili and turmeric

and cook briefly. Add steamed beans and salt and stir-fry quickly until coated with spices and lightly crisped. Serve hot.
Serves 4

STIR-FRIED GREEN BEANS WITH GARLIC

2 tablespoons oil
1 pound green beans, broken in half
6 cloves garlic, chopped
½ teaspoon salt
1 tablespoon soy sauce

Heat oil in a wok and stir-fry beans and garlic for 5 minutes. Keep heat high to singe beans.

Add seasonings, cover wok, lower heat, and stew for 5 minutes.
Serves 4
Variation: For *Stir-Fried Broccoli with Garlic,* replace beans with broccoli, using the flowers and the stems, which have been pared and sliced into thin sticks.

QUICK CREAMED GREEN BEANS

4 ounces mushrooms, chopped (a heavy cup)
1 small onion, chopped
2 tablespoons oil
1½ pounds green beans, broken into 1-inch segments (about 6 cups)
½ cup water
¼ cup nonfat dry milk powder
3 tablespoons arrowroot or cornstarch
1½ cups milk
¼ teaspoon salt
pepper
½ teaspoon dry mustard
cheese (optional)

Sauté mushrooms and onion in oil in a 2-quart pot for about 2 minutes until limp. Add beans and water, bring to a boil, cover, and cook over low heat for 10 minutes until just tender.

Dissolve dry milk powder and starch in milk. Stir into hot beans and cook over low heat, stirring frequently, until thickened and just ready to boil.

Season with salt, pepper, and mustard; stir in some cheese to melt, if desired.
Serves 6
Minor Protein
Variations: For other *Quick Creamed Vegetables,* omit mushrooms or retain as desired, and replace beans with corn, fresh lima beans, carrots, cauliflower, broccoli, parsnips, turnips, acorn squash, or potatoes. Peel vegetable if necessary, cut into small bite-size pieces, and cook as for beans, increasing cooking time as required so that vegetable is just tender. Thicken with milk and starch as directed and season as above, or vary the taste with paprika, curry powder, or, for a slightly sweet creamed vegetable dish, a dash of honey or molasses and cinnamon, nutmeg, or ginger.

Arrowroot can be replaced with ⅓ cup whole wheat flour in any version of this recipe although the sauce will be less delicate. If flour is used, allow thickened sauce to boil gently for 2 minutes.

Menu Suggestions: You may want to serve this over grain, potatoes, or biscuits to take advantage of the creamy sauce.

ATLANTIC AVENUE GREEN BEANS

The secret of this dish lies in the combined flavor of olive oil with sun-ripened fresh tomatoes, so only attempt it when tomatoes are in season. Serve with plenty of bread so that none of the sauce goes to waste.

3 tablespoons olive oil
1 small onion, chopped
8 medium tomatoes, peeled (if desired) and diced
1 pound green beans, trimmed at the ends
salt

Heat oil in a large, heavy skillet and sauté onion until wilted. Add tomatoes and cook until they begin to disintegrate.

Add whole beans, cover, and cook over low heat for about 45 minutes until vegetable is very tender.

Remove cover and let cool for a few

minutes so vegetable is warm, not hot, when it is served. Salt to taste.

Serves 4

Note: If you don't mind a little peel in the sauce, it is a lot easier not to peel the tomatoes.

Variations: Beans can be replaced with snow peas, eggplant, okra, or almost any vegetable; adjust cooking time accordingly.

CRISP FRIED BEETS

beets
oil or butter
lemon wedge

Scrub beets. Peel only if skin is tough. Shred in a food processor or hand grater. Heat fat to just cover the surface of a skillet or wok. When hot, add shredded beets and stir-fry for 3 to 5 minutes. Beets should retain their crispness. Season lightly with lemon and serve hot.

1 pound beets serves 4

STEAMED BEETS

Scrub beets and remove tops and long roots without cutting into bulb. Steam whole until bulb can be pierced. This will vary from 30 to 45 minutes, depending on the size and age of the beets.

When beets are cool enough to handle, skin will slip off readily with gentle pressure.

1 pound beets serves 4

FRESH ORANGE BEETS

1 pound beets
¼ cup fresh orange juice
1 tablespoon lemon juice
¼ teaspoon nutmeg
1 tablespoon butter

Cook beets until tender as directed for Steamed Beets. Peel and slice. You will have about 2 cups.

Add remaining ingredients to beets in a skillet or small saucepan and heat through until butter melts and beets are hot.

Serves 4

RUSSIAN BEETS

Lightly spiced beets in a warm, creamy yogurt sauce.

1 pound beets
2 tablespoons honey
2 tablespoons cider vinegar
1 tablespoon butter
½ tablespoon whole wheat flour
½ cup yogurt

Cook beets as directed for Steamed Beets. Peel and cut into bite-size pieces.

Combine beets in a saucepan with honey, vinegar, and butter and heat until butter melts.

Combine flour with yogurt to form a smooth paste and stir into beets. Cook over low heat, stirring, until thick and creamy. Serve hot.

Serves 4

SLICED BAKED BEETS

1 pound beets, trimmed, peeled, and thinly sliced (about 2 cups)
1 tablespoon honey
¼ teaspoon salt
⅛ teaspoon nutmeg
2 tablespoons lemon juice
1 small onion, chopped
¼ cup water
1 tablespoon butter

Preheat oven to 350° to 375°F.

Layer beets in a shallow baking dish. Top evenly with honey, salt, nutmeg, lemon juice, and onion. Pour on water, dot with butter, cover and bake for about 40 minutes until tender.

Serves 4

Note: If desired, onion can be replaced with ¼ cup chopped celery.

WHITE BROCCOLI MOZZARELLA

A well-chosen accompaniment for pasta, grain, and bean entrées which do not stress cheese.

1 pound broccoli
1 tablespoon olive oil
1 large clove garlic, chopped
½ cup water

½ teaspoon salt
1 teaspoon basil
1 teaspoon oregano
½ cup sliced olives
1½ cups shredded mozzarella cheese

Cut broccoli into thin trees. Heat oil in a large skillet and brown garlic lightly. Add broccoli, water, and seasonings, bring to a boil, cover, and simmer for 15 minutes until tender.

Stir in olives; just before serving, top with cheese and cover over low heat to melt.

Serves 4
Minor Protein

AMERICAN WHOLEFOODS BROCCOLI HOLLANDAISE

Classic hollandaise is a rich, butter-based sauce of a rather temperamental nature. The American wholefoods version, although not as rich, is a similarly flavorful, creamy lemon dressing that can enhance a number of freshly steamed vegetables for side dish or appetizer service.

1 large bunch broccoli
3 tablespoons lemon juice
1 cup ricotta cheese
¼ teaspoon salt
2 egg yolks

Slice broccoli into small trees and steam for about 10 minutes until just tender.

Using a wire whisk, beat lemon juice gradually into ricotta cheese in a saucepan or the top of a double boiler. When smooth, beat in salt and egg yolks.

Place over boiling water or over very low heat, preferably protected with a heatproof pad. Stir with a whisk until heated through, about 10 minutes. Do not boil. Serve warm spooned over vegetables.

Serves 4
Minor Protein

Variations: To prepare sauce with cottage cheese, puree until perfectly smooth in a processor fitted with a plastic mixing blade or in a blender, gradually adding the lemon juice. Add salt and egg yolks and process quickly to incorporate. Cook as above.

For other *Vegetables Hollandaise,* replace broccoli with cauliflower, green beans, asparagus, potatoes, or beets, all steamed until barely tender.

STEAMED BROCCOLI SALAD

Fresh-cooked broccoli, dressed and served at room temperature.

1 pound broccoli (about 4 cups)
½ cup Basic Oil and Vinegar Dressing, seasoned to taste (page 287)
Vegetable garnish of choice:
    1 tomato, cut in bite-size pieces (optional)
    1 cup cooked beans (optional)
    4 thin slices sweet red onion
    6 pitted black olives, sliced
    1 pimiento, cut in strips

Cut broccoli into bite-size pieces, peeling stems if tough. Steam for 8 to 10 minutes until barely tender. Place steamed broccoli in a shallow bowl and cover with dressing. Add one or more vegetable garnishes of choice and mix to coat with dressing. Let marinate at room temperature until ready to serve, or chill to keep.

Serves 4

Note: The salad can also be prepared using leftover cooked broccoli. The inclusion of the beans makes a small protein contribution to the meal and, when needed, grated Parmesan can be sprinkled on top.

Variation: Replace broccoli with cauliflower. Garnish with minced parsley for a touch of color.

BROCCOLI STALK SALAD

When you've used the buds, this is a good way to serve the remaining stems. Used in this manner, a little bit of broccoli goes a long way; 2 to 3 stalks can serve up to 4 as a side dish.

broccoli stalks
olive oil
wine vinegar
salt
pepper
oregano (optional)
garlic (optional)

Peel stalks and cut into long, thin sticks. Steam for 5 minutes.

Dress with oil and vinegar in a ratio of 2 tablespoons oil to 1½ tablespoons vinegar. Season with a pinch of salt, pepper, and, if desired, a sprinkle of oregano and a split clove of garlic. Serve at room temperature.

STEAMED BRUSSELS SPROUTS

Here are some popular serving suggestions for a generally unpopular vegetable.

Steam whole for 10 minutes if small, 20 if large. Serve under Cheese Sauce, or Curry Cream on rice, or dress with oil and vinegar and herbs to make a salad.

A 10-ounce container serves 4

BUTTER-STEAMED BRUSSELS SPROUTS

10-ounce container brussels sprouts
2 tablespoons butter
fresh parsley
2 tablespoons water
salt
pepper

Wash and quarter sprouts through core. Melt butter in a skillet, wok, or saucepan and stir-fry sprouts for 5 minutes.

Add lots of fresh parsley and water; cover and steam until tender, about 10 minutes. Surfaces will brown slightly.

Season to taste with salt and pepper.
Serves 4

COMPANY CABBAGE

Pan-fried cabbage and carrots garnished with walnuts.

2 tablespoons butter
¾ pound cabbage, sliced thin (about 6 cups)
2 medium carrots, shredded
4 scallions, sliced
½ teaspoon salt
1 teaspoon prepared mustard
¼ cup coarsely chopped walnuts
paprika

Melt butter in a wok or large skillet and stir-fry vegetables for 5 minutes until cabbage is translucent.

Add salt, mustard, and nuts and toss well.

Sprinkle top with paprika and serve hot.
Serves 4

SPICED CABBAGE

This Chinese-style cabbage makes an excellent side dish at an Oriental meal. Since it should be served at room temperature, it can be made ahead of other dishes that require last-minute preparation.

1 tablespoon peanut oil
1 pound cabbage, cut in strips ½ to 1 inch wide and 1½ inches long (about 8 cups)
2 tablespoons white or rice vinegar
1 tablespoon soy sauce
1 tablespoon honey
1 teaspoon salt
¼ teaspoon cayenne

Heat oil in a wok and stir-fry cabbage for 3 minutes. Make sure vegetable is well coated with oil.

Combine remaining ingredients in a large serving bowl. Stir in cabbage and mix well to coat with dressing. Serve at room temperature.
Serves 4 to 6

QUICK SAUERKRAUT

Sauerkraut is actually made by long-term salt pickling of cabbage. This cooked dish has a taste much like sauerkraut but is both quickly made and salt-free.

1 pound cabbage, coarsely shredded (5 to 6 cups)
¼ cup cider vinegar
2 cups plus 1 tablespoon water
1 tablespoon honey
1½ teaspoons whole wheat flour

Combine cabbage, vinegar, 2 cups water, and honey in a 2-quart pot. Bring to a boil and cook partially covered for 20 minutes.

Mix flour to a paste with remaining

tablespoon water. Stir into hot cabbage and cook, stirring, until thickened.

Serves 4 to 6

COOKED COLESLAW

A Pennsylvania-Dutch selection that is especially nice in the winter in place of a cold salad.

1½ tablespoons oil
4 cups coarsely shredded cabbage
½ teaspoon salt
1 tablespoon honey
2 tablespoons cider vinegar
½ teaspoon prepared mustard
½ cup yogurt

Heat oil in a large skillet or wok. Add cabbage, stir to coat with fat, and salt. Cover and cook for 10 minutes.

Stir in honey, vinegar, and mustard and, when well blended, cover and remove from heat.

Stir yogurt into warm cabbage just before serving.

Serves 4 to 6

CABBAGE NOODLES IN TOMATO BROTH

A low-calorie, low-carbohydrate substitute for spaghetti.

¾ pound cabbage, cut into strips about 1½ inches wide to resemble noodles (about 6 cups)
1 cup tomato juice
½ teaspoon honey
1 small clove garlic, chopped
pinch dried basil
butter
½ tablespoon nutritional yeast or tomato paste (optional)

Combine cabbage in a pot with tomato juice, honey, garlic, and basil. Bring to a boil, cover, and simmer for 10 minutes.

Add a small pat of butter and thicken, if desired, by stirring in yeast or tomato paste.

Serves 2 as a pasta substitute, 4 as a vegetable accompaniment

Menu Suggestions: Serve in bowls with bean, grain, or nut balls, or cubes of mozzarella cheese. Pass grated Parmesan for topping at the table.

FRIED CABBAGE AND POTATOES, INDIAN STYLE

One of the most delicious Indian vegetable dishes.

3 tablespoons oil
1 medium onion, chopped
1 teaspoon mustard seeds
4 large potatoes, unpeeled, cut in ½-inch dice
8 cups coarsely shredded cabbage (about 1¼ pounds)
1 teaspoon minced fresh ginger or ¼ teaspoon powdered
½ teaspoon cumin
½ teaspoon turmeric
½ teaspoon cayenne
1½ teaspoons salt
1 tomato, chopped
juice of 1 lemon

Heat oil in a large, heavy skillet and sauté onion with mustard seeds until seeds pop.

Add potatoes to skillet and cook, stirring occasionally, for about 5 minutes. Add cabbage, spices, and salt. Stir to mix evenly and cook, uncovered, about 25 minutes, stirring occasionally until vegetables are tender and golden. Pay close attention during the last 5 to 10 minutes to prevent overcooking.

Just before serving, stir in tomato and lemon juice.

Serves 6 to 8 as one of several selections

Note: Can be held awhile and reheated if necessary. Add tomato and lemon, however, just before serving.

Menu Suggestions: Include with a variety of selections at an Indian dinner or serve with an omelet, chapatis, and yogurt for a homey meal.

BRAISED RED CABBAGE

1 tablespoon butter or oil
1 small clove garlic, chopped
1 small onion, chopped
1 pound red cabbage, coarsely chopped (about 5 cups)
2 tablespoons tomato paste
⅓ cup water
¼ teaspoon salt
1 tablespoon lemon juice
3 tablespoons yogurt

Heat fat in a large skillet and sauté garlic and onion for about 3 minutes to soften. Add cabbage and stir to coat. Add tomato paste mixed with water and salt. Cover and cook over low heat, stirring a few times, about 20 minutes, or until tender.

Remove from heat and stir in lemon juice. Just before serving stir in yogurt.
Serves 4

CARROTS WITH WALNUTS

6 medium carrots
¼ cup water
2 tablespoons soy sauce
¼ cup walnut pieces

Slice carrots into thin disks. Combine with water in a small saucepan, bring to a boil, cover, and cook until just tender, 10 minutes.

Add soy sauce and walnuts and cook, stirring, over medium-high heat until moisture evaporates.
Serves 4
Variation: For *Carrots with Sunflower Seeds,* replace walnuts with sunflower seeds.

FRENCH CARROTS AND CELERY

3 cups combined carrots and celery, cut into thin strips 1 to 2 inches long
2 tablespoons butter
1 teaspoon wine vinegar
1 teaspoon Dijon or sweet French mustard

Combine vegetables and butter in a saucepan. Cover and stew over medium heat for 10 minutes until vegetables are just tender. Stir in vinegar and mustard.
Serves 4
Variations: Carrots or celery can be replaced by similarly cut summer squash, parsnips, green pepper, or leeks.

SWEET GINGER CARROTS WITH RAISINS

Ginger and carrots are such good companions that two side dishes using these ingredients are offered here.

1 pound carrots, diced (about 3 cups)
⅛ teaspoon salt
1 teaspoon honey
¼ cup raisins
¼ teaspoon ground ginger
¼ cup water

Combine all ingredients in a 1-quart pot, bring to a boil, cover, and simmer over low heat until just tender, about 15 minutes.
Serves 4

FRESH GINGER CARROTS

2 tablespoons butter
1 pound carrots, cut in matchsticks (about 3 cups)
2 teaspoons chopped fresh ginger

Melt butter in a skillet or wok and stir-fry carrots and ginger for 5 to 8 minutes until tender but still crunchy and beginning to brown. Serve hot.
Serves 4

BAKED CAULIFLOWER

Cauliflower baked in a light crumb coating.

1½ pounds cauliflower
1 cup rye or whole wheat cracker crumbs
¼ cup wheat germ
1 teaspoon salt
1 teaspoon paprika
pepper
¼ cup whole wheat flour
3 eggs beaten with 2 crushed cloves garlic
lemon wedges

Break cauliflower into florets and steam for 5 minutes, or until barely tender. Drain well and pat dry.

Preheat oven to 375°F.

Combine cracker crumbs, wheat germ, salt, paprika, and pepper.

Put whole wheat flour in a paper bag and add cauliflower pieces, a few at a time; shake to coat with flour.

Dip each flour-coated piece in egg to cover. Lift with tongs and allow excess egg to drip back into the bowl.

Shake egg-coated pieces in a paper bag containing some of the cracker crumb mixture. Replenish mixture if it gets damp or used up.

Transfer each coated piece to a wire rack to dry, or place directly in a shallow 2-quart baking dish that is well oiled.

Bake for about 25 minutes, or until coating is firm and lightly browned.

Serve with a garnish of lemon wedges.

Serves 6
Minor Protein
Note: For a more flavorful coating with added protein, add ⅓ cup finely grated Parmesan cheese, 2 tablespoons minced parsley, and 1 teaspoon oregano to the cracker crumb coating mixture. This dish can be assembled in advance and chilled, which gives the coating a chance to set before baking.

CAULIFLOWER WITH YOGURT

Although Indian in style, this is not too spicy. A good accompaniment to Western as well as Indian meals.

1 teaspoon oil
¼ teaspoon mustard seeds
¼ teaspoon cumin
½ teaspoon chili powder
1 small to medium cauliflower (about 1 pound), divided into florets
¼ teaspoon turmeric
½ teaspoon salt
¼ cup water
¼ cup yogurt

Heat oil in a 2- to 3-quart pot or wok. Add mustard seeds and cumin and fry until seeds pop. Add chili powder and cook for 30 seconds. Add cauliflower, turmeric, salt, and water, and stir to mix evenly. Cover and cook for 10 to 15 minutes until cauliflower is just tender.

Remove from heat and uncover. While still warm, but not hot, stir in yogurt until vegetable is evenly coated. Serve warm or at room temperature.

Serves 4

BARBECUED CORN

About as American as you can get, particularly when it's cooked under an open sky.

Place unshucked corn on a grill 4 to 6 inches above the coals. Roast for 10 minutes, turning a few times. Shuck, using a mitt to protect your hands, and return to heat for about 5 minutes, turning until lightly browned on all sides.

For delayed service, roast for about 10 minutes as described, then move to the side of the grill. Just before serving, husk and brown.

CREAMED CORN O'BRIEN

Creamy corn brightened with green pepper.

1 tablespoon butter
1 medium onion, chopped
½ cup chopped green pepper
2 cups corn kernels
1 tablespoon whole wheat flour
½ cup milk
salt
pepper

Melt butter in a skillet. Add onion and green pepper and sauté until tender, about 3 minutes.

Add corn, cover, and cook over low heat for about 5 minutes.

Combine flour with milk and stir into corn. Cook and stir until thickened and boiling gently, about 3 minutes. Season with salt and pepper to taste.

Serves 4
Minor Protein

CURRIED CORN

1 tablespoon oil
1 medium onion, chopped
1 small clove garlic, minced
½ cup diced sweet red or green pepper
½ teaspoon turmeric
½ teaspoon coriander
½ teaspoon cumin
2½ cups corn kernels
¼ cup water
½ teaspoon salt
2 tablespoons chopped fresh parsley
1 tablespoon lemon juice

Heat oil in a skillet and sauté onion and garlic until softened, about 3 minutes. Add red or green pepper, turmeric, coriander, and cumin, and sauté for 2 minutes.

Add corn and water, cover, and cook for 5 minutes. Stir in salt, parsley, and lemon juice and serve.

Serves 4 to 6

SUCCOTASH

An updated version of a native American dish.

1 medium onion, chopped
1 tablespoon oil
2 cups fresh lima beans
¼ cup water
2½ cups corn kernels
½ cup milk
2 teaspoons whole wheat flour
¼ cup yogurt
¼ teaspoon salt
paprika

Sauté onion in oil in a 1-quart pot for 3 to 5 minutes until tender. Add beans and water, bring to a boil, cover, and cook for 15 minutes until beans are just tender.

Add corn and milk, cover, and cook for 5 minutes.

Mix flour completely into yogurt, stir into vegetables, and cook over low heat, continuing to stir until thick, about 5 minutes. Do not boil.

Season with salt and mash gently with a fork to crush corn kernels. Sprinkle with paprika.

Serves 4
Minor Protein
Variations: If desired, replace lima beans with cooked soybeans or replace some of the limas with green beans.

CORN OYSTERS

Tiny puffed pancakes that make a delicious accompaniment to any summer meal.

4 ears fresh corn
2 eggs, separated
2 tablespoons nonfat dry milk powder
¼ teaspoon salt
¼ cup wheat germ
2 tablespoons butter/oil

Score corn kernels by running the tip of a knife through them. Cut kernels from cob, retaining both the pulp and the "milk."

Beat egg yolks with powdered milk and salt. Add corn and wheat germ and mix well.

Beat egg whites until stiff and fold into yolk mixture.

Heat fat in a large skillet. Drop batter by tablespoons into hot pan. Cook over moderate heat until crust begins to form, about 5 to 7 minutes. Turn and cook until lightly browned on the other side, 5 minutes longer. This amount cooks in 2 batches.

Makes 24 tiny pancakes; serves 4 to 6
Minor Protein
Note: If desired, add up to 1 cup shredded cheese to the batter.

SAUTÉED CUCUMBERS

Most people never think of cooking cucumbers, but they are delicious this way.

2 large cucumbers
½ teaspoon salt
¼ teaspoon paprika
¼ cup whole wheat flour
3 tablespoons oil or a mixture of oil and butter
yogurt or Tofu Sour Cream (page 289)

Peel and slice cucumbers. Combine in a bag with seasonings and flour and shake to coat.

Heat fat in a large skillet. Add cucumber and cook until tender, about 5 minutes per side.

If you have more than a panful to cook, keep the cooked cucumbers warm in a 300°F. oven while preparing the rest.

Serve soon after cooking. Top, if desired, with a dollop of yogurt or Tofu Sour Cream.

Serves 4

ITALIAN SAUTÉED CUCUMBERS

2 medium cucumbers
2 tablespoons butter or a mixture of oil and butter

1 clove garlic, chopped
1 teaspoon oregano
2 tablespoons chopped fresh basil, or
   2 tablespoons chopped fresh parsley plus ½ teaspoon dried basil
2 tablespoons grated Parmesan
   cheese
¼ teaspoon salt

Peel cucumbers and cut in ½-inch dice.

Heat fat in a skillet. Sauté garlic for 1 minute, then add cucumber, oregano, and basil. Sauté, stirring occasionally, until softened but still crunchy, about 10 to 15 minutes.

Sprinkle with cheese, salt to taste, and serve hot.

Serves 4

Variation: Replace some or all of the cucumber with zucchini but do not peel it.

BAKED HERBED EGGPLANT

Slices of eggplant with an herbed crumb topping are an easy and excellent accompaniment for pasta, grain, or even bean entrées.

1 medium eggplant (1 to 1½ pounds),
   cut in ½-inch thick rounds
¼ cup olive oil
1 large clove garlic, minced
½ teaspoon oregano
¼ teaspoon dried basil
½ teaspoon salt
pepper
2 tablespoons butter, melted
1 tablespoon minced fresh parsley
½ cup dried whole grain bread
   crumbs
¼ cup wheat germ

Preheat oven to 375°F.

Place eggplant rounds in a single layer on an oiled baking sheet.

Combine olive oil, garlic, oregano, basil, salt, and lots of pepper in a small bowl.

Brush eggplant with herbed oil and bake for 15 minutes. Turn, brush again, with herbed oil, and bake 10 minutes longer.

Add melted butter, parsley, bread crumbs and wheat germ, to the remainder of the herbed oil. Spoon on top of the eggplant. Bake 5 minutes longer, or broil for 2 to 3 minutes to brown.

Serves 4

Note: If desired, add 2 tablespoons grated Parmesan cheese to the bread crumbs.

EGGPLANT AU GRATIN

Eggplant baked in and eaten out of the shell.

1 tablespoon oil
1 small clove garlic, minced
1 small eggplant (1 pound)
salt
pepper
½ teaspoon oregano
⅓ cup combined grated Swiss and
   Parmesan cheeses

Preheat oven to 375°F.

Mix oil and garlic and let stand while preparing eggplant.

Cut eggplant in half lengthwise. Loosen meat from skin using a grapefruit knife to make a thin shell. Cut meat into cubes without removing from shell.

Brush cut surface of eggplant with garlic oil; sprinkle lightly with salt, generously with pepper and oregano.

Place cut-side up in a baking dish, surround with water to a depth of ¼ inch, cover and bake for about 40 minutes until very soft.

Top with cheese and bake uncovered for 5 minutes to melt. Eat out of the shell.

Serves 2

Minor Protein

RATATOUILLE

Ratatouille is a very basic vegetable dish from the Provence region of France. Although the proportions may vary, there are three essentials to the recipe: eggplant, olive oil, and garlic. Many people seem to be fond of this dish, as it appears often on restaurant menus and at parties.

    4 tablespoons olive oil
    1 large clove garlic, chopped
    1 large or 2 medium onions, sliced
    1 medium eggplant (about 1½ pounds), cut in half lengthwise and then in ¼-inch-thick half moons
    2 medium green peppers, cut in thin strips
    3 small zucchini (about 1 pound), cut in rounds
    4 medium tomatoes, cut in half lengthwise, then sliced thin
    1 teaspoon salt
    pepper

Heat 3 tablespoons oil in a 15-inch skillet and sauté garlic for 1 minute to soften.

Layer vegetables in the order listed, sprinkling the layers with salt and a generous amount of pepper. Drizzle remaining 1 tablespoon oil on top.

Cover pan and cook over low heat for 35 to 40 minutes until tender. Uncover and cook 10 minutes longer in order to evaporate some of the liquid.

Serve warm, at room temperature, or cold.

Serves 6

Note: This dish reheats well and actually improves with time.

CAMPFIRE RATATOUILLE

The ratatouille vegetables—zucchini, onion, eggplant, green pepper, and tomato—take on an excellent smoked flavor when cooked outdoors over an open fire or barbecue grill. The foil packets used as the cooking vessel can act as the serving dish as well.

    1 medium zucchini
    1 small eggplant
    1 tomato
    1 green pepper
    1 small onion
    pepper
    oregano
    soy sauce
    lemon juice

Cut zucchini, eggplant, and tomato into small chunks. Cut green pepper into strips and onion into rings. You should have 6 to 8 cups of vegetables.

Prepare four 12-inch squares of heavy-duty aluminum foil or double layers of regular foil. Divide vegetables evenly and place in the center of each foil sheet. Fold up edges to form a bowl around them.

Season each packet with some pepper, oregano, a few dashes of soy sauce, and lemon juice. Enclose completely in foil, folding the edges several times to seal.

Place directly in the coals, or on a flaming campfire, and cook for 20 minutes. Lift a packet from the heat and open it. If the vegetables are tender and lightly charred, they are ready to eat.

Distribute the packets and let everyone eat directly from the foil dish, or transfer the contents to plates. Be sure to let the vegetables cool a little before tasting, however, as they will be very hot.

Serves 4

Variations: You can experiment with lots of vegetables cooked in this manner. Diced potatoes can be added to the packet, and string beans, cauliflorets, and broccoli would also mix well; add cubes of tofu to create a *Shish Kebab in a Bag.*

EGGPLANT AND POTATO CURRY

This lightly spiced dish is intended as one part of an Indian dinner.

    ¼ cup oil
    1 large onion, thinly sliced
    2 cloves garlic, chopped
    1 tablespoon finely chopped fresh ginger
    1 teaspoon cumin
    ¼ teaspoon turmeric
    ¼ teaspoon cayenne
    1 medium eggplant (1½ pounds), cubed

½ cup water
¾ teaspoon salt
1½ pounds potatoes
1 cup yogurt

Heat 2 tablespoons oil in a 3-quart pot and sauté onion, garlic, and ginger for 3 to 5 minutes until softened. Add cumin, turmeric, and cayenne and cook 1 minute longer.

Add remaining 2 tablespoons oil and eggplant cubes and cook, stirring, until oil is absorbed and eggplant begins to cook.

Add water and salt, cover and cook until very tender, stirring once or twice, or about 20 minutes.

Meanwhile, scrub potatoes, cut into quarters, and steam until tender, 15 to 20 minutes. Remove peel after cooking and cut into bite-size pieces.

Stir cooked potatoes into cooked eggplant. Cool slightly and gently mix in yogurt.

Serves 4 to 6
Minor Protein
Variations: This vegetable-potato curry can be made with a variety of vegetables replacing some or all of the eggplant, including carrot, string beans, cauliflower, or squash; use approximately 6 cups of vegetables and adjust the cooking time as required.

Menu Suggestions: A salad (raita) and a bean dish (dal), or India Salad with Curry Dressing should be included on the menu, as well as bread and a chutney.

STEAMED EGGPLANT NOODLES

A low-calorie, low-carbohydrate pasta substitute.

1½ pounds eggplant

Peel eggplant and cut in lengthwise slices about ¼ inch thick. Cut each slice into sticks ¼ inch thick.

Place strips of eggplant in a vegetable steamer and steam for 15 minutes until tender but not mushy. Top with sauce of choice and serve.

Serves 4
Menu Suggestions: Eggplant noodles can be served as a side dish with tomato sauce, cheese sauce, Cashew Gravy, Tahini Gravy, Mushroom Sauce, or any similar topping. Or, prepare as an entrée topped with ricotta cheese and sauce by substituting eggplant noodles for the pasta in the Green Linguini with Red or White Mushroom Sauce recipes.

COLD EGGPLANT AND YOGURT

A cool dish that provides a contrast to a spicy entrée.

1 medium eggplant (1 to 1½ pounds)
4 scallions, sliced
½ teaspoon salt
2 tablespoons minced parsley
3 tablespoons oil
4 tablespoons lemon juice
¼ cup sliced olives
1 cup yogurt

Peel eggplant, cut in 1-inch cubes, and steam for about 7 minutes until just tender but not mushy. Cool slightly.

Toss eggplant in a bowl with scallions, salt, parsley, oil, lemon juice, and olives. Mix well, cover, and let stand at room temperature for 30 minutes, or chill for several hours.

Stir in yogurt just before serving.
Serves 4 to 6
Minor Protein

COLD GINGER EGGPLANT

A vegetable dish easily made ahead for Chinese meals. Although the list of ingredients is long, this is really easy to prepare, involves no last-minute work, and is appreciated by anyone who enjoys Chinese cooking.

1 large or 2 small eggplants (total 2 pounds)
4 scallions, sliced
¼ cup chopped parsley
2 tablespoons oil
1½ tablespoons minced fresh ginger
2 cloves garlic, chopped
1 tablespoon lemon juice
1 tablespoon white or rice vinegar
1 tablespoon soy sauce
1 tablespoon honey
2 tablespoons sherry
1 teaspoon Chinese sesame oil
1 tablespoon toasted sesame seeds

Broil eggplant over gas, wood, or charcoal flame until skin is charred and inside is quite soft. Turn so that all sides cook. This will take about 15 minutes, depending on the size of the eggplant and the flame. Cool after cooking. When it can be handled, remove skin and "string" eggplant by peeling off sections with your fingers from stem to blossom end. Make each "string" the width of a finger or less. Place in a serving bowl. Add scallions and parsley.

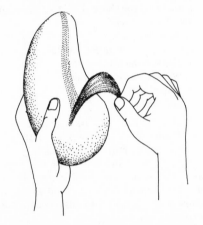

Dressing can be made while eggplant cools or whenever convenient. Heat oil in a skillet or saucepan and sauté ginger and garlic for about 1 minute until lightly colored. Add lemon, vinegar, soy sauce, honey, and sherry, bring to a boil, and stir until honey melts. Remove from heat and stir in sesame oil.

When dressing cools, pour over eggplant and mix well. Sprinkle with sesame seeds. Serve at room temperature.
Serves 6

STEAMED GREENS

In many parts of the world, spring is greeted by city and country folk alike who comb the fields, roadsides, and vacant lots for the first spring greens. Under the tutelage of their parents, children learn at a very young age to identify many wild edibles. If you can spot dandelion greens (before the flowers come), lambsquarter, sorrel, wild mustard, and the like you too can take part in this spring rite. If not, you can still enjoy cooked greens by preparing this dish with romaine, spinach, kale, chard, collard greens, beet greens, mustard greens, chickory, or any other leafy greens you can get hold of, preferably in a varied mix.

1 pound greens
1 tablespoon oil
1 clove garlic, chopped
salt
pepper
lemon wedges

Clean greens well and tear or shred with a knife into small pieces. (You will have about 12 cups.)

Heat oil in a large pot and cook garlic until it begins to sizzle but does not color. Add greens, cover, and cook for 5 minutes until wilted. Stir, replace cover, and continue to cook until greens are tender, 5 to 15 minutes, depending on what you have used.

Season with salt and pepper and serve with a wedge of lemon for additional seasoning at the table.
Serves 4

STIR-FRIED GREENS, CHINESE STYLE

1 pound Chinese bok choy, Swiss chard, collards, or other similar dark leafy greens
2 tablespoons oil
1 tablespoon soy sauce
1 tablespoon lemon juice
1 teaspoon honey
pinch salt (omit if broth is salted)
¾ cup vegetable broth
1 tablespoon arrowroot or cornstarch
2 tablespoons water
1 teaspoon Chinese sesame oil

Clean greens thoroughly and cut into 1-inch lengths. (You will have about 12 cups.)

Heat oil in a large skillet or wok and stir-fry greens until shiny and just beginning to soften, about 3 minutes. Add soy sauce, lemon juice, honey, a pinch of salt, and broth; bring to a boil, cover, and simmer until tender, 5 to 15 minutes, depending on the choice of greens.

Mix starch and water to a paste. Stir into greens and cook until sauce thickens. If too thick, add 1 to 2 tablespoons water.

Transfer to a serving dish, coat with sesame oil, and serve while still warm.

Serves 4

SAUTÉED MUSHROOMS

This dish offers the rich flavor of stuffed mushrooms without all the work.

2 tablespoons oil
1 tablespoon butter
1 large clove garlic, minced
4 scallions, thinly sliced
¾ pound mushrooms, sliced (about 4 cups)
¼ cup dried whole wheat bread crumbs
1 teaspoon oregano
½ teaspoon dried basil
¼ cup minced parsley
2 tablespoons sherry or dry white wine
few dashes soy sauce
few dashes hot pepper sauce
¼ teaspoon salt
pepper
2 tablespoons grated Parmesan cheese

Heat fat in a 10- to 12-inch skillet and sauté garlic and scallions for 2 to 3 minutes. Add mushrooms and cook 5 minutes longer until just tender.

Add everything but the cheese and cook for 3 to 5 minutes until most of the moisture is absorbed.

Remove from heat, sprinkle with cheese, stir, and serve.

Serves 4

CREAMY MUSHROOMS AND ONIONS

Serve as a side dish or a luscious topping for baked potatoes, bean burgers, grains, etc.

2 tablespoons butter or oil
1 medium onion, chopped
¾ pound mushrooms, sliced (about 4 cups)
2 tablespoons minced parsley
1 to 2 cups yogurt (preferably at room temperature)
salt
pepper

Heat fat in a large skillet or wok and sauté onion over medium-high heat until just beginning to color. Add mushrooms and stir-fry for 3 to 5 minutes until just tender. Add parsley; cook briefly and remove from heat.

Gradually stir in yogurt to desired degree of creaminess; the more you add, the more like gravy this will be. Season to taste with salt and pepper.

Serves 4
Minor Protein
Variations: The fat adds to the savoriness of this dish; however, those seeking a reduction can use just 1 tablespoon. For those unconcerned about fat content, up to ¼ cup sour cream can replace as much yogurt.

CREOLE OKRA

Spicy okra, New Orleans style.

1 large onion, chopped
1 clove garlic, chopped
2 tablespoons oil
1 pound okra, sliced into wheels (about 3½ cups)
½ cup diced green pepper
1 inch hot chili pepper, chopped (optional)
2½ cups diced fresh tomato, or 2 cups canned, lightly drained
4 sprigs parsley
4 fresh basil leaves or ¼ teaspoon dried
½ teaspoon salt

Sauté onion and garlic in oil until transparent, 3 to 5 minutes. Add okra and peppers and cook for 5 minutes.

Add remaining ingredients, cover, and simmer until okra is tender, about 15 minutes.

Adjust salt to taste and, if hot pepper was omitted, season to taste with hot pepper sauce.

Serves 4

CRISP FRIED ONIONS

Crunchy onion rings are fun to nibble by themselves or can be used to top grains, beans, or casseroles. These onions are the standard garnish for Kosheri, the Egyptian rice-macaroni-and-bean dish.

onions
milk
oil
whole wheat flour

Cut onions into ¼-inch-thick rings, allowing 1 medium onion for each 2 servings. Soak in milk to cover.

Heat oil to a depth of ¼ inch in a heavy skillet.

Drain onions and shake in a paper bag with whole wheat flour to coat, then drop into hot oil. Fry until crisp and golden, turning once to brown both sides. Drain on absorbent paper.

If more onions will be cooked, keep these warm in a 250° to 300°F. oven.

GLAZED ONIONS

Tiny "pearl" onions with a soy sauce–honey glaze make a flavorful garnish for beans or grains.

1 pound small onions (about 2 dozen 1½-inch onions)
2 tablespoons oil
½ tablespoon soy sauce
1 tablespoon honey

Remove papery outer layer from onions.

Combine whole onions with remaining ingredients in a saucepan, cover, and cook over low heat for 20 to 25 minutes until tender. Stir and shake pan occasionally to keep cooking even and prevent sticking or burning.

Serves 4 to 6

ONION-APPLE-RAISIN SAUTÉ

A pleasant accompaniment to noodle–cheese dishes or bean entrées.

2 large onions
2 large tart apples
2 tablespoons oil
3 tablespoons raisins

pinch cinnamon
pinch ginger

Cut each onion into 8 crescents. Peel apples and cut each into 16 wedges, removing core and pits.

Heat oil in a wok or large skillet. Stir-fry onions and apples for 5 minutes until onion is transparent. Add raisins and seasonings, cover, and cook over low heat until tender, about 5 minutes.

Serves 4

Variation: For *Curried Onion–Apple–Raisin Sauté,* add 1 teaspoon curry powder along with other seasonings.

NUTTED BAKED ONIONS

Cooking onions makes them surprisingly mild and sweet. Baked onion halves are a lovely treat, good for entertaining but really only practical to make when you are serving a crowd, or when they can be made simultaneously with something else in the oven.

4 large Spanish or Bermuda onions
1 cup water or vegetable broth
1 teaspoon salt (reduce if broth is salted)
2 teaspoons honey
1 teaspoon minced lemon peel
½ teaspoon paprika
1 tablespoon butter
½ cup chopped walnuts, pecans, or a mixture of nuts and dried whole grain bread crumbs

Preheat oven to 350°F.

Cut onions in half crosswise, or across the imaginary core (see "On Cooking: Preparing Vegetables"). Cut a thin slice from rounded end so onion stands firm with the broad-side up. Place side by side in a baking dish that holds the onions comfortably.

Combine water or broth, salt, honey, lemon peel, paprika, and butter in a small saucepan and bring to a boil. Pour over onions, cover, and bake for 50 minutes.

Uncover, top with nuts or crumbs, spoon any liquid in the bottom of the pan on top, and bake uncovered 10 to 15 minutes longer until lightly browned.

Serves 8

PARSNIP CURRY

Parsnips are a rather uncommon vegetable in most homes. As they are sweet and delicate in flavor (similar to both carrots and winter squash), the lack of interest in them is surprising. Most recipes for carrots and orange-fleshed squash can be adapted to parsnips (see the variation of Orange-Glazed Carrots, page 51). Here is a recipe specifically designed for the parsnip that is very tasty and makes a good accompaniment to almost every bean or grain entrée.

½ cup chopped onion
1 tablespoon oil
½ teaspoon cumin
1 teaspoon chili powder
1½ teaspoons turmeric
⅛ teaspoon cayenne (more
for a spicy curry)
½ cup water
½ teaspoon salt
1 pound parsnips, peeled and cut in
cubes or 1½-inch sticks (about 3½
cups)
⅓ cup thin strips green pepper
¼ cup chopped peanuts

Sauté onion in oil in a 1½-quart pot for 5 to 8 minutes until golden. Add spices and cook, stirring, for 1 minute. Add water, salt, and parsnips, bring to a boil, cover, and simmer over low heat for 20 to 30 minutes until vegetable is tender but not mushy. Sauce will become quite thick.

Garnish with pepper strips and peanuts before serving.

Serves 4 to 6
Variations: Some or all of the parsnip can be replaced with carrot or peeled winter squash.

PEAS AND MUSHROOMS

Fresh green peas are so delicious eaten raw, directly from the pod, that we hesitate to cook them. If you are so inclined, here is one way to do it nicely.

2 teaspoons butter
½ cup diced mushrooms
1½ pounds fresh peas, shelled (1½
to 2 cups)
¼ cup milk
sprig parsley
¼ teaspoon thyme

Melt butter in small saucepan and sauté mushrooms for about 3 minutes until liquid begins to run. Add remaining ingredients, cover, and cook over low heat for about 10 minutes until just tender.

Serves 4
Variations: (1) Replace mushrooms with scallions, tiny pearl onions, or chopped celery. (2) Replace some or all of the peas with carrots diced pea-size. (3) Replace peas with fresh corn kernels. Add ¼ cup chopped pimiento and omit thyme.

PLANTAIN CAKE

A dense but delicate breadlike vegetable cake that is rich in protein and an excellent accompaniment to rice–bean dinners or thick bean soups. The extra effort required to make something unusual is really rewarded in this dish.

2 medium-size ripe plantains (about 1
pound)
2 tablespoons oil
1 tablespoon wheat germ
1½ cups shredded mild white cheese
(mozzarella, Muenster, or Jack)
1 teaspoon cinnamon
4 eggs, separated
2 tablespoons honey

Peel plantains and cut into 4-inch sections. Cut each chunk lengthwise into slices barely ¼ inch thick. Heat oil in a large skillet and sauté plantains in batches until golden, turning as necessary until evenly cooked. This will take up to 10 minutes per batch. Pat cooked pieces dry with absorbent paper.

Preheat oven to 350°F. Grease a deep 9- to 10-inch glass pie plate with butter and coat with wheat germ. Shake out any excess.

Toss cheese with cinnamon. Beat egg yolks until thick and lemon-colored. Beat in honey. Beat egg whites until stiff. Fold in yolks.

Spread ⅓ egg mixture over bottom of prepared dish, using a spatula to make an even layer. Cover with half the plantain pieces and ¾ cup cheese. Spread with another layer of egg, the remaining plantain, remaining cheese, and finally the rest of the egg.

Bake for about 30 minutes, or until well browned. Serve warm or at room temperature.

Serves 6

Minor Protein

Note: While plantains can be cooked and kept a short time before assembly, the rest of the work should be done just before baking. If it is necessary to prepare this dish in advance, it is best to complete the baking and then serve it at room temperature or reheat it for a few minutes.

FRIED PLANTAINS

Plantains are large cooking bananas that can be used while in the green, yellow, or speckled stage. Although they are very starchy, they nonetheless are a traditional South American accompaniment for rice and bean dishes. For lighter service, try them with eggs instead of potatoes.

oil

plantains, preferably ripe (yellow or speckled with brown)

Heat enough oil to cover the surface of a skillet.

Peel plantains and cut on the diagonal into slices ¼ to ½ inch thick.

Sauté in hot oil, browning on both sides and pressing into the pan with a spatula to enhance browning.

Pat with absorbent paper to remove any excess fat after cooking. Serve hot.

1 pound plantains (or 2 medium) serves 4

Note: If plantains are unavailable, you can use unripe green bananas.

BASIC MASHED POTATOES

The addition of yogurt to mashed potatoes lends a very special flavor.

1½ pounds potatoes
½ teaspoon salt
⅛ teaspoon pepper

½ cup yogurt
¼ cup nonfat dry milk powder

Cut potatoes into quarters and steam for 15 to 20 minutes until tender. (You may peel them or not after cooking, depending on personal preference.)

Puree potatoes in a food mill, in a food processor using the plastic blade, in the blender, or whip by hand using a beater or wire whisk.

Beat in remaining ingredients until light and fluffy.

Makes about 3 cups; 4 to 6 servings

Minor Protein

Note: For calorie counters, ½ cup mashed potatoes from this recipe furnishes only 85 calories (and 4 grams protein). If butter is essential to your enjoyment of mashed potatoes, top with melted butter to taste.

Variation: For *Surprise Mashed Potatoes,* nourishing enough to provide Major Protein as a main course, stir a little crushed garlic and 4 ounces (1 cup) diced cheese into the fresh, hot, mashed potatoes. Cheese cubes will melt slightly, forming goey strands in the potato puree.

PAN-ROASTED POTATOES

Steamed, then roasted potatoes combine the best of both tastes, creating a creamy interior under a very crisp crust. If you don't mind using the oven, these are a lot less work to fix and clean up after than home fries and, in our opinion, better eating.

1½ pounds potatoes
2 tablespoons butter or part oil and butter

Preheat oven to 375°F.

Scrub potatoes, cut into even-sized chunks, and steam for 10 minutes until partially tender.

Coat with butter in a baking dish and bake for 30 to 40 minutes until well browned outside and fork-tender. Turn occasionally for even browning. Particularly large pieces may need more time.

Serves 4

Note: Oven temperature can be raised as high as 400°F. or made as low as 350°F. to accommodate other foods; adjust timing accordingly.

FRENCH FRIES

There are two essentials for making french fries properly: the right oil and the right variety of potatoes. Since an exceptionally high temperature is needed for frying potatoes, the oil must be fresh and able to withstand heat in order to avoid a burned or stale flavor. The potatoes should be mealy in texture, rather than the waxy variety preferred for potato salad, or the french fries will be insipid.

scrubbed, unpeeled Maine or Idaho potatoes (about 6 ounces per serving)
peanut, corn, or soy oil

Chill potatoes if possible.

Heat oil in a wok as for deep-fat frying or in a large, heavy skillet to a depth of ¼ inch. Bring temperature to 390°F. on a fat thermometer or to the point where a 1-inch cube of bread turns golden in 20 seconds.

Cut potatoes into sticks about ⅓ inch thick. Pat surface dry with toweling. Place a few at a time in hot fat and at the same time raise the heat a little to keep it steady. When the temperature stabilizes, add more potatoes.

Cook until potatoes are golden, turning as necessary. If oil is properly heated, potatoes should cook in about 5 minutes. Remove as they brown, adding more to take their place. Be sure to keep some potatoes in the oil throughout cooking or the temperature will rise rapidly. The object is to add fresh pieces as previous ones brown, keeping a good balance so heat goes neither too low nor too high.

Drain well. This can be done effectively by shaking the cooked potatoes in a brown paper bag.

If necessary, keep warm in a 300°F. oven until ready to serve.

Note: If this seems too complex, you might prefer to try Oven Fries.

Variations: Rather than serving french fries American style with catsup, we recommend the European manner with vinegar (which dramatically reduces the need for salt), or the Dutch style with mayonnaise.

OVEN FRIES

If you don't like frying, but do like fried potatoes, this could be your answer. Oven-frying of potatoes means less oil, less work, less money, and less mess.

1 pound potatoes
1 tablespoon oil
½ teaspoon paprika

Preheat oven to 450°F.

Scrub but do not peel potatoes. Cut as for french fries into sticks about ⅓ inch wide. Thinner fries can be made for crunchy "potato sticks"; thicker pieces will retain more potato taste and texture.

Toss potato pieces in a bowl with oil to coat. Add paprika and mix well (this enhances the color).

Spread on an oiled baking sheet and bake for 10 minutes. Loosen with a spatula, shake to keep from sticking, and bake 20 to 30 minutes longer. When done the outside will be firm to the touch, but they will be tender inside. The thinner sticks may be done sooner. Shake several times during baking to keep loose.

Serve, seasoning with salt to taste.

Serves 3 to 4

Note: Instead of salting potatoes, sprinkle with grated cheese during the last few minutes of baking. Oven Fries freeze quite successfully. Restore by placing in the broiler for 3 to 5 minutes.

HOME FRIES

Made from precooked potatoes, these are partially crisp on the surface.

1½ tablespoons oil
1½ tablespoons butter
1 large onion, chopped
4 cups diced cooked potatoes
salt
pepper

Heat fat in a heavy skillet and brown onion lightly. Add potato and continue to cook, mashing into fat with the bottom of a spatula and turning occasionally until they begin to brown, about 20 minutes.

Season to taste and serve.

Serves 4

Note: Home Fries can be kept warm in a low oven or by keeping the skillet barely warm with the use of a flame tamer. Do not cover the pan.

HASH BROWNS

Hash Browns are softer and moister than Home Fries.

1 tablespoon butter
1 tablespoon oil
4 cups diced cooked potatoes
1 tablespoon grated onion
1 tablespoon chopped parsley
½ teaspoon paprika
¼ cup milk
salt
pepper

Heat fat in skillet and add potatoes and onion. Cook, stirring occasionally, for 15 minutes.

Add parsley, paprika, and milk, turn potatoes with a spatula, and cook 5 minutes longer. Season to taste with salt and pepper.

Serves 4

Note: To keep warm until serving, cover pan.

DIJON POTATO SALAD

A French potato salad best made while potatoes are still warm so they absorb the dressing.

1 pound potatoes
3 tablespoons oil (part olive preferred)
¼ cup wine vinegar
2 teaspoons Dijon mustard
¼ teaspoon salt
⅛ teaspoon pepper
½ teaspoon dried chervil
¼ cup minced fresh parsley

Scrub potatoes, quarter, and steam for about 15 minutes until tender but not soft.

Beat remaining ingredients together in a bowl that will hold the salad.

When potatoes are cool enough to handle, remove peel and slice into dressing. Mix gently to coat.

Serve at room temperature. If made well in advance, store in refrigerator but try to remove a half hour before serving.

Serves 4

RICOTTA POTATO SALAD

A delicate potato salad with a protein bonus.

1¼ pounds potatoes, steamed, peeled, and sliced (about 4 cups)
1 cup ricotta cheese
½ cup yogurt
1 teaspoon prepared mustard
1 to 2 tablespoons water (optional)
2 scallions, chopped
2 tablespoons chopped green olives
2 tablespoons chopped sweet red or green pepper
salt
pepper

Have potatoes at room temperature or chilled.

Mix ricotta, yogurt, and mustard until creamy. If very thick, add water to make a thick mayonnaise consistency.

Fold vegetables into dressing and season to taste with salt and pepper.

Serves 6

Minor Protein

SPICED SPINACH

Much more interesting than ordinary creamed spinach.

2 tablespoons oil
½ cup chopped scallions
1 teaspoon minced fresh ginger
½ teaspoon chili powder
1 pound spinach, finely chopped (about 6 cups)
½ teaspoon salt

Heat oil in a large skillet and quickly brown scallions. Add ginger and chili powder and cook for 1 minute. Add spinach and salt, cover and cook over low heat for 5 minutes. Stir and serve while still hot.

Serves 4

Menu Suggestions: Serve as the vegetable with nut or bean roasts or as part of an Indian meal.

CHEDDAR-STUFFED SWEET POTATOES

4 medium sweet potatoes (about 6 ounces each)
1 cup grated cheddar or cheese of choice
¼ cup yogurt
paprika

Preheat oven to 350° to 375°F.

Bake potatoes as described in "Short-Order Cooking" (page 53).

Hold potatoes in a kitchen towel, cut a slice from the top, and scoop out pulp, leaving the shell intact.

Mash pulp with ¾ cup cheese and yogurt until light. Stuff back into shells, top with remaining cheese, and sprinkle with paprika.

Return to the oven for 5 minutes to melt cheese.

Serves 4

Minor Protein

ORANGE–SWEET POTATO CASSEROLE

Sweet potatoes and oranges baked in honey with a soft wheat topping.

2 unpeeled oranges, sliced ¼ inch thick
2 pounds sweet potatoes, peeled and sliced under ¼ inch thick (about 8 cups)
½ cup orange juice
¼ cup honey
2 tablespoons butter
¼ cup wheat germ

Preheat oven to 375°F.

Cut each orange slice in half and make alternate layers of potato and orange in a greased, shallow 2-quart casserole, beginning with potato and ending with orange.

Pour on orange juice and honey; dot with 1 tablespoon butter.

Cover and bake for about 30 minutes, or until potato is tender.

Uncover, sprinkle with wheat germ, dot with remaining tablespoon butter, and return to the oven for 10 minutes.

Serves 6 to 8

Note: Temperature can be varied from 350° to 400°F. if other foods are cooking in the oven. The rind on the orange will be soft enough to eat after baking, but if you do not have access to untreated oranges you may prefer to discard it.

FAR EAST SWEET POTATOES

Matchsticks of sweet potatoes stir-fried with vegetables and bean sprouts, seasoned with orange and spices, and topped with crunchy peanuts. A suitable side dish for all occasions; however, as this should be served immediately, it is best chosen when the other dishes do not require last-minute attention.

¾ pound sweet potatoes, peeled and sliced into matchsticks (about 3 cups)
1 medium onion, cut in crescents
½ cup diagonally sliced celery
½ cup sliced mushrooms
½ cup bean sprouts
1½ teaspoons minced fresh ginger
¼ teaspoon ground coriander
⅓ cup orange juice
1 tablespoon oil
1 to 2 teaspoons soy sauce
¼ cup chopped peanuts

Assemble vegetables in separate piles. Add ginger and coriander to orange juice.

Heat oil in a wok or large skillet and stir-fry sweet potatoes for 5 minutes. Add onion crescents and celery and stir-fry another 5 minutes. Add mushrooms and sprouts and stir-fry for 1 minute.

Pour juice over vegetables. It should bubble right up. When juice evaporates, add soy sauce to taste, top with nuts, and serve.

Serves 4

CANDIED SWEET POTATOES

A casserole of sweet potatoes baked in a syrup of maple-sweetened apple juice and topped with pecans. The perfect holiday choice.

2 pounds sweet potatoes, peeled and sliced ¼ inch thick (about 8 cups)
2 tablespoons maple syrup
½ cup apple juice or cider
¼ teaspoon salt
1 tablespoon butter
¼ to ½ cup chopped pecans

Preheat oven to 350°F.

Mix sliced potatoes with syrup, juice, and salt in a shallow 2-quart casserole. Dot top with butter, cover, and bake for about 45 minutes until tender.

Uncover, sprinkle with nuts, and bake 15 minutes longer.

Serves 6

Note: Temperature can be adjusted to accommodate other foods in the oven, and baking time can be increased or decreased as necessary.

SUNFLOWER SQUASH

A good choice with Mexican food.

1 to 1½ pounds winter squash
1 tablespoon oil
1 small onion, chopped
¼ cup sunflower seeds
¼ cup water
2 tablespoons soy sauce

Peel squash and cut in 1-inch cubes to make 3 to 4 cups.

Heat oil in a wok and sauté onions and sunflower seeds for about 3 minutes until onion is transparent. Add squash and sauté for 5 minutes longer.

Add water and soy sauce, cover, and cook over moderate heat for 20 to 30 minutes until squash is very tender.

Uncover and raise heat slightly to evaporate any liquid. The finished dish should be dry and quite soft.

Serves 4

SWEET BAKED SQUASH

Winter squash is naturally sweet and baking brings out its delicate nuttiness.

orange-fleshed winter squash
butter
honey or maple syrup (optional)

Preheat oven to 350° to 375°F.

Cut squash in half lengthwise from stem to blossom end. Scoop out seeds.

Place cut-side down in a shallow baking pan and surround with about ½ inch of water to prevent scorching. Bake for 30 to 40 minutes, or until barely tender.

Invert squash, rub surface with butter and, if desired, about ½ teaspoon sweetening per half. Return to the oven for 10 to 15 minutes until flesh is tender and cut surface browned.

1 small acorn squash serves 2; a large acorn or hubbard or butternut squash serves 4

Note: A light sprinkling of cinnamon and/or nutmeg can be used for additional seasoning.

STUFFED WINTER SQUASH

A hint of sweetness with an apple–bread crumb stuffing.

2 acorn squash
1 small onion, chopped
1 large stalk celery, chopped
1 apple, peeled and chopped
2 tablespoons chopped parsley
½ cup fresh whole grain bread crumbs
¼ cup wheat germ
½ cup ground nuts or seeds, any combination
2 tablespoons chopped raisins
2 tablespoons oil

Preheat oven to 350° to 400°F.

Cut squash in half lengthwise and scoop out seeds. Combine remaining ingredients and pack into squash hollows, mounding if necessary.

Place squash in a baking dish, surround with ½ inch hot water, cover, and bake for about 30 minutes until flesh is almost tender.

Remove cover and bake for 10 to 15 minutes until squash is tender and stuffing browns.

Serves 4

Minor Protein

BASIC STEAMED SPAGHETTI SQUASH

Spaghetti squash looks very much like honeydew melon with a firm, light green to yellow skin and a large, slightly oblong shape. Beneath the inedible skin is a firm, pale flesh that becomes stringlike in texture on cooking, giving the vegetable the characteristics that allow it to be compared to spaghetti. The flavor of the squash itself is rather innocuous, making it a perfect recipient for the same sauces you enjoy on pasta. We suggest you try it with pesto or tomato sauce and cheese; if it appeals, experiment with it in casseroles, soups, stews, etc., as a replacement for, or addition to, pasta.

1 large spaghetti squash (about 3 pounds)

Cut squash in half lengthwise through the stem end and, if large, divide it into chunks that will fit into the steamer. Remove seeds.

Steam for 15 to 20 minutes until flesh is just tender and you can separate it into strands with a fork.

Scrape flesh off the shell or loosen into strands if you wish to serve it in its shell; drain off liquid that accumulates. This liquid can be saved for vegetable broth.

Top with sauce of choice or season to taste with salt, pepper, grated cheese, and a little butter.

Makes about 4 cups "spaghetti"; serves 2 generously

Note: Try to cook "al dente" so vegetable resists a little when chewed; overcooked spaghetti squash is like too soft spaghetti.

LEMON SQUASH AND CARROTS

A delicate blend of yellow crookneck squash and carrots.

2 cups thinly sliced yellow squash
1½ cups thin, diagonal slices of carrot
1 small lemon, unpeeled and thinly sliced
1 tablespoon honey
½ cup water
¼ teaspoon cinnamon

Combine all ingredients in a saucepan and bring to a boil. Cover and simmer over low heat for about 8 minutes until carrots are barely tender.

Serves 4 to 6

HERBED SQUASH

The mild-flavored squash is perked up by the addition of a few herbs.

4 small yellow crookneck squash
¼ cup water
2 sprigs parsley
2 sprigs dill
½ teaspoon dried rosemary
½ teaspoon salt

Slice squash into rounds.

Combine water, herbs, and salt in a small saucepan. Bring to a boil.

Add squash to liquid, cover, and cook over low heat for 5 to 10 minutes until crisp-tender.

Serves 4

FRIED ZUCCHINI

A crunchy coating on the outside of the zucchini slices makes this vegetable as welcome at mealtime as french fries.

2 medium zucchini (1¼ to 1½ pounds)
1 egg
about 1 cup cornmeal
salt
pepper
oil

Cut zucchini into 4-inch segments. Cut each segment lengthwise into slices ¼ inch thick.

Beat egg in a shallow bowl. Season cornmeal with salt and pepper on a plate.

Dip each slice of zucchini in egg to coat, then dredge with seasoned meal.

When coating is completed, heat enough oil to generously cover a heavy 15-inch skillet. Brown zucchini in hot oil, about 5 minutes on each side, and drain on absorbent paper. You will probably have to do two or three panfuls to accommodate this amount. The early batches can sit at room temperature while the rest cooks; allowing the zucchini to cool slightly before serving actually enhances the flavor.

Serves 4

Menu Suggestions: A suitable accompaniment for most pasta, grain, or bean entrées, as well as egg and cheese dishes.

FRIED GREEN TOMATOES

Crumb-crusted green tomatoes have long been popular with American farm families as a way of enjoying the first and last tomatoes of the season. Today's lackluster commercial tomatoes can be uplifted in this manner as well.

**4 medium green or under-ripe red
    tomatoes
1 egg
about 1½ cups cornmeal
salt
pepper
oil**

Slice each tomato into 3 or 4 slices about ¼ inch thick.

Beat egg in a shallow bowl. Combine cornmeal and seasonings on a plate.

Dredge each tomato slice with cornmeal, dip in egg, and coat completely with cornmeal.

Heat enough oil to generously cover the surface of a large, heavy skillet. Sauté tomatoes until browned, 3 to 5 minutes per side. Service for 4 will require two pans or cooking in shifts.

Serves 4

Variations: Baking is more convenient if you are preparing this for a crowd. Place coated slices on a well-oiled baking sheet, drizzle with a little oil if desired, and bake in a 375°F. oven for 15 minutes.

For an entrée or a sandwich filling, place a slice of cheese on each cooked tomato round and melt. For a satisfying main dish, serve on pasta or rice with a blanket of Cheese Sauce.

BAKED PARSLEY TOMATOES

Any time that tomatoes aren't already on the menu during their season, pop some into the oven or roast them on the grill to accompany the entrée. They are good almost any way you fix them, including whole or cut in half and sprinkled with herbs, bread crumbs, or a little grated cheese and chopped fresh basil.

**4 ripe tomatoes
2 tablespoons pumpkin seeds
1 cup minced parsley
3 cloves garlic, chopped
2 tablespoons butter
salt
pepper**

Cut tomatoes crosswise into halves and place cut-side down on a grill or in a baking dish set in a 350°F. oven. Cook for about 10 minutes to soften slightly.

Meanwhile sauté pumpkin seeds in a dry skillet until popped and golden. Remove from skillet.

Add parsley, garlic, and butter to skillet, cover, and cook over medium heat for 5 minutes. Season with salt and pepper to taste.

Turn tomatoes cut-side up, spoon on parsley–garlic butter, and top with seeds.

Serve while still hot.

Serves 4

TOMATO WITH CHÈVRE

Thick tomato slices with creamy French goat cheese and fresh basil broiled on top.

**4 medium to large tomatoes
4 ounces French goat cheese such as
    Montrachet or Boucheron
¼ cup chopped fresh basil**

Cut each tomato into 3 thick slices. Arrange in a single layer in a shallow ovenproof pan. Cut cheese into small pieces and place evenly over tomato slices. Top with basil.

Broil for 3 to 5 minutes, until cheese is delicately browned. Serve at once.

Serves 4

Minor Protein

Variation: By replacing the goat cheese with farmer cheese a more subtle dish will be achieved, since farmer cheese lacks the intense saltiness of most goat cheeses.

GREEK STUFFED TOMATO

Mint seasons the bean-grain stuffing, making this a very refreshing summer side dish. Since it is served at room temperature, baking can be done well in advance during the cooler morning hours.

4 medium tomatoes
½ cup cracked wheat
½ cup hot water
1 scallion, chopped
1 tablespoon chopped fresh mint or 1 teaspoon dried
½ teaspoon salt
½ cup cooked chick-peas, drained
2 tablespoon olive oil

Preheat oven to 350°F.

Slice top from tomatoes, scoop out pulp and juice, and reserve. Invert tomato shells to drain.

Pour hot water over cracked wheat in a bowl and let stand for about 10 minutes to absorb liquid.

Add scallion, seasonings, and chick-peas to cracked wheat and stuff into tomato shells. Place in a baking dish.

Puree reserved tomato pulp and juice in a food mill, blender, or processor and pour over tomatoes and bottom of baking dish. Drizzle oil over each tomato.

Bake for 35 minutes. Remove from oven, spoon any liquid in pan over tomatoes, and cool to room temperature.

Serves 4
Minor Protein
Note: This is an excellent dish for summer entertaining since it can be prepared in quantity ahead of time.

SIMPLE VEGETABLE STIR-FRY

One of the fastest and most healthful ways to prepare vegetables is by stir-frying them in a wok or a large skillet. Here is the procedure we often use. For individual seasoning, offer Chinese mustard at the table.

2 tablespoons oil
1 clove garlic, split in half
1 medium onion, cut in thin crescents, or 6 scallions, cut in 1-inch lengths
¼ cup almonds, raw cashew pieces, peanuts, or pumpkin seeds
½ cup sliced mushrooms (optional)
4 cups any one, or combination of the following vegetables:
    asparagus, cut in 2-inch lengths
    green beans, trimmed at the ends
    snow peas, strings removed
    broccoli, cut in thin trees
    cauliflower, florets or sliced thin
    green pepper, cut in strips
    Chinese greens, cut in strips
    celery, cut in 2-inch matchsticks
    carrots, cut in 2-inch matchsticks
1 tablespoon soy sauce
1 teaspoon vinegar

Heat 1 tablespoon oil in a wok. Stir-fry garlic and onion for 1 minute over medium-high heat until lightly colored.

Add remaining 1 tablespoon oil. Stir-fry nuts and vegetables for 5 minutes. Vegetables should remain crisp.

Add soy sauce and vinegar and stir to coat. Serve at once.

Serves 4

QUICK VEGETABLE MEDLEY

A mosaic of shredded vegetables with your choice of seasonings.

3 cups shredded raw vegetables from the following list (include at least two colors):
    potato
    sweet potato
    carrot
    winter squash
    zucchini
    parsnip
    turnip
1 teaspoon salt
½ cup water
1 tablespoon butter
pinch nutmeg, ginger, cumin, curry powder, or soy sauce

Combine vegetables, salt, and water in a saucepan. Bring to a boil, cover, reduce heat, and cook for 5 minutes until tender. Season with butter and anything else you wish.

Serves 6

Note: This medley can be mixed with cooked grains for stuffing vegetables or omelets. Pureed with milk and heated, it becomes a light soup.

VEGETABLE CRUMB SAUTÉ

Vegetables and crumbs are mixed together in this dish; the unusual addition of cracked wheat adds a very nice crunch to the texture.

½ cup hot water
¼ cup cracked wheat
2 tablespoons oil/butter
1 clove garlic, minced
2 cups shredded or minced raw vegetables:
   carrot
   potato
   zucchini
   parsnip
   cauliflower
½ cup ground sunflower seeds
2 slices whole grain bread, crumbled
¼ cup wheat germ
1 teaspoon nutritional yeast (optional)
bean sprouts (optional)
salt to taste

Pour hot water over cracked wheat and let stand while preparing everything else.

Heat fat in a 10- to 12-inch skillet and sauté garlic briefly. Add vegetables and stir-fry until crisp and to your taste.

Press all moisture out of the cracked wheat and add to the skillet with the remaining ingredients. Cook until lightly browned, stirring with a fork to distribute all ingredients evenly.

Serves 4

Minor Protein

STEAMED VEGETABLES WITH SALSA CRUDA

A mellow, raw tomato sauce, which can be spiced to taste, tops a mixture of steamed vegetables and toasted pumpkin seeds.

3 medium potatoes (about 1 pound), cut in quarters
4 medium carrots, cut in chunks
½ pound green beans, trimmed
2 stalks celery, cut in 1-inch pieces
2 medium zucchini, cut in chunks
¼ cup pumpkin seeds
1 cup Salsa Cruda (page 308)
½ cup yogurt

Steam potatoes for 10 minutes; add carrots, beans, and celery and steam for 5 minutes; add zucchini and steam 5 minutes longer, or until all vegetables are tender.

While vegetables steam, toast seeds in a dry skillet until they pop. Do not overbrown.

Stir yogurt into Salsa Cruda. Sauce can be prepared while vegetables cook or well in advance, and can be made either mild or hot, depending on individual preference.

Toss cooked vegetables with seeds. Spoon sauce over all.

Serves 4 generously

Minor Protein

Menu Suggestions: Serve as an accompaniment to Cheese Enchiladas, Bean Tacos, Chili Rellenos, or Green Rice with Stuffed Chilies. For a light meal, the vegetable dish itself can serve as the entrée, accompanied by a couple of Nachos or Harvest Corn Bread and Lemon Greens.

MASHED COMBINATION VEGETABLES

More delicate than mashed potatoes.

1½ pounds vegetables of choice, including:
   potatoes
   sweet potatoes
   winter squash
   carrots
   parsnips
   turnips
   Jerusalem artichokes
1 tablespoon butter
1 small onion, chopped
salt
pepper

Peel vegetables, cut in large chunks, and steam for about 20 minutes until tender. Puree in a food mill or mash with a potato masher or wire whisk.

Melt butter in a small saucepan, add onion, and cook until lightly colored. Mix in mashed vegetables and heat through. Season with salt and pepper to taste.

Serves 4

Variations: (1) Add ½ to 1 cup shredded sharp cheddar, Gouda, Edam, or similar cheese to seasoned mashed vegetables. Mix well, cover, and heat long enough to melt. (2) Sprinkle plain or cheese-flavored mashed vegetables with a few caraway seeds.

FRUIT CURRY

A well-seasoned, savory fruit dish can serve as a vegetable accompaniment. This one is of Asian origin.

1 tablespoon oil
1 tablespoon butter
1 tablespoon turmeric
1 teaspoon cumin
2 tablespoons minced or grated fresh ginger
1 bay leaf
2 cardamom pods, crushed to release seeds
1 large onion, chopped
½ cup diced tomato
2 medium apples, peeled and sliced (about 2 cups)
2 large bananas, peeled and sliced (1½ to 2 cups)
¼ cup water
juice of 1 lemon
3 tablespoons peanut butter
pinch salt

Heat fat in a large skillet and sauté spices over low to medium heat for about 3 minutes. Add onion and tomato and sauté until onion softens, 3 to 5 minutes.

Add fruit and water, cover, and cook until just tender, 5 to 8 minutes.

Stir lemon juice into peanut butter to form a smooth paste, add to fruit, and warm through, stirring to spread peanut butter evenly.

Season with just a pinch of salt.

Serves 4 to 6

Protein Complement

Menu Suggestions: Serve this flavorful curry with Skillet Vegetables with Yogurt and Cheese or Very Quick Curried Chick-Peas or Indian Lentils, rice, and chapatis or pita bread.

BEAN ACCOMPANIMENTS

By following the "bean pot" concept—cooking up a large volume of beans for use over several days—the preparation of bean accompaniments becomes quick and simple. Home-cooked beans are so tasty that they may be presented with very little embellishment, but for added interest and variety in meal planning beans can be given a lift with a light sauce or seasoning. Although people tend to think of bean dishes as winter food, cold marinated beans are excellent warm-weather fare.

When the "bean pot" is empty, you can use canned beans, but be sure to adjust the salt in the recipe if presalted.

For the fundamentals of bean preparation, turn to "On Cooking: Basic Bean Cookery"; other pertinent information on the use of beans can be found in "Food Handling and Storage," "The Protein Principle," and in "The New American Menu." The information about menu planning is especially important in using bean accompaniment recipes, as the protein value of bean dishes is greatly enhanced when they are served in a meal that contains grains, nuts, seeds, eggs, or dairy foods.

BEANS WITH STEWED ONIONS

Simple cooked beans generously seasoned with onions make a flavorful side dish.

2 large onions, coarsely chopped
2 to 4 tablespoons oil (at least part olive preferred)
4 cups cooked beans, drained
salt
pepper

Combine onions and oil in a saucepan or skillet; cover and stew over low heat for 10 minutes until onions are tender.

Stir in beans, season with salt if beans are unsalted, add pepper to taste, and heat through.

Serves 6

Protein Complement

Menu Suggestions: This becomes an attractive main dish when combined with Bulgur Dumplings.

CHICK-PEAS WITH GRAVY

1 medium onion, chopped
1 clove garlic, chopped
1 tablespoon oil
¼ cup tahini
1 to 2 tablespoons soy sauce
½ cup water or bean cooking liquid
3 cups cooked chick-peas, drained
lemon wedge

Sauté onion and garlic in oil until lightly browned, about 5 minutes over medium-high heat.

Combine tahini, soy sauce, and liquid using only 1 tablespoon soy sauce if liquid is salty, 2 if you are using water. Mix until smooth.

Add tahini mixture and chick-peas to onion and cook over moderate heat, stirring until thick and creamy and just beginning to boil, 3 to 5 minutes.

Squeeze in lemon juice and serve.

Serves 4

Major Protein

QUICK CURRIED BEANS

This medium-hot dry curry can be used as a complementary vegetable with grain main dishes or as a side dish at an Indian dinner. Very quick and easy to prepare.

1 large onion, chopped
1 large clove garlic, chopped
2 tablespoons oil
1 tablespoon curry powder
1 teaspoon paprika
½ teaspoon ground ginger
4 cups cooked beans with a little bean liquid

2 cups chopped, peeled tart apple
2 tablespoons soy sauce
1 tablespoon lemon juice

Sauté onion and garlic in oil until tender, about 5 minutes. Add spices, stir, and cook briefly.

Add beans, apple, and soy sauce, and simmer uncovered for 15 minutes, or until apple is tender. Stir occasionally to prevent sticking.

When cooking is completed, stir in lemon juice and serve.

Serves 6

Protein Complement

INDIAN LENTILS (DAHL)

The standard accompaniment to all Indian vegetable curries.

1 large onion, chopped
2 cloves garlic, chopped
1 tablespoon oil
½ teaspoon crushed red pepper
½ teaspoon turmeric
1 teaspoon cumin
1 cup dried lentils
2 cups water
½ teaspoon salt

Sauté onion and garlic in oil in a 1- to 2-quart pot. When softened, add spices and cook for 1 minute longer.

Add lentils and water. Bring to a boil, cover, and simmer over low heat until tender, 45 minutes to 1 hour.

Stir occasionally while cooking and add salt any time after the first 20 minutes.

Serves 4

Protein Complement

Menu Suggestions: In addition to accompanying any Indian meal that does not already contain beans, Dahl can be coupled with a rice-vegetable dish and a yogurt salad to make a complete dinner. Consult "Condiments" for a quick chutney to serve with the meal.

ITALIAN BEANS AND GREENS

1 large clove garlic, split in half
¼ cup olive oil
1 pound romaine lettuce, coarsely shredded (about 10 cups)

1 tablespoon chopped parsley
3 cups cooked chick-peas or fava beans, drained
1 cup liquid from beans, or water
2 tablespoons tomato sauce, pulp, or juice, or 1 tablespoon tomato paste
1 teaspoon salt (omit if beans are salted)
pepper

Brown garlic lightly in oil in a large pot. Add lettuce and parsley, cover, and cook over low heat for 10 minutes until wilted.

Add remaining ingredients, cover, and simmer for 15 minutes, or until beans are tender.

Serves 6
Protein Complement
Menu Suggestions: A good complement for pasta, pizza, any vegetable-cheese combination, or cornmeal entrées such as Polenta and Corn Dodgers.

BEAN PISTOU

Fresh and dried beans combined in a rich garlic and herb sauce.

2 cups string beans
2 cups cooked soybeans or chick-peas
1 cup Tomato Pesto (page 319)

Trim ends of string beans and snap into 1- to 2-inch lengths. Steam for 5 minutes.

Heat cooked dried beans, drain of all excess moisture, and combine in a serving bowl with warm green beans.

Pour Pesto on top and serve.

Serves 4
Minor Protein
Menu Suggestions: An ideal summer meal with a cold rice or pasta salad, fresh sliced tomatoes, bread and cheese.

TWO-TONE MEXICAN BEANS

A two-layer bean dish: one whole and lightly sweetened, the other mashed and spicy. A dollop of yogurt or sour cream on top of the beans is an appropriate garnish.

3 cups cooked kidney or pinto beans, drained
2 tablespoons bean cooking liquid

1 tablespoon molasses
1 tablespoon oil
1 small onion, chopped
1½ teaspoons chili powder

Place half the beans in a saucepan with bean liquid and molasses. Cook over medium heat for about 5 minutes until warm and dry.

Heat oil in a small skillet, brown onion and chili powder, and cook the remaining beans, mashing gently with a fork until thick and dry.

To serve, place some of the mashed beans on each plate. Top with cooked whole beans.

Serves 4
Protein Complement

ORIENTAL SOYBEANS

A mild, slightly sweet and gingery bean that is a good companion to rice.

2 cups cooked soybeans, drained
½ cup cooking liquid
1 medium onion, chopped
1 cup chopped, peeled apple
¼ teaspoon ground ginger
2 tablespoons molasses
1 tablespoon soy sauce

Combine all ingredients in a saucepan. Bring to a boil and simmer, uncovered, for 10 to 15 minutes. The apple should still be slightly crisp when done.

Serves 4
Protein Complement

Baked Beans

The traditional baking of beans by long, slow oven cookery, particularly suited to wood cookstoves, grew out of the religious restrictions on Sunday cooking for Pilgrim women who would put the beans in to cook on Saturday night so that by Sunday evening supper would be ready. Sunday night beans became so popular in Boston that at one time there were community ovens, conveniently set up in local taverns, where you could bring your prepared pan of beans in the morning and retrieve them in time for the evening meal.

Today this type of cooking is no longer practical, but the flavor of baked beans can be reproduced by simmering the beans with the appropriate seasonings and combining this, if desired, with a short baking. The resulting bean dish has a subtle difference in texture but is nonetheless a well-flavored adaptation.

Although the lower the heat and the longer the cooking time, the more traditional the recipe, if the oven is in use for other cooking, beans are adaptable. Ideally, the partially cooked, seasoned beans should not be exposed to temperatures above 300°F. during an oven stay exceeding six hours. But really the only rule that must be followed closely when the beans are in the oven is to keep the pan covered until the last 30 to 45 minutes and not to let the heat go above 350°F. or the beans will be dry and tough.

The following baked bean recipes are adapted to modern kitchen practices. Recipes can be multiplied or divided without any problem; as baked beans freeze well, it may be worth your while to expand the recipe and prepare enough for another meal.

Note: For the 3 cups cooked beans required for these recipes, soak and cook ½ pound of the bean specified according to the techniques described in "On Cooking: Basic Beans."

If preferred, baking can be omitted entirely and ingredients can be combined on top of the stove and simmered slowly, uncovered, until sauce is thick and the beans soft, approximately 45 minutes.

BOSTON-STYLE BAKED BEANS

3 cups cooked navy, pea, or great northern beans, drained
liquid from cooked beans
tomato paste or juice
1 large onion, thinly sliced
1 tablespoon cider vinegar
2 tablespoons molasses

1 teaspoon dry mustard
1 teaspoon salt (omit if beans are salted)
2 tablespoons oil

Preheat oven to 300° to 350°F.

Moisten beans in a shallow 1-quart casserole with about ½ cup of their cooking liquid, or water if necessary, seasoned with a little tomato paste or juice according to personal taste.

Add onion, vinegar, molasses, and seasonings. Pour oil evenly over surface.

Cover and bake for about 30 minutes; uncover and bake for about 30 minutes longer until liquid is reduced and beans are quite tender. Watch to prevent excessive drying out.

Serves 4
Protein Complement
Menu Suggestions: For a New England dinner serve with hot, steamed or baked Boston Brown Bread (which can be bought canned or made at home in the oven along with the beans) and a crisp slaw. For a more substantial meal, precede this with a mixed vegetable-grain soup.

APPLE–BEAN BAKE

3 cups cooked kidney or similar beans, drained
3 medium apples, peeled and sliced (2½ to 3 cups)
2 tablespoons molasses
2 tablespoons cider vinegar
¼ cup apple juice

Preheat oven to 350°F.

Combine beans with apples in a shallow 1½- to 2-quart casserole. Pour on molasses, vinegar, and apple juice.

Cover and bake for about 30 minutes until apple is tender. If too liquid, remove cover and continue to bake until some of the sauce evaporates. On the other hand if the beans become too dry during cooking, add some bean liquid or a little apple juice.

Serves 4 to 6
Protein Complement
Menu Suggestions: A good companion to rice-and-vegetable dishes. The addition of salad or Cooked Coleslaw completes the meal.

BAKED MEXICAN LIMA BEANS

3 cups cooked dried lima beans, drained
1 teaspoon salt (omit if beans are salted)
1 large onion, chopped
1 large clove garlic, chopped
3 tablespoons chopped canned green chilies, including some jalapeños if desired
½ teaspoon dry mustard
1 teaspoon chili powder
1 tablespoon molasses or honey
2 tablespoons cider vinegar
½ cup tomato juice, puree, mashed canned pulp, or diluted tomato paste

Preheat oven to 300° to 350°F.
Combine all ingredients in a 1-quart casserole. Cover and bake for 30 minutes. Uncover and bake 30 minutes longer, or until beans are very tender and surrounded by a rich gravy.
Serves 4
Protein Complement
Variation: For *Texas Baked Beans,* replace limas with navy, pea, or great northern beans.
Menu Suggestions: Serve with a cornmeal breadstuff, such as tortillas, tacos, Harvest Corncake, or Corn Cheese Pancakes. Or serve as a double entrée with Cheese Enchiladas or Chili Rellenos. For a Texas Baked Bean Dinner, serve with corn bread, cucumber salad, and watermelon.

BEAN–CHEESE SALAD

Prepare salad in advance so that flavor has time to develop.

2 cups cooked beans, drained
2 stalks celery, chopped
¼ cup chopped parsley
2 small or 1 large tomato, chopped
3 ounces brick, Jack, Muenster, or similar mild cheese, cubed (about ⅔ cup)
¼ cup cider vinegar
¼ cup oil
2 teaspoons honey
salt (omit if beans are salted)
pepper

In a serving bowl, mix beans, celery, parsley, tomato, and cheese.
Beat together remaining ingredients until honey "melts." Pour over bean mixture.
Let marinate for 30 minutes or longer.
Serves 6
Minor Protein
Note: Omit tomatoes if they are out of season.

AVOCADO–BEAN SALAD

2 cups cooked beans, drained
¼ cup minced onion
¼ cup wine vinegar
¼ cup oil
½ teaspoon salt (omit if beans are salted)
¼ teaspoon dried oregano
¼ teaspoon paprika
1 small clove garlic, split in half
2 cups peeled, bite-size avocado cubes
fresh spinach or romaine

Combine beans, onion, vinegar, oil, and seasonings, and let marinate.
When ready to serve, add avocado and mound on a generous bed of greens.
Serves 4
Protein Complement

MIDEAST CHICK-PEA SALAD

This salad can be prepared in advance or just before serving.

¼ cup minced parsley
¼ cup minced onion
1 large clove garlic, minced
6 tablespoons lemon juice
5 tablespoons olive oil
⅛ teaspoon cayenne
½ teaspoon salt (omit if beans are salted)
3 cups cooked, drained chick-peas, at room temperature

Combine all ingredients except beans and mix well. Add beans and stir to coat. Adjust seasoning to taste.
Serves 6
Protein Complement
Variations: (1) Substitute scallion

for onion; (2) Substitute wine vinegar for lemon juice; (3) Replace cayenne with ¾ teaspoon finely chopped hot chili pepper; (4) Add one tomato, cut in bite-size pieces; (5) Add ½ teaspoon dried oregano.

For *Greek Bean Salad*, replace chickpeas with cooked white beans. Garnish with olives, top with crumbled feta cheese if desired, and sprinkle liberally with pepper.

GRAIN, DUMPLING, AND PASTA ACCOMPANIMENTS

Most plain cooked whole grains, including brown rice, millet, cracked wheat (bulgur), barley, and buckwheat (kasha) have a delicate nutlike flavor that makes them enjoyable by themselves. However, for those who prefer more elaborate fare, it is worth knowing how to dress up some of these grains.

The following recipes utilize both uncooked and cooked grains. For background information on preparation, see "On Cooking: Basic Grains." Additional advice for handling of grains is included in "Food Handling and Storage"; suggestions for maximizing their value are given in "The Protein Principle."

Grains

Seasoning Grains

When cooking grains as a side dish, you may want to add some flavoring to the cooking medium. For example, grains can be cooked in the liquid drained from canned tomatoes or in a tomato broth made by combining equal parts of tomato juice and water. The addition of tomato may extend the cooking time a few minutes. Similarly, the broth from cooked vegetables or soaked dried mushrooms makes a tasty cooking water.

Herbs and spices added to the cooking liquid can make a grain side dish more interesting. For seasonings such as cumin, curry powder, turmeric, oregano, dill, basil, and thyme, use ½ to 1 teaspoon per cup of uncooked grain. Add 1 tablespoon dried or up to ¼ cup minced fresh parsley per cup of uncooked grain. For color, add ⅛ teaspoon saffron per cup of uncooked grain. For added aroma, put a piece of cinnamon in the cooking pot.

Any amount of chopped onion, celery, mushroom, carrot, or green pepper can be sautéed in a little oil in the pot before the grain is added. When the vegetable has softened a bit, add grain, stir well to coat with the flavorful oil and vegetables, then add boiling water, and cook as usual.

Raisins can be added at any time during cooking. Nuts, sesame seeds, or chopped olives are a nice addition to the pot when the grain is almost cooked.

If you want a decorative effect, make a grain ring by mixing 2 tablespoons butter into each 4 cups hot cooked grain; pack grain into an oiled 1-quart ring mold and let sit, in a pan of warm water until ready to unmold.

Restoring Leftover Grains

To add flavor to leftover grains, reheat in a pan with sautéed mushrooms, onions, fresh chopped parsley, or mix in grated cheese once grain is warmed through. If grain is bland, season it with soy sauce.

Try mixing several different grains together when you reheat them. Any combination of rice, millet, barley, cracked wheat, and kasha is more interesting than any one grain alone.

For a crunchy topping, toast sunflower seeds, pumpkin seeds, sliced almonds, or cashew pieces in a dry skillet and scatter them on top of the cooked grain.

BREAD STUFFING

In addition to giving stale bread a purpose, stuffing makes a delicious and inexpensive accompaniment to vegetable entrées. It is especially appealing to children.

4 cups whole grain bread cubes (from 6 ounces bread)
¾ teaspoon poultry seasoning, or ½ teaspoon thyme plus ¼ teaspoon sage
1 tablespoon dried or 3 tablespoons minced fresh parsley
1 tablespoon nutritional yeast
½ teaspoon salt
generous amount pepper
½ cup chopped onion
3 tablespoons melted butter/oil
¼ to ½ cup one or more of the following (optional):
    chopped celery
    chopped apple
    dried fruit
¼ to ½ cup one or more of the following protein-contributing foods (optional):
    wheat germ
    chopped nuts
    grated cheese
    nonfat dry milk powder
1 to 2 tablespoons soy sauce
½ cup boiling water or vegetable broth
1 egg beaten (optional)

Preheat oven to 350°F.

Mix bread cubes with seasonings. Add onion, fat, and any of the optional ingredients you wish.

Pour soy sauce and boiling water over all and stir to moisten completely. If stuffing seems too dry, add additional liquid. Stir beaten egg into stuffing mixture if you wish a lighter stuffing.

Place in a greased 1-quart baking dish, cover, and bake for 20 minutes. Uncover and bake 10 minutes longer.

Serves 4
Minor Protein
Note: For pre-made *Stuffing Mix,* dry bread to make croutons and combine with seasonings. Store in an airtight container. Prepare as above, using a little more liquid to moisten.

For *"Stove-Top Stuffing,"* cook stuffing mixture in a covered skillet on top of the stove for 20 to 30 minutes. Toss mixture with a fork several times during cooking. Remove cover during the last few minutes to dry slightly.

The preferred way to reheat leftover stuffing is by steaming it over boiling water in a vegetable steamer for 5 minutes. If reheating is done in the oven, add a little milk to prevent stuffing from drying out.

Menu Suggestions: If you include one or more of the optional protein ingredients suggested in the recipe, the stuffing served with Brown Gravy and perhaps a bean salad and cranberry sauce can be a meal in itself.

STEAMED BARLEY

Plain barley is best cooked over steam.

1 cup uncooked barley
1 quart water
1 teaspoon salt

Bring water and salt to a boil.

Sprinkle barley into water and simmer, uncovered, for 20 minutes. Drain through a fine strainer or vegetable steamer.

Place partially cooked grain in a vegetable steamer, set over boiling water, cover, and steam (as for vegetables) for 30 minutes until grain is tender to the bite.

Makes 3½ cups; serves 6
Protein Complement

STEAMED BARLEY SALAD

An excellent salad for picnics, buffets, and barbecues because it does not spoil easily in hot weather.

2 cups hot, steamed barley (as per previous recipe using a heavy ½ cup of grain)
¼ cup lemon juice
¼ cup oil
½ cup chopped cucumber
¼ cup sliced scallion
½ cup chopped parsley
1 cup diced tomato

Mix hot barley with lemon juice and oil. Stir in vegetables. Chill for at least 1 hour. Remove from refrigerator a little before serving so salad is not ice cold; season generously with pepper and, if your palate requires, lightly with salt.

Serves 6
Protein Complement

MUSHROOM AND BARLEY SALAD

¼ pound mushrooms
3 tablespoons lemon juice
3 tablespoons oil
pinch salt
¼ cup chopped or sliced green olives
1½ cups cooked barley

Slice or chop mushrooms into chunky pieces. (You should have a scant 1¼ cups.)

Make a dressing of lemon juice, oil, and salt. Pour over mushrooms and let marinate for 15 to 30 minutes.

Add olives and barley to mushrooms; mix well. Can be served at once, kept for 1 hour at room temperature, or refrigerated until needed.

Serves 4
Protein Complement

FLUFFY KASHA

Buckwheat groats deserve this special handling to make the light, nutty grain that is so popular in eastern Europe.

1 cup uncooked buckwheat groats
1 egg, lightly beaten
2 cups boiling water
½ teaspoon salt

Mix buckwheat with beaten egg to coat.

Toast grain in a dry 1-quart saucepan, stirring until each grain is separate and dry. Add boiling water and salt; cover and cook over low heat until the liquid is absorbed and the grain is tender, about 15 to 20 minutes.

Fluff grain with a fork after cooking; replace cover and let sit until ready to serve.

Makes about 4 cups; serves 4
Minor Protein
Variations: For *Protein-Enriched Kasha,* stir ¾ cup yogurt gently into the hot cooked grain, mixing until yogurt is no longer visible. This adds a pleasant, tangy overtone to the flavor of the grain.

For *Onion Kasha,* sauté 1½ cups chopped onion in 2 tablespoons oil in the saucepan before adding the grain. When onion begins to brown, add buck-wheat–egg mixture and "toast" until dry. Proceed as basic recipe directs.

For *Mushroom Kasha,* add ½ pound sliced mushrooms with or instead of the onion.

For *Kasha Varnishkes,* prepare Onion Kasha and at the same time cook 4 ounces (about 2 cups) small pasta (bow ties or shells) in boiling salted water until tender. Drain and toss with cooked kasha. Serve plain or with a topping of cottage cheese and yogurt as a main dish.

KASHA KNISHES

A traditional knish has a pastry covering surrounding the savory grain filling. In this simplified version, the tender grain mixture is encased in a crunchy wheat germ coating.

3 medium potatoes (about 1 pound)
2 tablespoons oil
1 large onion, chopped (at least 1 cup)
1 cup buckwheat groats
2 cups boiling water
1½ teaspoons salt
pepper
2 eggs
about ¼ cup wheat germ

Quarter potatoes and steam until tender, about 15 to 20 minutes. Press through a sieve or food mill. Do not puree in a food processor.

While potato cooks, heat oil in a 1-quart pot and sauté onion until golden. Add buckwheat and sauté for 2 to 3 minutes, stirring to coat with oil and onion.

Pour boiling water over kasha; cover and cook over low heat until liquid is absorbed and grain is tender, 15 to 20 minutes.

Preheat oven to 350° to 375°F.

Combine cooked kasha, sieved potatoes, seasonings, and 1 beaten egg. Shape into 8 balls, using about ½ cup for each.

Beat remaining egg. Roll each ball in wheat germ, dip in egg, and coat generously with more wheat germ.

Place knishes on an oiled baking

sheet and bake about 25 minutes until firm and golden.

Serves 8
Minor Protein
Note: For *Miniature Knishes* suitable for hors d'oeuvres, shape into tiny balls using about 2 tablespoons mixture for each. Coat as directed and bake. Check progress after 15 minutes, as baking time will be reduced. Wrap any extra knishes in foil and freeze. Reheat in the oven without thawing or unwrapping.

OAT PILAF

Very nice with eggs.

2 tablespoons oil
½ cup chopped onion
1½ cups oats
1 egg, lightly beaten
¾ cup vegetable broth, or water seasoned with Tomato Cubes (page 430) or tomato juice, or plain water
¼ cup chopped parsley
½ teaspoon dried basil
½ teaspoon oregano
¼ teaspoon salt (omit if broth is salted)

Heat oil in a small saucepan and sauté onion for 3 to 5 minutes until tender.

Mix oats with egg, add to onion, and cook, stirring, until each grain is separate and dry.

Add liquid and seasonings; simmer uncovered, stirring a few times until grain is swollen and tender, about 5 minutes. Cover until ready to serve.

Serves 4
Minor Protein
Variation: For *Oat–Vegetable Pilaf,* add up to ½ cup any or all of the following along with the onion: chopped green or red pepper, mushrooms, celery, zucchini.

VIENNESE RICE

Sautéeing the grain in butter before cooking enhances the nutty taste.

2 tablespoons butter
1½ cups uncooked brown rice

½ teaspoon salt (omit if liquid is salted)
3 cups water, broth, or liquid drained from canned tomatoes

Melt butter in a 2-quart pot and sauté rice for about 5 minutes, stirring occasionally, until it begins to color.

Add remaining ingredients, bring to a boil, cover, and simmer over low heat about 45 minutes until tender.

Makes about 5 cups; serves 6
Protein Complement

PEANUT RICE

Nuts and spices enhance the flavor of basic cooked rice. A particularly nice dish with curries.

1 cup uncooked brown rice
2 cups water
¼ cup peanuts
½ teaspoon salt
¾ teaspoon cumin
good pinch turmeric

Cook rice in water in your usual manner. Halfway through cooking, add nuts and seasonings. Continue cooking until tender.

Serves 4
Minor Protein

NUTTED RICE WITH RAISINS

1 cup uncooked brown rice
2 cups water
2 tablespoons pumpkin seeds
¼ cup raisins
¼ cup sliced almonds
¼ teaspoon cinnamon

Combine rice and water in a saucepan, bring to a boil, cover, and cook over low heat until tender and liquid is completely absorbed, about 45 minutes.

Place pumpkin seeds in a dry skillet over medium heat and toast until they brown and pop.

Add toasted pumpkin seeds, raisins, almonds, and cinnamon to cooked rice and toss gently with a fork or chopsticks. Replace cover until ready to serve.

Serves 4
Minor Protein

GREEK SPINACH RICE

A typical way of preparing rice in Greece is to cook it in a broth flavored with olive oil and vegetables. The thick, soupy stew that results is eaten luke-warm, as is most Greek food, which has a significant effect in developing the flavor.

2 pounds spinach
¼ cup olive oil
1 small onion, chopped
4 soft tomatoes, or ½ cup tomato pulp, or 4 Tomato Cubes (page 430), or 2 tablespoons tomato paste
2 teaspoons salt
pepper
large bunch dill
2 to 2½ cups water
1 cup uncooked brown rice

Trim spinach and tear it into small pieces; sauté in oil with onion in a 3-quart pot. When spinach is limp, press the tomatoes through a sieve over the pot, or add the pulp or cubes as indicated. (If tomato paste is preferred, mix it with the water before adding.) Add seasonings and liquid; bring to a boil.

Stir rice into boiling liquid, cover, and cook over low heat for about 1 hour until tender. Stir occasionally and add more water if needed to make the consistency of thick soup. Remove cover after cooking to cool; serve lukewarm.

Serves 4 to 6

Minor Protein

Note: Interestingly, spinach enhances the quality of the protein in this dish.

Variation: For *Greek Eggplant Rice,* replace spinach with a 1- to 1½-pound eggplant cut in 1-inch cubes. Sauté in oil with onion for about 5 minutes, then proceed as above.

Menu Suggestions: Rice prepared in this manner makes a very good accompaniment to beans, eggs, or any feta cheese dish. We enjoy this dish so much that we often make it the focal point of the meal enhancing the protein value by adding beans and cheese to an accompanying salad.

AROMATIC RICE WITH GREEN BEANS

Rice cooked with vegetables, nuts, and spices.

1 tablespoon butter
½ cup sliced mushrooms
1 cup uncooked brown rice
2 cups boiling water
½ pound string beans (as young and fresh as possible)
1 stick cinnamon
¾ teaspoon ground ginger
¾ teaspoon salt
2 tablespoons slivered almonds
2 tablespoons chopped peanuts

Melt butter in a 2-quart pot. Sauté mushrooms for 1 minute, then add rice and sauté, stirring, for 2 to 3 minutes until faintly colored.

Add remaining ingredients, cover, and cook over very low heat until grain is tender and dry, about 45 minutes.

Serves 4

Minor Protein

Variation: For a change, omit the mushrooms and add ½ cup raisins to the sautéed grain along with the remaining ingredients.

HINDU PULAO

The combination of rice, vegetables, and spices knows many variations. This version is cooked with the whole spices left in; they are removed at the table as they are discovered. This highly aromatic dish is an excellent accompaniment to spicy curries.

2 tablespoons butter or oil
¾ cup chopped onion
1½ cups uncooked brown rice
3 cups water
1 teaspoon salt
2-inch stick cinnamon
1 bay leaf, crushed
¼ teaspoon peppercorns
4 to 6 cardamom pods, lightly crushed
½ cup cashews, slivered almonds, or a combination
¼ cup slivered sweet red or green pepper

Heat fat in a 2- to 3-quart pot and sauté onion for about 10 minutes until browned. Add rice and stir to coat with oil and onion. Sauté for 2 to 3 minutes.

Add water and seasonings, bring to a boil, cover, and simmer over low heat for 45 to 50 minutes until rice is tender.

Brown nuts in a dry skillet. When rice is cooked, fluff with a fork; toss in nuts and raw pepper slivers just before serving.

Serves 6

Minor Protein

Note: Although cardamom is definitely preferred, if you do not have it, you can use cloves instead.

GARDEN RICE

A variety of fresh vegetables cooked with rice.

1 tablespoon oil
1 small onion, chopped
1 clove garlic, chopped
½ sweet red or green pepper, chopped
1 small carrot, chopped
1 tomato, diced
½ cup zucchini sticks or cauliflorets
1 cup green peas, edible pod peas, or green beans cut in 1-inch segments
½ cup bean sprouts
¾ cup uncooked brown rice
1¼ cups water
2 tablespoons soy sauce
1 bay leaf
½ teaspoon salt

Heat oil in a 3-quart pot and sauté onion and garlic for about 5 minutes until tender. Add pepper, carrot, tomato, and zucchini or cauliflower, and sauté, for 5 minutes longer.

Add peas, sprouts, rice, water, soy sauce, and bay leaf; bring to a boil, cover, and cook gently for 15 minutes. Add salt, replace cover, and cook until tender, about 40 minutes.

Serves 4

Minor Protein

Menu Suggestions: For an outdoor summer barbecue, set the pot over a wood or charcoal fire. For the entrée, try Outdoor Mixed Grill. Serve with Eggplant Cutlets for an indoor dinner.

RICE WITH SNOW PEAS

The rice for this dish is cooked separately from the vegetables and the two are tossed together just before serving.

1 cup uncooked brown rice cooked in 2 cups water (3 cups cooked brown rice)
2 tablespoons oil
2 cups (about ½ pound) fresh snow peas, strings removed
8 medium mushrooms, sliced
4 scallions, thinly sliced
½ cup thinly sliced fresh water chestnuts, Jerusalem artichoke, or zucchini rounds
¼ cup slivered almonds
¼ teaspoon salt
pepper

Cook rice. Heat oil in a wok or skillet. Stir-fry vegetables and almonds for 3 to 5 minutes until mushrooms are barely tender. Season with salt and pepper. Stir hot rice into vegetables and serve.

Serves 4

Minor Protein

Note: If you use cold precooked rice for this dish, reheat it for 5 minutes in a vegetable steamer before combining it with vegetables.

DIRTY RICE

A wonderful way to add interest to the rice accompanying bean entrées. The addition of imported dry mushrooms, if available, gives this dish a very robust flavor.

2 tablespoons oil or butter
1 large clove garlic, chopped
4 scallions, sliced
½ cup nuts (pumpkin seeds, sunflower seeds, pine nuts, cashew pieces, almonds, singly or combined)
½ cup coarsely chopped fresh mushrooms or soaked dried mushrooms (preferably an imported variety)
2 tablespoons soy sauce
4 cups cooked brown rice

Heat fat in a 2-quart pot. Sauté garlic for 1 minute; add scallions and sauté for 1 minute longer. Add nuts and cook until they are lightly colored. Add mushrooms and cook for about 2 minutes, or until they are slightly softened. Add soy sauce, cover, and simmer for 5 minutes.

Stir rice into mushroom mixture to coat evenly. Heat through. If serving is delayed, keep warm in a covered pot. Can be reheated if necessary.

Serves 6
Minor Protein

CREAMY TAHINI RICE

1½ tablespoons oil
1 medium onion, chopped
1 cup mixed nuts (sunflower seeds, pumpkin seeds, peanuts, almonds, cashews)
3 cups cooked brown rice
2 tablespoons soy sauce
⅓ cup tahini
⅓ cup water

Heat oil in a large skillet. Add onion and nuts and sauté for about 5 minutes until nuts are lightly colored.

Stir in rice, soy sauce, tahini, and water. Cook gently until heated through and sauce is thick and creamy around the grain.

Serves 4 to 6
Minor Protein

RICE WITH EGG AND LEMON

2 eggs
½ cup grated Parmesan cheese
2 tablespoons lemon juice
¼ cup chopped parsley
1¼ cups brown rice cooked in 2½ cups water, or 4 cups reheated cooked brown rice
1 tablespoon butter (optional)

Beat eggs until frothy. Beat in cheese and gradually add lemon juice. Stir egg mixture and parsley into hot rice and cook briefly over low heat to melt cheese without toughening the egg. Top with butter if desired and cover to melt.

Serves 4 as a base, 6 as a side dish
Minor Protein

Menu Suggestions: Serve as a base for vegetable stew or Fried Green Tomatoes, or as a side dish with vegetable entrées.

RICE PATTIES

Cold cooked rice can be shaped into a patty and sautéed to make a base for stews and sauces that has greater interest than just plain rice. This is an easy way to reheat and use leftovers.

about ½ cup cooked brown rice per person
whole wheat flour
oil

With moist hands, compress grain into 1 large or 2 small patties (holds best with shorter grains). Dredge patties in flour.

Heat enough oil to cover the surface of a skillet and, when hot, brown patties on each side. Press gently with a spatula to keep shape and enhance cooking. Flip several times if necessary until done.

Protein Complement

SUSHI RICE

Cold tangy rice, rolled into compact bundles and held together with a lettuce leaf. Offer with a tofu dish or eggs, as part of a cold vegetable platter, or as a warm-weather snack.

1 cup cooked brown rice (short grain preferred)
1 tablespoon vinegar
salt
8 paper-thin slices cucumber or carrot made using a vegetable peeler
½ teaspoon Chinese Mustard (page 307)
8 large leaves romaine

Season rice with vinegar and a little salt if unsalted. This can be done just before assembly, or in advance just after rice is cooked. Chill until needed.

Coat each slice of cucumber or carrot with some mustard.

Soften each romaine leaf by dipping it in boiling water for a few seconds until it can easily be rolled. Remove with tongs and place flat, outside down, on a kitchen towel.

Place 2 tablespoons rice in the center of each leaf. Top with mustard-coated vegetable. Fold sides of leaf over rice, then roll the ends over the filling to form a tight, compact bundle. Continue, using all the leaves and filling. Place in a single layer on a dish and chill until serving time. Allow at least 15 minutes to chill, or prepare well in advance (these can be kept for several days).

Makes 8 rolls; serves 2 to 4
Protein Complement

BASIC RICE SALAD

There are a number of foods you can marinate with rice to create an excellent cold grain salad. Below you will find our basic recipe with some suggestions for embellishment. If the salad is prepared using warm rice, the dressing penetrates the grain more easily, making a more flavorful dish, but even leftover, chilled cooked grain will make a very satisfactory salad. The longer the salad stands, the deeper the flavor penetrates. However, if it is to marinate longer than an hour, refrigeration is recommended. Chilled salad should be removed from the refrigerator about 30 minutes before serving since its flavor is best when at room temperature. Because this salad contains no mayonnaise, it is a wise choice for picnics, buffets, and warm-weather service.

2 cups cooked brown rice
salt
3 tablespoons oil
3 tablespoons lemon juice or a mixture of lemon juice and vinegar
¼ cup chopped parsley
¼ cup chopped red onion
up to 1 cup of the following (singly or in combination):
    cooked beans
    artichoke hearts
    avocado wedges
    thin raw carrot rounds
    raw or cooked peas
    diced celery
    diced cooked cauliflower or broccoli

    lightly cooked asparagus
    raw zucchini or cucumber strips
    diced radish
    feta cheese and olives
    hard-cooked egg wedges
fresh chopped garlic (optional)
tomato wedges
pimiento or Antipasto Peppers (page 310)

Season rice to taste with salt. Stir in oil, lemon, parsley, onion, and any of the alternate ingredients. If dry, add additional oil and lemon. Let stand to develop flavor.

To serve, place salad in a bowl or on a flat plate and top with freshly chopped garlic if desired. Garnish edges with tomato wedges and center with pepper strips.

Serves 4 to 6
Protein Complement; Minor Protein when beans, feta cheese, or egg is added

Note: Rice salad makes a good filling for hollowed-out tomatoes or halved sweet pepper shells.

CREAMY RICE SALAD

2 cups cooked brown rice
¼ teaspoon salt (omit if grain is salted)
¾ cup yogurt
2 tablespoons mayonnaise
¼ cup chopped sweet red or green pepper
¼ cup chopped scallion
½ cup raw peas, grated carrot, chopped cucumber, cooked corn, or any other vegetable of choice

Combine all ingredients. If prepared in advance, chill until serving time, but remove from the refrigerator before serving so salad is not ice cold.

Serves 4 to 6
Minor Protein
Variation: For *Creamy Barley Salad,* substitute cooked barley for rice.

COLD CORN, RICE, AND BEANS

A delicious warm-weather dish, especially when made with ripe summer tomatoes and fresh corn. All the components of this dish can be prepared well in advance, and put together just before serving.

3 ears fresh corn (1½ cups corn kernels)
½ cup cooked beans, drained
2 medium tomatoes, chopped
2 tablespoons cider vinegar
2 tablespoons oil
2 tablespoons chopped parsley
¼ cup chopped, canned green chilies pepper
¼ cup mayonnaise
¼ cup yogurt
1 tablespoon lemon juice
½ teaspoon paprika
2 cups cooked brown rice, at room temperature

Cut corn kernels from cob and cook in a covered pot with just a little water for 5 minutes until tender but still crunchy. Drain.

Mix corn with beans, tomato, vinegar, oil, parsley, chilies, and a good grinding of pepper. Let marinate for 30 minutes to 1 hour at room temperature (longer in the refrigerator).

Combine mayonnaise, yogurt, lemon juice, and paprika. When ready to serve, mound rice on a serving plate. Top with corn–bean mixture. Spoon yogurt dressing over all.
Serves 4 to 6
Minor Protein
Note: The proportion of corn and beans can be varied but should equal a total of 2 cups.
Menu Suggestions: An excellent accompaniment to Stuffed Squash Blossoms, Chili Rellenos, or an omelet.

SPANISH WHEAT

Cracked wheat in a flavorful tomato sauce.

1 tablespoon oil
1 small onion, chopped
½ large green pepper, chopped
few rings hot chili pepper, chopped (optional)
1 cup cracked wheat

2 cups undrained canned tomatoes, fresh chopped tomatoes, or tomato puree
½ teaspoon each oregano, basil, chili powder, and salt

Combine oil, onion, peppers, and cracked wheat in a pot and cook over medium heat, stirring occasionally, for about 5 minutes. Add remaining ingredients, cover, and cook over low heat until grain is tender, 20 to 25 minutes.
Serves 4
Protein Complement
Variations: For *Super Spanish Wheat,* add 1 cup shredded cheddar or Jack cheese when cooking is completed; cover and heat to melt. Or, top leftovers with cheese in a shallow baking dish and heat in a 350°F. oven.

For *Spanish Rice,* substitute brown rice for cracked wheat and cook about 1 hour.

ORANGE–WHEAT SALAD

A refreshing summer grain accompaniment.

3 cups cold cooked cracked wheat (see Note)
¼ cup sliced scallions
1 cup cooked beans, drained
2 tablespoons mayonnaise
2 tablespoons yogurt
2 tablespoons lemon juice
juice of 1 orange
½ teaspoon salt
1 orange, peeled and sectioned

Mix cold grain with scallions and beans until evenly combined.

Mix mayonnaise, yogurt, lemon juice, orange juice, and salt to make a smooth dressing. Pour dressing over grain mixture and stir well. Mix in orange sections.
Serves 4 to 6
Minor Protein
Note: To prepare grain, sauté 1 cup cracked wheat in 1 tablespoon oil until lightly colored. Add 2 cups boiling water and ½ teaspoon salt, cover and cook over low heat for 15 to 20 minutes until grain is tender and all liquid

absorbed. Remove cover to let steam escape, then refrigerate.

Menu Suggestions: Recommended with cooked vegetable entrées, such as Eggplant Ratatouille Pie or Cauliflower Puff.

PEANUT-BUTTERED GRAIN

Liven up leftovers by adding just a hint of peanut butter flavor. Use as an accompaniment to vegetable–cheese combinations.

2 tablespoons oil
2 medium onions, chopped
3 cups cooked kasha, brown rice, millet, or cracked wheat
3 tablespoons soy sauce
3 tablespoons peanut butter

Heat oil in a large skillet and sauté onions for 5 to 7 minutes until lightly colored. Add grain, tossing with a fork to break up clumps.

Add soy sauce and peanut butter and cook, stirring gently with fork, until hot and evenly blended.

Serves 4 to 6
Minor Protein
Variation: Make *Peanut-Buttered Beans and Grain* by adding 2 cups cooked beans and enough cooking liquid to moisten.

SAVORY GRAIN CRACKERS

A chewy, flavorful cracker that can be made from any leftover grain as a delicious accompaniment to soups or salad. Excellent topped with a spoonful of cottage cheese or spread with a bit of butter.

2 cups cooked leftover grain (rice, barley, millet, cracked wheat, kasha)
2 tablespoons minced onion
1 teaspoon mixed dried herbs (parsley, basil, oregano, thyme, chervil, etc.)
2 tablespoons soy sauce
about ½ cup whole wheat flour

Preheat oven to 400°F.
Combine all ingredients and knead with hands to form a smooth dough that holds together. If too crumbly, add a little water.

Form into 1-inch balls, place on an oiled baking sheet, and flatten with the prongs of a fork dipped into hot water to keep them from sticking.

Bake for about 15 minutes until brown and firm. Serve hot.

Makes 20 crackers; serves 4
Protein Complement
Note: If grain is highly seasoned, omit herbs and onion. Extras can be refrigerated and reheated in the broiler or toaster oven for a few minutes before serving.

Dumplings

A dumpling is a mass of dough cooked by boiling or steaming. The use of dumplings as an accompaniment to stews and soups is renowned in Poland, Hungary, Austria, Czechoslovakia, and parts of Germany. At one time in the culinary history of America "chicken and dumplings" were common fare.

Dumplings can be made from bread, crackers, potatoes, flour, or cereal grains. They are leavened with eggs, baking powder, or yeast. The addition of some fat to the dough adds to their tenderness. Wheat germ, nonfat dry milk powder, and nutritional yeast enhance the food value. Thus, a dumpling added to a bean or vegetable dish can bring important nourishment as well as lend texture. Most dumplings are bland in taste, but they gain rich flavor by soaking up the broth they are served in.

Dumplings may be a main dish, as are Ricotta-Spinach Dumplings and Gnocchi. Bread Meat, another dumpling with great nutritional qualities and meatloaf-like taste, can be served on its own or as part of a stew. In this section, you will find recipes for other favorite dumplings, such as Matzo Balls and Corn Dodgers.

The important basic rule in dumpling cookery is to use a large, broad pot to allow room for the dough to swell without crowding. The cooking liquid should be just at a simmer; vigorous boiling will tear the dumplings apart.

Dumplings may be cooked directly in the soup or stew they are served in, or they may be cooked separately, drained, and added later. If you are at all uncertain about making them, cooking separately is advised. One way to determine the results beforehand is to run a sample test, dropping a single dumpling into simmering water and judging the outcome. If the dumpling does fall apart, add a little flour to the rest of the batter and run the test again.

Frequent lifting of the lid during cooking tends to make dumplings heavy, so keep the pot covered, as the recipe recommends. If you can't resist peeking, you might choose a pot with a glass cover or get a glass pie pan that fits snugly on top of a pot, a good do-it-yourself cover for curious cooks.

The first time you make dumplings you may feel a little insecure, but once you have mastered the recipe you will feel comfortable with dumplings forever.

EGG DUMPLINGS

These very light dumplings should be cooked directly in the soup or stew, so be sure to begin with a broad pot to give them plenty of room.

2 eggs, separated
1 tablespoon milk
¼ teaspoon salt
3 tablespoons whole wheat flour

Beat egg yolks with milk, salt, and flour until smooth. Beat egg whites until stiff. Fold yolk mixture into whites until evenly blended.

Drop batter by rounded tablespoons into simmering soup or stew. Cover and cook without peeking for 10 minutes. Serve at once.

Makes about 20 dumplings; serves 4 to 6
Minor Protein

BREAD DUMPLINGS

The ingredients are similar to those of Bread Meat, but they are shaped into individual balls. Although Bread Dumplings may seem heavy to the touch, they are quite tender in the mouth.

4 slices whole grain bread
1 egg, beaten
1 tablespoon minced onion
½ teaspoon salt
½ teaspoon sage or nutmeg
¼ cup nonfat dry milk powder
¼ cup wheat germ

Soak bread in cold water to cover until very soft, then squeeze dry. Mash with a fork and mix in remaining ingredients. Let sit a few minutes to absorb any moisture.

Bring stew, soup, or a large pot of salted water to a gentle simmer. For use in stew, shape a tablespoonful of dough lightly into a ball and drop into simmering liquid. For soups, make small marble-size balls.

Add the dumplings without crowding; cover and simmer for 15 minutes without raising the lid. If cooked separately from the dish they will be served in, skim them from the pot with a slotted spoon and drain. Serve immediately after cooking.

Makes 12 large or 24 small dumplings; serves 4
Minor Protein
Note: Dough for dumplings can be prepared in advance, but cooking should take place just before serving; reheating makes dumplings hard.

MATZO BALLS

An integral part of Jewish cuisine, matzo balls are served in chicken broth during Passover and, for the lucky, at other times of the year as well. We are very fond of these dense but tender cracker dumplings and serve them in any light vegetable broth. They are especially good in Tamari Broth with Greens, even if the combination is somewhat untraditional.

4 whole wheat matzos
2 eggs
2 tablespoons oil
½ teaspoon salt
6 tablespoons seltzer or plain water

Crush the matzos into fine crumbs in the blender, processor, or with a rolling pin. You should have 1 cup crumbs.

Beat eggs with oil and salt. Stir in crumbs. Add seltzer and mix to a smooth batter. Chill for 30 minutes or longer.

To cook, bring 3 quarts of water to a boil in a wide 5-quart pot. Add 1 teaspoon salt. Shape chilled dough into 1-inch balls using a light hand. Drop into simmering water. When they rise, cover and simmer for 30 minutes. Drain.

To serve, place in bowls and cover with hot soup; if matzo balls have cooled down before they are served, place them in the soup pot and reheat for a few minutes.

Makes 12 to 14 dumplings; serves 4 to 6

Minor Protein

Note: These dumplings can be cooked ahead of time, chilled in a covered container, and reheated in the soup for service as described. Similar dumplings can be made using any whole grain cracker.

CORN DODGERS

Cornmeal dumplings cooked in "pot likker" were very popular at one time in the South and each household had its favorite recipe passed down from one generation to the next. Our Corn Dodger recipe makes a light, tender dumpling that can be used to complement bean stews. This same recipe can be used for a version of Italian Gnocci, or to fashion a Corn Pierogi, as described in Variations, below.

1 cup cornmeal
2 tablespoons nonfat dry milk powder
1 teaspoon baking powder
½ teaspoon salt
1 egg
1 tablespoon oil
¼ cup water

Combine dry ingredients in a mixing bowl. Add egg, oil, and water to dry mixture and beat gently until smooth. Batter will be thick.

Drop by the tablespoonful into a large pot of simmering salted water or broth. Cover and cook for 15 minutes. Drain and serve.

Makes 12 dumplings; serves 4

Minor Protein

Variations: For *Italian Corn Gnocchi,* add ¼ cup grated Parmesan cheese to the batter. These dumplings can be used in stews or served with tomato sauce and additional grated cheese.

For *Corn Pierogi,* top dumplings with sautéed onions, cottage cheese, and yogurt or sour cream. This makes a nice lunch or dinner entrée.

For a sweet and creamy breakfast or lunch treat, line a baking dish with ½ cup cottage cheese per serving, top with sliced dumplings, sprinkle with cinnamon and a drizzle of honey, and broil for 5 minutes until bubbly. Serve hot with a garnish of yogurt.

Uneaten Corn Dodgers can be drained and kept in a covered dish in the refrigerator for 3 to 5 days. To reheat, slice and place side by side in a shallow baking dish, cover surface with grated Parmesan, and broil for 5 minutes until brown and bubbling. This is very much like Italian polenta.

BULGUR DUMPLINGS

These chewy grain balls are a typical Armenian lenten treat that are used to garnish vegetable or brothy bean soups and stews.

1½ cups hot water
1 cup cracked wheat
½ teaspoon salt
1 cup whole wheat flour
1 tablespoon nutritional yeast (optional)
2 quarts simmering salted water or vegetable broth

Pour hot water over cracked wheat in a mixing bowl and let stand for at least 10 minutes to absorb liquid. Press out all excess moisture. Add salt, flour, and yeast and let stand for at least 5 minutes.

Form into small marble-size balls with a teaspoon and drop into simmering water or broth. Cover and cook for 20 minutes. Drain with a slotted spoon and use as desired, or as described below.

Makes about 40 small dumplings; serves 4 to 6

Protein Complement

Menu Suggestions: Try Bulgur Dumplings with such entrées as Spinach and Chick-Peas with Feta, Algerian Chick-Peas with Cheese Croquettes (they can substitute for the Cheese Croquettes), or add to Italian Beans and Greens to transform it into a main dish. Good too, on a bed of Beans with Stewed Onions with a wedge of lemon or a dash of catsup.

Pasta

As we have seen, pasta is the focal point of many entrées. Since half-portions of a pasta main dish can serve as a side dish, our pasta accompaniments are somewhat sparse.

In this section, we give special attention to homemade pasta. The difference between commercial and homemade noodles is as great as the gap between the hard tomatoes available in winter and the juicy, vine-ripened fruit of summer. What's more, pasta making is a project that is fun to do and surprisingly simple. If you can make bread or assemble a pie crust, the preparation of pasta will be a breeze. The only prerequisite is some work space; if your counter space is not adequate, move your pasta making to a kitchen or dining room table. A pasta machine eliminates the hand kneading of dough and makes rolling easier, but is by no means essential.

Making Pasta

The best flour for making pasta is one with a high gluten content. This makes the noodles chewy rather than mushy. If you are given a choice, "hard" rather than "soft" wheat should be selected. Bread flour is more suitable than all-purpose flour; pastry flour is inappropriate. You will find that the exact amounts of flour and liquid in all pasta recipes are subject to slight variations

due to differences in flours and atmospheric conditions; the damper the weather, the more flour you will need.

One tablespoon of nutritional yeast can be added to the flour in any pasta recipe. This greatly enhances its nutritional value; even a Protein Complement like Basic Whole Wheat Pasta will be elevated to Minor Protein status. The directions for preparing the dough are given in the Basic Whole Wheat Pasta recipe and are suitable for both hand- and machine-made pasta.

Thorough kneading is important to develop the strands of gluten; do not skimp on this step. Letting the dough rest before hand rolling makes the pasta easier to work; it can then be rolled much thinner for tender noodles. If this step is curtailed or even eliminated, the job will become more difficult.

Once the dough is rolled, it can be cut into any shape. Broad lasagne noodles are the simplest; since commercial whole wheat lasagne noodles are the least acceptable of the whole grain varieties, this would be a good choice for your first expedition into pasta making. Broad noodles, from ½ to ¾ inch wide, can be cut to any length. For fettuccine, cut long strips about ¼ inch wide. One of the nicest decorative pasta shapes you can fashion is the bow tie; it is made by cutting the dough into 2-inch by 1-inch pieces and pinching them in the center to create a bowlike effect. Making spaghetti is the most tedious cutting job; since whole grain spaghetti is available in the market you might put your effort into the less common varieties.

Pasta can be cooked fresh, frozen, or left at room temperature to dry.

Basic Pasta Cooking

Pasta should be served as soon as possible after cooking. If it sits around after it has been drained, it can become gummy, and reheating has a softening effect. Try to time the cooking so that the pasta is ready just in time for service. If you miscalculate, the best approach is to remove the pot from the heat a few minutes before the pasta is fully cooked and let it remain in the hot water until ready to serve or sauce. This works especially well with whole grain pasta, which does not get overcooked as easily as the refined varieties.

Unless otherwise directed in the recipe, standard cooking proportions are as follows:

2 quarts water, brought to a boil
1 teaspoon salt (reduce or omit if necessary)
½ pound pasta

Add the pasta to boiling salted water and begin timing as soon as the water returns to a boil. Allow 5 minutes for fresh pasta and taste. Allow 10 minutes for dried pasta and taste. If it is not done, continue to test at 1-minute intervals until cooked to personal taste.

Pasta should be cooked uncovered so that the liquid can be kept at a gentle boil; vigorous boiling makes pasta mushy. To conserve energy, however, the water should be brought to a boil originally in a covered pot.

Drain pasta immediately after cooking. Rinse off the surface starch by dousing with cold water in a colander, then coat with hot sauce, or proceed according to recipe directions.

If you find sticking a problem, a tablespoon of oil can be added to the pot during cooking, but if you add the pasta gradually and keep the water simmering, it should not stick. If it is not to be served immediately after draining, a little oil or butter stirred in will reduce stickiness.

The easiest way to warm up pasta once it has been chilled is to put it in a colander and pour very hot tap water over it until the temperature is raised. If this is not sufficient, place cooked pasta in a vegetable steamer and reheat over boiling water for a minute or two.

BASIC WHOLE WHEAT PASTA

2 cups whole wheat flour
½ teaspoon salt
1 tablespoon oil
½ cup water

Mix flour and salt and work in oil with fingers.

Pour in water and blend with fingers, kneading until dough holds together. If dough begins to crumble, add a tablespoon of water and work it in. You should not have to add more than 2 additional tablespoons of water.

When dough can be formed into a mass, place it on a board wiped with oil and knead with the heel of your hand, turning, for a full 10 minutes, until it is as stiff and smooth as modeling clay. If you are using a pasta machine, omit this step and run the dough through the rolling blade, folding it over itself several times as it is ejected and repeating the rolling. Begin with the widest opening, gradually decreasing the width until the elasticity of the dough has built up and it is ready for final rolling.

If preparing dough without a machine, cover the well-kneaded ball of dough with a damp cloth and let it rest about 30 minutes. This makes rolling much easier, so that you can make thin noodles. (This is not necessary with a machine.)

To roll dough by hand, divide it into about 6 pieces, then roll with a pin on a flat surface, going out from the center in all directions until the dough is as thin as you can make it. Dough can be turned over during rolling as many times as necessary to facilitate the process. To roll dough in the machine, divide into 4 pieces and pass through rollers, successively decreasing the thickness until it is at the #5 to #4 setting, which is about the thinnest it can successfully be rolled without tearing. If tearing occurs, dust with flour, fold in thirds, and repeat successive rolling process.

After rolling, cut as desired, using a knife or machine blade, and shake noodles gently to free them from one another.

Noodles can now be cooked, wrapped for freezing, or spread on a well-aerated surface, like a screen or rack, to dry.

Makes about ¾ pound fresh pasta or 6 servings (about ½ pound dried)
Protein Complement

SOY–WHOLE WHEAT NOODLES

The addition of soy flour to the dough elevates the quality of the pasta protein.

2 cups whole wheat flour
¼ cup soy flour
½ teaspoon salt
½ tablespoon oil
½ cup water

Combine flours and salt in a large bowl. Make a well in the center and add oil and water. Knead into a single mass, using your hands.

Place dough on an oiled work surface and knead a full 10 minutes, as for Basic Whole Wheat Pasta, or follow the directions for preparing pasta using a machine.

Let rest, then roll, cut, and use as in Basic Whole Wheat Pasta recipe.
Makes about 14 ounces fresh pasta; serves 6
Minor Protein
Note: Salt is added to the dough for flavor and can be omitted if necessary. Oil makes the dough more pliable but can also be omitted if necessary.

EGG NOODLES

4 cups whole wheat flour
1 teaspoon salt
4 eggs
¼ to ⅓ cup water

Combine flour and salt in a large bowl. Make a well in the center and add eggs and ¼ cup water. Mix with a wooden spoon and then with your hands until the dough forms a mass. If too dry, add additional water.

Turn dough out onto an oiled work surface and proceed according to directions for Basic Whole Wheat Pasta.
Makes about 2 pounds fresh noodles; serves 12
Minor Protein

RICOTTA NOODLES

The addition of ricotta cheese makes a tender, nutritious noodle.

½ cup ricotta cheese
1 tablespoon oil (olive preferred)
1 egg

¼ teaspoon salt
1½ to 2 cups whole wheat flour

Beat together ricotta, oil, egg, and salt. Add flour, kneading with your hands to form a stiff dough. Knead by hand or machine and proceed according to directions for Basic Whole Wheat Pasta.
Makes about ¾ pound fresh pasta; serves 6
Minor Protein

YOGURT NOODLES

Noodles with the gentle tang of yogurt.

2 cups whole wheat flour
½ teaspoon salt
1 cup yogurt

Combine flour and salt in a mixing bowl. Stir in yogurt to form a dough.

Knead on a floured board, adding more flour if necessary to form a smooth dough. Five minutes' kneading is adequate for this noodle.

Roll *without* a resting period, as described for Basic Whole Wheat Pasta, and cut into desired shapes.
Makes about ¾ pound fresh pasta; serves 6
Note: Exact amounts of flour and yogurt will vary slightly due to the difference in consistencies of both flours and yogurts.

FRESH CHINESE FRIED NOODLES

This is the way to make real Chinese noodles to top chow mein.

about ¾ pound fresh pasta dough, as for Basic Whole Wheat Pasta or Soy–Whole Wheat Noodles
oil

Cut pasta dough into noodles about ¾ inch wide and 1 inch long.

Heat oil in a wok for deep frying or in a large, heavy skillet to a depth of about ¼ inch. Test heat by adding a fresh noodle; if it rises to the top and puffs almost immediately, it is at the right temperature. If the noodle browns before it has a chance to puff, it is too hot.

Add noodles without crowding and fry until golden, turning so both sides color lightly. When done, remove with a mesh spoon and drain on absorbent paper.

Cool to room temperature before serving. Store for future use in tightly covered container.

Makes 10 to 12 cups fried noodles; serves 12

Minor Protein or *Protein Complement* (depending on pasta dough)

SPAGHETTI WITH GARLIC

½ pound spaghetti
2 tablespoons olive oil
2 large cloves garlic, chopped
oregano (optional)

Cook spaghetti in boiling salted water for 10 to 12 minutes to taste.

During the last few minutes that pasta cooks, heat oil in a small heatproof pan or metal measuring cup and cook garlic until it just colors, about 3 minutes over moderate heat. Do not overcook.

Drain spaghetti and toss in a serving dish with hot garlic oil. Sprinkle with a little crushed oregano for added flavor, if desired. Serve at once.

Serves 4
Protein Complement

PASTA WITH BROCCOLI

Soft flecks of broccoli and good-quality olive oil penetrate the pasta, giving this dish its rich taste.

1 large bunch broccoli (1½ to 2 pounds)
½ pound spaghetti or linguine
5 tablespoons olive oil
½ teaspoon salt
pepper
grated Parmesan cheese (optional)

Divide broccoli into small florets to make 4 to 6 cups. Reserve stems for Broccoli Stalk Salad or serve with American Wholefoods Hollandaise. Steam florets for 10 minutes until quite tender.

While broccoli steams, cook pasta for 10 to 12 minutes to taste. Drain.

Return pasta to cooking pot and add broccoli, oil, salt, and a generous amount of pepper. Stir well so that broccoli is almost completely broken up. Serve with grated Parmesan.

Serves 4 to 6
Minor Protein with cheese
Note: Olive oil is essential to the flavor of this dish. If other oil is used, steep with garlic for more flavor.

Menu Suggestions: A good accompaniment to any eggplant entrée, or to Manicotti or Mushroom Custard.

PEANUT BUTTER PASTA

Pasta with a light peanut flavor.

½ pound spaghetti
½ cup chopped onion
½ cup slivered green pepper
1 tablespoon oil
½ cup warm water
4 tablespoons peanut butter
2 tomatoes, diced
1½ cups tomato juice
½ teaspoon oregano
coarsely chopped peanuts

Cook spaghetti in boiling salted water for 10 to 12 minutes to taste. Drain.

While spaghetti cooks, sauté onion and pepper in oil for about 5 minutes until wilted. Stir water gradually into peanut butter until smooth and add to pan with tomatoes, tomato juice, and oregano. Bring to a boil, stirring occasionally to make a smooth sauce.

Spoon hot sauce over pasta and top with chopped peanuts.

Serves 4
Minor Protein

NOODLES WITH SESAME PASTE

A cold noodle dish with a sesame sauce and spicy bean sprout topping that is a Chinese Szechuan specialty.

½ pound linguine
1 tablespoon Chinese sesame oil

Spiced Bean Sprouts
1½ cups mung or soybean sprouts
3 tablespoons lemon juice
1 teaspoon hot pepper sauce

Sesame Sauce
  3 tablespoons tahini
  1 tablespoon peanut butter
  1 teaspoon honey
  2 tablespoons white or rice vinegar
  2 tablespoons soy sauce
  ½ teaspoon Chinese sesame oil
  pinch cayenne (optional)

Cook pasta in boiling salted water until tender, 10 to 12 minutes. Drain and mix with sesame oil in serving bowl, stirring well to coat. Cool to room temperature.

To prepare sprouts, place in a pot with water to cover, bring to a boil for 1 minute, drain and cool under cold running water. Drain well. Toss with remaining sprout ingredients and let marinate at room temperature for at least 15 minutes.

Combine all sauce ingredients, mixing until smooth. If very thick, add hot pasta water to reduce to consistency of thick cream. Cayenne can be omitted for a milder dish.

Just before serving pour sauce over pasta, toss to coat, and top with Spiced Bean Sprouts.

Serves 4 to 6
Minor Protein
Note: The elements of this dish can be prepared well in advance; it is therefore a useful addition to a Chinese meal where there are many last-minute operations.

SWEET NOODLE PUDDING

An easy casserole for a big party.

  1 pound whole grain noodles
  6 tablespoons butter
  6 eggs, beaten
  1 teaspoon cinnamon
  ½ cup honey
  1 cup raisins
  2 large apples, peeled, cored, and sliced

Preheat oven to 350°F.
Cook noodles in boiling salted water for 8 to 10 minutes until barely tender. Drain and toss with 4 tablespoons butter to melt.

Combine noodles, eggs, ½ teaspoon cinnamon, ¼ cup honey, raisins, and apples in a greased 9 x 13-inch baking dish. Sprinkle with remaining ½ teaspoon cinnamon, drizzle with ¼ cup honey, and dot with remaining 2 tablespoons butter.

Bake for about 50 minutes until top is browned.

Serves 10 to 12
Minor Protein

FRENCH PASTA SALAD

A good party choice for buffet dining.

  1 can (14 ounces) artichoke hearts in water
  3 cups cold, cooked fettuccine
  ¼ cup mayonnaise
  ¼ cup yogurt
  1½ tablespoons tomato juice
  capers
  fresh chopped parsley

Drain artichokes, rinse under cold water, and drain again. Cut in half and toss with pasta in a serving dish. Mix mayonnaise, yogurt, and tomato juice and pour over pasta just before serving. Garnish with capers and parsley.

Serves 4
Minor Protein
Menu Suggestions: This can also serve as the first course preceding a soufflé or a vegetable entrée.

PASTA, ARTICHOKES, AND CHICK-PEAS WITH LEMON DRESSING

A cold pasta salad with a creamy lemon dressing that uses leftover pasta and precooked beans.

  2 cups cooked small pasta (shells, spirals, or elbows)
  1½ cups cooked chick-peas, drained
  1 can (14 ounces) artichoke hearts in water, drained and cut in fourths, or 1 to 1½ cups sliced cooked fresh artichoke hearts
  ¼ cup mayonnaise
  ¼ cup yogurt
  1½ tablespoons lemon juice
  1 teaspoon fresh snipped dill, or 1 tablespoon minced parsley

Mix pasta, chick-peas, and artichokes in a serving bowl. Combine mayonnaise, yogurt, and lemon juice and pour over pasta. Stir well. Sprinkle with herb of choice.

Serves 4 to 6
Minor Protein

MACARONI AND LEBAN

Leban is the Arabic name for yogurt. This cold pasta salad, popular in Lebanon, is a good addition to a Mideast meal or a cold buffet.

2 cloves garlic
1 teaspoon salt
2 teaspoons dried mint
2 cups yogurt
2 cups cooked pasta, drained
¼ cup pine nuts, pumpkin seeds, sunflower seeds, or cashews

Pound garlic with salt and mint, using a mortar and pestle. When mashed, stir into yogurt. Add cooked pasta.

Sauté nuts in a dry skillet until lightly colored. Sprinkle on top of pasta. Serve at room temperature.

Serves 6
Minor Protein

SAVORY PASTRY ACCOMPANIMENTS

Instead of a simple breadstuff, savory pastries can accompany the meal. You might think of them as glamorized bread, contributing the same elements plus a bit more.

The savory pastries presented in this section may be based on pre-made baked goods, such as bread or tortillas, or they may be fashioned from a dough made expressly for this purpose.

Additional savory pastry accompaniment possibilities are included in "Savory Pastry Entrées" and "Short-Order Cooking," where offerings such as Bean-

Stuffed Pita Pockets, Fresh Tomato Pita Pizza, Mexican Pizza, Quick Calzone, Sealed Sandwiches, Cornish Pasties, and more can be served with soup, salad, or some other suitable entrée simply by reducing the portion size.

NACHOS

Nachos are cheese-topped corn tortillas served plain or topped with a touch of hot Mexican sauce. They are a quick and handy accompaniment to rice-and-bean entrées and a good snack too.

1 corn tortilla
2 to 3 tablespoons shredded Jack cheese
cumin
canned chilies (optional)
spicy Mexican sauce (optional) such as Chili Sauce (page 308) or Quick Mexican Hot Sauce (page 58)

Place tortilla on a baking sheet or, for individual preparation, the tray of the toaster oven. Top with cheese and a light sprinkling of cumin. Arrange strips of chili pepper on top if desired.

Broil until cheese is bubbly. Eat as soon as the tortilla is cool enough to hold. Generally it is cut in 4 wedges for easy handling, and a little hot sauce is spooned on top.

Minor Protein

Note: If you are using frozen tortillas, no defrosting is necessary.

BREAD TURNOVERS WITH CHEESE

A convenient way to add protein to a soup, salad, or vegetable plate.

1 cup grated cheese
⅓ cup cottage cheese
¼ cup minced parsley
1 egg, lightly beaten
8 slices whole grain bread
milk

Combine cheeses, parsley, and most of the egg to form a thick filling. Save a little of the egg for brushing the turnovers later on. Chill cheese mixture until ready to bake.

Preheat oven to 400° to 425°F.

Cut crusts from bread and roll flat in all directions. Place 1 tablespoon cheese filling on half and fold into a triangle. Press edges with a fork to seal. Place on an oiled baking sheet.

Beat reserved egg with a little milk and paint tops of turnovers.

Bake for 12 to 15 minutes until browned.

Makes 8 turnovers; serves 4 to 8
Minor Protein

Note: Filling mixture can be made well in advance but the actual assembly should be done just before baking.

ARMENIAN BEAN PIES

Open rounds of pita with a flavorful bean topping.

1 cup cooked kidney or other pink bean, drained
1 small onion, minced
¼ cup minced green pepper
1 small tomato, chopped
2 tablespoons minced parsley
1 small clove garlic, minced
¼ teaspoon cayenne
¼ teaspoon nutmeg
1 tablespoon tomato paste or juice
1 tablespoon lemon juice
salt (omit if beans are salted)
2 whole wheat pita breads
1 tablespoon oil
yogurt

Preheat oven to 450°F.

Grind beans or mash with a fork if very tender. Mix with vegetables and seasonings, salting to taste.

Cut pita into 2 flat circles by punching with the tines of a fork around the circumference and gently prying apart. Spread bean mixture to cover surface of rounds, using about ¼ cup for each. Drizzle with oil.

Place on a baking sheet and bake for 10 minutes until crisp. Serve with dollop of yogurt on top.

Serves 4 as an accompaniment; 2 as an entrée
Minor Protein

Menu Suggestions: Use to add protein to vegetable-based entrées, or make this the entrée with a side of cooked grain or a cold grain salad like Macaroni and Leban, plus a fresh vegetable salad.

VEGETABLE ROLLS

A simple slice of bread makes an available and versatile envelope for a filling, which, in this recipe is shredded vegetables.

1 medium onion, thinly sliced
1 cup shredded spinach or cabbage
½ cup shredded carrot
¼ cup slivered green pepper
½ cup shredded zucchini or eggplant (optional)
2 tablespoons oil
2 tablespoons soy flour
2 tablespoons tomato juice or water
½ teaspoon salt
pepper
8 slices whole grain bread
1 tablespoon butter
sesame seeds

Combine vegetables in a pot with 1 tablespoon oil and cook, covered, for 10 minutes to soften.

Make a paste of soy flour and tomato juice and stir into vegetables. Cook over low heat for 2 to 3 minutes until thickened. Season with salt and pepper and let cool.

Preheat oven to 375°F.

Flatten each slice of bread with a rolling pin. Spread a rounded tablespoon of vegetables in a strip down the center of each and roll to cover.

Combine remaining tablespoon oil and butter in a shallow baking dish and place it in the oven to melt. Roll vegetable rolls in the hot fat and leave seamside down in the pan. Sprinkle top with sesame seeds.

Bake for about 20 minutes until browned. If desired, rolls can be turned after 10 minutes for more even coloring, but this is not essential. Serve hot or at room temperature.

Makes 8 rolls; serves 4 to 8

GREEK FETA BISCUITS

Feta cheese baked inside biscuit dough is appropriate to any Greek meal, but is particularly suitable when Greek Artichokes and Dill or Greek Spinach Rice is made the focal point of the meal.

Yogurt Biscuit Dough (page 326)
⅔ cup mashed feta cheese
1½ tablespoons minced parsley
1 egg, lightly beaten
milk or water
sesame seeds

Preheat oven to 425°F.

Roll dough ⅛ inch thick and cut into 4-inch rounds. A 1-pound coffee or wheat germ can makes a perfect guide. Reroll trimmings to give you 10 rounds.

Mix feta with parsley and most of the egg, reserving a little for a glaze.

Place 2 teaspoons (¾ tablespoon) filling in the center of each round. Fold all four ends to the center over the filling, stretching gently if necessary. Pinch to make a sealed square. Place biscuits seam-side down on an oiled baking sheet.

Beat remaining egg with a little milk or water. Paint the tops of the biscuits with this mixture and sprinkle with sesame seeds. Bake for 10 to 12 minutes. Serve warm.

Makes 10 biscuits; serves 5 to 10

Minor Protein

Note: Freeze any leftovers after baking. Thaw at room temperature and reheat for 5 minutes in a 350° to 400°F. oven.

RUSSIAN VEGETABLE TURNOVERS

Piroshki is the Russian name for individual turnovers. The filling can be anything from meat to kasha to vegetables. This one is made with a biscuit dough crust.

For the Filling
3 cups raw vegetables including:
  ½ cup thinly sliced onion
  1 to 1½ cups shredded greens (beet tops, celery tops, spinach, cabbage)
  ½ to 1 cup shredded carrot
  ¼ cup sliced mushrooms
  any other shredded vegetables of choice
1 tablespoon oil
1 tablespoon dill weed
½ teaspoon salt
2 tablespoons soy flour
2 tablespoons water
3 to 4 tablespoons cream cheese

For the Dough
1½ cups whole wheat flour
3 teaspoons baking powder
½ teaspoon salt
3 tablespoons oil
¾ cup cottage cheese
⅓ cup milk

To prepare filling, combine vegetables, oil, and dill in a pot, cover and cook for 10 minutes. Add salt and a paste of soy flour and water and cook, stirring, for 2 to 3 minutes until thick. Cool while you prepare the dough.

For dough, combine flour, baking powder, and salt in a bowl and stir in oil. Add cottage cheese and milk and stir to make a soft dough.

Knead dough gently on a well-floured surface. Roll or pat into a large rectangle ⅛ inch thick. Cut into 2-inch rounds, reroll trimmings, and continue till you have made 24 rounds.

Preheat oven to 425°F.

Top half the rounds with 1 tablespoon vegetable filling. Take a scant teaspoon cream cheese, press flat, and place over vegetables. Top with a plain round of dough and pinch edges to seal.

Place on an oiled baking sheet and bake for 15 to 20 minutes until lightly colored. Serve warm.

Makes 12 turnovers; serves 6 to 12

Minor Protein

Note: Turnovers can be assembled in advance and kept in the refrigerator until ready to bake. Cover with a damp towel to prevent drying and remove from refrigerator while preheating oven. Turnovers can also be frozen, unbaked, for up to 3 months. Remove pastries from the freezer while oven preheats. Unwrap and bake for 20 minutes.

BEAN PASTRY TURNOVERS

A tender, flavorful cooked bean dough with a complementary cheese filling.

1¼ cups cooked beans, drained
1 cup whole wheat flour
1 teaspoon baking powder
½ teaspoon salt (omit if beans are salted)
2 tablespoons oil
about ¼ cup milk
1½ cups grated cheddar or Jack cheese

Preheat oven to 375°F.
Grind beans to a dry pulp. Mix with flour, baking powder, salt if needed, oil, and enough milk to form a dough.

Knead gently on a floured surface, adding more flour or milk as necessary to make a dough that is easy to handle.

Roll half the dough at a time into a rectangle ⅛ inch thick. Cut into 8 squares. Top each with a rounded tablespoon of cheese, fold into a triangle, and seal edges by pressing. Roll and fill remaining dough.

Place on an ungreased baking sheet and bake until firm and light brown, about 20 minutes.

Makes 16 turnovers; serves 4 to 8
Minor Protein

EMPANADAS

Small pastries like these, filled with meat or beans, are popular throughout South America.

pastry for two 9-inch shells, preferably Plus Pastry (page 399) or Cheddar Pastry (page 229)
1 cup cooked beans, drained
2 tablespoons minced onion
2 tablespoons chopped raisins
½ teaspoon cumin
½ teaspoon paprika
¼ teaspoon cayenne
1 tablespoon oil
4 olives, cut into 4 slices each
1 pimiento, cut in 16 strips

Preheat oven to 400°F.
Chill pastry until filling is assembled.
Chop beans coarsely. Add onion, raisins, seasonings, and oil, and mix well.

Divide pastry in half. Roll each half until thin. Cut into 4-inch rounds, the size of a 1-pound coffee or wheat germ can. Reroll outtakes. Each half of dough should make about 8 rounds.

Place a rounded tablespoon filling in center of each round. Top with olive slice and pimiento strip. Moisten edges, fold in half moons over filling, and pinch edges to seal. Cut a small slit in the top of the crust.

Bake on an ungreased baking sheet for about 15 minutes until golden. Serve warm.

Makes 16 turnovers; serves 8
Minor Protein
Note: Assembled unbaked pastries can be covered and refrigerated or frozen. Frozen empanadas can be cooked exactly like fresh ones.

PISSALADIÈRE NIÇOISE

Throughout southern France these onion-filled pizzas are displayed in patisseries where you can purchase an individual tart or a slice of a large pie for a midday snack.

¼ Pizza Dough recipe (page 219)
2 tablespoons olive oil
1 slice garlic
1½ cups thinly sliced onion
2 cups diced tomato
⅓ cup grated Parmesan cheese
pepper
2 pimientos, cut in strips
4 to 6 black olives, sliced

Let dough rise for 2 hours or longer, as directed in the recipe.

Heat oil in a large skillet, add garlic and onion, cover, and stew over low heat for about 15 minutes until onions are soft. Add tomato to onions, uncover pan, and cook for 10 to 15 minutes until soft.

Roll dough, place on an oiled 9-inch pie tin, and press to make a thin crust on the bottom, going about ¾ up the sides. Cover bottom with 3 tablespoons cheese.

Fill with onion–tomato mixture. Season generously with pepper and sprinkle with remaining cheese. Arrange pimientos lattice-fashion on top and place olive pieces in spaces. Let sit for 15 minutes. Preheat oven to 425°F. Bake for 15 minutes, reduce heat to 350°F. and bake 15 to 20 minutes longer until edges are lightly colored. Serve hot or at room temperature.

Serves 4
Minor Protein
Note: If you wish to make a full or half recipe of dough, you can chill the leftovers and make Pizza or Calzone later in the week; dough can be frozen and kept for a month. Pissaladière recipe is easily multiplied to make 2, 3, or even 4 pies to serve at a buffet or company meal. It can be reheated in a 350°F. oven for about 10 minutes.

POTATO KNISHES

These crusty mounds of potato dough with a savory onion center are an especially nice addition to a vegetable plate or any primarily vegetable entrée.

Potato Dough (page 206)
oil
3 large onions, chopped
egg

Prepare dough as recipe directs. If prepared specifically for knishes, reserve a little of the egg for the glaze.

Heat enough oil to cover the surface of a large skillet and cook onions slowly until they brown. Let cool to room temperature.

Preheat oven to 375°F.

Divide dough into 18 pieces and, using a well-floured surface, shape each into a flat circle, 2 to 2½ inches around.

Place 1 tablespoon browned onions in the center of circles and fold dough over filling to completely cover. Form into small rounds.

Place filled dough on an oiled baking sheet. Beat some egg with an equal amount of water and brush over the surface.

Bake for 25 to 30 minutes until firm and lightly colored. Serve hot.

Makes 18 knishes; serves 9 to 18
Minor Protein
Note: Knishes can be refrigerated

before baking and reheated, or frozen after baking. Recipe can be divided, and part of the dough can be used for Gnocchi, Semel Bresel, or Hot Potato Turnovers (recipe follows).

HOT POTATO TURNOVERS

Potato dough, filled with cheese, fries up crisp outside with a soft gooey center.

Potato Dough (page 206)
1 cup shredded, mild melting cheese like Jack, Gouda, or mozzarella
oil/butter

Divide dough into 18 pieces and shape each into a flat 3-inch circle on a well-floured surface.

Place a scant tablespoon of cheese on half of each round. Fold to form a half moon. Pinch edges to seal and make sure there are no holes in the dough.

Heat enough oil, alone or with butter, to cover the surface of a large, heavy skillet. When hot, brown turnovers on each side, cooking as many as will fit comfortably into the pan at one time.

Serve hot. If necessary, cooked turnovers can be kept warm in a 325°F. oven while another batch cooks, but they are best served as soon as possible.

Makes 18 turnovers; serves 6 to 9
Minor Protein; if 3 turnovers are consumed at a sitting, *Major Protein*
Note: Assembled turnovers can be refrigerated until ready to cook, or can be kept frozen, uncooked, for about 3 months. Cook without thawing until nicely browned.

CREAM PUFFS

A cream puff shell is lovely to look at and very versatile, adapting to a wide variety of fillings. For an appetizer, a large or mini cream puff shell filled with Tabouli or Deviled Tofu Salad is a promising beginning to any meal; creamed vegetables or minced cooked vegetables bound with Russian dressing also make suitable fillings. For a light lunch or savory pastry accompaniment, the shell can be filled with egg salad, Tofu "Chicken" Salad, or Tofu à la King. And, of course, cream puffs can also appear at dessert with a sweet pudding or fruit filling inside.

1 cup water
½ cup oil
1 cup whole wheat flour
½ teaspoon salt
4 eggs

Preheat oven to 425°F.

Combine water and oil in a saucepan and bring to a boil. Add flour and salt all at once and stir with a wooden spoon until mixture forms a mass. Remove from heat and let cool for 2 minutes.

Beat in eggs one at a time, adding the next egg when the mixture is no longer glossy.

Place on an oiled, floured baking sheet in mounds—a scant ¼ cup for large cream puffs or about 1 tablespoon for mini puffs. Leave 2 inches between mounds.

Bake for 15 minutes. Reduce heat to 375°F. and bake 15 minutes longer, or until surface is dry.

Cool, then cut off lids and remove any soft dough from the center. Fill just before serving.

Makes 12 large or 36 mini cream puffs

Note: If cream puffs are allowed to sit around, they may lose some of their crispness. To recrisp, place in a 375° to 400°F. oven for about 5 minutes. Cream puffs can be frozen as soon as they cool. To use, thaw at room temperature (which occurs within half an hour of removing them from the freezer), then recrisp as above. A large cream puff holds ¼ cup filling; a mini puff holds a generous tablespoon of filling.

Variation: For *Cheese Puffs,* add 1 cup shredded Swiss cheese to the cream puff batter and bake as usual. These can be eaten plain or filled.

SAVORY FARMER PUFFS

This is a gentle cheese–vegetable filled cream puff that is suited for service with

salad, soup, or even for lunch instead of a sandwich.

4 large Cream Puffs (page 283)
½ cup farmer cheese
½ cup shredded cheese of choice
½ cup diced tomato
minced fresh parsley or dill
3 to 4 tablespoons yogurt
salt
pepper

Remove a slice from the top of each prepared cream puff and hollow out the center if necessary.

Mash farmer cheese; stir in shredded cheese until evenly blended. Fold in tomato and herbs to taste and add yogurt as needed to form a soft, creamy mixture. Season with salt and pepper to taste.

Pack cheese mixture into cream puff shells and serve.

Serves 4
Minor Protein

YOGURT SALAD PUFFS

A yogurt–vegetable filling in cream puffs makes a nice luncheon entrée or dinner appetizer.

1 cup chopped peeled cucumber
1 teaspoon salt
2 cups yogurt
½ cup walnut pieces
2 tablespoons thinly sliced scallion or fresh dill
3 sliced radishes
¼ teaspoon hot pepper sauce
6 large Cream Puffs (page 283)

Sprinkle cucumber with ½ teaspoon salt and let stand for 15 minutes or longer to extract moisture. Drain well.

Drain any liquid from yogurt so it is as thick as possible. Combine yogurt with drained cucumber, remaining salt and other ingredients. Chill.

Just before serving, spoon yogurt into cream puffs.

Serves 6
Minor Protein

STUFFED CHAPATIS

The chapati, the staple bread of India, is made from a simple flour-and-water dough rolled into a thin pancake and cooked on top of the stove. The preparation of the chapati dough is explained fully in "Bread Baking and Cracker Making"; it is probably the easiest of all breads to prepare. In India, the dough is often filled before cooking, as here, transforming it into a savory pastry.

Chapati Dough (page 323)
1 cup cooked rice or millet
½ cup finely chopped raw or cooked vegetables
1 teaspoon curry powder
salt
pepper

Let dough rest about 30 minutes, then divide it into 12 equal portions, shaping each into a ball. Roll very thin, as for Chapatis, making a 4- to 5-inch round with each ball of dough.

Combine remaining ingredients, seasoning to taste with salt and pepper. Place a rounded spoonful of filling in the center of each pancake, fold into half moons, press edges, and roll lip slightly to seal.

Heat a heavy skillet or griddle without any fat (or if you have a wood stove with a flat top, get the surface hot). Cook the stuffed chapatis for about 1 minute on each side until speckled with brown. Using tongs, press the edges against the hot cooking surface briefly so they cook too.

While hot, spread with a little butter and serve.

Makes 12 "turnovers"; serves 4
Protein Complement
Note: These should be cooked just before serving since they don't have the same quality if reheated. Preparation can be done ahead of time and the stuffed chapatis can be kept at room temperature or in the refrigerator. In either place, cover with a damp cloth to prevent drying.

Variations: Other common chapati fillings include mashed beans, shredded raw carrots, minced cooked vegetables, or mashed potatoes, plain or seasoned to taste with curry spices or blended curry powder. About 1½ cups of filling are needed for 12 balls of dough.

CONSUM

The Italians have a savory pastry very much like the stuffed chapati, which they call consum. In this version, the dough is filled with seasoned sautéed greens.

Chapati Dough made with part soy flour (page 323)
1 pound mixed greens, including some bitter varieties like escarole, chicory, and broccoli rape mixed with mild greens like cabbage, spinach, and chard
1 tablespoon oil
1 clove garlic, minced
salt
pepper

Let dough rest for 30 minutes; then divide into 12 balls and roll into thin 4- to 5-inch rounds.

While dough rests, chop greens coarsely. Heat oil in a large pan and cook garlic briefly; then add greens and stir until wilted. Cover and cook 5 to 10 minutes longer until greens are tender. Season to taste with salt and pepper and let cool.

Place a spoonful of greens in the center of each pancake. Fold into half moons, pinch edges, and roll lip slightly to seal.

Cook in a hot, dry skillet, griddle, or the top of a wood stove (as for Stuffed Chapatis) until all surfaces are speckled with brown. Serve hot.

Makes 12 "turnovers"; serves 4
Variation: When Consum are shallow-fried in oil (like Fried Dumplings, see following recipe), they are called Cassoni and are quite delicious.

Menu Suggestions: These savory bundles make a perfect accompaniment to most Italian entrées, particularly those featuring beans or vegetables and a ricotta cheese filling or topping.

FRIED DUMPLINGS

When stuffed chapatis are fried in oil, they puff up, creating crisp dumplings very similar to egg rolls. The filling can be composed of leftover cooked grains, beans, or vegetables. The choice of seasoning can be suited to the rest of the meal and the dumplings can be dipped in a sauce for extra flavoring at the table.

Several suggestions for Fried Dumplings follow. Directions for preparing the dough and assembly can be found in the recipe for Stuffed Chapatis (page 323). Allow 1½ cups of filling for 12 dumplings.

To cook, heat oil to a depth of ¼ inch in a heavy 15-inch skillet. When quite hot, add half the dumplings so they fit comfortably, and fry for 3 to 5 minutes until golden on both sides. Drain on absorbent paper.

For *Fried Chinese Dumplings,* prepare a filling of cooked rice, slivered scallions, any shredded or cooked vegetables, and crumbled tofu. Season with soy sauce. Serve the dumplings with Chinese Mustard, Sweet Chinese Dipping Sauce, or "Duck" Sauce.

For *Fried Italian Dumplings,* prepare a filling of cooked rice, minced garlic, shredded mozzarella or provolone cheese, and grated Parmesan cheese. Serve plain or with tomato sauce.

For *Fried Mexican Dumplings,* fill with mashed cooked or refried beans seasoned with chili powder and cayenne. Use Guacamole as a condiment or make a sauce of yogurt seasoned lightly with sour cream.

Minor Protein

Note: Dumplings can be assembled in advance and chilled or frozen. Frozen dumplings can be fried without thawing.

SALADS AND DRESSINGS

Noah Webster says salad is "any cold dish of meat, shellfish, fruit or vegetables with mayonnaise or other dressing." This definition serves as a starting point but does not do justice to the great variety of salads that can be composed nor to the contrast of tastes and textures they offer.

The rest of the meal must be considered in planning when to serve the salad. Sometimes it may whet the palate for the meal when no formal appetizer is planned; at other times it offers a cleansing break between the appetizer and the entrée. This is now the trend in American restaurants. In the European tradition, a simple green salad is more likely to appear after the entrée as a means of preparing the palate for dessert. In our home, we generally put the salad on the table just before the main course so that it can be eaten whenever we or our guests prefer. With a one-dish casserole, a rice and bean entrée or similar composite dish, we like to use the salad as an accompaniment, since it adds interest to the plate. In fact, we often serve two different salads with the entrée.

Although many people may think that the salad section of a cookbook is of minimal importance, at our table the salad is frequently the distinguishing feature of the meal. Do not skimp when it comes to salads; they should be offered generously.

Fine Points of Salad Making

A mixed vegetable salad really needs no recipe, for you can hardly go wrong in your choice of ingredients. There are, however, a few details that will make salads even more enjoyable.

Wash salad ingredients in cold water. This keeps them crisp.

Dry all salad ingredients thoroughly. Clinging water dilutes the dressing. If you are unable to do the job effectively with towels, try a salad spinner. It can turn a tedious task into a few-second operation.

Salad ingredients in bite-size pieces are easier to handle. Having to cut greens with a knife and fork can be awkward and messy. It is also a good idea to shred any vegetables that are difficult to chew, such as carrots, turnips, and raw beets. Cut raw cauliflower and broccoli into small bits.

Salad greens should be dressed just before serving to keep them from becoming limp, unless, of course, a "wilted" salad is the objective. Most other vegetables benefit from at least brief marination in the dressing. The recipes in this section specify when the salad should be dressed.

Excellent salad dressings can be made with light, polyunsaturated oils like safflower or sunflower oil. They can be either used alone or combined with cooking oils like corn, soy, peanut, and olive. Many oils come in different grades, ranging from the minimally processed unrefined oil, which retains a good deal of the characteristic flavor and nutrient content, to cold-pressed oil, which tends to be mild in taste with only trace amounts of nutrients, to chemically expressed oil which is the most highly processed, neutral in flavor, and provides no nutrients other than fat and calories. Additional specialty oils, such as French walnut, may be selected for salads, but unless they are minimally refined and retain a distinct flavor there is no real reason to use them.

By blending yogurt, tofu, cottage cheese, or nuts into the salad dressing, a noticeable amount of protein can be added to the meal.

As a gauge, 1 cup of most dressings is adequate for a salad for 6 to 8.

If salad dressing is prepared in advance, be sure to mix it well before using in order to recombine the ingredients. Having bottles of homemade dressing on hand in the refrigerator is the surest way to encourage salad eating.

Remember, the salads offered here are by no means definitive. They are merely meant to suggest the many ways in which vegetables and flavoring agents may be combined. Use them to trigger your imagination. A well-designed salad should be as appealing to your eyes as it is to your taste buds, so consider color and texture in making your choices.

Salad dressings begin this section, followed by salads that have a predominant ingredient, listed alphabetically. Salads with more varied ingredients come next, and the section ends with fruit salads that can be served with the meal.

Dressings

BASIC OIL AND VINEGAR DRESSING

The classic proportion of oil to vinegar is 3 to 1. We prefer a ratio closer to 2 to 1, which is less delicate but more flavorful.

¼ cup wine or cider vinegar
¼ teaspoon salt
dash Dijon mustard
pepper
½ to ¾ cup oil

Using a fork or wire whisk, beat vinegar with salt, mustard, and pepper. Gradually beat in oil until the dressing is slightly creamy and diluted to taste. Dressing ingredients can also be combined in a jar and shaken together in lieu of beating, but the gradual addition of oil makes a creamier dressing.
Makes ¾ to 1 cup dressing

Note: Substituting fresh lemon juice for some of the vinegar produces a mellower dressing. Substituting all lemon juice imparts a distinct lemon taste. If the dressing is too sharp and you do not wish to add more oil, it can be diluted with a little water.

Variations: For *Garlic Dressing,* add 1 minced clove garlic.

For *Herb Dressing,* add ½ teaspoon dried chervil, ¼ teaspoon dried or 1 tablespoon fresh basil, 1 tablespoon fresh dill or parsley, using any one or several in combination. A split clove of garlic can also be added.

For *Italian Dressing,* add a split clove of garlic and ¼ teaspoon each dried basil and oregano. Use wine vinegar and at least part olive oil.

For *Creamy Dressing,* beat in up to 3 tablespoons yogurt.

For *Soft Cheese Dressing,* beat in 3 tablespoons crumbled feta or blue cheese.

288 · COOKING IN THE WHOLEFOODS STYLE

For *Rich Parsley Dressing,* combine ¼ cup parsley with the vinegar and seasonings in a blender or processor fitted with a steel blade. With the motor running, add oil in a steady stream through the feeder cap until dressing is creamy and parsley is finely minced.

For *Chunky Cottage Cheese Dressing,* add 1 tablespoon minced parsley, 1 minced scallion, and ¼ cup cottage cheese. Shake well so that ingredients are well distributed but tiny lumps of cheese remain. This is especially good on tomato salads and mixed greens.

FRENCH TOMATO VINAIGRETTE

½ tablespoon tomato paste
2 tablespoons wine vinegar
6 tablespoons oil

Beat all ingredients with a fork until smooth.
Makes ½ cup dressing
Variations: For *Creamy French Tomato Vinaigrette,* beat in ¼ cup yogurt.

For *Italian Tomato Vinaigrette,* add ¼ teaspoon dried basil and ⅛ teaspoon oregano.

For *Mexican Tomato Vinaigrette,* replace wine vinegar with cider vinegar and add ½ teaspoon chili powder.

NO-OIL TOMATO JUICE DRESSING

Appropriate for those who want a fat-free dressing. To accommodate those who want a richer or more traditional dressing, serve a separate cruet of oil. Once the salad is dressed and served, oil can be poured on to taste.

½ cup tomato juice
2 tablespoons lemon juice
½ teaspoon honey
1 teaspoon celery seed, or 1 tablespoon chopped chives
pepper

Mix ingredients together, adding a generous amount of pepper.
Makes ⅔ cup dressing; serves 4

SWEET AND SPICY DRESSING

¼ cup catsup
6 tablespoons lemon juice
6 tablespoons oil
½ teaspoon dry mustard
2 tablespoons minced onion

Combine all ingredients, mixing or shaking until well blended.
Makes 1 cup

FRESH MAYONNAISE

Once you are accustomed to having fresh mayonnaise, it's hard to go back to the store-bought kind.

1 egg
½ teaspoon dry mustard
½ tablespoon lemon juice
½ teaspoon salt
1 cup oil (safflower or sunflower preferred)

Break egg into a deep bowl and put mustard on top. Beat in lemon juice, using a fork or wire whisk. Beat in salt.

Beat in oil in a slow, steady stream without stopping until mayonnaise thickens, or "grabs." This is easiest to do with two people, one to beat and one to pour. Keep chilled and use within a month.
Makes 1 cup
Note: For *Fresh Mayonnaise in a Machine,* combine egg, mustard, lemon juice, and salt in a blender or a processor fitted with a plastic mixing blade. Add ¼ cup oil all at once, blend, and then add remaining oil in a slow, steady stream through the feeder cap until it becomes mayonnaise.
Variation: Mayonnaise can be made with yolks only, replacing each whole egg with two yolks.

AVOCADO MAYONNAISE

If the minimum amount of oil is used, the pronounced lemon flavor makes a dressing that is excellent on plain green salads. When the full amount of oil is used, the delicately flavored dressing is an appealing binder for potato salad.

2 tablespoons diced avocado
2 tablespoons lemon juice
6 to 8 tablespoons oil

Puree avocado and lemon juice in a blender or a processor fitted with a plastic mixing blade. With machine running, add oil in a steady stream until dressing is thick and creamy.
Makes ½ cup

CASHEW MAYONNAISE

Nuts, rather than egg, hold this dressing together.

2 tablespoons sunflower seeds
2 tablespoons cashew pieces
¼ cup water
2 tablespoons lemon juice
¼ cup oil (olive preferred)
¼ teaspoon salt

Grind nuts to a powder in a blender or processor. Add water and lemon juice and puree until smooth. With machine running, slowly pour in oil until dressing is thick. Season with salt, adjusting to taste.
Makes about ⅔ cup
Protein Complement

TOFU MAYONNAISE

A thick, creamy dressing made with tofu can be seasoned in the same manner as traditional mayonnaise and used to dress salad greens or to bind salad ingredients. The great advantage of this dressing is that it is lower in fat and calories and adds protein to the salad.

½ pound tofu (1 large or 2 small cakes)
2 tablespoons lemon juice or cider vinegar
½ teaspoon salt
¼ teaspoon prepared mustard
3 tablespoons oil
2 to 4 tablespoons water

Pat tofu dry with a paper towel and combine in a blender or a processor fitted with a steel blade with lemon juice, salt, and mustard. Process until creamy. With machine running, add oil

through feeder cap, then water, until mayonnaise is of desired consistency.
Makes 1 cup
Minor Protein
Variation: For *Tofu Sour Cream,* omit mustard and water to make a thicker dressing. Increase tartness, if you wish, by stirring in another tablespoon of lemon juice.

THOUSAND ISLAND DRESSING

¼ cup yogurt
2 tablespoons mayonnaise
2 tablespoons catsup
2 tablespoons minced green pepper
1 tablespoon minced pimiento
1 tablespoon minced green or black olives

Combine all ingredients and mix until evenly blended.
Makes ⅔ cup
Variation: Use ¼ cup Zucchini or Green Tomato Relish in place of minced vegetables.

GREEN GODDESS DRESSING

½ cup mayonnaise (commercial, homemade, or Tofu Mayonnaise, page 289)
½ cup yogurt
1 tablespoon lemon juice
¼ cup minced parsley
1 minced scallion

Combine ingredients and mix until smooth.
Makes 1 cup
Minor Protein
Note: If regular mayonnaise is used, yogurt can be replaced with Tofu Sour Cream.

AVOCADO DRESSING

1 clove garlic
½ medium avocado
2 tablespoons lemon juice
2 tablespoons mayonnaise
2 tablespoons yogurt
⅛ to ¼ teaspoon hot pepper sauce

Cut garlic and rub over surface of a shallow bowl. Mash avocado in this container. (You should have ¼ cup mashed avocado.) Beat remaining ingredients into avocado until smooth. If too thick, thin with 2 to 4 tablespoons water to make consistency of thick cream.

Makes about ⅔ cup

Note: Before it is thinned with water, this mixture can serve as a dip for raw vegetables.

CREAMY NUT DRESSING

A delicious dressing for sliced fresh tomato or any cold cooked vegetable.

> ¼ cup almonds, cashews, and sunflower seeds, ground to meal
> 3 tablespoons mayonnaise
> 3 tablespoons yogurt
> 1 teaspoon lemon juice
> minced fresh basil or parsley (optional)

Combine all ingredients and mix until smooth.

Makes ½ cup

Minor Protein

CREAMY BLUE CHEESE DRESSING

> ¼ cup wine vinegar
> ¼ teaspoon salt
> pepper
> ½ cup oil
> 2 to 4 tablespoons yogurt
> ¼ cup crumbled blue or Roquefort cheese

Combine vinegar, salt, and pepper.

Beat in oil in a slow, steady stream, then add yogurt (use the full amount for a less piquant, creamier dressing). Stir in cheese.

Makes 1 cup

Minor Protein

CREAMY HERB DRESSING

Particularly good on mixed greens topped with cold cooked broccoli, beets, artichoke hearts, green beans, and similar leftovers.

> 1 cup cottage cheese
> ½ cup yogurt
> ¼ cup mayonnaise
> 1 tablespoon lemon juice

> 2 teaspoons mixed dried herbs (basil, parsley, chervil) or 2 tablespoons fresh

Puree ingredients until smooth in a blender or processor.

Makes 1½ cups; serves 6

Minor Protein

LEMON–TAHINI DRESSING

A creamy, flavorful dressing.

> ¼ cup tahini
> ¼ cup lemon juice
> ¾ cup oil (part olive and part safflower preferred)
> ¼ cup water
> 1 teaspoon soy sauce
> ¼ teaspoon salt
> 1 tablespoon minced dill and/or parsley (optional)

Using a fork, wire whisk, blender, or food processor, mix ingredients together until smooth and creamy.

Makes 1½ cups; serves 8 to 10

Protein Complement

Variation: For a more flavorful dressing, use a blender or a processor fitted with a steel blade and add 1 slice onion, 1 small stalk celery with leaves, and 1 wedge green pepper. Process until smooth.

CREAMY TOMATO DRESSING

Excellent to dress a platter of raw vegetables.

> ½ cup tomato juice
> ¼ cup cottage cheese
> 1 tablespoon lemon juice
> ½ teaspoon curry powder

Puree ingredients in a blender or a food processor fitted with a plastic mixing blade.

Makes about ¾ cup; serves 4

Minor Protein

CREAMY TOFU GARLIC DRESSING

The East–West restaurant in New York City serves a salad with a dressing like this one that is so delicious it is not unusual for people to order two at a single sitting.

8 ounces tofu (1 large or 2 small squares)
2 tablespoons cider vinegar
1 tablespoon lemon juice
¼ teaspoon dry mustard
pinch salt
1 tablespoon soy sauce
1 clove garlic, minced
¼ cup oil
about ⅓ cup water

Combine tofu, vinegar, lemon juice, mustard, salt, soy sauce, and garlic in a blender or a processor fitted with a plastic or steel blade. Puree until smooth. With machine running, add oil through feeder. Gradually add water until dressing is of thick pouring consistency.

Makes 1 cup dressing; serves 6 to 8
Minor Protein

CREAMY CARROT DRESSING

¼ cup oil
1 carrot, diced
1 tablespoon sesame seeds
1 tablespoon peanuts
1 clove garlic
1 tablespoon soy sauce
⅓ cup yogurt

Combine oil, carrot, seeds, nuts, garlic, and soy sauce in a blender or processor fitted with a steel blade. Process until smooth. Add yogurt and blend briefly.

Makes about ¾ cup; serves 4
Minor Protein

ORANGE–HONEY DRESSING

An appropriate dressing for a dinner fruit salad or any mixed green salad.

2 tablespoons orange juice concentrate, thawed
½ tablespoon wine vinegar
½ tablespoon honey
¼ teaspoon dry mustard
⅛ teaspoon salt
⅓ cup safflower or sunflower oil

Combine ingredients and shake or beat until evenly blended.

Makes ½ cup; enough for 4
Variation: For *Creamy Orange–Honey Dressing,* add 2 tablespoons lemon juice, ¼ cup yogurt, and 1 tablespoon mayonnaise to ¼ cup of Orange–Honey Dressing. Serve on mixed greens; serves 4 to 6.

Salads

GREEN BEAN AND TOMATO SALAD

1 pound green beans, cut into 1- to 2-inch lengths (about 4 cups)
2 medium tomatoes
2 tablespoons wine vinegar
1 teaspoon soy sauce
6 tablespoons oil (part olive preferred)

Steam beans for 10 minutes until just tender. Cut tomatoes into thin wedges, making 12 to 16 per tomato.

Combine vinegar and soy sauce in a large shallow bowl and beat in oil until creamy. Add beans and tomato and let marinate for at least 1 hour at room temperature. If prepared in advance and chilled, remove 30 minutes before serving. Salad should be eaten at room temperature.

Serves 4 to 6

MARINATED GREEN BEANS WITH COTTAGE CHEESE

Serve at any meal that needs a protein boost.

1 pound fresh green beans
¾ cup diced mushrooms (optional)
¾ cup Light Italian Tomato Dressing (page 57)
1 to 1½ cups cottage cheese

Trim ends of beans and steam for 5 minutes. Mix beans, mushrooms, and dressing in a shallow bowl and let marinate while you prepare the rest of the meal.

Place a ¼-cup mound of cottage cheese on each serving plate. Top with marinated beans and pour on dressing from the bowl.

Serves 4 to 6
Minor Protein

COLD BEET SALAD

Add this to a cold salad platter or serve as an accompaniment to a sandwich.

1 cup chopped cooked beets
1 cup chopped cucumber
2 chopped hard-cooked eggs
4 scallions, thinly sliced
¼ cup yogurt
1 tablespoon sour cream
lemon juice
salt
pepper

Combine all ingredients, adding lemon juice, salt, and pepper to taste.
Serves 4
Minor Protein

BEET SALAD WITH BLUE CHEESE

4 medium beets (about 1 pound)
1 carrot, shredded
2 tablespoons crumbled blue cheese
½ cup Creamy Blue Cheese Dressing (page 290)

Cook beets until tender. When cool enough to handle, remove peel and chill until needed. (This can be done a day in advance.)

Slice beets and arrange on a serving plate. Top with shredded carrot and blue cheese. Pour on dressing just before serving.
Serves 4
Minor Protein

COUNTRY COLESLAW

½ cup yogurt
3 tablespoons wine or cider vinegar
2 tablespoons honey
½ teaspoon salt
1¼ pounds cabbage, finely shredded (about 5 cups)
½ cup shredded carrot

Combine yogurt, vinegar, honey, and salt in a bowl large enough to hold the coleslaw. When smooth, add vegetables and toss. Taste and, if too sharp, add a little yogurt; if too bland, add a dash more vinegar.
Makes 1 quart; serves 6
Variation: For a more varied coleslaw, add ½ cup slivered green pepper and 4 thinly sliced scallions.

PUERTO RICAN CABBAGE SALAD

We learned to love this salad in Puerto Rico, and never tired of it, even though we ate it day after day.

1 pound cabbage, chopped (about 5 cups)
2 small tomatoes, diced
3 ribs celery, chopped
3 tablespoons oil
2 tablespoons cider vinegar
½ teaspoon salt
¼ teaspoon hot pepper sauce

Combine all ingredients and toss together. Refrigerate until ready to serve.
Serves 6

GREEK COLESLAW

The most important requirement in preparing Greek Coleslaw is that you work the shredded vegetable with your hands.

1 clove garlic (optional)
¾ pound cabbage, coarsely shredded (about 4 cups)
juice of ½ lemon

If a little garlic flavor is desired, cut garlic clove and rub it into the salad bowl, then discard. Fill bowl with shredded cabbage and knead with your hands until cabbage softens. Squeeze in lemon juice and toss.
Serves 4

COLESLAW PIE

This grated vegetable "cake" combines layers of shredded vegetables with crackers, creating a salad you can eat out of hand. It is easily wrapped for packing into lunch boxes and is an interesting addition to a buffet table.

3 cups shredded vegetables made from:
    1 carrot
    ½ green pepper
    cucumber or zucchini
    beets
    cabbage
    2 scallions

1 teaspoon salt
2 tablespoons cider vinegar
whole grain rye or caraway rye crackers

Shred vegetables in a drum grater, cheese grater, or food processor. Press to extract any moisture and drain. Toss with salt and vinegar.

Place crackers in a single layer in an 8-inch square pan. Break pieces to fill any gaps. Top crackers with half the vegetable mixture. Cover with another layer of crackers, another layer of vegetables, and finally a top layer of crackers.

Place waxed paper on top and press down firmly so liquid rises. Chill for several hours up to several days. Cut in squares to serve.
Serves 6

CABBAGE RAITA

Raita is an Indian relish generally used as a contrast to curries.

1 cup yogurt
½ teaspoon salt
1 teaspoon cumin
½ pound cabbage, finely shredded (about 2 cups)

In a serving bowl, beat yogurt with salt and cumin, using a fork. When it flows freely, stir in cabbage. Chill until ready to serve and bring to the table very cold.
Serves 6
Minor Protein

CARROT RAITA

Carrot salads are often featured in Indian cooking. This one, which is a bit spicy and very refreshing, is also good with Mideast or even American meals.

2 cups yogurt
½ teaspoon salt
2 carrots, coarsely grated
½ teaspoon cumin
¼ teaspoon cayenne

Stir yogurt and salt into grated carrot until evenly mixed. Sprinkle cumin and cayenne on top.
Serves 4
Minor Protein

SWEET CARROT RAITA

This carrot salad is just a little sweet and just a little spicy. It provides an excellent contrast to vegetable–grain entrées and is the recommended accompaniment to Moroccan Couscous.

2 cups finely chopped or grated carrots
2 tablespoons lime juice
1 tablespoon honey
¼ teaspoon cayenne

Combine all ingredients, mixing well and pressing lightly to make juicy. Adjust seasoning so raita is mildly sweet and mildly hot.

Serve at room temperature. If made in advance and chilled, remove from refrigerator at beginning of meal preparation so salad is not too cold.
Serves 6

CARROT–PEANUT SALAD

4 good-sized carrots, grated (about 2½ cups)
½ cup peanuts, finely chopped
3 tablespoons yogurt
3 tablespoons mayonnaise

Combine all ingredients and mix well. Serve as is or on a bed of mixed shredded greens.
Serves 4
Minor Protein

YOGURT–CUCUMBER SALAD

A versatile salad that goes well with both Mideastern and American cuisines.

1½ cups peeled, thinly sliced cucumber
1 cup yogurt
½ to 1 tablespoon crushed dried mint
dash lemon juice

Gently mix all ingredients, adjusting mint to personal taste. If possible, prepare in advance so flavors have a chance to develop.
Serves 4
Minor Protein
Variations: Cucumber can be grated and pressed to extract moisture for a slightly varied texture. Dried mint can be replaced with 2 to 4 tablespoons fresh

mint, or the flavor can be altered entirely by adding parsley, dill, or a little cumin to taste, or by adding 2 thinly sliced scallions.

MIDEAST RELISH

1 cup chopped peeled cucumber
½ teaspoon salt
¼ cup minced scallion
¼ cup yogurt, or yogurt combined with sour cream

Combine cucumber, salt, and scallion and let stand at room temperature to extract moisture. Drain and top with yogurt.
Serves 4

CUCUMBERS WITH CREAMY COTTAGE CHEESE

A rich, creamy salad that is a particularly good accompaniment to a meal in need of more protein.

1 medium cucumber, peeled and diced
¼ teaspoon salt
1½ cups cottage cheese
1 tablespoon lemon juice
2 tablespoons parsley leaves
2 small or 1 large scallion
lettuce leaves

Place cucumber in a bowl and sprinkle with salt.

Combine remaining ingredients except lettuce in a processor fitted with a steel blade or in a blender. Puree until smooth. If too stiff for blender, add 1 tablespoon yogurt, but try to keep as thick as possible.

Mix cottage cheese dressing with cucumber. Chill. Serve on lettuce leaves.
Serves 4 to 6
Minor Protein

CUCUMBER CUCHUMBER

A typical Indian salad.

3 cucumbers, peeled and diced (about 3 cups)
2 tablespoons minced pickled hot peppers
1 teaspoon salt
juice of 1 lime

Combine all ingredients and mix well.
Serves 6 to 8

CUCUMBER SALAD WITH SPICY DRESSING

A good salad to serve with Chinese food.

2 medium cucumbers
2 tablespoons soy sauce
2 tablespoons white or rice vinegar
2 teaspoons honey
¼ teaspoon salt
½ teaspoon hot pepper sauce
1 tablespoon Chinese sesame oil

Peel and slice cucumbers. Combine everything but the cucumber and mix well to dissolve honey and salt. Stir cucumber into dressing; let stand while preparing the meal in order to develop maximum flavor.
Serves 4

CUCUMBER MOUSSE

A refreshing gelatin salad especially designed for summer entertaining.

1 large cucumber
1 envelope or 1 tablespoon unflavored gelatin
1 cup cottage cheese
2 to 4 tablespoons yogurt
½ teaspoon salt
1 tablespoon chopped fresh dill or chives
greens
tomato wedges
olives

Peel cucumber and grate to make 1 cup. Place in a strainer and let liquid drain into a bowl. Squeeze to extract as much juice as possible and add water to this to make ½ cup liquid. Sprinkle gelatin over liquid and let stand for a few minutes to soften. Then place over low heat and stir to dissolve.

Combine cottage cheese and yogurt in a blender or processor and puree until smooth. For a firm mousse, use only 2 tablespoons yogurt; add more for a softer set.

Mix pureed cottage cheese with cucumber, dissolved gelatin, salt, and herbs. Pour into a 2-cup mold or 4 individual dishes and chill for several hours, until firm.

To serve, unmold on a bed of greens. Surround with tomato wedges and olives.

Serves 4
Minor Protein

PINEAPPLE–CUCUMBER MOLD

1 can (20 ounces) crushed pineapple in unsweetened juice
1 small cucumber
⅛ teaspoon salt
1 tablespoon lemon juice
apple juice
1 envelope or 1 tablespoon unflavored gelatin
yogurt
mint leaves

Drain pineapple and press out as much liquid as possible. Reserve juice.

Peel cucumber, grate, sprinkle with salt, and let sit in a bowl for a few minutes to extract moisture. Squeeze and add liquid to pineapple juice.

Add lemon juice to the accumulated liquids and enough apple juice to make 1¾ cups of fluid.

Sprinkle gelatin over ¼ cup of the liquid and let stand for a few minutes to soften. Cook, stirring, over low heat to dissolve. Combine with remaining liquid and chill for 20 to 30 minutes, or until the consistency of thick egg whites.

Fold grated cucumber and 1 cup of the crushed pineapple into the gelatin. (The remaining pineapple can be used for garnish or saved for another purpose.) Turn mixture into a 3-cup mold, 8 x 8-inch metal pan, or 6 individual molds. Chill for several hours until firm.

To serve, unmold and garnish with yogurt, a few mint leaves, and some of the reserved pineapple, if desired.

Serves 6

CAULIFLOWER DINNER SALAD

5 cups torn greens
2 cups small cauliflower pieces (about ½ pound)
4 thin slices red onion

8 olives, sliced
¼ cup crumbled blue cheese
¼ teaspoon Dijon mustard
pinch salt
pepper
1 tablespoon lemon juice
1½ tablespoons wine vinegar
6 tablespoons oil

Line shallow salad bowl with greens. Top with cauliflower, onion, olives, and blue cheese. Combine remaining ingredients to make a dressing. Pour over salad just before serving and toss.

Serves 4
Minor Protein

LEMON GREENS

This is the simplest of all salads and very refreshing with a heavy or spicy meal.

crisp greens such as romaine, escarole, chicory, either singly or mixed
lemon wedges

Shred greens coarsely with a knife. Put on a serving plate. Squeeze fresh lemon juice over greens to coat without drowning. Toss. Chill or serve at once.

CHEESE SALAD WITH WALNUT DRESSING

Especially nice as an accompaniment to a plain pasta entrée.

3 cups chopped greens
½ cup sliced olives
1 cup mixed strips of cheese including provolone, mozzarella, cheddar, or Swiss
1 cucumber, peeled and sliced
3 tablespoons olive oil
salt
pepper
½ cup walnuts
¼ cup water
2 tablespoons lemon juice
garlic sliver (optional)
sliced red onion

Combine greens, olives, cheese, and cucumber in a serving bowl. Toss with oil and season with salt and pepper.

Prepare a dressing by pureeing nuts with water, lemon juice, a pinch of salt and garlic, using the blender or processor. If you do not have either, grind the nuts with a drum grater and beat in the other ingredients. (If desired, a few chunks of walnut can remain.)

Mix dressing with salad before serving and garnish with onion.

Serves 6
Minor Protein

CHEESE AND GREENS

A dish to serve at any meal that is not rich in dairy products.

    6 cups soft leafy greens, torn into bite-
      size pieces
    6 ounces Swiss, provolone, cheddar,
      or other cheese of choice cut into
      julienne strips
    ¼ cup oil
    salt
    pepper
    2 teaspoons wine vinegar

Mix greens with cheese. Dress at the table with oil, salt, pepper, and a hint of vinegar.

Serves 4
Minor Protein

ORANGE-SECTION SALAD

Despite the fruit, this is not a sweet salad. Serve at a rice and bean dinner.

    6 cups torn greens (preferably ro-
      maine with a little escarole or some
      other dark "bitter" green)
    2 oranges, peeled and sectioned
    thin slices sweet Spanish or red Ber-
      muda onion
    3 tablespoons fresh orange juice
    2 tablespoons wine vinegar
    6 tablespoons oil (safflower preferred)
    ⅛ teaspoon salt
    ½ teaspoon minced orange rind

Combine greens, oranges, and onion in a salad bowl. Combine remaining ingredients to create the dressing and toss with the salad just before serving.

Serves 4

CAESAR SALAD

The distinctive flavor of any Caesar salad comes from the union of garlic, barely cooked egg, Parmesan cheese, croutons, and anchovies. If you choose to omit the anchovy in favor of capers, an extremely flavorful salad can still be achieved.

    1 clove garlic, split
    1 tablespoon lemon juice
    1 teaspoon soy sauce
    3 tablespoons olive oil
    1 large head romaine lettuce (about 8
      cups in pieces)
    1 egg
    2 tablespoons grated Parmesan cheese
    ½ cup whole wheat croutons
    8 anchovies, cut in pieces or mashed
      (optional)
    2 tablespoons capers (optional)
    pepper

Rub salad bowl generously with garlic and discard. Add lemon juice, soy sauce, and oil and beat with a fork until smooth and creamy. Tear lettuce into pieces and place in the bowl.

Cook egg in the shell for 1 minute in boiling water, break over greens, and toss. Add cheese, croutons, anchovies and/or capers, as desired, and a generous grinding of pepper. Toss and serve.

Serves 4
Minor Protein

Note: If anchovies are omitted, increase cheese to ¼ cup and be sure to add capers.

STEAMED SALAD

A lightly cooked salad that offers a nice change on a cold day.

    1½ tablespoons lemon juice or cider
      vinegar
    3 tablespoons oil
    ¼ teaspoon salt
    ½ teaspoon prepared mustard
    pepper
    6 cups mixed greens in small, bite-size
      pieces, including lettuce, spinach,
      chicory, mustard greens, or others
      of choice
    ½ cup shredded beets or carrots
      (optional)

Combine lemon juice, oil, salt, mustard, and pepper in a deep pot. Add vegetables, toss, cover, and place over low heat. After a minute, stir lightly.

Replace cover and cook 1 to 2 minutes longer until just wilted. Transfer to a serving bowl.

Serves 4

Note: Dressing ingredients can be replaced with ¼ cup pre-made oil and vinegar dressing.

FRENCH MUSHROOM SALAD

3 tablespoons lemon juice
2 teaspoons Dijon mustard
¼ teaspoon salt
pepper
½ cup olive oil
½ pound mushrooms, sliced paper-thin (about 2½ cups)
watercress or soft greens

Combine lemon juice, mustard, salt, and pepper in a shallow bowl. Beat in oil slowly, using a fork or wire whisk to make a thick, creamy dressing.

Add mushrooms to dressing and mix well. Serve immediately on a bed of watercress or soft leaf lettuce, or chill in a bowl and place on greens just before serving.

Serves 4

TOMATO–MUSHROOM SALAD

Equally suited as an appetizer or a side dish.

lettuce
2 tomatoes
salt
pepper
2 tablespoons oil
¼ teaspoon dried basil
¼ teaspoon oregano
1 cup sliced mushrooms
1 tablespoon lemon juice
pickled hot peppers
olives

Line serving plate with lettuce leaves. Cut tomatoes into half slices and overlap slices attractively on lettuce. Sprinkle with salt, pepper, 1 tablespoon oil, basil, and oregano.

Arrange mushroom slices over tomato. Sprinkle with remaining oil and lemon. Garnish with peppers and olives. Salad can be served immediately or left at room temperature for about 30 minutes.

Serves 4

ONION–RADISH RELISH

An Indian condiment that can be transformed for service with a variety of Mideast or grain–bean entrées by adding yogurt.

¼ cup minced onion
¼ cup minced green pepper
½ cup coarsely chopped radish
¼ teaspoon salt
⅛ teaspoon cayenne
¼ teaspoon paprika
2 teaspoons lemon juice

Combine all ingredients. Serve immediately, let sit at room temperature for several hours, or refrigerate for as long as 3 days.

Makes 1 cup; serves 6

Variation: Add ¼ to ½ cup yogurt until creamy and mellow in taste.

CHINESE RADISH SALAD

Add some jazz to a simple Chinese dinner with this quickly made salad. Even those who generally don't pay radishes much attention are surprised by how good they are in this dressing.

½ pound radishes (about 1¼ cups)
½ teaspoon salt
2 teaspoons soy sauce
1 tablespoon molasses
2 tablespoons vinegar
1 teaspoon Chinese sesame oil

Trim radishes. Using the flat side of a Chinese cleaver or a heavy knife, gently crush them so they split (do not use so much force that they actually break into pieces). Sprinkle with salt and let stand for 10 minutes. Rinse and drain.

Combine remaining ingredients to make the dressing. Pour over radishes and marinate until ready to serve. Salad can be served at once or made well in advance.

Serves 4 to 6

CAUCASUS SALAD

Inspired by Russian cuisine, this salad is meant to accompany potato and buckwheat dishes or to be served as part of an hors d'oeuvres platter.

⅔ cup thinly sliced radishes
⅔ cup thinly sliced cucumber (peel if waxed)
2 scallions, minced
¼ teaspoon salt
1 sprig fresh dill, snipped
¼ cup yogurt

Combine all ingredients and toss to mix. If prepared in advance, chill before serving.
Serves 4

SPINACH SALAD

Spinach and mushrooms are a perfect match.

8 cups spinach (about ½ pound)
¼ pound mushrooms, sliced (about 1¼ cups)
4 scallions, sliced
¼ cup pumpkin seeds
soy sauce
½ cup Basic Oil and Vinegar Dressing (page 287) or any dressing of choice

Combine spinach, mushrooms, and scallions in a salad bowl.

Toast pumpkin seeds in a dry skillet and when they pop, remove from heat, season lightly with soy sauce, and toss into the salad. Toss with dressing when ready to serve.
Serves 4
Minor Protein
Note: For Main Dish Spinach Salad, double the portion sizes and add:

tomato wedges
diced avocado
2 to 4 ounces crumbled feta cheese or 2 to 4 slices Cheeson cut in strips
4 sliced hard-cooked eggs
alfalfa sprouts

TOASTED SEEDS AND SPINACH SALAD

A blend of spinach and apples enhanced by the smoky flavor of toasted seeds.

1 tablespoon sesame seeds
1 tablespoon pumpkin seeds
1 cup sliced apple
lemon juice
4 cups spinach
1 tablespoon cider vinegar
3 tablespoons oil
¼ teaspoon soy sauce

Toast seeds in a dry skillet until lightly browned and pumpkin seeds pop. Shake skillet occasionally for even cooking. Be careful not to overcook.

Douse apple slices with a little lemon juice to prevent browning. Combine spinach, toasted seeds, and apple in a salad bowl. Combine vinegar, oil, and soy sauce to make a dressing. Pour over salad, toss, and serve.
Serves 4

SPINACH–BEAN SPROUT SALAD

An Oriental salad that is suited to many Western-style meals.

Soy–Sesame Dressing
1 tablespoon sesame seeds
¼ cup lemon juice
1 tablespoon soy sauce
¼ cup oil
1 tablespoon chopped sweet onion

Salad
6 cups torn spinach
2 cups mung or soybean sprouts
¼ cup thinly sliced white radish

Toast sesame seeds in a dry skillet for about 1 minute until aromatic. Combine with remaining dressing ingredients and let stand at least while you assemble the salad.

Put spinach in a shallow serving bowl. Put sprouts in a strainer and pour boiling water over them to soften slightly. Rinse with cold water to cool rapidly, and drain. Arrange over spinach along with radish. Just before serving, add dressing and toss to mix.
Serves 6
Minor Protein
Note: If waterchestnuts, jicama, or raw Jerusalem artichokes are available, peel and slice onto the salad with radish.

WILTED SPINACH SALAD

4 cups spinach (about ¼ pound)
4 to 6 thin slices red onion, separated into rings
1 tablespoon sesame seeds, toasted in a dry skillet
3 tablespoons oil
1 tablespoon wine vinegar
¼ teaspoon salt
¼ teaspoon Dijon mustard

Place spinach in a salad bowl and top with onion and sesame seeds.

Combine remaining ingredients in a small saucepan and bring to a boil. Pour hot dressing over the salad at once and toss. Serve immediately.
Serves 4

SPINACH–YOGURT SALAD

A delicious accompaniment to a Mid-eastern dinner.

½ pound spinach
2 tablespoons lemon juice
¼ teaspoon salt
1 cup yogurt
1 teaspoon dried mint

Drain spinach after cleaning to remove as much water as possible. Discard the tough parts of the stems, then place the spinach in a pot, cover, and cook over moderate heat for 5 to 10 minutes to wilt.

Cool spinach enough to handle and squeeze out as much moisture as possible. (The liquid can be saved for soup stock.) Chop the spinach; you should have about 1 cup. Mix spinach with lemon juice, salt, and yogurt in a serving bowl. Sprinkle mint on top.
Serves 4
Minor Protein
Note: This dish can remain at room temperature for about an hour in cool weather, but if made well in advance or in hot weather, refrigerate until ready to serve.

YOGURT SQUASH

Serve as a salad accompaniment to grains and beans or as part of a Greek smorgasbord.

1 cup yogurt
2 cups shredded unpeeled zucchini (from about a 10-ounce squash)
½ teaspoon salt
½ teaspoon cumin seeds
½ cup minced green pepper
½ tablespoon lemon juice

Place yogurt on cheesecloth or a linen napkin in a colander and let drain for about 30 minutes.

Mix shredded zucchini with salt, place in a strainer, and let drain for about 30 minutes. Squeeze to extract moisture.

Meanwhile, toast cumin seeds in a dry skillet until lightly colored. Cool and grind in a mortar and pestle or pound with a rolling pin.

Mix yogurt, squash, green pepper, lemon juice, and ½ teaspoon of freshly ground cumin. Sprinkle with remaining cumin and chill until ready to serve. If desired, good olive oil can be drizzled on the surface of the salad just before serving.
Serves 4
Minor Protein
Note: Freshly toasted and ground cumin seeds are essential to the flavor of this salad. Servings are relatively small, as this is generally one of several dishes on the menu, meant to tantalize the palate. Double the recipe for 6 larger servings.

ITALIAN TOMATO SALAD

Be sure to have plenty of whole grain bread around to sop up the delicious dressing.

3 medium to large tomatoes
1 celery heart (use a stalk if hearts are unavailable)
2 to 3 thin slices red onion
1 clove garlic, cut
12 to 16 olives
salt
oregano
minced fresh or dried basil
4 tablespoons olive oil
2 tablespoons wine vinegar
pepper

Cut tomatoes into wedges. Slice celery thin and cut onion rings in half.

Rub a glass serving bowl with garlic and add tomatoes, celery, onion, and olives. Season lightly with salt and a generous pinch of oregano and basil.

Drizzle oil, then vinegar over vegetables, and mix gently. Top with fresh ground pepper. Serve at room temperature.

Serves 4

Note: Salad can be served immediately, but marinating improves it. It can be kept for several hours at room temperature but should be covered to help preserve the nutrients. If chilled, remove from refrigerator at least 15 minutes before serving.

Variation: If you need to add protein to the meal, cut 4 ounces mozzarella cheese into sticks and marinate with tomatoes.

GREEK TOMATO AND CUCUMBER SALAD

2 tomatoes
1 cucumber
2 tablespoons capers
2 scallions, sliced
salt
pepper
½ teaspoon oregano
1½ tablespoons lemon juice
3 tablespoons olive oil

Slice tomatoes thin and cut each slice in half. Peel cucumber, if waxed, and slice thin. Alternate layers of tomato and cucumber in a shallow serving dish or flat plate. Top with capers and scallions.

Salt lightly, pepper generously, and crush dried oregano over the top. Pour on lemon juice and oil. Mix gently just before serving.

Serves 4

Note: For Minor Protein, crumble 3 to 4 ounces feta cheese on top.

TOMATO SLICES WITH SWEET-AND-SOUR ONION DRESSING

A sweet touch for tomatoes when they're in season.

1 cup chopped sweet Spanish onion
1 teaspoon honey

2 teaspoons cider vinegar
12 to 16 thick tomato slices

Combine onion, honey, and vinegar. Spoon over tomato slices at serving time.

Serves 4

TOMATO PACHADI

A chopped tomato salad of Indian descent.

3 medium tomatoes, chopped
½ medium onion, finely chopped
1 tablespoon crushed dried mint
1 teaspoon honey
½ teaspoon salt
1½ cups yogurt

Combine all ingredients at the beginning of meal preparation so the salad has a chance to stand.

Serves 6
Minor Protein

VIRGIN MARY SALAD

A molded spicy tomato salad that is fitting for parties.

1 envelope or 1 tablespoon unflavored gelatin
1¾ cups tomato juice
¼ teaspoon salt
½ teaspoon honey
½ teaspoon soy sauce
¼ to ½ teaspoon hot pepper sauce
2 tablespoons lemon juice
1 cup finely chopped cabbage
½ cup chopped celery
2 tablespoons chopped green pepper

Sprinkle gelatin over ½ cup tomato juice and let stand for a few minutes to soften. Place over low heat and stir to dissolve.

Stir remaining juice, salt, honey, soy sauce, pepper sauce, and lemon juice into dissolved gelatin. Chill for 20 to 30 minutes until it reaches consistency of thick egg whites.

Fold vegetables into thickened gelatin, turn into a 3-cup mold or bowl, and chill for several hours until firm. Unmold on a bed of greens to serve.

Serves 6

TURNIP SLAW

Turnip slaw makes a good second salad at a meal instead of a cooked vegetable.

It also goes well on a buffet table and makes an unusual sandwich garnish. The flavor is quite interesting, and although it is probably not the kind of dish most people would eat in huge amounts, it will be appreciated in the middle of winter when the produce aisle doesn't have much to recommend.

2 medium turnips (about ¾ pound)
¼ cup yogurt
2 teaspoons cider vinegar
1 teaspoon honey
¼ teaspoon salt
1 tablespoon minced parsley

Peel turnips and shred. (You should have 2 cups.) Mix yogurt, vinegar, honey, and salt to make the dressing and combine with turnip. Garnish with parsley.
Serves 4

DELI-STYLE HEALTH SALAD

This is the standard mixed vegetable salad sold at the delicatessen counter. You can save yourself some money by preparing it at home.

2 cups cucumber chunks (peel only if waxed)
2 stalks celery, thinly sliced
½ cup thinly sliced carrot rounds
½ cup thinly sliced onion
¼ cup chopped sweet red or green pepper
½ cup sliced olives
2 teaspoons honey
½ cup cider vinegar
¼ teaspoon salt
½ cup water

Combine vegetables in a large, shallow container. Mix honey with vinegar until dissolved. Add salt and water. Pour over vegetables.

Marinate salad in the refrigerator for 3 hours or longer. Stir occasionally if vegetables are not completely covered by the marinade.
Serves 6

SALADE NIÇOISE

The marinated vegetables, which are the basis of this southern French dish, can be served as they are, or can be tossed with greens, which is more typical of the restaurant versions.

4 tablespoons combined lemon juice and wine vinegar
½ cup oil (at least some olive preferred)
½ teaspoon salt
1 teaspoon dried chervil
pepper
2 cups sliced cooked potatoes (warm or cold)
2 cups cooked green beans, cut in 1-inch lengths (warm or cold)
1 tomato, cut in bite-size pieces
2 tablespoons capers
few slices red onion
8 or more olives
4 to 6 cups soft greens (optional)

Make a dressing of lemon juice, vinegar, oil, salt, chervil, and generous amounts of pepper, and toss with all the ingredients except the greens in a deep serving bowl. Just before serving, mix in greens if desired.
Serves 4
Note: This can be prepared in advance or just before serving, whichever is most convenient.

TURKISH COUNTRY SALAD

This bean, cheese, and vegetable salad is equally good as a side dish or as a stuffing for pita pockets.

2 cups shredded romaine, or a mixture of romaine and escarole
1 cup coarsely chopped, peeled cucumber
2 medium tomatoes, coarsely chopped
¼ cup thinly sliced sweet Spanish onion
¾ cup slivered or crumbled white cheese (preferably mizithra or ricotta pecorino, but string cheese, mozzarella, feta, or a combination will do)
1 to 1½ cups cooked white beans, drained
¼ cup olive oil
2 tablespoons lemon juice
fresh ground pepper
olives

Toss vegetables, cheese, and beans together in a serving dish. Dress with oil and lemon juice and mix well. Add lots of pepper, salt only if an unsalted cheese is used, and garnish with olives.

Serves 4 to 6
Minor Protein
Note: Do not be limited by the specific ingredients or measurements; they can be varied to suit tastes and the availability of ingredients.

TABOULI

This chopped parsley and grain salad has become one of the most widely recognized Arabic dishes in the United States. Serve it in scoops of lettuce leaves or pita bread.

¼ cup cracked wheat
¾ cup hot water
2 cups chopped parsley
¼ cup chopped fresh mint
½ cucumber, peeled and diced
1 tomato, diced
2 scallions, sliced thin
3 tablespoons lemon juice
3 tablespoons oil
¼ teaspoon salt
olives (optional)

Soak wheat in water for about 15 minutes to soften. Drain well, squeezing out all moisture.

Toss parsley, mint, cucumber, tomato, scallion, and soaked wheat together in a serving dish. Coat with lemon juice, oil, and salt and mix well. Garnish with olives if desired. Chill salad if it is not served soon.

Serves 4
Note: The chopping of so much parsley is a time-consuming job that can be greatly reduced if you have a food processor.

ISRAELI SALAD

Chopped vegetables with herbs and feta cheese.

4 cups chopped greens (preferably a mixture of soft leaf lettuce and crisp romaine and cabbage)
2 scallions, thinly sliced

½ cup chopped green pepper
1 cup chopped tomato
¾ cup crumbled feta cheese (about 4 ounces)
¼ teaspoon dried basil
¼ teaspoon oregano
olives
salt
pepper
2 tablespoons olive oil
2 tablespoons lemon juice

Combine vegetables in a serving dish. Top with crumbled cheese, herbs, and olives. Salt lightly, pepper generously, pour on oil and lemon juice, toss, and serve.

Serves 4
Minor Protein
Variation: Omit oil and lemon juice and serve with Lemon–Tahini Dressing.

INDIA SALAD WITH CURRY DRESSING

soft leaf lettuce
4 artichoke hearts, canned in water, cut in sixths
1 tart apple, cut in wedges
1 cup cooked chick-peas, drained
4 red Bermuda onion slices, separated into rings
¼ cup chopped peanuts
1 tablespoon lemon juice
2 tablespoons oil
¼ cup yogurt
¾ teaspoon curry powder
pinch salt

Tear lettuce leaves into bite-size pieces and arrange in a salad bowl. Place artichokes, apple wedges, and chick-peas on top. Cover with onion rings and sprinkle with peanuts.

Combine the remaining ingredients to make the dressing. If flavor is too mild, add more curry powder to taste. Pour dressing over salad at serving time.

Serves 4
Minor Protein

ORIENTAL SALAD PLATTER

Oriental food preparation involves artistry almost above all else. Set out a beautiful plate—how you use the ingredients here is as important as what you use.

Arrange an assortment of any of the following on a serving platter or on individual plates:

> green and red pepper strips
> thin celery sticks
> thin cucumber strips
> shredded cabbage, spinach, or romaine
> bean sprouts
> thin radish slices
> cooked drained chick-peas
> slivered scallion
> thin zucchini sticks
> paper-thin mushroom slices
> raw peas
> thin tofu sticks
> Rolled Omelet Slices (page 73)
> pear wedges
> orange sections

Serve with Sweet and Spicy Dressing (page 288) or Gado Gado Sauce (page 149).

Potential *Protein Complement* or *Minor Protein* depending on ingredients and dressing

JULIENNE VEGETABLES AND CHEESE

> 1 small to medium zucchini (about ½ pound), cut in thin 2-inch sticks
> 2 celery stalks, cut in thin 2-inch sticks
> ¼ pound firm cheese (Swiss, cheddar, Gouda, mozzarella or slicing ricotta), cut in thin 2-inch sticks
> 2 tablespoons lemon juice
> ½ teaspoon Dijon mustard

> 4 tablespoons oil (some olive oil preferred)
> pepper
> salt
> ¼ cup coarsely chopped walnuts

Toss vegetables with cheese in a serving bowl.

Make a dressing with lemon juice, mustard, oil, pepper, and salt if cheese is not salty. Mix dressing into vegetables and top with nuts.

Serves 4 to 6
Minor Protein

CARROTS, PEAS, AND CHEESE

> 1 cup raw green peas
> ½ cup diced carrot
> ¼ cup diced cheddar cheese
> 2 tablespoons chopped sweet onion
> ¼ cup Basic Oil and Vinegar Dressing (page 287) seasoned generously to taste with mustard

Combine peas, carrots, cheese, and onion in a bowl with the dressing. (Carrots and cheese should be cut the size of the peas.) If possible, this should sit for at least 15 minutes before being served.

Arrange on a bed of greens to serve.
Serves 4
Minor Protein
Note: Salad can be made hours in advance and chilled.
Variations: Zucchini cut into small dice and/or cooked corn kernels can be used to replace some of the vegetables or can be added for a larger salad.

CABBAGE–CARROT–BEAN SALAD

> ¼ teaspoon salt
> ¼ teaspoon dry mustard
> 1 tablespoon fresh dill
> 2 tablespoons lemon juice
> 5 tablespoons oil
> 1 cup cold cooked beans
> 1 cup shredded cabbage
> 1 cup shredded carrots
> 2 scallions, thinly sliced

In a serving bowl, combine salt, mustard, dill, and lemon juice. Beat in oil, a tablespoonful at a time, until smooth and creamy.

Add vegetables to the bowl and stir until well coated. Serve at once or refrigerate until ready to serve.

Serves 4
Protein Complement

MEXICAN BEAN AND CORN SALAD

This makes good use of leftover cooked corn on the cob. It is a delicious accompaniment to Cheese Enchiladas, Chili Rellenos, or any egg- or cheese-based entrée.

1 cup cooked corn (cut from 2 average ears)
1½ cups cooked kidney or pinto beans, drained
2 cups shredded lettuce
¼ cup sliced or chopped black olives
2 tablespoons chopped canned green chilies
½ cup Mexican Tomato Vinaigrette (page 288)

Toss the vegetables together in a serving dish. Pour on dressing and mix well.

Serves 4 to 6
Minor Protein
Note: If there is no cheese elsewhere on the menu, ½ to 1 cup diced Jack or cheddar can be added to the salad.

DUTCH SALAD

A mixed vegetable salad composed of little bits of many things.

1 cup cooked diced beets
1 cup cooked diced potatoes
¼ cup thinly sliced onion
1 small tart apple, diced
2 hard-cooked eggs, diced
½ cup diced Gouda, Edam, cheddar, Muenster, or similar cheese
¼ cup diced pickle
⅛ teaspoon salt
3 tablespoons cider vinegar
3 tablespoons oil
mayonnaise

Combine first 4 ingredients with eggs, cheese, and pickle and season with salt. Dress with vinegar and oil, mixing gently but thoroughly. Just before serving, garnish with dollops of mayonnaise.

Serves 4
Minor Protein
Variation: Replace beets with 1 cup diced tomato.

CRISP SHREDDED SALAD

1 cup shredded, peeled rutabaga or turnip
1 cup thinly sliced celery
4 scallions, slivered or sliced thin
4 radishes, sliced thin
2 cups shredded romaine
6 tablespoons oil
2 tablespoons wine vinegar
½ teaspoon salt
¼ teaspoon pepper
½ teaspoon dry mustard
½ teaspoon dried basil

Combine vegetables and chill until serving time. Combine remaining ingredients for dressing. Dress salad and toss just before serving.

Serves 4

PEAR SALAD

4 pears, cut up
¼ cup sunflower seeds
2 tablespoons currants or raisins
1 tablespoon honey
2 tablespoons lemon juice
2 tablespoons water
¼ teaspoon ground ginger

Combine pears, seeds, and raisins. Combine remaining ingredients to make dressing and pour over pears.

Serves 4

WALDORF SALAD

2 medium tart apples, peeled (if desired) and chopped
1 tablespoon lemon juice
1 large stalk celery, chopped
¼ cup sunflower seeds
3 tablespoons chopped dates or ¼ cup raisins
2 tablespoons mayonnaise
6 tablespoons yogurt

Toss apple with lemon juice. Add all other ingredients and toss to mix. Serve within the hour or chill until needed.
Serves 4 to 6
Minor Protein

CRUNCHY PEACH SALAD

Serve this in the summer instead of the apple-based Waldorf Salad.

1½ cups diced peaches
1 large stalk celery, chopped
¼ cup coarsely chopped or slivered almonds
¾ cup yogurt
½ tablespoon honey
1 tablespoon lemon juice
¼ teaspoon cinnamon
¼ teaspoon ground ginger

Combine all ingredients and stir gently but thoroughly. Serve at once or chill until needed.
Serves 4
Minor Protein

CREAMY DINNER FRUIT SALAD

Although this mixture of fruits might appear unusual, it is a good combination for a side dish or appetizer.

1 small avocado, peeled and diced
1 large grapefruit, peeled and sectioned
1 cup cantaloupe cubes or balls
juice of ½ lemon
pinch salt
½ cup yogurt
1 tablespoon honey

Combine fruit in a bowl, sprinkle with lemon juice and salt, and chill until serving time. Beat yogurt with honey until smooth. At serving time, spoon fruit salad into individual bowls and top with yogurt dressing.
Serves 4

TROPICAL FRUIT PLATTER

Exotic fruit served on a platter, then garnished to taste with coconut, banana chips, and a peanut dressing.

large soft lettuce leaves
1 papaya or cantaloupe, seeds and peel removed and meat sliced
1 avocado, peeled and sliced
1 kiwi, peeled and sliced in wedges or rounds
2 oranges, peeled and sectioned
½ pineapple, cut from rind and diced
½ cup strawberries, blueberries, or cherries
1 lime or lemon
½ cup banana chips
½ cup shredded, unsweetened coconut

Peanut Cream Dressing
½ cup yogurt
1½ tablespoons peanut butter
2 tablespoons orange juice
2 tablespoons lime juice
½ teaspoon honey
1 teaspoon grated fresh ginger

Line serving platter with lettuce leaves. Arrange fruit in separate mounds on top of lettuce. Cut lime or lemon and sprinkle a little of the juice over the papaya or melon and avocado. Place banana chips and coconut in separate small bowls.

Combine ingredients for dressing, mixing until uniformly blended. Place fruit platter, bowls of garnish, and dressing on the table and let everyone help themselves.
Serves 6
Minor Protein
Variation: Curry Cream (page 41) can replace Peanut Cream Dressing.
Menu Suggestions: Tropical Fruit Platter is a nice accompaniment to any bean–grain entrée, especially those baked as loaves. It also goes well with simple sandwiches, even a plain cheese or Grilled Open-Face Tofu Sandwich.

Condiments

The purpose of a condiment is to season or "give relish." Herbs, spices, vinegar, oil, salt, and pepper are the most rudimentary members of this group.

In addition to these common seasonings, most cultures have developed their own specialties which have become standard table features: the mustard and catsup, delicatessen pickle and hot sauce of the American table; the "salsa" of Mexico; the olives of Greece; the vegetable pickles of Asia and the Arab countries; the chutneys of India; the soy sauce and hot mustard of the Orient; and the mayonnaise of the Netherlands.

Those condiments that can be prepared in a relatively short time for immediate use are presented in this chapter. Condiments that can be "put up" for future use are found in "The Food Factory."

GOMASIO

The oriental combination of salt and toasted ground sesame seeds is used like conventional salt at the table but provides much less sodium.

4 tablespoons sesame seeds
1 teaspoon salt

Toast seeds in a dry skillet until they just begin to color. Use low heat and shake the skillet often. Watch closely, as they can burn surprisingly fast. While still hot, grind in a blender or food processor, or pound fine with a mortar and pestle. When crushed, add salt and process or pound a few seconds longer to coat salt with oil from the seeds.

Makes ¼ cup

Note: Do not prepare more than this amount at one time (except for quantity cooking), so that the sesame salt is always fresh.

SUN BUTTER

During the years we have been writing about food, many people have written to tell us how they make their own spread in order to improve the ratio of unsaturated to saturated fats found in standard butter. Here is our version of Sun Butter, a creamy, spreadable blend of butter and oil, with the virtues of both.

1 stick butter (¼ pound)
¼ cup safflower or similar light oil

Place butter in the container of a food processor fitted with a plastic mixing blade or, lacking this, the blender. Run the machine to break the butter up as much as possible.

With the machine running, gradually add oil. When evenly blended and smooth, transfer to a suitable container for refrigerator or freezer storage. The mixture will be quite soft but will set on chilling. Use as you would butter.

Makes ¾ cup spread

Note: To improve the keeping qualities and food value of Sun Butter, squeeze the oil from a 100 IU vitamin E capsule into the container while blending.

Variations: For *Creamy Herb Butter,* mix 1 tablespoon fresh minced herbs, such as parsley, basil or dill, into the soft Sun Butter before chilling; or use 1 teaspoon dried herbs including those mentioned or our favorite, chervil.

SAVORY NUT BUTTER

Delicious as a spread or for seasoning steamed vegetables.

6 tablespoons mixed nuts and seeds (recommended combination: sunflower seeds, sesame seeds, almonds, and a few peanuts)
¼ cup chopped celery

¼ cup butter
⅛ teaspoon salt

Grind nuts to a powder in a blender or processor. Add celery, butter, and salt, and process until smooth. If the blender is used, you may have to work in the remaining ingredients with a fork.

Makes a heavy ½ cup
Note: A half cup Savory Nut Butter provides 700 calories and 12 grams protein as compared to 800 calories and no protein in butter.

BIALY BUTTER

An onion spread to use in place of butter, either by itself on bread or crackers or as a seasoning spread before filling a sandwich with cottage cheese, bean spreads, sliced egg, etc.

½ pound onions, sliced thinly in half rings (about 2 cups)
1 tablespoon oil
pinch salt or ½ teaspoon soy sauce
2 tablespoons soy flour
¼ cup water

Sauté onion in oil in a skillet, stirring occasionally, for about 5 minutes, or until limp. Cover and cook over low heat about 20 minutes longer, or until onions are soft enough to mash with a fork. Add salt or soy sauce and mash until pulpy.

Mix soy flour to a paste with water. Stir into onion and cook, continuing to stir about 3 minutes until mixture is thick and the soy flavor mellows.

Chill before serving and store in the refrigerator.

Makes ⅔ cup

CHINESE MUSTARD

1 teaspoon Chinese mustard powder
1 teaspoon water

Dissolve mustard powder in water. Add additional water if necessary; mustard should be rather thin. Let stand for at least 15 minutes before using or mustard will be bitter.

Makes enough mustard for 2 to 4 servings

ORIENTAL DIPPING SAUCE

Use for tempura and steamed dumplings.

2 tablespoons soy sauce
2 tablespoons water
1 teaspoon white or rice vinegar
¼ teaspoon minced fresh ginger
1 small clove garlic, minced (optional)

Combine all ingredients and mix well.
Makes ¼ cup; serves 4
Variation: If desired, ½ teaspoon unrefined sesame oil can be added if sauce is to be used for steamed dumplings.

SWEET CHINESE DIPPING SAUCE

Use with tempura, Steamed Egg Rolls, tofu dishes, Spring Lettuce Rolls, and similar Oriental dishes.

2 tablespoons soy sauce
2 tablespoons honey
1½ tablespoons sherry
½ clove garlic in one piece

Combine all ingredients in a small saucepan and bring to a boil. Remove from heat and let cool to room temperature.

Serves 4 to 6

"DUCK" SAUCE

For egg rolls and crisp Chinese noodles, and to create a Chinese restaurant aura.

1 cup cut-up peeled peaches
2 tablespoons honey
1½ tablespoons cider vinegar
1 tablespoon soy sauce

Combine all ingredients in a small saucepan and simmer for about 5 minutes until barely softened. Puree in a blender, processor, or food mill and chill.

For long-term storage, freeze in ¼-cup units and defrost at room temperature as needed.

Makes ¾ cup

TARTAR SAUCE

½ cup mayonnaise
¼ cup yogurt
1 tablespoon chopped capers
¼ cup Zucchini or Green Tomato Relish (page 440) or chopped Bread and Butter Pickles (page 439)
1 teaspoon prepared mustard

Combine all ingredients and mix thoroughly.
Makes 1 cup

TOUCH-OF-HONEY CATSUP

This quick homemade catsup has only ½ tablespoon of sweetening per half cup in the form of honey, as compared to 2½ to 3 tablespoons sugar and/or corn syrup in commercial varieties.

6 tablespoons tomato paste
2 tablespoons lemon juice or cider vinegar
½ teaspoon soy sauce
1½ teaspoons honey
1 tablespoon water

Mix all ingredients together until smooth. Store in the refrigerator for long-term use.
Makes about ½ cup

QUICK COCKTAIL SAUCE

A jazzed-up version of catsup.

½ cup Touch-of-Honey Catsup (recipe above)
one or more of the following:
    ¼ teaspoon hot pepper sauce
    1 tablespoon horseradish
    up to 1 tablespoon grated onion
    2 to 3 tablespoons minced celery
    2 to 3 tablespoons minced green pepper
    2 to 3 teaspoons minced olive
    1 tablespoon chopped pickle

Add any or all of the above seasonings to the catsup and mix well.

SALSA CRUDA

A standard feature of the Mexican table, this mild raw tomato sauce is used to season eggs, tortillas, tacos, beans, and plain steamed vegetables.

1 large tomato (about ½ pound)
1 tablespoon minced onion
1 canned green chili, cut in strips
1 generous tablespoon minced parsley
1 teaspoon lemon or lime juice

Secure tomato on a long-handled fork or skewer and roast over a flame until the skin is charred all over. (This gives the sauce its smoky flavor.) Puree, skin and all, in a blender or processor until fairly smooth. Combine puree with remaining ingredients and let stand for at least 15 minutes to develop flavor. Use as soon as possible. Leftovers can be refrigerated for a few days; for longer storge, see Note below.
Makes 1 cup; serves 4
Note: To keep more than a day or two, bring sauce to a boil and simmer for 2 to 3 minutes. Store in a covered jar in the refrigerator.
Variation: For *Spicy Salsa,* add chopped jalapeño peppers to taste. One small minced garlic clove can also be added, if desired.

CHILI SAUCE

A basic Mexican condiment used hot, cold, or at room temperature on tacos, enchiladas, tostados, beans, rice, eggs, and just about anything that needs to be spicy.

2 tablespoons oil
1 large onion, chopped
1 clove garlic, minced
2 tablespoons chili powder
1 cup water
½ teaspoon salt
¼ teaspoon oregano
1 tablespoon vinegar

Heat oil in a small skillet or saucepan and sauté onion and garlic for 3 to 5 minutes until limp but not colored. Add chili powder and cook for ½ minute. Add remaining ingredients, bring to a boil, and simmer for 20 minutes. Use at once or transfer to a jar, cover, and refrigerate for use as needed over the next month.
Makes 1¼ cups

Note: The spiciness of the sauce can be increased by adding cayenne pepper along with chili powder. To make a tomato-flavored chili sauce using this base, combine with an equal volume of tomato pulp or puree and simmer until slightly thickened.

RAW CREOLE SAUCE

This spicy tomato relish can be served as a garnish on rice, burgers, beans, or any plain vegetable.

1 pound ripe tomatoes, cut in pieces
1 teaspoon peeled, coarsely chopped fresh ginger
2 tablespoons cut up onion
¼ teaspoon cayenne
2 teaspoons lemon juice

Combine all ingredients in a blender or processor fitted with a steel blade. Blend to an even but coarse texture. Serve at room temperature. Refrigerate for storage and use within a few days.
Makes 2 cups; serves 4 to 6

SPICY TUNISIAN SAUCE

This flavorful raw tomato relish, is the traditional condiment for Couscous and Kosheri and is an important flavoring agent in Tunisian Sandwiches. It can be used as well for a spicy falafel dressing, as is customary in Israel, or on any stuffed pita or chapati roll.

2 medium tomatoes, peeled and finely chopped
¼ cup minced parsley
2 scallions, minced
1 medium clove garlic, minced
¼ teaspoon salt
½ teaspoon crushed dried red pepper (pizza type)
½ teaspoon cumin
2 tablespoons olive oil

Combine all ingredients and let flavors blend at room temperature. If not used within several hours, refrigerate and use within a few days.
Makes 1⅓ cups sauce; enough for 4 to 6
Note: This is a rich, oily sauce. If

necessary, oil can be reduced to 1 tablespoon.
Variation: For *Fiery Sauce,* add ¼ to ½ teaspoon hot pepper sauce to taste.

CRANBERRY SAUCE

2 cups cranberries
½ cup apple juice
½ cup honey
1 teaspoon grated or minced orange rind

Combine cranberries, apple juice, and honey in a saucepan and simmer for 5 minutes until berries pop. Remove from heat and stir in rind. Cool to room temperature, then chill in a covered container.
Makes 1½ cups
Note: Will keep for two weeks in the refrigerator.
Variation: For *Crunchy Cranberry Relish,* add up to ½ cup walnuts or pecans and/or ½ cup chopped celery to the cooked mixture.

RAW RAISIN CHUTNEY

Sweet and spicy.

1 cup raisins
1 tablespoon chopped fresh ginger
½ teaspoon cayenne
½ teaspoon salt
juice of 1 lemon
about ¼ cup water

Combine all ingredients in a blender or a processor fitted with a steel blade and puree to a thick paste. Add water as needed.
Serves 4 to 6
Note: Can be stored in the refrigerator for up to a week.

COOKED RAISIN CHUTNEY

Sweet, spicy, and long-lasting.

1 cup raisins
½ inch fresh ginger, chopped, or ¼ teaspoon powdered
1 teaspoon cayenne
½ teaspoon salt
¼ cup cider vinegar
2 teaspoons honey
¼ cup water

Combine all ingredients in a saucepan and cook for 10 minutes until softened. Puree in a blender or processor and cool to room temperature. Keeps for several weeks under refrigeration.

Serves 4 to 6

COCONUT SAMBAL

A cooling condiment from Ceylon to be served with curries along with chutney, pickles, nuts, rice, and fruit and vegetable salads.

1 cup dried unsweetened coconut
6 tablespoons milk
½ teaspoon chili powder
¼ teaspoon salt
2 teaspoons lime or lemon juice

Place coconut in a small mixing bowl and, using a fork, toss lightly with milk. Let sit for a few minutes. Add remaining ingredients and mix lightly. (Sambal should be fluffy, not a paste.) Serve at once.

Serves 8

ANTIPASTO PEPPERS

Home-roasted sweet peppers, familiar to many as canned pimientos, add a flavorful accent to salads.

2 sweet red or green peppers, or one of each
2 tablespoons lemon juice
1 tablespoon wine vinegar
3 tablespoons olive oil
⅛ teaspoon salt
pepper
1 clove garlic, split (optional)

Peel peppers by charring skin under a broiler or over a direct flame. Turn often until skin blisters all over. When cool enough to handle, peel with a sharp paring knife. Cut peppers in half and remove seeds and thick membranes. Slice each half into 6 strips, each about ½ inch wide.

Combine remaining ingredients to make a marinade; add peppers and let stand at room temperature for several hours.

Note: Will keep about a month under refrigeration.

QUICK PICKLES

A crunchy pickle with a simple brine that can be replenished so that there is always a fresh supply of pickles in the refrigerator.

2 unwaxed or peeled cucumbers
1 small onion
1 small clove garlic, minced
1 tablespoon fresh dill, or 1½ teaspoons dill seed
1 cup hot water
2 tablespoons honey
1 tablespoon salt
3 tablespoons cider vinegar

Slice each cucumber lengthwise into 8 sticks. Slice onion into rings. Alternate layers of cucumber and onion in a broad nonmetal dish. Scatter garlic and dill on top.

Mix water with honey and salt to dissolve; add vinegar and pour this brine over the cucumber. Cover and refrigerate for at least 6 hours before using.

Makes 16 pickles

Note: When ready to replenish the pickle container add 1 tablespoon vinegar and 1 rounded teaspoon honey to the brine and add more sliced cucumbers and onion as needed. Prepare a fresh solution after 2 or 3 batches have been made.

PICKLED BEETS

Pickled beets are especially good with mild, creamy dishes, providing a contrast of taste and texture to foods sauced with yogurt, sour cream, cottage cheese, or a smooth gravy. The national cuisines that specialize in beet dishes also feature mushroom and potato dishes, so, as you would expect, they are all suited to the same menu.

1 pound beets, steamed (see directions, page 234)
1 small onion, thinly sliced
¼ cup cider vinegar

¼ cup water (from steaming beets, or
   plain water)
1 tablespoon honey
½ teaspoon salt
4 cloves
½ bay leaf

When beets are cool enough to
handle, peel and slice. Cut each slice
in half. Place in a shallow casserole
or bowl.

Combine remaining ingredients in a
saucepan, bring to a boil, cover, and
cook for 5 minutes. Pour over beets.
Chill for at least 1 hour before serving.
To store, keep in a covered container
in the refrigerator.

Serves 4
Note: Pickled beets keep for 2 to 3
weeks with refrigeration.

ITALIAN VEGETABLE MARINADE

Serve these brined vegetables alone,
add them to an antipasto, or use to
garnish a salad.

**3 cups mixed vegetables from the fol-
   lowing:**
      carrots cut in ¼-inch rounds
      celery cut in ½-inch pieces
      radishes cut in halves or thick
        slices
      turnip cut in ¼-inch-thick fans
      cabbage cut in strips
      onion cut in rings
      green beans cut in 1-inch pieces
      green pepper chunks
      cauliflorets
1 cup water
¼ cup cider vinegar
1 teaspoon salt
½ teaspoon oregano
¼ teaspoon pepper sauce
split clove garlic (optional)

Combine water, vinegar, and seasonings in a pot and bring to a boil. Add
vegetables; cover and simmer for 15
minutes. (Vegetables should still be

firm.) Cool to room temperature and
chill for at least 2 hours.

Makes 1½ pints
Note: Keeps for several weeks in the
refrigerator.

NAMASU

Japanese raw vegetable pickles that are
lightly sweet and tangy.

2 cups sliced raw vegetables including:
      carrot
      radish
      celery
      peeled parsnip
      peeled turnip
      cabbage
½ teaspoon salt
2 tablespoons honey
2 tablespoons vinegar

Combine vegetables of choice in a
shallow bowl. Sprinkle evenly with salt.
Mix honey with vinegar and, when dissolved, pour evenly over vegetables.
Cover and refrigerate for 24 hours before serving.

Makes 1 pint
Note: Keeps for about 2 weeks in
the refrigerator.

QUICK TURNIP PICKLES

A spicy, flavorful pickle used in the
Arab world to perk up couscous as well
as other grain and bean entrées.

2 medium turnips
½ teaspoon salt
1 tablespoon lime juice
⅛ teaspoon cumin
⅛ teaspoon cayenne

Peel turnips and slice into thin
rounds. Slice each round in half. Toss
turnips in a bowl with salt and lime
juice. Cover and let marinate for
several hours at room temperature.
Shortly before serving, combine cumin
and cayenne and add to the pickles.

Serves 4

Sauces and Gravies

In this section we offer sauces and gravies that are meant to generously bathe foods, providing them with flavor and contrasting texture. (Those sauces that are used sparingly, as a seasoning, we have chosen to include in the preceding chapter, "Condiments.") Some of the familiar and classic sauces of the world, including basic white sauce and tomato-based sauces, are explained in detail. Some new-fashioned sauces, both hot and cold, are introduced. Many of the dishes in this book are not really complete without an appropriate gravy, and there are many simple foodstuffs that can be enhanced with an accompanying sauce.

As the preparation of most sauces is relatively simple and speedy, these recipes can be mastered with very little effort. It is essential that the pot used for cooked sauces be a good, even conductor of heat. A sauce prepared in a thin pot with hot spots can scorch readily. The heat used in cooking should be low to moderate, and when constant stirring is called for, it is best done with a wire whisk. A wooden spoon is also useful because it can be left in the pot without becoming hot. All sauce recipes can be adjusted to your needs by multiplying or dividing.

Some additional last-minute sauces can be found in "Short-Order Cooking," while "The Food Factory" offers two convenient sauce mixes.

Starch-Thickened Sauces

The use of starch to thicken a liquid is the simple principle behind many seemingly exotic sauces; French béchamel and standard turkey gravy both rely on a single concept, and once you are familiar with this cooking rule you can make a wide variety of sauces with confidence. The proportions to use are outlined below; the manner in which you put them together can be varied, as explained in the instructions which follow, to suit the dish you are working with.

The Medium Sauce proportions are used for most purposes. The Thin Sauce is the basis of creamed or thickened soups, while the Thick Sauce is the foundation for a soufflé and the binder used in croquettes, loaves, and fillings.

Arrowroot and cornstarch are preferred for delicate sauces, especially those used on pasta and vegetables. Flour is more suited to the gravies for heavy foods like burgers, loaves, pot pies, and such.

Note: If a completed sauce is too thin, a small amount of additional starch can be made into a paste with water or the principal liquid and stirred in, cooking over low heat until thickened. If a completed sauce is too thick, stir in liquid to thin it to the desired consistency.

If a sauce must be kept for a short time before using, set it on top of a double boiler or place the saucepan inside a larger pot and surround it with gently boiling water to keep it warm.

Starch-thickened sauces thicken on cooling and congeal further when chilled. If reheating is necessary, it should be done over extremely low heat, preferably using a heatproof pad (flame tamer), double boiler, or a saucepan set in a boiling water bath (as used to keep the sauce warm; see above).

Classic Technique

The classic method of sauce preparation is to heat the fat (butter or oil) in

STANDARD SAUCE BASE

Consistency	Fat (optional)	Starch	Liquid
Thin	1 tablespoon	½ tablespoon arrowroot or cornstarch, or 1 tablespoon whole wheat flour	1 cup
Medium	1 tablespoon	1 tablespoon arrowroot or cornstarch, or 2 tablespoons whole wheat flour	1 cup
Thick	2 tablespoons	1½ tablespoons arrowroot or cornstarch, or 3 tablespoons whole wheat flour	1 cup

a small saucepan and stir in the starch to make a smooth paste. The liquid is then added gradually, stirring constantly, over low to moderate heat. Cooking and stirring continue until the sauce thickens. When arrowroot or cornstarch is used, the sauce will reach maximum thickness before it comes to a boil and should be removed from the heat before boiling actually occurs, as extreme temperatures cause thinning. When flour is the thickening agent, the sauce should be simmered a minute or two to cook out the raw starch taste. When this technique is used, the fat cannot be omitted. Sauce preparation will take about 10 minutes.

Modified Classic Technique

A slightly faster method calls for combining all but a few tablespoons of the liquid with the fat (which is optional) in the saucepan and heating gently until warm. The remaining liquid, which must be cold, is combined with the starch thickener to make a smooth paste. This is added to the warmed liquid, and stirring and cooking continue until the sauce becomes thick, as in the standard method. This technique requires less of the cook's attention and the preparation time is under 10 minutes.

WHITE SAUCE

Prepare 1 cup Medium Sauce using milk as the liquid and at least part butter for the fat. Season with ¼ teaspoon salt, pepper, and ½ to 1 teaspoon herbs of choice. If nothing more will be done to the sauce, 1 tablespoon sherry or cooking wine can enhance the flavor.

BÉCHAMEL

Rather than using all milk for the sauce, a combination of milk and broth (vegetable, chicken, meat, or fish) can be used. This makes a lighter sauce, preferred by some.

VELOUTÉ

When only stock is used, a sauce known as Velouté is produced. Often a tempered egg yolk is added to this sauce for enrichment.

CHEESE SAUCE

A White or Béchamel Sauce is the beginning of a Cheese Sauce. For each cup sauce add ½ to 1 cup shredded or diced cheese after thickening. One-quarter teaspoon dry mustard or nutmeg can be used for seasoning if desired. If cheese does not melt readily, stir over low heat until creamy. In France this sauce is known as Mornay.

BROWN GRAVY

A basic sauce for bean, grain, and vegetable loaves.

1 tablespoon arrowroot or cornstarch
1½ tablespoons soy sauce
1 cup water
2 tablespoons nonfat dry milk powder

Make a paste of starch and soy sauce in a small saucepan. Add remaining ingredients, stirring to dissolve milk powder. Stir over moderate heat until gravy thickens and just reaches the boiling point, but does not boil.

Makes 1 cup; serves 4

Variations: Instead of all water and powdered milk, ½ cup milk and ½ cup water can be used.

For *Chicken-Style Gravy,* add ¼ teaspoon poultry seasonings.

MUSHROOM GRAVY

1 tablespoon oil
1 cup thinly sliced mushrooms
1½ tablespoons arrowroot or cornstarch
1½ tablespoons soy sauce
1 cup water
2 tablespoons nonfat dry milk powder

Sauté mushrooms in oil in a small saucepan for about 5 minutes until tender. Stir in starch and gradually add remaining ingredients, continuing to stir over moderate heat until gravy thickens.

Makes about 1¼ cup; serves 4

TAHINI GRAVY

A dairy-free sauce that is excellent on roasts as well as on plain rice or noodles.

2 teaspoons arrowroot or cornstarch
1½ tablespoons soy sauce
1 cup water or vegetable stock
2 tablespoons tahini

Make a paste of starch and soy sauce. Gradually stir in liquid and cook over moderate heat until gravy thickens. Stir in tahini and warm through without boiling.

Makes about 1 cup; serves 4
Protein Complement

ONION SAUCE

A delicate sauce for grains, bean balls, and steamed vegetables.

2 cups thinly sliced or chopped onion
2 tablespoons oil
1 tablespoon arrowroot or cornstarch
1½ cups milk
½ teaspoon thyme
½ teaspoon salt
pepper

½ cup yogurt (preferably at room temperature)

Sauté onion in oil in a small saucepan until softened and just beginning to color. Sprinkle starch over surface, stir until smooth, and gradually add milk. Stir over moderate heat until sauce thickens. Season, remove from heat, and stir some of the hot sauce into the yogurt. Stir this tempered yogurt into the remaining hot sauce.

Makes 2 cups; serves 4 to 6
Minor Protein

Note: If reheating is necessary, keep heat extremely low and do not boil.

Variations: For *Mushroom Sauce,* replace onion with 2 cups sliced or chopped mushrooms. If desired, sour cream can be substituted for some of the yogurt. Add steamed vegetables to the completed sauce for a *Mushroom–Vegetable Stew.*

CASHEW GRAVY

Thick and rich with a plain, homey taste. Ideal for grain loaves, burgers, and vegetable loaves.

6 tablespoons unroasted cashews
1¼ to 1½ cups water
1 tablespoon arrowroot or cornstarch
2 teaspoons soy sauce
salt
lemon juice

Grind nuts to a powder in a blender or processor. Gradually blend in 1¼ cups water to make a smooth "milk."

Mix starch with a little of the cashew milk in a saucepan to make a thin paste. Stir in remaining cashew milk and soy sauce and cook gently until thickened. If too thick, add the additional ¼ cup water. Season with salt and a little lemon juice to taste.

Makes about 1½ cups; serves 4 to 6
Protein Complement

Variations: For a rich *Brown Cashew Gravy,* increase soy sauce to 1 tablespoon.

For a delicious *Tomato Cashew Gravy* for plain rice, thin Cashew Gravy with ¼ to ½ cup tomato juice or the broth from canned tomatoes.

Sauce can be made fairly thin so that it is absorbed by the rice rather than blanketing it.

CREAMY PIMIENTO SAUCE

For bean loaves and burgers, or to dress up plain rice.

1 tablespoon oil
1 small onion, minced
2 tablespoons whole wheat flour
1 cup milk
½ cup cut-up pimientos (from 3 whole pimientos or 1 jar, 4 ounces drained weight)
2 tablespoons water
½ teaspoon honey

Heat oil in a small saucepan and sauté onion for about 3 minutes until limp. Stir in flour and gradually add milk. Cook, stirring, until sauce thickens and comes to a boil. (This will take about 10 minutes on moderate heat).

Combine pimiento, water, and honey in a blender or a processor fitted with a steel blade and puree until smooth. Stir pimiento puree into thickened white sauce and simmer for 5 minutes.
Makes 1½ cups; serves 4
Minor Protein

INSTANT SAUCE BALLS

Any broth can be thickened for a more substantial soup or a gravy by the addition of these sauce balls. Vegetables cooked in broth can similarly be turned into a stew or creamed filling, and a thin soup can be made robust and creamy with almost no effort.

¼ cup butter, at room temperature
½ cup whole wheat flour

Mash butter gently with a spoon so it is pliable. Work in flour, using your fingers, and knead to form a smooth "dough." Form into 8 balls, using 1 tablespoon for each.

Use at once as directed, chill for use later in the day, or place on a metal pan and freeze for use within the next 3 months. When frozen hard, transfer to a plastic freezer bag, press out all the air, seal, and return to the freezer.
Makes 8 balls

Instant Sauce

For light thickening, add 2 sauce balls per quart of liquid.

For a creamy soup or thin gravy, add 1 ball per cup of liquid.

For a rich gravy, add 2 balls per cup of liquid.

Slice small pieces of fresh or frozen sauce ball over a pot of liquid that is barely simmering. Stir gently as the nuggets soften and thicken sauce. Simmer for 1 minute.

Tomato Sauce

Canned American and Italian-style tomato sauces are so widely used in this country that the taste and texture of the homemade version may seem unfamiliar. Homemade tomato sauce, made from fresh or canned tomatoes, is entirely different from these ready-made varieties and can elevate a simple pasta dish from ordinary to special.

The ideal sauce is made from fresh tomatoes, but unless they have been vine-ripened they will not be of rich enough color, flavor, or substance to make a full-bodied sauce. It is worthwhile preserving sauce in volume, or at least putting up some good summer tomatoes for use in sauce later in the year, especially if you grow your own. Instructions are provided in "The Food Factory."

When fresh or home-preserved tomatoes are not available, a very good sauce can be made from commercially canned tomatoes. Canned Italian plum tomatoes offer more pulp for thick-bodied sauces; however, California peeled tomatoes (the variety most commonly sold in this country) make a pleasant if somewhat thinner sauce that can be given more authority with the addition of tomato paste. Whole canned tomatoes, although more costly per pound, are more meaty than cut canned tomatoes and therefore give a higher sauce yield.

Contrary to tradition, it is not necessary to simmer tomato sauce for hours; this practice actually destroys important nutrients. An average of 30 to 45 minutes (depending on the tomatoes and the recipe) will suffice to produce a sauce of good consistency.

General Guidelines

The variability of tomatoes, coupled with individual taste preferences, makes precise guidelines for tomato sauce preparation impossible. The recipes in these pages should be used with the following points in mind:

• To reduce cooking time and insure a meatier sauce, drain tomatoes well before you begin. When using fresh tomatoes, cut and let stand for 15 minutes or simmer for 10 minutes, then pour off the liquid that accumulates. This broth can be saved for other cooking uses.

• If, at the end of the specified cooking time, the sauce is thin and runny, tomato paste may be used to thicken it. Mix in a teaspoonful at a time and simmer for 5 minutes. If it is still too thin, repeat the process. Do not add too much at one time and be sure to let it simmer a little after each addition. If you are preparing the sauce for storage, either in the freezer or refrigerator, wait to add the tomato paste until the sauce is reheated. Sauces thicken somewhat in the chilling process.

• Another thickening alternative is to add nutritional yeast, up to 1 tablespoon per quart, which will give the sauce a creamy texture.

• Sauce made from canned tomatoes is quite hearty, in contrast to the light, fresh taste of sauce made from ripe tomatoes. Some dishes demand the robust quality that canned tomatoes provide. An ideal compromise when making a mostly canned tomato sauce is to add one or two fresh chopped tomatoes to the pot during the last 10 minutes. This gives a special lift; it is also a good way to perk up stored sauces when they are reheated.

• Different varieties of fresh and canned tomatoes vary in their ratio of pulp to liquid, in acidity and sweetness, and, if canned, in saltiness as well. Thus, the measurements in the recipes are approximate and seasoning must be guided by taste. A sauce that is too sharp can be softened with just a bit of honey.

• Butter can really enrich and mellow the flavor of tomato sauce. If this appeals to you, stir in 1 tablespoon for each 2 cups sauce just before you take it off the heat. If sauce is to be stored, do not add butter until serving.

Freshly made tomato sauce can be stored in the refrigerator for about a week. Freezing is recommended for longer storage.

For most purposes, ½ to ¾ cup sauce will suffice per serving.

For backup, there are good kitchen-quality sauces on the market that contain no sweetening or thickeners.

LIGHT FRESH TOMATO SAUCE

A delicate sauce for pasta or burgers.

2 tablespoons oil
2 medium onions, chopped
1 green pepper, chopped
2 pounds tomatoes, diced, undrained (about 5½ cups)
1½ teaspoons salt
1 teaspoon honey

Heat oil in a 1½- to 2-quart pot. Cook onion and green pepper until tender but uncolored. Add tomatoes, salt, and honey and cook over moderate heat for 15 to 20 minutes until tender but not falling apart.

Makes about 1 quart; serves 8

Note: For use on bean burgers, sauce can be sweetened with 1 to 2 teaspoons molasses for a pleasing contrast.

MARINARA SAUCE

A full-bodied sauce with a gentle, sweet flavor. A good all-around sauce that can be used in combination dishes or on pasta.

1 large clove garlic, minced
1 large onion, chopped
½ cup sliced carrots

2 tablespoons oil
4 cups well-drained tomato pulp
1 to 2 teaspoons dried or 1 to 2 tablespoons fresh basil
1 to 2 teaspoons oregano
1 teaspoon salt, or to taste
pepper
1 tablespoon butter (optional)

Stew garlic, onion, and carrots in oil in a covered 1½- to 2-quart pot for 10 minutes. Add tomatoes and seasonings, replace cover, and simmer for 20 to 30 minutes until carrots are cooked enough to puree. Puree in a food mill (this gives the thickest texture), blender, or processor fitted with a steel blade.

Return to pot, adjust seasoning, and cook uncovered for about 10 minutes to thicken. Add pepper just before serving, and butter if desired.

Makes 3 cups sauce

Note: If sauce is to be served on plain pasta, adding butter to the sauce is recommended.

ITALIAN TOMATO SAUCE

1 large clove garlic, minced
1 large onion, chopped
½ cup sliced green or Italian pepper
2 tablespoons oil (at least part olive preferred)
4 cups well-drained tomato pulp
1 teaspoon honey
1 to 2 teaspoons dried or 1 to 2 tablespoons fresh basil
1 to 2 teaspoons oregano
1 teaspoon salt, or to taste
pepper
dry red wine (optional)

Sauté garlic, onion, and pepper in oil for about 5 minutes until softened. Add tomatoes, honey, basil, oregano, and salt; cover and simmer for about 20 minutes.

Puree in a food mill (for full-bodied texture), blender, or processor fitted with a steel blade. Return to pot, adjust seasoning, and simmer uncovered for about 10 minutes to thicken. Add pepper and 2 to 4 tablespoons wine, if desired, and cook briefly.

Makes 3 cups sauce

Note: If desired, pureeing can be

omitted for a more textured sauce. Mash tomatoes lightly with a fork during the last 10 minutes of cooking as sauce thickens.

Variation: For *Mushroom–Tomato Sauce,* add ½ to ¾ pound mushrooms, cut in quarters, to the pureed sauce and simmer for about 15 minutes until tender.

ENCHILADA SAUCE

A Mexican tomato sauce for use on enchiladas, tacos, chili rellenos, and similar dishes.

1 clove garlic, minced
1 medium onion, chopped
½ cup slivered green pepper
½ to 1 teaspoon minced hot chili pepper (depending on your preference for spiciness)
2 tablespoons oil
1½ teaspoons chili powder
4 cups drained tomato pulp
½ teaspoon oregano
¼ teaspoon cumin
¾ teaspoon salt

Sauté garlic, onion, and peppers in oil for about 5 minutes until softened. Add chili powder and cook briefly. Add tomato pulp and seasonings; cover and cook for 20 minutes until vegetables are tender. Uncover and cook 10 minutes longer, or until thickened to desired consistency. Mash gently with a fork.

Makes about 1 quart

Note: This is a well-textured sauce that can be pureed if desired to a smooth, even consistency.

NEW AMERICAN CREAMY TOMATO SAUCE

A thick creamy sauce without any dairy ingredients. An excellent choice over plain grains or pasta, especially with a garnish of chopped peanuts and slivered green pepper.

1½ tablespoons oil
1 medium onion, chopped
¼ cup peanut butter
½ cup warm water
1½ cups tomato juice
dash soy sauce
1 teaspoon catsup (optional)

Heat oil in a saucepan and sauté onion for 3 to 5 minutes until just tender. Mix peanut butter with warm water until smooth and stir into cooked onion. Stir in tomato juice. Bring to a boil, stirring occasionally, and cook for 3 to 5 minutes until thick and hot. Season to taste with soy sauce or catsup.
Makes 2 cups; serves 4
Protein Complement
Variation: Sauté ½ cup green pepper strips along with the onion. Add ½ teaspoon basil with juice for seasoning.

TOMATO–MUSHROOM BURGER SAUCE

Serve on grain, nut or bean burgers, or roasts.

1 small onion, chopped
1 large clove garlic, chopped
2 tablespoons oil
½ pound mushrooms, sliced (about 2⅓ cups)
½ cup catsup
½ cup tomato juice
2 teaspoons soy sauce

Sauté onion and garlic in oil for 2 to 3 minutes to soften. Add mushrooms and sauté 3 to 5 minutes longer until lightly cooked. Stir in remaining ingredients and heat through.
Makes 1½ cups; serves 4 (enough for 6 to 8 burgers)
Variation: For a milder version of this sauce, replace catsup and tomato juice with 1 cup tomato puree.

SWEET RED PEPPER SAUCE

A mild red sauce that contains no tomatoes; a welcome change on grain burgers, loaves, or plain pasta and grains.

1 large onion, sliced or chopped
1 tablespoon oil
16 ounces canned pimiento, drained (8 whole)
1 cup water
1 tablespoon lemon juice
½ teaspoon salt
1 teaspoon honey
3 tablespoons minced fresh parsley or 1 tablespoon dried

1 teaspoon dried basil
1 teaspoon oregano

Sauté onion in oil in a small saucepan until limp. Puree pimientos with water in a blender or processor until pulpy. Pour pimiento puree and remaining ingredients into the pot with onion and simmer for 5 minutes.
Makes about 2½ cups; serves 6 on burgers, 4 on plain pasta or grain
Variation: For *Fiery Red Pepper Sauce,* add ⅛ teaspoon cayenne to cooked onion and cook briefly before adding remaining ingredients.

PESTO

Pesto is a popular Italian sauce that has built its reputation on fresh herbs, garlic, and high-quality cheese. It is traditionally served on hot pasta, but also greatly enhances fresh tomatoes and cooked vegetables, especially spaghetti squash. A little bit added to Minestrone transforms the soup to Pistou.

½ cup grated Parmesan cheese
¼ cup pine nuts, soy nuts, or sunflower seeds mixed with a few walnuts
2 cups lightly packed basil leaves or a combination of basil and parsley
¼ teaspoon salt
2 cloves garlic, crushed
¼ cup oil (at least part olive)

After grating the cheese in a food processor fitted with a steel blade or in a blender, add nuts and grind finely. Add herbs, salt, and garlic and puree to a thick paste. (In using the blender it may be necessary to stop the machine and push the herbs down several times.) With the machine running, gradually add oil until the sauce is smooth and creamy.
Makes about 1 cup; serves 4
Minor Protein
Note: Fresh basil is essential to this recipe but it can be combined with parsley in any convenient proportion.
The food processor is really the best tool for making pesto. The blender requires frequent starting and stopping.

With a longer time investment, the sauce can actually be pounded in a mortar and pestle, which is the traditional manner of preparation.

To store sauce in the refrigerator, cover with a thin layer of oil to prevent contact with the air, cover with a lid, and chill. For long-term storage, spoon into ice cube trays and freeze. Defrost at room temperature.

Variations: For a more delicate sauce, dilute with 2 to 3 tablespoons yogurt or ricotta cheese.

For *Tomato Pesto,* omit nuts and blend in ¼ cup tomato paste before adding the oil.

SPICY PEANUT SAUCE

A sauce with a gentle bite to serve on grains, steamed potatoes, or other cooked vegetables.

- **1 small onion, chopped**
- **2 tablespoons chopped green pepper**
- **1 tablespoon oil**
- **1 cup chopped tomato**
- **¼ teaspoon salt**
- **½ teaspoon chopped jalapeño pepper or ⅛ teaspoon cayenne**
- **⅓ cup peanuts, ground into meal (about ½ cup)**
- **¼ cup water**

Sauté onion and green pepper in oil for about 5 minutes until tender. Add tomato and cook 5 to 10 minutes longer, until mushy. Stir in salt, hot pepper, and peanut meal. Gradually add water, stirring to make a creamy sauce. Heat through and adjust spices to taste.
Serves 4
Protein Complement

NO-COOK COLD CHEESE SAUCE

This cheese sauce does not need any cooking and is meant to be served at room temperature over cooked vegetables or even on grains. The food itself can be warm, room temperature, or chilled.

- **4 ounces cheddar or Gouda-type cheese, diced (about 1 cup)**
- **1 cup yogurt**
- **1 tablespoon lemon juice**
- **½ teaspoon prepared mustard**
- **2 small scallions, cut up**

Process cheese in a blender or processor fitted with a steel blade to grate. Feed in remaining ingredients in the order listed and process until smooth.
Makes 1½ cups; serves 4 to 6
Minor Protein

YOGURT–TAHINI SAUCE

A slight variation on the standard falafel sauce, this one can be used in its place or spooned over plain cooked beans stuffed into pita pockets.

- **2 tablespoons lemon juice**
- **¼ teaspoon salt**
- **¼ cup tahini**
- **¼ cup water**
- **½ cup yogurt**
- **1 small clove garlic, crushed**
- **⅓ teaspoon cumin**

Beat lemon juice and salt into tahini with a fork until thick. Slowly beat in water until mixture loosens and turns creamy white. Stir in yogurt and seasonings. Sauce will resemble thin mayonnaise in consistency.
Makes 1 cup; serves 4
Minor Protein

PEANUT BUTTER–VEGETABLE SAUCE

Serve over raw or cooked vegetables, especially carrots, broccoli, beets, green beans, or baked sweet or white potatoes. Unlikely as the combination may seem, it is extremely tasty.

- **½ cup yogurt, or 6 tablespoons yogurt plus 2 tablespoons sour cream**
- **2 tablespoons peanut butter**
- **2 teaspoons prepared mustard**
- **dash fresh lemon juice**

Gradually stir yogurt into peanut butter until well blended; add remaining ingredients.
Makes about ⅔ cup; serves 2 to 4
Minor Protein

Bread Baking
and Cracker Making

The word "bread" has, among its many definitions, the expected technical one, "an article of food made from flour or meal by moistening, kneading, and baking," and the more surprisingly basic one of "food, sustenance." We can think of no other item in our diet that is so befitting of this latter definition.

Fresh muffins and biscuits, dense whole grain loaves, crisp flatbreads, spicy corn bread, crusty French and Italian bread, chapatis, pita, and tortillas are traditional breadstuffs that typify their native cuisines.

Unfortunately, the false concept that bread is a fattening, non-nutritious filler, combined with the industrial mass-production of breadstuffs that has resulted in a very undistinguished product, has made many people today shun what should be a cornerstone of every meal. With the emphasis on increasing our intake of unrefined grain foods, however, this decline in bread eating should be reversed.

A trip to the market can provide many acceptable choices for your table, but the best bread in all respects is the wholefoods bread manufactured in home kitchens.

A basic grain food, breads are a complement to beans and nuts and are themselves improved by the addition of milk, eggs, or cheese either to the recipe or to the meal.

FLATBREADS

The making of crackers requires little skill or time. They are made much like pie dough, combining flour, shortening, flavoring ingredients, and liquid. Some call for leavening and others do not. The only time-consuming part of this job is the rolling of the dough, which can take place immediately after it is mixed or can be put off by refrigerating the mixture and rolling and baking it as convenient.

As baking time is generally quite short, you can often make fresh crackers for a meal in under 30 minutes.

The shelf life can be extended over several weeks by storing the crackers at room temperature in covered containers.

CRACKED WHEAT CRACKERS

A crunchy cracker with a distinguished nutty wheat flavor.

¼ cup raw cracked wheat
¾ cup hot water
1 cup whole wheat flour
½ teaspoon salt
½ teaspoon baking soda
½ teaspoon baking powder
2 tablespoons oil
¼ cup water

Pour hot water over wheat in a small bowl and soak for 10 minutes. Press out liquid and reserve.

Mix soaked wheat, flour, salt, and leaving. Add oil, reserved water, and additional water as needed to make a dough that is soft but can be handled. Let dough rest for 10 to 15 minutes, then knead gently on a lightly floured surface.

Preheat oven to 425°F.

Place dough on an oiled, floured baking sheet and roll with a pin, then press with palms to a thin rectangle 10 inches by 12 inches. Prick all over with a fork and score into 2-inch squares with a dull-bladed knife.

Bake for about 15 minutes until light

brown. Do not overbake. Cool on a rack and break along scored lines.

Makes 30 2-inch crackers; about 7 ounces
Protein Complement

RYE–WHEAT THINS

½ cup whole wheat flour
½ cup rye flour
¼ teaspoon salt
2 tablespoons oil
½ tablespoon honey
¼ cup yogurt

Preheat oven to 400°F.

Combine flours and salt. Add oil, honey, and yogurt and stir to form a smooth dough. Divide dough into four pieces and roll each as thin as possible on a lightly floured surface. Pieces should be less than ⅛ inch thick. Trim rough edges with a knife.

Slip a thin-bladed knife under the dough to loosen it from the work surface and transfer it to an ungreased baking sheet. Score into 1½-inch squares with a knife or the tines of a fork.

Bake for 8 to 10 minutes until just beginning to color. Check frequently during the last few minutes, as crackers can burn easily and quickly.

Makes about 40 1½-inch squares (or enough dough to cover 1 baking sheet)
Minor Protein
Variation: For *Caraway Thins,* sprinkle caraway seeds on the surface of the rolled dough and roll them in before baking.

RYE FLATBREADS

2 cups rye flour
½ teaspoon salt
2 teaspoons baking powder
¼ cup nonfat dry milk powder
2 tablespoons oil
about ⅔ cup water

Preheat oven to 400°F.

Mix dry ingredients in a bowl. Mix in oil and water to make a stiff dough. Use hands to get dough to hold together. Knead on a floured surface for about 5 minutes until smooth.

Divide into four pieces and roll each very thin, less than ⅛ inch, and about

8 inches square. Place rolled dough on an oiled, floured baking sheet. (You may need two sheets for this amount or you may have to bake in two shifts.) Prick all over with a fork.

Bake for about 12 minutes until lightly colored. Cool on a rack.

Makes 10 ounces; four 8-inch squares
Minor Protein

CHEESE CRISPS

Because they have a higher protein content than many breadstuffs, Cheese Crisps are a perfect accompaniment to soups and salads and also make a rewarding snack.

2 cups grated cheddar cheese (about ½ pound)
6 tablespoons whole wheat flour
1 tablespoon oil
¼ teaspoon salt
1 tablespoon cold water
paprika

Preheat oven to 450°F.

Combine all ingredients but the paprika and work with hands to form a stiff paste. Roll thin on a pastry cloth or floured work surface. Cut into shapes by hand or with a cookie cutter. Reroll outtakes and cut.

Place on an oiled baking sheet. Sprinkle surface lightly with paprika. Bake for 5 to 8 minutes until light brown. Do not overbake. Let cool for about 30 seconds, then loosen and transfer to a cooling rack.

Makes 30 2-inch crackers
Minor Protein
Note: If crackers soften during storage, reheat in a 450°F. oven for a few minutes.

CORN CHIPS

Good as a snack as well as a cracker.

1 cup cornmeal
½ cup whole wheat flour
1 teaspoon nutritional yeast
¼ teaspoon salt
¼ cup nonfat dry milk powder
½ teaspoon paprika
1 tablespoon oil
1 teaspoon soy sauce
about ⅓ cup water

Preheat oven to 375°F.

Combine dry ingredients. Add remaining ingredients and mix until dough holds in a ball. Use your fingers and knead a bit in the bowl to make uniform.

Divide dough into 4 pieces and roll each as thin as possible, less than ⅛ inch. Transfer dough to an oiled baking sheet dusted with cornmeal. Bake for 10 minutes. Cool on a rack. Break into pieces.

Makes 8 ounces
Minor Protein
Variation: If desired, sprinkle crackers lightly with salt before baking.

CORN CRISPS AND CORN PONES

Our American ancestors learned how to make these from the Indians. Corn Crisps are thin and crunchy, as the name implies. Corn Pones are thick and chewy in the center. Make some of each for variety at the table.

2 cups cornmeal
½ teaspoon salt
1⅓ to 1½ cups boiling water
2 tablespoons oil

Preheat oven to 400°F.

Combine cornmeal and salt in a bowl. Stir in 1⅓ cups boiling water to make a thick batter. Let stand for several minutes to absorb liquid. Stir in oil. If dry, add more water.

For Corn Pones, drop batter by the soupspoonful (about 2 tablespoons) onto a well-oiled baking sheet. For Corn Crisps, drop by the tablespoon onto a well-oiled baking sheet and spread into thin 2½- to 3-inch rounds.

Bake for about 15 minutes until edges of Pones are brown and Crisps are golden all over. Spread with butter while still warm and offer honey to spread on the Corn Pones as well.

Serves 6; makes 20 crisps or 12 pones
Protein Complement
Note: These are best when freshly made and still warm.

OATCAKES

This is the kind of bread that you are likely to develop a fondness for and one that can take on special meaning (remembrances of childhood and oatcakes past). It is basically a bland, rather dry, flat biscuit, but the rich oatiness makes it much more appealing than this description would suggest. It is easy to make with pantry staples and can be cooked either in the oven or on top of the stove. Oatcakes are the traditional accompaniment to Colcannon and Irish stew and are pleasing with any salad or vegetable entrée.

2 cups oats ground to "flour" in a blender or processor (makes 1½ cups)
½ teaspoon baking powder
½ teaspoon salt
1¼ cups oats
2 tablespoons oil
6 to 8 tablespoons hot water

Combine oat "flour," baking powder, salt, and 1 cup of oats. Stir in oil and enough hot water to make a ball of dough.

Divide dough in half. Spread remaining ¼ cup oats on work surface and roll each ball of dough around in the oats to coat. With a rolling pin, roll each ball to a circle about 9 inches in diameter. Edges will be ragged. Cut each circle into 4 wedges.

To cook, place on an oiled, floured baking sheet and bake in a 350°F. oven for about 15 minutes, or in a 400°F. oven for about 10 minutes, until firm and lightly colored. Or, heat a heavy skillet, add oatcakes, cover and cook for 5 to 8 minutes per side until crisp and lightly colored.

For best eating, serve hot with butter. Save leftovers for snacking with butter and honey or jam.

Makes 8 wedges; serves 4 to 6
Protein Complement
Note: If necessary, baking powder can be omitted; oatcakes will be hard rather than flaky or crumbly.

BREAD WITHOUT AN OVEN

Chapatis, the standard Indian bread staple, and tortillas, their South American counterpart, are peasant breads that can easily be made in simple kitchens. Both can be prepared without an oven, on a hot heavy skillet, griddle, or the flat surface of a wood-burning stove. The result is a thin, flexible pancake with a characteristic grain flavor—not surprising since, other than flour, only minimal amounts of oil, salt, and water go into the recipe.

Puris are made from the chapati recipe by deep-frying the dough; the West Indians take another approach to flat pancake bread by adding a leavener and more flavoring ingredients. The early American settlers had breads adapted to their rustic life-style, represented here by Native American Seed Cakes.

While these specialty breads are an almost indispensible part of various ethnic meals, they need not be limited to traditional service. All the breads in this section combine surprisingly good eating with easy preparation. We enjoy them rolled around beans, cooked vegetables, egg salad, a combination of cheese, avocado, and sprouts (in fact, almost any sandwich filling), or eaten hot from the stove, spread lightly with butter, as an accompaniment to soup, stew, or salad.

You will find many menu suggestions for their use throughout this book. You may also recognize that the dough used for chapatis is also used to make pasta, fried Chinese noodles, and the envelope for boiled and fried dumplings, pirogen, and ravioli.

Although all these breads are best fresh and warm, they can be cooked frozen, and reheated. Or the preshaped, uncooked dough can be refrigerated for several days or frozen for a few weeks, as long as it is kept tightly wrapped to prevent drying.

All recipes are easily multiplied or divided.

CORNMEAL TORTILLAS

In Mexico, most people now go to the tortilla shop rather than taking the time to prepare fresh homemade tortillas. We would not argue that when tortillas are available commercially it is really not worth the trouble to make them at home; however, if you cannot get them when needed, it is useful to know how to assemble them using basic pantry ingredients.

2 cups fine cornmeal
½ cup whole wheat flour
½ teaspoon salt
⅔ to ¾ cup water

Combine dry ingredients in a mixing bowl and work in enough water to form dough into a ball. Knead for about 5 minutes to form a uniform dough. (Because cornmeal contains little gluten, dough will not become elastic as chapati dough does.) Cover and let rest for 15 minutes or longer.

Divide into 12 balls and roll each, from the center out, into a thin 5- to 6-inch round. If dough sticks, flour surface well or dust with cornmeal. Turn over several times, loosening the tortilla from the work surface with a knife blade.

Cook on a hot, ungreased skillet, griddle, or the top of a wood-burning stove, browning on one side, then turning and cooking the other side until speckled. Tortillas can be turned several times and pressed lightly with a spatula, which may make them puff slightly. Wrap in a cloth after cooking to keep them warm and soft, and, if desired, spread them lightly with butter.
Makes 12 tortillas; serves 4 to 6
Protein Complement

CHAPATIS

A soft, freckled Indian bread.

1 cup whole wheat flour
¼ teaspoon salt
1 tablespoon oil
¼ cup water

Combine flour and salt in a mixing bowl. Work in oil, using your fingers. Pour in water and blend with fingers, kneading until dough holds together. If flour begins to crumble, add a tablespoon of water. You should not have to add more than 2 additional tablespoons.

When dough holds in one mass, place on a work surface wiped with oil and knead for a full 10 minutes until smooth and elastic like clay.

Cover with a damp cloth or invert a mixing bowl over the dough; let stand at room temperature for about 30 minutes, if possible, before rolling. This makes rolling easier.

Divide into six balls. Roll from center out, keeping as round as possible, into a thin 6-inch circle. Continue for all balls, keeping unrolled dough and rolled chapatis covered to prevent drying.

Heat a large, heavy skillet or griddle, or cook on top of a wood-burning stove. When hot, place chapati on the ungreased surface and cook for about 1 minute until bread puffs up slightly in places and bottom is lightly colored. Turn and cook other side until spotted with brown. If necessary, chapati can be turned several times until well freckled. Pressing lightly with a spatula during cooking will make chapatis puff.

As each chapati is removed from the cooking surface, stack and wrap in a cloth napkin or towel to keep warm and pliable. Serve warm, as soon after cooking as possible.

Makes 6 breads; serves 3 to 6

Protein Complement

Note: Prepared chapati dough can be divided into balls and stored in a covered container in the refrigerator.

Variations: For *Spiced Chapatis,* add ¼ teaspoon cayenne, ¼ teaspoon cumin, and ¼ teaspoon turmeric.

Rye Chapatis can be made by substituting rye flour.

DHAL POUREE ROTI

This skillet bread is of West Indian origin. A leavening agent is used to produce a large soft round that is the perfect accompaniment to curries and can easily be folded around a favorite filling. The spiced ground split-pea filling rolled into the dough adds to the flavor and nourishment.

For the Dough
2 cups whole wheat flour
2 tablespoons nonfat dry milk powder
½ teaspoon salt
1½ teaspoons baking powder
2 tablespoons oil
¾ cup plus 2 tablespoons water

For the Filling
⅓ cup dry split peas (yellow preferred)
1 cup water
pinch saffron (optional)
¼ teaspoon cayenne
¼ teaspoon salt

To prepare dough, combine dry ingredients in a mixing bowl. Cut in oil as for pastry. Stir in water all at once to make a soft dough. Rub surface with oil, cover with cloth, and let rest for about 1 hour.

While dough rests, combine peas, water, and saffron and bring to a boil. Cook for 2 minutes, remove from heat, and drain. Grind to a coarse meal in a food processor or blender. Add seasonings.

Divide dough into 6 balls. Working on a floured surface, flatten with the palm of the hand. Place a rounded tablespoon of pea mixture in the center and fold edges over to completely encase. When all balls are filled, roll one at a time on a floured surface to a thin 9- to 10-inch round.

Heat a large, heavy skillet or griddle or use the flat top of a wood-burning stove. Wipe with oil and, when quite hot, brown breads one at a time, cooking both sides. To keep warm and moist, pile and cover with a damp cloth after cooking. Serve warm.

Makes 6 breads; serves 4 to 6

Minor Protein

NATIVE AMERICAN SEED CAKES

This easily prepared breadstuff is best described as a cross between a cracker and a pancake. Give the seed cakes a try as an accompaniment to your next hearty soup or vegetable stew dinner.

¾ cup whole wheat flour
1 teaspoon baking powder

¼ **teaspoon salt**
2 tablespoons oil
½ **cup sunflower and/or pumpkin**
  seeds, ground to meal
1 teaspoon honey
¼ **cup water**

Combine flour, baking powder, and salt in a mixing bowl. Cut in oil. Add remaining ingredients and work to a smooth dough. Knead briefly in the bowl to blend evenly. Cover and let stand for 30 minutes if possible. As long as the dough does not dry out, the resting period can be extended.

Divide dough into 16 to 18 even pieces and roll each into a round about 2 inches in diameter and ¾ inch thick. Keep covered until ready to cook.

Heat enough oil to generously cover the surface of a 15-inch skillet. When hot, brown the seed cakes, allowing about 2 to 3 minutes per side. Blot with absorbent paper and serve warm with butter. This number of seed cakes will probably require two pans or cooking in separate batches.

Makes 16 to 18 breads; serves 4 to 6
Minor Protein

QUICK BREADS

The term "quick breads" denotes those baked goods leavened with baking powder, baking soda, or eggs. They are no more complicated to make than a casserole or a vegetable or meat loaf. Muffins, biscuits, corn bread, fruit and nut loaves, all typical examples, can be mixed in less than 15 minutes. Baking time can be just as short, although for a loaf you may need as much as a full hour in the oven. Some varieties even provide the option of stove-top cookery on a heavy skillet or griddle, or by steaming.

There is nothing special you need to buy for quick breads since most of the ingredients are probably already pantry staples—flour, eggs, fresh or dried milk, baking powder and soda, oil and sweetening. You may need a muffin or loaf pan, and if you really want to go all out, a spider pan, popover pan, and cornstick mold. It is possible, however, to get by with a standard baking sheet and other ovenproof pans.

If you follow the directions here for preparing the batter, you should experience all the pleasures of high-quality baked goods. Two techniques that enhance their execution are explained more fully so that you will know why you do what you do.

• *Mix dry and liquid ingredients separately.* The leavening ingredient (baking powder or baking soda) remains inert as long as it is kept dry. Once it comes in contact with liquid, leavening begins, and within a short time its power is spent. If the gases that cause the bread to rise escape, the batter will sink. Luckily, the crust formed during baking traps these gases. This is why, unless otherwise directed, it is best not to start the reaction until you are ready to put the bread in to bake. If you do want to prepare things ahead of time, halt the operation just before the liquid ingredients go into the dry mixture. With fairly dry doughs (biscuit dough, for example), this is less important than it is with the damp batters used for muffins and quick loaf breads.

• *Mix thoroughly but gently until all ingredients are moistened.* "Gently" is a key word here, for to obtain a tender crumb you do not want to overdevelop the gluten in the flour. Heavy handling, as in the kneading of yeast breads, strengthens this wheat protein, making a strong framework to support the greater leavening power of the active yeast. Most quick breads, however, are more cakelike in texture, a quality achieved by delicate handling. Biscuit dough can withstand more handling than muffin and loaf batters.

The recipe for biscuits and muffins can be halved, but we always make a full batch, freezing the extras; a backlog of baked goods in the freezer means a quick meal on future occasions. The unbaked batter can also be frozen for a short time as described in the introductory recipe notes.

<table>
<tr><td>

REFRESHING TECHNIQUES FOR AGING BREAD, ROLLS, BISCUITS, MUFFINS, ETC.

Place on a steaming basket set in a pot with an inch of boiling water. Cover and steam for one minute.

or

Dampen a brown paper bag with water. Place breadstuff inside. Bake in 350°F. oven until the bag is dry.

</td></tr>
</table>

Biscuits

To cut biscuit dough, use an empty food tin or a glass of the desired diameter. For a smooth edge, dip in flour first. Recombine outtakes. Alternately, to eliminate rerolling and to speed production, cut biscuit dough into squares, using a knife dipped in flour.

For pre-split biscuits, roll dough ¼ inch thick and cut into 20 to 24 pieces. Put some softened butter on top of half the pieces, cover with remaining pieces, and bake as usual.

To freeze unbaked biscuit dough conveniently, cut rolled dough with empty frozen-concentrate juice cans that have both ends removed. Fit rounds gently into cans, cover ends with foil, and freeze. To use, push dough out from one end, break apart, and bake. If still frozen at baking, increase baking time by about 5 minutes. Use dough within two weeks.

Prebaked frozen biscuits can be restored by unwrapping and baking on an oiled pan in a warm (300° to 325°F.) oven for 15 to 20 minutes. Use a toaster oven when defrosting a few biscuits at a time.

BASIC BISCUITS

Our version of one of the oldest American foods.

2 cups whole wheat flour
¼ cup wheat germ
4 teaspoons baking powder
½ teaspoon salt
¼ cup oil
1 tablespoon honey or molasses
about ⅔ cup milk

Preheat oven to 425°F.

Combine dry ingredients. Stir in oil until mixture is crumbly. Add sweetening and enough milk to make a soft dough.

Pat or roll dough gently until it is ½ inch thick. Cut into 2-inch squares or rounds. Reshape outtakes. Place on a baking sheet or pan wiped with oil, leaving an inch between for crusty biscuits; have sides touching for a tender crust. Bake for about 15 minutes until browned.

Makes 10 to 12 biscuits
Minor Protein
Variations: For *Cottage Cheese Biscuits,* reduce milk to about ½ cup and gently knead 1 cup cottage cheese into dough.

For *Soy Biscuits,* replace 1 cup whole wheat flour with 1 cup soy flour, omit wheat germ, and use ½ cup water instead of the milk.

For *Yogurt Biscuits,* reduce baking powder to 2 teaspoons, add ½ teaspoon baking soda, and replace milk with yogurt.

TOMATO–CHEESE BISCUITS

1 cup whole wheat flour
1 cup cornmeal
½ teaspoon salt
2 teaspoons baking powder
¼ teaspoon baking soda
½ cup packed grated sharp cheddar cheese
¼ cup oil
½ cup tomato juice

Preheat oven to 425°F.

Combine cheese with dry ingredients. Continue as for Basic Biscuits.

Makes about 16 2-inch biscuits
Minor Protein
Note: As an alternative to baking, these biscuits can be cooked on a hot griddle or heavy skillet that has been wiped with oil. Cook 5 to 8 minutes per side, or until nicely colored and firm.

POT OF GOLD BISCUITS

Flavored with grated sweet potato. Good for holiday entertaining.

2 cups whole wheat flour
2 teaspoons baking powder
¼ teaspoon baking soda
½ teaspoon salt
¼ cup oil
¼ pound sweet potato, peeled and shredded (about ¾ cup)
½ cup orange juice
1 tablespoon honey

Preheat oven to 425°F.
Combine dry ingredients and cut in oil. Stir in sweet potato. Add juice and honey and stir to a smooth dough. When firm enough to handle, knead briefly (about 30 seconds). Pat to a ½-inch thickness and cut into 1½-inch squares. Bake on an oiled baking sheet or pan for 12 to 15 minutes.
Makes 12 1½-inch biscuits
Protein Complement

Muffins

If you wish to eliminate the egg from any muffin recipe, replace it with ½ teaspoon baking powder. Nonfat dry milk powder can be omitted and milk can be used instead of water.

Wipe the muffin tin generously with oil before filling so muffins can be removed easily. Generally batter is added to fill muffin cups two-thirds full; for oversized muffins (the kind you find in diners), cups can be filled almost to the top. If you wipe the top of the tin with oil, the batter that overruns to make the dome will not stick.

If any of the cups in the muffin tin are empty, fill them half full with water before baking. This keeps the tin from scorching.

Bake until the surface is lightly colored and a toothpick inserted in the center comes out clean. Remove muffins from tin shortly after baking. Serve warm or wrap as soon as they cool down to keep fresh.

The prepared batter can be stored in the refrigerator in a covered container for several days and used to bake muffins as needed. (Do not keep longer than 5 days.) As the batter ages, there will be a slight reduction in leavening and the resulting muffin will gradually become more dense and moist.

For longer storage, spoon unbaked muffin batter into cupcake liners in muffin tin, filling cups two-thirds full, and freeze. When solid, remove from tin and wrap individually in foil or all together in a heavy plastic bag. Use within two weeks.

To use frozen batter, unwrap and insert filled cupcake liners in muffin tin. Bake in a 300°F. oven until batter rises to the top of the tin. Increase heat to 425°F. and bake 5 to 10 minutes longer, or until golden. Or, thaw batter-filled liners in the muffin tin at room temperature for about an hour and bake as usual.

To restore frozen baked muffins, unwrap, return to oiled muffin tin, and bake in a 300°F. oven for 15 to 25 minutes (time varies with size) until heated through. Or, place muffin in a foil wrapper in a 350° to 375°F. oven for 15 to 20 minutes until well heated. A toaster oven works best for defrosting a few muffins.

If muffins are defrosted at room temperature, place in a warm oven (or toaster oven) for 5 minutes for better flavor. Or, split and toast.

WHOLE WHEAT MUFFINS

2 cups whole wheat flour
2 tablespoons wheat germ
½ teaspoon salt
3 teaspoons baking powder
6 tablespoons nonfat dry milk powder
3 tablespoons oil
1 egg, lightly beaten
1 cup water
¼ cup honey

Preheat oven to 400°F.
Combine dry ingredients. Make a well in the center and add the liquid ingredients. Stir just enough to moisten. Spoon batter into oiled muffin cups, fill-

ing ⅔ for medium muffins and almost to the top for large ones. Bake for 15 to 20 minutes.

Makes 12 medium or 9 large muffins
Minor Protein
Variations: Add ¼ cup raisins, chopped dates and/or nuts to batter.

To make *Corn Muffins,* replace 1 cup whole wheat flour with 1 cup cornmeal; omit wheat germ.

For *Cheese Muffins,* add ½ cup grated sharp cheddar cheese and ⅛ teaspoon cayenne to flour mixture. Reduce honey to 2 tablespoons.

WHEAT GERM MUFFINS

Our favorite all-purpose muffin.

1½ cups whole wheat flour
1 cup wheat germ
½ teaspoon salt
3 teaspoons baking powder
6 tablespoons nonfat dry milk powder
1 cup water
1 egg, lightly beaten
3 tablespoons oil
2 tablespoons honey

Preheat oven to 400°F.
Combine dry ingredients. Make a well in the center, add liquid ingredients, and stir to moisten. Batter will be quite thick. Spoon into oiled muffin cups, filling ¾ for medium muffins, to top for large ones. Bake for 20 to 25 minutes.

Makes 10 to 12 muffins
Minor Protein
Note: For a sweet muffin, increase honey to ¼ cup.

BRAN MUFFINS

2 tablespoons oil
¼ cup molasses
1 egg
¾ cup milk
1 cup bran
1 cup whole wheat flour
2 teaspoons baking powder
⅛ teaspoon baking soda
½ teaspoon salt
¼ cup raisins

Preheat oven to 375°F.
Beat oil, molasses, egg, and milk together until smooth. Stir in bran and let it absorb liquid.

Combine remaining ingredients and stir into bran mixture until thoroughly moistened. Spoon into oiled muffin tin and bake for about 20 minutes.

Makes 12 muffins
Minor Protein

PEACH MUFFINS

Add a special touch to your muffins during peach season.

1 cup peeled diced fresh peaches
1 recipe Whole Wheat Muffins, Wheat Germ Muffins or Bran Muffins (omit raisins)

Prepare muffin batter as directed. Stir peaches into batter and bake as directed for muffin recipe selected.

SPICED PEAR MUFFIN

1⅔ cups whole wheat flour
⅓ cup soy flour
1 teaspoon cinnamon
¼ teaspoon nutmeg
½ teaspoon salt
1 tablespoon baking powder
1 cup diced, peeled pears
1 egg, lightly beaten
3 tablespoons oil
2 to 4 tablespoons honey
¾ cup water

Preheat oven to 400°F.
Combine dry ingredients and pears. Make a well in the center and add liquid ingredients. Stir to moisten. Spoon into oiled muffin cups and bake for 20 to 25 minutes.

Makes 9 muffins
Minor Protein

APPLE–OAT MUFFINS

An exceptionally light and tender muffin that is very good with bean dishes.

1 cup whole wheat flour
¾ cup oats
½ teaspoon salt
3 teaspoons baking powder

1 cup milk
1 egg, lightly beaten
3 tablespoons oil
3 tablespoons molasses
1 cup grated apple

Preheat oven to 400°F.
Combine dry ingredients. Make a well in the center and add milk, egg, oil, and molasses. Stir until moistened. Mix in apple. Spoon into oiled muffin cups and bake for 15 to 20 minutes.
Makes 12 muffins
Minor Protein
Note: To prevent browning, grate apple just before adding liquid to dry ingredients. Peel or not, as desired. Grate in a processor or drum grater or chop fine by hand.

SUNFLOWER–RYE MUFFINS

A wheat-free muffin.

1½ cups rye flour
⅓ cup sunflower seeds, ground into meal (about ½ cup)
3 teaspoons baking powder
½ teaspoon salt
½ teaspoon cinnamon
6 tablespoons nonfat dry milk powder
3 tablespoons oil
3 tablespoons molasses
1 egg, lightly beaten
1 cup water

Preheat oven to 400°F.
Combine dry ingredients. Make a well in the center and add liquid ingredients. Stir until moistened. Spoon into oiled muffin cups. Bake for about 20 minutes.
Makes 9 to 12 muffins
Minor Protein

ALL-SOY MUFFINS

1½ cups soy flour
2 teaspoons baking powder
½ teaspoon salt
¼ cup nonfat dry milk powder
¼ cup coarsely chopped peanuts
¼ cup raisins
1 egg, separated
1 tablespoon oil
2 tablespoons honey
1 teaspoon minced orange rind
1 cup water

Preheat oven to 350°F.
Combine flour, baking powder, salt, milk powder, peanuts, and raisins. Make a well in the center and add egg yolk, oil, honey, orange rind, and water. Stir until smooth.
Beat egg white until stiff and fold into batter. Spoon batter into well-oiled muffin cups, filling halfway. Bake for 30 minutes.
Makes 10 muffins
Minor Protein

RICE–CORN MUFFINS

1 cup cooked brown rice
1 cup cornmeal
2 teaspoons baking powder
½ teaspoon salt
2 tablespoons oil
1 tablespoon honey
1 egg, lightly beaten
¾ cup milk

Preheat oven to 400°F.
Combine rice, cornmeal, baking powder, and salt. Make a well in the center and add remaining ingredients. Stir until moistened. Spoon into oiled muffin cups and bake for 20 minutes.
Makes 8 muffins
Minor Protein

SWEET CORN MUFFINS

A sweet muffin with a cakelike crumb. Good enough to serve for dessert.

2½ cups cornmeal
1 tablespoon baking powder
¼ teaspoon salt
⅓ cup oil
⅓ cup honey
1½ cups milk

Preheat oven to 375°F.
Combine dry ingredients. Make a well in the center and add oil, honey, and milk. Stir until batter is smooth. Pour into an oiled muffin tin, filling almost to the top. Bake for 20 to 25 minutes.
Makes 12 muffins
Minor Protein
Variations: For crunchy *Golden Temple Muffins,* fashioned after the millet-flecked muffins served in the

Golden Temple of Conscious Cookery Restaurants, add ¼ cup uncooked millet to the batter.

For *Double Corn Muffins,* reduce honey to 3 tablespoons for a less sweet muffin and add ½ cup corn to the batter.

Corn Bread

There are many excellent recipes for making corn bread as well as corn muffins. Some are dry and crumbly in texture, some are tender, and some are almost custardy inside. We offer a few of our favorites, which vary in texture and ingredients.

If possible, choose a heavy metal pan to obtain a good crust. Rub the pan generously with oil and heat in the oven for 5 minutes before adding batter. Corn bread is always best fresh and still warm from the oven. Leftovers can be saved for the next day—a real treat for breakfast—but will taste best if warmed briefly in the oven or toasted. Unless otherwise stated in the recipe, corn bread is not recommended for freezing.

HOUSE CORN BREAD

We like this recipe so well we have repeated it in all of our books.

> **1 tablespoon butter**
> **1 tablespoon oil**
> **¾ cup cornmeal**
> **1 egg, lightly beaten**
> **½ teaspoon baking soda**
> **½ teaspoon salt**
> **1½ cups yogurt**
> **1 tablespoon honey**

Preheat oven to 425°F.

Combine butter and oil in a 9-inch baking pan or a shallow 1-quart casserole. Place in the oven for 5 minutes to melt.

Mix remaining ingredients together and pour into the hot baking dish. Return to the oven for 30 minutes until set. Cut into 3-inch squares to serve.

Makes nine 3-inch pieces
Minor Protein

Note: If you wish to bake bread in a spider pan, rub compartments generously with oil-impregnated paper towel and heat as above. Omit butter and add the 1 tablespoon oil to the batter itself. To double the recipe, use a 9 x 13-inch pan.

Variation: For *Savory Onion Corn Bread,* omit honey, increase salt to ¾ teaspoon, and add ⅓ cup chopped onion to the batter.

APPLE–CORN STICKS

The Puerto Ricans have a corn bread specialty called *serullos,* made by frying the batter so that the outside is crisp and the inside is soft and creamy. Despite the fact that our batter is baked, it produces a bread with the same textural contrasts. These Apple-Corn Sticks are delicious served hot with bean entrées.

> **1 cup cornmeal**
> **¼ teaspoon salt**
> **2 teaspoons baking powder**
> **1 tablespoon honey**
> **1¼ cups milk**
> **1 cup sliced, peeled apple**
> **1 tablespoon oil**
> **cinnamon**

Preheat oven to 375° to 400°F.

Combine dry ingredients. Add honey, 1 cup milk, and apple, and stir to a smooth batter.

Pour oil into an 8-inch-square baking dish and heat in the oven. Pour batter into the hot pan, pour remaining ¼ cup milk over the surface, and sprinkle with cinnamon.

Bake for about 30 minutes until set and crisp on top. Cut into 4 x 2-inch sticks.

Makes 8 sticks; serves 4
Minor Protein

HARVEST CORN CAKE

Practically a meal unto itself. The perfect accompaniment to bean soups.

> **1½ cups cornmeal**
> **¼ cup soy flour**
> **⅓ cup nonfat dry milk powder**

2 teaspoons baking powder
½ teaspoon salt
¼ cup chopped green pepper
½ cup fresh or frozen corn kernels
¼ cup chopped onion
1 cup shredded cheddar or Jack cheese
1 egg, lightly beaten
1 cup water
3 tablespoons oil
1 tablespoon molasses

Preheat oven to 375°F.

Combine dry ingredients, vegetables, and ½ cup cheese. Make a well in the center and add egg, water, oil, and molasses. Stir gently but thoroughly until batter is smooth.

Pour into an oiled, deep 9- to 10-inch glass pie pan or a shallow 1-quart baking dish. Sprinkle with remaining cheese. Bake for about 20 minutes, or until set and lightly browned. Let cool at least 5 minutes before serving, but eat warm.

Serves 6
Minor Protein
Note: Leftovers can be frozen successfully.

Quick Bread Loaves

A loaf of quick bread is generally sweet but not as sweet as a dessert bread, and may be served with a main course of beans, grain, soup, or salad, or used to make sandwiches, including such favorites as cream cheese on date-nut bread or peanut butter on banana bread. Quick breads are especially nice for entertaining.

If the batter for the bread is thick, spread it evenly in the pan, pushing the batter into the corners. Rap the pan firmly on a counter to settle the batter. Then push the sides up slightly with a spatula, making a slight groove in the center. This minimizes cracking, although generally some cracking is typical in these breads.

Although the following recipes are for a single loaf, all can be doubled to produce an extra loaf for the freezer. A

frozen loaf should be used within six months. It will take about 25 minutes for a foil-wrapped loaf to thaw in a 300°F. oven, or two to three hours at room temperature.

BANANA BREAD

1½ cups whole wheat flour
¼ cup wheat germ
1 teaspoon cinnamon
2 teaspoons baking powder
½ teaspoon baking soda
¼ teaspoon salt
½ cup chopped nuts (optional)
¼ cup oil
½ cup honey
¾ teaspoon vanilla
1 cup mashed banana
1 egg, lightly beaten

Preheat oven to 350°F.

Combine dry ingredients including nuts. Combine wet ingredients and stir into dry mixture until thoroughly combined. This will make a thick batter.

Spread in an oiled, floured, 8½ x 4-inch loaf pan. Bake for 45 to 50 minutes, or until a toothpick inserted comes out clean. Cool for 10 minutes in the pan; transfer to a cooling rack and cool completely before cutting.

Makes 1 loaf
Minor Protein
Variation: For *Pumpkin Bread,* replace banana with pumpkin puree. Add ½ cup chopped dates if desired.

PUMPKIN SEED BREAD

A tender, sweet loaf containing no eggs or dairy products.

1 cup whole wheat flour
⅓ cup soy flour
¼ cup sunflower or pumpkin seeds, ground into meal (about ⅓ cup)
2 teaspoons baking powder
⅛ teaspoon baking soda
1½ teaspoons cinnamon
½ teaspoon nutmeg
⅓ cup oil
¼ cup honey
2 tablespoons molasses
1 cup pumpkin puree

Preheat oven to 350°F.

Mix dry ingredients in a large bowl. Mix wet ingredients in a small bowl. Add wet to dry and mix gently but thoroughly. (Batter will be very thick.) Spread into an oiled, floured 8½ x 4-inch loaf pan. (Pan will be about half full.)

Bake for 45 minutes, or until a toothpick inserted comes out clean. Cool for 10 minutes in the pan and transfer to a rack to cool completely before cutting.

Makes 1 loaf
Minor Protein
Note: For decoration, a few sunflower or pumpkin seeds can be sprinkled on top before baking. For a pleasing dessert, pour warm fruit sauce over sliced Pumpkin Seed Bread.

CRANBERRY BREAD

A large, heavy loaf that is extremely flavorful, especially when spread with butter or cream cheese.

2 cups whole wheat flour
½ cup wheat germ
¼ teaspoon salt
¼ cup nonfat dry milk powder
2 teaspoons baking powder
½ teaspoon baking soda
½ cup chopped pecans
1 cup cranberries, washed and patted dry
1½ teaspoons minced orange rind
¾ cup honey
1 egg, lightly beaten
2 tablespoons oil
½ cup orange juice

Preheat oven to 350°F.

Combine dry ingredients, nuts, and cranberries. Combine orange rind, honey, egg, and oil, and add along with juice to dry mixture. Mix gently but thoroughly until completely moistened. (This will be a thick batter.) Spread batter into an oiled, floured 8½ x 4-inch loaf pan.

Bake for about 50 minutes, or until a toothpick inserted comes out clean. Cool for 15 minutes in the pan; transfer to a rack and cool completely before slicing.

Makes a 2-pound loaf
Minor Protein

BOSTON BROWN BREAD

Brown Bread is the classic accompaniment to baked beans. The traditional method of steaming the bread for several hours, which seems extravagant in terms of present-day fuel costs, was really not so in a century when the wood stove was kept going all day long for heat. If you have a wood stove, steaming the bread is still feasible; if not, Boston Brown Bread can be oven-baked and still maintain its unique texture.

1 cup cornmeal
1 cup rye flour
1 cup whole wheat flour
1 teaspoon salt
1 teaspoon baking soda
2 cups buttermilk or sour milk*
⅔ cup molasses
½ to 1 cup raisins (optional but preferred)

Combine dry ingredients. Make a well in the center and add milk and molasses. Mix thoroughly until batter is smooth with no dry spots. Stir in raisins.

Pour into well-oiled cans, as described below. Do not fill more than ¾ full with batter.

For steaming, cover top with a double thickness of oiled waxed paper and secure with a rubber band. Place on a wire rack in a pot deep enough to cover once the bread cans are inside. Add enough boiling water to reach halfway up the cans. Cover pot and steam small breads for 1½ to 2 hours, medium breads for 2½ hours, and large breads for 3 hours. Don't be too concerned about overcooking. When cool enough to handle, loosen with a knife around the sides and remove from can. If difficult to loosen, remove the opposite end and push.

To bake, pour into oiled cans, but do not cover. Bake in a 350°F. oven for 35 to 45 minutes for small breads, 45 to 50 minutes for medium breads, and 1 hour for large loaves, or until a broom straw inserted in the center comes out clean.

* To make sour milk, combine 1⅞ cups milk and 2 tablespoons vinegar and let stand for 10 minutes to "sour."

Cool for about 15 minutes in the can, then remove as for steamed bread.

Serve bread while still warm, slicing thin. As this is a moist, spongy bread, it will be easier to cut with dental floss than with a knife.

Makes 2½ pounds bread, or 4½ to 5 cups batter, divided as desired

Minor Protein

Note: Brown Bread is baked in cans rather than in traditional baking tins. The following cans will hold the batter as inndicated: for small loaves, use 1 cup batter in a 10-ounce baking powder can; for medium loaves, use 2 cups batter in an 18-ounce juice can; for large loaves, use 3 cups batter in a 1-pound wheat germ or coffee tin.

To reheat Brown Bread, wrap in foil and steam for 5 minutes.

To freeze extra loaves, cool completely at room temperature, wrap in foil, and freeze. To use, place, still wrapped, in a vegetable steamer and steam for 20 to 30 minutes. Open foil and probe with a toothpick to test for doneness. If pick can be inserted to the center without resistance, bread is ready. Otherwise, close foil and continue to steam. Longer steaming will have no adverse effects.

YEAST BREADS

Each time we make yeast bread after a period of abstention we are reminded how easy it is. The difficult part always turns out to be the reading of the recipe. While there is a lot you should *know,* there is really very little *to do.*

The preparation of yeast dough is a kitchen event that welcomes children. Unlike other baking, which requires precise measuring and delicate handling, this operation thrives on manipulation— the more willing hands the better. An after-school bread-baking session has a fourfold effect: it entertains, it educates, it excites the appetite, and finally, it delivers fresh, warm nourishment to the table.

The necessary background information precedes the recipes. Once this has been digested, the mystery of baking will be reduced to proper proportions, and following any recipe will be a simple matter of assembling the ingredients, making the dough, letting it rise, and baking the bread. Among our recipes you will find yeast breads that do not require kneading and some that are so quick-rising that they can be ready for the oven in an hour.

Most recipes can easily be doubled or halved to accommodate individual household needs. Make it standard policy, however, to bake something for now and something for the freezer. It takes very little extra time, maximizes oven use, and insures something on hand for the future.

When to Begin

Baking yeast bread takes about three to six hours from start until the loaf comes out of the oven. There are a few short-cut recipes that reduce this to two hours. Of course, you don't spend all this time working with the bread; in fact, your physical involvement may be no more than 20 to 30 minutes, with rising and baking accounting for the remainder of the time. Each recipe is followed by rising and baking times, so you can gauge properly.

Before you decide on a recipe, read it through to determine at what stages you will be needed so that you are available when the time comes. For some breads, your presence will be required at one- or two-hour intervals; other breads can be left unattended all day or overnight.

Basic Yeast Bread Procedures

1. The first step, after you have assembled all the ingredients, is to *soften the yeast.* All recipes here are made with granulated dry yeast. If you use compressed yeast cakes instead, you will need a ⅔-ounce cake for each 2 teaspoons of yeast in the recipe.

If possible, remove the yeast from the refrigerator about an hour ahead of time to bring it to room temperature. This will enhance its activity.

Sprinkle the yeast (or crumble cakes) into warm water as the recipe directs. The ideal temperature for the water is 105° to 115°F. (80° to 85°F. for compressed cakes). If the water is too cool, activity will be suppressed; if it is too hot, the yeast may be inactivated.

If sweetening is added at this time, use only the amount indicated. While a little bit speeds yeast growth, too much will inhibit it. Similarly, salted water should not be used as it, too, suppresses yeast activity.

After about five minutes, the yeast should be dissolved and the surface frothy. Mix, preferably with a chopstick or wooden utensil, to combine evenly.

2. *Mixing the dough* takes place as soon as the yeast is ready. Using the *conventional* bread-making procedure, the remaining sweetening, salt, shortening, milk or other liquid, eggs, if used, other flavoring ingredients, and the entire load of flour are added to the yeast.

You will notice that we use dry milk powder, rather than liquid milk, exclusively. If you wish to use fluid milk, it must be scalded, then cooled before use. The scalding is done to destroy bacteria and enzymes that interfere with the yeast; the cooling is to protect the yeast against killing temperatures.

Flour is added by beating with a wooden spoon until the dough is too stiff to stir, at which time the mixing spoon is abandoned and the hands take over. When the dough is stiff enough to hold a shape, it is turned out of the bowl onto a floured work surface and the remaining flour is added, as necessary, by kneading it in by hand.

An alternative method of bread-making, which we favor, is known as the *sponge method*. With this technique, only the sweetening and part of the flour are combined with the yeast initially, and this mixture, known as the "sponge," is covered and set to rise. Following this initial rising, the remaining ingredients are added as in the conventional method just explained. There are several rising periods in the sponge method; this may increase preparation time, but it also enhances yeast activity and makes a lighter, higher-rising product.

3. *Kneading* takes place at various points in the bread-making process, depending on the recipe. Some recipes forego this step altogether, but, in general, a kneaded bread has a better texture. The purpose of this step is to incorporate more flour and to stretch the gluten in the flour so that it forms elastic-like bands that trap the leavening gases during rising and baking to create a large, light loaf. Breads that are not kneaded, as well as breads with low-gluten flours, like rye, corn, and buckwheat, will be dense with a crumbly crumb.

Ideally, kneading should continue for 10 minutes. This is most comfortably managed if the work surface is mid-thigh or top of the thigh in height. If your table or counter is higher than this, use a little platform to elevate yourself. If you are baking many loaves at once, you may have to knead the dough in batches. (Although 10 minutes seems unusually long when kneading, stick with it; the resulting fine texture of the bread is a just reward.)

The basic rhythm of kneading is to stretch the dough away from you, using the heels of your hands, then fold it back on itself, give it a quarter turn, and repeat until it is springy and evenly textured throughout. It is impossible to over-knead or knead too rigorously. Punching, slapping, and pounding the dough are all permissible.

While you are kneading, the work surface should be kept well floured to keep the dough from sticking, but try not to add more flour than the recipe calls for, as extra flour makes the bread heavier. Although recipes often specify kneading until the dough is "smooth and satiny," whole grain bread always retains a bit of its stickiness. Remember, add flour only as needed to keep it from adhering to the board and your hands.

4. Rising may take place one, two, or three times. The object is to give the yeast a chance to grow, and to do this, warmth is required. Best growth rate is between 74° and 80°F.—an ideal place might be near a heat duct, over the refrigerator, in a pilot-lit oven with the door ajar, next to the clothes dryer, or just in a warm, draft-free spot on the counter. Personally, we find the warm water bath (below) to be the most reliable rising environment.

No matter where it is set, the dough must be protected from drying out. This is accomplished by placing it in a deep bowl two to three times the size of the dough itself. Usually, the bowl is lightly oiled and the dough is turned in the oil to coat the surface. To protect the top, wet a dish towel or linen napkin, wring it out so that it is just damp, and drape it over the bowl. The towel not only keeps the surface from getting dry and crusty but also holds in the warmth.

WARM WATER BATH RISING

Place dough in a greased ceramic or glass bowl. Place the bowl in a pot with enough warm water to reach three-quarters up the bowl. The water in the bath should be just warm enough to touch. If you have to draw your fingers out quickly, it is too hot. Cover the dough with a damp towel and let rise as directed.

Note: In using the sponge method, you run the risk of the sticky batter clinging to the cloth covering during rising. Should this occur, scrape the batter back into the bowl before adding other ingredients. Rinse the cloth in cold water and wring it out to reuse.

Rising time varies with the recipe, but one to two hours is most usual for the first rising period. When it is sufficiently leavened, the dough will about double in size, and if you stick your finger into it, it will retain the imprint. If you cannot get to it right away, it can be left to rise on extra hour or two without harm. After two hours, however, it should be "punched down" to

keep it from souring. If need be, it can be left to rise several more times, but be sure to punch it down again every two hours. If you find you will not get to finish the job in the next six to eight hours, it is better to refrigerate the dough until you can proceed properly. When it is set to rise after chilling, allow extra time, as the dough will first have to warm up to room temperature.

5. After the dough rises sufficiently, it is *punched down* to ready it for another rising, or for shaping. You can just punch out the air with a fist, but removing the dough from the bowl and kneading it for a minute to expel all the air is more thorough.

6. Bread can be *shaped* in a number of ways. If you let the dough rest for about 5 to 10 minutes after it is punched down, it will be easier to mold.

If you are using a loaf pan, divide dough into loaf portions, shape into balls, and flatten by patting and slapping with your hands. Stretch dough so it is about twice the length and width of the pan. Fold sides into the center, making dough equal to the width of the pan. Press gently to remove any air holes.

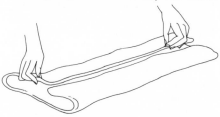

Fold ends into center to equal pan length. Press out air and pinch seams to seal. Dough should only half fill the pan.

Other breads are simply molded in a mound or long cylinder and placed flat on the baking sheet. Rolls can be shaped according to any of the variations in the Basic Roll recipe (page 345).

7. *Final rising* usually precedes baking. Once again, the dough should be placed in a warm spot and covered to prevent crust formation.

8. The *final touches* will depend on what kind of surface you want. Brushing the dough with beaten egg or egg yolk before baking will keep the crust tender. A milk wash will enhance browning. Brushing it with water will give a hard, crisp surface. An egg white coating will make a crisp and glossy loaf. A glaze of egg yolk or white is often used before sprinkling the surface with seeds, chopped onion, or other garnish to help them adhere.

If you want a crisp crust, you can also set a pan of hot water on the floor of the oven, or open the door two or three times during baking and mist the bread with a plant sprayer.

9. *Bake* bread in a preheated oven as near the center as possible. Leave a few inches between loaves for heat to circulate. (Try to bake pieces of the same size in each oven load so that the baking time is the same for all.)

10. When the bread is *done,* it will have an even, golden color and a firm crust. When tapped on the bottom, the bread should sound hollow, although, if it is baked inside a pan, it will be hard to determine this until it is removed. Do not poke a toothpick or skewer into the bread to test it as you would a cake, for the steam that keeps it high will be released too soon. Bread should be turned out of the pan when it is removed from the oven, and cooled on a rack.

If you wish to keep the crust of the bread soft, you can butter it when it comes from the oven.

Rolls can be eaten soon after they emerge, but a loaf should be allowed to cool down. If it is cut too early, the inside may be damp.

11. *To store* fresh baked bread, let it cool first to room temperature. If wrapped while still warm, moisture will be trapped inside, making the bread damp and encouraging bacterial growth.

Helpful Hints

Although the recipe measure for flour is given in cups, flour is generally bought by the pound. There are about 3 to 3½ cups of whole wheat flour per pound.

The better the flour, the better the bread. If possible, purchase "bread" flour made from hard winter or hard spring wheat, as it has a higher gluten content than all-purpose flour.

Unbaked yeast dough can be kept in the refrigerator for about 5 days and can be frozen for about one month. After this period, leavening ability diminishes and flavor changes occur. If you know in advance you will be freezing the dough, you may want to use 1½ to 2 times the yeast called for in the recipe. Once thawed, the dough must be used within 24 hours.

Wear an apron or smock to protect your clothes.

To clean utensils and the work area where dough has collected, use cold water first to flush off the starch.

M. F. K. Fisher, the noted food commentator, has written in *The Art of Eating* about bread baking: "It does not cost much. . . . It leaves you filled with peace, and the house filled with one of the world's sweetest smells. But it takes a lot of time. If you can find that, the rest is easy. And, if you cannot find it, make it, for probably there is no chiropractic treatment, no yoga exercise, no hour of meditation in a music-throbbing chapel, that will leave you emptier of bad thoughts than this homely ceremony of baking bread."

PITA BREAD

Pita is the bread staple of the Middle East, a simple round of dough with a pocket inside, perfect for stuffing to make a neat sandwich. This is an especially convenient bread to prepare, since it can be left to rise from 2 to 10 hours without any attention.

1 tablespoon yeast
1 cup plus 2 tablespoons warm water
1 teaspoon salt
1 teaspoon honey
1 tablespoon oil
2½ to 3 cups whole wheat flour

In a large mixing bowl, sprinkle yeast over 2 tablespoons warm water and let stand for 5 minutes to dissolve. When bubbly, add remaining 1 cup water, salt, honey, oil, and about 2 cups flour, or enough so you can begin kneading.

On a floured surface, work in remaining flour as necessary to make a smooth dough, kneading for 5 to 10 minutes. Place dough in an oiled bowl, cover, and set to rise in a warm place for 2 to 10 hours.

About 40 minutes before baking, punch down dough and divide into 8 balls. Roll each into a 5- to 6-inch round, ⅛ inch thick. Place on a baking sheet sprinkled with flour or cornmeal, cover with a cloth, and set in a warm place to rise for 30 minutes.

Preheat oven to 425°F. when bread is almost risen.

Bake for 10 to 12 minutes until puffed. Remove and wrap in a cloth to steam slightly and keep soft. Serve hot or at room temperature. For storage of more than a day, freeze.

Makes 8 breads

Rising: first period, 2 to 10 hours; second period, 30 minutes. *Baking:* 10 to 12 minutes.

Note: For less resistance during rolling, let balls rest for 5 to 10 minutes, or pound a few times with a rolling pin.

STANDARD WHOLE WHEAT BREAD

A simple whole wheat bread with no embellishments, designed for one quick rising right in the baking pan.

2 tablespoons yeast
2½ cups warm water
¼ cup honey
⅓ cup oil
1 tablespoon salt
½ cup wheat germ
about 7½ cups whole wheat flour

Sprinkle yeast over ½ cup warm water in a small bowl and let stand to soften and dissolve.

While yeast softens, combine remaining 2 cups water with honey, oil, salt, wheat germ, and about 2 cups flour. Beat by hand or at low speed with an electric mixer until smooth. Beat in dissolved yeast.

Beat in remaining flour until you have to discard the tools and knead by hand.

Knead on a floured surface for 10 minutes. Shape into two oiled 8½- to 9-inch loaf pans, cover, and let rise in a warm spot for about 40 minutes until doubled.

Preheat oven to 375°F. Shortly before bread has risen completely.

Bake for about 40 minutes, or until nicely browned. Remove from pan and cool completely before slicing.

Makes two 1½-pound loaves

Rising: 40 minutes. *Baking:* 40 minutes.

Protein Complement

Note: To delay baking, shape into loaves, cover, and refrigerate until 1 hour before baking. Let rise in a warm spot, then bake.

Variations: For *Whole Wheat Sticks,* take ¼ dough and divide into 13 pieces, about 1 ounce each. Roll on a floured surface into logs about 6 inches long and ½ inch wide. Moisten surface by patting with wet hands and roll in poppy seeds, caraway seeds, cumin seeds, dill seeds, or sesame seeds to coat. Place on an oiled baking sheet; cover and let rise until doubled, about 45 minutes. Bake in a 400°F. oven for

15 minutes. Eat warm or cool completely.

For *Braided Rolls,* divide ¼ dough into 8 pieces, each about 1½ ounces. Divide each piece into thirds and roll on a floured surface into ropes about 7 inches long. Pinch three ropes together at one end, braid loosely, and pinch the other end. Fold ends under. Pat top with wet hands and invert in poppy seeds to coat. Place on an oiled baking sheet; cover and let rise until doubled, about 45 minutes. Bake in a 400°F. oven for 15 minutes. Eat warm or cool completely.

One-fourth dough recipe can also be used to make an 8-inch square of *Onion-Cheese Pan Bread* (recipe follows). All three of these roll recipes produce a chewy, open crumb much like crusty bakery rolls. Like the commercial rolls, these go stale quickly and should be either consumed the day of baking or frozen. However, the dough used to make the rolls can be kept in the refrigerator for a few days, shaped as needed, allowed to rise for an hour, and baked for fresh rolls daily.

ONION-CHEESE PAN BREAD

Your favorite bread dough can be made into flavorful onion–cheese squares and served still warm with the meal. What's left makes a delicious accompaniment for breakfast eggs.

dough for 1 Standard Whole Wheat loaf or other bread of choice
½ cup chopped onion
1 tablespoon oil
½ teaspoon celery seed
½ teaspoon paprika
1 cup shredded cheddar cheese

Prepare dough according to the recipe and press to cover the bottom of an oiled 9 x 13-inch pan or two 8- or 9-inch squares. Cover and let rise in a warm spot until doubled, 40 to 60 minutes.

Preheat oven to 375°F. at end of rising period.

Sauté onion in oil until tender and mix with seasonings. Scatter lightly over dough. Cover surface with cheese. Bake for 20 to 25 minutes until fully baked. Serve while still warm or at room temperature, cutting bread into "squares" about 4 inches by 2 inches.
Makes 16 "squares"
Rising: 40 to 60 minutes. *Baking:* 20 to 25 minutes.

Minor Protein

Note: If the dough recipe you select is designed for two loaves, you can make a loaf of bread at the same time you bake the pan bread. If you wish, you can also make only half the Onion–Cheese Pan Bread and make rolls or a mini-loaf with the remainder of the dough.

Store leftovers in the refrigerator for a day and reheat them in a toaster oven. For longer storage, cut into pieces and freeze, defrosting as needed for "fresh" bread another time.

CRACKED WHEAT BREAD

Crunchy kernels of wheat in a tender whole wheat loaf.

2 tablespoons yeast
½ cup warm water
¾ cup cracked wheat
2 cups hot water
about 6 cups whole wheat flour
½ cup nonfat dry milk powder
2 tablespoons oil
2 tablespoons honey
2 teaspoons salt

In a large mixing bowl sprinkle yeast over warm water to soften. In a separate bowl pour hot water over cracked wheat.

In about 5 minutes, when yeast is dissolved, beat in 3 cups flour and the remaining ingredients, including the cracked wheat and the soaking water. Add additional flour so dough can be kneaded, turn onto a floured surface, and knead for 10 minutes, adding remaining flour as needed.

Place dough in an oiled bowl; cover and let rise in a warm spot for 1 hour, or until doubled. Punch down, cover, and let rise for 30 minutes.

Punch down again, divide dough in half, and let rest for 10 minutes. Shape into two oiled 8½ x 4-inch loaf pans; cover and let rise for 1 hour longer.

Preheat oven to 375°F. near the end of the third rising.

Bake for about 45 minutes, or until nicely browned. Remove from pan and cool completely before slicing.

Makes two 1½-pound loaves

Rising: first period, 1 hour; second period, 30 minutes; third period, 1 hour. *Baking:* about 45 minutes.

Minor Protein

BUTTERMILK BREAD

Large, tender loaves.

> **2 tablespoons yeast**
> **½ cup warm water**
> **2 cups buttermilk**
> **¼ cup oil**
> **¼ cup honey**
> **2 teaspoons salt**
> **about 5½ cups whole wheat flour**

Soften yeast in warm water. When dissolved, stir in remaining ingredients, adding as much flour as possible in the bowl and kneading in the rest as necessary. Knead for 5 to 10 minutes.

Cover dough in an oiled bowl and let rise for 1 hour, or until doubled. Punch down and let rest for 10 minutes.

Shape into two loaves; cover and let rise for 45 minutes until doubled.

Preheat oven to 375°F. near the end of the second rising.

Bake for 35 to 40 minutes until nicely browned. Remove from pan and let cool completely before slicing.

Makes two 1½-pound loaves

Rising: first period, 1 hour; second period, 45 minutes. *Baking:* 35 to 40 minutes.

Minor Protein

HERBED OAT BREAD

A tender crumb with light herb seasoning. Bake some as a loaf and some as cloverleaf rolls.

> **1 tablespoon yeast**
> **¼ cup warm water**
> **¾ cup oats**
> **1 cup hot water or scalded milk**
> **2 tablespoons butter or oil**
> **2 tablespoons honey**
> **¾ cup mixed grains (¼ cup soy flour, 2 tablespoons wheat germ, and the remainder rye, if available, or whole wheat flour)**
> **1½ teaspoons salt**
> **1 teaspoon celery seed**
> **1 teaspoon caraway or dill seed**
> **½ teaspoon sage**
> **¼ teaspoon nutmeg**
> **¼ cup nonfat dry milk powder (if water was used)**
> **1 egg**
> **2½ cups whole wheat flour**

Sprinkle yeast over warm water in a small bowl to soften. In a large bowl pour hot water or milk over oats and let stand for about 10 minutes until liquid is well absorbed and oats soften.

To softened oats, add shortening, honey, mixed grains, salt, herbs, milk powder, egg, softened yeast, and 1½ cups flour. Beat with a wooden spoon.

Spread most of remaining 1 cup flour on work surface and knead dough for about 5 minutes, adding more flour as necessary. Cover dough in an oiled bowl and let rise in a warm spot for 1 hour until doubled.

Punch down. Shape into two farmer's loaves by simply forming into two 6- to 7-inch rounds on an oiled baking sheet. Or, shape some or all of the dough into cloverleaf rolls by dividing each half of dough into 10 2-inch balls, placing them in oiled muffin cups, and cutting a cross ¼ inch deep in the top with scissors.

Cover loaves and rolls and let rise for 1 hour until doubled.

Preheat oven to 400°F. near the end of the second rising. Bake rolls for 15 minutes, loaves for about 30 minutes or until browned.

Rolls can be eaten while still warm, but when loaves come from the oven, rub surface with butter and let cool before serving. This bread is best sliced thin on the diagonal like a London broil.

Makes two 14-ounce loaves, or 20 cloverleaf rolls (or a combination)

Rising: first period, 1 hour; second period, 1 hour. *Baking:* rolls, 15 minutes; loaves, about 30 minutes.

Minor Protein

FRENCH BAGUETTES

This is the long, crusty French bread based on the *pain de campagne* (country bread) produced by the famous Poilâne bakery of Paris. A thicker Italian loaf and small heroes can be made using the same recipe.

1½ tablespoons yeast
1½ cups warm water
3 to 3½ cups whole wheat flour
1½ teaspoons salt

This bread is made using the sponge method. Sprinkle yeast over warm water in a large bowl and let sit for 5 to 10 minutes until bubbly. Beat in 1½ cups flour and 1 teaspoon salt. Cover and let rise in a warm spot for 2 to 12 hours.

Add remaining ½ teaspoon salt to sponge and as much remaining flour as possible in the bowl. Knead in remainder of flour on a work surface, continuing for about 10 minutes, or until dough is smooth and soft.

Cover in an oiled bowl and let rise in a warm place for 1 to 2 hours, or until doubled. If baking is delayed, bread can be left to rise longer but must be punched down every 1 to 2 hours.

About 30 to 40 minutes before baking, punch down, let rest for 5 minutes, and shape into a long, thin baguette. To do this, divide dough into two balls. Flatten each ball and fold into thirds. Flatten again and fold into thirds in the other direction. Flatten, fold in half lengthwise, and roll and stretch on work surface to form a loaf 12 inches long and about 1½ inches in diameter. Place seam-side down on a baking sheet dusted with cornmeal. Cover and let rise for 30 to 40 minutes.

Preheat oven to 450°F.

Just before baking, cut a few slanted gashes with a razor or very sharp knife, if desired. Bake for 15 minutes, reduce heat to 350°F. and bake 20 to 30 minutes longer, or until just starting to color. For a crisp crust, bread should be steamed during the first 15 minutes, either by placing a deep pan with boiling water on the oven floor, by spraying water into the oven with a plant mister after the 1st, 5th, and 12th minute of baking, or by brushing the bread with water just before baking and several times during the first 15 minutes. If a basin of water is used for steaming, remove when the heat is turned down.

Bread can be served warm but should be allowed to cool for at least 15 minutes.

Makes two 12-ounce, 1-foot-long loaves

Rising: sponge rising, 2 to 12 hours; first rising, 1 to 2 hours; second rising, 30 to 40 minutes. *Baking:* 35 to 45 minutes.

Protein Complement

Note: Longer rising of the sponge within the suggested time span gives a more characteristic flavor.

Variations: For *Italian Bread,* shape loaf in the same manner but use all the dough to form one large loaf. Increase baking at 350°F. to about 40 minutes, or until golden.

For *Hero Rolls,* divide dough into 4 to 6 portions and shape as for baguettes, making each loaf 2 inches wide and 6 to 8 inches long. Decrease baking at 350°F. to 20 minutes, or until color looks right.

CHEESE BREAD

This high protein bread makes an especially good sandwich.

2 tablespoons yeast
1½ cups warm water
3 tablespoons honey
2 teaspoons salt
3½ to 4 cups whole wheat flour
½ cup nonfat dry milk powder
2 cups grated cheddar cheese

Sprinkle yeast over ½ cup water in a large bowl and let stand for about 5 minutes until frothy. Add remaining water, honey, salt, 2½ cups of flour, and dry milk, and mix until smooth. Add cheese and enough additional flour to make a dough that can be kneaded. Knead on a floured surface for 5 to 10 minutes, adding remaining flour as necessary. Cover in a greased bowl and let rise in a warm spot for 1½ hours until doubled.

Punch down. Shape into two oiled 8½ x 4-inch loaf pans; cover and let rise for 1 hour.

Preheat oven to 375°F. near the end of the second rising.

Bake for 35 to 45 minutes. Remove from pan and cool completely before slicing.

Makes 2 loaves, about 1 pound each
Rising: first period, 1½ hours; second period, 1 hour. *Baking:* 35 to 40 minutes.

Minor Protein
Variation: For *Cheese Bread Wedges,* place dough for one loaf in an oiled 9-inch pie pan instead of a loaf pan, and score surface into 6 wedges with a fork. Cover and let rise as for a loaf. Bake in a 375°F. oven for 25 to 30 minutes. Separate on scored lines and split through the middle for pie-wedge sandwiches.

CHALLAH

Challah is the traditional Jewish Sabbath specialty—a large, light, slightly sweet braided loaf.

1½ tablespoons yeast
1 cup warm water
3 tablespoons honey
½ cup nonfat dry milk powder
about 4 cups whole wheat flour
¼ cup oil
1 teaspoon salt
3 eggs

In a large bowl sprinkle yeast over warm water and let sit for about 5 minutes until frothy. Beat in honey, milk powder, and 2 cups flour to form a sponge. Cover and let rise in a warm spot for 1 to 2 hours.

Stir down sponge and add oil and salt. Beat in eggs, one at a time, and stir in enough remaining flour to make a dough you can knead.

Knead on a well-floured surface, adding flour as necessary but keeping dough as light as possible. Knead for 5 minutes. Dough should be fairly soft. Cover dough in an oiled bowl and let rise for 1 to 2 hours until doubled.

Punch down, divide in half, and shape into braids. To make a braid, divide each half into three pieces and roll into ropes about 15 inches long and 1 inch thick. Pinch three ropes together at one end and fold under ½ inch; plait loosely. Pinch the ropes together at the end and tuck under ½ inch. Repeat with remaining ropes for second loaf.

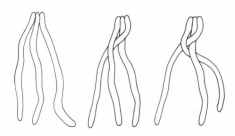

Place braids on an oiled, floured baking sheet; cover and let rise for 1 hour.

Preheat oven to 425°F.

Just before baking, brush surface of dough with an egg wash made by mixing 1 tablespoon of egg with water. The egg for the wash can be reserved from the

3 eggs used in the batter. Sprinkle surface with poppy seeds.

Bake for 15 minutes; reduce heat to 325°F. and continue baking for 20 to 30 minutes until golden and hollow when tapped on the bottom. Cool on a rack before slicing.

Makes 2 braids, 1 pound each

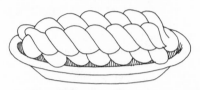

Rising: sponge rising, 1 to 2 hours; first rising, 1 to 2 hours; second rising 1 hour. *Baking:* 35 to 45 minutes.

Minor Protein

Note: If desired, milk powder can be omitted although it makes for a tenderer crumb. To delay baking, shape dough as directed, cover, and refrigerate until 1 hour before baking. Let rise for 1 hour in a warm place and bake as directed.

Half the challah dough can be used for making Brioche (see following recipe) by kneading 1½ tablespoons butter into the dough and proceeding as directed for Brioche.

BRIOCHE

A brioche is a rich, gently sweetened French creation that is traditionally shaped into individual buns resembling oversized mushrooms. The dough itself is a rich version of challah dough and can be made with one less rising period.

1½ tablespoons yeast
1 cup warm water
3 tablespoons honey
½ cup nonfat dry milk powder
about 4 cups whole wheat flour
¼ cup oil
3 tablespoons butter, at room temperature
1 teaspoon salt
3 eggs

Prepare sponge as directed for Challah (see page 341). Add remaining ingredients, including butter, kneading in flour as in the preceding recipe.

Divide dough in 16 to 18 pieces and shape into brioche as follows: Form most of each piece into a ball which fills an oiled muffin cup about ⅔ full. Press gently into the cup. Form remaining small piece into a tiny ball. With fingers, make an indentation in the center of the large piece and insert ball.

Cover muffin tin with cloth and let rise in a warm spot for about 30 minutes until doubled.

Preheat oven to 425°F.

Before baking, brush with egg wash by diluting 1 tablespoon egg (reserved from the eggs used in the dough) with a little water.

Bake for about 10 minutes until lightly colored; reduce heat to 325°F. and bake 10 to 15 minutes longer. Remove from pan and cool on a rack.

Makes 16 to 18 brioche

Rising: sponge rising, 45 minutes; pan rising, 30 minutes. *Baking:* 20 to 25 minutes.

Minor Protein

Note: To delay baking, cover and refrigerate shaped brioche until 30 to 40 minutes before baking. Remove to a warm spot to rise.

Dough can be allowed to rise before shaping, as in Challah recipe, if you wish to use part for brioche and part for the braided bread.

Brioche can be shaped and frozen in the pan prior to baking. When solid, remove from pan and wrap and freeze for future use. To bake, thaw at room temperature for 1 to 1½ hours, let rise for about 30 minutes in a warm spot until doubled, and bake as usual. Use frozen dough within a month.

CRUSTY SANDWICH ROLLS

Big rolls for making a sandwich that demands a crusty exterior and cares little for the crumb beneath. Ideal for Tunisian Sandwiches, Pan Bagnia, or a simple fried egg sandwich.

2 tablespoons yeast
1½ cups warm water
2 teaspoons honey
¼ cup oil
2 teaspoons salt
3½ to 4 cups whole wheat flour

Dissolve yeast in water combined with honey. Add remaining ingredients to yeast mixture and knead for 8 to 10 minutes.

Cover in an oiled bowl and let rise in a warm spot for 45 minutes.

Punch down, let rest for 5 minutes, then divide into 8 pieces. Roll each on a floured surface to an 8- or 9-inch round. Fold edges of round into center, making soft folds in the dough and pressing gently in the center so the edges join. Press gently to form ridges and valleys where the dough pleats, compressing slightly to form a 5- to 6-inch round.

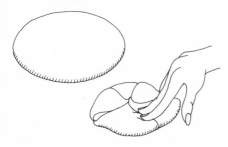

Place on an oiled baking sheet, cover, and let rise for 1 hour.

Preheat oven to 425°F.

Bake for 10 minutes with a pan of hot water on the floor of the oven beneath the baking sheet. Remove water after 10 minutes, turn heat to 350°F., and bake 15 minutes longer.

Remove from oven and wrap in a towel for a few minutes to steam. Let cool. Cut for sandwiches just before filling.

Makes 8 sandwich-size rolls

Rising: first period, 45 minutes; second period, 45 minutes. *Baking:* 25 minutes.

Protein Complement

ENGLISH MUFFINS

Far superior to any you can buy.

1 tablespoon yeast
1½ cups warm water
2 teaspoons honey
1 teaspoon salt
¼ cup nonfat dry milk powder
¼ cup soy flour
about 3½ cups whole wheat flour
3 tablespoons oil

Dissolve yeast in ¼ cup water in a large bowl. Add remaining water, honey, salt, milk powder, soy flour, and 2 cups whole wheat flour. Beat smooth, cover, and let rise in a warm place for 1½ hours.

Punch down, pour in oil, and fold in 1 cup flour as you would fold egg whites into a batter. Turn out onto a work surface covered with some of the remaining ½ cup flour and knead for about 5 minutes, flouring as necessary to form a smooth dough.

Cover in a greased bowl and let rise for 1 hour.

Punch down, let rest for 10 minutes, then roll ½ inch thick and cut into 3-inch rounds. (A tuna can with ends removed makes a perfect cutter.) Reroll outtakes.

Place muffins on a surface dusted with cornmeal; cover and let rise once more until doubled, about 45 minutes.

To cook, heat a heavy griddle, skillet, or baking sheet on top of the range; place muffins on top and cook over low heat about 6 minutes per side, or until brown on top and bottom. Turn only once. To serve, split with the tines of a fork and toast.

Makes 15 muffins

Rising: first period, 1½ hours; second period, 1 hour; third period, 45 minutes. *Cooking:* about 12 minutes.

Minor Protein

Note: Those muffins you wish to store should be cooled completely after browning, wrapped in airtight packages, and frozen. To use, defrost at room temperature or in the toaster oven as for commercial varieties; split and toast.

PUMPKIN PAN ROLLS

A soft dinner roll.

1½ tablespoons yeast
1½ cups warm water
¼ cup molasses
¾ cup pumpkin puree
½ cup nonfat dry milk powder
5 cups whole wheat flour
1½ teaspoons salt
¼ cup oil

Soften yeast in warm water for about 5 minutes until frothy. Beat in molasses, pumpkin, milk powder, and 2½ cups flour to make a sponge. Cover and let rise in a warm spot for 1 hour. (Use quite a large bowl, as this dough really balloons.)

Gently fold salt, oil, and another 1½ cups flour into sponge. When too stiff to mix by hand, turn onto a work surface covered with ½ cup flour. Knead, adding the rest of the flour as necessary to keep the dough from sticking. When fairly smooth, knead for a full 5 minutes.

Cover dough in an oiled bowl and let rise for 1 hour until doubled.

Punch down, let rest for 5 minutes, divide dough in half, and shape into rolls as follows: Form each half of dough into a log about 1½ inches thick. Slice into 1½-inch lengths, lay cut-side down, and pat into even rounds. Place side by side in an oiled baking pan so pieces are almost but not quite touching. An 8- or 9-inch square pan will hold about 9 rolls.

Cover pan and let rise for about 20 minutes.

Preheat oven to 425°F.

Bake for 12 to 15 minutes. Serve warm or at room temperature, leaving rolls in the pan to cool.

Makes about 22 1½-ounce rolls
Rising: sponge rising, 1 hour; first rising, 1 hour; second rising, 20 minutes. *Baking:* 12 to 15 minutes.

Minor Protein

Note: To delay baking, cover rolls in a pan and refrigerate until 30 to 45 minutes before baking. Remove to a warm spot to rise.

Variations: For *Squash Rolls,* replace pumpkin with mashed winter squash (a good outlet for leftover cooked squash).

For *Pumpkin* or *Squash Loaf,* divide dough in half and shape into two oiled 8½ x 4-inch bread pans. Cover and let rise for 30 to 45 minutes. Bake in a 375°F. oven for about 40 minutes, or until golden.

NO-KNEADING, FAST-RISING DOUGH

The following recipe, which does not require kneading or hours of attention, makes a very tender and flavorful bread with many variations. The dough can be divided in various ways in one baking and also holds up well under refrigeration, allowing you to bake fresh rolls for several days.

1½ tablespoons yeast
1 cup warm water
¼ cup oil
1½ teaspoons salt
2 tablespoons honey
1 egg
½ cup nonfat dry milk powder
3 cups whole wheat flour

Sprinkle yeast over ¼ cup warm water and, when dissolved, add remaining ¾ cup water, oil, salt, honey, and egg. Beat smooth, using a wooden spoon. Beat in dry milk and 2 cups flour, then gradually mix in remaining 1 cup flour until it is completely absorbed into dough. Dough will be somewhat sticky.

Cover and let rest for 15 minutes. Shape as for one or more of the variations below; cover and let rise in a warm spot for 45 minutes to 1 hour.

Preheat oven to 400°F.

Bake according to instructions for the specific variation.

Makes 16 to 18 rolls

Rising: about 1 hour. *Baking:* 10 to 20 minutes, depending on the variation.

Minor Protein

Note: To reserve dough for later use, cover and chill until 1½ hours before baking. Shape as desired, set in a warm spot to rise, and bake as directed. Dough can be shaped before chilling if more convenient.

Variations: For *Finger Rolls,* pat dough into an oiled 8-inch square pan using floured hands to minimize sticking. Using a sharp knife, cut in half down the center, then cut each half into 4 x 1-inch fingers. Wipe knife with oil if sticky. Cover and let rise as directed, then bake for 15 to 20 minutes until golden. Serve hot, pulling bread apart along knife lines. Prebaked bread can be frozen, but fingers should not be torn apart until ready to serve.

For *Cloverleaf Rolls,* press about 2 tablespoons dough into cups of an oiled muffin tin, filling each halfway. With scissors, cut a cross in the dough about ¾ of the way down. Cover and let rise as directed until dough reaches the top of the tin. Bake for 12 to 15 minutes until golden. If desired, a nugget of butter can be placed in the center crevice before baking.

For *Cinnamon Rolls,* prepare a mixture of 6 tablespoons honey and ½ teaspoon cinnamon and warm it until honey becomes thin. Mix well to incorporate cinnamon. Place 1 tablespoon dough in each cup of an oiled muffin tin. Flatten to cover bottom. Drizzle ½ teaspoon honey mixture over each. Top with another tablespoon dough flattened slightly to completely cover.

Drizzle again with ½ teaspoon honey. Muffin cups should be filled halfway. Cover and let rise as directed until dough reaches top of tin. Bake for 12 to 15 minutes, or until lightly browned. Serve warm or reheat briefly for best flavor.

For *Bread Sticks,* use refrigerated dough because it is easier to handle. Pinch off about 2 tablespoons dough or a 2-inch ball and roll into a log about 5 inches long and just under ½ inch around. Roll in sesame, caraway, poppy, or dill seeds. Place 1 inch apart on an oiled baking sheet. Cover and let rise as directed. Bake for 10 to 12 minutes, or until nicely browned. Serve warm or at room temperature.

For *Crusty Rolls,* shape dough into 2-inch balls and flatten slightly on an oiled baking sheet. Refrigerated dough will be easier to handle. Cover and let rise as directed. Place a deep pan of boiling water on the floor of the oven during baking or spray with a plant mister after 5 minutes and 8 minutes. Bake about 12 minutes, or until nicely browned.

BASIC ROLL DOUGH

While rolls can be formed from any bread dough, the dough geared specifically to rolls is generally a little sweeter and richer due to an increase in fat or the addition of an egg. Milk also makes the dough finer textured.

1½ tablespoons yeast
1¼ cups warm water
2 tablespoons honey
½ cup nonfat dry milk powder
1½ teaspoons salt
⅓ cup soy flour (if unavailable, replace with wheat germ)
3 to 3¼ cups whole wheat flour
¼ cup oil
1 egg

In a large bowl dissolve yeast in water. Beat in honey, milk powder, ½ teaspoon salt, soy flour, and 1½ cups whole wheat flour to make a sponge. Cover and let rise in a warm spot for 1 to 2 hours.

Beat sponge down and beat in remaining 1 teaspoon salt, oil, egg, and another cup flour. Knead in remaining flour as necessary until dough is smooth and has been worked for 5 to 10 minutes.

Cover in an oiled bowl and let rise for 1 to 2 hours.

Punch down, let rest for 5 minutes, and shape according to variation suggestions below; cover and let rise on an oiled baking sheet for 30 to 40 minutes until just about doubled.

Preheat oven to 425°F.

Bake for 10 to 15 minutes until golden.

Makes 10 Burger Buns; 24 Butterflies; 32 Crescents; 16 Plain or Parker House Rolls

Rising: sponge rising, 1 to 2 hours; first rising, 1 to 2 hours; second rising, 30 to 40 minutes. *Baking:* 10 to 15 minutes.

Minor Protein

Note: To delay baking, dough can be allowed to rise two or three more times before shaping but must be punched down every 1 to 2 hours. Or, dough can be shaped and refrigerated, then allowed to rise about an hour in a warm spot before baking.

Variations: For *Burger Buns,* roll dough ½ inch thick and cut into 4-inch rounds using a 1-pound coffee or wheat germ tin. Reroll outtakes and continue to shape rolls until all dough is used. Cover, let rise, and bake as directed. To keep buns soft, rub top with butter when removed from oven and wrap loosely with a kitchen towel until cool.

For *Butterflies,* divide dough into 4 pieces and roll each into a 12 x 6-inch rectangle ¼ inch thick. Melt ¼ cup butter and brush 1 tablespoon over each rectangle. Roll as a jelly roll. Cut into 2-inch lengths, flatten gently with flat of a knife blade or rolling pin, and place seam-side down on an oiled baking sheet. Cover, let rise, and bake as directed.

For *Crescents,* divide dough into 8 pieces and shape each into a ball. Roll from center out into 7- to 8-inch rounds. Cut each into 4 wedges. Melt ¼ cup butter and use to brush surface of dough. Roll from wide end to tip, curve to form half moons or crescents, and place tip underneath on an oiled baking sheet. Leave about 2 inches between crescents. Cover, let rise, and bake as directed. For large crescents, divide into 4 balls, roll into 12-inch rounds, and shape as for small rolls.

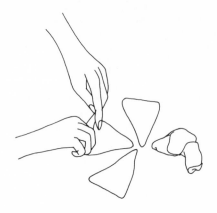

For *Parker House Rolls,* roll dough ½ inch thick and cut into 2- to 3-inch rounds. Crease with the dull side of a knife blade a little to one side of center. Brush small side with some melted butter and fold over wider piece. Cover, let rise, and bake as directed. For *Plain Rolls,* cut as for Parker House rolls and leave flat.

SOFT PRETZELS

Whole wheat dough in pretzel form makes a lighthearted bread for any meal.

1 tablespoon yeast
1 cup warm water
1 tablespoon molasses
1 teaspoon salt
1 cup rye flour
1½ to 2 cups whole wheat flour
salt
1 egg beaten with 1 teaspoon water
coarse salt (optional)
sesame or poppy seeds

Sprinkle yeast over ¼ cup water in a large bowl to soften. When frothy, add remaining water, molasses, salt, rye flour, and enough wheat flour to make a stiff dough.

Knead in remaining flour as necessary, working dough for 5 to 10 minutes. Cover in an oiled bowl and let rise in a warm place for 1 hour until doubled.

Punch down and let rest for 10 minutes. Divide into 13 balls, 1½ inches in diameter. Roll to thin coils about 16 inches long, and shape into pretzels, pinching all places where dough overlaps.

Place pretzels on a floured surface and let rise *uncovered* for about 30 minutes until light.

Bring about 2½ quarts water to a boil in a wide 5-quart pot. Add 1 tablespoon salt. Drop pretzels a few at a time into boiling water and cook for 2 to 3 minutes, turning when they float, until they swell and are springy. Drain well and place on an oiled baking sheet. Preheat oven to 425°F.

Brush pretzels with beaten egg wash. Sprinkle with salt if desired and some sesame or poppy seeds. Bake for 15 to 20 minutes until crisp and nicely browned.

Makes 13 pretzels

Rising: first period, 1 hour; second period, 30 minutes. *Boiling:* about 3 minutes per batch. *Baking:* 15 to 20 minutes.

Protein Complement

Note: If desired, dough can be chilled after shaping. Remove to room temperature for 30 minutes before boiling. For warm pretzels in the future, boil as directed, drain well, and wrap for freezing. To use, place frozen pretzel in a cold oven set at 425°F. and bake for 25 minutes, or until browned. Use within 3 months.

Variation: For *Rye Bread Sticks,* roll dough into 13 sticks, each 6 inches long. Place on an oiled baking sheet, cover and let rise for 30 minutes. Omit boiling procedure, brush with egg, sprinkle with seeds, and bake as for soft pretzels. Serve warm.

Snacks

Some people have the ability to go from one meal to the next without putting anything into their mouth. For others, it is essential to nibble throughout the day. It really makes little difference which schedule you follow, as long as what you are eating is not excessive and has good food value.

If you are a nibbler, you need not resort to commercial confections; simple snacks can be made from most anything in your wholefoods pantry. Particularly handy are the old standbys of fresh and dried fruit, nuts, seeds, hardcooked eggs, cheese and crackers, and sticks of raw vegetables, plain or covered with peanut butter or cottage cheese. Newer ideas might include stuffed grape leaves, seasoned beans, Marinated Mushrooms or Artichoke Hearts, or one of our spreads from the "Appetizers and Hors d'Oeuvres" section.

But, despite all the sensible snacks around us, items similar to candy, pretzels, and chips are especially tantalizing. Thus, we offer some excellent choices in this category, none of them overloaded with sugar, salt, and hydrogenated fat.

We received an interesting tip from one mother who wrote to tell us that she keeps a special container in the refrigerator filled with appropriate snacks for her child. Anything inside the container can be eaten at will; anything outside can be eaten on request only. You may wish to adopt this idea with refrigerator and room-temperature canisters geared to the needs of individual household members—a dieter's snack, a surprise for the kids, a late-night tidbit, etc.

POPPED CORN

Probably the first American snack food, popcorn is high in fiber, low in calories, and devoid of fat, salt, and sugar (before it is seasoned, in any event).

Place popping corn in a popcorn maker or large pot with a tight cover. (It is not necessary to have any fat in the pan.)

Cook over medium-high heat, shaking so kernels don't burn. Be patient and listen for popping to begin. Once popping has started, don't peek or corn is liable to start flying.

Keep shaking. When popping stops, remove from heat.

1 cup unpopped corn yields 10 to 12 cups popped corn

Note: If popcorn is freshly made, it needs no embellishment.

CURRY POPCORN AND NUTS

A seasoned popcorn mixture with a lingering bite. An "adult" snack that is good to have at parties.

2 tablespoons oil
½ teaspoon turmeric
1 teaspoon cumin
1 tablespoon sesame seeds
½ cup peanuts
½ cup unroasted cashews
½ cup popping corn
¼ cup shredded, unsweetened coconut
½ teaspoon salt
¼ teaspoon cayenne
¼ teaspoon cinnamon

Heat the oil in a large, broad pot with a tight-fitting lid. Sauté turmeric, cumin, sesame seeds, peanuts, and cashews over medium heat for 1 to 2 minutes until aromatic but not more than very lightly colored.

Add popping corn, cover, turn heat to high, and cook, shaking until popping is over, about 5 minutes. Remove from heat and toss in coconut and remaining seasonings. Let cool to room

temperature before serving. To keep, store in an airtight container.
Makes about 7 cups
Protein Complement

POPCORN BALLS

Fun for kids to shape for a snack or party treat.

8 cups popped corn
1 cup mixed peanuts and sunflower seeds
½ cup honey
½ cup molasses
1 tablespoon oil
1 tablespoon cider vinegar
½ teaspoon salt

Preheat oven to 350°F.
Combine popped corn and nut-seed mix in a large bowl. Combine remaining ingredients in a saucepan and heat briefly until well combined. Stir and pour over popcorn mixture, tossing to coat completely.
Spread in a shallow 9 x 13-inch baking dish or two smaller pans. Bake for 15 minutes.
Remove from oven and, when cool enough to handle but not yet cold, shape into 2-inch balls or other desired forms. Cool completely. Wrap individually in plastic wrap to keep.
Protein Complement

ROASTED CHICK-PEAS

Much lower in fat than nuts, these are a traditional snack food in Greece and all over the Middle East. They are sometimes available in specialty stores, but are simple enough to make at home. Can also be used as a garnish with a sandwich instead of potato chips.

2 cups dried chick-peas
4 cups water
¼ cup oil
1 teaspoon salt

Combine chick-peas in a pot with water, bring to a boil for 2 minutes, cover, remove from heat, and let stand for 1 hour or longer.
Preheat oven to 350°F.

Drain soaked chick-peas and spread on absorbent paper to dry. Place in a single layer in a large, shallow baking pan. Drizzle with oil. Shake to coat.
Bake for about 45 minutes, shaking the pan occasionally, until lightly browned.
Shake the hot roasted chick-peas in a brown paper bag with the salt. When cool, store in airtight containers. Keeps for weeks.
Makes 3 cups
Protein Complement
Variation: For *Soy Nuts,* replace chick-peas with dried soybeans. After soaking, rub with fingers to remove husks and split beans in half. If husks are difficult to remove, return to boil for 1 minute and, when cool enough to handle, proceed with husking.

"SNACKS"

The value of nuts and seeds increases when they are munched ensemble rather than individually on separate occasions. There are many prepackaged "snacks" utilizing this principle; also known as "trail mix" and "gorp," they are the best picnic-hiking-lunchbox stuffers around.

The exact proportion of ingredients is not crucial. We prefer a larger quantity of sunflower and pumpkin seeds because they are lower in fat than other nuts. The addition of soynuts and/or wheat germ insures good protein.
• As a general guideline, combine several cups of sunflower and pumpkin seeds with about a quarter as much sesame seeds. Add about 1 cup each of almonds, peanuts, unroasted cashews, soynuts, and wheat germ.
• For a sweet mix, add 1 cup of raisins and about the same amount of chopped dates.
• You can also add some shredded unsweetened coconut, carob chips, banana chips, diced dried pineapple, diced dried apple, or dried apricot, peach, and pear halves.
• Keep this mix in airtight containers for a handy snack.
Minor Protein

DRY-ROASTED NUTS

Lightly roasting nuts bring out a rich, deep flavor.

unroasted nuts and seeds of choice

Add enough nuts to fit comfortably in an ungreased skillet and place over moderate heat. Roast until lightly browned, about 5 minutes. If pumpkin seeds are being roasted, watch (and listen) for them to swell and pop. Shake pan occasionally for even browning and keep an eye on them as soon as they begin to color, as they darken all of a sudden.

Cool completely before storing in airtight containers.

Protein Complement

Variation: For *Soy-Roasted Nuts,* dilute 2 teaspoons soy sauce with 1 teaspoon water for every ¾ cup nut/seed mixture. Standing away from pan in case it spatters, stir with dry-roasted nuts, cooking about 30 seconds until liquid evaporates.

CURRY NUTS

Good as a snack, a condiment with Indian food, a sandwich accompaniment, or a garnish for rice.

1 tablespoon oil
1½ to 2 teaspoons curry powder
1 cup mixed nuts and seeds, including peanuts, sliced almonds, unroasted cashews, walnuts, sunflower and pumpkin seeds

Heat oil in a skillet and cook curry powder briefly, using the full amount for a spicier nut. Add nuts and stir-fry until lightly browned, 3 to 5 minutes. Cool before eating or storing.

Makes 1 cup (as a garnish serves 6 to 8)

Protein Complement

Variation: For *Chili Nuts,* replace curry with ⅛ teaspoon cayenne and 1½ teaspoons chili powder.

BEER NUTS

Crunchy peanuts with a sweet, smoky flavor.

1½ cups peanuts
3 tablespoons honey
1 teaspoon soy sauce
1 teaspoon oil

Preheat oven to 250°F.

Place nuts in a single layer in a shallow baking pan. Place in the oven for 15 minutes.

Combine remaining ingredients and stir into hot nuts. Return to oven for 15 to 20 minutes until mixture is bubbling and quite thick and nuts are nicely colored. Watch to prevent burning.

Spread mixture on a well-oiled plate and let cool completely. When cool, break apart with fingers and serve in a bowl. Store in airtight containers, but use within a week as these quickly lose their freshness.

Makes about 2 cups or 10 ounces

Protein Complement

ROASTED CHESTNUTS

The chestnut vendor offering hot, charcoal-roasted chestnuts on the streets of many cities symbolizes the coming of winter. This seasonal treat can be enjoyed by a cozy fire at home as well. Chestnuts can be roasted in a popcorn basket over an open fire, in a shallow baking dish inside the oven, or in a skillet on top of the range. The first method is preferred, for the charred, crunchy portions that result from the uneven cooking are really part of the appeal.

To cook chestnuts, the shell must be slit first to prevent bursting. Using a small, sharp paring knife, cut a cross on the flat side of the nut, piercing the shell completely.

For *fireplace cookery,* place nuts in a long-handled basket or popcorn popper without crowding and hold it just above the flame. Shake occasionally so that all sides are exposed to the heat. Be patient and do not put the basket directly in the flame or the outside will char before the inside becomes tender. Chestnuts should cook through in about

15 minutes. When the shells have blackened, transfer the nuts to some newspaper until they are cool enough to handle. Peel and eat them while still warm.

For *baking,* preheat oven to 350°F., place slit nuts in a single layer in a baking dish and bake for 30 minutes. When sufficiently cooked, shells and inner skin are easily removed.

To cook chestnuts on *top of the stove,* slit as above, place in a heavy skillet without crowding, and cook over moderate heat, shaking the pan a few times until shell appears cooked and nuts become aromatic and can be peeled without trouble.

A properly cooked chestnut will be a little resistant on the surface but soft and almost creamy within.

1 pound in shell serves 4 to 8

CRUNCHY PRETZELS

It's fun to make pretzels at home, especially for the young.

¾ cup warm water
1 tablespoon yeast
1 teaspoon honey
2 tablespoons oil
1 teaspoon salt
about 1¾ cups whole wheat flour
1 egg
⅓ cup sesame seeds
½ teaspoon coarse salt (optional)

Combine water, yeast, and honey in a large mixing bowl and let stand for about 10 minutes until dissolved and bubbly.

Add oil, salt, and as much of the flour to the yeast as necessary to form a dough that can be kneaded. Turn out onto a floured work surface and knead, adding flour as necessary, for 8 to 10 minutes.

Cover in a bowl and let rise in a warm place for 45 minutes. Punch down, divide in two balls, and let rest for 5 to 10 minutes to facilitate rolling.

Roll each piece of dough to an 8 x 12-inch rectangle. Cut in 24 strips, 8 x ½-inches. Fold each strip in half, then roll to a thin 10-inch coil. Place on a greased baking sheet in a twisted pretzel shape, leaving 1 inch between each pretzel. Cover and let rise in a warm place for 45 minutes.

Preheat oven to 425°F. near the end of the second rising.

Beat egg and paint on surface of the pretzels. Mix sesame seeds with coarse salt if a salted pretzel is desired and sprinkle on each pretzel.

Bake for 12 to 15 minutes. Transfer to racks to cool.

Makes 48 pretzels or about 1 pound
Rising: first period, 45 minutes; second period, 45 minutes. *Baking:* 12 to 15 minutes.

Note: Pretzels will probably need to be baked in two batches.

GRANOLA BARS

A baked nut crunch.

1½ cups oats
¾ cups mixed sunflower seeds, sesame seeds, chopped peanuts, almonds, and unroasted cashews
2 tablespoons wheat germ
⅛ teaspoon salt
¼ cup oil
¼ cup honey plus molasses to equal ⅓ cup
¼ teaspoon vanilla

Preheat oven to 350°F.

Toast oats in a heavy, dry skillet for about 5 minutes until they begin to color. Stir to promote even cooking.

Mix oats with nuts and seeds, wheat germ, and salt in a bowl. Add remaining ingredients and stir to moisten.

Cover a baking sheet with foil or wax paper. Wipe with oil. Shape the nut mixture on the oiled paper into an 8 x 10-inch rectangle ¼ inch thick. Pat with moistened hands to compress.

Bake for 12 to 15 minutes until lightly colored.

Let cool for 5 minutes to bond; score with the tongs of a fork into pieces, invert on a cooling rack, and peel off paper. Let cool completely, then break into sections.

Makes one cookie-sheet full
Minor Protein

COCONUT KISSES

A cross between a cookie and a candy.

2 egg whites
¼ cup honey
¼ teaspoon almond extract
½ cup sunflower seed meal
1 cup shredded, unsweetened coconut

Preheat oven to 375°F.

Beat egg whites until stiff. Gradually beat in honey. Whites will soften slightly. Fold in remaining ingredients.

Drop by rounded teaspoonfuls onto a baking sheet covered with unglazed paper, such as brown grocery bags.

Bake for 12 to 15 minutes until nicely colored. Remove from oven, let stand a minute or two to set, then remove with a spatula and cool completely on a rack.

Makes 3 dozen kisses
Minor Protein
Variation: For *Peanut Kisses,* omit almond extract, sunflower seed meal, and coconut and add ½ cup wheat germ and 1 cup chopped peanuts.

FUDGE

A delicious, rich confection.

¼ cup honey
2 tablespoons oil
1½ tablespoons cocoa mixed with carob powder in any proportion
¼ cup peanut butter
½ teaspoon vanilla
1 cup oats
¼ cup nonfat dry milk powder
½ cup chopped dates, nuts, coconut as desired

Mix honey, oil, cocoa, carob, and peanut butter in a small saucepan and bring to a boil. Cook and stir less than a minute.

Remove from heat and beat in remaining ingredients until evenly blended. Knead with hands, if necessary, to form a uniform mixture. If too dry, add up to 1 tablespoon hot water.

Press into a ½-inch-thick rectangle on a wax paper-lined surface. When thoroughly cooled, cut into pieces of desired size. For more than 1 to 2 days' keeping, wrap and refrigerate.

Makes about ¾ pound; 16 1½-inch squares
Minor Protein

HALVAH

Commercially, halvah is made by blending sesame butter (tahini) with sugar syrup. We have fortified the mixture a little, but the flavor in still the same.

¼ cup tahini
3 tablespoons honey
⅓ cup wheat germ
¼ cup sunflower seeds, ground into meal (about ⅓ cup)

Combine all ingredients until evenly mixed. Shape into two logs, 1 inch in diameter and 6 inches long. Cover with plastic wrap and store in the refrigerator. Cut pieces as needed.

Makes two 6-inch logs
Minor Protein

FROZEN PINEAPPLE

A sugarless ice pop.

cubes or spears of fresh or canned pineapple
lollipop sticks or toothpicks with sharp tip removed

Insert a handle into each piece of pineapple. Wrap in plastic wrap and freeze. Eat frozen off the stick.

FROZEN BANANA POPS

Half a banana frozen on a stick with a carob fudge and peanut covering pleases all ages.

2 tablespoons hot water
⅓ cup carob powder
2 teaspoons honey
8 ice cream sticks
4 bananas, peeled and cut across the middle
½ cup finely chopped or ground peanuts

Make a fudgy coating by stirring hot water into carob until a thick, smooth consistency is reached. Add a bit more water or carob as needed for a thick syrup; it should be neither so thin that it runs nor so thick that it's pasty. Add honey to taste.

Insert an ice cream stick into each banana half and dip into syrup to coat completely. Roll in peanuts. Place coated bananas on foil and freeze. When hard, wrap completely and return to the freezer.

Makes 8 pops

FROZEN JUICICLES

Ice cubes are fun to eat even when they have no flavor. These juice cubes are a delightful summer treat. Hold them in paper towels or cups for eating out of hand.

1½ cups juice
1 ice cube tray

Pour juice into an ice cube tray. Freeze for several hours until firm.

Makes 12 cubes

Note: Especially good juice choices include pineapple, orange, and apple–berry blends. Grape is not recommended, as it stains badly if it drips on clothing or furniture.

Desserts

To most of us "dessert" means two things—pleasure and pounds—and for good reason. Almost all desserts are merely treats for the senses: caloric concoctions of sugar, cream, butter, pastry flour, eggs, and liqueur. The momentary ecstasy is often replaced by a lingering layer of fat to remind us of our unresisted temptation.

Fortunately, this does not have to be the rule, for there is actually a way "to have your cake and eat it too." The trick is to make the dessert an integral part of the meal.

Despite all the pleasure food provides, its primary function is to keep our bodies in good working order; the object in menu planning is to assemble foods to fulfill this purpose. All too often, the dessert addict skimps on the rest of the meal in anticipation of what is to come, sacrificing personal nourishment.

If menu planning is employed cleverly, however, the dessert can be designed to complement other foods in the meal and provide nutrients that might otherwise be missed. The key is to think of the entire meal as a unit. For example: since the combination of beans and grains provides high-quality protein, a grain-based dessert will be a bonus to a bean-based entrée. More specifically, split pea soup, chili, or simple baked beans can all be enhanced by a grain dessert such as Indian Pudding, rice pudding, or even oatmeal cookies.

Cheese and milk help elevate the quality of a largely vegetable meal. Italian Cheesecake, rich with ricotta, can provide the protein lacking in a salad, pasta, or eggplant main dish. While Honey-Vanilla Pudding or Coconut Custard Pie can be the perfect follow-up to a steamed vegetable plate, these dairy-rich desserts should not appear on a menu featuring meat, eggs, or cheese.

Cakes and cookies that emphasize nuts and seeds, like French Nut Cake, Greek Lenten Cake, Traditional Peanut Butter Cookies, or Almond Drops, can elevate both grain and bean dishes. Heavy meals accentuating beans and grains, dairy, or meat are best followed by fruit, especially if the vegetable component is skimpy.

There are hundreds of ways this concept can be put to use, balancing desserts against meals and incorporating the more nourishing desserts into menus that are not quite ample.

The desserts that can do the job are in this section, and the best part is that they are all delicious.

A Few Words About Honey

Because so many people question the use of honey instead of sugar, the following facts deserve to be noted:

• Honey is a wholefood and no chemicals are used in its production. Sugar, on the other hand, is exposed to a variety of chemical agents during processing.

• Honey, unlike sugar, is not irritating to the lining of the stomach.

• More than half the carbohydrate in honey is in the form of simple sugars which turn directly into glucose, or blood sugar, without any digestive action.

• Honey is sweeter than sugar; thus, less is needed for the same degree of sweetness. However, honey also contains about one third more calories than an equal measure of sugar.

• Raw or unpasteurized honey, unlike sugar, contains very small amounts of minerals and B vitamins.

• Like sugar, honey probably contributes to tooth decay.

• Raw honey contains an enzyme that has been tentatively traced to botulism in infants under one year old. Therefore, only cooked honey should be used for infant feeding, if sweetening is necessary at all. In general, it is best to avoid sweetened foods in children's diets.

There is really no one "honey," for color, flavor, and consistency can vary widely, depending on the plant the bees chose for their nectar. For general cooking and baking, the common American clover or wildflower honeys are the mildest in taste, the most reasonably priced, and well suited to all recipes.

For those who wish to savor their true potential there are dozens of other honeys from all over the world, among them, pine blossom, acacia (often touted as the world's finest), wild thyme (the most common Greek variety), lotus, mint, eucalyptus, heather, buckwheat (rich and strong), orange blossom, alfalfa, sage blossom, linden, manzanita, and leatherwood, to name just a few. Most of these are far too precious to be used in any way other than as a spread, much as you would employ jam, or perhaps for sweetening tea.

BLENDED SWEETENERS

By combining honey with molasses or maple syrup, the distinctive flavors of these unrefined sweeteners can be mellowed for more delicate desserts.

FRUIT DESSERTS

Fresh fruit in season is at the top of the list of dessert choices. A sweet juicy peach, a bowl of ripe strawberries, a delicate pear, and a crisp winter apple are all exquisite treats of nature. Our penchant for embellishment, however, often dictates something more and there is a variety of resources for adding enticement to fruit. We present dessert ideas here that are fruit-based and light enough to follow a generous meal. They are of particular value to those who do not pay much attention to fresh produce in other forms.

BAKED APPLE

The best apples for this dessert are Rome Beauty, Northern Spy, and those marketed as "baking" varieties. While Macintosh and other similar eating varieties can be used, Delicious are definitely not recommended for baking.

1 medium to large apple per serving
honey or maple syrup
raisins (optional)
crushed pineapple (optional)
chopped nuts (optional)
apple juice

Preheat oven to 350° to 375°F.

Remove core from apple, leaving bottom intact so that the hollow can be filled. Cut a thin slice from the top to flatten it. If desired, peel can be removed from top half, but this is not necessary.

Drizzle sweetener of choice into the hollow, allowing about 1 teaspoon per apple. Fill with optional ingredients as desired. Place in a baking dish and surround with a little apple juice or water to a depth of about ½ inch to prevent scorching.

Bake for about 30 minutes. Probe with a fork or skewer to determine doneness. Apple should be tender but not mushy when baking is completed. If not yet ready continue to bake. Some apples, depending on type and size, require up to 45 minutes. Serve warm, at room temperature, or chilled. If desired, apple can be garnished with a dollop of yogurt, sour cream, or Clotted Cream.

Note: If you are preparing dessert for fewer than 6, you may want to use the Steamed Apples recipe in "Short-Order Cooking."

MACAROON-TOP APPLES

Apples with a sweet, airy topping.

4 cups peeled sliced apples
¼ cup plus ⅓ cup honey
¼ teaspoon cinnamon
2 tablespoons butter
1 egg
½ teaspoon vanilla extract
½ teaspoon baking powder
¼ teaspoon salt
½ cup whole wheat flour

Preheat oven to 375°F.
Combine apples, ¼ cup honey, and cinnamon in a greased 9-inch baking dish or glass pie plate. Bake for 20 minutes.
Meanwhile prepare topping by creaming remaining ⅓ cup honey with butter. Beat in egg and vanilla. Add baking powder, salt, and flour, and stir until smooth.
Spread topping mixture over surface of hot apples. Return to oven for about 30 minutes until crust is golden. Serve warm or cold.
Serves 6

APPLE CRUMBLE

Deep-dish apples with crumb topping.

3 medium apples, peeled and cut in bite-sized pieces
2 tablespoons raisins
2 tablespoons almond halves
½ teaspoon cinnamon
¾ cup oats
¼ cup whole wheat flour
pinch salt
2 tablespoons oil
½ cup apple juice
3 tablespoons honey or maple syrup

Preheat oven to 350°F.
Combine apples, raisins, almonds, and cinnamon in an oiled, shallow 1-quart baking dish. Combine oats, flour, and salt with oil and mix until crumbly. Cover apples with crumbs.
Combine apple juice with sweetening, heating gently if necessary to blend. Pour evenly over the crumbs.
Bake until apple is fork-tender, 30 to 40 minutes. Serve warm, either plain or

with a topping of sweetened yogurt, whipped cream, or ice cream.
Serves 4
Note: Casserole can be assembled in advance and refrigerated before baking. Leftovers should be stored in the refrigerator. If desired, reheat in a 300°F. oven for 10 minutes before serving.

APPLE–BANANA BETTY

1¾ cups fresh whole grain bread crumbs
¼ cup wheat germ
1 teaspoon cinnamon
4 medium apples, peeled and sliced thin
4 firm bananas, peeled and cut in ¼-inch rounds
⅓ cup honey
¼ cup maple syrup
2 tablespoons butter

Preheat oven to 350°F.
Combine bread crumbs, wheat germ, and cinnamon. Place one-third mixture in the bottom of a buttered, shallow 2-quart baking dish or deep 9- to 10-inch pie plate. Top with half the fruit, another one-third crumbs, remaining fruit, and remaining crumbs.
Heat together honey, maple syrup, and butter until butter melts and pour evenly over fruit–crumb mixture. Cover and bake for 20 minutes. Uncover and continue baking for 10 to 15 minutes until apple is tender.
Serves 6 to 8
Variation: For *Peach–Banana Betty,* replace apples with 2 pounds peeled, sliced peaches.

FRESH BLUEBERRY BUCKLE

A cross between a pudding and a cake.

5 tablespoons butter
⅓ cup plus ¼ cup honey
1 egg
½ teaspoon vanilla extract
1⅓ cups whole wheat flour
1 teaspoon baking powder
⅛ teaspoon salt
⅓ cup milk
2 cups fresh blueberries
¼ teaspoon nutmeg

Preheat oven to 375°F.

Cream 3 tablespoons butter with ⅓ cup honey. Beat in egg and vanilla.

Combine 1 cup flour, baking powder, and salt. Add alternately to egg mixture with milk. Stir gently but thoroughly.

Pour batter into a buttered 9-inch baking pan. Top with blueberries.

Combine remaining 2 tablespoons butter with remaining ⅓ cup flour and nutmeg until crumbly. Sprinkle over berries. Pour remaining ¼ cup honey evenly on top.

Bake for about 40 minutes until well browned. Serve warm but not hot, with yogurt, sour cream, Soy Whipped Cream, Whipped Ricotta Topping, or similar topping. Or, chill and serve cold.

Serves 6

BANANES AUX PECANES

A Louisiana Creole dessert.

4 bananas
1 cup chopped pecans
⅓ cup molasses
1 tablespoon butter

Peel bananas and slice in half crosswise. Slice each half lengthwise into four piece (32 slices in all).

Layer half the bananas in a greased 1-quart baking dish. Cover with pecans and top with remaining bananas. Pour molasses over all. Cut butter into bits and arrange on top.

Broil 6 inches from the heat for about 10 minutes, or until bananas begin to brown. Serve warm.

Serves 6

BAKED BANANAS
AND CHEESE

A combination of banana chunks, firm cheese curds, and a thin, sweet sauce. Not much to look at, but very tasty.

2 tablespoons butter
4 medium bananas, peeled and sliced in half lengthwise and crosswise
1 cup cottage cheese
2 tablespoons honey
6 tablespoons milk
cinnamon

Preheat oven to 350°F.

Melt butter in a shallow 8- or 9-inch baking dish by placing it in the preheating oven. Roll banana pieces in butter and arrange in the dish.

Combine cottage cheese and honey and spread over bananas. Pour milk over all and sprinkle generously with cinnamon.

Bake for 20 minutes until banana is tender and sauce bubbly. Let cool a few minutes before serving.

Serves 4
Minor Protein

CRANBERRY PUDDING

Tart berries in a sweet cakey batter, set off nicely with a dressing of Whipped Ricotta Topping, Soy Whipped Cream, Yogurt Cream, Foamy Custard Sauce, or a similar topping.

1 cup whole wheat flour
2 teaspoons baking soda
½ cup molasses
¼ cup hot water
2 cups cranberries

Preheat oven to 350°F.

Mix flour with baking soda. Stir in molasses and hot water all at once. When smooth, stir in cranberries.

Pour into a buttered 9-inch or shallow 1½-quart baking dish. Bake for about 30 minutes until brown on top and set. Serve warm or at room temperature with topping of choice.

Serves 6

CRANBERRY CRUNCH

The tart berries are a succulent contrast to the sweet, crumbly streusel topping.

2 cups cranberries
⅓ cup honey plus 2 tablespoons
½ cup oats
¼ cup whole wheat flour
½ teaspoon cinnamon
1 tablespoon oil
1 tablespoon butter
1 tablespoon molasses

Preheat oven to 350°F.

Combine berries and ⅓ cup honey

in a small pot and boil gently until berries pop, about 5 minutes. Pour into an 8- or 9-inch glass baking dish. (It is best to avoid metal, which imparts a taste to the berries.)

Combine oats, flour, and cinnamon and cut in oil and butter with a pastry blender or wire whisk to an even consistency. Scatter on top of berries. Mix remaining 2 tablespoons honey with molasses and drizzle evenly over topping.

Bake for 30 minutes, or until golden on top. Serve warm, at room temperature, or chilled, either plain or with yogurt, Yogurt Cream, sour cream, Soy Whipped Cream, or a similar topping.
Serves 6
Variation: For *Cranberry-Apple* Crunch, reduce cranberries to 1½ cups and cook as above. Add 1 cup chopped, peeled apple to cooked berries in the baking dish and proceed as directed.

MARINATED FIGS

Figs are one of the sweetest of fruits; set to marinate in juice, they produce a dessert of elegant simplicity.

12 dried golden figs (about ½ pound)
2 tablespoons raisins
1¼ cups apple juice
2 tablespoons lemon juice

Combine figs, raisins, and apple juice in a small saucepan. Bring to a boil and simmer for just 1 minute. Remove from heat, add lemon juice, and set in the refrigerator to chill. Let marinate for at least 8 hours (and preferably a full day) before serving.
Serves 4 to 6
Note: Figs can be cut up in the serving dish before they are presented, or can be served whole with a knife and fork. For more elegant presentation, top figs with a small portion of fine-quality ice cream.

MANGO JAM

In the tropics, where guavas and papayas and mangoes are plentiful, these luscious fruits make a delicious ending to a meal. When mangoes are in season, you can preserve them for several weeks in a thick puree. This jam, served very cold with crackers and slices of a mild white cheese like mozzarella, is a popular Puerto Rican sweet.

4 mangoes
½ cup honey
1 cup water
rind and juice of 1 lemon

Peel mangoes and slice meat from pit. Combine honey, water, lemon rind and juice in a saucepan and bring to a boil. Add fruit and cook over low heat, mashing gently until thickened, about 20 minutes. Transfer to a jar and chill. (It will keep for several weeks.) Serve very cold.
Makes about 3 cups; serves 8 or more

POACHED PEACHES AND CREAM

1½ cups water
½ cup maple syrup
1 teaspoon vanilla extract
6 peaches, peeled and cut in quarters or slices
yogurt

Combine water, maple syrup, and vanilla in a saucepan and bring to a boil. Add peaches and simmer for 15 to 20 minutes until peaches are tender but still hold their shape.

Remove fruit from syrup and boil down for 10 minutes until slightly thickened and somewhat reduced. Pour over fruit and chill. To serve, place drained peaches in serving dishes, tart shells, cream puffs, or on plain cake slices. Mix syrup with plain yogurt to taste and spoon over fruit.
Serves 4 to 6

PEARS IN VANILLA SYRUP

4 firm pears
1½ cups water
½ cup maple syrup
1 teaspoon vanilla extract

Quarter pears from stem to blossom end and cut away core.
Combine water, maple syrup, and

vanilla in a 2-quart saucepan and bring to a boil. Add pear pieces and simmer partially covered for 30 minutes. Turn pears over in the syrup and cook 15 to 30 minutes longer, or until spoon-tender. If they cook dry, add ¼ cup more water. When done, syrup will be quite thick and reduced.

Serve hot or cold, plain or with a dollop of yogurt.

Serves 4 to 6

Variation: For *Caramel Pears,* omit vanilla. This slight change gives a dramatically different flavor.

CRUMB-CRUSTED PEARS

1½ pounds pears, peeled and sliced (about 4½ cups)
1½ tablespoons lemon juice
¼ cup honey
¾ teaspoon cinnamon
½ teaspoon nutmeg
½ cup whole wheat flour
4 tablespoons butter
2 tablespoons maple syrup

Preheat oven to 350°F.

Combine pears, lemon juice, honey, ½ teaspoon cinnamon, and nutmeg in a 9-inch pie plate (preferably glass or ceramic).

Mix flour with remaining ¼ teaspoon cinnamon. Cut in butter with a pastry blender or wire whisk until uniform and crumbly. Sprinkle over pears. Drizzle maple syrup over all.

Bake for about 35 minutes, or until pears are tender. Serve warm or at room temperature.

Serves 4 generously

Note: To serve 6, add another ½ pound (about 1½ cups) pears.

ROAST PINEAPPLE

Use this technique to improve a disappointing pineapple.

1 pineapple
2 tablespoons honey
cinnamon

Quarter pineapple after removing top. Leave meat in each quarter in one hunk, loosened from the rind. Prick surface of meat liberally with a fork. Drizzle 1½ teaspoons honey over each quarter. Sprinkle liberally with cinnamon. Broil for 5 minutes until hot and bubbly. Cut in slices and serve.

WINTER FRUIT SALAD

A salad that takes advantage of the best offerings of the season and is equally good as an accompaniment or dessert.

3 apples, peeled and diced
2 grapefruit, peeled and sectioned
4 oranges, peeled and sectioned
2 cups diced fresh pineapple
¼ cup raisins
¼ cup shredded unsweetened coconut
⅓ cup sunflower seeds

Combine all ingredients in a large bowl. Cut fruit over the bowl to retain all the juices. If desired pour additional orange juice or some apple juice over the salad.

Serves 8

Note: Other suitable winter fruits for the salad include pears, bananas, and avocado. Use these to replace or add to the above to make about 8 cups. When pomegranates are available, squeeze a wedge of the fruit in a citrus juicer and add the liquid to the salad for a colorful syrup.

BAKED FRUITS ALASKA

An elegant low-calorie dessert.

1 cantaloupe
fresh peaches, cut up
berries
1 egg white
½ teaspoon honey
⅛ teaspoon vanilla extract

Preheat oven to 450°F.

Cut cantaloupe in half and scoop out seeds. If melon is small, cut in half crosswise rather than from end to end to make a deeper hollow. Cut a thin slice from rounded ends so melon halves sit comfortably. Fill cavity with peaches and berries.

Beat egg white until stiff. Fold in honey and vanilla. Spread over cantaloupe halves to completely seal the fruit within the mountain of meringue.

Bake for 5 to 8 minutes until golden. Serve at once.

Serves 2

SUMMER FRUIT COBBLER

5 to 6 cups mixed peaches, nectarines, berries, and plums, peeled if desired and cut in bite-size pieces
¾ cup honey
1 cup cornmeal
1 teaspoon baking powder
¼ teaspoon salt
½ cup milk
1 tablespoon lemon juice
2 tablespoons butter

Preheat oven to 375°F.

Combine fruit with ¼ cup honey in a shallow 2-quart baking dish or a 9 x 13-inch pan.

Mix cornmeal, baking powder, and salt. Stir in milk and let sit a minute or so until batter is thick. Drop by spoonfuls evenly over fruit.

Heat together remaining ½ cup honey, lemon juice, and butter just until butter melts. Pour over batter and fruit.

Bake for 30 minutes until crust is firm. Cool and serve at room temperature, adding a few spoonfuls of yogurt, if desired, to each plate.

Serves 6

Fruit Juice Gels

One flaw often overlooked in packaged gelatin desserts, even beyond their total lack of nourishment other than calories, is the fact that they have discouraged cooks from making similar desserts from scratch. Unlike the thickened, commercial sugar-and-water concoction, a natural fruit juice thickened with a gelling agent can provide real nutritional value along with the fun.

There are several gel products available, all quite simple to use. Unflavored gelatin is the most common and in our experience gives the most consistent results. However, gelatin (including the kosher kind) is made from animal bones, which some people find objectionable.

Agar, a seaweed derivative, offers a nonanimal alternative. It is available granulated or pressed into bars, also known as *kanten*. One of the advantages of agar is that it gels at room temperature, although for storage of more than a day the finished product must be refrigerated. Among the disadvantages are its cost (generally much higher than gelatin) and its temperament. In our own use, we have found that agar flakes are likely to produce tough, chewy areas in the gel; a friend finds her agar gels are often too thin.

FRUIT JUICE GEL (GELATIN)

Any fruit juice can be used in this manner with the exception of fresh or frozen pineapple which inhibit the gelling action.

1 envelope unflavored gelatin
2 cups juice

Sprinkle gelatin over ½ cup juice in a saucepan. Place over low heat and stir constantly for 3 to 5 minutes until gelatin dissolves. Remove from heat, stir in remaining cold juice, pour into individual dishes or a single mold, and chill until set.

Makes 2 cups; serves 4

Variations: A mixture of juices works quite well; among our favorites: ½ cup apple juice and 1½ cups orange juice; 1 cup canned pineapple juice and 1 cup orange juice; 1 cup grape juice and 1 cup apple or orange juice. Some of the premixed combinations like strawberry–apple and boysenberry–apple are also recommended.

For *Fruited Gel,* chill mixture for 20 to 30 minutes until thickened to the consistency of unbeaten egg whites. Fold in up to 1 cup fresh, frozen, or canned fruit. Chill until set.

FRUIT JUICE GEL (AGAR)

1½ teaspoons granulated agar
2 cups juice

Sprinkle agar over juice in a saucepan. Let stand for a few minutes to soften, then bring to a simmer and cook, stirring to dissolve. Simmer for 5 minutes.

Pour into serving dishes or a single mold. Although thickening will take place at room temperature, chilling is recommended as it speeds the process and gels taste best cold anyway.

Makes 2 cups; serves 4
Variations: Prepare with any juice you wish or make a fruited version as directed above.

PUDDINGS AND FROZEN DESSERTS

Puddings and frozen desserts, many of them dairy-based, are more filling than fruit desserts. They are a valuable adjunct to the protein in many main dishes, but, with few exceptions, should not follow an egg or cheese entrée.

HONEY–VANILLA PUDDING

A soothing, delicate dessert that is hardly more complicated than an instant mix.

3 tablespoons arrowroot or cornstarch
2 cups milk

¼ cup honey
1 teaspoon vanilla extract

Dissolve the starch in ¼ cup milk. Combine remaining milk and honey in a saucepan and scald. Add the starch mixture and stir over low heat until pudding thickens. Remove arrowroot pudding before boiling begins. If thickened with cornstarch, simmer for 30 seconds.

Stir in vanilla, pour into a large bowl or 4 individual dishes, and cool to room temperature before chilling.

Makes 2 cups; serves 4
Minor Protein
Note: To prevent a film from forming on top of the pudding, a bit of butter can be placed on the surface to melt during cooling.

Variation: For *Butterscotch Pudding,* reduce honey to 3 tablespoons and add 2 tablespoons molasses. Reduce vanilla to ¼ teaspoon and stir in 1 tablespoon butter at the same time.

HONEY–CHOCOLATE PUDDING

An obvious but pleasing honey taste is melded with the chocolate.

3 tablespoons cocoa
2½ tablespoons arrowroot or cornstarch
2 cups milk
⅓ cup honey
½ teaspoon vanilla extract

Make a paste of cocoa, starch, and ¼ cup milk. Combine remaining milk and honey in a saucepan and scald.

Stir some of the hot milk mixture into the cocoa paste, then return to the saucepan and stir over low heat until thick. If thickened with arrowroot, remove from heat before boiling begins. If thickened with cornstarch, simmer very gently for about 30 seconds.

Stir in vanilla, pour into a large bowl or 4 individual dishes, cool to room temperature, then chill.

Makes 2 cups; serves 4
Minor Protein
Variation: For *Chocolate Pudding Pie,* increase starch to 3 tablespoons, or add 1 egg beaten with a little of the thick hot pudding to temper, and cook

without boiling for 1 minute. Pour into prebaked crust. Cool to room temperature, then chill.

Carob Pudding can be made by replacing the cocoa with carob powder and reducing the honey to ¼ cup. In our opinion, however, carob in this form is quite cloying. A good compromise would be to substitute carob for some of the cocoa, thereby reducing the chocolate but still retaining much of the flavor.

TAHINI CUSTARD

A delicious nondairy pudding that enhances the value of a meal that features beans.

2 cups apple juice
2½ tablespoons honey
2½ tablespoons arrowroot
2 tablespoons water
¼ cup tahini

Combine apple juice and honey and bring to a boil. Make a paste of arrowroot and water. Stir into hot juice and cook over low heat until thick. Stir in tahini and cook until smooth. Pour into a large bowl or 4 individual dishes, cool to room temperature, then chill.

Makes 2 cups; serves 4
Protein Complement

EGG-WHITE ALMOND CUSTARD

A gentle flan that is particularly welcome after a rice and bean meal.

3 eggs
2 cups milk
¼ cup maple syrup
¼ cup finely ground almonds (from about 3 tablespoons whole)
pinch salt

Separate eggs and let whites come to room temperature. Refrigerate or freeze yolks for other use.

Bring milk to the boiling point, add maple syrup and almond meal, and cook gently for 1 minute. Remove from heat and cool to lukewarm, about 10 minutes.

Preheat oven to 325°F. Beat egg whites until frothy; add salt and continue beating until stiff. Fold whites gently but thoroughly into cooled milk mixture until evenly blended.

Pour into a shallow 9-inch baking dish or flan mold. Place in a larger pan and surround with hot water. Bake for 40 to 45 minutes, until a butter knife inserted 1 inch from the center emerges clean. Cool to room temperature, then chill promptly for several hours before serving.

Serves 6
Minor Protein
Note: Make well in advance so flan can chill, as this should be very cold when served. If you are looking for a use for the egg yolks, try making a batch of Spritz Cookies.

BAKED VANILLA CUSTARD

Known as flan in many countries.

3 eggs
¼ cup honey
2 cups milk
¼ cup nonfat dry milk powder
⅛ teaspoon salt
1 teaspoon vanilla extract

Preheat oven to 325°F.

Combine all ingredients and beat with wire whisk or rotary beater until smooth. Pour into 6 custard cups and place in a baking dish. Surround with hot water to a depth of 1 inch.

Bake for 40 to 50 minutes until set but on the soft side. Remove cups from water bath, cool in a rack to room temperature, then chill.

Serves 6
Minor Protein
Note: Despite the fact that many custard recipes call for scalding the milk, this is only necessary with raw (unpasteurized) milk. However, if milk is hot, baking time will be reduced to 35 or 40 minutes.

The amount of fresh milk can be reduced by half if the dry milk powder is increased to ½ cup and the remainder of the liquid is furnished by 1 cup water. At least half whole milk should be used.

If desired, 3 whole eggs can be replaced with 2 eggs and 2 yolks for a more tender custard, or 2 eggs and 2 whites for a stiffer custard.

To test for doneness, a butter knife can be inserted into a custard cup near the edge. If the knife emerges clean, the custard is ready, even though the center may still be soft. If the center is as firm as the edge when tested, the cups should be transfered to an ice-water bath rather than cooled on a rack in order to halt cooking and keep the custard tender.

As soon as the custard has cooled down, it should be refrigerated since bacteria favor this warm, egg-rich environment.

Variation: For *Baked Chocolate/ Carob Custard,* prepare mixture for Baked Vanilla Custard but add 3 tablespoons cocoa, carob powder, or any combination, increase the honey by 1 tablespoon, and decrease the vanilla to ½ teaspoon. To insure even blending, mix the cocoa/carob with a little of the milk before combining the ingredients. All-carob baked custard is excellent.

LEMON SPONGE PUDDING

A delicate lemon custard on the bottom and an airy sponge cake on top. A delicious and refreshing dessert that can be served warm or cold.

3 eggs, separated
⅓ cup honey
¼ cup lemon juice
1 cup milk
1 teaspoon minced lemon rind
3 tablespoons whole wheat flour

Preheat oven to 325°F.

Beat together egg yolks, honey, lemon juice, milk, rind, and flour. Beat egg whites until stiff and fold into yolk mixture. Pour into a greased 8-inch-square baking pan or 4 to 6 greased custard cups. Place in a hot water bath.

Bake for 45 minutes, or until brown on top and a butter knife inserted into

the custard comes out clean. Remove from water bath and cool on a rack. Serve while still warm or chill as soon as possible after cooling.

Serves 4 to 6
Minor Protein

TOP-OF-THE-STOVE RICE PUDDING

2 cups cooked brown rice
2 eggs, lightly beaten
2 cups milk
6 tablespoons honey or ⅓ cup maple syrup
½ teaspoon cinnamon
½ teaspoon nutmeg
¼ to ½ cup raisins
½ teaspoon vanilla extract (omit with maple syrup)

Combine all ingredients except vanilla in a saucepan. Cook over low heat, stirring constantly until thick. Take care not to boil. Cooking will take 10 to 15 minutes. (If desired, pudding can be prepared in the top of a double boiler or in a pot set on a heatproof pad; with this method, cooking takes about 30 minutes, but requires less attention.) Stir in vanilla after cooking.

Pour pudding into single bowl or individual dishes. Serve warm or chill as soon as pudding has cooled down.

Serves 6
Minor Protein
Variation: For *Baked Meringue Topping,* separate eggs and prepare pudding with yolks only. Beat whites until stiff and fold in 1 teaspoon honey or maple syrup and ¼ teaspoon vanilla. Place pudding in a shallow 8- or 9-inch baking dish and spread with meringue. Bake in a 300°F. oven for 15 to 20 minutes until light brown. Cool to room temperature, then chill.

For *Baked Rice Pudding,* combine all ingredients in a greased 8- or 9-inch baking dish and bake in a 350°F. oven for about 30 minutes until nicely browned.

BREAD PUDDING

Bread pudding is a rather unappetizing name for a dessert that is as delightful as baked custard, quite nourishing, and has been a part of American culinary history for generations.

5 to 6 cups diced whole grain bread
1 cup raisins
4 eggs, beaten
½ cup nonfat dry milk powder dissolved in 4 cups milk, or 1½ cups powdered milk dissolved in 4 cups water
½ cup honey or maple syrup
2 teaspoons vanilla extract
½ teaspoon cinnamon
2 tablespoons wheat germ
1 tablespoon butter

Mix bread and raisins in a greased 9 x 13-inch or 2-quart baking dish. Beat eggs with milk, sweetening, and vanilla. Pour over bread and let stand for 15 minutes to soften and absorb the liquid.

Preheat oven to 350°F. Sprinkle surface of pudding with cinnamon and wheat germ. Dot with butter.

Bake for about 30 minutes until custard is set and top is lightly browned. Serve warm or cold, plain or with a little milk or cream.

Serves 10 to 12
Minor Protein
Note: This is a good outlet for bread and even cakes that are drying out; it can be made with several varieties of bread mixed together.

INDIAN PUDDING

One of the best winter desserts we know of is this traditional New England cornmeal pudding. Served warm, it is excellent plain and unsurpassed with a little vanilla ice cream on top. Make plenty, for the chilled leftovers are also a treat.

⅔ cup yellow cornmeal
5 cups milk
2 tablespoons butter
½ cup molasses
¼ cup honey
½ teaspoon salt
½ teaspoon ginger
1 teaspoon cinnamon
2 eggs, lightly beaten
¾ cup raisins (optional but good)

Preheat oven to 350°F.

Combine cornmeal and 1 cup milk in a saucepan and stir until smooth. Add 3 more cups milk and cook over medium heat, stirring, until mixture thickens and comes to a boil. Simmer for 2 minutes. Remove cornmeal from heat and stir in butter, sweetening, and spices.

Beat a little of the hot mixture into the eggs, then slowly return to the remainder of the hot cornmeal, stirring to prevent eggs from cooking. Stir in raisins.

Pour into a greased, shallow 2-quart (9 x 13-inch) baking dish. Pour remaining 1 cup milk evenly over top. Bake for 45 minutes to 1 hour until set and browned on top. Serve warm or at room temperature. Chill leftovers.

Serves 8 to 10
Minor Protein

STRAWBERRY ICE

This particular ice appeals more to adults than children. It can be nicely presented by using the edge of an ice cream scoop or sturdy spoon to shave the ice into the dessert dishes.

1½ cups sliced strawberries
2 tablespoons honey
2 tablespoons orange juice
1 egg white

Puree berries with honey and orange juice. Freeze in a 1-pint container, then whip frozen berry puree until light with an electric mixer or in a blender or processor.

Beat egg white until stiff and fold into whipped puree. Return to pint container and freeze for at least 2 hours.

Makes 1 pint; serves 4 to 6
Note: About 30 calories per half cup.

FROZEN STRAWBERRY YOGURT

2 cups unsweetened frozen strawberries
2 tablespoons orange juice
3 tablespoons honey
1 cup yogurt

Puree berries, orange juice, and honey in a blender or processor fitted with a steel blade. Add yogurt and process quickly until well mixed.

Pour into a shallow 8- or 9-inch metal pan and chill for about 2 hours until firm.

Return to the blender or processor, breaking into chunks. Puree again until smooth. This may require a little stopping and scraping until yogurt begins to soften. When the mixture is as creamy as soft custard, pack it into a 1-pint freezer container and freeze solid. Remove from the freezer for 10 to 15 minutes before serving to soften.

Makes 1 pint; serves 4 to 6
Minor Protein
Note: About 100 calories per serving.

PEACH SHERBET

1½ cups peaches canned in unsweetened juice and drained
¼ cup reserved peach juice
1 cup yogurt
¼ cup honey

Combine all ingredients in a blender or processor fitted with a steel blade and process until only tiny pieces of fruit remain.

Pour into a shallow 8- or 9-inch metal pan and freeze until firm around the edges, about 1 hour. Transfer to a bowl and beat with an electric or rotary beater until smooth and fluffy.

Pack into a 1-pint freezer container and freeze solid. Remove from freezer for 10 to 15 minutes before serving to soften slightly; mash with a fork.

Makes 1 pint; serves 4 to 6
Minor Protein
Note: About 130 calories per serving.

FROZEN APPLE CREAM

The iciness of this frozen dessert is very appealing.

1 cup plain yogurt
2 tablespoons maple syrup
1 cup unsweetened applesauce
¼ teaspoon cinnamon
2 tablespoons walnut pieces

In a 1-pint freezer container mix yogurt and maple syrup until smooth. Combine applesauce, cinnamon, and nuts in a separate dish. Spoon on top of the yogurt and swirl in with a fork, spatula, or knife so that applesauce is marbled through yogurt rather than evenly mixed.

Cover and freeze. Serve when still slightly mushy, within 3 to 4 hours, or if frozen firm, let soften for about 10 minutes at room temperature before serving. Frozen Apple Cream is best at a slushy consistency.

Serves 4
Minor Protein
Note: Only about 100 calories per serving.

HONEY–LEMON MILK SHERBET

Cool and refreshing.

2 egg whites
½ cup honey
2 cups milk
½ cup lemon juice
½ teaspoon minced lemon rind

Beat egg whites with a rotary or electric mixer until stiff. Gradually beat in honey, milk, lemon juice and rind.

Pour into a shallow 8- or 9-inch metal pan and freeze for about 2 hours until icy but not hard.

Transfer to a large bowl and beat again until smooth and slushy but not melted. Pack into freezer containers and freeze until firm.

Makes about 5 cups; serves 6 to 8
Minor Protein
Note: About 65 calories per ½ cup made with skim milk; 80 with whole milk.

BUTTERMILK SHERBET

1½ cups buttermilk
1 cup fresh or drained canned crushed pineapple
2 tablespoons honey
1 teaspoon lemon juice

Combine all ingredients and freeze in a shallow metal tray for about 2 hours until firm but not hard.

Whip in a blender, or processor fitted with a steel blade, or with an electric mixer until the consistency of soft snow.

Pack in a freezer container and freeze solid.

Makes 3 cups; serves 6
Minor Protein
Note: About 65 calories per half-cup serving.
Variation: Replace pineapple with ⅔ cup orange juice.

BANANA CREAM

A creamy frozen fruit dessert that is as pleasing to the palate as ice cream, but with much less fat and sugar.

1 ripe banana
1 tablespoon orange juice
1½ tablespoons honey
1 cup ricotta cheese

In a blender or processor puree banana with orange juice and honey. When smooth, add ricotta and process until smooth and light.

Transfer to a 1-pint container and freeze. Serve firm but not quite hard. If frozen solid, let stand at room temperature for about 10 minutes before serving.

Makes 1 pint; serves 4
Minor Protein
Variations: For *Strawberry Cream,* replace banana with 1 cup fresh cut-up berries; 2 tablespoons honey may be needed, depending on the sweetness of the fruit.

For *Peach Cream,* replace banana with 1 cup peeled fresh peach pieces and increase honey to 2 tablespoons. Or, use 1 cup drained peaches canned in unsweetened juice and replace orange juice with 1 tablespoon canning liquid.

FRESH STRAWBERRY ICE CREAM

This is truly delicious and every bit as rich as the finest ice cream on the market.

1 cup fresh strawberries
¼ cup nonfat dry milk powder
6 tablespoons honey
½ cup yogurt
½ teaspoon vanilla extract
1 cup heavy cream

Puree fruit in a blender or processor with milk powder and honey until smooth and milk is no longer grainy. Stir in yogurt and vanilla. Freeze.

When firm but not hard, beat fruit mixture in a bowl until smooth. Whip cream. Fold the two mixtures together. Transfer to a freezer container and freeze until firm.

Makes 1 quart
Variation: For *Peach Ice Cream,* replace berries with 1 cup diced fresh or drained canned peaches.

MAPLE–WALNUT ICE CREAM

Rich and delicious.

¼ cup nonfat dry milk powder
6 tablespoons maple syrup
½ cup yogurt
1 cup heavy cream
⅓ cup walnut pieces

Beat nonfat dry milk powder into maple syrup, using a rotary or electric mixer until creamy and grains of milk powder "melt." Fold in yogurt. Freeze.

When the mixture is firm but not hard, beat until smooth. Whip cream. Fold the two together. Fold in nuts. Transfer to a freezer container and freeze solid.

Makes 1 quart

BAKED GOODS

The Making of a Baker

Baking and cooking are two quite different endeavors and people do not always show equal talents for both. This distinction exists even among professionals, and fine restaurants will usually employ a separate "pastry chef."

While a good cook can be guided by instinct and inspiration, a successful baker is much more dependent on precision. The recipe is like a blueprint and the end product is as good as one's ability to follow directions and not succumb to the temptation to improvise.

Accurate measuring implements and a reliable oven are essential.

Because baking is governed by precise instructions, anyone can achieve some degree of competence by paying close attention to a reliable recipe. Since a mistake, once made, may be difficult to correct, the next few pages are intended to save you from discouraging errors; you can benefit from some of our unfortunate experiences. For those of you who may be making a bold foray into the baker's domain for the first time (or trying again for that matter), we have brought together much of our accumulated knowledge about baking, with particular emphasis on using wholefoods ingredients.

While this will, we hope, eliminate failure, if you are not pleased with the end product, you may be cheered by the knowledge that there is hardly a baked item that cannot be "saved" by dunking it in a favorite beverage.

Know Your Ingredients

Flour

Flours differ in texture and in their ability to absorb moisture. Some are coarse and grainy, others fine and soft. Unless otherwise stated, the flour used in our recipes is a commercial all-purpose whole wheat. If you can get a more finely ground or softer whole wheat pastry flour, it will make a more delicate cake and a flakier pie crust, but you may need to use one to two extra tablespoons for every cup measure called for.

Sifting is generally not required, but flour should be stirred before measuring as it will pack down during storage. If a recipe instructs you to sift flour before measuring and you choose not to, decrease the amount used by one tablespoon per cup.

If you do not use the soy flour called for in some recipes, replace it with an equal amount of whole wheat flour. Results will be slightly coarser and drier. Do not add more soy flour than a recipe specifies, but if you wish to add some where it is not already indicated, follow the recommendations in "On Cooking: Fortifying Foods."

Sweetening

Mild-flavored clover and wildflower honeys, unsulfured molasses, and Grade B maple syrup are preferred in baking. You will find that we often use more than one sweetener in a recipe. While this may seem bothersome, it has the pleasant effect of toning down distinctive tastes so that no one predominates in the end.

Liquid sweeteners all attract moisture, keeping baked goods from staling rapidly. In most cases, you can expect cookies made with liquid sweeteners to be chewy rather than crisp.

Despite the fact that we have provided numerous kitchen-tested offerings, there will undoubtedly be some who wish to adapt old favorites to wholefoods ingredients. If you intend to do some experimenting, the following table is helpful, but we do not guarantee the results will always be as expected since many variables enter into baking conversions.

Sugar Substitutes in Baking

Replace each cup granulated sugar with one of the following:

> ½ to ¾ cup honey[1]
> ⅔ to ¾ cup maple syrup[1]
> ¾ cup molasses[2]
> ½ cup honey plus ¼ cup molasses[2]
> ½ cup honey plus ¼ maple syrup[1]

For each cup liquid sweetener used, reduce the liquid in the recipe by ¼ cup. If the recipe does not contain any

[1] For each cup honey or maple syrup used, ⅛ teaspoon baking soda will help the end results, although it is not crucial. When either of these are used with molasses, adjust leavening for "molasses only" as described in Note 2.

[2] For each cup molasses used, you must add ½ teaspoon baking soda and decrease the baking powder in the recipe by 2 teaspoons. If less than 1 cup of molasses is added, convert proportionately, that is ¼ teaspoon baking soda with ½ cup molasses, etc.

liquid, add ¼ cup additional flour per cup of liquid sweetening.

Shortening

Our baking is done exclusively with butter and liquid oil, preferably a light variety like corn or safflower. Butter adds to the flavor of baked goods and makes crisp cookies and flaky pie crusts. Oils, which are probably more healthful, make cakes and cookies chewier and pie crusts crunchy rather than flaky. A combination of oil and butter can give very nice results, especially if you first cream the two together in the blender or with the mixing blade of the food processor to a soft shortening consistency.

Leavening

Baking powder, baking soda, yeast, eggs, and entrapped air all affect the ultimate height of baked goods. Because both baking powder and baking soda are high in sodium, some people restrict their use. Low-sodium potassium-based substitutes are available and do an adequate job, but people with a very sensitive palate may be able to detect a trace of bitterness.

For even distribution of baking powder or baking soda in a batter, add them through a flour sifter or strainer.

The beating of a batter helps incorporate air, adding to the lightness of a cake, but this should only be done when indicated in the recipe. Batters that contain minimal liquid, fat, or sweetening will produce tough baked goods if overhandled.

The beating of eggs also helps leaven baked goods. Rising is further enhanced by beating the egg whites separately and folding them into a batter. Any time you omit or reduce baking powder or soda, whip the egg whites separately to help lighten cakes and cookies.

Liquid Ingredients

When fruit juices are used instead of water in baking they add to the sweetness, as well as the food value, and thus there is less need for concentrated sweeteners. At the same time, the acidity they add must be balanced by baking soda. If you are making such a conversion on your own, add ¼ teaspoon baking soda per ½ cup fruit juice and reduce the baking powder by 1 teaspoon.

Milk makes the inside of baked goods more tender and the surface crisp and brown. As you will notice, in our recipes we generally add nonfat dry milk powder to the dry ingredients and use water as our liquid. If you wish, you can replace the two with an equal volume of fluid milk.

Nuts and Seeds

Nuts and seeds, in pieces or as "meal" (see "On Cooking: Nut and Seed Meals"), add to the taste, texture, and food value of baked goods. One type of nut or seed can generally be substituted for another if you run short with only a slight difference in flavor, but this may result in a dramatically altered nutritional content. We have balanced the choice of nuts and seeds when they appear in a recipe so as to maximize nutrition as well as taste. A reliable table of food values, as well as the abbreviated figures on page 518 will help you to recognize the impact of any changes you may make.

Proper Techniques

A good baker has a sharp eye, a strong arm, and a light hand. The proper way to measure both liquid and dry ingredients is discussed in detail in "On Cooking: How to Measure." Be sure you understand measuring fully before you begin baking.

The terms used to describe each step in baking are quite precise in meaning. *Whipping,* for example, means beating hard at an increasingly fast pace until a light, delicate structure entraps the maximum volume of air. *Beating* also implies vigorous action. Nowadays mechanical aids such as the electric mixer and in some cases the food processor can replace the traditional wire whisk and wooden spoon, so that less time and physical effort are consumed. However, if a recipe calls for a specific tool, you should assume this is done for a purpose. Other important procedures like separating, whipping, and folding egg whites are found in "On Cooking: Egg Handling."

One additional instruction that often appears in baking is to *add dry and liquid ingredients alternately, mixing smooth after each addition*. To do this, begin with the dry ingredients and add the liquid as needed to make the batter smooth. The thicker the batter is, the gentler you should be when you mix; however, make sure all ingredients are completely moistened and evenly blended and that no lumps remain unless the recipe specifies otherwise.

Preparing the Pan

There are many opinions as to which method of preparing a pan is best and most recipes contain pertinent instructions. Because of their high fat content, pies are baked in ungreased pans, as are those cookies that are rich in fat. Sponge cakes and angel food cakes, which want to cling to the sides of the pan for support as they rise, are also generally baked in untreated pans.

Most other items are baked in *greased* or *greased and floured* pans, or pans *lined with paper*. These latter two instructions are explained below, but no matter what the instructions, the fat used to grease a pan must be one that withstands high temperatures. Soy and peanut oil are both good choices; butter burns easily and is usually not recommended. Some people wipe baking pans with a liquid lecithin, a substance that performs well but is messy to use.

Flouring a pan produces a thin, brown crust, which is not always desirable, but since flouring almost guaran-

tees easy removal of the cake from the pan, we prefer this approach. Using a pan with an insertable bottom also facilitates removal.

To *grease and flour* a pan, wipe the bottom and sides (unless otherwise directed) with oil to form a thin, even coating. Sprinkle flour lightly over the pan and shake it about until it adheres to the greased surfaces. Dump out excess flour.

To *grease and line with paper*, wipe the bottom of the pan with oil, then cover with a piece of wax paper cut to fit. Wipe the surface of the paper with oil. When peeled off, a little of the crust will probably adhere to the paper.

Inside the Oven

The oven should always be brought to the specified temperature before the baking pan is introduced. Cookies and unfilled pie crusts will not be harmed if they have to sit a few minutes, so you can wait until they are assembled, if you wish, before lighting the oven. Filled pies and cakes, however, are more temperamental and it is generally better to have the hot oven ready for them than vice versa. If you are uncertain how long it will take to assemble a recipe, light the oven after all ingredients have been readied and after the dry ingredients have been mixed together, but before they have been mixed with the liquid portion.

If you bake in a glass pan, the heat of the oven should be decreased by 25°F., as glass increases exterior browning; if unadjusted, baked goods may be overdone on the surface before the inside is properly cooked.

The weight of the pan may also affect baking, since heavier pans are better heat conductors than thin, light, less expensive ones, resulting in more even cooking. To create a more hefty pan and approximate the conditions in a professional bakery, place a cookie sheet under any baking pan. This has an added advantage: if you've miscalculated and the pie filling or cake batter overflows, it won't spill onto the bottom of the oven. (If this does happen, sprinkle the mess immediately with salt.)

Remember, never stack baking sheets in the oven, as this impedes air circulation. If cakes or pies are to be baked on two or more levels, stagger them so that one is not directly above another. If several pans are placed on one rack, it is important to leave space so that the air can circulate around them. Pans on upper levels will bake more quickly, as hot air always rises. Because heat may vary at the sides, back, and front of the oven, foods may cook at different rates, depending on their placement. Testing different spots with an oven thermometer will help you judge relative baking time.

Due to this variability in ovens, our recipe baking times are given only as a guide; you should check progress about 5 to 10 minutes before the specified baking time. When baking is almost complete, peek every two to three minutes until the baked goods are done to your satisfaction. Unfortunately, every time you open the oven heat is lost, so try not to be overanxious.

You will find more specific baking advice within the individual categories of baked goods.

One Last Message

You are now fortified with all you need to know in order to become a competent baker. But you should realize that, due to the ingredients preferred in wholefoods cookery, exact replicas of white sugar–white flour pastries are not always possible. Rather than trying to imitate the less adaptable baked goods and being disappointed, you should strive for new specialties that stand on their own. You will find yourself equipped

with more than enough selections in the pages that follow.

COOKIES

If you have never baked before, cookies are a good place to begin. Cookies are much less "temperamental" than cakes or other pastries, and most recipes are uncomplicated. If you have any questions, be sure to read the preceding introduction to baked goods. Then assemble all your ingredients and you're ready to begin.

The Batter

There are several different types of cookie batter:

(1) the *drop batter,* which should more accurately be called a "push" batter since it will need assistance to get it off the spoon;

(2) the *bar batter,* which has a thick pouring consistency (its most familiar form is brownie batter);

(3) and *rolled dough,* which is firm enough to roll and handle without sticking to your hands and the pastry cloth, and usually requires an hour or two of chilling.

Then there are variations of these basic batters, including:

(1) *slice batters,* which are molded and chilled so they can be sliced for baking;

(2) *the ball batter,* which is really a stiff drop batter that is generally chilled, formed into balls, placed on baking sheets, and flattened prior to baking as directed;

(3) and, finally, *press cookies,* which are also made from chilled dough, fashioned into fancy shapes on the baking sheet with the aid of a cookie press, pastry bag, or a sturdy plastic bag with a corner cut off.

If you prefer to make a drop batter into a rolled dough, just add additional flour, generally 2 to 2½ tablespoons per cup. Similarly, if you reduce the flour in a rolled cookie recipe, you can make drop cookies from it.

Baking powder is often used in making cookies and creates a better-textured product. Some people object to this ingredient and it can be omitted, but when it is, the cookies tend to be compact and hard rather than crunchy.

The Baking

The size of cookies can be increased or decreased from the recipe recommendations, but all the cookies on the sheet should be the same size for even baking.

The distance between cookies on a baking sheet varies with the size of the cookie and how runny the batter is. A one-inch border is the average spacing for rolled cookies that do not expand and for small drop cookies. Large drop cookies, which spread over a greater area, should be placed two inches apart.

Make sure you use a pan without sides or only a tiny lip. If you have less than a baking sheetful, cookies can be placed on the inserts of loose-bottom pans or on inverted pie tins. If you want to reuse the cookie sheets for the next batch, scrape off any clinging crumbs and wipe lightly with oil. Run cold water over the back to cool sheets down so that the succeeding cookies do not bake too rapidly.

Check cookies often during baking, and if they appear to be browning too fast, reduce the oven heat by 25 degrees. It is always better to under-bake cookies slightly, and many people actually prefer them this way; cookies that are over-cooked will be hard and bitter-tasting. Properly baked cookies will have a pale but obvious color and will be a little soft when they are removed from the oven. They become firm as they cool.

The recipe will generally tell you how soon to remove cookies from the baking sheet. Most are allowed to sit a minute or two; those that are particularly delicate may need to rest until they harden, while very sticky ones must be removed at once to be manageable. To do the least amount of damage when removing cookies, use a thin-bladed spatula. If you repeatedly have trouble removing cookies from the baking sheet, you can line it with foil and later you'll only have to peel off the paper.

Some people say that cookies can be cooled on a plate, but we do not agree. We recommend transferring them to a cooling rack or a similar surface that allows air circulation so they become properly crisp; never pile warm cookies on top of each other or they will stick.

Cookies for the Future

Unbaked cookie dough can be kept in the refrigerator for two to three weeks if you do not wish to do all your baking at once. Be sure to keep dough well covered to prevent it from drying out. Unbaked dough can also be frozen for six to nine months. Slice-and-bake cookie doughs are particularly suitable for freezing. Shape dough first into a roll, then wrap and freeze it. When you are ready to bake, slice the frozen dough with a sharp knife and bake as soon as the oven is ready. (If you wish, pack the dough into clean, empty frozen juice concentrate cans with the ends removed; seal them with foil and when ready to use, just push out the dough and slice along the edge of the can.)

Rolled and pressed cookies should be shaped before freezing, then frozen in a single layer, and stacked later with paper between the layers for easy removal.

Drop batters are the most difficult to contend with. If you wish to freeze unbaked drop cookies, shape the dough on greased baking sheets and freeze it. When frozen, transfer it to appropriate freezer containers. These cookies, can also be baked without defrosting.

You may also bake cookies and freeze them for long-term use. Cool completely before wrapping and use within 6 months for best quality.

BASIC COOKIE DOUGH

Many different cookies can be made from this one basic recipe. You can even divide the dough and make several varieties at one time.

¼ cup butter
¼ cup oil
¾ cup honey
1 egg
¼ teaspoon salt
selected flavorings (see variations below)
1 teaspoon baking powder
1¾ to 2 cups whole wheat flour

Preheat oven to 350°F.
Cream butter, oil, and honey until smooth and creamy. Beat in egg, salt, and the flavorings indicated in specific variations below.

Mix baking powder with flour and add to creamed mixture to make a smooth drop batter. Chill or not as convenient.

Drop by heaping teaspoonfuls onto a greased baking sheet and bake for about 12 minutes until firm. Remove from sheets when cookies emerge from the oven and cool on a rack.

Makes about 3½ dozen 2-inch cookies

Variations: For *Orange Cookies,* add 2 tablespoons undiluted orange juice concentrate as the flavoring. Flatten each cookie on the baking sheet by making a thumb print in the center. Dust with cinnamon.

For *Vanilla Cookies,* add 1 teaspoon vanilla extract. Flatten each cookie on the baking sheet using wet fingers. Dust with cinnamon.

For *Lemon–Nut Cookies,* add 2 tablespoons fresh lemon juice and ½ teaspoon minced rind as the flavorings. Add ½ to ¾ cup mixed sunflower seeds and chopped walnuts with the flour.

For *Coconut Cookies,* add ½ teaspoon vanilla extract and ½ to ⅔ cup shredded unsweetened coconut as the flavorings.

For *Peanut Cookies,* add ¾ cup chopped peanuts with flour. Leave as nuggets on the baking sheet or press with wet fingers to flatten.

For *Pecan Chip Cookies,* add ½ teaspoon vanilla extract and 2 tablespoons orange juice as the flavorings. Use 2 full cups flour and add ¾ cup chopped pecans and 1 cup chocolate or carob chips or pieces chopped from a solid block.

For *Sunflower–Date or Carob Chip Cookies,* add ½ teaspoon vanilla extract and 2 tablespoons orange juice as the flavorings. Use 2 full cups flour and add ¾ cup sunflower seeds and 1 cup carob chips or chopped dates.

For *Light Spice Cookies,* add ½ teaspoon vanilla extract, 1 teaspoon cinnamon, and ¼ teaspoon nutmeg as the flavorings. Use 2 full cups flour.

TOLL-FREE COOKIES

The updated chocolate chip cookie.

½ cup butter
½ cup honey
2 tablespoons orange juice
½ teaspoon vanilla extract
1¼ cups whole wheat flour
½ teaspoon baking soda
⅛ teaspoon salt
½ teaspoon cinnamon
1 egg, lightly beaten
½ cup combined sunflower seeds and walnut pieces
1 cup raisins or carob or chocolate chips

Preheat oven to 375°F.
Cream butter and honey until smooth and fluffy. Beat in orange juice and vanilla.

Combine flour, baking soda, salt, and cinnamon and add to the creamed mixture alternately with the beaten egg. Stir in nuts and raisins or chips.

Drop by rounded teaspoonfuls onto an ungreased baking sheet. Bake for 10 to 12 minutes until golden. Transfer to a rack and cool.

Makes 3½ dozen 2-inch cookies
Note: Freeze baked cookies for long-term keeping.

HONEY GRAHAMS

2 cups whole wheat flour
2 tablespoons nonfat dry milk powder

¼ teaspoon salt
½ teaspoon baking soda
½ teaspoon cinnamon
¼ teaspoon nutmeg
¼ cup oil
3 tablespoons honey
2 tablespoons molasses
¼ cup water

Preheat oven to 300°F.

Combine dry ingredients in a mixing bowl. Stir in oil. Pour in honey, molasses, and water and mix until smooth, kneading gently with hands to form a ball of dough. If too dry, add water; if too wet to roll, add flour.

Divide dough in half and roll each half on a lightly floured surface into a rectangle ⅛ inch thick. Transfer to an oiled, floured baking sheet and score with the tines of a fork or a dull knife blade into 1½ x 2-inch sections or pieces of other desired size. Prick evenly all over with a fork.

Bake for 20 minutes until firm but still pale gold in color. Transfer to a rack to cool.

Makes 60 1½ x 2-inch cookies

Note: These cookies keep for a very long time in a covered tin.

COTTAGE CHEESE COOKIES

A plain cookie that is a good companion to fruit or pudding.

1½ cups whole wheat flour
2 teaspoons baking powder
¼ teaspoon salt
¼ cup butter
6 tablespoons honey
½ cup cottage cheese
1½ teaspoons vanilla or almond extract
cinnamon (optional)

Preheat oven to 400°F.

Combine flour, baking powder, and salt. Cut in butter. Add honey, cottage cheese, and extract, and mix thoroughly, kneading with hands, to form a dough. Shape into two logs, each 2 inches around and about 4 inches long. Wrap in plastic wrap and chill.

Slice dough as thin as possible. The best way to do this is to hold a long piece of dental floss or heavy thread taut beneath dough and cross the ends over the dough with a quick, pulling motion.

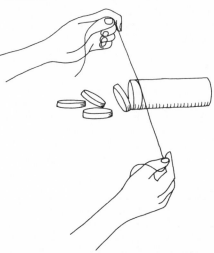

Place on a lightly oiled baking sheet, dust cookies lightly with cinnamon for some color, if desired, and bake for about 10 minutes, or until lightly browned. Cool on a rack.

Makes about 44 2-inch cookies

Note: If preferred, chilled dough can be rolled flat, ¼ inch thick, and cut into shapes with a cookie cutter.

Dough can also be shaped into logs and frozen for future baking. Wrap foil over plastic-wrapped logs or pack directly into cleaned frozen juice concentrate cans with ends removed, covering ends with foil or other freezer paper. Slice while frozen and bake as directed.

Variations: For a decorative effect, a dollop of fruit butter or jam can be put in the center before baking, or coarse unrefined sugar can be sprinkled lightly on top.

SHORTBREAD

A rich butter-flavored cookie.

1½ cups whole wheat flour
⅛ teaspoon salt
4 tablespoons butter
2 tablespoons oil
3 tablespoons honey
1 tablespoon maple syrup
½ teaspoon vanilla extract

Preheat oven to 350°F.

Combine flour and salt.

In a blender or processor fitted with a plastic blade, whip butter, oil, honey, maple syrup, and vanilla until smooth and creamy, the consistency of soft margarine.

Mix butter mixture into flour, using hands if most convenient, until dough is uniform and holds together. Pat dough gently to an even layer in an oiled 8-inch-square pan.

Bake for about 25 minutes until edges are lightly browned. While still warm, score into 2-inch squares with the prongs of a fork. Cool completely in the pan, then remove and divide along scored lines.

Makes 16 2-inch cookies

Note: Double the recipe can be baked in a 9 x 13-inch pan or jelly-roll pan.

Variation: For *Scotch Oat Shortbread,* replace 1 cup flour with 1 cup oats.

WALNUT DATE-TOPPED SHORTBREAD SQUARES

A rich, festive cookie.

For the Base

1 cup whole wheat flour
2 tablespoons butter
2 tablespoons oil
2 tablespoons honey
1 tablespoon maple syrup
¼ teaspoon vanilla extract

For the Topping

2 tablespoons whole wheat flour
⅛ teaspoon salt
½ teaspoon cinnamon
¼ teaspoon baking soda
½ cup chopped dates
½ cup chopped walnuts
⅓ cup orange, pineapple, or apple juice
2 tablespoons honey
½ teaspoon vanilla extract

Preheat oven to 350°F.

Place flour for the base in a mixing bowl and cut in butter and oil. Stir in honey, maple syrup, and vanilla and mix with hands to form a smooth dough.

Press base into an oiled 8-inch square pan. Bake for 15 minutes until barely firm and a little colored at the edges.

While base bakes, prepare topping by combining flour, salt, cinnamon, baking soda, dates, and nuts, then stirring in juice, honey and vanilla.

Spread topping over partially baked crust. Return to the oven for 15 minutes; topping will not be quite set when done.

Cool and cut into squares to serve.

Makes 9 big squares

Note: Double the recipe can be baked in a 9 x 13-inch pan. To cut sticky dried dates, dip scissors or knife into some flour first.

BANANA DROP CAKES

Large, soft cookies.

1¾ cups whole wheat flour
¼ cup soy flour
1 tablespoon baking powder
⅔ cup nonfat dry milk powder
½ teaspoon salt
1 teaspoon cinnamon
½ teaspoon nutmeg
⅔ cup chopped walnuts
⅓ cup sunflower seeds
½ cup unsweetened carob chips (optional)
2 eggs, lightly beaten
½ cup oil
⅔ cup honey
1½ cups mashed banana (3 medium bananas)

Preheat oven to 350°F.

Combine first seven ingredients with nuts, seeds and chips in a mixing bowl. Make a well in the center; add remaining ingredients and stir until smooth.

Drop by heaping soupspoons onto an oiled baking sheet. Bake for 10 to 12 minutes until firm. Let set for 1 minute in the pan, then transfer to a rack to cool.

Makes 32 cookies

Variation: For *Banana Bars,* spread batter in an oiled 9 x 13-inch pan. Bake in a 350°F. oven for about 20 minutes, or until a toothpick inserted comes out clean. Cool in the pan and cut into bars to serve. These are delicious topped with Whipped Orange–Sesame Cream.

GINGER COOKIES

Crunchy and spicy.

½ cup molasses
1 tablespoon oil
½ teaspoon baking soda
1 teaspoon hot water
1½ teaspoons ginger
½ teaspoon cinnamon
1¾ cups whole wheat flour

Preheat oven to 350°F.
Combine molasses, oil, baking soda dissolved in hot water, ginger, and cinnamon. Add enough flour to make a dough firm enough to roll. Use hands if necessary to work in.
Roll thin on a floured surface and cut into shapes with a cookie cutter.
Baked on a greased baking sheet for about 10 minutes. Cool on a rack.
Makes about 2 dozen cookies

JUMBO WALNUT COOKIES

⅓ cup butter
¼ cup oil
½ cup maple syrup
5 cups whole wheat flour
¾ cup walnuts, ground fine (with a
  few small pieces remaining if desired)
1 teaspoon cinnamon
½ teaspoon nutmeg
½ teaspoon salt
½ cup orange juice
1 cup honey
1 teaspoon baking soda

Cream butter, oil, and maple syrup. Combine flour, walnut meal, cinnamon, nutmeg, and salt. Combine orange juice, honey, and baking soda in a separate container. Add these two mixtures alternately to the creamed shortening to make a thick, evenly blended dough. Chill for several hours, or about 20 minutes in the freezer.
Preheat oven to 350°F.
Take one fourth the dough from the refrigerator at a time and roll gently on a well-floured surface until ¼ inch thick. Cut into 3-inch rounds. (A 6½-

ounce tuna can with ends removed serves well as a cutter.) Lift with a spatula and transfer to an oiled, floured baking sheet. Continue with all dough, rerolling outtakes.
Bake for about 12 minutes until lightly colored but still on the soft side. Cool for 5 minutes on a baking sheet, then transfer to a rack to cool.
Makes about 40 cookies
Note: As this makes a lot of big cookies you may want to freeze part of the dough or some of the baked cookies for the future. The recipe can also be cut in half.
Variation: For *Great Big Honey-Molasses Cookies,* omit ground walnuts, replace the ½ cup maple syrup used in the creamed mixture with ½ cup honey, and replace the 1 cup honey combined with the orange juice with 1 cup molasses.

MR. BILL COOKIES

Gingerbread men for a new generation.

5 cups whole wheat flour
1 teaspoon baking soda
1 teaspoon baking powder
½ teaspoon nutmeg
1 teaspoon cinnamon
1½ teaspoons ground ginger
¼ cup oil
¼ cup melted butter
½ cup honey
1 cup molasses
¼ cup milk

Combine first six ingredients in a bowl. Combine oil, butter, honey, molasses, and milk separately, pour into the dry ingredients, and mix with a wooden spoon to form a stiff dough. After the initial mixing, dough can be kneaded with hands to combine if easier. Chill for 1 hour or longer.
Preheat oven to 375°F.
Take one fourth the dough from the refrigerator at a time and roll on a well-floured surface ¼ inch thick for chewy cookies, ⅛ inch for crisp ones. Cut into men or other desired shapes.
Transfer with a spatula to an oiled, floured baking sheet, arranging them close together but not touching. About

one fourth the dough can be accommodated per sheet.

Bake for 10 minutes. Loosen from pan while still hot, let sit a few minutes, then transfer to a rack to cool.

Makes about 60 4-inch men, or 3 pounds cookies

Note: To make your own cut-out for Mr. Bill, draw a 4-inch figure on cardboard, cut it out, and lay it on top of rolled dough. Cut around pattern with a small paring knife. If you wish to decorate him, press in pieces of raisins for eyes, slivered almonds for mouth, peanut halves or sunflower seeds for buttons, etc., before baking.

For fewer cookies, cut the recipe in half (no adjustments needed).

RICH ALMOND COOKIES

Lots of ground almonds go into the dough for a very rich cookie that is especially appealing to adults.

1½ cups almonds
1¼ cups whole wheat flour
¼ cup butter
¼ cup oil
¼ cup honey
½ teaspoon vanilla extract

Chop ¼ cup almonds in blender, processor, or drum grater and set aside. Grind remaining 1 cup to a fine meal.

Mix almond meal with flour. Work in butter and oil, then honey and extract to make a well-blended dough. This can be done by hand or by mixing together with the plastic blade of the food processor until dough forms a mass. (Dough will be a bit sticky.) Chill for 1 hour or longer.

Preheat oven to 350°F.

Pinch off 1 teaspoon dough at a time and shape into small, fat ovals about 2 x 1 x ¼ inches. Press tops into

reserved chopped almonds and place on an ungreased baking sheet.

Bake for 12 to 15 minutes until lightly browned. Cool on pan for about 10 minutes, then transfer to a rack to cool completely.

Makes 4 dozen small cookies

Variation: For *Rich Walnut Cookies,* replace almonds with a mixture of 1 cup walnuts and ½ cup sunflower seeds.

ALMOND DROPS

No added fat or flour. These are tiny cookies, so watch yourself—before you know it, you can eat the whole batch.

1 cup almonds
2 egg whites
¼ cup honey
½ teaspoon vanilla extract
¼ teaspoon almond extract
about 1 teaspoon nutmeg

Preheat oven to 350°F.

Grind almonds to meal. Mix to a smooth paste with egg whites, honey, and extracts.

Drop by teaspoons onto an oiled, floured baking sheet. Sprinkle with nutmeg.

Bake for 6 to 8 minutes until firm but still rather pale. Loosen from baking sheet and, when firm enough to move, transfer to a rack to cool.

Makes about 3 dozen 1-inch cookies

SPRITZ COOKIES

A rich butter cookie made with pressed dough.

½ cup butter
½ cup honey
2 tablespoons maple syrup
2 egg yolks
1½ teaspoons almond extract
⅛ teaspoon salt
2 cups whole wheat flour

Preheat oven to 400°F.

Cream butter, honey, and maple syrup. Beat in egg yolks, extract, and salt. When smooth, stir in flour to make a stiff dough.

Force through a pastry bag in 3-inch lengths onto an ungreased baking sheet. Shape each piece into an "S" or "O" and press with wet fingers to flatten, making ridges in the spaces between the fingers.

Bake for 10 minutes until lightly browned at the edges but still quite pale. Cool on a rack.

Makes about 3 dozen cookies

Note: If you don't have a pastry bag, you can fashion a "shooter" by cutting the corner off a sturdy plastic bag and forcing the dough through the hole.

Variation: One whole egg can replace 2 egg yolks, although the yolks are preferred.

MANDELBROT

This Jewish specialty is a dry, lightly sweetened almond bread that falls somewhere between coffee cake and zwieback. A perfect dunker.

1 egg
¼ cup honey
2 tablespoons oil
⅛ teaspoon salt
1 teaspoon lemon juice
¼ teaspoon almond extract
1¼ cups whole wheat flour
1½ teaspoons baking powder
⅓ cup coarsely ground almonds

Preheat oven to 375°F.

Beat egg with honey until foamy. Beat in oil, salt, lemon juice, and almond extract. Add flour, baking powder, and nuts, and mix well to form a stiff, evenly blended dough.

Pat into a loaf 3 inches wide, 8 inches long, and 1 inch thick on an oiled, floured baking sheet.

Bake for 20 to 25 minutes until lightly browned. Cool slightly and, while still warm, slice into bars ½ inch wide.

Makes one 8-inch loaf; 16 slices

TRADITIONAL PEANUT BUTTER COOKIES

⅔ cup honey
⅓ cup oil
1 cup peanut butter
1 egg
¼ teaspoon salt (omit if peanut butter is salted)
½ teaspoon vanilla extract
¼ cup nonfat dry milk powder
1½ cups whole wheat flour
1 teaspoon baking powder

Preheat oven to 375°F.

Beat honey, oil, and peanut butter together until smooth. Beat in egg, salt, vanilla, and milk powder.

Combine flour and baking powder. Add to peanut butter mixture, using your hands if necessary to form a thick but not dry dough. If soft, add up to ¼ cup more flour.

Form into 1½-inch balls, using about 1 tablespoon for each. Place on a lightly oiled baking sheet and flatten with a fork dipped in hot water or your thumb.

Bake for 10 to 12 minutes until top begins to color. Do not overbake. Remove from pan and cool on a rack.

Makes about 4 dozen 2-inch cookies

PEANUT BUTTER–OAT COOKIES

A barely sweet cookie, totally wheat-free and about the simplest of all baked treats.

¼ cup honey
¼ cup maple syrup
¼ cup peanut butter
2 eggs
1 teaspoon vanilla extract
2½ cups oats

Preheat oven to 350°F.

Beat together honey, maple syrup, peanut butter, eggs, and vanilla, using a fork, wire whisk, or rotary beater. When smooth, stir in oats.

Drop by rounded teaspoons onto an oiled baking sheet. Flatten slightly with fingers.

Bake for 10 to 12 minutes until lightly colored. Let sit for about 30 seconds on the baking sheet, then transfer to a rack to cool.

Makes about 40 1½-inch cookies

Variations: Add up to ½ cup sunflower seeds or currants.

APPLE ROCKS

Nuggets of apples, dates, nuts, and oats.

¼ cup butter
¼ cup oil
½ cup honey
2 eggs
1 cup chopped dates
1 cup chopped peeled apple
½ cup oats
½ cup chopped walnuts
¼ cup wheat germ
½ teaspoon cinnamon
¼ teaspoon salt
1¼ cups whole wheat flour
½ teaspoon baking powder

Preheat oven to 350°F.

Cream butter, oil, and honey. Beat in eggs. Stir remaining ingredients into egg mixture, combining the flour and baking powder together before they are added so baking powder is evenly distributed.

Mix batter smooth. Drop by teaspoons onto a greased baking sheet.

Bake for 15 to 20 minutes until lightly browned. Slide spatula under cookies while still hot to loosen and, when firm, transfer to a rack to cool.

Makes 4 to 5 dozen cookies

SOFT OATMEAL COOKIES

½ cup whole wheat flour
1½ cups oats
1 teaspoon baking powder
¼ cup chopped walnuts
⅓ cup butter (at room temperature)
⅓ cup honey
1 egg

1 teaspoon vanilla extract
½ cup raisins (optional)

Preheat oven to 375°F.

Combine flour, oats, baking powder, and nuts. Beat together butter, honey, and egg. Stir into oat mixture. Add raisins if desired.

Drop by tablespoons onto an oiled baking sheet. Pat each cookie down lightly to form rounds ¼ inch thick.

Bake for 12 to 15 minutes until lightly browned. Leave on the baking sheet for a few minutes to cool, then transfer to a rack.

Makes 16 cookies

Variation: Replace walnuts with pecans or shredded, unsweetened coconut.

CARROT COOKIES

Too bad rabbits can't bake.

1 cup whole wheat flour
1 teaspoon baking powder
⅛ teaspoon salt
1 cup rolled oats
¼ cup sunflower seeds
¼ cup walnut pieces
¼ cup raisins
1 cup shredded carrot
½ cup honey
½ cup oil
¼ teaspoon vanilla extract

Preheat oven to 375°F.

Combine flour, baking powder, salt, and oats, and mix well. Stir in seeds, nuts, raisins, and carrots.

Beat together honey, oil, and vanilla. Stir into flour mixture until well moistened.

Drop by rounded teaspoons onto an oiled baking sheet. Flatten with fingers, compressing dough so cookies hold together.

Bake for 10 to 12 minutes until lightly colored. Let sit for 1 minute on the sheet, then transfer to a rack to cool.

Makes about 40 cookies

DRIED FRUIT BARS

A flour and oat crust with softened dried fruit sandwiched inside. A relative of fig newtons.

For the Crust
1 cup whole wheat flour
1 cup oats
½ teaspoon baking soda
⅛ teaspoon salt
⅓ cup oil
¼ cup honey

Filling #1—Prune–Orange
1½ cups cut-up dried prunes
¼ cup orange juice
2 tablespoons honey

Filling #2—Date
1 cup chopped dates
¼ cup water
2 tablespoons honey

Filling #3—Fig
1 cup chopped figs
¼ cup apple juice
2 tablespoons honey

Filling #4—Apricot
1½ cups diced dried apricots
¼ cup orange or apple juice
2 tablespoons honey

Preheat oven to 350°F.

For the crust, combine flour, oats, baking soda, and salt. Stir in oil and honey until well blended.

Combine dry fruit and liquid for filling of choice in a small saucepan. Simmer for about 5 minutes until soft and thick. Stir in honey.

Pat half of crust into a greased 8-inch-square pan, making a thin layer. Spread filling to cover, getting it into the corners too. Pat remaining dough into an 8-inch square on wax paper and invert over filling. Remove paper.

Bake for 20 to 25 minutes until firm and golden. Cool in the pan. Cut in small squares to serve.

Makes 25 1½-inch squares

DATE BARS

Light in texture but chock full of dates and nuts.

2 eggs
¼ cup honey
1 cup chopped dates
½ cup walnut pieces
½ teaspoon vanilla extract
6 tablespoons whole wheat flour
½ teaspoon baking powder

Preheat oven to 325°F.

Beat eggs until light. Beat in honey. Add dates, nuts, and vanilla.

Combine flour and baking powder and stir into date mixture until evenly blended.

Pour into a well-oiled 8- or 9-inch square pan. Bake for 20 to 25 minutes until lightly browned on top. Cool in the pan. Cut into squares or bars to serve.

Makes 16 2-inch squares, or 32 bars, 2 x 1 inches

Note: To double, use 3 eggs, double remaining ingredients, and bake in a 9 x 13-inch pan.

To cut sticky dried dates, dip scissors or knife in flour first.

NIKKI'S NEW BROWNIES

Our well-loved brownie recipe is even better now with combined unrefined sweeteners.

3 squares (3 ounces) unsweetened baking chocolate
6 tablespoons milk
3 eggs
¾ cup honey
⅓ cup maple syrup
1½ teaspoons vanilla extract
½ teaspoon salt
1 cup whole wheat flour
¼ cup oil
¾ cup walnut pieces

Preheat oven to 350°F.

Combine chocolate and milk in a small saucepan or the top of a double boiler and cook over very low heat or a flame tamer until chocolate is creamy. Remove from heat and let cool a little.

Beat eggs with honey, maple syrup, and vanilla. Beat in cooled chocolate and remaining ingredients. Pour into an oiled 9 x 13-inch baking pan.

Bake for 25 minutes. Cool in the pan and cut into squares to serve.

Makes 18 brownies

CHOCOLATE NUT SQUARES

A delicate chocolate cookie, much like a thin brownie.

1 ounce (1 square) unsweetened baking chocolate
¼ cup butter
½ cup honey
1 egg
¼ teaspoon vanilla extract
6 tablespoons whole wheat flour
⅛ teaspoon salt
⅔ cup finely chopped walnuts or hazelnuts

Preheat oven to 400°F.
Combine chocolate and butter in a small saucepan and melt over very low heat. Remove from heat and beat in honey, egg, vanilla, flour, and salt.
Spread batter thinly into two greased 8-inch-square pans. Sprinkle with nuts.
Bake for 10 to 12 minutes. Do not overbake. Cool a minute in the pan, then cut into 2-inch squares. When completely cool, remove from the pan.
Makes 32 2-inch squares

RUGELACH

Eastern Europe is the home of rugelach, a popular miniature filled pastry.

For the Pastry
1½ cups whole wheat flour
½ teaspoon salt
2 teaspoons baking powder
¼ cup butter (at room temperature)
⅓ cup honey
½ cup cottage cheese

Fruit–Nut Filling
⅓ cup chopped walnuts
½ cup chopped raisins
2 tablespoons wheat germ
¾ teaspoon cinnamon

Poppy Seed Filling
3 tablespoons honey
2 to 3 tablespoons poppy seeds

Combine flour, salt, and baking powder. Cut in butter with a pastry blender or wire whisk. If you find it easier, work in butter with your fingers.
Stir honey and cottage cheese into flour mixture and knead gently with hands until dough holds together in a ball. If too dry, add more cottage cheese. Cover with plastic wrap or place in a plastic bag and chill for a few hours. When ready to assemble, take out ingredients for selected filling.
Preheat oven to 400°F.
Divide dough into thirds, shape into balls, and roll each ball into a thin 9-inch round from center out.
For *Fruit–Nut Rugelach,* cut each circle into 8 wedges and, if not very thin, roll each wedge in all directions to make broad triangles. Combine filling ingredients, sprinkle some on each triangle, and roll from broad end to tip to enclose filling. Bend slightly to form a crescent.
For *Poppy Seed Rugelach,* roll each circle as thin as possible initially and spread each uncut round with 1 tablespoon honey. Sprinkle generously with poppy seeds. Cut into 8 wedges and roll from broad end to tip to enclose filling. Bend slightly to form a crescent.
Place rugelach on an ungreased baking sheet and bake for about 10 minutes until lightly browned. Cool on a rack.
Makes 24 rugelach

HAMENTASCHEN

Hamentaschen are a tradition of the Jewish holiday, Purim. The cookie is shaped to resemble the three-cornered hat worn by the evil Hamen.

Cookie Dough
3 tablespoons butter
3 tablespoons oil
3 tablespoons honey
1 egg yolk
½ teaspoon grated or minced lemon rind
1¼ to 1⅓ cups whole wheat flour

Prune Filling
1 cup chopped dried prunes
¼ cup orange juice
¼ cup honey
1 egg white

Cream butter, oil, and honey for dough. Beat in egg yolk and lemon rind.

Add flour as needed to make a stiff dough. Chill for at least 2 hours.

For filling, combine prunes, orange juice, and honey in a saucepan and simmer for about 10 minutes, mashing with a fork, until thick.

Preheat oven to 375°F.

Roll dough about ⅜ inch thick and cut into 3-inch rounds. (A 6½-inch tuna can with the ends removed works well as a cutter.) Reroll outtakes.

Transfer rounds to an oiled baking sheet and place 1 tablespoon filling in the center of each. Form into triangles by rolling up sides to wall in the filling; pinch the corners to hold. Some filling should be visible in the center.

Beat egg white with a spoonful of water. Paint over tops of cookies.

Bake for 12 to 15 minutes, or until golden. Cool on a rack.

Makes 10 cookies

CAKES

Cake baking is a more exacting science than cookie making, but throughout history cakes have been held in such high esteem that the precision they demand is clearly worth your while. The introduction to baked goods contains background information that will enhance your success.

Preparation and Handling

Although it is not essential, it is preferable to have all ingredients at room temperature before you assemble a cake. Thus, the first thing you should do is remove the eggs, flour, oil, and other appropriate ingredients from the refrigerator, as far as an hour ahead if convenient.

Cake batters come in a variety of consistencies, all of which must be mixed smooth so that the ingredients are well moistened and no lumps remain. Most often they have a thick pouring consistency, but some coffee cake and kuchen batters are so thick they must be spread with a spatula or spoon. Cake batters made with lots of beaten egg whites may be light and cloudlike in appearance.

To settle cake batter evenly in the pan and remove air holes, you may want to give the filled pan a good bang on the counter. Do not, however, do this with cakes that are leavened with beaten egg white, for they depend on entrapped air for their lightness, and rough handling will reduce the volume.

Since cakes rise more in the center than they do at the sides, for a more level surface you can push the batter lightly up at the edges and leave a slight depression in the middle. If your loaf cake cracks as it rises, don't be alarmed; this is practically unavoidable because of the depth of the pan.

Baking Guidelines

If you find yourself without the proper pan, consult "Baker's Math" (page 511) to find the best substitute. To allow for rising, a cake pan should not be more than two thirds full. If you have no other choice, a 9-inch pan can replace an 8-inch pan; the resulting cake will be a bit thinner (and vice versa). Remember, however, that the size and shape of the pan will influence the baking time. With a wider pan than specified, less time is needed. A batter baked in a tube pan, which conducts heat from both the inside and outside, will cook faster than the same amount of batter in a pan lacking a center well. Cake batter baked in small pans, such as cupcakes, not only will cook more quickly but will require a hotter oven to prevent internal drying. And, when baking in a clear glass pan, the oven temperature should be reduced by 25 degrees.

Cakes are more delicate than other baked goods and must be regarded with respect during baking. Place them on a rack in the middle of the oven and try not to peek until baking time is almost over.

When baking is completed, a toothpick or piece of straw (from a new broom) inserted into the center will come out clean. If it is damp and coated with batter, baking should be continued. A cake that is adequately baked will spring back when lightly pressed. If it is removed from the oven too soon, the cake will be damp and likely to fall. A cake that is overbaked will be dry, if not actually burned.

Cooling

Sheet cakes, brownies, and coffee cakes are generally cooled in the pan where they will stay fresh longer. Cakes rich in fat, and those that are to be iced, are allowed to rest in the pan for 10 minutes, and are then transferred to a rack to cool. Cakes have a tendency to split if removed from the pan too soon; if they are left to cool completely in the pan, however, they may become soggy.

To remove cake, run the thin blade of a spatula or blunt knife around the inside of the pan and carefully loosen the bottom edges. Invert the pan on a rack or plate and shake it if necessary so that the cake falls out. If cake does not come loose, insert a thin spatula around the cake again, prying the bottom, and invert once more. As soon as the cake comes free, turn it right-side up on a rack and let it cool completely before frosting or cutting.

Note: While cookie and pie recipes can be multiplied or divided logically, this is not always true for cakes. It is best not to alter cake recipes, but if you do multiply the recipe, do not increase the salt proportionately.

YELLOW YOGURT CAKE

An excellent basic cake with a moist, dense, but tender crumb that contains no fat other than what's in the eggs and the yogurt.

> **2 eggs**
> **¾ cup honey**
> **1 cup yogurt**
> **1 teaspoon vanilla extract**
> **1¾ cups whole wheat flour**
> **1 teaspoon baking powder**
> **½ teaspoon baking soda**
> **⅛ teaspoon salt**
> **1 recipe Buttercream or Chocolate Cream Frosting (pages 414–415)**
> **chopped walnuts**

Preheat oven to 350°F.

Beat eggs until very light. Beat in honey. Add yogurt and vanilla and beat until creamy.

Combine flour, baking powder, baking soda, and salt, making sure baking powder and baking soda are evenly mixed and not caked. Fold into egg mixture gently but thoroughly. Pour into an oiled, floured 8-inch-square pan.

Bake for 30 to 35 minutes. Cool for 10 minutes in the pan, then remove to a rack to cool completely.

Frost when cool, and sprinkle chopped walnuts on top.

Makes one 8-inch square; serves 9 to 12

Variations: For *Orange–Apricot Cake,* which needs no icing, prepare Yogurt Cake batter and add ¼ cup chopped dried apricots. Bake as usual. Stir 2 tablespoons honey into ½ cup orange juice to dissolve. When cake comes from the oven, prick the cake surface all over with a toothpick and gradually pour orange juice on top. Leave in the pan to cool and absorb juice. Cut and serve from the pan.

YOGURT SPICE CAKE

A lightly spiced cake to serve plain or with a whipped topping.

> **2 eggs**
> **½ cup honey**
> **¼ cup molasses**
> **1 cup yogurt**

1¾ cups whole wheat flour
1 teaspoon baking soda
¼ teaspoon salt
1 teaspoon cinnamon
½ teaspoon nutmeg
⅛ teaspoon ginger

Preheat oven to 350°F.
Beat eggs until very light. Beat in honey and molasses. Beat in yogurt until creamy.

Combine remaining ingredients, making sure baking soda is evenly distributed. Fold into egg mixture gently but thoroughly. Pour into an oiled, floured 8-inch-square pan.

Bake for 30 to 35 minutes. Cool for 10 minutes in the pan, then remove to a rack to cool completely.

Makes one 8-inch square; serves 9 to 12

YOGURT POUND CAKE

A rich version of Yellow Yogurt Cake that is extremely tender and flavorful.

2 cups plus 2 tablespoons whole wheat flour
1 teaspoon baking soda
1 teaspoon baking powder
½ teaspoon cinnamon
⅛ teaspoon ground cardamom, or the crushed seeds from 2 pods (optional)
½ cup butter
¾ cup honey
3 eggs
1 teaspoon almond extract
1 cup yogurt

Preheat oven to 350°F.
Mix dry ingredients. Cream butter and honey in a large bowl. When smooth, beat in eggs one at a time. Beat in extract.

Add dry ingredients to creamed mixture alternately with yogurt, stirring smooth after each addition. Pour batter into an oiled, floured 9 x 5-inch loaf pan. Rap on counter to remove air.

Bake for 50 to 60 minutes until top is golden and cake tests done. Cool for 10 minutes in the pan, then remove to a rack.

Makes one 2-pound loaf

ALMOND SPONGE TORTE

A light nut cake that contains no flour.

2 eggs, separated
3 tablespoons honey
1 tablespoon maple syrup
½ cup almonds, ground to meal
½ tablespoon lemon juice
pinch salt

Preheat oven to 350°F.
Beat egg yolks until thick. Gradually beat in honey and maple syrup. Stir in almond meal and lemon juice.

Beat whites in a separate bowl until stiff, adding a pinch of salt when they become foamy. Fold into yolk mixture. Spread in a greased, floured 8-inch layer-cake pan.

Bake for about 20 minutes until puffed and brown. Turn off oven, leave door open, and let sit for 10 minutes. When cake has settled, remove from pan and cool.

Makes one 8-inch round; serves 6
Variation: For *Almond Sponge Tarts,* prepare one-half Cookie Dough Crust (page 398) and use to line 6 muffin cups. Chill. Fill with Almond Sponge Torte batter and bake as above. Remove tarts from the pan to cool.

GIANT "TWINKIE"

An excellent birthday cake.

The Cake
4 eggs
½ cup honey
1 teaspoon vanilla extract
¾ cup whole wheat flour
¾ teaspoon baking powder
¼ teaspoon salt

Buttercream Filling
¼ cup butter
2 tablespoons safflower or other light oil
¼ cup honey
1 teaspoon vanilla extract
¼ cup nonfat dry milk powder
¼ cup ice water
1 teaspoon lemon juice

Preheat oven to 375°F. Oil and flour a 10 x 15-inch jelly-roll pan.
Beat eggs with an electric mixer at

high speed until very foamy. Slowly pour in honey, continuing to beat. Add vanilla. Sift flour, baking powder, and salt directly over eggs and fold gently but thoroughly until batter is smooth. Pour batter into prepared pan and spread evenly.

Bake for 12 to 15 minutes, or until golden and springy. Cool in the pan for 10 minutes, loosen with a spatula, and turn out onto a flat surface to cool completely.

To prepare filling, cream together butter, oil, and honey. This can be done with an electric mixer or in a food processor fitted with a plastic blade. Beat in vanilla.

In a small mixing bowl combine milk powder and ice water. Beat, preferably with an electric mixer, until foamy. Add lemon juice and continue to beat until consistency of whipped cream. This may take as long as 10 minutes. When whipped, add creamed butter mixture and beat at high speed until smooth and thick like buttercream.

Cut cake into two pieces. Spread filling evenly over one piece. Top with remaining cake. Cut into squares to serve.

Makes one 8 x 10-inch cake; 20 2-inch squares

Variation: For *Individual "Twinkies,"* cut cake into 2½ x 1½-inch pieces. Wrap individually in plastic wrap and store in the refrigerator. For long-term storage, freeze.

DEVIL'S FOOD CAKE

A rich cake for special occasions.

2 cups whole wheat flour
½ cup cocoa, carob powder, or a mixture
1 teaspoon baking powder
½ teaspoon baking soda
¼ teaspoon salt
¼ cup oil
¼ cup butter
1 cup honey
2 eggs
1 teaspoon vanilla extract
1 cup buttermilk

Preheat oven to 350°F.

Place flour in a bowl and sift in cocoa or carob, baking powder, baking soda, and salt. Mix well.

In a separate large bowl cream oil, butter, and honey. Beat in eggs, one at a time, and vanilla until mixture is light and fluffy.

Add flour mixture alternately with buttermilk to creamed mixture, stirring gently but thoroughly after each addition. Batter will be like chocolate pudding in consistency. Spread batter into two greased, floured 9-inch layer-cake pans. Rap on counter to level.

Bake for about 25 minutes until cake tests done. Do not overbake. Cool in the pan for 10 minutes, then transfer to a rack to cool completely.

Frost and fill with Whipped White Icing, Whipped Ricotta Topping, or Chocolate Cream Frosting and Filling. If desired, add a layer of sliced fruit to the filling.

Makes one 9-inch layer cake; serves 8

"DEVIL DOGS"

½ recipe for Devil's Food Cake (above)
Buttercream "Twinkie" Filling (page 383)
cocoa

Preheat oven to 350°F. Oil a 12 x 15-inch jelly-roll pan and dust with cocoa. Shake out excess.

Pour batter into pan and spread evenly with a spatula. Bake for 12 to 15 minutes. Cool in the pan for 10 minutes; loosen with a spatula and turn out onto a flat surface to cool completely.

Cut cake in half and spread one piece with Buttercream Filling. Cover with remaining cake.

Cut into 2½ x 1½-inch bars, wrap individually in plastic wrap, and store in the refrigerator. For long-term storage, freeze.

Makes about 20 Devil Dogs

Menu Suggestions: For a party, leave uncut and serve as a Giant Devil Dog.

MARBLE CAKE

3 tablespoons butter
2 tablespoons oil
¾ cup honey
2 tablespoons maple syrup
1 egg
½ teaspoon vanilla extract
¼ teaspoon salt
2 cups minus 2 tablespoons whole wheat flour
½ teaspoon baking soda
2 teaspoons baking powder
1 cup yogurt
2 tablespoons cocoa
1 teaspoon cinnamon
2 tablespoons orange juice

Preheat oven to 350°F.
Beat butter, oil, honey, and maple syrup together until smooth. Beat in egg, vanilla, and salt.
Combine flour with baking soda and baking powder. Add to egg mixture alternately with yogurt, beating smooth after each addition. Pour two-thirds batter into a greased, floured 8½-inch loaf pan.
Make a paste of cocoa, cinnamon, and orange juice, and stir into remaining batter. Pour dark batter over batter in pan and cut in with a knife, making swirls to create a marbled effect.
Bake for 50 to 60 minutes until cake tests done. Cool in the pan for 10 minutes, then transfer to a rack to cool completely.
Makes one 8½-inch loaf; 8 thick slices

GINGERBREAD

½ cup sour milk or ½ cup sweet milk mixed with ½ tablespoon vinegar and left at room temperature for 10 minutes to "sour"
1 teaspoon baking soda
¾ cup molasses
¼ cup oil
1 egg
⅛ teaspoon salt
1 teaspoon ginger
½ teaspoon cinnamon
2 cups whole wheat flour
¼ cup raisins

Preheat oven to 350°F.
Prepare sour milk if necessary. Dissolve baking soda in molasses in a mixing bowl. Beat in remaining ingredients, including the sour milk. Pour into a greased, floured 8- or 9-inch pan. Bake for 30 to 35 minutes. Cool in the pan.
Serves 8 or 9
Variation: For *Apple-Topped Gingerbread*, line the bottom of the baking dish with wax paper. Melt 2 tablespoons butter, combine with ¼ cup molasses, and spread over paper. Peel and thinly slice 1 good-sized apple and arrange over bottom of the pan. Pour in gingerbread batter and bake as directed. Cool in the pan for 10 minutes, invert on a rack, peel off paper, and cool completely.

FRENCH NUT CAKE

This is an extremely rich cake. Slice thin to serve.

1⅓ cups whole wheat flour
3 tablespoons sunflower seeds, ground into meal (about ¼ cup meal)
⅔ cup walnuts, ground into meal (about ¾ cup meal)
1½ teaspoons baking powder
¼ cup butter
¼ cup oil
1 cup honey
2 eggs
½ teaspoon almond extract
½ teaspoon vanilla extract
pinch salt
¼ cup milk

Preheat oven to 325°F.
Combine flour, nut meals, and baking powder.
In a large bowl, cream butter, oil, and honey. Beat in eggs one at a time. Beat in extracts and salt.
Add flour mixture and milk alternately to creamed mixture, stirring smooth after each addition. Pour batter into an oiled, floured 8½-inch loaf pan.
Bake for 1¼ hours until cake tests done with a toothpick. Cool in the pan for 20 minutes, then remove to a rack.
Makes one 8½-inch loaf; 16 half-inch slices

APPLESAUCE CAKE

Unlike many other cakes, only one bowl is required for mixing this one.

2 tablespoons butter
2 tablespoons oil
½ cup molasses
1 egg
1 cup unsweetened applesauce
1 tablespoon orange juice
1 teaspoon cinnamon
¼ teaspoon salt
¾ teaspoon baking soda
½ cup raisins
1½ cups whole wheat flour

Preheat oven to 350°F.

Beat together oil and butter until smooth and soft. Beat in molasses, egg, applesauce, orange juice, cinnamon, and salt. Add soda and stir to dissolve.

Dredge raisins with some of the flour and add along with remaining flour, stirring gently to form a smooth batter. Pour into a greased, floured 8-inch loaf pan.

Bake for 1 hour until firm. Cool in the pan for 10 minutes, remove to a rack, and cool completely.

Makes one 8-inch loaf; about 10 slices

Variation: For *Egg-Free Applesauce Cake,* omit egg and add ½ teaspoon baking powder to flour.

APPLE BABKA

A moist apple cake leavened with yeast that improves as the days go by.

1 tablespoon yeast
¼ cup warm apple juice
½ cup honey
¼ cup oil
2 eggs, beaten
¼ teaspoon salt
1 teaspoon vanilla extract
2 cups whole wheat flour
2 cups shredded apple
¼ cup chopped walnuts
¼ cup raisins or chopped dates
1 tablespoon maple syrup
cinnamon

Dissolve yeast in apple juice. Beat together honey, oil, eggs, salt, and vanilla. Stir in yeast. Add flour, apple, nuts, and dried fruit and stir into a smooth batter.

Place batter in an oiled loaf pan, cover with a cloth, and let rise in a warm spot for 1 hour.

Preheat oven to 375°F. Drizzle maple syrup over the loaf, sprinkle with cinnamon, and bake for 1 hour. Cool completely in the pan before eating.

Makes one 9-inch loaf; serves 8 to 12

ZUCCHINI LOAF CAKE

This is one of the best uses for zucchini.

1 egg
⅓ cup oil
½ cup honey
2 tablespoons molasses
½ teaspoon cinnamon
½ teaspoon vanilla extract
1 cup shredded, lightly packed zucchini
1½ cups whole wheat flour
2 tablespoons soy flour
2 tablespoons nonfat dry milk powder
1½ teaspoons baking powder
⅛ teaspoon baking soda
¼ teaspoon salt
½ cup combined sunflower seeds and chopped walnuts

Preheat oven to 350°F.

Beat egg in a large mixing bowl. Beat in oil, honey, molasses, cinnamon, and vanilla in that order. Stir in zucchini.

Combine remaining ingredients except seeds and nuts and add to zucchini mixture, stirring. When mixture is smooth, stir in seeds and nuts. Turn into an oiled, floured 8-inch loaf pan.

Bake for about 50 minutes, or until cake tests done. Cool for 10 minutes in the pan; transfer to a rack and cool completely.

Makes one 8-inch loaf; 10 slices

CARROT CAKE

This cake stays fresh for days.

½ cup oil
1 cup honey
2 eggs
½ teaspoon vanilla extract
2 cups shredded carrot
2 cups whole wheat flour
¼ cup nonfat dry milk powder
1 teaspoon cinnamon
¼ teaspoon salt
1 tablespoon baking powder

Preheat oven to 375°F.
Beat oil with honey until thick and smooth. Beat in eggs one at a time, then vanilla. Stir in carrot.
Combine remaining ingredients in a mixing bowl and stir into wet mixture until completely moistened and evenly blended. Pour into an oiled 9 x 13-inch baking pan.
Bake for about 30 minutes, or until cake tests done. Cool in the pan. Serve plain or ice with Cream Cheese Frosting.
Makes 1 large sheet cake; serves 16 to 20
Note: If cake is frosted, it must be stored in the refrigerator; you may want to ice only part of it, or prepare icing and spread on each piece just before serving if cake is designed for several days' feeding.

BANANA CAKE

A rich, moist cake that keeps well and feeds many. No icing is needed, but cake can be enhanced with sweetened yogurt if desired.

2 cups whole wheat flour
¼ teaspoon salt
2 teaspoons baking powder
½ teaspoon baking soda
¼ cup oil
¼ cup butter, cut in pieces
1 cup honey
2 eggs
1 teaspoon vanilla
1 cup mashed banana (2 to 3 bananas)
¼ cup yogurt
¼ to ½ cup walnut pieces (optional)

Preheat oven to 375°F. for a sheet cake; 350°F. for a loaf.
Combine flour, salt, baking powder, and baking soda.
In a large bowl beat together oil, butter, honey, eggs, and vanilla until smooth and foamy. Beat in mashed banana.
Add combined dry ingredients and yogurt alternately to sweetened banana mixture, stirring gently after each addition until smooth and well moistened. Stir in nuts. Pour batter into a greased and floured 9 x 13-inch cake pan or a 9-inch loaf.
Bake large cake pan in a 375°F. oven for 30 to 40 minutes, or until cake tests done. Bake loaf in a 350°F. oven for about 1 hour, or until it tests done. Let large cake cool in the pan; cool loaf in the pan for 10 minutes, then remove and cool completely on a wire rack before slicing.
Makes 1 large loaf or 1 sheet cake; serves 16

COUNTRY-FRESH PEAR CAKE

This delicious but homey cake, inspired by the fall larder, is dense, moist, and rich despite a minimum of eggs and butter.

2 eggs
¼ cup milk
½ cup honey
¼ cup molasses
pinch salt
1½ cups whole wheat flour
2 pounds pears, peeled, cored, and sliced very thin (about 5 cups)
2 tablespoons butter

Preheat oven to 350°F.
Beat eggs with milk in a large mixing bowl. Beat in honey and molasses. Add salt and flour and mix thoroughly. Stir sliced pears into the batter to coat.
Butter and flour a 9-inch round layer cake or springform pan, preferably one with a removable bottom. Spread batter in the pan. Dot top with butter.
Bake for 45 to 50 minutes until surface is lightly colored. Cool in the pan

and remove sides to serve. Cake can be eaten warm, at room temperature, or chilled (which we like best). Slice thin to serve and, if desired, top with a dollop of Yogurt Cream.

Serves 10

PINEAPPLE UPSIDE-DOWN CAKE

The Topping
2 tablespoons butter
¼ cup honey
4 slices canned unsweetened pineapple (from a 7-ounce can)
8 pecan or walnut halves

The Cake
2 eggs, separated
¼ cup honey
2 tablespoons pineapple juice (drained from canned fruit)
½ cup whole wheat flour
½ teaspoon baking powder
pinch salt

Preheat oven to 350°F.

Line a 9-inch layer cake or square cake pan with wax paper. For topping, melt butter, combine with honey, and spread over the paper. Arrange pieces of pineapple artistically in the pan. Place nuts in the open spaces.

To make the cake, beat egg yolks in a mixing bowl until light. Beat in honey and juice. Sift flour and baking powder over the honey mixture and fold to completely blend.

Beat egg whites stiff, adding salt when they become foamy. Fold into flour batter. Spread batter over pineapple in the baking pan.

Bake for 30 minutes until golden. Cool for 10 to 15 minutes in the pan, invert, and peel off paper. Cool completely. Don't worry if cake sinks a little.

Serves 6

Note: If recipe is doubled, bake in a 9 x 13-inch pan.

Variation: For *Peach* or *Apricot Upside-Down Cake,* choose fruit canned in unsweetened juice. Use the liquid to replace the pineapple juice in the cake batter.

FRUIT SHORTCAKE

Old-fashioned strawberry shortcake is so easy to make and so delectable, why limit the recipe to strawberries?

The Shortcake
2 cups whole wheat flour
4 teaspoons baking powder
¼ teaspoon salt
3 tablespoons butter
2 tablespoons oil
2 tablespoons honey
about ½ cup milk
1 tablespoon melted butter

The Filling
3 to 4 cups pitted cherries, cut-up strawberries, peaches, or nectarines, sliced pears, crushed pineapple, or whole blueberries
juice of ½ orange
1 tablespoon honey

The Topping
1½ to 2 cups Whipped Ricotta Topping (page 411), Soy Whipped Cream (page 411), Yogurt Cream (page 411) or other whipped topping of choice

Preheat oven to 425°F.

Combine flour, baking powder, and salt in a mixing bowl. Cut in the solid butter and oil. Add honey and enough milk to make a soft dough.

Pat half the dough into an oiled 9-inch pie plate or square baking dish. Cover with melted butter. Pat remaining dough into a top layer. Score into six wedges or rectangles with the tines of a fork.

Bake cake for 15 minutes. Cool in the pan.

While cake bakes, prepare fruit, using only one or a combination. Mix with juice and honey and let marinate.

Prepare topping as close to serving as convenient; if prepared more than a few minutes in advance, chill.

To serve, divide cake along scored lines. Separate layers and spoon some fruit filling on bottom half. Cover with the top of the shortcake and spoon on the whipped topping.

Serves 6

FRUIT KUCHEN OMA

A biscuit crust, a fruit filling, and a creamy yogurt topping.

The Crust
2 cups whole wheat flour
¼ cup wheat germ
2 teaspoons baking powder
½ teaspoon baking soda
½ teaspoon salt
¼ cup oil
1 tablespoon honey
⅔ cup yogurt

The Fruit Filling
4 cups peeled sliced apples, pears, peaches, or unpeeled sliced plums, or pitted cherries
2 teaspoons lemon juice
½ cup honey
½ teaspoon cinnamon

The Topping
1 egg
1 cup yogurt
1 tablespoon maple syrup

Preheat oven to 425°F.

For crust, mix flour, wheat germ, baking powder, baking soda, and salt. Stir in oil, then add honey and yogurt to make a soft dough. Press evenly into a thin layer in an oiled, floured 10 x 15-inch jelly-roll pan.

For filling, combine fruit with lemon juice, honey, and cinnamon and mix well. Lift fruit from mixing bowl with a slotted spoon and arrange over crust to completely cover. Reserve any of the honey mixture left in the bowl.

Bake for 12 to 15 minutes until the edges of the dough are golden but not brown.

Beat egg, yogurt, and maple syrup in the bowl that held the fruit so that any leftover honey is incorporated into the topping.

Remove kuchen from the oven and reduce the temperature to 325°F. While the oven is cooling down, spread topping evenly over the fruit, using a big spoon.

Return to the oven for 20 to 25 minutes, or until topping is set. Serve warm but not hot, or let cool completely.

Serves 8 to 12

FRESH PEACH CAKE

A moist, dense, very tender cake topped with sweet fruit in season.

1 egg
¼ cup honey
pinch salt
½ cup yogurt
½ teaspoon almond extract
1 cup whole wheat flour
½ teaspoon baking soda
2 cups sliced fresh peaches (peeled or not, as preferred)
¼ teaspoon cinnamon
2 tablespoons maple syrup

Preheat oven to 375°F.

Beat egg with honey. When smooth, beat in salt, yogurt, and extract until evenly blended. Mix flour with baking soda and stir in gently but thoroughly.

Pour batter into an oiled 8-inch-square or 9-inch round pan. Spread to cover evenly. Top batter with sliced peaches placed close together over the entire surface. Sprinkle evenly with cinnamon and drizzle with maple syrup.

Bake for 30 minutes, or until cake tests done. Cool in the pan.

Serves 6 to 8

Variations: Peaches can be replaced with nectarines or apricots.

FRESH FRUIT COFFEE CAKE

½ cup cottage cheese
½ cup milk
2 tablespoons oil
¼ cup honey
1¼ cups whole wheat flour
2 teaspoons baking powder
2 cups sliced, peeled apples, pears, or peaches or whole blueberries
¼ teaspoon cinnamon
2 tablespoons sliced almonds
3 tablespoons maple syrup
1 tablespoon butter

Preheat oven to 375°F.

Puree cottage cheese until smooth in a food mill, processor, or blender, adding some of the milk if necessary. Mix puree with milk, oil, and honey.

Combine flour and baking power and add to pureed cottage cheese mixture to form a thick batter. Spread batter in an oiled 8-inch-square pan.

Arrange fruit, overlapping slightly, on top of the dough. Sprinkle evenly with cinnamon, nuts, and maple syrup. Dot with butter.

Bake for 25 to 30 minutes. Cool in the pan.

Serves 6

STREUSEL COFFEE CAKE

A coffee cake with a layer of nuts and raisins in the middle and a sweet cinnamon topping. Most coffee cakes become dry after the first day; this one is excellent toasted and lightly buttered.

The Cake
¾ **cup cottage cheese**
¾ **cup milk**
3 **tablespoons oil**
6 **tablespoons honey**
2 **cups whole wheat flour**
3 **teaspoons baking powder**

Streusel Filling
⅓ **cup chopped walnuts**
¼ **cup raisins**
2 **tablespoons wheat germ**
1½ **teaspoons cinnamon**
2 **tablespoons maple syrup**

Cinnamon Topping
3 **tablespoons maple syrup**
2 **tablespoons wheat germ**
½ **teaspoon cinnamon**
1 **tablespoon butter**

Preheat oven to 375°F.

Puree cottage cheese in a processor or blender, adding a little milk if necessary to make a smooth puree. Stir in remaining milk, oil, and honey.

Stir flour and baking powder into cottage cheese mixture gently but thoroughly. (This will make a thick batter.) Spread half the batter into an oiled 9-inch-square pan.

To make the filling, sprinkle nuts, raisins, wheat germ, and cinnamon evenly over the batter. Drizzle with 2 tablespoons maple syrup.

Pat remaining batter on top, spreading to cover filling. Surface will be rough. Top cake with remaining 3 ta-

blespoons maple syrup, 2 tablespoons wheat germ, and ½ teaspoon cinnamon. Dot with butter.

Bake for 25 to 30 minutes. Leave in the pan and serve warm or at room temperature.

Makes 12 2-inch pieces

FRUITCAKE

If you think you don't like fruitcake, try this one—it's sure to change your mind, for it's chock full of real dried fruits instead of the bizarrely colored glacéed bits used in most fruit cakes.

1 **cup pitted dates, cut up**
1¼ **cups diced dried apples**
1 **cup dried apricot halves, cut in quarters**
1 **cup walnut halves**
¾ **cup whole wheat flour**
½ **teaspoon baking powder**
¼ **teaspoon salt**
3 **eggs**
¼ **cup honey**
½ **cup molasses**
1 **teaspoon vanilla extract**

Preheat oven to 300°F.

Combine dried fruit and nuts. Combine flour, baking powder, and salt and add to dried fruit mixture. Stir well.

Beat eggs, then beat in honey, molasses, and vanilla. Add to fruit mixture and stir until all ingredients are well moistened.

Spoon into a well-greased 6-cup tube or ring mold. Bake for 1 hour. Cool in the pan for 10 minutes, then turn onto a rack and cool completely.

Makes 1 large ring

Note: Fruitcake can be baked in a variety of pans, ranging from small muffin tins (baking time will be about 30 minutes) to an 8-inch loaf pan or square. To determine if the cake is done, insert a toothpick and, when it comes out clean, take the cake out of the oven.

This cake stores very well, making it ideal for gift giving or mailing at holiday time. Wrap in foil to retain moistness. If desired, douse with rum, wrap, and age a few weeks.

GREEK LENTEN CAKE

This cake was created by the Greeks to serve during Lent when dairy products and rich oils are forbidden. It contains no dairy products, no eggs, and no shortening, yet is still a very flavorsome cake. It can be enhanced with Raisin Sauce, fruit butter, or warm applesauce spooned on each piece.

1½ cups whole wheat flour
1 teaspoon baking powder
½ teaspoon baking soda
¼ teaspoon salt
¼ cup chopped walnuts
¼ cup raisins
1 cup orange juice
½ cup tahini
¼ cup honey

Preheat oven to 350°F.
Combine flour, baking powder, baking soda, salt, walnuts, and raisins in a large mixing bowl.
In a separate bowl, beat orange juice gradually into tahini, then beat in honey. Stir tahini mixture into dry mixture until thoroughly moistened. Spread batter in an oiled, floured 8- or 9-inch-square pan.
Bake for about 25 minutes until lightly browned on top and cake tests done. Cool in the pan and serve warm or at room temperature.
Serves 9

ARABIC YOGURT CAKE

A sweet, dense, very moist cake that is sold from large pans on the street throughout the Middle East. You might want to give it a try sometime when you're serving Mideastern food.

The Cake
½ teaspoon baking soda
¼ cup orange juice
¼ cup honey
⅛ teaspoon salt
½ cup yogurt
1 cup cornmeal

The Syrup
1 tablespoon butter
2 tablespoons honey
1 tablespoon water
¼ teaspoon ground cardamom (if unavailable, use cinnamon)

Dissolve baking soda in orange juice in a mixing bowl. Add honey, salt, and yogurt and stir until smooth. Stir in cornmeal and, when well blended, cover and let stand for 2 hours.
Preheat oven to 350°F.
Butter a shallow 9-inch pan and spread with batter. Bake for about 30 minutes until lightly browned.
Combine syrup ingredients in a small saucepan and heat until butter melts and syrup is thin.
When cake is baked, cut in half in pan, then cut each half in thirds. Pour syrup evenly over the surface. Let cool completely in the pan and cut into small pieces to serve.
Serves 12

CAROB AND CHOCOLATE CUPCAKES

Your choice of all carob, all chocolate, or a combination of the two.

2 tablespoons butter
2 tablespoons oil
½ cup honey
1 egg
1 teaspoon vanilla extract
⅛ teaspoon salt
1¼ cups whole wheat flour
¼ cup ground walnuts
6 tablespoons carob powder and/or cocoa
2 teaspoons baking powder
¼ teaspoon baking soda
½ cup milk

Preheat oven to 375°F.
Beat butter with oil until creamy. Beat in honey until smooth, then egg, vanilla, and salt.
Combine flour, walnuts, carob/cocoa, baking powder, and baking soda, and add to cream mixture alternately with milk until batter is smooth. (If carob, cocoa, or either of the leavening agents is lumpy, sift them into the mixture.) Spoon batter into an oiled or paper-lined muffin tin.

Bake for 20 minutes. Ice when cool with Buttercream Frosting, Whipped White Icing, or any other icing you wish.

Makes 10 cupcakes

Note: The easiest way to ice cupcakes is to dip tops in a bowl of frosting, then lift them with a quick turn of the wrist to create a swirled effect.

CARROT CUPCAKES

A light cupcake made without wheat or milk.

> 3 eggs, separated
> ⅓ cup honey
> ½ cup grated carrot
> ½ cup finely chopped walnuts
> ½ cup soy flour
> ½ teaspoon cinnamon

Preheat oven to 350°F.

Beat egg yolks with honey until thick. Add carrot, nuts, soy flour, and cinnamon. Beat egg whites until stiff and fold into carrot batter. Spoon into well-oiled or paper-lined muffin cups and bake for 25 minutes. Ice or not as desired.

Makes 12 cupcakes

DOUBLE DONUTS

Donut making is a nice afternoon activity; with these you'll be doubly rewarded in taste and food value.

> 1 egg
> ¼ cup honey
> 2 tablespoons maple syrup
> 1 tablespoon oil
> ½ teaspoon vanilla extract
> 1¾ cups whole wheat flour
> ½ cup soy flour
> ¼ teaspoon salt
> ¼ teaspoon baking soda
> 1½ teaspoons baking powder
> ½ teaspoon cinnamon
> ¼ cup yogurt
> oil for deep frying

Beat together egg, honey, maple syrup, oil, and vanilla.

Combine flours, salt, baking soda, baking powder, and cinnamon and add to egg mixture alternately with yogurt to form a stiff dough. Knead gently with hands, and chill if possible.

Sprinkle surface of dough with flour to prevent sticking and roll on a well-floured surface until ⅓ inch thick. Cut with a donut cutter or use a 6½-ounce tuna can with the ends removed to make 3-inch rounds and cut a hole in the center with a thimble. Donuts can also be made by forming dough into coils and attaching the ends (coiled donuts can be made in any size).

Heat about ⅓ cup oil in a wok to 375°F. Fry donuts until golden on each side. If oil is the correct temperature, 1 minute per side should suffice. Do not crowd the pot; you should be able to fry 1 large or 3 mini donuts at a time. Drain on grocery bags and let cool completely before eating.

Makes 8 large donuts (about 3½ inches across) or *24 mini donuts* (about 2 inches across)

Note: Homemade donuts are delicious but do not keep well; eat what you wish within a few hours of frying and freeze the rest for another time. Defrost at room temperature.

LEMON–ORANGE REFRIGERATOR LAYER CAKE

A delicious, rich party cake with four layers, each filled with a lemon–orange custard.

The Cake
> 2 eggs, separated
> ¼ cup lemon juice
> 2 teaspoons minced lemon peel
> ½ cup honey
> ¼ teaspoon salt
> 1 cup sifted whole wheat pastry flour
> 1 teaspoon baking powder

The Filling
> ¼ cup cornstarch or arrowroot
> ¼ cup lemon juice
> 1 cup orange juice
> ½ cup honey
> 2 eggs, separated

Preheat oven to 350°F.

Beat egg yolks for cake until light and lemon-colored. Gradually beat in lemon juice, rind, honey, and salt. Mix flour with baking powder and sift over the egg mixture. Fold gently until evenly mixed and well moistened.

Beat egg whites stiff and fold into batter. Spread batter into two oiled, floured 8- or 9-inch layer cake pans with removable bottoms.

Bake for 20 minutes until firm and brown. Remove sides of pan and cool.

To prepare the filling, mix starch with lemon juice until smooth. Add orange juice and honey and cook in a double boiler or over a heatproof pad (flame tamer), stirring frequently until very thick, about 20 minutes. As mixture thickens, stir constantly. A wire whisk is best for this. Remove from heat when thick, and before mixture boils.

Beat egg yolks and gradually temper with some of the hot filling. Mix tempered egg back into the remaining filling and return to double boiler, stirring continuously without boiling, for 2 minutes.

Cool filling for 10 minutes. Beat egg whites until stiff and fold into cooled filling until smooth and creamy.

With cakes still attached to the bottom of the pans, slice through the middle to make two layers from each. Remove bottom layers from pan.

Place one of the top halves top-side down on a plate. Cover with about ½ cup filling, place another cake layer on top, and continue filling and layering, placing the other top piece top-side up last. Cover cake with remaining lemon-orange filling.

Insert toothpicks in the top and drape with foil or plastic wrap to prevent drying. Chill several hours before cutting.

Makes one 8- or 9-inch four-layer cake; serves 10 to 12

Note: Prepare well in advance, as there are several steps and cake should chill several hours before being served.

ITALIAN CHEESECAKE

The Italians make cheesecake with ricotta cheese and the result is a dessert that is creamy, light, and especially nourishing.

1 cup dry bread, cracker, or cookie crumbs
2 tablespoons oil or melted butter
1 tablespoon plus ⅔ cup honey
4 eggs
4 cups ricotta cheese
2 teaspoons vanilla extract
2 tablespoons whole wheat flour
2 teaspoons slivered lemon peel
2 tablespoons slivered almonds
1 tablespoon pumpkin seeds

Combine crumbs, fat, and 1 tablespoon honey. Press on the bottom of a 9-inch springform pan and chill.

Preheat oven to 325°F.

With a rotary or electric beater, mix eggs, one at a time, into ricotta until smooth and creamy. Beat in remaining honey, vanilla, and flour. Fold in lemon peel and almonds. Pour batter into chilled crust. Scatter seeds on top.

Bake for 1 hour until just firm and lightly colored on top. Turn oven off, open door, and leave cake to cool for 30 minutes. Then cool completely and chill before serving.

Makes a 9-inch cake; serves 10 to 12
Major Protein

Note: Prepare in advance, as cake should be well chilled before being served. One tenth of this cake furnishes 15 grams protein and 290 calories.

CREAMY CHEESECAKE

This no-crust cheesecake is heavier than Italian cheesecake and richer as well, but it is much less cloying than the traditional cream cheese cake.

2 cups ricotta cheese
8 ounces cream cheese
1½ cups yogurt
4 eggs
¾ cup honey
1½ teaspoons vanilla extract
3 tablespoons whole wheat flour
3 tablespoons arrowroot or cornstarch

Preheat oven to 325°F.

Using an electric mixer or rotary beater whip ricotta, cream cheese, and yogurt together until smooth and creamy. Beat in eggs, one at a time, then honey, vanilla, flour, and arrowroot. Pour into a buttered, floured 9- or 10-inch springform.

Bake for 1¼ to 1½ hours until firm and lightly colored. Turn oven off and let cheesecake sit for 2 hours. If top seems too deeply browned at the end of the baking period, leave oven door slightly ajar during the cooling-down period. Refrigerate for several hours before serving.

Makes a 9- to 10-inch cake; serves 10 to 12

Minor Protein

Note: Prepare in advance, as cake should be well chilled before being served.

If springform leaks (as many do), wrap in foil to prevent a messy oven.

One tenth of this cake furnishes 12 grams protein and 280 calories.

PUDDING CHEESECAKE

A no-bake cheesecake. The texture is as creamy as pudding and the flavor is sweet and soothing.

Crust
  ⅓ **cup combined almond and sunflower seed meal**
  ⅓ **cup whole grain cookie or cracker crumbs**
  ⅓ **cup wheat germ**
  2 tablespoons oil
  1 tablespoon honey

Filling
  4 eggs, separated
  1¼ cups skim or whole milk
  2 envelopes unflavored gelatin
  ⅛ teaspoon salt
  4 cups ricotta cheese, cottage cheese, or a combination
  ½ cup honey
  1 tablespoon lemon juice
  1 teaspoon minced lemon peel
  1 teaspoon vanilla extract
  ¼ cup chopped dates
  ½ cup drained crushed pineapple

Combine crust ingredients and press into the bottom of a 9-inch springform. Chill.

To make the filling, beat egg yolks with milk in a small saucepan. Sprinkle on gelatin and salt. Place over low heat and cook, stirring constantly, until gelatin dissolves and mixture thickens slightly. Do not boil.

If using cottage cheese, puree smooth in a processor or food mill.

In a large bowl, beat cheese with a rotary or electric beater until smooth and light. Gradually beat in honey, lemon juice, peel, and vanilla. Add gelatin mixture and stir until evenly blended. Stir in dates and well-drained pineapple.

Chill mixture until it is the consistency of unbeaten egg whites or until it mounds slightly when dropped from a spoon. This will take about 15 minutes. In the meantime, clean up and whip egg whites until stiff.

Fold egg whites gently but thoroughly into gelatin mixture. Pour into chilled crust and chill for several hours until firm. To serve, loosen from pan with a thin knife, release spring, and remove sides.

Makes a 9-inch cake; serves 12 or more

Minor Protein

Note: One twelfth of this cake furnishes 14 grams protein and 240 calories.

PIES AND INDIVIDUAL PASTRIES

It seems more people are intimidated by making pie crusts than by any other cooking procedure, but since it is hardly any quicker to make crusts from a mix, it is a skill worth acquiring.

Most crusts require nothing more than adding a measured amount of fat to a measured amount of flour and getting the whole thing to hold together with a few spoonfuls of water. With a properly prepared work surface and a little practice, rolling the dough for shaping is equally as easy, but beginners may want to start out with a crumb crust or a "cookie" crust, which can simply be pressed into its form. With only this small effort, your pastry can become an object of pride and accomplishment.

Roll the Dough with Confidence

1. To keep the crust light, add liquid sparingly, just enough to hold the flour in a ball without crumbling.

2. Work on as cool a surface as possible, especially when the crust contains butter. A marble slab is a baker's dream.

3. Pastry can be rolled on any flat surface. Many people line the work area with wax paper to prevent sticking. For a nonstick job, we recommend a canvas pastry cloth and a cotton rolling pin cover.

4. Handle dough as little and as gently as possible, unless you are advised otherwise. A sweetened mixture can be handled more and sometimes you will even be instructed to knead it gently.

5. Some doughs are chilled before rolling in order to harden the fat. Only those containing butter benefit from this treatment, although it is perfectly safe to chill any dough if it is a matter of convenience. Keep it well covered to prevent drying out.

6. Roll only one crust at a time; keep remaining pastry covered so that the surface does not dry out.

7. Roll quickly, applying gentle pressure, from the center out, like the spokes of a wheel.

8. If dough is resistant to rolling after chilling and develops cracks, whack it several times with the rolling pin to soften it.

9. Never press any dried dough back into pastry, as these pieces will remain hard and tough even after baking.

10. Roll dough to a thickness of ⅛ inch for pies and ⅜ to ¼ inch for individual tarts. Make a circle at least 1 inch larger than the pan if pastry will have a fluted edge. Invert tin on the dough to gauge the size.

11. To transfer rolled dough to a pie plate, sprinkle lightly with flour and transport it rolled around the pin.

12. Place pastry gently in the pan and do not stretch it or it will shrink during baking.

13. Press any cracks smooth with moist fingers. Patches can be made with leftover pieces of pastry, moistening edges to be joined and pressing gently in place.

14. Once the pastry is in the pan, you may push it out gently from the center to make the bottom thin and the sides somewhat thicker to support the filling. This is more important for individual tarts or for pies baked in pans with removable sides.

15. If there is a time lapse before filling or baking, the pastry-lined pan should be covered and chilled. If butter has been used, you can put the crust into the freezer for a few minutes prior to baking for added flakiness. Crumb crusts that are not baked before filling must be chilled thoroughly first to get them to hold together.

Single-Crust Pies

To finish the edge of a single-crust pie, trim evenly 1 to 1½ inches beyond the rim. Fold this edge over itself for a high-standing ridge. "Flute" by pushing the dough toward the outer edge with the index finger of one hand, at the same time pressing inward with the thumb and index finger of the other hand. A high edge like this will keep the filling from bubbling over.

Where there is only a bottom shell, prebaking is possible for a crisper crust. To prebake, prick the bottom and sides evenly with the prongs of a fork to prevent puffing, line with paper, and fill with dried beans, grains, or special pie weights if directed (this is known as "baking blind"), and place in a 425°F. oven. Bake until barely colored if pastry is to be returned to the oven with its filling, or continue until golden if this is its final baking. Time varies from 10 to 15 minutes. Except for heat loss, there is no harm in opening the oven while the shell bakes, so check frequently to avoid over-browning.

Two-Crust Pies

You cannot prebake the shell of a two-crust or lattice-top pastry and thus you must face the fact that pie dough absorbs liquid from the filling and often becomes soggy. To remedy this, you can try any of the following; all help, none are totally effective.

• Brush the crust with melted butter before filling.
• Paint the crust with beaten egg, egg yolk, or egg white and let dry before filling.
• Dust the crust with cornstarch before filling.
• Sprinkle the crust with finely ground nuts or bread crumbs before filling.
• Thicken the filling before placing it in the crust.

Since pie filling shrinks during baking, it should form a nice mound in the shell before you cover it.

The top crust should have a few slashes to allow steam to escape. Or, you can insert a few pieces of tubular macaroni to vent off the gas and prevent boiling over, or, if you prefer, buy one of the little ceramic blackbirds sold for this purpose.

To put the pie together, lay the top crust gently over the filling without stretching; trim the edges even with the bottom layer and flute as explained for the single crust, or simply seal the edges together by pressing with the back of the tines of a fork. If you moisten the edge of the bottom crust with water before attaching the top crust, the edges will adhere with less effort.

If you fear the filling will overflow at the rim, make an extra strong seal by leaving a larger overhang of crust and folding one layer over the other. Most books tell you to fold under so the top crust rolls over the bottom, but if you go the opposite way, folding the bottom crust over the top crust in toward the center of the pan, any spillage will run into the pie, not the oven.

If the edges of the pie appear to be cooking too quickly, take a strip of foil and cover the rim loosely. Remove during the last few minutes to complete browning.

Lattice Pies

The decorative basket-weaving of pastry on top of a pie filling is characteristic of certain tarts, and although it can be omitted, it adds a lovely touch. Some people find it easier to weave a lattice off the pie, on a piece of cardboard or wax paper, sliding the assemblage gradually off the board, over the filling, and pinch the strips where they adjoin the bottom crust so the lattice will adhere. The edge can then be finished as for any single- or double-crusted pie.

French Tart Tins

These special pans designed for quiche and tarts have fluted sides and a flat bottom insert that can be removed to expose the decorative pastry walls. This gives your homemade pastries a very professional look, yet the effort is really quite minimal—the dough is just pressed lightly into the fluted areas and trimmed level at the top. For service, the outer rim is removed, which makes it quite easy to slice and lift each piece from the tin.

Tarts

Individual tart shells can be made with most pastry doughs. Pastry for a single 9-inch crust will make 8 to 10 tarts, depending on size.

For small tart molds or for shaping on the inside of a muffin tin, divide dough into about 10 small balls and roll each into a 4-inch circle. Ease into mold.

For large tarts, you can use the back of a muffin tin as a mold. Divide dough into 8 balls and roll into 5-inch circles. Press gently onto an inverted muffin tin. Make the walls slightly thicker than the bottom; trim the top level with the flat of the pan or pinch slightly to form a ridge along the outside.

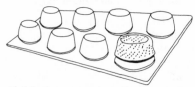

Prick tart shells all over and bake in a 425°F. oven for about 10 minutes, or until lightly browned. Cool for 5 minutes in the pan, then lift gently from the mold and cool on a rack.

Fill tarts as close to serving as convenient.

Turnovers

Turnovers are similar to double-crusted pies in that the filling is entirely encased in the crust. The simplest way to make a perfect seal is with a small pastry "press." The tool itself only costs a couple of dollars and makes an excellent mold for ravioli, steamed dumplings, and similar items in which a filling is placed at intervals on one piece of dough, covered with another layer of dough, then cut into a shape and pinched at the edges in a one-step operation.

Alternately, a single piece of dough can be cut to size, the filling placed on half, and the remainder "turned" over and the edges pinched with the fingers, pressed with the tines of a fork, or gently rolled to form the seal. As with double-crusted pies, it helps to moisten the crust lightly before sealing.

Making Pastry in Advance

Pie dough stores well in the refrigerator and freezer if it is tightly wrapped. Since making an extra crust or two adds only a few more minutes to the job, it is advisable to prepare something for future use. Unbaked pie dough will keep up to two weeks in the refrigerator, and about six months in the freezer. You will get best freezing results with those doughs that are relatively high in fat. A very low fat content may mean a cardboard crust after baking.

There are many techniques for freezing pie dough. For convenience it is best to roll the dough first or you will have to wait an hour or more for it to thaw before it is usable. The dough can be shaped into the pie tin and frozen, but this may tie up your baking tin and make an awkward-size package for the freezer. To make better use of the space, roll the dough into circles large enough to flute the edges later on. Place the pastry on a piece of wax or freezer paper set on cardboard for support. You can freeze up to six crusts together if you separate them with paper so that they can be taken apart later. Wrap the entire package in heavy-duty foil, label it and freeze. To use, thaw at room temperature until pliable (about 15 minutes), keeping a layer of wax paper above and below to prevent condensation of moisture on the surface. When softened, ease into the pie tin, trim the top, and proceed as usual.

Leftover Pastry

If you have a small amount of extra dough, you can turn it into rough pastry cookies by rolling it about ⅜ inch thick, brushing it with honey diluted slightly with milk, sprinkling cinnamon and finely chopped nuts liberally over the surface, pricking it well with a fork, and baking it in a hot (400° to 450°F.) oven until lightly colored. The "cookies" cook quickly, so be sure to check on their progress in about 8 minutes.

Pie Fillings

Although we offer a variety of recipes in this chapter, you may wish to devise a filling of your own. A 9-inch shell will hold 2 to 3 cups of pre-made filling or 4 to 6 cups of filling baked in the shell. (Fresh filling shrinks.)

Individual tart shells hold from ¼ to ⅓ cup filling each.

Yeast Pastries

Using our Foundation Sweet Dough (page 406), you can put together a variety of sweet rolls and croissants. To prepare a whole series of treats, the dough can be kept in the refrigerator for a week and fashioned into something new each day.

CRUMB CRUST

A crumb crust is the simplest to produce, but it must be well chilled or baked before it is filled.

¼ cup oil or melted butter
1¼ cups dry whole grain bread, cracker, or cookie crumbs, including up to ¼ cup wheat germ in the mixture
2 tablespoons honey

Stir oil into crumbs. Mix in honey until evenly blended. Press on the bottom and sides of a 9-inch pie pan. Chill before filling, or prebake in a 350°F. oven for 8 to 10 minutes until just beginning to color. Do not overbake.
Makes one 9-inch crust

NUT AND CRUMB CRUST

¾ cup finely ground nuts (from ⅔ cup nuts)
½ cup fine dry bread, cracker, whole wheat cookie crumbs, or whole wheat flour
2 tablespoons oil or melted butter
1 tablespoon honey (optional)

Combine nut meal and crumbs and stir in oil or butter. Add honey if desired. Press into a 9-inch pie pan or springform. If using a springform, press crumbs over the bottom and slightly up the sides to form a lip. Chill or bake in a 350°F. oven for 8 to 10 minutes. Do not overbake.
Makes one 9-inch crust
Note: A combination of nuts is best. We prefer some sunflower seeds mixed with either almonds, walnuts, hazelnuts, or pecans.

COOKIE DOUGH CRUST

A cookie dough crust is a rich pie dough that is easy to produce, can withstand handling, and, if you prefer, can be pressed into shape rather than rolled.

1½ to 1¾ cups whole wheat flour
1 teaspoon baking powder
⅛ teaspoon salt
3 tablespoons butter

3 tablespoons oil
1 egg, lightly beaten
2 tablespoons honey
½ teaspoon vanilla extract or ½ teaspoon minced lemon peel

Combine 1½ cups flour, baking powder, and salt. Cut in butter and oil until evenly blended. Beat egg with honey and add to flour along with flavoring.

Work together to form a uniform dough that can be handled. If too sticky, add remaining flour a tablespoon at a time.

To use dough immediately, press into a thin layer in the pan as the recipe directs. To roll dough, cover and chill for at least 30 minutes.

Chill shell before filling. For a baked shell, place in a 375°F. oven for about 15 minutes until golden.

Makes two 9-inch shells, or one deep-lattice or double-crusted pie

Note: This dough freezes very successfully.

To prepare crust in a processor, combine dry ingredients in the work bowl fitted with a plastic blade. Add butter and oil through the feeder and process quickly to cut in. With the machine still running, add egg, honey, and flavoring and process until dough forms a ball. If sticky, add additional flour by hand as needed.

Variation: For *Cookie Dough Tart Shells*, divide into 8 to 10 balls and press over the bottom and up the sides of an inverted muffin tin. Chill for at least 10 minutes, then prick all over with a fork and bake as directed above. Let cool for 10 minutes, then remove gently from tin to cool completely.

STANDARD PASTRY

A good all-around dough that is easy to assemble and makes a flavorful, crunchy crust. This basic recipe provides enough pastry for several baking projects.

3½ cups whole wheat flour
½ teaspoon salt
⅛ teaspoon baking soda

½ cup butter
¼ cup oil
½ tablespoon honey
¼ cup lemon juice
⅓ to ½ cup water

Combine flour, salt, and baking soda in a large bowl.

Combine butter, oil, and honey in a processor fitted with a plastic blade or a blender and whip to the consistency of soft margarine.

Cut whipped shortening into flour mixture until evenly dispersed into tiny balls.

Add lemon juice and water as needed, until dough holds together in a ball. Roll for immediate use, or chill for future use.

Makes pastry for three 9-inch shells, or two double-crusted 9-inch pies, or 24 to 30 tarts

Note: For use within a week, keep tightly wrapped in the refrigerator and roll as needed. For longer storage (up to 3 months), shape, wrap, and freeze.

For an extra flaky crust, add 1 teaspoon baking powder to the dry ingredients.

PLUS PASTRY

A soy-enriched dough that has an excellent texture and flavor.

2¼ cups whole wheat flour
¼ cup soy flour
¼ teaspoon salt
¼ cup butter
¼ cup oil
about ½ cup cold water

Combine flours and salt. Cut in butter and oil. Stir in water as needed to form a dough that holds. Roll, ease into a pie pan, and use or freeze as needed.

Makes two 9-inch shells or about 18 tarts

Note: To prepare in a processor, combine flours and salt in the work bowl fitted with a plastic mixing blade. Add butter and oil through the feeder and process quickly until evenly dispersed. With the machine running, add water through the feeder until dough forms a mass.

TENDER PIE CRUST

An excellent crust for fruit tarts or to hold a creamed vegetable filling.

1½ cups whole wheat flour
pinch salt
¼ cup oil
2 tablespoons butter
2 tablespoons yogurt
1 tablespoon honey
3 tablespoons cold water (only if needed)

Combine flour and salt in a bowl. Cut in oil and butter until mixture resembles a coarse meal. Add yogurt, honey, and water, if needed, to form into a ball.

If possible, chill for about an hour before rolling or freeze for 10 minutes to make rolling easier.

Makes two 9-inch shells, or a deep double-crusted pie, or a pie with a lattice top, or 12 to 14 tarts

Note: Freezer storage is not recommended.

CREAMY CHEESE PASTRY

A tender low-fat crust that is easy to roll and can be used in pies, tarts, and turnovers, especially when a thin crust is needed.

1½ cups whole wheat flour
½ teaspoon salt
½ teaspoon baking powder
4 tablespoons butter, at room temperature
¾ cup ricotta or small curd cottage cheese, well drained

Mix flour, salt, and baking powder in a bowl. Cut in butter until thoroughly blended.

Work in cheese with fingers, kneading gently to form a ball. If too dry, add another tablespoon cheese. Chill for 30 minutes before rolling.

Roll dough, half at a time, using a pastry cloth for best results. Tears can be mended easily by pressing on a thin overlay of dough.

Makes pastry for two 9- to 10-inch shells, or 16 to 20 tarts, or 30 small turnovers

Note: For use within 1 week, store in the refrigerator; shape and freeze for storage up to 3 months. This pastry has a higher protein and lower fat content than most others.

CHEESE CRUST

Transform your favorite dough into a Cheese Crust for vegetable or fruit pies.

pastry for a 9- or 10-inch shell
½ cup grated cheddar cheese

Roll pastry to a 12-inch circle. Sprinkle cheese over surface.

Roll like a jelly roll, fold ends in to meet in center, and flatten with hands. Fold in half and flatten again. Fold in half once more, shape into a ball, and chill for 10 to 30 minutes.

Roll and use as desired.

Makes one 9- or 10-inch shell

APPLE CRUMB PIE

1 unbaked 9-inch pie crust made from Standard or Plus Pastry (page 399)

The Filling
6 cups peeled, sliced apples
1 to 2 tablespoons lemon juice
½ teaspoon cinnamon
½ teaspoon nutmeg
1 tablespoon arrowroot or cornstarch
¼ to ⅓ cup honey
2 tablespoons maple syrup

The Crumb Topping
⅓ cup whole wheat flour
¼ teaspoon cinnamon
3 tablespoons butter
2 tablespoons maple syrup

Prepare pie shell first and chill until ready to fill.

Preheat oven to 425°F.

Mix apples with lemon juice (using maximum amount if apples are sweet) and spices.

Stir starch into honey to dissolve (use the larger amount of honey if apples are very tart). Add to apples along with maple syrup. Mix well. Transfer to pie shell just before baking.

Mix flour and cinnamon for topping. Cut in butter until mixture resembles coarse meal. Sprinkle over apples in pie shell. Drizzle maple syrup over all.

Bake pie for 10 minutes. Reduce heat to 350°F. and bake 30 minutes longer, or until crust is golden and apples are tender. Serve warm or at room temperature.

Makes one 9-inch pie

Note: All parts of the pie can be prepared in advance but should be assembled just before baking.

Variations: A variety of *Fruit Crumb Pies* can be made by substituting pears, peaches, or cherries for the apple, or combining the apple with cranberries. For sour cherries or a combination with cranberries, use ⅓ cup honey.

DUTCH APPLE PIE

A lattice-topped deep pie baked in a straight-sided pan.

1 recipe Cookie Dough Crust (page 398)
2 pounds apples, peeled and thinly sliced (5 to 6 cups)
1 to 2 tablespoons lemon juice
1 teaspoon cinnamon
¼ cup honey
¼ cup maple syrup
2 tablespoons raisins

Prepare pastry. Use two-thirds dough to line a 9-inch springform or pan with a removable bottom, covering the bottom and 1 inch up the sides. Chill pastry-lined pan and remaining dough. Preheat oven to 375°F.

Toss apples with lemon juice, using the maximum amount if apples are very sweet. Add remaining ingredients.

Prepare lattice strips with unrolled pastry. Pile apple mixture into shell and top with lattice strips.

Bake for 45 to 55 minutes until crust is lightly browned. Cool for 10 minutes in the pan, then remove sides and finish cooling. Serve at room temperature or chilled.

Makes one deep 9-inch pastry

WALNUT–PEACH PIE

An open-face peach pie made with sweet fruit of the season.

1 unbaked 9-inch pie crust made from Tender Pie Crust, Plus, or Standard Pastry (pages 400, 399)
4 cups peeled, sliced peaches
2 eggs
⅓ cup honey
2 tablespoons butter
½ cup coarsely chopped walnuts
¼ teaspoon cinnamon

Preheat oven to 400°F.

Line pie pan with crust, prick all over with a fork, and bake for 10 minutes. Cool slightly while oven heat is reduced to 325°F.

Fill shell with peaches. Beat eggs with honey and pour over fruit. Dot with butter, cover with nuts, and sprinkle with cinnamon.

Bake for 35 to 40 minutes until filling is set. Cool before cutting.

Makes one 9-inch pie

DEEP-DISH STRAWBERRY-RHUBARB PIE

When our delicious strawberry-rhubarb filling was so juicy it could hardly be contained in a pie shell, a friend had the excellent idea of deep-dish service.

5 cups strawberries and rhubarb combined in any proportion (about equal parts is recommended)
3 tablespoons arrowroot or cornstarch
⅔ cup honey
pastry for a 2-crust pie made from Standard Pastry (page 399) or other pastry of choice, chilled
honey and milk (optional)

Slice rhubarb into ½-inch lengths, place in a bowl, and pour on boiling water to cover. Let stand for 10 minutes, then drain and pat dry. Hull strawberries and cut in halves or quarters, depending on size.

Preheat oven to 375°F.

Dissolve starch in honey, combine with fruit, and place in a shallow 1½-

quart baking dish or 6 individual 1-cup pans. Roll pastry and lay over fruit; do not seal at the edges, but flute for appearance if desired. Make a few slits in the crust.

Bake for about 40 minutes until crust is golden. The surface of pastry can be brushed lightly with honey thinned with a little milk toward the end of baking to enhance browning.

Makes 6 servings
Variations: For *Sour Cherry Pie,* replace strawberries and rhubarb with 5 cups pitted sour cherries.

FRESH FRUIT TART

  1 prebaked 9-inch tart shell made with Cookie Dough Crust (page 398) or Creamy Cheese Pastry (page 400)
  3 tablespoons honey
  3 tablespoons arrowroot or cornstarch
  1¼ cups orange juice
  2 tablespoons lemon juice
  4 cups assorted cut-up fresh fruit

In a saucepan combine honey with starch and gradually stir in orange juice until smooth. Cook over medium heat, stirring continuously, until mixture thickens and comes to a boil. If thickened with arrowroot, remove from heat immediately; if cornstarch is used, boil gently for 1 minute. Remove from heat, stir in lemon juice, and let cool to room temperature.

Drain any liquid from fruit and combine with cooled orange juice mixture. Fold gently until fruit is evenly distributed. Place fruit filling in crust and chill several hours before serving.

Makes one 9-inch tart

FRESH FRUIT TART WITH CHEESE FILLING

A creamy cheese layer fills the crust. On top is a glaze made with fresh summer fruit.

  1 prebaked 9-inch tart shell or 12 individual shells made with Cookie Dough Crust (page 398) or Creamy Cheese Pastry (page 400)

Cheese Filling
  8 ounces cream cheese
  6 tablespoons yogurt
  1 teaspoon vanilla extract
  1 tablespoon honey

Fruit Glaze
  3 cups fresh strawberries, blueberries, or peeled sliced peaches singly or in combination
  2 tablespoons honey
  1 tablespoon cornstarch or arrowroot
  2 tablespoons lemon juice

For filling, combine all ingredients and whip in a processor fitted with a plastic blade or with a rotary or electric mixer until light and creamy. Use to fill baked tart shell or individual shells about halfway.

For glaze, mash 1 cup of the fruit with a fork and mix with honey, starch, and lemon juice in a small saucepan. Stir over low heat until mixture is thick and translucent.

Arrange remaining peach slices, whole blueberries, and strawberries cut in half (or quarters for individual tarts) over surface of cheese filling. Spread with glaze. Chill for several hours to set.

Makes one 9-inch tart or 12 individual tarts

CANNED FRUIT PIE OR TARTS

If you can fruit at home, this is a good way to enjoy it when fresh fruit is not available. Otherwise, commercially canned fruit in unsweetened juice can be chosen.

  1 prebaked 9-inch shell or 8 prebaked tarts
  2½ cups drained, canned fruit (from two 1-pound cans)
  4 teaspoons arrowroot or cornstarch
  1 cup canning liquid
  1 to 2 tablespoons honey
  1 cup Yogurt Cream (page 411), Whipped Ricotta Topping (page 411) or Soy Whipped Cream (page 411)

Slice fruit if unsliced.
In a saucepan, mix starch with a

little of the canning liquid to make a smooth paste. Stir in remaining liquid. Cook, stirring continuously until thick and translucent. Add honey to taste. Mix thickened syrup with fruit and chill.

Place in a crust to serve and top with whipped topping of choice.

Makes one 9-inch pie or 8 tarts

Variations: Suggested fruits for filling include peaches, pears, apricots, plums, or pineapple. If you wish to make this pie with fresh fruit, slice and poach 4 cups fresh fruit in ¼ cup apple juice until just tender, about 10 minutes. Drain, reserving liquid. Add orange juice to liquid to make 1 cup and proceed as for canned fruit.

APRICOT–RAISIN TART

A large-pan pastry with a dried fruit filling.

Pastry for two 9-inch crusts made from Standard or Plus Pastry (page 399)
3 cups dried apricots
2 cups apple juice
1½ cups raisins
½ cup honey
1 tablespoon cornstarch or arrowroot
⅛ teaspoon salt
2 tablespoons lemon juice
1½ tablespoons butter

Prepare dough and chill while preparing filling.

Combine apricots and juice in a saucepan and bring to a boil. Cover and simmer for 5 minutes until just tender. Add raisins, honey mixed with starch, salt, and lemon juice. Cook, stirring, until thick, 3 to 5 minutes. Add butter, remove from heat, and let cool.

Preheat oven to 375°F.

Roll pastry extremely thin and use to line a 10 x 14-inch jelly-roll pan. Make lattice strips with any extra. Spread fruit over pastry and arrange lattice strips decoratively on top.

Bake for about 30 minutes until golden. Do not overbake, as raisins burn easily.

Makes one 10 x 14-inch tart

Variations: Dried prunes or peaches can be added with the apricots.

VIENNESE PLUM TART

Almond paste topped with fresh prune-plums.

1 unbaked 9-inch tart shell made from Tender Pie Crust (page 400)
Almond Paste
1 cup finely ground almonds
⅓ cup honey
½ teaspoon cinnamon
¼ teaspoon vanilla or almond extract
1 egg, lightly beaten

Plum Topping
about 10 prune-plums
2 tablespoons honey
2 tablespoons butter

Line tart pan with removable bottom with pastry. Chill for at least 1 hour or prebake in a 425°F. oven for 10 minutes and cool before filling.

Combine ingredients for almond paste until evenly mixed. Spread in crust.

Cut plums in half, remove pits, and place close together on top of pie. Combine honey and butter in a heatproof dish, melt, and pour evenly over fruit.

If shell has not been prebaked, set pie on a baking sheet and place in a 450°F. oven for 15 minutes; then reduce heat to 375°F. (or alternately place prebaked filled crust in at this temperature) and bake for about 35 minutes until fruit is tender. Cool to room temperature to serve.

Makes one 9-inch tart

PECAN PIE

One of the sweetest pies around and one of the best. For real luxury, serve with a whipped topping.

1 unbaked 9-inch pie shell made from Standard or Plus Pastry (page 399)
2 tablespoons butter
3 eggs
½ cup honey
⅓ cup maple syrup
1 teaspoon vanilla extract
pinch salt
1½ cups broken pecans

Prepare crust and chill while preparing filling.

Melt butter and let cool.

Preheat oven to 400°F.

Beat eggs in a mixing bowl with a wire whisk or rotary beater. Beat in honey, maple syrup, vanilla, and salt. Add cooled butter and nuts.

Pour into pastry. Bake for 10 minutes, reduce heat to 350°F., and bake for 25 minutes, until set but not dry. Cool to room temperature before serving.

Makes one 9-inch pie

Minor Protein

Note: You will need about 2 cups whipped topping for 8 pieces of pie. Whipped Ricotta Topping or Yogurt Cream are suitable, as of course is fresh whipped heavy cream.

PUMPKIN PIE

The traditional Thanksgiving Day dessert, but don't wait until then to enjoy it.

1 unbaked 9-inch crust made from Nut and Crumb recipe (page 398) or any rolled pastry of choice
1½ cups fresh or canned pumpkin puree
¼ teaspoon salt
1 cup milk
2 eggs, beaten
½ cup molasses
2 tablespoons honey or maple syrup
1 teaspoon cinnamon
½ teaspoon nutmeg
¼ teaspoon ginger
½ teaspoon vanilla extract

Prepare crust and chill until filling is ready.

Preheat oven to 450°F.

Combine remaining ingredients in the order listed, beating with a fork or wire whisk.

Pour filling into chilled crust and bake for 15 minutes. Reduce heat to 350°F. and bake for 40 minutes. Cool at room temperature. Serve plain or with a whipped topping.

Makes one 9-inch pie

Minor Protein

Note: Cornmeal Crust (page 228) is terrific for Pumpkin Pie but must be prebaked, as described in the crust recipe, before filling. After pumpkin filling is added, baking can continue in a 350°F. oven for about 45 minutes.

Variations: For a delicate *Pumpkin Custard,* omit crust and pour filling mixture into 6 greased custard cups. Set in a water bath and bake in a 325°F. oven for 40 to 50 minutes (see directions for Baked Vanilla Custard page 362). Or, cook on top of the stove as for Quick-Cooking Custard, page 60.

For *Mock Pumpkin Pie,* replace pumpkin with 2 cups cooked soybeans or other mild-flavored bean. Puree smooth in a food mill or processor and use as pumpkin puree. Omit salt from recipe if beans are salted. Sweeten as for Pumpkin Pie or replace sweetening with ¾ cup honey.

COCONUT CUSTARD PIE

A tender, delicate custard baked inside a crust.

1 unbaked 9-inch pie crust made from any recipe
3 eggs
2 cups milk
½ cup nonfat dry milk powder
¼ cup honey
1 teaspoon vanilla extract
⅛ teaspoon salt
½ cup shredded, unsweetened coconut

Preheat oven to 425°F.

Prick crust all over with a fork and bake for 10 minutes. Lower temperature to 325°F.

Beat together eggs, milk, milk powder, honey, vanilla, and salt. Use a fork or wire whisk so as not to incorporate too much air.

Sprinkle coconut over partially baked crust. Pour in custard mixture.

Bake for 30 to 35 minutes until a knife inserted in custard comes out clean. Cool to room temperature, then chill promptly.

Makes one 9-inch pie

Minor Protein

LEMON MERINGUE PIE

Lemon Meringue Pie is wonderful to eat, but preparing it is filled with many moments of tension. As this is a delicate pie with many steps, we recommend that you be comfortable as a pastry chef before you attempt it.

1 9-inch crust made from pastry of choice
4 eggs, separated
½ cup plus 1 tablespoon honey
⅛ teaspoon salt
⅓ cup orange juice
1 cup water
⅓ cup cornstarch or arrowroot
1 tablespoon butter
⅓ cup lemon juice
1 tablespoon minced lemon peel
½ teaspoon vanilla extract

Preheat oven to 425°F.

Prepare crust, prick well with a fork, line with wax paper, and fill with rice, beans, or pie weights to bake "blind." Bake for 10 minutes; remove weights and paper and return crust to the oven for 5 to 8 minutes until the bottom is firm and lightly browned. Remove from oven and cool completely.

Prepare filling after shell has been baked.

Reserve egg whites and yolks in separate bowls to warm to room temperature.

In saucepan combine ½ cup honey, salt, orange juice, and ½ cup water. Heat to melt honey and bring to a boil.

Mix starch with remaining water to make a smooth paste. Stir into hot honey mixture and cook over low heat, stirring constantly, until quite thick. Do not boil. Taste, and if starchy, cook for 2 to 3 minutes longer (10 minutes in the top of a double boiler).

Beat egg yolks and temper by gradually beating in some of the hot mixture. Then add yolks to saucepan and cook very gently, stirring until thick. Do not boil. Stir in butter to melt, then lemon juice and peel. When smooth, remove from heat. (From start to finish, filling will take about 20 minutes to make, during which time your attention is required.)

Stir filling several times to speed cooling. When no longer hot, preheat oven to 325°F. When oven is ready, pour cooled filling into crust.

Beat egg whites stiff. Beat in remaining tablespoon honey and vanilla.

Dump egg whites in center of the pie and spread to completely cover filling; smooth over pastry at the edges to seal completely.

Bake for 15 to 20 minutes until evenly browned. Remove from oven and cool completely at room temperature away from drafts. When cool, and not before, transfer to the refrigerator.

Makes one 9-inch pie

FROZEN WHIPPED STRAWBERRY CREAM PIE

A pie you can keep in the freezer so there is always something on hand for entertaining.

1 baked 9-inch Crumb or Nut and Crumb Crust (page 398)
1 pint strawberries
2 tablespoons orange juice
3 tablespoons honey
1½ cups ricotta cheese

Puree 1½ cups strawberries in a blender or processor. Add orange juice, honey, and ricotta and process until smooth and creamy. Taste for sweetening and adjust to taste. Fold in remaining berries cut in small pieces.

Pour filling into prebaked crust. Cover with foil and freeze until firm, at least 2 to 3 hours.

To serve, let stand at room temperature to soften to taste. Some people like it in the partially frozen stage, in which case 30 minutes at room temperature is about right. An hour at room temperature will defrost filling to a soft, creamy texture. Try it both ways. It can also be left in the refrigerator a few hours to soften.

Makes one 9-inch pie
Minor Protein
Note: For best eating, consume within a month, although pie can keep as long as three months and still be quite satisfactory.

Variations: For *Frozen Whipped*

Banana Cream Pie, replace strawberries with 2 bananas, pureeing them both for the filling. Reduce honey to 2 tablespoons.

For *Frozen Whipped Peach Cream Pie,* replace strawberries with 2 cups peeled fresh peaches and use in the same manner as the berries.

QUICK APPLE–DATE TARTS

The filling for the tarts has three important features: it is simple to prepare, has no added sweetening, and is absolutely delicious.

8 large individual tart shells, baked
6 cups diced peeled apple
1½ cups chopped dates
3 tablespoons butter
1½ teaspoons minced lemon peel

Combine apple, dates, butter, and lemon peel in a saucepan, cover, and cook gently until apples are tender but not mushy, 8 to 10 minutes. Stir once or twice during cooking and taste for doneness.

Spoon filling into baked tart shells if you wish to eat them warm, or let it cool at room temperature and spoon into tart shells just before serving.

Makes 8 individual tarts

APPLE TURNOVERS

pastry for 9-inch crust made with rolled recipe of choice
honey
about ½ cup applesauce
cinnamon
milk

Preheat oven to 425°F.
Roll crust to a thin rectangle. Cut into 4-inch squares or rounds.

Spread each piece of pastry lightly with honey. Place 1 tablespoon applesauce in the center, sprinkle with cinnamon, and bring one side over the other in a triangle, rectangle, or half moon as preferred. Seal edges by pinching with fingers or pressing with the tines of a fork. Moisten with water if necessary to hold.

Thin a little honey with milk and wipe over tops of turnovers.

Bake on an ungreased baking sheet for 10 minutes. Reduce heat to 350°F. and bake for 15 to 20 minutes until firm and lightly browned.

Serve when cool enough to handle or let cool to room temperature.

Makes 6 to 8 turnovers

Variation: To make *Extra Flaky Pastry* for turnovers, roll and cover with ¼ cup butter cut into bits. Roll as a jelly roll, bring ends together in the center, flatten, fold in half, flatten, fold in half again, flatten once more, and chill for 10 minutes. Reroll and cut as described above.

DESSERT CREAM PUFFS

A three-step process, well worth the time.

8 large Cream Puffs (page 283)
2 cups Honey-Vanilla Pudding (page 361)
1 recipe Carob Fudge Sauce (page 413)

Prepare cream puffs and let cool completely before filling.

Prepare pudding and chill.

Prepare sauce, cooking until thicker than syrup but not so thick it can't be easily poured. Sauce can be made just before serving, so it is warm, or can be reheated later on.

When ready to serve, spoon ¼ cup pudding in each shell. Cover with lid and drizzle 1 to 2 tablespoons warm fudge sauce on top.

Serves 8
Minor Protein

FOUNDATION SWEET DOUGH

One basic yeast dough can be used to fashion a variety of sweet rolls suited to both dessert and breakfast.

1½ tablespoons yeast
1 cup warm water
2 eggs
¾ teaspoon salt
⅓ cup honey

¼ cup oil
½ cup nonfat dry milk powder
¼ cup soy flour
about 4 cups whole wheat flour

Sprinkle yeast over ¼ cup warm water and let stand for 5 to 10 minutes until frothy. Stir to dissolve.

In a large bowl, beat eggs with salt, honey, and oil. Add dissolved yeast, remaining water, milk powder, soy flour, and whole wheat flour as required to form a dough that can be kneaded.

Turn dough onto a floured work surface and knead for about 10 minutes. Cover in an oiled bowl and let rise in a warm spot for 1 to 1½ hours until doubled.

Punch dough down and shape as directed in specific recipes; or refrigerate for use over the week.

Makes about 2½ pounds dough (enough to prepare two of the following recipes)

Rising time: 1 to 1½ hours.

Note: If the techniques of working with yeast dough are new to you, read about Yeast Breads in "Bread Baking."

Variations: Seven recipes using this one basic dough follow. You may want to make this recipe as *Seven-Day Dough* and assemble something different daily for a full week. To serve 4 people, with enough for occasional guests or the freezer, double the Foundation Sweet Dough recipe, refrigerate, and divide as follows:

Kolache: 10 ounces dough for 6 buns (half the recipe)

Cinnamon Buns: 10 ounces dough for one 8-inch pan (half the recipe)

Snails: 5 ounces dough for 4 danish (one fourth the recipe)

Fruit Twist: 20 ounces dough for 1 loaf (full recipe)

Cheese Danish: 10 ounces dough for 4 danish (half the recipe)

Bear Claws: 10 ounces dough for 4 danish (half the recipe)

Croissants: 15 ounces dough for 6 rolls (three fourths the recipe)

Total: 80 ounces dough or double the basic recipe.

KOLACHE

Kolache are Polish coffee buns with a sweet center. They are the simplest of the sweet dough rolls to prepare.

½ recipe Foundation Sweet Dough
6 tablespoons fruit butter or honey-sweetened preserves
2 tablespoons honey
2 tablespoons milk

Divide dough into 12 balls. Flatten each into rounds 2½ inches in diameter and ¼ inch thick. Place 2 inches apart on an oiled baking sheet.

Make a depression in the center of each round with two fingers. Fill with ½ tablespoon fruit butter or preserves. Cover with a cloth and let rise in a warm spot for 30 to 45 minutes until light.

Preheat oven to 425°F. near end of rising period.

Dissolve honey in milk and brush over each roll before baking. Bake for 10 to 12 minutes until golden. Transfer to a rack to cool. Eat warm or at room temperature.

Makes 12 buns

First rising: To make Foundation Sweet Dough, 1 to 1½ hours; *second rising,* 30 to 45 minutes.

Note: If desired, Kolache can be assembled, covered, and chilled until 40 minutes before baking. Let rise in a warm spot and bake as directed.

CINNAMON BUNS

Slices of filled, rolled Sweet Dough create attractive pinwheels with a lightly sweetened cinnamon filling.

½ recipe Foundation Sweet Dough
2 tablespoons peanut butter
¼ cup honey
1 teaspoon cinnamon
¼ cup chopped walnuts
1 tablespoon wheat germ

Roll dough to an 8 x 16-inch rectangle.

Heat peanut butter with honey and cinnamon until smooth and creamy. Spread over dough. Sprinkle evenly with walnuts and wheat germ.

Roll dough along the 16-inch side

jelly-roll fashion. Slice about ½ inch thick. Place slices with cut surface down on an oiled 9 x 12-inch baking pan or two 8-inch squares, spacing evenly with a little room between.

Cover with a cloth and let rise in a warm spot for about 40 minutes until light.

Preheat oven to 425°F. near end of rising period.

Bake for 10 to 12 minutes until golden. Serve warm.

Makes 24 to 32 small buns

First rising: To make Foundation Sweet Dough, 1 to 1½ hours; *second rising,* 40 minutes.

Note: If desired, buns can be assembled, covered, and chilled until 40 minutes before baking. Let rise in a warm spot and bake as directed.

By preparing buns in two 8-inch pans you have the option of freezing half, unbaked, for use within the month. Defrost at room temperature, about 2 hours, and let rise an additional 30 to 40 minutes, or until light, before baking.

SNAILS

Coils of sweet dough with a sweet nut topping.

½ recipe Foundation Sweet Dough
2 tablespoon butter
¼ cup honey
1 teaspoon cinnamon
¼ cup finely chopped walnuts

Roll dough into a 9 x 16-inch rectangle. Cut into strips 1 inch wide and 16 inches long. Roll strips into thin ropes and form into loose coils on an oiled baking sheet. Tuck end underneath and leave 2 inches between coils.

Heat butter with honey and cinnamon. Stir in nuts. Drizzle 1 teaspoon topping on each coil and spread with back of spoon to cover.

Cover with a cloth and let rise in a warm spot for 30 to 40 minutes until light.

Preheat oven to 425°F. near end of rising.

Bake for 10 to 12 minutes. Cool on a rack.

Makes 16 Snails

First rising: to make Foundation Sweet Dough, 1 to 1½ hours; *second rising,* 30 to 40 minutes.

Note: If desired, Snails can be assembled, covered, and chilled until 40 minutes before baking. Let rise in a warm spot and bake as directed.

FRUIT TWIST

A large braided loaf with a fruit filling and Buttercream Glaze. A typical coffee cake and holiday loaf.

½ recipe Foundation Sweet Dough
1 cup chopped peeled apple
2 tablespoons raisins
3 tablespoons chopped walnuts
½ teaspoon cinnamon
2 tablespoons molasses
1 tablespoon honey
1 tablespoon milk
½ recipe Buttercream Glaze (page 414)

Roll dough into a 9 x 16-inch rectangle.

Combine apple, raisins, walnuts, cinnamon, and molasses. Place in a strip 16 inches long and 3 inches wide in center of dough.

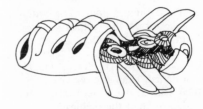

Cut dough in 1-inch wide strips from outer edge to filling. Fold dough strips over filling and pinch lightly where they meet. Cover with a cloth and set to rise in a warm spot for 30 to 40 minutes until light.

Preheat oven to 400°F. near end of rising.

Dissolve honey in milk and brush over lacing of dough. Bake for about 15 minutes until golden. Cool on a rack. When cool, spread thinly with Buttercream Glaze.

Makes 1 large loaf

First rising: to make Foundation Sweet Dough, 1 to 1½ hours; *second rising,* 30 to 40 minutes.

Note: If desired, Fruit Twist can be assembled, covered, and chilled until 40 minutes before baking. Let rise in a warm spot and bake as directed.

CHEESE DANISH

½ recipe Foundation Sweet Dough
1 cup pot cheese, farmer cheese, or dry-curd cottage cheese
¼ cup cream cheese
¼ cup honey
½ teaspoon vanilla extract
2 tablespoons chopped raisins
1 egg, separated
2 tablespoons slivered almonds

Roll dough to an 8 x 16-inch rectangle. Cut into eight 4-inch squares. As you work with each, press or roll gently to enlarge slightly.

Combine cheeses, honey, vanilla, raisins, and egg yolk and blend evenly. Place about 2 tablespoons in the center of each square of dough. Bring the corners to the center. Where edges align, lift over filling and pinch to form a seal. Leave an opening in the center, but seal the outside corners well to prevent leaking.

Cover with cloth and let rise in a warm spot for 30 to 40 minutes until light.

Preheat oven to 425°F. near end of rising period.

If edges have separated during rising, stretch and press together once more. The expansion of the dough in the oven will cause them to open, but this initial seal will contain the filling.

Beat egg white with a little water to loosen and paint the entire top of each Danish, cheese center and all, with the egg wash. Sprinkle some almonds over the center of each.

Bake for 12 to 15 minutes until golden. Cool completely on a rack before serving.

Makes 8 Danish

First rising: to make Foundation Sweet Dough, 1 to 1½ hours; *second rising,* 30 to 40 minutes.

Note: If desired, Danish can be assembled, covered, and chilled until 40 minutes before baking. Let rise in a warm spot and bake as directed.

BEAR CLAWS

A sweet dessert pastry filled with nuts and raisins, shaped like a claw, and decorated with Buttercream Glaze.

½ recipe Foundation Sweet Dough
3 tablespoons melted butter
6 tablespoons honey
1 teaspoon cinnamon
¼ cup chopped walnuts
¼ cup chopped raisins
1 teaspoon minced lemon peel
½ recipe Buttercream Glaze (page 414)

Roll dough into a thin 9 x 24-inch rectangle.

Brush surface with 2 tablespoons melted butter, spread with honey, and top evenly with cinnamon, nuts, raisins, and lemon peel.

Fold dough along short side in thirds, like a letter.

With a sharp knife, cut into eight 3-inch-wide sections. Pinch outside edges lightly and place seam-side down on an oiled baking sheet, spacing the pieces 2 inches apart. Make two 1-inch long cuts on seamless folded edge and separate slightly to form claw.

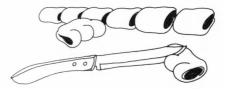

Brush tops with remaining melted butter. Cover and let rise in a warm spot for 40 minutes until light.

Preheat oven to 400°F. near end of rising period.

Bake about 15 minutes until golden. Cool on a rack. When cool, spread thinly with Buttercream Glaze.

Makes 8 large claws

First rising: to make Foundation Sweet Dough, 1 to 1½ hours; *second rising* 40 minutes.

Note: If desired, Claws can be assembled, covered, and chilled until 40 minutes before baking. Let rise in a warm spot and bake as directed.

If you plan to freeze them, do not add icing.

CROISSANTS

If you have any doubts about the ability to turn out high-quality pastries using whole wheat flour, try these. Although the preparation of the rich butter dough for these flaky rolls is not a quick operation and requires care and patience, the result is well worth the effort.

½ recipe Foundation Sweet Dough
⅓ cup butter

Divide dough into two equal portions and prepare one at a time, as it is easier to handle this way.

Working on a well-floured surface, roll one portion of dough into an 8- or 9-inch square. Take half the butter and knead into a flat cake. Place in the center of the dough. Fold two sides of dough over butter and press edges to seal. Roll lengthwise.

Turn dough over so seam is down; fold in thirds again in the opposite direction. Roll once more along the seam.

Flip dough over, fold, roll, and fold once more. Chill for 15 minutes. While dough is chilling, repeat this procedure with the second portion of the dough and the remaining butter.

Remove chilled dough and repeat the process of rolling and folding. The object of all this is to keep the butter inside an envelope of dough. Therefore, folding is always done with the idea of putting an additional layer of dough where butter is closest to the surface.

Eventually you lose track and when butter starts to peek through, final rolling should take place. Chill for 15 minutes first.

Place chilled dough on a lightly floured surface. Roll each piece into a 6 x 12-inch strip. Cut in two squares and each into two triangles. Roll or press each triangle with hands to make two long and one shorter side. Roll short side to tip and curve slightly to form a crescent.

Place with tip down 2 inches apart on an ungreased baking sheet. Cover with a cloth and let rise in a warm spot for about 30 minutes until light.

While oven preheats to 425°F., refrigerate croissants for 15 minutes to harden butter. Bake for 12 minutes. Eat warm.

Makes 8 large croissants

First rising: to make Foundation Sweet Dough, 1 to 1½ hours; *second rising,* 30 minutes. *Chilling:* 30 minutes during shaping and 15 minutes before baking.

Note: If desired, croissants can be shaped, covered, and chilled until 45 minutes to 1 hour before baking. Let rise in a warm spot until light, chill again for 15 minutes, bake as directed.

If there are leftovers, reheat them briefly before serving for best enjoyment. If you freeze some, defrost in a hot oven without thawing, baking for about 10 minutes until crisp.

FINISHING TOUCHES

The topping on the strawberry shortcake, the hot fudge on the ice cream sundae, the frosting on the cake are all accessories that give the dessert a finishing touch. Unfortunately, with few exceptions, the traditional recipes that serve this function overemphasize sugar and cream and offer little beyond their taste appeal.

It is possible, however, to combine aesthetic delights and wholefoods style with only minor compromises. In this section you will find many garnishes for desserts that actually add to their food value, and although some are on the sweet side, they are not excessively so. When we have included recipes high in fat, like the one for whipped cream, it is primarily to encourage the use of the real thing rather than a commercial chemical substitute. We hope you recognize by now that such foods do not have to be eliminated, just used with consideration.

In addition to the specific recipes given here, do not forget that the addition of plain honey, honey-sweetened preserves, honey- or maple syrup-sweetened yogurt, sour cream–yogurt mixtures sweetened with molasses, and sliced fruit marinated in orange juice or a little liqueur can glorify puddings, plain cakes, muffins, biscuits, or crackers.

CLOTTED CREAM

The souring of buttermilk at room temperature has the surprising effect of mellowing its natural tangy taste, transforming the low-fat milk into a thick, mild cream, much like crème fraîche in consistency and flavor. Clotted Cream is excellent with fresh berries, as well as other fruit desserts.

2 cups buttermilk

Pour buttermilk into a glass container and leave at room temperature for 8 to 12 hours until it becomes thick.

Pour through a colander lined with two layers of cheesecloth set over a bowl. Let stand for another 8 to 12 hours to drain.

Scrape curds from cheesecloth and refrigerate. Use within a few days for best flavor. (Use whey for cooking vegetables or as a base for soup.)
Makes ½ cup cream
Minor Protein
Note: If you do not have cheesecloth, drip-coffee filters can be used.

YOGURT CREAM

Use like whipped cream on top of warm apple desserts, Cranberry Crunch, plain cakes, tarts, pies, and fresh fruit.

¼ cup cream cheese
½ cup yogurt
about 1 teaspoon honey, maple syrup, or molasses

Mash cream cheese with a fork. Beat in yogurt until smooth and creamy. Sweeten lightly. If desired, a little vanilla extract can also be added, or a dusting of cinnamon or nutmeg can be used on top.
Makes about ¾ cup; serves 4
Minor Protein
Note: This dessert topping is relatively high in fat, furnishing 3.5 grams and about 45 calories per 2 tablespoons.

WHIPPED RICOTTA TOPPING

Ricotta cheese, often used as a sweet filling in Italian pastries, can also be turned into a light whipped topping.

1 cup ricotta cheese
2 tablespoons cream cheese
2 tablespoons yogurt
1 to 1½ tablespoons honey
1 teaspoon vanilla extract

Combine ricotta, cream cheese, and yogurt in a mixing bowl and whip until smooth and fluffy, preferably with an electric mixer. Beat in honey to taste and add vanilla.
Makes about 1¾ cups; serves 6 to 8
Minor Protein
Note: Contains half the fat of whipped cream when made with whole milk ricotta; contains only one third the fat of whipped cream when made with partially skim milk ricotta.

SOY WHIPPED CREAM

A nondairy whipped topping with very good flavor.

8 ounces tofu
1 teaspoon vanilla extract
1½ tablespoons honey
2 tablespoons oil

Combine tofu, vanilla, and honey in a blender or processor fitted with a plastic blade. Process until smooth. With the machine running, gradually add oil through the feeder cap.
Makes ⅔ cup; serves 4 to 6
Protein Complement

REAL WHIPPED CREAM

1 cup chilled heavy or "whipping" cream
vanilla extract
honey or maple syrup

If possible, have bowl and beater well chilled as well as cream.

Pour cream into a deep bowl at least twice its volume in capacity. Copper is the best material for whipping cream if you have a choice.

Using a wire whisk, or a rotary or electric beater, begin to slowly whip cream, moving the beater around in the bowl for even whipping. As cream begins to thicken, pick up the pace until it becomes quite fast.

Whip to desired consistency, but stop before cream turns to butter. (Under-whipping is certainly preferable to over-whipping). Add a few drops vanilla and fold in just a little honey or maple syrup for faint sweetening. Use whipped cream as soon as possible after preparation, as it is not very stable.

Makes 2 cups
Note: Two tablespoons of whipped cream furnish about 52 calories and 5.5 grams fat.

WHIPPED ORANGE–SESAME CREAM

A thick, rich nondairy topping that is delicious on plain cakes.

3 tablespoons orange juice
2 tablespoons honey
¼ cup tahini
⅓ cup light oil (safflower or sunflower)

Gradually beat orange juice and honey into tahini until smooth. Slowly beat in oil, pouring in a steady stream as if you were making mayonnaise, until "cream" is thick. This is most easily done in the blender or processor, adding the oil through the feeder cap. If done by hand, use a wire whisk and have a helper pour in the oil as the whipping takes place.

Makes ⅔ cup
Protein Complement

FRESH PEACH SAUCE

For plain cakes, puddings, and ice cream.

4 small or 2 large peaches (about 10 ounces)
1½ teaspoons arrowroot or cornstarch
½ cup orange juice
1 to 3 tablespoons honey
¼ teaspoon cinnamon
⅛ teaspoon nutmeg

Peel, pit, and puree peaches in a blender, processor, or food mill. You should have ½ cup puree.

Mix starch with a little orange juice to form a smooth paste. Combine in a saucepan with peach puree, remaining juice, and 1 tablespoon honey.

Stir over low heat until mixture thickens. If using arrowroot, remove from heat before mixture boils. If using cornstarch, boil briefly and gently.

Remove from heat and add spices. Taste and add more honey if necessary. Amount needed will vary depending on the sweetness of the peaches. Serve warm, at room temperature, or chilled.

Makes 1 cup; serves 4

FRESH STRAWBERRY SAUCE

For ice cream, yogurt, or plain cakes, or spooned over cottage cheese or ricotta for breakfast, snack, or dessert.

1½ cups cut strawberries
¼ cup honey
¼ cup water

Puree berries in a blender or processor. Combine puree, honey, and water in a saucepan and bring to a boil for 1 minute. Chill.

Makes 1½ cups
Note: Sauce can be frozen. Let thaw at room temperature.

BLUEBERRY SAUCE

1½ cups blueberries
¼ cup honey
1 tablespoon lemon juice

Combine all ingredients in a saucepan and bring to a boil. Simmer for 3 minutes. Chill before using.

Makes 1¼ cups

RAISIN SAUCE

An easy-to-prepare sauce for spooning warm over gingerbread, pound cake, and plain or toasted coffee cake that is beginning to get stale.

½ cup raisins
1½ cups water
2 tablespoons honey
1 tablespoon butter
1½ teaspoons arrowroot or corn-starch
1 teaspoon lemon juice

Combine raisins and water in a saucepan and simmer uncovered for 10 minutes. Stir in honey.

In a separate pot melt butter, stir in starch, then gradually add hot raisin mixture. Stir over low heat for 3 to 5 minutes until thickened. Add lemon juice. Serve at once, or keep warm in the top of a double boiler.

Makes 1 cup; serves 4

FOAMY CUSTARD SAUCE

A light sauce, reminiscent of eggnog, that is delicious over plain cakes, bread pudding, and cranberry desserts. Meant for those who like to spend time in the kitchen, as it requires continuous attention.

1 cup milk
2 tablespoons honey
2 eggs, separated
½ teaspoon vanilla extract
cinnamon and nutmeg (optional)

Scald milk in a saucepan or the top of a double boiler set directly on the heat. Stir in honey.

Beat egg yolks with a bit of the hot milk to temper, then add to milk and place back on the stove in top of a double boiler. Cook and stir until slightly thickened so that sauce coats the spoon, about 10 to 15 minutes. Do not boil. Remove from heat and stir in vanilla.

Beat egg whites until completely foamy. Beat custard sauce into the foamy whites.

Serve at once or chill. Sauce will thicken on chilling and should be stirred well before use. If desired, sprinkle cinnamon and nutmeg lightly over the sauce when serving.

Makes about 1½ cups; serves 6
Minor Protein

CAROB SYRUP

Use as a dessert sauce or a beverage syrup.

¼ cup carob powder
¼ cup nonfat dry milk powder
3 tablespoons honey
½ cup water
½ teaspoon vanilla extract

Make a smooth paste of carob, dry milk, honey, and water. Bring slowly to a gentle boil and simmer for 5 minutes. Remove from heat and stir in vanilla. Serve warm or store in the refrigerator for future use.

Makes ⅔ cup

Variations: For *Carob Fudge Sauce,* simmer for 10 minutes to a fudgy consistency.

For *Rich Cake Sauce,* beat in 2 tablespoons butter with the vanilla.

For a nondairy beverage syrup, omit milk powder.

For *Chocolate Syrup,* replace carob with cocoa and increase honey to ¼ cup for bittersweet syrup, 6 tablespoons for sweet milk chocolate syrup. If desired, part carob and part cocoa can be used.

HOT WET NUTS

A special treat for homemade sundaes.

2 tablespoons butter
½ cup chopped nuts
¼ cup maple syrup
2 tablespoons water

Melt butter in a small skillet and brown nuts lightly over low heat. Stir in maple syrup and water and simmer for 2 minutes.

Makes ⅔ cup; serves 6

BUTTERCREAM GLAZE

A thin icing for donuts, Danish, and loaf cakes.

¼ cup honey
1 tablespoon butter
⅓ cup nonfat dry milk powder
½ teaspoon vanilla extract
about 1 tablespoon water

Beat honey with butter until creamy. Beat in milk powder and vanilla and let stand to absorb the milk. If necessary, add water to make a soft icing. Spread thinly.

Enough for 12 Danish or donuts, 2 loaf cakes, or a large braided Fruit Twist

Note: Glazed cakes, like iced cakes, should be stored in the refrigerator. Unlike sugar frostings, which harden when chilled, this glaze will remain soft.

10. If desired, sprinkle with coconut, nuts, or other decoration while still moist, or place a few whole berries or thin twists of orange decoratively on top.

11. When frosting has set, carefully pull out the wax paper strips.

THE FROSTING ON THE CAKE

1. Be sure both cake and frosting are cool before beginning.

2. Brush any loose crumbs from cake.

3. Choose a flat plate 2 to 3 inches larger than the cake.

4. Cut four strips of wax paper 10 inches long and 3 inches wide and place, overlapping, around the edges of the plate.

5. If cake has more than one layer, choose the thickest for the bottom. Set it in the center of the plate so that it rests on the wax paper strips.

6. If filling a layer cake, spread filling almost but not quite to the edge, using a flexible metal spatula. Top with second layer, and repeat if multiple layers are involved.

7. When final cake layer is on top, cover lightly with frosting, again stopping just short of the edge. Then spread sides of the cake with a thin coating of frosting.

8. Spread a layer of frosting along the top edge down over the sides.

9. Pile remaining frosting on top and spread lightly toward the edge, swirling as you spread.

BUTTERCREAM FROSTING

½ cup honey
2 tablespoons butter
1 teaspoon vanilla extract
½ to 1 cup nonfat dry milk powder

Beat honey with butter until thick and creamy. Beat in vanilla.

Continue to beat, adding milk powder, 1 tablespoon at a time, until icing is of desired spreading consistency. Amount needed varies with the moisture content of the honey.

Before using the icing, let it sit for a while (while cake bakes or cools) to absorb the milk powder. Spread sparingly on cake, as this icing is quite sweet.

Enough for top and sides or top and one layer of an 8- or 9-inch cake

Minor Protein

Variations: For *Spice Frosting,* flavor with cinnamon and nutmeg to taste.

For *Carob* or *Chocolate Frosting,* reduce vanilla to ½ teaspoon and beat in 1½ tablespoons carob powder, cocoa, or a combination.

Top iced cake with chopped walnuts.

ORANGE FROSTING

For cupcakes or as a thin icing on carrot, zucchini, or other plain cakes.

**3 tablespoons honey
2 tablespoons orange juice
½ to ⅔ cup nonfat dry milk powder**

Mix honey with orange juice. Beat in milk powder a little at a time until smooth. Add enough milk powder to get a thin frosting. Drizzle over cupcakes or cake.

Enough frosting for 12 cupcakes, 1 large sheet cake, or 2 loaves
Minor Protein

WHIPPED WHITE ICING

A favorite for cupcakes.

**6 tablespoons honey (¼ cup plus 2 tablespoons)
1 egg white
1 teaspoon vanilla extract
1 teaspoon lemon juice**

Boil honey without stirring for about 5 minutes, until it reaches the soft-ball stage (238°F.). Remove from heat.

Beat egg white with an electric beater until soft peaks form. Gradually pour in the heated honey, continuing to beat for about 3 minutes, or until icing is of thick spreading consistency. Beat in vanilla and lemon juice.

Use at once, or store in the refrigerator where icing will keep for 2 days.

Makes 1½ cups (enough for 16 cupcakes)

Note: To ice cupcakes, invert in a bowl of frosting and lift out quickly with a twist of the wrist to give a swirled effect.

Variations: Lemon can be replaced with 1 teaspoon orange juice concentrate or some crushed sweet berries.

CREAM CHEESE FROSTING

A pleasant icing that is much less sweet than most.

**4 ounces (½ cup) cream cheese
4 teaspoons honey (1 tablespoon plus 1 teaspoon)**

**¼ teaspoon vanilla extract
about 1 tablespoon yogurt**

Beat all ingredients together with an electric mixer until light and creamy. If too thick, add an additional teaspoon yogurt. Spread on cake with a spatula.

Makes a scant ⅔ cup (enough for a 9 x 13-inch sheet cake)

Note: Icing can be refrigerated in a covered container for several days. Once a cake is iced, it must be stored in the refrigerator if it is not eaten within a few hours.

A cream cheese-frosted cake can be garnished with ¼ cup chopped nuts.

CHOCOLATE CREAM FROSTING AND FILLING

A very rich mixture to be used on plain cake or on Devil's Food Cake for party fare.

**3 tablespoons cocoa
¼ cup honey
1 tablespoon warm water
3 ounces (6 tablespoons) cream cheese
¼ cup yogurt
1 teaspoon vanilla extract
1½ cups nonfat dry milk powder**

Beat together cocoa, honey, and warm water, using an electric mixer.

Beat in cream cheese, yogurt, vanilla, and ¼ cup milk powder in this order until thick and creamy. Continue until all milk powder is absorbed and frosting is rich and thick. Frost cake immediately, as icing hardens on standing.

Makes about 1⅓ cups (enough to fill and frost a 9-inch layer cake)

Minor Protein

Note: If you wish to garnish the cake with chopped nuts, do so while the icing is still soft.

To garnish with pieces of fruit, wait until icing hardens.

For a more elaborate filling, put a layer of crushed pineapple or sliced fresh berries or cherries on chocolate filling before adding the second layer of cake.

THICK FUDGE FROSTING AND FILLING

This fudgy mixture can be stored in the refrigerator and is especially suited for spreading on crisp apple or pear slices or sandwiching between two plain cookies for quick dessert treats.

⅓ cup honey
¼ cup cocoa
6 tablespoons nonfat dry milk powder
½ cup water
⅛ teaspoon salt
1 tablespoon butter
½ teaspoon vanilla extract
¼ to ½ cup walnuts (optional)

Combine honey, cocoa, milk powder, water, and salt in a small saucepan. Bring to a boil over medium heat; simmer for 10 to 15 minutes, without stirring, until mixture is thickened.

Remove from heat, add butter and vanilla, and beat with an electric mixer until thick and creamy, about 5 minutes. Stir in nuts if desired. Store in the refrigerator.

Makes ¾ cup

Variation: For carob version, replace cocoa with carob powder and reduce honey to ¼ cup; a mixture of cocoa and carob can also be used.

Beverages

Many people who, like W. C. Fields, disdain water as a beverage find sparkling water much more to their taste. Both imported and domestic naturally sparkling mineral waters have become very popular. Certainly, they are pleasant, refreshing, noncaloric drinks, but it is unlikely that they possess the curative powers that many attribute to them. Moreover, many are not as naturally "sparkling" as they claim and may have had the carbonation adjusted.

This is not to dissuade you from their use, but to make you aware of their true nature and also to inform you of an alternative that is not so very different from costly mineral waters. That alternative, "seltzer" water, commonly available on tap at soda fountains, is a carbon dioxide-charged water. After several decades of relative obscurity, it is enjoying a commercial rebirth. Seltzer is more highly charged than most natural sparkling waters. It is like club soda in flavor and bubbliness but does not contain any added sodium salts or artificial flavorings.

Excellent homemade soda pop can be prepared using charged water, as in the following recipe. You may even want to start making charged water at home with a seltzer maker and carbon dioxide pellets that are sold for this purpose.

SELTZER FIZZ

The American Wholefoods soda pop; any juice can be turned into a carbonated beverage by mixing it with seltzer.

juice of choice, including apple, orange, pineapple, grape, and various fruit blends
seltzer

Fill a glass about two-thirds with juice. Add seltzer until juice is diluted to taste and quite fizzy. Exact proportions vary, depending on the juice as well as your own preferences, but a general ratio of 2 parts juice to 1 part sparkling water is about right.

VEGETABLE COCKTAIL

A blend of tomato juice and fresh vegetables for a "salad in a glass."

1 slice green pepper
1 scallion
½ medium cucumber, peeled
3 sprigs parsley
2 cups tomato juice
1 teaspoon lemon juice
ice

Cut up vegetables and combine in a blender or processor fitted with a steel blade. Add ½ cup tomato juice and blend until smooth. Add remaining juice and lemon juice and blend briefly to combine.

Serve over ice to thin, as this is somewhat thicker than plain juice.

Makes about 3 cups; serves 4
Note: Best consumed soon after preparation; if stored, keep in a covered container and shake well before serving.

LEMONADE

It is just as easy to make real fresh lemonade as it is to reconstitute the frozen concentrate.

3 tablespoons honey
1 cup warm water
½ cup lemon juice (about 2½ lemons)
2 cups cold water

Dissolve honey in warm water. Add lemon juice and cold water, and chill.

Makes about 1 quart
Variations: For a delicious *Fruit Punch*, combine lemonade with orange juice, apple juice, cherry apple, grape, and similar sweet fruit juices to taste.

For *Lemon-Limeade*, use ¼ cup lemon juice and ¼ cup lime juice.

CRANBERRY JUICE COCKTAIL

2 cups cranberries
3 cups water
about ⅓ cup honey
1 teaspoon lemon juice

Combine berries and water in a saucepan and simmer for 15 minutes to extract juice. Mash gently with a spoon to aid the process.

Strain juice through a sieve and once again crush berries to release juices without actually pushing the pulp through the strainer.

Add honey and lemon juice while still hot. Stir to melt. Taste and if too tart, adjust honey to taste. Chill.

Makes 1½ pints

Note: Cranberry juice can be either served straight or mixed with apple, orange, or grape juice.

After juice is extracted, about ½ cup pulp will remain. To make *Cranberry Jelly,* add about 1 tablespoon honey to this pulp.

Both the juice and the jelly made with the pulp will keep up to two weeks with refrigeration.

FRESH FRUIT DRINK

A blend of fresh fruit and juice with unlimited possibilities.

1 cup diced fresh fruit of choice (berries, melon, nectarines, or peeled peaches or plums)
½ cup fruit juice of choice (orange, pineapple, apple, grape)
¼ cup ice

Puree fruit in a blender or processor fitted with a steel blade, adding juice to make puree smooth. Gradually add ice and process until completely dissolved.

Makes 1¼ cups; serves 2

Variation: For a *Fresh Fruit Fizz,* process fruit and juice as described, add ¼ cup carbonated water, and serve over ice.

PARTY PUNCH

No need for canned or dry mix beverages.

2 cups orange juice
2 cups apple juice
1 cup grape juice
2 cups seltzer or ice

Combine the juices. Just before serving, add seltzer or ice.

Makes 1½ quarts

Variation: For *Virgin Sangria,* add 1 cup sliced seasonal fruit to the juices and let marinate.

JANE'S SCHLURPY

A blender drink with an icy head that makes a hot weather treat.

1½ cups one or a combination of juices (orange, grape, pineapple, apple, or other favorites)
1½ cups ice or 12 ice cubes

Combine juice and ice in a blender and process at high speed until most of the ice is liquefied. Pour into tall glasses. An icy head will rise.

Makes 3 cups (serves 2 generously, 4 more sparingly)

ORANGE JULIA

Like drinking a creamsicle.

1½ cups orange juice
1 teaspoon honey
¼ teaspoon vanilla extract
2 tablespoons nonfat dry milk powder
2 ice cubes

Combine all ingredients in a blender or processor and run at high speed until ice is liquefied. Or, whip with a beater or shake in a jar until ice melts. Serve at once.

Serves 2

CAROB DRINK

Mrs. Goldbeck's "Yoohoo."

1 overflowing soupspoonful Carob Syrup (nondairy version, page 413)
4 tablespoons nonfat dry milk powder
cold water
cracked ice

Combine syrup and dry milk powder in a jar with enough cold water and ice to equal 1 cup. Shake well until blended and most of ice is desolved.

Serves 1
Minor Protein

THICK SHAKE

Rich enough to eat with a spoon.

½ cup sliced strawberries, banana, peach, cantalope, or other fruit of choice
¾ cup combined apple and orange juice
¼ cup nonfat dry milk powder
4 ice cubes

Puree fruit in a blender or processor fitted with a steel blade.

Add remaining ingredients and whip until ice dissolves and mixture is light and thick. Pour into glasses. Eat with a spoon.

Makes 2 cups; serves 2
Minor Protein
Variation: For a shake you can drink, increase juice to 1 or 1½ cups, or add ½ cup yogurt or milk.

HERB TEA AND CEREAL "COFFEE"

There is a wide variety of herbs that can be used for tea, and as most are caffeine-free, they are often preferred to black-leaf teas and coffee. Herbs are not without their own effects, however. Some, like camomile, are relaxants. Some, like peppermint, are noteworthy for their soothing effect on the digestive system. Both ginseng and maté are potent stimulants. Other herbs act as appetite depressants, laxatives, sedatives, etc. Because they are of plant origin, some may also cause allergic reactions in sensitive individuals.

While it is best to be aware of the potential medicinal properties of the herbs you select for tea, by and large the herbal blends on the market do not adversely affect most people.

The preparation of herb tea is similar to that of regular tea. Because herbs swell considerably in water, a tea strainer is more practical than a teaball when using loose or bulk herbs. Allow a rounded teaspoonful for each cup of boiling water. This will make one large mug or two small teacups. (When a pot of tea is desired, use 2 tablespoons herbs per quart of water.) About 3 minutes' brewing time is recommended.

To prepare iced herb tea, increase the proportion to 3 tablespoons herbs per quart of boiling water (2 teaspoons per cup) and brew for 5 minutes. Remove herbs and then chill.

Herb teas lack the bitterness of leaf teas and can generally be served without sweetening or with only a bit of honey. If you wish to sweeten iced herb tea, this is best done before chilling. One teaspoon honey per quart of tea should suffice.

The roasted cereal grain blends that are sold as coffee substitutes are more full-bodied than herb teas, have neither the stimulating effect of coffee nor the medicinal properties of herbs, and make quite a satisfying hot or even iced drink.

As not all cereal coffees are the same, you may want to try several to find the one that appeals most. The addition of a little honey imparts a certain mellowness, while sweetening with molasses makes cereal coffees more robust. With the addition of milk, the resulting "coffee" will be suited to children as well as grown-ups.

The Food Factory

Most people consider "manufactured foods" those items they buy. If you think about it, though, the breads, cakes, and cookies you bake, a fresh tomato sauce, or a homemade soup are all similarly "manufactured." The advantage in having them commercially made, of course, is convenience—you do not need the time or inclination to do the job yourself.

For many people, however, home production of food is an enjoyable pastime, and the fact that most of it can be done far below the cost of commercial counterparts simply compounds the pleasure. This section is intended as an introduction to the food production possibilities that exist within your own home: yogurt making, sprout growing, home preservation of fruits and vegetables by freezing, canning, pickling, and preserve-making, and the preparation of convenience mixes.

Making yogurt and growing sprouts are the simplest jobs in the food factory, requiring no expertise and little equipment. Both are designed to become routine kitchen tasks that can provide you with a continuous supply of inexpensive protein and a fresh vegetable.

Mixes for soup, sauces, and baking can also save time and steps. It is not very difficult to assemble a few mixes, when you have free time, and keep them on hand for more hurried meals.

Putting up food is usually a seasonal activity, in full swing when high-quality produce is readily available. Discussed here are the basics of home freezing, canning, pickling, and preserve-making, with special emphasis on the easiest and most efficient techniques; of special interest are the many fruits and vegetables that can be "directly frozen" without processing. Another interesting approach freezes foods into "ice cubes" for convenient retrieval.

While the freezing and canning ideas discussed here are in no way a complete guide to either subject (that would constitute a book in itself), we have included the essential highlights.

Consider as you read this section that catsup, pickles, relishes, fruit butters, and preserves not only add to your own table but also are welcome gifts. They are truly the finest gourmet foods—products of labor and love that are hard to equal.

YOGURT MAKING

Yogurt may well be the oldest manufactured dairy product, although its invention was probably unintentional. It was apparently discovered about eleven centuries ago in the Middle East as travelers carrying milk with them in animal-skin sacks found that it had thickened and had excellent eating qualities. Today, although the process is more refined, the principle is the same—milk is exposed to specific bacteria and then placed in a warm spot to culture.

Home Production of Yogurt

Yogurt is a very important and versatile food. It is one of the few and certainly the simplest sources of protein that can be manufactured at home. By following the instructions given here, you should have no problems in making your own yogurt, and you will save money at the same time. To give an idea of the economical aspects of making yogurt at home, 1 cup of milk yields 1 cup of yogurt, yet an 8-ounce cup of commercial yogurt may cost almost as much as a full quart of milk. You can reduce the cost even further by making yogurt with nonfat dry milk.

Yogurt may be made from cow's milk (the most common in this country) or ewe's milk (more common in the Middle East) or, for that matter, from the milk of any species including goats, yaks, or reindeer.

Two bacteria are used in the production of yogurt: *Lactobacillus bulgaris* and *Streptococcus lactis,* either singly or together. The bacteria can be purchased as a dried starter or can be transferred directly from one batch of yogurt to the next, as is the case in the directions that follow.

When fresh fluid milk is used to make yogurt it must be scalded first, as the bacteria naturally present in milk can inhibit the activity of the yogurt-producing bacteria. When canned milk or reconstituted dried milk is used to make yogurt, this scalding can be omitted, for the heat used in making these milk products renders them sterile.

Although yogurt can be made in any sterile container that is kept warm, a temperature-controlled yogurt maker will yield more consistent results. Alternately, you can incubate yogurt in a thermos bottle, in a container placed in an oven with the pilot light on, in a ceramic crock wrapped in a blanket or newspapers or nestled in a styrofoam chest, or in various other suitable spots. It is essential, however, that the temperature be constant throughout the culturing process. (For this reason, it is not a good idea to place incubating yogurt near a heat register because of the fluctuations from warm to cold.)

The best temperature for culturing yogurt is around 115°F. It should take about 4 to 5 hours to culture yogurt at this temperature. When cultured at lower temperatures (for example, 80°F.), the process takes longer, perhaps 8 to 12 hours. The longer the

period of development, the greater the pungency of the yogurt.

Yogurt should be chilled before it is used. This will set or stabilize the curd, increase the thickness a bit, and end the culturing stage.

Step-by-Step Yogurt Making

Here are the directions for making about a quart of yogurt using two different methods, the first based on fresh milk, the second featuring nonfat dry milk (NFDM).

Ingredients
nonfat dry milk (optional)
milk
yogurt starter

Equipment
saucepan
dairy or candy thermometer (optional)
incubation container

1. Although fluid milk is the basis, if you desire extra protein and nutrients and a richer-tasting yogurt, begin by dissolving ½ cup nonfat dry milk in 1 quart fluid milk.

2. Heat milk until it is *just about to boil.* Remove from heat and let cool to 115°F. (Use a dairy or candy thermometer, or wait until a few drops placed on your wrist feel warm but not hot.)

3. Place 2 tablespoons fresh, unflavored yogurt in the sterile container in which you plan to incubate the yogurt. This acts as the "starter." (Adding more yogurt will *not* speed the process.)

4. Stir a little of the warm milk into the yogurt until it is smooth. This will raise the temperature slowly and prepare it for the rest of the milk.

5. Stir in the remaining milk and mix thoroughly so that the yogurt is distributed throughout.

6. Cover and transfer to a yogurt maker or other incubating spot.

7. Do not disturb the yogurt for the

next 4 hours. Yogurt should not be moved unnecessarily during the culturing process; doing so may produce a thin yogurt or separation of the curds and whey.

8. When you think the yogurt is sufficiently cultured, lift the container gently from the incubator. Tilt it slightly to gauge the consistency. For a thicker yogurt, incubate for another hour or so, but if it's fairly firm or you are otherwise satisfied, transfer to the refrigerator and chill for several hours before using.

EASY NFDM YOGURT

Requires no cooking.

1. Dissolve the amount of nonfat dry milk recommended for a quart of milk (1 to 1⅓ cups) in *only 3 cups* warm water. Use a wire whisk or rotary beater to mix.

2. Follow preceding yogurt-making directions, starting with step #3 above. Pour milk through strainer as it is added to the culturing jar to be certain no undissolved lumps remain.

Generations of Yogurt

When your yogurt supply begins to get low, you can prepare a new batch using the previous one as your starter. Some strains of yogurt are reported to have been kept alive for generations through careful handling. However, if after a while, your own yogurt is not working as quickly as it used to in culturing new yogurts, purchase a good commercial yogurt and begin again. The bacteria in your home brew may have become exhausted, especially if it has been exposed to unsterile conditions that might introduce competing bacteria.

There is some disagreement as to the effect of freezing temperatures on the bacteria; because some bacteria may be destroyed by extreme cold, yogurt that has been frozen is not a reliable starter. Also, if the yogurt has been heated, it will not be able to foster a new culture. In fact, if the scalded milk is mixed with the starter while it is still very hot, it may kill off the yogurt-producing bacteria.

GROWING SPROUTS

Many people associate sprouts only with Chinese food or the nestlike garnish atop a salad in health food restaurants. However, this food is a growing part of the American table, and can be found today in the produce department of many supermarkets (produced by a new breed of small farmer).

Sprouts can also be made year-round in your kitchen, providing a constant supply of fresh greens. They are extremely easy to grow and are worth the effort since they supply both protein and the nutrients that we are accustomed to getting only from the freshest of vegetables.

Sprouts reflect the food value of the original seed or bean, but because some of the starch is consumed as energy in the sprouting process, bean sprouts contain less carbohydrate than the original beans and increased amounts of vitamins A and C. Their protein contribution is nothing to be scoffed at either; 1 cup of soy sprouts, for example, which furnishes a mere 48 calories, has as much protein as a large egg.

These miniature vegetables vary in taste, depending on the bean or seed from which they originate. The most familiar are alfalfa sprouts, which taste much like fresh green peas. Mung, a popular Oriental sprout, is juicy and succulent with a mild, beany taste. Soy sprouts are crisp and have a nutlike flavor. Wheat berries produce a sweet sprout, whereas radish seed sprouts are peppery. Lentils, garbanzo beans, and fenugreek are a few other commonly sprouted seeds, each with its own distinctive taste. Your favorite dried bean can be used to grow sprouts, while other seeds may be obtained from health food stores, some supermarkets, and mail order outlets (see page 425). Any seed may be sprouted *as long as it is not treated with fungicides* (beware: many packaged garden seeds are).

Equipment

The sprouting process is akin to what happens routinely in a garden: the seeds are put in contact with water in an environment conducive to growth. The simplest and most common device for sprouting is a glass jar with a piece of mesh, cheesecloth, or fine netting across the mouth. Canning jars are especially suited, as the outer rim of the two-piece lid will hold the material in place. The size of the jar is determined by how many seeds you are sprouting, but it should be no smaller than one pint. We have seen sprouting jars as large as one gallon in homes and restaurants.

Many other sprouting devices exist, ranging from special caps that fit canning jars, to mesh bags, to sprouting trays, some of which can even be stacked in layers for continuous or varied crops.

Step-by-Step Sprouting

---

1. Soak the seeds in a generous amount of water. For a 1-quart jar use about 1½ tablespoons fine seeds, or about ¼ cup beans, and about four times their volume in water. If you are using the jar method, soaking can be done right in the sprouting jar. Soak for 6 to 12 hours to allow for maximum water absorption and swelling.

2. After the initial soaking, drain the seeds by inverting the mesh-covered container, allowing the liquid to run off. Some people use this water for soup or for feeding plants. Be sure the holes in the mesh are small enough to keep the seeds from passing through. (If you are sprouting in something other than a jar, drain the seeds through a fine strainer and transfer them to your sprouter.)

3. The seeds can now be set to germinate in their container. While they are growing, they must be kept moist (but not wet) and well aerated. To meet these requirements, for the next few days rinse the seeds with cool water through the mesh. Pour the water out and keep the jar upside down to drain. Rinse twice each time and at least twice a day. Shake the jar so the seeds spread out and have room to grow. Leave the sprouter on an inverted slant in a dish to permit additional draining.

4. Keep in a warm, dark place. A kitchen cabinet is a convenient setting, or you may choose to place the sprouting jar right on the counter so you'll remember to rinse the seeds. To create darkness, throw a kitchen towel over the sprouter, but leave the mesh cover unblocked so that air can flow through. (This keeps the sprouts from becoming waterlogged and rotting.) The more frequently the seeds are washed the better the sprouts will grow. Post a sign on the cabinet if you're afraid you'll forget the daily rinsing.

5. Within three to five days, the sprouts will be adorned with tiny tails and ready to eat. On the last day you may put them in the light to develop chlorophyll, but only for a few hours or they will turn bitter. If you will not be able to put them away in time, skip this step.

Because of the temperature, growth may be a little slower in winter and faster in summer. The precise time to harvest your sprouts is largely a matter of judgment and personal taste. Some people say the shoot should be no longer than the seed; this does not help much in the case of alfalfa sprouts, which at half an inch dwarf the tiny seed and are still fine eating. We prefer to taste day by day, and when sprouts

Jar Sprouting

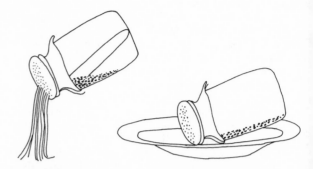

Soak seeds directly in sprouting jar.

Cover jar with cheesecloth, fine netting, mesh or other material small enough to keep seeds from passing through. Secure in place with a rubber band, the outer rim of a two-piece ball jar lid, or a commercial sprout cover, etc.

Rinse and drain sprouts through mesh several times a day. Shake jar to distribute seeds, and store in a warm, dark place with the jar tilted in an inverted position. This will allow excess moisture to run off, so be sure and keep a dish underneath to catch the liquid. Try to spread the seeds all along the sides of the jar to keep them from crowding.

Strainer Sprouting

Soak seeds in any container.

Pour contents through a strainer woven small enough to contain seeds. Spread the seeds evenly over the surface to keep them from crowding.

Rest the strainer in a pot or bowl so that excess liquid can drain off. Rinse two to three times daily. Keep in a warm dark place or cover with a towel so light stays off the germinating seeds.

are long enough to be crunchy and pleasant in flavor, we consider it time to halt their growth. When sprouts grow too long, the flavor becomes bitter (which is not harmful, only distasteful, but will guide you for next time). With most seeds, sprouts will be past their prime once leaves appear at the end of the shoot.

6. The last step is readying the sprouts for storage. With most sprouted seeds a final rinsing, draining, and placement in the refrigerator in a covered container completes the process. Some of the beans, however, contain loose hulls; while these are an excellent source of fiber, they may detract from the texture and appearance of many dishes. To remove these hulls before storing, place the sprouts in a large enough bowl of water to cover them generously. Swish them around until most of the hulls float to the top. Skim with a strainer, drain the sprouts carefully, and store them in a covered container in the refrigerator.

Using Sprouts

You will discover lots of ways to use sprouts in this book, but you needn't wait for a recipe to try them out. The simplest way to serve them is raw in salads or as a green instead of lettuce on sandwiches or tacos. You can also use them:

• stir-fried with any vegetables as the Chinese do

• instead of celery in egg salad

• combined with cottage cheese for a crunchy salad or sandwich filling

• in potato salad or coleslaw

• added to stews and soups during the last 10 minutes of cooking

Note: Only alfalfa sprouts do not cook well and only soy sprouts must be cooked or blanched before eating.

Mail Order Seed Suppliers

Jung Quality Seeds
Randolph, Wis. 53956

Mellinger's
2310 W. South Range Road
North Lima, Ohio 44452

Morgan & Thompson
Box 100
Farmingdale, N.J. 07727

Nichol's Garden Nursery
1190 N. Pacific Highway
Albany, Ore. 97321

L. L. Olds Seed Co.
Box 7790
Madison, Wis. 57707

Vermont Bean Seed Co.
Garden Lane
Bomoseen, Vt. 05732

Walnut Acres
Penns Creek, Pa. 17862

PUTTING UP PRODUCE

Because we prefer to use fresh produce in season, we do not spend much time canning and freezing. However, we do put up for later use some foods that we grow ourselves or have difficulty obtaining year round. Our criteria for selecting fresh produce for storage are:

• Foods that have a short season, during which they are of superior taste.

• Foods that can be frozen or canned without a great deal of work or expensive equipment.

• Foods that maintain good enough flavor and texture during processing to justify the work involved.

Because at present most of the pickled foods on the market are laden with salt and chemical ingredients, we also do a little home pickling. And to take the place of highly sugared jams and canned fruit, we put up a few jars of homemade preserves, fruit butters, and fruit in syrup if we can get the produce in quantity at a reasonable cost.

Homemade Frozen Foods

Freezing has several distinct advantages over the other principal methods of home food preservation. It requires the least amount of labor, it does the least damage to texture and flavor, and it preserves the food value best. In terms of fuel efficiency, however, it may be the most costly.

Selecting Foods for Home Freezing

The majority of fresh produce can be frozen successfully, with a few notable exceptions, among them, potatoes, leafy greens, radishes, and other foods that have a very high moisture content.

Some foods must be blanched before freezing to halt enzyme activity which would diminish color, flavor, and texture during storage. Some foods are best precooked entirely before they are frozen. Conveniently, current research has disclosed that a number of foods can also go straight into the freezer with no more than a cleaning and tight wrapping. It is this last group, which can be directly frozen, that receives most of our attention, since this is such an effortless way to store foods for the future.

FOODS SUITABLE FOR DIRECT FREEZING

avocado	onion
bananas	peaches
berries	peppers
celery	pineapple
coconut	rhubarb
corn	"Soup 'n' Greens"
cucumber	cubes
herbs	whole tomatoes

It is important to remember that frozen foods will never be any better than they were prior to storage. Therefore, there is little sense in putting up bland strawberries, starchy corn, or herbs that are past their prime.

Equipment

The tools needed for home freezing are minimal and are those commonly employed for other kitchen tasks. For most of the foods just mentioned you will need only:
- suitable freezer packaging, including plastic containers with tight-fitting lids, plastic freezer bags, and heavy-duty aluminum foil

For the slightly more involved jobs you will need:
- a 3-quart or larger pot with a cover
- a steaming basket or colander
- a food mill
- soft kitchen towels
- ice cube trays

For all freezing jobs it is also wise to have:
- freezer tape
- a waterproof marker

Preparing Food for Freezing

Foods should be dried as thoroughly as possible before freezing. A soft kitchen towel does an excellent job. Pat gently to prevent damage.

In using plastic bags or foil, remove as much air as possible by gently compressing the filled package or using a vacuum pump. Or, air can be sucked out of the bags through a straw.

In using solid containers, leave ½ inch of head room for expansion during freezing. Any exceptions to this will be noted in the specific recipe instructions.

Be sure to label packages with indelible ink, including the date of packaging, so they can be used in sequence. Most properly prepared home-frozen produce will keep well for 8 to 12 months if held at 0°F. or below.

Flash Freezing

Flash freezing is recommended for foods that you want to use in varying amounts rather than in a solid mass. It is most appropriate for berries, beans, sliced onion, pre-cut peppers, etc.

Spread the food on a shallow metal tray with enough room between individual pieces to permit circulation of air. Place uncovered in the freezer until food is frozen solid. When hard, which will vary from one to three hours depending on the size of the food and the temperature in your freezer, transfer to plastic freezer bags or containers and seal.

Direct Freezing

Avocado—Avocados can be pureed and frozen for later use in guacamole, soups, salad dressings, and such. Remove peel and either mash with a fork or process in the blender or food processor; leave pulp slightly chunky or continue until creamy, depending on intended uses. Add 1 tablespoon lemon juice or ¼ teaspoon powdered ascorbic acid per quart to preserve color. Pack into containers. To eliminate pockets of air, press the avocado pulp into the corners as you pack; seal, label, and freeze.

Bananas—Bananas can actually be frozen unwrapped in their own skins for short-term preservation. Use within three months for baking or pureed desserts, or just unzip the peel and eat out-of-hand for a novel snack.

Pureed frozen bananas can be used later in baking and frozen desserts. Pack in measured amounts for your favorite recipe. To each cup mashed banana add ½ tablespoon lemon juice or ⅛ teaspoon powdered ascorbic acid to prevent darkening. Although the lemon should not adversely affect the flavor in baking, if you are concerned, use ascorbic acid, which imparts no flavor to food as used here. Pack into containers; seal, label, and freeze.

Berries—Remove any damaged or decaying berries. Wash berries gently, drain, and pat dry. Follow directions for Flash Freezing, page 426. Berries, including blackberries, blueberries, cranberries, strawberries, and even cherries can be prepared in this manner. (Cherries may be pitted prior to freezing if you wish.) Fresh berries can also be placed directly in freezer containers, leaving ½ inch head space, but this will not be as useful later on if you only want to use part of the pack at a time.

Celery—Save leaves and extra trimmings in plastic bags in the freezer for use in soups, stews, and other cooking. You can add to the bag or take from it as you like, but be sure to get all the air out before you close it again.

Cucumber—Cucumber is admittedly a strange choice for freezing, but gardeners often have such a windfall crop that it is a shame to waste it. Peel, scrape out the seeds, chop the meat, pack in ice cube trays, and place in the freezer. When solid, transfer the cubes for long-term storage into freezer bags. When your fresh supply is exhausted, crush a few cubes onto the salad just before serving; the slightly icy cucumber bits offer a refreshing contrast.

Coconut—Best preserved by shredding the meat, packing it in its own milk, leaving ½ inch head space for pints and 1 inch for quarts, and freezing.

Corn—There is nothing as good as fresh corn eaten moments after harvest. If you can freeze it while it is still sugar-sweet, it is worth the space it takes in the freezer. The procedure is quite simple. Without detaching the husks, ease them open and remove the silky fibers. Replace the husks around the ears; if very bulky, remove some of the outer layers. Wrap each ear in foil for extra protection if you wish (this is not mandatory), then place the ears in freezer bags, close, and store. Cook without defrosting. Even if kernels alone are desired, freeze on the cob and cut them off while still frozen as needed.

Herbs—Parsley, basil, dill, chives, and other favorite cooking herbs freeze better than they dry. One simple approach is to wash and pat them dry, then wrap them in small bunches in foil packets. Combine the packets in a plastic freezer bag. The herbs should be crushed frozen into the pot, using the same amount you would if they were fresh.

HERB CUBES

A favorite trick of ours is to puree herbs in the blender or processor with only as much water as necessary to make a coarse puree and then pack them into ice cube trays. When solid, they are transferred to plastic freezer bags. These Herb Cubes are ideal seasoning ingredients for soups, stews, and sauces. A cube or two added to the water when cooking grains or pasta insures a well-flavored dish.

Onion—Chopped or sliced onion for cooking purposes can be stored in the freezer but should be used within three to six months. "Flash freezing" is recommended so small amounts can be used as needed.

Peaches—Peaches can be peeled, sliced, packed in freezer bags with all the air sucked out, and used later for frozen desserts, fruit shakes, and sauces. They do not work as well for baked desserts unless you don't mind soft rather than plump fruit in pies, cobblers, etc. Use within three months.

Peppers—Both sweet and hot peppers, left whole, cut in chunks, sliced, or diced can be frozen for use in cooking. Just pack into freezer bags and seal.

Pineapple—If you find some sweet ones, they are worth preserving. Remove the skin, eyes, and core. Slice, dice, crush, or cut as desired. Pack tightly so the pineapple's juice fills the air spaces. Leave ½ inch head space in pints; 1 inch in quarts.

Rhubarb—Cut in 1- to 2-inch pieces or freeze stalks whole. Double-wrap for extra protection.

"SOUP 'N' GREENS" CUBES

Collect odds and ends of carrots, parsnips, celery, the outer leaves of greens, and other mild vegetable trimmings. Combine in the blender or food processor with enough water to make a coarse puree. Freeze in ice cube trays, then transfer to freezer bags for long-term storage. Two cubes can replace ¼ cup liquid in any soup or stew, or in the water used to cook grains.

Tomatoes—Tomatoes can be frozen very successfully for use in cooking. There are a number of freezing techniques for them and you may want to try several, depending on future intentions. The procedure you choose may also hinge on how much time you have and how much space is available in your freezer when tomato season comes around.

Whole Frozen Tomatoes: The quickest way to preserve tomatoes for future cooking unfortunately takes up the most freezer space. That is: simply washed, patted dry, and packed whole into freezer bags, removing all the air with a vacuum pump or straw. Tomatoes prepared this way can be used later whole or cut up to take the place of fresh or canned tomatoes in cooking. If you wish to peel them before use, run the unthawed fruit under very hot tap water for a few seconds. The skins will crack, facilitating removal.

Because of their high water content, the texture of tomatoes frozen in this manner is adversely affected; the flavor, however, is well preserved, making them fit for soups, stews, and casseroles. They are less suitable for making tomato sauce, although this is feasible with plum tomatoes, which have a higher ratio of pulp and less natural moisture.

For best results, use within three to six months.

Other techniques for freezing tomato products appear on pages 429–430.

Processing for Freezing

All other produce must be blanched or cooked completely before freezing. Some are worth the effort because of the convenience they provide later on.

Cauliflower, pumpkin, stewed tomatoes, tomato puree, tomato cubes, tomato sauce, green tomato sauce, and tomato broth, all require some heat treatment before freezing.

Blanching is a quick heat treatment that inhibits the foods' enzyme activity. It can be done in a boiling water bath or with steam heat. To blanch in a water bath, bring a large potful of water to a boil, plunge food in for the specified length of time, drain in a colander, and rinse quickly with cold water. Pat dry and freeze as directed.

For steam blanching, place foods in a steamer basket set over an inch of boiling water; cover and steam for the recommended time period. Remove at once, rinse under cold running water until completely cooled, pat dry, and proceed according to the recipe.

Cauliflower—Freezing cauliflower is worthwhile in season when large, fresh heads are available at a good price.

1. Remove leaves and part of stem, leaving just enough to hold the head together.

2. Soak in cold salted water to draw out any insects. Drain.

3. Tie each head in a 12-inch square of doubled cheesecloth. This makes it easier to handle.

4. Place on a steaming rack over boiling water and cook for 5 to 8 minutes, or until you can barely pierce it with a fork.

5. Remove from steamer and rinse under cold water to cool quickly and completely. Drain well and pat outside dry.

6. Leaving cheesecloth intact, double-wrap in heavy-duty foil and freeze.

Frozen cauliflower can be used directly from the freezer by steaming it for about 5 minutes, until heated through and barely tender. It can also be coated with crumbs and baked, as in Baked Cauliflower, but it must be defrosted first. If you remove the foil and soak the cheesecloth-wrapped head in a sink full of cold water, thawing will proceed quite rapidly.

Pumpkin—Preserve your Halloween jack-o-lantern by cutting it into chunks, steaming it until tender, scooping the pulp from the skin, mashing and packing it into containers in the amounts needed for your favorite recipe. Leave ½ inch head space for pints or less; 1 inch in larger containers.

Tomatoes—Stewed Frozen Tomatoes: Cooking tomatoes prior to freezing increases storage life up to 9 to 12 months and condenses their volume so that they occupy less freezer space. For best results, the tomatoes should be peeled, so this method involves a little time.

1. To peel tomatoes, bring a large kettle of water to a boil. Plunge tomatoes into the kettle a few at a time and, when skins crack (within ½ to 2 minutes, depending on the tomato), lift out into a strainer or colander, rinse under cold water until cool enough to handle, and pull off skins with your fingers or a small paring knife.

2. Remove the core and cut the tomatoes into quarters. Place in a saucepan (add a few fresh basil leaves if available) and simmer gently, stirring occasionally so that cooking is even. Continue until just softened. Timing will vary with the size of the load, but this is a fairly rapid process, averaging 15 minutes.

3. Ladle the stewed tomatoes into freezer containers, leaving ½ inch head space; seal, label, and freeze. Later they can be used in any recipe calling for undrained canned tomatoes, or can be cooked down further for tomato sauce.

Tomato Puree: If you have a food mill, this is a very easy procedure, as the peeling step is eliminated. Just wash tomatoes, cut in wedges, and place in a saucepan. Cover and cook until soft and liquid. Stir a few times for even cooking. When the mixture reaches the boiling point (in about 15 minutes), it will be ready for pureeing.

Set up the food mill, using the medium-hole disk, over a big bowl or other suitable container. Ladle tomatoes into the top and rotate the handle, forcing them into the bowl and retaining the peel in the mill. Remove peel every so often to keep the mill from clogging. Stir the puree well and transfer to freezer containers leaving ½ inch head space in pints, 1 inch in quarts; cover, label, and freeze. This puree makes a fine soup base or can be cooked down later for sauce.

TOMATO CUBES

Frequent reference is made in this book to Tomato Cubes, one of our favorite flavoring aids made with the fine-tasting fresh tomatoes that abound in summer. Tomato cubes are made from the Tomato Puree above, but instead of being frozen as a block in containers, the puree is spooned into ice cube trays and placed directly in the freezer until solid. Once frozen, the cubes are transferred to freezer bags, closed tightly, and returned to cold storage.

Throughout the winter, when a gravy, soup, or stew needs a lift, we just drop in a couple of cubes. Two cubes can replace ¼ cup tomato juice or one diced fresh tomato in a recipe.

Tomato Broth and Drained Tomato Pulp: This is a variation of the preceding Tomato Puree recipe. The end result is twofold: a thin tomato-flavored broth excellent for soup stock and cooking grains, and a thick pulp that can quickly be transformed into sauce later on by defrosting it over heat in a pot with sautéed onions, garlic, chopped pepper, and herbs.

To proceed, cut tomatoes into chunks or wedges as for puree and cook in a covered saucepan until liquid runs freely. Stir once or twice for best heat penetration.

To separate the broth from the pulp, place the food mill (using the medium disk), a colander, or a strainer over a large bowl. Transfer the tomatoes slowly and carefully, letting liquid drain into the bowl and conserving the pulp. Remove broth to freezer containers, leaving ½ inch head room for pints and 1 inch for quarts. Press remaining pulp through mill or strainer, discard peel, and pack into freezer containers, leaving ½ inch head room. Both store well for up to a year.

Tomato Sauce: If you wish, you can make tomato sauce in large batches for freezing, using any of the fresh tomato sauce recipes in the "Sauces" section. This, however, is the least satisfactory approach, as onions, garlic, and herbs all undergo curious flavor changes during freezer storage. Thus, the excellence of the sauce is altered. For this reason, we recommend that you make your tomato sauce as needed from the stewed tomatoes, drained pulp, or puree in your freezer pantry.

Yield: It is difficult to give an exact yield, as tomatoes differ widely in their water content. The following figures give approximate volumes to help ensure that you will have enough storage containers on hand.

4½ pounds tomatoes = 1 quart drained pulp plus 1½ pints (3 cups) broth, or 2 quarts stewed tomatoes, or 2 quarts tomato puree.

You will get a slightly higher yield of drained pulp (about 1½ quarts) if plum tomatoes are used.

Green Tomatoes—If you garden, you will undoubtedly have a glut of green tomatoes at the end of the season. One excellent freezer item that takes advantage of this surplus is Green Tomato Sauce, a chunky puree that makes a flavorful topping for tacos, omelets, steamed vegetables, plain beans, or unseasoned rice. As you will not use large quantities at any one time, it is best to freeze this sauce in half-pint containers.

GREEN TOMATO SAUCE

1 medium onion, cut up
1 clove garlic
1 hot chili pepper
1½ pounds green tomatoes, cut up
  (about 5 cups)
¼ cup parsley
2 fresh basil leaves
1 teaspoon salt

Combine all ingredients in a processor fitted with a steel blade or in the blender. It may be necessary to process in batches in the blender or add some of the tomatoes after partial processing. Puree until evenly mixed but still somewhat chunky. If necessary, when using the blender, a little water can be added to get the machine going.

Transfer to a pot and bring to a quick boil.

Use what you need and freeze the rest in half-pint containers, leaving ½ inch head room.

Makes 8 half-pints (each half pint serves 2 to 4)

Whenever possible, use foods directly from the freezer. Frozen vegetables can be steamed or put directly into soups or stews without thawing. Purees and sauces can also be heated from the frozen state, but be sure to pack them in flexible wide-mouth containers to facilitate their removal.

If defrosting is required, allow from 5 to 7 hours in the refrigerator, from 2 to 4 hours at room temperature, or about an hour in a cold water bath.

Canning

In canning, foods are packed into sterile containers and then sealed airtight, using heat to destroy any existing bacteria and drive off oxygen so that no new organisms can grow.

There are two different methods of canning. The simplest is *canning by steam or hot water.* It is successful only for foods that are highly acidic, such as fruits, most tomatoes, and foods packed in an acid brine of vinegar or lemon juice.

Low-acid vegetables and meats require higher temperatures to destroy harmful organisms. *Canning under pressure* is required for this job and a special pressure canner, which resembles a large pressure cooker, is a mandatory piece of equipment. This is a costly tool appropriate only for gardeners who wish to put up a large portion of their harvest.

The handful of recipes provided here require only an inexpensive steam or water-bath canner.

Selection of Food

In the pages that follow are the formulas for making home-canned tomatoes, vegetable soup, catsup, brined spaghetti squash, canned fruit, and fruit purees. This pretty much covers what you can put up by water-bath canning except, of course, for the many pickles and preserves that we describe later on.

Because of the limitations of nonpressure canning, only foods with a high acid content are acceptable, i.e., those with a pH below 4.5; most tomatoes and fresh fruit are in this category. Not all tomatoes are suitable, however, because of individual differences and new varieties. Tomatoes advertised as "low acid" are better preserved by freezing. Overripe tomatoes and tomatoes with large cracks or any sign of mold should not be canned, as these conditions indicate reduced acidity. Pears and apricots also approach the borderline of safety.

If there is any doubt about the acidity of these foods, you may want to add ¼ teaspoon powdered citric acid or 1 tablespoon white vinegar or lemon juice per pint (½ teaspoon citric acid or 2 tablespoons vinegar or lemon per quart). Citric acid, also known as "sour salt," is available in powdered form in drugstores, and as coarse crystals in food markets. Crush crystals before measuring. (These instructions are repeated whenever appropriate to individual recipes, as is alternate advice for increasing the acidity of fruits canned in liquid.)

As with freezing, only foods in top condition should be considered for canning. Any mold- or insect-damaged specimens should not be used. Canning should be done as soon after harvesting as possible to maximize flavor and food value.

Equipment

A *water-bath canner* is a deep pot fitted with a removable wire basket to keep the jars off the bottom and permit water to circulate under and around them.

A *nonpressure steam canner* is a fairly recent innovation consisting of a perforated tray, which holds the canning jars, set in a shallow pot that is filled with rapidly boiling water and covered with a high metal dome. This device traps the steam, which in turn heats the food inside the jars. (The manufacturer calls this a "fruit canner.")

Proper *canning jars and lids* are the only other essentials for the operation. Although some books suggest recycling jars saved from commercially processed food, the only ones that are really appropriate are those manufactured specifically for home canning. Most practical are jars with two-piece, screw-top lids, which come in pint and quart sizes with regular or extra-wide mouths. Both pints and quarts will be useful for small families. For feeding four or more, quarts alone are sufficient. As long as the jars are not nicked, they can be reused. For proper seal, only unused lids should be employed.

Other useful items to have on hand include:

- tongs
- paring knives
- chopsticks
- pot holders
- canning jar lifter
- ladle
- colander
- clean kitchen towels
- timer
- funnel
- measuring implements
- wire cooling rack

Preparing the Utensils

To keep canned foods bacteria-, yeast-, and mold-free, the jars, lids, and other utensils that come directly in contact with the food itself should be sterilized.

The usual approach to sterilizing is to put clean jars in a large pot filled with water reaching at least one inch above the jars. The water-bath canner may be used for this purpose. Bring to a boil, then cook for 10 to 15 minutes. Turn off the heat, but let the jars remain until needed to prevent recontamination. When the time comes for filling, lift jars from the water bath with sterile tongs, drain, and invert on a clean towel for a few minutes.

A new approach utilizes the automatic dishwasher. Running the clean canning jars through the hot-wash cycle of the dishwasher, without soap, provides adequate sanitation and is much less tedious. Stop the machine before the drying cycle, but leave the jars inside until needed.

The lids must also be sterilized briefly before use. This procedure will be described on the packing box and may vary slightly with the brand. If no other instructions are given, place center inserts in a pot with water to cover, bring just to the boiling point, and remove immediately from heat. Let stand until jars are ready to seal. The outside bands do not need heat treatment, although it will not harm them.

The other tools that come in contact with the food should also be sterilized—the ladle, tongs, paring knife, fork or spoon, chopsticks, and the funnel. This is done in the same manner as described above for the jars.

Preparing the Food

Specific instructions needed to ready foods for canning are provided in the individual recipes. No matter what recipe you follow, it is most important that the fresh produce be thoroughly cleaned in cold running water before it is used. Do not soak it, as this depletes the food value, but rinse as many times as needed, and use a vegetable brush to dislodge any dirt.

Filling the Jars

When the above steps have all been completed, packing begins. Using a sterile ladle, a funnel, or other suitable tool, transfer food into warm, sterilized jars, filling to within ½ inch of the top, unless otherwise directed. Remove air bubbles that occur by compacting food with a nonmetallic utensil like a chopstick or a narrow plastic spatula and probing the spaces between the food and the jar.

Wipe the rim and screw threads of the jar with a clean cloth. Remove the flat lid from the hot water bath with tongs, drain, and place over the top of the jar. Screw outside band on firmly as far as you can without using force. *Do not retighten this screw band.*

Heat Processing

Heat processing should begin as soon after filling as possible.

If you are using a water-bath canner, it can be preheating while the food is being prepared and packaged. You will need enough water in the pot to cover the jars by at least an inch. As the jars will displace some of the liquid, it is best to fill the pot initially about two-thirds full with water and at the same time bring an extra supply to boil in the tea kettle. If the canner was used to sterilize the jars, it will already have some warm water in it, so as soon as the sterilized jars have been removed, begin reheating (always with the cover on). It may take as long as 30 minutes to bring the necessary amount of water to a boil, so it is best to start early and if the pot is ready before the food, it can be turned off, then quickly brought back to a boil when the time comes.

If you have a nonpressure steam canner the job will proceed more quickly and you will not have the chore of lifting an enormous potful of water before or after processing. (A filled water-bath canner is too heavy for most people to manage. It is best to bring the water to the pot already in place on the stove, and to empty it in stages after it has cooled down.)

As directed in the flyer that accompanies the canner, put two quarts of water in the bottom section of the steam canner, insert the perforated tray, and, with the dome cover in place, bring to a boil. This will take about 10 minutes and is easily evidenced when steam escapes through the holes in the sides of the dome.

When the boiling point is reached, processing can begin.

1. Place jars in the wire basket of the water-bath canner, or between the holes on the steaming tray if a steam canner is used. Make sure jars do not touch each other or the sides of the canner.

2. Replace lid, and when water returns to a rolling boil, or when steam appears once again through the holes in the steam canner, begin timing.

3. As soon as the processing time specified in the recipe directions is over, turn off the heat. Carefully lift the lid away from you to divert the steam and, using a bottle lifter or tongs, remove jars one at a time. Hold jars upright; tilting may impede the airtight seal.

4. Set the jars aside to cool where they will not be in the way for several hours. A wire rack makes the best cooling surface, but a soft kitchen towel folded thick will also do. Transfer the jars to the cooling area directly from the canner, leaving room between them for air to circulate.

If there are more jars to process, reheat the water in the canning vessel, replacing lost water as needed.

Testing the Seal

As jars cool, you may hear them "pop," a sign that the airtight seal is being formed. When jars are at room temperature, you can test the seal by checking for a slight indentation in the center of the lid. Press gently with your fingers. If you can push the lid down, the seal has *not* been formed. Canning duds must be reprocessed or placed in the refrigerator for storage and first use.

Storage

Jars that are properly sealed can be transferred to their storage place. This is generally not done until at least 12 hours after processing to guarantee the seal. The screw bands can be left in place or removed. Removal is recommended, as rust and mold growth have an affinity for the tiny air space between the band and the jar. While this will not harm the contents, it is unsightly. Keep jars in a cool place, out of direct light.

A Word of Encouragement

Reading these instructions might give the impression that canning is a complicated, time-consuming process. In practice, however, in a well-organized space it proceeds quite comfortably. Those who feel unsure might try canning with an experienced friend the first time. By the second round it will be a lot less mysterious.

Favorite Canning Recipes

CANNED TOMATOES

If you have a large freezer you may not need to consider canning tomatoes. If not, you will welcome these jars midwinter for soups, stews, and fresh-flavored tomato sauce. (Before proceeding, make sure you have read the general directions for canning.)

To prepare the tomatoes, wash them then plunge them into boiling water to peel as described in the directions for Frozen Stewed Tomatoes (page 429). As soon as the skins are cracked and

the tomatoes cool enough to handle, remove the peel, using a small paring knife.

Pack immediately into warm, sterile jars. Large tomatoes may be halved or quartered, others can be left whole. As the jar is being filled, compress gently to surround the tomatoes with liquid and remove air bubbles. A chopstick works well for this.

If available, a clean leaf of fresh basil can be added to each jar. Salt can be added if desired, using ½ teaspoon per pint jar, 1 teaspoon per quart.

Fill jars to within ½ inch of the top; cover and heat-process for 35 minutes for pints, 45 minutes for quarts. Cool and store as explained in the general directions.

The exact yield is difficult to predict; it varies, depending on the tomatoes and how you pack them; *2 to 3 pounds will generally yield 1 quart.*

Note: Remember, do not use special low-acid varieties or overripe tomatoes for canning. If you suspect tomatoes have a lower than average acid content, you can increase their acidity by sprinkling ¼ teaspoon powdered citric acid or 1 tablespoon white vinegar or lemon juice over the tomatoes in a pint jar (doubling these amounts for quarts).

MIXED VEGETABLE SOUP

Put up jars of this tomato-based soup for the post-tomato season. A food mill is preferred for pureeing, so there is no need to peel the tomatoes or seed the cucumber beforehand. However, if you prefer to use a blender or food processor, you will have to peel the tomatoes and scape the seeds from the cucumber before cooking them.

5 pounds tomatoes, cut up (about 12 cups)
3 cucumbers, peeled and cut up (5 to 6 cups)
6 carrots, cut up (about 2½ cups)
4 stalks celery with tops, cut up (about 2 cups)
1 green pepper, diced (about 1 cup)
4 sprigs parsley
8 basil leaves

3 cups water
¼ cup lemon juice
2 tablespoons honey
4 teaspoons salt

Combine vegetables, herbs, and water in a 6-quart pot and bring to a boil. Cover and simmer for about 40 minutes, or until tender enough to puree.

Press soup through a sieve or the fine blade of a food mill. Discard skins and seeds. Return soup to pot and add lemon juice, honey, and salt. Bring just to a boil.

Ladle into warm, sterilized quart or pint jars with ½ inch head space. Process for 10 minutes in boiling water bath or steam canner.

To use soup, empty contents of jar into a saucepan, bring to a boil and simmer for 10 minutes. If too sharp, add a small glob of honey or melt a pat of butter on top.

Makes 4½ quarts

CATSUP

This home version is mellower than commercial varieties and contains no refined sweetening, which they do. Even with the added honey there are only 2.5 teaspoons of sweetening per cup as compared to approximately 5.8 tablespoons (about seven times more) in the leading factory-made catsup.[1] As an added plus, our updated method involves far less work and cooking time than do traditional recipes.

2½ pounds ripe tomatoes, peeled and cut up (about 6 cups)
½ medium onion
1-inch piece hot pepper or green pepper wedge
¼ cup cider vinegar
1½ tablespoons honey
½ teaspoon salt
1 small bay leaf
¾ inch cinnamon stick
1 slice garlic
¼ teaspoon whole cloves
½ teaspoon celery salt

[1] *Consumer Reports*, March, 1978.

Combine tomatoes, onion, and pepper in a blender or processor fitted with a steel blade and process until smooth.

Pour this tomato puree into a 2-quart pot and add vinegar, honey, salt, and remaining seasonings tied in a cheesecloth bag. Bring to a boil and simmer uncovered, stirring occasionally, for 45 minutes until sauce is reduced and thickened.

Remove seasoning bag, ladle catsup into warm sterilized half-pint jars, leaving ¼ inch head space, and process in steam canner or boiling water bath for 10 minutes.

Makes 2 half-pints

Note: To multiply the recipe, the blender or processor will have to be filled more than once.

Once opened, catsup must be refrigerated and should be used within a month.

BRINED SPAGHETTI SQUASH

By increasing the acidity of a vegetable, water-bath canning is possible. We use this technique for spaghetti squash, which we relish for use in Spaghetti Squash Rémoulade.

9 pounds spaghetti squash (2 large or 3 medium)
2 tablespoons salt
2½ cups white vinegar
2½ cups water

Cut squash into wedges to fit the steaming basket; scoop out seeds. Steam for 15 minutes, or until just tender but not soft. Scrape strands from peel and pack into warm, sterilized quart jars until three fourths full.

Combine salt, vinegar, and water, and heat to boiling point. Pour hot brine to cover squash, leaving ½ inch head room. Push down with a sterilized utensil to remove air pockets and surround vegetable with liquid. Process in steam canner or boiling water bath for 10 minutes.

Before using, drain thoroughly and rinse with cold water.

Makes 4 quarts

CANNED FRUIT

Because of its high acid content, most fruit is suited to water-bath or steam canning. Basically, the procedure for preserving in syrup or juice does not change from one fruit to another, but the amount needed per jar will vary, depending on the size of the fruit and how they are prepared. Below are two basic recipes. The same techniques can be used to prepare cherries, pineapple, etc., when they are available. Select only prize specimens with good flavor.

CANNED PRUNE-PLUMS IN SYRUP

Allow approximately 10 ounces un-pitted plums and ¾ cup syrup for each pint jar.

¼ cup honey
2 cups water
2 pounds prune-plums

Combine honey and water in a saucepan and heat to melt honey. Add washed, unpeeled plums and simmer for 5 minutes.

Divide fruit evenly among warm, sterilized jars. Cover with hot syrup (use ladle or pour through funnel), leaving ½ inch head room. Process in steam canner or boiling water bath for 15 minutes for pints, 25 minutes for quarts.

Makes 3 pints
Note: Recipe can be multiplied.

CANNED PEACHES IN SYRUP

Allow approximately 1 pound peaches and ½ cup syrup for each pint jar.

5 pounds peaches
2 cups water
½ cup honey

Plunge peaches into boiling water and blanch for 1 minute. Drain, rinse under cold water, and peel. Cut peaches in half and discard pits.

Heat water and honey in a saucepan until honey melts. Add peach halves and simmer for 3 minutes.

Transfer to warm sterilized jars, leaving ½ inch head space. Process in steam canner or boiling water bath for 15 minutes for pints, 25 minutes for quarts.

Makes 5 pints
Note: Recipe can be multiplied.

Variation: For *Canned Peaches in Juice,* proceed as for Canned Peaches in Syrup but replace water and honey with 2½ cups apple juice.

CANNED PEARS AND APRICOTS

Because the acidity of these two fruits varies, often bringing them close to the borderline of safety in water-bath canning, for extra insurance, replace ¼ cup water in the syrup pack recipe with lemon juice. For juice packing, use 2¼ cups apple juice plus ¼ cup lemon juice.

FRUIT PUREE

Fruit purees come in handy as sauces for puddings and plain cakes, or they can be cooked down later to make fruit butters. Fruit puree can be made with apples (for applesauce), peaches, plums, pears, berries, or a combination of fruit.

Canning in half-pint or pint jars is recommended for convenience. Allow about 8 cups sliced fruit for 4 half pints or 2 pint jars. Again, the exact weight will vary, depending on the fruit used as well as on the amount of residue (i.e., peel, pits).

3½ to 4 pounds fruit
honey (optional)

Wash and slice fruit, discarding pits. Cook over low heat in a covered pot until soft enough to puree (approximately 15 to 20 minutes).

Puree in a food mill; discard peel. Add 1 tablespoon honey per cup, if desired. The need for sweetening varies with the fruit and personal preference.

Pour into warm, sterilized jars, leaving ¼ inch head space in half-pints, ½ inch in pints. Process for 10 minutes in steam canner or boiling water bath.

Makes 4 half-pint jars
Note: If you wish to make the puree

in a blender or food processor, fruit must be peeled prior to cooking.

Pickling

Pickling, the preservation of food using vinegar and/or salt, is a practice that is centuries old. It predates canning and freezing by several thousand years. Today we do not rely on preservation by pickling for practical purposes but rather for the provocative effect pickled foods have on our taste buds.

There are several different methods of pickling. Food may be dry-packed in salt, which promotes natural fermentation (sauerkraut is the best-known example). A long-brining method may also be used, in which the food is submerged in a saltwater solution for several weeks, then "finished" in a pickling solution (the traditional way barrel pickles are made). Finally, food may be "quick-pickled" by packing it fresh in jars containing a vinegar solution. This last method, the least time-consuming and very satisfactory for many foods, is the one we use.

Produce for Pickling

Although most people associate the word "pickle" with the cucumber, many fruits and vegetables can be preserved using pickling techniques. Relishes made with zucchini or green tomatoes, zucchini bread-and-butter pickles, dilled vegetables, and a variety of pickled vegetables, including hot peppers, are just a few examples.

As is the case with all other storage methods, the foods selected should be perfect and must be put up as soon after harvest as possible. Cucumbers, especially, suffer from waiting around, and hollow specimens may be the result if pickling is delayed. Produce that is young or slightly underripe is preferred to produce left on the plant too long.

Try to use uniform pieces in each jar. Produce that shows minor blemishes or is of irregular shape should be saved for sliced pickles and relishes.

For making whole, sliced, or chunky cucumber pickles, it is best to choose a variety bred specifically for pickling. These tend to have thinner skins and are more uniform in shape and size.

Clean all produce thoroughly with lots of cold water and a vegetable brush. Handle gently so the skins do not bruise.

Other Pickling Ingredients

Vinegar is an important ingredient in all quick pickles, acting as the main preservative, since bacteria do not thrive in a highly acidic environment. Use only commercial vinegar, which is 4 to 6 percent acetic acid (or 40 to 60 grain), because the acid content of homemade vinegars is often unknown or unreliable. The recipe will specify whether plain white vinegar, cider, malt, or wine vinegar is preferred. Avoid lengthy boiling of the vinegar, as this can lower the acid content.

Salt has a preservative action in long-brined pickles, but in quick pickling its chief use is as a flavoring ingredient. Although relishes can be made with any type of salt, for other pickles the product marketed specifically as "pickling salt" gives the most reliable results. Plain and iodized table salts tend to cloud and discolor pickles, due to the presence of additives; kosher and coarse salts are apt to dissolve slowly and lump.

The use of *soft water* is preferred, although it is less crucial in quick pickling. If your water is high in iron, the foods you pickle may darken unattractively. You can soften water with a high calcium and magnesium carbonate content by boiling it, skimming off the surface scum, and letting it sit for 24 hours. The sediment that forms at the bottom can be left behind by ladling out the water from the top, or by pouring it off through cheesecloth, being careful not to agitate the sediment.

Bottled distilled water can also be used for pickling.

When *honey* is called for, select a light, mild-flavored type such as alfalfa, clover or wildflower. Stronger honey will overpower other tastes.

The *herbs and spices* that are used for pickling should be as fresh as possible. Old seasonings impart a stale, musty flavor. While ground seasonings are all right for relishes, they can cause darkening in pickles; thus, whole pickling spices are preferred when making pickles.

Equipment

The utensils used to prepare the food are of major importance in pickling. Choose only stainless steel, enamelware, or glass. Iron, brass, copper, and aluminum utensils will react adversely with the salts and acids in the pickling mixture.

Quick pickling depends on the same equipment as canning:

- heat-resistant jars with sealable lids (generally quarts, pints, and half-pints)
- a water bath or nonpressure steam canner
- ladle
- paring and chopping knives
- funnel
- pot holders
- measuring implements
- colander
- timer
- long-handled spoon
- good cutting surface
- clean kitchen towels
- wire rack
- large pot for cooking

A food scale will also come in handy, but in its absence, the Table of Weights and Measures (see pages 512–519) can be utilized as a guideline.

Pickle Packing and Processing

Although the pickling solution itself is designed to prevent bacterial growth, brief heat processing is favored to destroy any organisms that might have survived, as well as to seal the jar so that it cannot be invaded during storage.

Heat processing can be done in either a water-bath canner or nonpressure steam canner as described in "Canning" (pages 431–434).

To summarize, the food is packed into warm sterile jars to within ½ inch of the top, then covered with the pickling solution, leaving ¼ inch head room. Relishes and bread-and-butter type pickles that are already dispersed in the pickling liquid require a ¼-inch airspace at the top. The rim is then wiped clean and the lid secured in place. The jars are placed in the canner, prepared according to the general directions for canning (see page 433), and processed as the recipe directs. Most pickles are heat-treated for only about 10 minutes for pints and up to 20 minutes for quarts. (Individual recipes may vary slightly from this formula.)

When processing is completed, jars are set to cool. Avoid tipping them, as this may break the seal. When thoroughly cooled, check the seal, then label and store in a dark, cool spot in your pantry.

If less than a jar's worth is left after the pickles are packed into their containers, refrigerate the excess and use within a few weeks.

Once the pickle jar is opened, refrigeration is required. Pickling liquid should cover solid portions at all times, so do not use the brine as a flavoring ingredient until you have used up the pickles.

Favorite Pickling Recipes

Those foods that flood the market as the growing season draws to a close are all good candidates for pickling. Zucchini, cucumbers, and green tomatoes are used in several pickles and relishes. A variety of other vegetables can also be processed for use on the hors d'oeuvres tray or as a salad garnish, such as Dilled Green Beans (which can be replaced with an equal volume of carrots, cauliflower, or any other vegetables you wish) and Mixed Vegetable Pickles. Pickled Hot Peppers are another important addition to our condiment pantry; they come in handy as a salad or antipasto ingredient and as an added spice in Mexican, Indian, and other "hot cuisine" dishes.

BASIC PICKLES

    4 to 6 pounds cucumbers
    4 cloves garlic
    4 tablespoons mixed pickling spice
    8 dill heads
    4 cups white vinegar
    4 cups water
    6 tablespoons salt

Pack cucumbers into 4 warm, sterilized quart jars, either keeping them whole or cut as desired. Slice 1 clove garlic into each jar and add 1 tablespoon pickling spice and 2 dill heads.

Combine vinegar, water, and salt in a pot and bring to a boil. Pour hot brine over cucumbers, leaving ½ inch head space. Process for 10 minutes in a steam canner or boiling water bath.

Let rest for 4 weeks before using.
Makes 4 quarts

BREAD-AND-BUTTER PICKLES

    10 cups sliced, unwaxed cucumbers
       (about 4 pounds)
    4 teaspoons salt
    2 large onions, sliced
    1 cup thin green pepper strips
    2 cups cider vinegar
    ¾ cup honey
    2 teaspoons dry mustard
    1 teaspoon turmeric
    2 teaspoons celery seed
    1 stick cinnamon

Salt cucumber slices and let stand for 1 hour or longer to extract moisture. Pour off accumulated liquid, rinse in cold water, drain, and pat dry.

Combine cucumber with remaining ingredients in a pot and boil for 5 minutes until cucumbers are "glassy."

Pack into warm, sterilized jars and process for 5 minutes in a steam canner or boiling water bath.
Makes 4 pints
Variation: Replace cucumber with sliced zucchini.

SWEET SUMMER SQUASH PICKLES

    about 9 yellow crookneck squash,
       sliced into rounds
    3 medium onions, sliced into rings
    1 tablespoon celery seed
    1¼ cups honey
    3 cups cider vinegar
    1½ cups water
    ½ cup salt

Make alternate layers of squash and onions in warm, sterilized pint jars. Add ½ teaspoon celery seed to each.

Combine remaining ingredients and bring to a boil. Pour hot brine over vegetables, leaving ¼ inch head space. Process in a steam canner or boiling water bath for 20 minutes.
Makes 6 pints

MIXED VEGETABLE PICKLES

    small green tomatoes or wedges
    cucumber chunks
    zucchini chunks
    carrot chunks
    green beans
    celery pieces
    small cauliflorets
    8 dill heads
    2 teaspoons mustard seed
    4 cloves garlic
    4 1-inch segments hot pepper or 2
       teaspoons cayenne (optional)
    2 cups white vinegar
    6 cups water
    6 tablespoons salt
    dill stalks

Pack vegetables in warm, sterilized quart jars. Add 2 dill heads, ½ teaspoon mustard seed, and 1 clove garlic per quart. Add a segment of hot pepper or ½ teaspoon cayenne to each quart if hot pickled vegetables are desired.

Combine vinegar, water, salt, and dill stalks, and bring to a boil. Remove dill stalks and pour hot brine over vegetables, leaving ½ inch head space. Process for 10 minutes in a steam canner or boiling water bath.

Let rest for 4 weeks before using.
Makes 4 quarts

DILLED GREEN BEANS

2 pounds young green beans
4 dill heads
1 teaspoon cayenne or crushed dried red pepper
2 cups white vinegar
2 cups water
3 tablespoons salt

Pack beans into warm, sterilized pint jars. Add 1 dill head and ¼ teaspoon pepper to each.

Combine vinegar, water, and salt and bring to a boil. Pour hot brine over beans, leaving ¼ inch head room. Process for 10 minutes in a steam canner or boiling water bath.

Let rest for at least 2 weeks before using.
Makes 4 pints

EGYPTIAN PICKLED TURNIPS

2 pounds turnips, peeled and cut in bite-size chunks (about 8 cups)
1 cup peeled sliced beets (about 6 ounces—1 large beet)
2 tablespoons chopped celery leaves
3 cups water
1 cup white vinegar
1 tablespoon salt

Divide turnips and beets evenly into warm, sterilized pint or quart jars. Add some celery leaves to each.

Bring water, vinegar, and salt to a boil and pour hot brine over vegetables, leaving ½ inch head space per quart, ¼ inch per pint. Process in a steam canner or boiling water bath for 10 minutes for pints, 15 for quarts.

Let rest for at least a week before using.
Makes 4 pints or 2 quarts

PICKLED HOT PEPPERS

hot peppers
2½ cups vinegar

Pack peppers into warm, sterilized pint jars.

Heat vinegar to 175°F., or just below boiling. *Do not boil.* Pour hot vinegar over peppers, leaving ¼ inch head space. Process in a steam canner or boiling water bath for 10 minutes.

Let stand for a week before using.
Makes 2 pints

ZUCCHINI RELISH

4½ pounds zucchini, chopped (about 16½ cups)
4 large onions, chopped (about 5 cups)
1 sweet red pepper, chopped
1 green pepper, chopped
3 tablespoons salt
2½ cups white vinegar
1 cup honey
½ teaspoon nutmeg
2 teaspoons celery seed
1 teaspoon turmeric
1 teaspoon dry mustard

Chop vegetables by hand or in a processor. Mix with salt in a large bowl and let stand for several hours or overnight to extract moisture. Drain, rinse with cold water, and drain thoroughly. (A salad spinner can be used for drying.)

Combine vegetables with remaining ingredients in a 5-quart pot and bring to a boil. Simmer uncovered for 20 minutes, stirring occasionally.

Ladle into warm, sterilized half-pint or pint jars, leaving ¼ to ½ inch head space. Process in a steam canner or boiling water bath for 10 minutes.
Makes 6 pints

GREEN TOMATO RELISH

3 pounds green tomatoes, chopped (about 7 cups)
2 medium onions, chopped (about 1½ cups)
1 large 6-ounce green pepper, chopped (about ¾ cup)
1 cup cider vinegar
6 tablespoons honey (¼ cup plus 2 tablespoons)
1 teaspoon celery seed

½ teaspoon cinnamon
1 teaspoon salt

Chop vegetables by hand or in a processor. Combine with remaining ingredients in a 3-quart pot and bring to a boil.

Simmer uncovered, for 20 minutes, stirring occasionally. Ladle into warm, sterilized half-pint or pint jars, leaving ¼ inch to ½ inch head space.

Process in a steam canner or boiling water bath for 10 minutes.

Makes 4½ pints

Preserves

Preserves, a term that encompasses jam, marmalade, conserves, and fruit butter, refers to a sweetened mass of fruit cooked to a thick spreading consistency. The combination of the natural fruit acids and the added sweetener works to discourage the growth of organisms that would otherwise spoil the fruit.

Jams preserved commercially contain about 55 percent sweetener. Recipes for homemade preserves often call for as much as three quarters of a pound of sugar per pound of fruit. Our interest in home storage is therefore limited to those products in which this exorbitant ratio can be reduced. We have found fruit butters to be the most acceptable way to minimize sweetening without sacrificing flavor. In the jam recipes we include here, honey is used instead of sugar with the proportion reduced to ¾ of a pound of sweetening per 3 to 4 pounds of fruit.

Because we minimize the sugar content, we heat-process our preserves so there is less risk of spoilage. When high concentrations of sweetening are employed, as in traditional recipes, this is not necessary. The paraffin seal recommended in older recipes is not required with heat processing, and when a non-pressure steam canner is used, the entire processing procedure takes only 10 minutes.

Before you begin, read the directions for canning on pages 431–434 so that you will be familiar with the sterilizing, packing, and heat processing steps, which are the same for plain canned foods, pickles, and preserves. As in canning and pickling, the jars and other equipment used to make preserves must be sterilized and the ingredients should be of excellent quality. The completed preserves should be allowed to cool in the same manner as other canned foods and the seals should be tested before storing.

Recipe directions are explicit, but since not all fruits have equal jellying strength, and since some honeys contain more moisture than others, cooking time may vary slightly from that given. If you are uncertain about the consistency of your preserves, cooking is completed when the mixture drops from a teaspoon in one mass, or when the fruit does not separate from the liquid on cooling. If about one fourth of the fruit is slightly underripe, a thicker preserve will be obtained. Conserves and preserves are softer than jams, but all will set up more firmly when chilled.

Leave ¼ inch head space when filling jars. If there is a lot of froth on the surface, skim it with a sterilized slotted spoon before sealing.

Some of our recipes vary from the traditional, but it is precisely this individuality that makes them worth trying. If curries are a favorite in your household, you may also want to add the chutney recipes to your repertoire, and rather than ponder what to do with all those green tomatoes in early fall, put up some Mince Filling to use in next Thanksgiving's pie.

FRUIT BUTTER

12 cups cut-up fruit (4 to 6 pounds)
¼ cup apple juice or orange juice
1 stick cinnamon
1 teaspoon nutmeg
¼ cup honey

Place fruit in a pot with juice; cover and cook for 15 to 20 minutes until soft enough to puree. Puree through the fine blade of a food mill, discarding skin and seeds. If very liquid, drain before pureeing and save the juice to drink. You should have about 6 cups puree.

Return puree to pot with remaining ingredients and simmer, stirring occasionally with a wooden spoon, until thick and reduced to about 4 cups. This will take from 1 to 1½ hours.

Ladle fruit butter into warm, sterilized jars and process in a steam canner or boiling water bath for 10 minutes.

Makes 4 half-pints
Variations: Prepare with apples, pears, plums, peaches, mangoes, cantaloupe, berries, or a mixture of fruit. If fruit is very tart, sweetening may have to be doubled.

PEACH–PLUM PRESERVES

3 pounds peaches, peeled and diced small (about 5 cups)
1 pound plums, peeled if desired and diced small (about 2 cups)
1 cup honey

Combine fruit with honey in a saucepan and bring to a boil. Simmer for 10 minutes, crushing fruit with the back of a wooden spoon.

Ladle into warm, sterilized jars. Process in a steam canner or boiling water bath for 10 minutes.

Makes 6 or 7 half-pints

SUMMER CONSERVE

3 cups peeled, diced peaches (about 1½ pounds)
3 cups diced cantaloupe
¼ cup lemon juice
1 cup honey

Combine all ingredients in a saucepan and boil gently for 30 minutes.

Ladle into warm, sterilized jars and process in a steam canner or boiling water bath for 10 minutes.

Makes 4 half-pints

PINEAPPLE–ORANGE PRESERVES

1 pineapple
4 oranges
1 cup honey

Cut pineapple from rind and chop. (You should have 4½ to 5 cups.)

Place pineapple in a saucepan. Peel oranges and cut in pieces over the pot to retain juice. Discard any pits. Add honey, bring to a boil, and simmer for 30 minutes, stirring occasionally.

Ladle into warm, sterilized jars and process in a steam canner or boiling water bath for 10 minutes.

Makes 4 half-pints

PINEAPPLE CHUTNEY

1 pineapple
1 teaspoon salt
½ cup raisins
¼ teaspoon cayenne
2 teaspoons peeled, minced ginger
2 cloves garlic, minced
2 tablespoons molasses
1½ cup cider vinegar

Cut pineapple from rind and chop. (You should have 4½ to 5 cups.) Mix with salt in a bowl and let stand for 1 hour. Drain in a colander but do not rinse.

Combine pineapple with remaining ingredients in a pot, bring to a boil, and simmer for 30 minutes.

Ladle into warm, sterilized jars and process in a steam canner or boiling water bath for 10 minutes. Store for 3 weeks before using.

Makes 4 half-pints

FRESH PLUM CHUTNEY

½ cup cider vinegar
½ cup honey
½ cup water
¼ teaspoon salt
1 cinnamon stick
2-inch piece ginger, peeled and minced, or 2 teaspoons ground ginger
¼ teaspoon crushed dried red pepper
½ teaspoon cloves
6 cups pitted diced prune-plums (about 2 pounds)
1 cup peeled, diced apple
⅔ cup raisins
¼ cup minced onion

Combine vinegar, honey, water, and seasonings in a 3-quart pot and bring to a boil. Add plums, apples, raisins, and onion and simmer over medium heat, stirring occasionally, until soft and thick, about 30 minutes. Mash gently with a wooden spoon.

Ladle into warm, sterilized jars and process in a steam canner or boiling water bath for 10 minutes. Store for 4 to 6 weeks before using.

Makes 5 half-pints

MINCE FILLING

4 cups diced green tomatoes (about 1¼ pounds)
4 cups peeled, diced tart apple (about 1½ pounds)
1 cup raisins
½ cup honey
½ cup molasses
2 tablespoons oil
¼ cup cider vinegar
½ teaspoon nutmeg
1 teaspoon cinnamon
½ teaspoon salt

Combine all ingredients in a 3- to 5-quart pot and simmer for 25 minutes.

Ladle into warm, sterilized pint jars, leaving ¼ inch head space. Process in a steam canner or boiling water bath for 10 minutes.

Makes 3 pints

Note: To make a dessert with filling, pour 1 pint into an 8-inch baking dish and cover top with pastry. Bake in a 400°F. oven for 12 to 15 minutes until brown. Eat while warm. Serves 4.

Signs of Spoilage

If you have followed the directions for canning, pickling, and preparing preserves, using unblemished produce and clean equipment, you should be rewarded with a fine-tasting product. Before using any home-canned food, however, examine it for signs of spoilage. Should you find any of the following, discard the contents rather than take chances:

- broken seals
- seepage around the seal
- mold, even a tiny bit, on the underside of the lid or anywhere in the contents (mold on the outside of the jar should be washed off before opening)
- gassy contents or spurting liquid when jar is opened
- cloudiness or a murky appearance to the food or in the surrounding liquid
- unnatural or unpleasant odor

Remember, too, that once the jar is opened, the contents must be refrigerated to prevent spoilage.

CONVENIENCE MIXES

Cooking from a mix is really nothing more than arriving in the kitchen after the ingredients have been put together but before they have been cooked. When time is short, mixes can be a great convenience, and for those cooks who are a bit uncomfortable with certain procedures, a mix lends the confidence and freedom to prepare a sauce or baked goods where they might otherwise hesitate to do so. We suggest, too, that if you have friends who appreciate good food, an extra mix is a thoughtful personal gift.

WHITE SAUCE MIX

White Sauce Mix makes foolproof gravy in less than 10 minutes. The combination of vegetable leftovers and a container of sauce mix in the pantry can be the source of many delicious casseroles and pot pies.

1 cup whole wheat flour
2½ cups nonfat dry milk powder
1 tablespoon salt

Combine all ingredients. Store in a covered container at room temperature. Shake well before each use to distribute ingredients evenly.

Makes 3 cups mix

QUICK WHITE SAUCE

Thin Sauce = 3 tablespoons mix plus 1 cup milk, water, or a combination

Medium Sauce = ⅓ cup mix plus 1 cup water or equal parts milk and water

Thick Sauce = ⅔ cup mix plus 1 cup water

Combine dry mix with enough of the liquid to make a smooth paste. Stir in remaining liquid and cook over moderate heat, continuing to stir frequently until sauce thickens and comes to a boil. Boil gently for 1 to 2 minutes.

Makes 1 cup

Minor Protein

Note: For a richer sauce, add ½ to 1 tablespoon butter per cup of sauce at the end of cooking and stir to melt.

Variations: For *Quick Cheese Sauce,* stir ½ cup grated cheese into 1 cup medium white sauce until melted.

For *Quick Tomato–Cheese Sauce,* prepare medium white sauce, using ¼ cup water to form the paste and ¾ cup tomato juice for the remaining liquid. After sauce has thickened stir in ½ cup shredded cheese to melt. A combination of cheddar and mozzarella cheeses is particularly good.

For *Quick Creamed Soups,* make a paste of ¾ cup mix and ½ cup water and stir gradually into 1 quart hot broth or soup stock of choice. Boil gently for 2 minutes.

For a homey cup of *Quick Cream of Tomato Soup,* combine 3 tablespoons mix with ¼ cup milk to make a smooth paste. Gradually stir in ¾ cup tomato juice and cook as usual.

MUSHROOM SAUCE MIX

"Prep" this mix for mushroom sauce on demand.

½ ounce (about ⅔ cup) dried mushrooms
1 cup whole wheat flour
2½ cups nonfat dry milk powder
1 tablespoon salt
1 teaspoon nutmeg
2 tablespoons nutritional yeast

Crush half the mushrooms until quite small and leave the remainder as they come.

Combine all ingredients and store in a covered container at room temperature. Mix thoroughly before each use.

Makes 3¾ cups mix

QUICK MUSHROOM SAUCE

Medium Sauce = 6 tablespoons mix plus 1 cup water

Thick Sauce = ¾ cup mix plus 1 cup water

Combine dry mix with some of the water to make a smooth paste, using about ¼ cup liquid to each 6 tablespoons mix. Add remaining water and stir continuously over moderate heat until sauce thickens and comes to a boil. Boil gently for 1 to 2 minutes to cook out the raw flour taste.

Makes 1 cup

Minor Protein

Variation: For a *Tangy Quick Mushroom Sauce,* prepare 1 cup medium sauce, remove from heat and stir in 1 tablespoon each yogurt and sour cream. If reheating is necessary, keep heat low and do not boil.

SUPER-QUICK CREAMED GREEN BEANS WITH CASHEWS

1 tablespoon oil
1 small onion, chopped
¼ cup cashew pieces
1 pound green beans, cut in 1- to 2-inch lengths
1½ cups water
¾ cup Mushroom Sauce Mix
2 to 4 tablespoons grated cheese (optional)

Heat oil in a 1½- to 2-quart pot and sauté onion and nuts for 2 to 3 minutes until nuts are lightly colored. Add beans and ½ cup water, cover and cook for 10 minutes until just tender.

Combine remaining 1 cup water with sauce mix. Stir into cooked beans and cook until thick and beginning to boil. Simmer 2 to 3 minutes longer. Add cheese if desired, stir to melt, and serve.

Serves 4

Minor Protein

POCKET SOUP

Those who enjoy an instant cup of broth but are dismayed by the use of flavor enhancers and the abundance of salt in commercial brands may welcome the chance to make their own soup mix.

2 tablespoons dried split peas
2 tablespoons cracked wheat
¼ cup dehydrated vegetable flakes (soup greens)
2 teaspoons sesame seeds
2 teaspoons sunflower seeds
1 teaspoon nutritional yeast
½ teaspoon salt

Grind split peas, cracked wheat, vegetable flakes, and seeds in blender until they are a fine powder. Combine ground mixture with yeast and salt. Store in a covered container at room temperature.

To use, add 1 heaping teaspoon soup mix to 6 ounces boiling water, or 2 level teaspoons to 1 cup boiling water. Stir, let sit a few minutes, and serve.

Makes ¾ cup dried soup mix (enough for 18 cups of soup)

Note: This is one of those times when the blender seems to do a much more efficient job than the food processor.

GOLDBECKS' MASALA (HOMEMADE CURRY POWDER)

Makes a mild to moderate curry.

2 tablespoons cumin seed
½ teaspoon crushed red pepper
½ teaspoon mustard seeds
½ teaspoon ground ginger
2 tablespoons ground coriander
2 teaspoons turmeric

Grind all ingredients together in a blender, processor, or spice mill or pound to a powder in a mortar and pestle. Store in an airtight container.

Makes ¼ cup seasoning mix

BURGER MIX

There are several good commercial mixes, but you may prefer to make your own, thereby reducing the cost of your meal.

½ cup dry chick-peas
¼ cup dry soybeans
¼ cup dry lentils
¼ cup peanuts
¼ cup sunflower seeds
¼ cup sesame seeds
¼ cup oats
¼ cup cornmeal
¼ cup wheat germ
2 tablespoons soy flour
1 tablespoon nutritional yeast
2 tablespoons dried parsley
1 teaspoon baking soda
1½ teaspoons salt

Grind the dry beans, nuts, seeds, and oats in the blender to consistency of coarse flour. For best results, process only ½ cup at a time. Combine mixture with remaining ingredients and mix well to distribute evenly. Store in a covered container at cool room temperature or refrigerate.

Makes 4 cups (enough for 8 burgers or 24 fritters)

Note: If you do not have the beans called for, others can be used as long as you have a total of 1 cup dried beans to begin with. Nuts and grains can also be varied with others in equal quantity. Cracked wheat, barley, rice, or millet can all be ground in the blender until they are a suitable texture.

BURGER MIX BURGERS

A delicious and tender burger that you can pan-fry or cook on the grill to enjoy on a bun or just by itself on a plate.

1 cup Burger Mix (recipe above)
⅓ cup hot water
dash soy sauce

Combine Burger Mix with water and a little soy sauce; mix well and let stand about 15 minutes to absorb the moisture. Shape into 2 patties.

Heat a heavy skillet and cover with a thin layer of oil. When hot, add burgers and cook 3 to 5 minutes or until bottom is brown. Turn, cover pan, and cook about 5 minutes longer, steaming the interior and browning the bottom at the same time.

Serves 1

Major Protein

Variations: For grilled burgers, place on a rack over hot coals and brown each side. For *Burger Mix Fritters*, form mixture into 6 balls and deep-fry in skillet or wok. These can be stuffed into pita pockets with salad and dressing and served like falafel.

Multipurpose Flour Mixes

Although muffins, biscuits, pancakes, and the like are not difficult to prepare from scratch, knowing that most of the measuring and mixing has already taken place is both psychologically encouraging and time-saving.

Following are three of our favorite mixes and some suggestions for their use. All should be stored in the refrigerator and used within three months for best results.

As directed in the recipes, the mix should be spooned lightly into the measure without compressing.

EXTRA LIGHT MIX

This particular mix gives a tender product with only the faintest trace of wheat flavor.

4 cups whole wheat flour
1 cup nonfat dry milk powder
2½ tablespoons baking powder
1½ teaspoons salt
½ cup oil

In a large bowl, blender, or processor fitted with a plastic mixing blade, combine the dry ingredients and mix well. Slowly add oil, mixing continually until it is completely absorbed.

Store in a closed container in the refrigerator and mix well before each use.

Makes about 7 cups; 1¾ pounds

QUICK LIGHT BISCUITS

2¼ cups Extra Light Mix, spooned into measure
½ cup water

Preheat oven to 425°F.

Add water to mix to form an even dough. Knead gently to combine. Pat into a rectangle ½ inch thick. Cut into eight 2-inch squares.

Bake for 15 to 20 minutes until golden. Serve while still warm.

Makes 8 biscuits

Minor Protein

QUICK LIGHT MUFFINS

3 cups Extra Light Mix, spooned into measure
1 cup water
1 egg, beaten
2 tablespoons honey

Preheat oven to 400°F.

Combine all ingredients and stir gently until completely moistened.

Spoon into an oiled muffin tin, filling each cup two-thirds full. Bake for 15 to 20 minutes.

Makes 8 muffins

Minor Protein

QUICK BREAD STICKS

These can be kept in a covered container and will surely be consumed before they have a chance to stale.

2½ cups Extra Light Mix, spooned into measure
½ cup cornmeal
½ cup water
3 to 4 tablespoons sesame seeds

Preheat oven to 400°F.

Combine mix and cornmeal in a bowl. Add water and stir to form a dough that holds together. Knead gently with mixture still in bowl in order to get dough to stick. If too dry, add a little water as needed.

Pinch off dough in small balls, about 1½ inches in diameter. Roll between your palms, pressing gently into "cigars" ½ inch wide and about 3½ inches long. Moisten sticks lightly with wet hands and roll in sesame seeds to cover.

Place on an oiled baking sheet and bake for about 20 minutes, or until golden. Serve warm, or cool completely and eat at room temperature.

Makes 16 breadsticks
Minor Protein

QUICK LIGHT PANCAKES

1¾ cups Extra Light Mix (page 446),
spooned into measure
1 cup water
1 egg, beaten
1 tablespoon honey

Combine all ingredients and stir gently until completely moistened. Drop by quarter cupfuls onto a hot pan that has been wiped with oil.

Cook until bottom is lightly browned and spatula slips underneath with ease. Flip and cook until bottom is set and freckled.

Makes 10 pancakes; serves 2
Minor Protein

QUICK-FRIED ONION RINGS

1 large Spanish onion
1½ cups Extra Light Mix, spooned
into measure
1 egg, beaten
¾ cup water
oil for deep frying

Cut onion into rings about ⅛ inch thick. Combine mix, egg, and water, and stir until smooth.

Heat oil in a wok for deep frying to 365°F.

Hold onion ring with tongs or drape on a fork, dip into batter, and ease into hot fat. Do not crowd the oil. Brown, turn, brown the other side, then drain on absorbent paper.

As cooking continues, place cooked onions in a shallow baking pan in a 300°F. oven to stay warm and crisp.

Serves 4 to 6
Note: Leftovers freeze very well and can be restored by spreading on an ungreased baking sheet and placing in a 400°F. oven for about 8 minutes until crisp.

Variation: High Protein Mix can be used in this recipe in place of the Extra Light Mix.

CHEESE PIE

A simplified quiche of sorts, in which the batter sinks to form a crust and the cheese custard rises to the top.

paprika
1 cup shredded Swiss cheese
½ cup chopped onion
3 eggs
1½ cups milk
½ cup Extra Light Mix, spooned into
measure
½ teaspoon prepared mustard

Preheat oven to 325°F.

Generously butter a 9-inch pie pan and sprinkle with about ¼ teaspoon paprika. Arrange cheese and onion in the pan.

Beat eggs with milk, mix, and mustard until smooth. Pour over cheese. Sprinkle evenly with paprika.

Bake for about 30 minutes, or until set. Let stand for 10 minutes before serving.

Serves 3 to 4 as an entrée, 4 to 6 as an accompaniment
Major Protein up to 4 servings; *Minor Protein* for more than 4

Variation: Cheese Pie may also be prepared with High Protein Mix.

QUICK POT PIE

Transform leftovers into something more exciting to eat.

6 cups cooked beans, vegetables, or
other leftovers in gravy
1½ cups Extra Light Mix, spooned
into measure
½ cup water
1 tablespoon honey (optional)

Preheat oven to 400°F.

Place mixture to be covered in a 1½- to 2-quart casserole or deep 9½- to 10-inch pie plate. Pan should be about three-fourths full.

Combine mix with water and honey and stir gently until well moistened.

Drop batter by spoonfuls evenly on top of baking dish.

Bake for 15 to 20 minutes until nicely browned.

Serves 4

Minor Protein or *Major Protein*, depending on filling used.

HIGH PROTEIN MIX

This has a higher protein value than the other mixes and a more pronounced grain flavor.

3 cups whole wheat flour
¼ cup soy flour
¾ cup wheat germ
1 cup nonfat dry milk powder
2½ tablespoons baking powder
1½ teaspoons salt
1 tablespoon nutritional yeast
½ cup oil

In a large bowl, blender, or processor fitted with a plastic mixing blade, combine the dry ingredients and mix well. Slowly add oil, continually mixing until it is completely absorbed.

Store in a closed container in the refrigerator and mix well before each use.

Makes about 7 cups; 1¾ pounds

QUICK PROTEIN BISCUITS

2½ cups High Protein Mix, spooned into measure
½ cup water

Preheat oven to 425°F.

Add water to mix to form an even dough. Knead gently to combine. Pat into a rectangle 1 inch thick. Cut into eight 2-inch squares.

Bake on a lightly oiled pan for 15 to 20 minutes until golden.

Makes 8 biscuits
Minor Protein

QUICK PROTEIN CRACKER BREAD

A crisp cracker that is a real treat with Camembert, Brie, or a vegetable spread. Stored in a dry, airtight wrapper, Cracker Bread will last several weeks.

2½ cups High Protein Mix, spooned into measure
½ cup water
sesame seeds

Preheat oven to 425°F.

Combine mix with water and knead gently to form a dough. Divide dough into 10 balls and roll each into a 4-inch round, ⅛ inch thick.

Place on an oiled baking sheet. Sprinkle with sesame seeds and press gently to help them stick.

Bake for 10 to 12 minutes until golden. Serve warm or cool.

Makes 10 cracker breads
Minor Protein

QUICK PROTEIN MUFFINS

3¼ cups High Protein Mix, spooned into measure
1 cup water
1 egg, beaten
2 to 4 tablespoons honey

Preheat oven to 400°F.

Combine all ingredients, adding the maximum sweetening for a sweet muffin, and stir gently until completely moistened. Spoon into an oiled muffin tin. Bake for 15 to 20 minutes.

Makes 8 muffins
Minor Protein

CORN MIX

A tasty mixture of corn and wheat.

2 cups whole wheat flour
2 cups cornmeal
1 cup nonfat dry milk powder
2½ tablespoons baking powder
1½ teaspoons salt
½ cup oil

In a large bowl, blender, or processor fitted with a plastic mixing blade, combine the dry ingredients and mix well. Slowly add oil, continually mixing until it is completely absorbed.

Store in a closed container in the refrigerator and mix well before each use.

Makes about 6½ cups; 1¾ pounds

QUICK CORN BISCUITS

1¾ cups Corn Mix (page 448), spooned into measure
¼ cup water

Preheat oven to 425°F.
Combine mix and water, kneading gently to form a dough that holds together. If too dry or crumbly, add a few drops water. Pat into rectangle ½ inch thick and score with a fork into six 2-inch squares. Do not break apart.
Place on an oiled baking sheet and bake for 15 to 20 minutes until nicely browned. Break apart to serve.
Makes 6 biscuits
Minor Protein

QUICK CORN CRISPS

A corn–wheat cracker for snacking or traditional cracker use. Stored in a covered tin these will keep a long time.

1¾ cups Corn Mix
¼ cup water

Preheat oven to 425°F.
Combine mix and water, kneading gently to form a dough that can be rolled. If too dry or crumbly, add additional water.
Roll on a lightly floured surface into a large rectangle that is ⅛ inch thick. (If you find it more comfortable, roll only half at a time.)
Transfer dough to an oiled, floured baking sheet and score with a fork into desired shapes and sizes for breaking apart later.
Bake for 10 minutes, or until golden. Cool on a rack and crack on lines.
Makes ½ pound crackers
Minor Protein

CORN FLATS

A tortilla-like bread that should be served warm, spread with butter if you wish; it goes well with Mexican, Indian, Chinese, or typically American soups, salads, and stews.

1½ cups Corn Mix, spooned into measure
¼ cup water

Stir water into mix to form a soft ball of dough that can be handled. Cover with a cloth and let rest for 15 to 30 minutes.
Divide into 4 balls. Roll each on a lightly floured surface into a thin circle, about 7 inches around.
Heat a griddle, heavy skillet, or use the top of a wood-burning stove. Wipe with an oil-moistened paper towel and, when quite hot, cook rounds one at a time, until each side is flecked with brown. To keep warm and pliable, stack and cover with a cloth. Serve while still hot.
Makes 4 breads; serves 2 to 4
Minor Protein
Note: To make individual flat breads, combine 6 tablespoons mix and 1 tablespoon water.

QUICK CORN MUFFINS

2¾ cups Corn Mix, spooned into measure
1 egg, beaten
2 tablespoons molasses or honey
1 cup water

Preheat oven to 400°F.
Place mix in a bowl. Add remaining ingredients and mix gently until completely moistened.
Spoon into an oiled muffin tin, filling two-thirds full for medium muffins, three-fourths for large ones.
Bake for 15 to 20 minutes until lightly browned.
Makes 8 to 10 muffins
Minor Protein

QUICK CORN–CHEESE PANCAKES

Serve for breakfast with syrup or make extra-large pancakes and fold around leftover stew, rice and beans, ratatouille, chili, or similar leftovers for a luncheon or evening meal.

1⅓ cups Corn Mix, spooned into measure
½ cup shredded cheddar cheese
1 egg, beaten
1 cup water

Combine mix and cheese. Add egg and water and stir until evenly blended. Let stand for 5 minutes to thicken.

Heat griddle or heavy skillet. When hot, wipe with oil and cook pancakes using ¼ cup batter for regular pancakes or ⅓ cup for large pancakes that can be folded over a filling. When spatula slips easily underneath, turn and cook the other side.

Keep warm, if necessary, by stacking on a plate and covering with a cloth.

Makes eight 4-inch pancakes, or six 6-inch pancakes; serves 2

Major Protein

Note: For two main-dish servings of filled pancakes, you will need 2 cups filling, and if mixture itself is not moist, 1 cup gravy as well. With a moist filling, you can top each pancake with a dollop of yogurt. Mushroom Sauce (also from a homemade mix) or tomato sauce both make excellent pancake toppings.

QUICK CORN FRITTERS

Corn fritters, served with maple syrup and thin Cheeson strips, provide an excellent brunch or light meal. Or, serve as an accompaniment to bean stews at dinner.

1½ cups Corn Mix (page 448), spooned into measure
1 egg
1 teaspoon molasses
⅓ to ½ cup water
⅔ cup corn kernels
oil for deep frying

Place mix in a bowl. Beat egg with molasses and add to mix along with ⅓ cup water. Stir to blend evenly into a thick batter. Add more water if necessary; batter should drop in a thick lump off the spoon. Stir in corn.

Heat oil in a wok or other suitable pot for deep frying to 365°F. Drop batter by rounded teaspoons into hot oil without crowding. Turn in oil to brown all surfaces. Drain on absorbent paper and serve warm.

Makes about 20 fritters; serves 4
Minor Protein

QUICK CORN-CRUSTED TOMATOES

Batter-coated tomatoes fried in a skillet until crisp on the surface and hot inside.

4 to 5 green or underripe red tomatoes
1½ cups Corn Mix, spooned into measure
1 egg, beaten
½ to ¾ cup water
whole wheat flour

Cut each tomato into 3 or 4 thick slices.

Combine mix with egg and ½ cup water, stirring gently to make a smooth, thick batter. Add more water if necessary for a batter of thick pancake consistency.

Heat enough oil to generously cover a heavy skillet. When hot, dredge tomato slices with flour, then coat with batter. Let excess batter drip back into bowl.

Place immediately into a hot pan and brown on both sides. Serve as soon as possible, keeping warm if need be in a 300°F. oven.

Makes 16 slices; serves 4 to 6
Minor Protein

Variations: The same batter can be used for *Quick Corn-Crusted Mushrooms* and for *Quick Cheese* or *Quick Tofu Sticks*. If desired, make some of each for a *Mixed Fry*. Only tofu needs to be dredged in flour before being coated with batter.

Planning the Menu

These sample menus are designed to help orient you in preparing wholefoods meals and to simplify what is often the cook's greatest dilemma—planning the menu. The menus are not meant to limit your choices, but rather to illustrate some appropriate food combinations. We have provided many possibilities within the menus so that the meal can reflect your personal taste preferences rather than ours and still be nutritionally and aesthetically balanced.

Included here are patterns for simple meals that are easily assembled, meals for both family and entertaining that call for a bit more time in the kitchen, party ideas, and international dinners. Naturally these are but a few of the myriad wholefoods meals available using the recipes in this book. Many more ideas are offered in the introduction to each main dish recipe section, as well as in the menu suggestions that often accompany recipes.

Note: Where recipes are specified, page references are included; where only the category is suggested, recipes can be selected by scanning the appropriate recipe section. Specific beverages are included only when they are an integral part of the meal.

SIMPLE WHOLEFOODS DINNERS

Chef's Special Salad (page 31)
salad dressing of choice
wholegrain muffin

Guacamole (page 46)
Tortilla Pyramid (page 37) or Broccoli
Tostados (page 37)
Lemon Greens (page 295) or tossed
salad with Light Mexican Tomato
Dressing (page 57)

Fluffy Stuffed Baked Potato (page 163)
raw vegetable sticks with
Pimiento-Cheese Dip (page 47)
wholegrain breadstuff

Quick Calzone (page 33) or
Individual Bean Pizza (page 34)
Tomato-Mushroom Salad (page 297) or
Italian Tomato Salad (page 299)

Quick, Creamy Onion Pie (page 45) or
Broccoli Custard Pie (page 225)
Orange-Glazed Carrots (page 51)
tossed salad with
Bottom-of-the-Bowl Dressing (page 57)

French-Toasted Cheese Sandwich
(page 34) or Souffléed Cheese
Sandwich (page 34) or
Croque Madame (page 124)
Favorite Fruit Salad (page 60) or
Crunchy Peach Salad (page 305)

Mom's Thick Split Pea Soup (page 100)
or African Bean Soup (page 103)
Rice-Corn Muffins (page 329) or House
Corn Bread (page 330)
Peanut Butter Complements (page 31)
or a mound of cottage cheese

Scrambled Eggs with Tomatoes
(page 131) or French Cheese Omelet
(page 132)
Tangy Coleslaw (page 46)
Oven Fries (page 249)
wholegrain toast
Vegetable Cocktail (page 417)

Fresh Tomato Pita Pizza (page 33) or
Pizza (page 220) or
Biscuit Crust Pizza (page 220)
Three-Bean Salad (page 65)
or Avocado-Bean Salad (page 261)

Tamari Broth with Greens (page 55)
assorted steamed vegetables with
Double Cheese Sauce (page 58) or
Yogurt-Tahini Sauce (page 319)
or Peanut Butter-Vegetable Sauce
(page 319)
whole grain or bread

Layered Tomato Casserole (page 45) or
Matzo Lasagne (page 45)
Steamed Broccoli (page 50)
or Pan-Fried Asparagus (page 51)
chick-peas seasoned with fresh-ground
pepper

Main Dish Stir-Fry (page 42)
over brown rice or rice crackers or
Woodstock Rice and Vegetables
(page 188)
chopped fresh cabbage with
Lemon-Tahini Dressing (page 290) or
Creamy Carrot Dressing (page 291)
Bread and Spread (page 50)
Herb Tea (page 419)

Creamed Corn Soup (page 56) or
Quick Tomato–Onion Soup (page 90)
Kidney Bean Luncheon Salad (page 28)
or Chopped Bean Liver (page 29) or
Tofu "Chicken" Salad (page 30)
sandwich

B.O.B. (page 43) or Sloppy Beans
(page 44) or Kidney Beans in
Cheddar Sauce (page 176)
Basic Biscuits (page 326) or
English Muffins (page 343) or
wholegrain toast
tossed salad with dressing of choice

Eggplant Cutlets (page 140) or
Eggplant Ratatouille Pie (page 242)
Cracked Wheat Pilaf (page 48)
Mideast Chick-Pea Salad (page 261)
Pita Bread (page 337)

Greek Lentil Soup (page 101)
Greek Coleslaw (page 292)
cubes of feta cheese or Greek Tomato
and Cucumber Salad (page 300)
wholegrain breadstuff

FAMILY AND COMPANY DINNERS

Vegetable Soup (page 92) or
Hot Borscht (page 93)
Cottage Cheese Cutlets (page 38) or
Rice Pancakes (page 38) or
Rice Cheeseburgers (page 197)
Butter-Steamed Brussels Sprouts
(page 236) or Curried Corn (page 239)
tossed salad with Creamy Nut Dressing
(page 290) or Creamy Tofu Garlic
Dressing (page 290)

Avocado Cocktail (page 76) or
Mushrooms in Garlic Butter (page 77)
Vegetables Mozzarella (page 140) or
Cauliflower Puff (page 150)
Brown Rice-a-Roni (page 49) or
Nutted Rice with Raisins (page 265)
mixed greens with Garlic Dressing
(page 287)

Baked Broccoli and Cheese Casserole
(page 152) or Baked Spinach and Feta
(page 153)
Fresh Ginger Carrots (page 238) or
Sweet Baked Squash (page 252)
Steamed Barley Salad (page 263) or
Orange–Wheat Salad (page 270)
Bran Muffins (page 328) or
All-Soy Muffins (page 329)

Bean Burgers (page 196) or Soyburgers
(page 196)
English Muffins (page 343) or
Burger Buns (page 346) or toast
Corn on the Cob (page 50) or
Crisp Fried Onions (page 246) or
Fried Zucchini (page 253)
Toasted Seeds and Spinach Salad
(page 298)

One-Pot Baked Macaroni and Cheese
(page 39) or Pasta with Creamy
Spinach (page 113)
Baked Parsley Tomatoes (page 254)
French Mushroom Salad (page 297) or
Cabbage-Carrot-Bean Salad (page 303)
Soy Biscuits (page 326) or
Herbed Oat Bread (page 339) or
Rye Bread Sticks (page 347)

Tomato–Bean Pâté (page 29) or
White Bean Pâté (page 66) or
Pea Pâté (page 67)
Rye Wheat Thins (page 321) or
Rye Flatbreads (page 321)
Fluffy Mushroom Omelet (page 133) or
Mushroom Soufflé (page 139)
Carrots with Walnuts (page 238)
Buttermilk Bread (page 339) or
Finger Rolls (page 345)

Stracciatella (page 91) or Minestrone
(page 96)
Mushroom Custard (page 128) or
Zucchini Frittata (page 135)
Spaghetti with Garlic (page 277) or
Pasta with Broccoli (page 277)
Italian Tomato Salad (page 299)
Garlic–Sesame Bread (page 49)

Vegetable Cottage Cheese (page 47) or
Protein Spread (page 69)
wholegrain crackers
Boston Roast (page 44) or Bean Birds
(page 203)
gravy of choice
Pan-Fried Cabbage (page 51) or
Baked Asparagus (page 232)
Pear Salad (page 304) or Waldorf Salad
(page 304)

Broccoli Tropicana (page 78) or
Celery Rémoulade (page 79) or
Schoolhouse Salad (page 79)
Tofu with Onions and Cheese (page 167)
or Tofu à la King (page 168)
Cottage Cheese Biscuits (page 326) or
brown rice
tossed salad with Light French Tomato
Dressing (page 57) or
No-Oil Tomato Juice Dressing
(page 288)

Poached Spinach–Potato Pâté (page 85)
Mushroom Rissoles (page 202)
Cashew Gravy (page 314)
French Carrots and Celery (page 238)
or Nutted Baked Onions (page 246)
Green Bean and Tomato Salad
(page 291) or Cheese Salad with
Walnut Dressing (page 296)
Braided Rolls (page 338)
or Parker House Rolls (page 446)

Baked Brie with Almonds (page 70)
or Fried Camembert (page 70)
Carrot Stew (page 141) or Vegetables
with Apricot Sauce (page 146)
whole grain of choice
Marinated Cucumber Salad (page 65)
or Yogurt–Cucumber Salad (page 293)

---

grapefruit half or Cold Stuffed Tomato
(page 47)
Liverish (page 202) or
Baked Rice Balls (page 201) or
Rice–Nut Loaf (page 205)
gravy of choice
Spiced Green Beans (page 232) or
Crisp Fried Beets (page 234)
Spinach Salad (page 298)

Baked Mushrooms (page 77) or
Stuffed Clam Shells Areganata (page 86)
or Stuffed Artichoke (page 82)
Pasta with Onion Sauce (page 114) or
Linguine Country Style (page 115)
Caesar Salad (page 296)
Italian Bread (page 340)

Golden Carrot Soup (page 100)
Cheese Steak (page 125) or
Cheese–Nut Roast (page 126) or
Cheese Croquettes (page 128)
Steamed Greens (page 244) or
Spiced Spinach (page 250)
Tomato–Mushroom Salad (page 297)
or Tomato Salad with
Sweet-and-Sour Onion Dressing
(page 300)

---

melon or Marinated Artichoke Hearts
(page 65)
Italian Vegetable Casserole (page 154)
Barbecued Corn (page 239) or
Corn Oysters (page 240)
tossed salad with Italian Dressing
(page 287)

American Wholefoods Broccoli
Hollandaise (page 235)
Basque Country Stew (page 180) or
Beans from Brittany (page 180)
Hi-Protein Crepes (page 213) or
Apple-Oat Muffins (page 328)
Steamed Salad (page 296)

CHILDREN'S PARTY SUGGESTIONS

Finger Foods

Toasted Noodles (page 52), Corn Chips
(page 321)
trimmed bread shapes spread with
Peanut Butter Complements (page 31),
Celery Cheddar Spread (page 30),
Cheese–Nut Spread (page 69),
Tofu Cream Cheese and Vegetables
(page 69)
Popped Corn (page 348),
Popcorn Balls (page 349), "Snacks"
(pages 348–53), Beer Nuts (page 350),
Granola Bars (page 351)

Table Foods

CLTs (page 27),
Fresh Tomato Pita Pizza (page 33),
Souffléed Cheese Sandwich (page 34),
Bean Tacos (page 36),
Bean Salad Pita (page 222)

Desserts

Banana Soft Serve (page 59),
Pineapple Sherbet (page 59),
Favorite Fruit Salad (page 60),
Frozen Pineapple (page 352),
Frozen Banana Pops (page 352),
Frozen Juicicles (page 353),
Frozen Strawberry Yogurt (page 364)

Cake

Monkeys in a Blanket (page 61),
Giant Twinkie (page 383),
Devil Dogs (page 384), Carrot Cake
(page 386) with Cream Cheese
Frosting (page 415), Carob and
Chocolate Cupcakes (page 391),
Lemon-Orange Refrigerator Layer Cake
(page 392)

Beverage

Seltzer Fizz (page 417),
Lemonade (page 417), Party Punch
(page 418)

ADULT PARTY SUGGESTIONS

Cold Hors d'Oeuvres

Homemade cheese spreads (page 69),
Spicy Cheese Rolls and Cheese Truffles
(page 72)
Guacamole (page 46),
raw vegetables with Dips (pages 63–64),
Baba Ghanouj (page 68),
Hummus (page 68),
Eggplant Caviar (page 78)
White Bean Pâté (page 66),
Mushroom Pâté (page 67),
Pea Pâté (page 67)
Deviled Tofu (page 30),
Tempeh Sandwich Salad (page 174)
Stuffed Lemon Eggs (page 72)
Curry Popcorn and Nuts (page 348),
Roasted Chick-Peas (page 349),
Chili Nuts (page 350)
Greek Olives (page 65),
Pickled Mushrooms (page 66),
Quick Pickles (page 310)

Hot Hors d'Oeuvres

Vegetable Derma (page 80),
Bite-Size Knish (page 84),
Mixed Grain Balls (page 201)
Cheese-Stuffed Mushrooms (page 52),
Filled Croustades with Salpicon
(page 80)
Nachos (page 279),
Russian Vegetable Turnovers
(page 281)
miniature Savory Farmer Puffs
(page 284)
Classic Cheese Quiche (page 74),
Onion Pie (page 75),
Pissaladière Niçoise (page 282)
Baked Vegetable Cheese (page 127),
Baked Vegetable Omelet (page 136),
Potato Pudding (page 155)

Cold Buffet

Celery Rémoulade (page 79),
Steamed Broccoli Salad (page 235),
Cold Eggplant and Yogurt (page 243),
Macaroni and Cheese Salad (page 48),
Cold Pasta and Broccoli (page 118),
Mushroom and Barley Salad (page 264),
Basic Rice Salad (page 269),
French Pasta Salad (page 278),

Tabouli (page 302)
Ricotta Potato Salad (page 250),
Carrot–Peanut Salad (page 293),
Deli-Style Health Salad (page 301),
Salade Niçoise (page 301)
Three-Bean Salad (page 65),
Tofu Antipasto Salad (page 86),
Bean-Cheese Salad (page 261),
Mexican Bean and Corn Salad
(page 304)
Favorite Fruit Salad (page 60)
Party Mousse (page 87),
Cucumber Mousse (page 294),
Pineapple-Cucumber Mold (page 295),
Virgin Mary Salad (page 300)

Hot Buffet

Chili (page 43),
Barbecued Tofu and Vegetables
(page 170),
Bean Moussaka (page 185),
Hawaiian Bean Loaf (page 204)
Pasta with Green Beans (page 115),
Spaghetti Fantasy (page 118),
Lo Mein (page 119)
Fruit Noodle Pudding (page 122),
Sweet Noodle Pudding (page 278)
Broccoli with Peanuts in
Sweet and Sour Sauce (page 147),
Atlantic Avenue Green Beans
(page 233)
Cauliflower with Yogurt (page 239)
Eggplant Ratatouille Pie (page 150),
Baked Spinach and Feta (page 153),
Cheese–Vegetable–Barley Bake
(page 154),
Vegetable Strudel (page 224)
Paella (page 190),
Rice with Snow Peas (page 267),
Spanish Wheat (page 270)

BARBECUE SUGGESTIONS

Here are some foods that can be cooked
on the grill.

Entrées

Vegetable Kebabs (page 172)
Outdoor Mixed Grill (page 173)
Tempeh Kebabs (page 42)
Bean Burgers (page 196)
Soyburgers (page 196)
Cashew Burgers (page 197)

Accompaniments

The Standard Baked Potato (page 53)
Baked Asparagus (page 232)
Barbecued Corn (page 239)
Campfire Ratatouille (page 242)
Baked Parsley Tomatoes (page 254)
Garden Rice (page 267)

HOLIDAY ENTERTAINING SUGGESTIONS

Cold Appetizer

Crackers and cheese spread of choice,
Pea Pâté (page 67),
Celery Rémoulade (page 70),
raw vegetable relish tray

Hot Appetizer

Baked Mushrooms (page 77),
Stuffed Clam Shells Areganata
(page 86)

Soup

Fresh Tomato Soup (page 93),
Pumpkin Soup (page 106)

Main Entrée

Bread-Stuffed Peppers (page 157),
Hot Open-Faced Tofu Turkey Sandwich
(page 168),
Hot Open-Faced Tempeh Sandwich
(page 174),
Mushroom Rissoles (page 202),
Bean Birds (page 203),
Rice-Nut Loaf (page 205)
served with Brown Gravy (page 313)
and Cranberry Sauce (page 309)

Vegetable Entrée

Cauliflower Puff (page 150),
Vegetables with Soufflé Sauce (page 150)

Accompaniments

Smothered Jerusalem Artichokes
(page 232),
Cheddar-Stuffed Sweet Potatoes
(page 251),

Candied Sweet Potatoes (page 252),
Stuffed Winter Squash (page 252)

Green Salad

Thousand Island Dressing (page 289),
Green Goddess Dressing (page 289)

Bread

Pot of Gold Biscuits (page 327),
Sunflower-Rye Muffins (page 329),
Pumpkin Seed Bread (page 331),
Cranberry Bread (page 332),
Herbed Oat Bread (page 339),
Pumpkin Pan Rolls (page 344)

Dessert

Macaroon-Top Apples (page 356),
Cranberry Crunch (page 357),
Pears in Vanilla Syrup (page 358),
Indian Pudding (page 364),
Walnut Date-Topped Shortbread
Squares (page 374),
Mr. Bill Cookies (page 375),
Spritz Cookies (page 376),
Chocolate–Nut Squares (page 380),
French Nut Cake (page 385),
Apple Babka (page 386),
Fruitcake (page 390),
Pecan Pie (page 403),
Pumpkin Pie (page 404),
Mince Pie (page 443)

Finale

Roasted Chestnuts (page 350),
fresh and dried fruit platter,
nuts in the shell

INTERNATIONAL DINNERS

One feature of *American Wholefoods Cuisine* is that it adopts, then adapts, the best examples of wholefoods cookery from kitchens around the world. As a matter of fact, one way to insure a varied diet is to eat as if you were dining in a different country each day.

In this section menus are laid out with choices for each course so that the meal can be put together as it might be in an ethnic home or restaurant. This gives you some freedom while assuring you a balanced meal.

You may want to introduce international dinners to your household by setting aside one night a week specifically for "ethnic" eating. And don't overlook these menus when you are entertaining, for they are bound to excite those who are suspicious of wholefoods and meatless dining but lean toward so-called gourmet meals.

The Latin Influence

Spain and Portugal are the progenitors of the Latin influence, which extends from Central and South America up into the American Southwest.

Here we find tomatoes, peppers, beans, rice, garlic, and onions central to many dishes. Dairy products are not accentuated, and those cheeses that do appear are mostly mild and often melted.

As the cooking style of the European Latin reached the New World, it meshed with Indian culinary customs and local commodities. Corn and hot spices became integral parts of the cuisine, and cooking techniques were adapted to a peasant farming culture. As a result, there are few hard-and-fast rules about seasonings and exact ingredients, only basic techniques and typical dishes, both of which are freely improvised on by the individual cook.

Except on feast days, dessert generally consists of fresh fruit or the soft baked custard know as flan.

For home cooking of these ethnic foods, you will want to stock fresh and/ or canned chilies, tortillas and tacos, such staple seasonings and condiments as garlic, oregano, cinnamon, cayenne, crushed red pepper, parsley, olives, and pimientos. Avocados, plantains, squash, pumpkins, melons, papayas, mangoes, and similar tropical delicacies are among the more specialized produce typical of this cuisine.

SPANISH SUPPER

Opener (choose one)
Spanish Garlic Soup (page 91)
Gazpacho (page 108)
White Gazpacho (page 108)

Entrée (choose one)
Huevos Rancheros (page 131)
Spanish Omelet (page 133)
Spanish-Style Chick-Peas over grain
(page 177)
Basque Country Stew (page 180)
Arroz con Queso (page 189)
Paella (page 190)
Super Spanish Wheat (page 270)

Accompaniment (choose one)
Green salad
Marinated Cucumber Salad (page 65)
Cheese Salad with Walnut Dressing
(page 296)

Bread
A crusty bread

Dessert (optional)
Broiled Orange (page 61)
Baked Vanilla or Chocolate Custard
(page 362)
Egg White Almond Custard (page 362)

MEXICAN FEAST

Opener (choose one)
Guacamole (page 46)
Avocado Cocktail (page 76)

Dairy Course (choose one)
Mexican Corn Soup (page 98)
Mexican Omelet (Tortilla) (page 135)
Chili Rellenos (page 158)
Cheese Enchiladas (page 217)

Bean Course (choose one)
Bean Tacos (page 36)
Refried Beans (page 54)
Mexican Bean Soup (page 103)
Mexican Vegetables (page 147)
Tacos with Special Bean Filling
(page 218)
Two-Tone Mexican Beans (page 259)
Mexican Bean and Corn Salad
(page 304)

Salad
Lemon Greens (page 295)
Pear Salad (page 304)
Crunchy Peach Salad (page 305)

Accompaniment (as desired)
Sunflower Squash (page 252)
Cornmeal Tortillas (page 323)
Brown rice

Condiment (as desired)
Quick Mexican Hot Sauce (page 58)
Salsa Cruda (page 308)
Chili Sauce (page 309)

Dessert (optional)
Fresh mango and papaya
Baked Vanilla or Chocolate Custard
(page 362)
Egg White Almond Custard (page 362)
Ginger Cookies (page 375)

PUERTO RICAN DINNER

*Opener or Accompaniment
(choose one or two)*
Pimiento–Cheese Dip with
raw green beans and tacos (page 47)
Green Banana Escabeche (page 84)
Fried Plantains (page 248)

Entrée (choose one)
Puerto Rican Rice and Beans (page 182)
Sopones (page 182)
Paella (page 190)

Accompaniment (choose one)
Green salad
Puerto Rican Cabbage Salad (page 292)
Orange-Section Salad (page 296)

Condiment
Hot pepper sauce

Bread (choose one)
Apple-Corn Sticks (page 330)
Pumpkin Pan Rolls (page 344)
Any crusty bread

Dessert (optional)
Quick-Cooking Custard (page 60)
Mango Jam (page 358)
Fresh or Roast Pineapple (page 359)

Baked Vanilla or Chocolate Custard
(page 362)
Coconut Custard Pie (page 404)

SOUTH AMERICAN MEDLEY

Entrée (choose one)
Black Bean Soup (page 102)
Colombian Potatoes (page 144)
Peruvian Mountain Potatoes (page 145)
Porotos Granados with Hot Sauce
(page 183)

Accompaniment (choose one or more)
Sliced tomatoes
Avocado wedges
Green salad
Quick Pickles (page 310)
Tropical Fruit Platter (page 305)

Bread (choose one)
Empanadas (page 282)
Warm cornmeal tortillas
Any crusty bread

Dessert (optional)
Melon or fresh pineapple
Baked Vanilla or Chocolate Custard
(page 362)
Egg White Almond Custard (page 362)
Pumpkin Custard (page 404)
Orange or Peanut Cookies (page 372)

BRAZILIAN DINNER

Entrée
Fejoida (page 184)
(black beans with orange segments,
rice, spicy onions, cooked greens)

Bread (choose one)
Plantain Cake (page 248)
Any crusty bread

Accompaniment (as desired)
Tomato slices
Avocado wedges

Dessert (optional)
Pineapple Sherbet (page 59)
Baked Vanilla or Chocolate Custard
(page 62)
Egg-White Almond Custard (page 62)
Coconut Cookies (page 372)
Coconut Custard Pie (page 361)

The Italian Kitchen

While some cuisines are distinctly foreign to the American palate, the cooking of Italy is quite familiar. Pasta with tomato sauce, pizza, ravioli, lasagne, and eggplant Parmesan are all accepted by even the least adventurous diner.

There is, however, a greater scope to Italian cooking if you pursue the more traditional home-cooked dishes; in the countryside, where fresh produce is abundant, and meat is not, vegetable, bean, and grain dishes have long been perfected. The Italians have worked wonders with eggplant, tomatoes, artichokes, mushrooms, peppers, coarse greens, chick-peas, and lentils. Although most people tend to regard Italy as a one-starch nation (wheat pasta), it is here that such mundane fare as cornmeal and potatoes have been gloriously transformed into polenta and gnocchi.

The basic requirements of the Italian pantry are not unusual: fresh garlic, fresh and dried basil, dried oregano, fresh and canned tomatoes, olive oil, pasta, high-quality grating Parmesan, romano, or locatelli, plus mozzarella, provolone, and ricotta cheeses. You may also wish to stock such canned condiments as olives, pimientos, capers, pickled peppers, and eggplant caponata.

ITALIAN FEAST I

*Antipasto (choose several to be
served on a platter of greens)*
Cheese-Stuffed Mushrooms (page 52)
Greek Olives (page 65)
Marinated Artichoke Hearts (page 65)
Eggplant Caponata (page 74)
Avocado–Bean Salad (page 261)
Italian Tomato Salad (page 299)
Antipasto Peppers (page 310)
Italian Vegetable Marinade (page 311)
Provolone strips
Plain chick-peas

Condiments
Oil
Vinegar
Grated Parmesan cheese

Entrée (choose one)
Frittata of choice (page 134)
Italian Gnocchi (page 207)
Pizza (pages 219–221)

Bread (as desired)
Parmesan Toast (page 49)
Italian Bread (page 340)

Dessert (optional)
Tortoni (page 59)
Strawberry Ice (page 364)
Italian Cheesecake (page 393)

ITALIAN FEAST II

Opener or Accompaniment (choose one)
Minestrone (page 96)
Stewed Artichokes, Italian Style
(page 230)
Italian Beans and Greens (page 258)

Entrée (choose one)
Spiedini (page 71)
Pasta with Pesto and Slivered Cheese
(page 114)
Italian Cheese Stuffing Balls (page 127)
Polenta (page 124)
Manicotti (page 213)
Calzone (page 221)

Accompaniment (choose one)
Marinated Zucchini Sticks (page 66)
Tomato–Mushroom Salad (page 297)
Italian Tomato Salad (page 299)

Dessert (optional)
Fresh grapes
Pineapple Sherbet (page 59)
Country-Fresh Pear Cake (page 387)

ITALIAN FEAST III

*Hot Appetizer or Accompaniment
(choose one)*
Stuffed Artichokes (page 230)
Sweet Stuffed Peppers, Italian Style
(page 83)
Stracciatella (Italian Egg-Drop Soup)
(page 91)
Italian Mushroom Soup (page 105)
Italian Sautéed Cucumbers (page 240)
Baked Herbed Eggplant (page 241)
Sautéed Mushrooms (page 245)

Cold Appetizer or Salad (choose one)
Marinated Artichoke Hearts (page 65)
Eggplant Caponata (page 77)
Broccoli Stalk Salad (page 235)

Entrée (choose one)
Red or White Cheese Ravioli
(page 121)
Lasagne (page 124)
Ricotta–Spinach Dumplings (page 127)
Eggplant Ratatouille Pie (page 242)
Eggplant Parmesan (page 151)
Eggplant Lasagne (page 151)
Eggplant Manicotti (page 162)

Pasta (choose one if entrée is not pasta)
Rice with Egg and Lemon (page 268)
Spaghetti with Garlic (page 277)
Pasta with Broccoli (page 277)

Bread (choose one)
Garlic Sesame Bread (page 49)
Italian Bread (page 340)
"Quick" Bread Sticks (page 446)

Salad (as desired)
Green salad

Dessert (optional)
Melon
Tortoni (page 59)
Pears in Vanilla Syrup (page 358)
Honey–Lemon Milk Sherbet (page 365)

French Cuisine

In our view, French cuisine is still the most refined; no matter what is presented, the French know how to do it with a delicate hand.

In our travels through the French countryside we have been struck by the French reverence for fresh greens, always dressed to perfection and never with a commercial dressing. While other vegetables are served sparingly in restaurants, they are given somewhat better treatment in homes. Most regions have at least a few enticing vegetable dishes that may be homemade or sold by vendors at the local markets.

The French excel in their treatment of eggs and in the production of cheese. French omelets and quiche are so light and tender they appear cloudlike, with subtle seasoning that titillates the palate. As you work your way south, though, the Provençal love of garlic and onions emerges in full force.

Good country breads are also to be found, although the traditional French baguette has suffered in recent years.

The foreign influences on French food today are primarily from Tunisia, Morocco, and Vietnam and are particularly evident on the Parisian Left Bank both in ethnic restaurants and in street-vendor food.

Desserts in France border on the divine—not just the rich pastries which are an even rarer indulgence than you might imagine, but also the beautiful wild berries and fresh sherbets which reflect the bounty of the rich French soil.

Because the basics of the French pantry parallel the American wholefoods pantry, dining "à la Française" can easily be a spur-of-the-moment idea.

FRENCH COUNTRY DINNER

Appetizer (choose one)
White Bean Pâté (page 66)
Celery Rémoulade (page 79)
French Mushroom Salad (page 297)

Entrée (choose one)
Spinach Quiche (page 74)
French Onion Soup, Country Style
(page 96)
Creamed Carrot and Zucchini Crepes
(page 214)

Accompaniment (choose one)
Ratatouille (page 242)
Green Salad with
French Tomato Vinaigrette (page 288)
Salade Niçoise (page 301)

As desired
Baguettes (page 340)
Cheese platter

Dessert (optional)
Fresh fruit platter
French Nut Cake (page 385)
Fresh berries with Clotted Cream
(page 411)

FRENCH MEDITERRANEAN MEAL

Opener (as desired)
Steamed Artichokes with Dipping Sauce
(page 81)

Entrée (choose one)
Aioli with Vegetables (page 41)
Pistou Soup (page 97)
Potatoes Niçoise (page 143)
Marseilles Spinach Stew (page 143)

Bread (choose one)
Pissaladière Niçoise (page 282)
Baguettes (page 340)
Brioche (page 342)

Salad
Green salad with oil and vinegar

Dessert (optional)
Fresh figs
Marinated Figs (page 358)
Yogurt with honey
Fresh Fruit Tarts (page 402)

GOURMET FRENCH DINING

Opener (choose one)
Mushroom Pâté (page 67)
Nanette's Vegetable Pâté (page 67)
Mushrooms in Garlic Butter (page 77)
Vegetables à la Grecque (page 78)
French Mushroom Soup (page 105)

Entrée (choose one)
Omelet Fines Herbes (page 132)
French Cheese Omelet (page 105)
Cheese Soufflé (page 138)
Fresh Tomato-Filled Crepes (page 214)

Accompaniment (choose one)
Baked Asparagus (page 232)
French Carrots and Celery (page 238)
Peas and Mushrooms (page 247)
Pan-Roasted Potatoes (page 248)

Salad (choose one)
Mixed greens with Herb Dressing
(page 287)
Mixed greens with
French Tomato Vinaigrette (page 288)

Bread
Baguettes (page 340)

Dessert (optional)
Fresh berries in season
Strawberry Ice (page 364)
Chocolate Nut Squares (page 380)
French Nut Cake (page 385)

LEFT BANK STREET FARE

Entrée (choose one)
Classic Cheese Quiche (page 74)
French Onion Soup (page 96)
Croque Madame (page 124)
Tunisian Sandwich (page 222)

Accompaniment (choose one)
Pickled Mushrooms (page 66)
Schoolhouse Salad (page 79)
French Fries (page 249)
Cold Steamed Artichoke with
French Tomato Vinaigrette Dressing
(page 288)

Dessert (optional)
Egg Crepes with honey or jam
(page 212)
Maple–Walnut or
Fresh Strawberry Ice Cream (page 366)
Croissants (page 410)

Northern and Eastern Europe

These are the countries where harsh climate curtails the fresh fruit and vegetable harvest, making inhabitants more dependent on hearty crops like cabbage, carrots, beets, cauliflower, and broccoli. Potatoes are such a staple that it is hard to create a meal without including them; beans, too, receive great attention in this part of the world, where long cooking brings welcomed warmth to the kitchen.

Bread is highly regarded throughout northern and eastern Europe, and the use of whole grains is accepted by everyone today, although at one time these "coarse breads" were considered a distinguishing feature of peasant and working class fare. Oats, rye, barley, and buckwheat are used as much as wheat to make the traditional dense, crusty breads, crisp flatbreads, savory pastries, dumplings, and grain-filled casseroles.

Dairy products are generally of high quality, for some of the best cheeses and finest yogurt and buttermilk come from this part of the world.

If your pantry is stocked with basic grains, beans, long-lasting vegetables and fruits, cheddar and Gouda-type cheeses, and some caraway, dill, and paprika, you shouldn't have any difficulty in producing the dinners that follow.

ENGLISH FARMHOUSE SUPPER

Entrée (choose one)
Cauliflower-Cheese Chowder (page 94)
Cheddar Soup (page 98)
Leek and Cheddar Soup (page 99)

Bread (choose one)
Cornish Pasties (page 224)
Cracked Wheat Bread (page 338)
Herbed Oat Bread (page 339)

Accompaniment (choose one or more)
Steamed potatoes
Turnip Slaw (page 300)
Quick Pickles (page 310)

Dessert (optional)
Baked Apple (page 355)
Shortbread (page 373)
Apple Crumb Pie (page 400)
Fresh berries with Clotted Cream
(page 411)

ENGLISH WHOLEFOODS DINNER

*Opener or Accompaniment
(choose one or two)*
Orange-Glazed Carrots or Parsnips
(page 51)
Quick Mixed Vegetable Soup (page 90)
Fresh Tomato Soup (page 93)

Entrée (choose one)
Cottage Pie (page 155)
Kidney Beans in Cheddar Sauce
(page 176)
Kedgeree (page 186)
Mushroom Rissoles with Brown Gravy
(page 202)
Filled English Pancakes (page 209)

Salad
Tossed green salad

Dessert (optional)
Steamed Apples (page 60)
Apple Rocks (page 378)
Apple Turnovers (page 406)
Yogurt with granola or muesli

IRISH FARM DINNER

Entrée
Colcannon (page 145)

Bread (choose one)
Oatcakes (page 322)
Buttermilk Bread (page 339)
Herbed Oat Bread (page 339)

Condiments (include all)
Quick Pickles (page 310)
Wedges of cheddar
Cider

Accompaniment (choose one if desired)
Onion–Apple–Raisin Sauté (page 246)
Turnip Slaw (page 300)
Waldorf Salad (page 304)

Dessert (optional)
Buttermilk Sherbet (page 365)
Shortbread (page 373)

GERMAN POTPOURRI

Because of the popularity of the potato
in this part of the world, it can be found
in every course, but in constructing your
menu be sure to choose only one potato
dish. For a lighter meal, skip the soup
or the entrée.

Soup (choose one)
Cream of Spinach Soup (page 99)
Mom's Thick Split Pea Soup (page 100)
Creamy Lima Bean Soup (page 104)

Entrée (choose one)
Quick Creamy Onion Pie (page 45)
Savory Noodle Pudding (page 122)
Farmer's Eggs (page 130)
German-Style New Potatoes (page 144)
German Bean Tzimmis (page 181)
with Bread Meat (page 206)

Accompaniment (choose one or two)
Pan-Fried Cabbage (page 51)
Vegetables with Rich Crumb Topping
(page 51)
Marinated Cucumber Salad (page 65)
Braised Red Cabbage (page 237)
Beet Salad with Blue Cheese (page 292)
Coleslaw Pie (page 292)
Dutch Salad (page 304)

Bread (choose one)
Rye Flatbreads (page 321)
Rye Bread Sticks (page 347)

Dessert (optional)
Honey-Vanilla Pudding (page 361)
Spritz Cookies (page 376)
Fruit Kuchen Oma (page 389)
Dutch Apple Pie (page 401)
Viennese Plum Tart (page 403)

EASTERN EUROPEAN TABLE

Opener (choose one or two)
Eggplant Caviar (page 78)
Schoolhouse Salad (page 79)
Hot Borscht (page 93)
Cold Creamy Borscht (page 110)
Cold Beet Salad (page 292)
Caucasus Salad (page 298)

Hot Vegetable (choose one)
Baked Mushrooms (page 77)
Russian Beets (page 234)
Eggplant au Gratin (page 241)

Grain Course (choose one)
Polish Pierogi (page 207)
Blintzes (page 214)
Mushroom and Barley Salad (page 264)
Fluffy Kasha (any variation) (page 264)
Kasha Knish (page 264)
Russian Vegetable Turnover (page 281)
Potato Knish (page 283)

Dessert (optional)
Mandelbrot (page 377)
Rugelach (page 380)
Apricot–Raisin Tart (page 403)

A Visit to Greece and the Middle East

Having spent many weeks in a Greek farming village, we have had the good fortune to be invited into the kitchen both to observe and to take part in daily food preparation. The celebration of many special occasions, including Easter, a christening, engagement, and "name" days, has exposed us to the customs as well as the delights of Greek cooking.

We have thus come to regard Greek food as our "second cuisine" and, through extension, have become quite at home with the foods of the other nations of the Middle East, which, despite their own definite characteristics, are very similar both in ingredients and style of service.

Greek and Middle Eastern meals are frequently made up of many small dishes, including several salads emphasizing beans, vegetables, yogurt, grains, and often nuts and seeds. To tantalize the palate, olives and pickled vegetables are almost invariably served, as are the flat, soft breads so perfect for sandwich stuffing. Cheese tends to be downplayed, and those that do appear, such as feta, are often made of sheep's milk and are sometimes quite salty.

Food is generally served at room temperature rather than hot or cold. This is true of soups, entrées, and even the customary thick coffee at the end of the meal.

At home, desserts are apt to be fresh, home-preserved, or dried fruits. Baking is reserved for celebrations, and the elaborate confections of filo dough and nuts, oozing with syrup, are often brought in from the bakery. Even when these desserts are assembled at home, the filo pastry itself is likely to be commercially made.

For your Greek and Mideast meals, you will want to have fresh garlic, dried oregano, fresh and dried mint, perhaps some cumin and fresh dill, yogurt, feta cheese, tahini, and cracked wheat, in addition to basic beans and produce and a few select condiments, such as olives, capers, pickled peppers, and stuffed grape leaves, if they are available.

GREEK DINNER

Opener or Accompaniment (choose one)
Greek Lentil Soup (page 101)
Greek Bean Salad (page 262)

Entrée (choose one)
Greek Stuffed Cabbage (page 82)
Bean Moussaka—omit opener
(page 185)
Zucchini Pancakes (page 195)
Greek Artichokes and Dill (page 231)
Greek Spinach Rice (page 266)

Accompaniment (choose one)
Greek Coleslaw (page 292)
Yogurt–Cucumber Salad (page 293)
Greek Tomato and Cucumber Salad
(page 300)
Feta cubes with fresh ground pepper

Bread (choose one)
Greek Feta Biscuits (page 281)
Pita Bread (page 337)
Any crusty bread

Condiment (as desired)
Greek Olives (page 65)

Dessert (optional)
Dried apricots, figs, or dates
Nuts in the shell
Roasted Chestnuts (page 350)
Marinated Figs (page 358)
Top-of-the-Stove or
Baked Rice Pudding (page 363)
Rich Almond Cookies (page 376)
Greek Lenten Cake (page 391)

ISRAELI "TOURIST SPECIAL"

Opener (choose one)
Baba Ghanouj (page 68)
Israeli Eggplant Spread (page 68)

Entrée
Falafel with Tahini Sauce (page 200)

Salad (choose one or more)
Mideast Relish (page 294)
Tabouli (page 302)
Israeli Salad (page 302)

Bread
Pita Bread (page 337)

Condiment (as desired)
Greek Olives (page 65)
Stuffed Grape Leaves (page 82)
(or use canned)
Pickled Hot Peppers (page 440)
Yogurt

Dessert (optional)
Favorite Fruit Salad (page 60)
Broiled Orange (page 61)

LEBANESE DINNER

Opener (choose one or more)
Baba Ghanouj (page 68)
Hummus (page 68)
Nikki's Special Kibbi (page 87)
Tabouli (page 302)

Entrée
Atlantic Avenue Green Beans
(page 233) with
Cracked Wheat Pilaf (page 48)

Accompaniment (choose one)
Turkish Squash (page 159)
Yogurt–Cucumber Salad (page 293)
Mideast Relish (page 294)
Spinach–Yogurt Salad (page 299)
Yogurt Squash (page 299)

Bread
Pita Bread (page 337)

Condiment (as desired)
Greek Olives (page 65)
Pickled Mushrooms (page 66)

Dessert (optional)
Halvah (page 352)
Tahini Custard (page 362)
Arabic Yogurt Cake (page 391)
Dried apricots and dates
Almonds and pistachio nuts

ARABIC DINNER

Entrée (choose one)
Mideast Carrot and Chick-Pea Puree
(page 105)

Algerian Chick-Peas with
Cheese Croquettes (page 181)
Kosheri (page 187)

Accompaniment (choose one)
Onion–Radish Relish (page 297)
Yogurt Squash (page 299)

Salad (choose one)
Mixed salad with
Lemon–Tahini Dressing (page 290)
Greek Tomato and Cucumber Salad
(page 300)

Condiment (as desired)
Greek Olives (page 65)
Quick Turnip Pickles (page 311) or
Egyptian Pickled Turnips (page 440)
Pickled Hot Peppers (page 440)

Bread
Pita Bread (page 337)

Dessert (optional)
Baked Rice Pudding (page 363)
Arabic Yogurt Cake (page 391)
Dried fruit
Yogurt with honey

MOROCCAN COUSCOUS DINNER

Appetizer
Moroccan Yogurt Soup (page 109)

Entrée
Moroccan Couscous (page 193)

Condiments (include all)
Cabbage Raita (page 293) or
Quick Turnip Pickles (page 311)
Sweet Carrot Raita (page 293)
Spicy Tunisian Sauce (page 309)

Bread (choose one)
Bread Turnovers with Cheese
(page 279)
Hot cheese-stuffed pita

Dessert (optional)
Marinated Figs (page 358)
Arabic Yogurt Cake (page 391)

Beverage
Mint Tea

The Orient

The cuisines of China and Japan are based largely on soy products and fresh vegetables, and most dishes are cooked quickly with only small amounts of fat. Thus, they are well suited to the principles of wholefoods cookery. Even when there is a long list of ingredients, you will find these dishes are relatively easy to execute once you have learned how to coordinate their preparation. Here you will find the Master Rule indispensible.

In planning the menu, choose at least a few dishes that can be made in advance and do not attempt more than two that require last-minute attention. If you wish, however, you can include several wok-cooked dishes in one meal by presenting them in sequence, retreating to the kitchen after each course, giving the diners time to recoup their appetites or to nibble on a selection of cold dishes. (Practiced cooks work with two woks.)

Our Chinese pantry includes the following special items which you will need for the recipes in this section.

* tofu
* bean sprouts
* fresh ginger
* hot Chinese mustard (English mustard powder can be used instead)
* Dried Chinese mushrooms. These are much stronger in flavor than the dried mushrooms commonly found in supermarkets and, although they tend to be costly, a little goes a long way. They must be soaked in hot water for 20 to 30 minutes to soften before use. (Save the soaking medium; it makes a good stock.)
* Rice vinegar. Less biting than white or wine vinegar; however, any white vinegar can be used in its stead.
* Vegetable broth. If you do not have fresh broth on hand, a powdered vegetable base can come in handy. Wholefoods outlets offer bouillon that contains no caramel coloring, MSG, or other flavor enhancers. Pocket Soup, page 445, provides a good instant homemade broth.
* Sesame seed oil. A strong-flavored oil made from roasted sesame seeds, it is not intended for cooking, but for seasoning. Small amounts added to soups, vegetable dishes, and salads give an authentic flavor that makes the difference between good and excellent when it comes to Oriental cooking. Available in Oriental groceries and natural food stores, this oil keeps well at room temperature and knows no substitute.

Other staples that are probably already on your shelf include cornstarch or arrowroot (interchangeable), soy sauce, sesame seeds, scallions, garlic, cooking sherry, cayenne, and agar or gelatin. Some specialty items will be useful for creative additions of your own. We especially recommend *cellophane* or *"bean thread" noodles* (translucent noodles, made from ground beans, that are dried and looped into skeins and last indefinitely on the pantry shelf); canned *bamboo shoots,* which can be replaced with canned hearts of palm (or even celery hearts in a pinch); canned *baby corn;* dried *tiger lily buds; hot chili oil;* and fresh *water chestnuts,* which are sweet and crunchy (and very ugly) and make the canned variety seem quite insipid. These are best replaced in a recipe, if need be, with fresh Jerusalem artichoke slices.

You will want a wok, possibly your vegetable steamer, and chopsticks—for unlike the spoon and fork, chopsticks help you savor *each* mouthful. The ubiquitous beverage is tea, served piping hot throughout the meal.

JAPANESE DINNER

Opener (choose one)
Tamari Broth with Greens (page 55)
Egg Drop Soup (page 55)

Entrée
Tofu–Vegetable Tempura with
Dipping Sauce (page 171)

Accompaniment (choose one)
Brown rice
Rice with Snow Peas (page 267)
Sushi Rice (page 268)

Salad (choose one)
Spinach–Bean Sprout Salad (page 298)
Oriental Salad Platter (page 302)
Namasu (Pickled Vegetables)
(page 311)

Dessert (optional)
Fruit Juice Gel (page 360)
Tahini Custard (page 362)

CHINESE DINNER I

Opener (choose one)
Steamed Chinese Dumplings (page 83)
Chinese Greens in Broth (page 91)
Chinese Hot and Sour Soup (page 107)

Main Course (choose one)
Egg Fu Yung (page 136)
Savory Smoky Tofu (page 169)
Spicy Bean Curd (page 169)

Vegetable Course (choose one)
Broccoli with Peanuts in
Sweet and Sour Sauce (page 147)
Stir-Fried Green Beans with Garlic
(page 233)
Simple Vegetable Stir-Fry (page 255)

Accompaniment
Brown rice

Salad (as desired)
Cucumber Salad with Spicy Dressing
(page 294)
Chinese Radish Salad (page 297)

Dessert (optional)
Pineapple Sherbet (page 59)
Jumbo Walnut Cookies (page 375)

CHINESE DINNER II

Opener or Entrée (choose one)
Spring Lettuce Rolls
(Sweet Dipping Sauce) (page 83)
Mu Shu Vegetables with
Mandarin Pancakes (page 216)

Entrée (choose one)
Savory Smoky Tofu (page 169)
Spicy Bean Curd (page 169)

Grain Accompaniment (choose one)
Rice with Snow Peas (page 267)
Noodles with Sesame Paste (page 277)

Vegetable Accompaniment (choose one)
Stir-Fried Green Beans with Garlic
(page 233)
Spiced Cabbage (page 236)
Cold Ginger Eggplant (page 243)
Stir-Fried Greens, Chinese Style
(page 244)
Cucumber Salad with Spicy Dressing
(page 294)

Dessert (optional)
Fresh pineapple
Fruit Juice Gel (page 360)

CHINESE DINNER III

Opener (choose one)
Steamed Egg Roll (page 73)
Chinese Hot and Sour Soup (page 107)
Egg Fu Yung (page 136)

Entrée (choose one)
Green Bean Chow Mein (page 146)
with rice or rice crackers
Vegetable Chop Suey (page 119)
Lo Mein (page 119)

Salad (choose one)
Cucumber with Spicy Dressing
(page 294)
Chinese Radish Salad (page 297)
Spinach–Bean Sprout Salad (page 298)

Condiment (as desired)
Fresh Chinese Fried Noodles (page 276)
Chinese Mustard (page 307)

Dessert (optional)
Maple-Walnut Ice Cream (page 366)
Ginger Cookies (page 375)

Asian Fare

Indian cuisine is one of our favorites, offering many different dishes to provide leisurely and varied dining. Although the blend of spices in curries can set the mouth on fire, in many dishes seasonings are prized more for their ability to produce interesting and unusual flavors.

There should be at least four different elements in a simple but well-balanced Indian meal, and six or seven in a more elaborate one. (These are our qualifications, not an official rule.) A simple Indian meal requires a grain dish, a bean or vegetable entrée, a cold salad (raita), and a chutney. Yogurt can be used to replace the salad or the chutney, or can be offered as a separate element. Chapatis or even pita bread can either fulfill the grain requirement or be served as an adjunct to a grain-based dish.

The components of an elaborate meal are presented in the Indian Dinner menu and include a wet curry, a dry vegetable, a bean dish (which can take the place of the wet or dry dish, if desired), a salad, a chutney, a grain and/or breadstuff, and, if not included as part of another dish, plain yogurt.

Typical Indian desserts are extremely sweet; your taste buds will probably be more appreciative of chilled fresh fruit or a light frozen dessert.

The Indian pantry is less exotic than you might imagine. Beans, grains, and familiar vegetables are all staples in Indian cooking, as are garlic, onion, and lemon. The more specialized seasonings you may need to stock include fresh and powdered ginger, cumin, turmeric, cinnamon, cayenne, crushed red pepper, chili powder, mint, mustard seed, peppercorns, and, for more esoteric dishes, cardamom and coriander.

Although our experience with other Asian fare is more limited, we have been particularly impressed with several Indonesian specialties. Because the entrées are largely sufficient in themselves, containing the grain, nut-bean, and vegetable components in a single dish, the Indonesian Dinner appears to be less opulent than the Indian Dinner. If desired, one of the Indian breadstuffs and a simple green salad can be added to the menu.

INDIAN DINNER

Wet Curry (choose one)
Vegetable–Cheese Curry (page 148)
Eggplant and Potato Curry (page 242)
Cauliflower with Yogurt (page 239)

Dry Vegetables (choose one)
Spiced Green Beans (page 232)
Fried Cabbage and Potatoes,
Indian Style (page 237)
Parsnip Curry (page 247)
Spiced Spinach (page 250)
Fruit Curry (page 257)

Bean Dish (choose one)
Very Quick Curried Chick-Peas
(page 54)
Dahi Vaddi (page 88)
Mulligatawny Soup (page 102)
Quick Curried Beans (page 258)
Indian Lentils (page 258)

Grain (choose one)
Peanut Rice (page 265)
Aromatic Rice with Green Beans
(page 266)
Hindu Pulao (page 266)
Brown rice

Salad (choose one)
Cabbage Raita (page 293)
Carrot Raita (page 293)
Cucumber Cuchumber (page 294)
Onion–Radish Relish (page 297)
Tomato Pachadi (page 300)

Chutney (choose one)
Raisin Chutney (cooked or raw)
(page 309)
Coconut Sambal (page 310)
Pineapple Chutney (page 442)
Fresh Plum Chutney (page 442)

Condiments (as desired)
Yogurt
Dry-Roasted Cashews (page 350)
Curry Nuts (page 350)

Bread (choose one)
Stuffed Chapatis (page 284)
Chapatis (page 323)
Dhal Pouree Roti (page 324)
Pita Bread (page 357)

Dessert (optional)
Melon
Pineapple Sherbet (page 59)
Halvah (page 352)
Baked Bananas and Cheese (page 257)

INDONESIAN DINNER

Opener or Accompaniment (choose one)
Cold Curry–Apple Soup (page 110)
Far East Sweet Potatoes (page 251)

Entrée (choose one)
Bami Goreng—
Indonesian Fried Noodles (page 120)
Nasi Goreng—
Indonesian Fried Rice (page 121)

Gado Gado (page 149)
Tempeh Kebabs with
Pineapple Barbecue Sauce (page 175)
over brown rice (page 503)

Dessert (optional)
Fresh coconut
Coconut Kisses (page 352)
Roast Pineapple (page 359)

THE
FOOD READER

The Wholefoods Pantry

American Wholefoods Cuisine will more easily become an integral part of your life if you set up a favorable environment for it. In a kitchen that is stocked with appealing wholefoods, it is easy to put together generous and satisfying meals. We have developed the pantry concept in recognition of one very basic quality of human nature: that is, people tend to do what is easy and convenient. Therefore, you can help overcome any natural resistance by making sure your kitchen is well stocked with the wholefoods that you like.

The kind of pantry you have depends on how much cooking you do and the number of people you cook for. The "short-order" cook will probably have a less extensive pantry than the "gourmet" cook, but each of these pantries will be adequate in its own right, simply reflecting different approaches to food. To help in organizing and storing foods, we have divided the pantry into dry, refrigerator, and freezer sections, as well as outlining a minimal pantry for those who want just the basics.

Despite the absence of chemical preservatives, wholefoods keep well if stored properly and used within a reasonable amount of time. By following the guidelines in "Food Handling and Storage," you will be able to maintain the quality of the food you buy.

We like the idea of leaving as many wholefoods as possible within view to encourage consumption; nuts, seeds, and dried fruits in jars or tins on an open shelf, a bowl of fruit ripening on the table, an assortment of natural cheeses in a storage box in the refrigerator, and whole grain crackers in the bread box or counter-top tin are all an invitation to dig in.

THE DRY PANTRY

The dry pantry is based on a room temperature of 55° to 70°F. and assumes that the fresh foods listed will be used within a recommended time span. You will sometimes find an (R) or an (F) following an entry. This indicates refrigerator or freezer storage is warranted at certain times. For example, flours, nuts, seeds, and their by-products purchased in amounts intended to last more than three months, are best held below 55°F. Once opened, most oils that will not be used within a month fare better with refrigeration. Prepared condiments, canned fruits, juices, etc., should also be refrigerated once opened. Baked goods in excess of immediate needs are best frozen. Depending on freezer capacity, local weather conditions, and personal cooking habits you may also maintain long-term storage of staples such as nuts, grains, coffee beans, cooking cheese, etc., in the freezer. The Storage at a Glance table on page 477 provides details.

Grains
* Barley
* Brown rice
* Buckwheat groats (kasha)
* Bulgur (cracked wheat)
* Millet
— Oats
* Wild rice

Flours
* Arrowroot/potato starch/cornstarch
* Buckwheat flour (R)
* Raw bran
* Rye flour (R)
* Soy flour (R)
* Triticale flour (R)
* Unbolted cornmeal (yellow preferred) (R)

Wheat germ (R)
Whole wheat flour (R)
Whole wheat pastry flour (R)

Whole Grain Breads
Bagels and bialys (F)
• Canned brown bread (R)
Corn bread (F)
English muffins (F)
Muffins (F)
Pita (F)
Rolls (F)
Whole Wheat and mixed grain loaves (F)

Whole Grain Crackers
• Brown rice
• Corn tacos and tostados
Croutons
Dried bread and cracker crumbs
Whole rye
Whole wheat
Whole wheat matzoh
Whole wheat pretzels

Pasta *Rice*
Whole grain spaghetti, macaroni, and noodles
Backup: Artichoke macaroni; High-protein spaghetti, macaroni; Spinach pasta

Cold Cereals
"Granola" types (R)
Whole grain of choice

Hot Cereals
• Oatmeal
• Rolled and crushed rye
(plus selections listed under Grains and Flours)

Beans (Dried and Canned)
Black-eyed peas (cow peas)
– Black (turtle)
Cannellini (white kidney)
– Chick-peas (garbanzos/ceci)
Fava
Kidney (red/chili)
• Lentils
Limas (butter beans)
Mung
• Peas, split green or yellow
Peas, whole green
• Pinto (pink)
Soy
White (great northern, navy, pea bean, French haricot, marrow)

Canned Vegetables
• Tomatoes
• Tomato paste
Tomato puree
• Tomato sauce

Fresh Vegetables
Ripening avocado
• Onions
• Potatoes
Ripening tomato
• Winter Squash

Fresh Fruit
Ripening varieties

Canned Fruit
Applesauce
Apricots
Peaches
Pears
Pineapple
Pumpkin

Bottled Fruit Juices
• Apple
Apricot
Berry
Grape
Grapefruit
Mango
Orange
Papaya
Peach
Pineapple
Pomegranate
• Prune

Vegetable Juices
• Carrot
• Tomato

Other Cold Beverages
Bottled water
Sparkling water (seltzer/mineral water)

Powdered Beverages
Carob powder
Cereal grain "coffee"
Cocoa
Coffee (R)
Dry milk powder
Herb tea
Leaf tea

Nuts, Seeds, etc.
• Almonds (R)
Unroasted cashews (R)
Filberts (hazelnuts) (R)

Peanuts (R)
Pecans (R)
Popping corn
Pumpkin seeds (R)
Sesame seeds
Soynuts
Sunflower seeds (R)
Walnuts (R)

Nut and Seed Butters
Peanut butter (R)
Tahini (R)

Oils
Corn (R)
Olive
Peanut
Safflower (R)
Soybean (R)
Sunflower (R)

Dried Fruit
Apples
Apricots
Cherries
Currants
Dates
Figs
Peaches
Pears
Prunes
Raisins

Mixes
Dried soup mix
Falafel and Burger Mixes
Mushroom Sauce Mix
White Sauce Mix

Miscellaneous
Baking powder
Baking soda
Sprouting seeds
Unflavored gelatin/agar
Vinegar

THE CONDIMENT PANTRY

Sweeteners
Fruit butter/jam (R)
Maple syrup (R)
Molasses
Honey
Unsweetened baking chocolate

Savory Seasonings
Catsup (R)

Gomasio (sesame salt) (R)
Horseradish (R)
Kelp
Liquid hot pepper sauce
Mayonnaise (R)
Miso
Mustard (R)
Nutritional yeast
Sherry (cooking wine)
Soy sauce

Prepared Condiments
Capers (R)
Caponata (R)
Chutney (R)
Grape leaves (R)
Olives (R)
Pickled peppers (R)
Other pickled vegetables (R)

Herbs and Spices
Basil
Bay leaf
Caraway seed
Cardamom
Cayenne
Celery seed
Chervil
Chili powder
Cinnamon
Cloves
Coriander
Cumin
Curry powder
Dill
Garlic
Ginger
Mint
Mustard, powdered and seeds
Nutmeg
Oregano
Paprika
Parsley
Peppercorns
Poppy seeds
Poultry seasoning
Red pepper, crushed
Rosemary
Sage
Tarragon
Thyme
Turmeric

Flavor Extracts
Almond
Vanilla

THE REFRIGERATOR PANTRY

- Eggs
  Milk
- Natural Cheese
  Spreadable Sun Butter
  Sweet (unsalted) butter
- Tofu
- Unflavored yogurt

Fruit
Apples
Berries
Grapefruit
Lemons
Limes
Oranges
Other ripe varieties

Vegetables
Carrots
Celery
Greens
Parsley
- Scallions
Sprouts
Others in season

Miscellaneous
Buttermilk
Cream
Half-and-half
Multipurpose flour mixes
Salad dressing
Shredded unsweetened coconut
- Sour cream
- Baking yeast

THE FREEZER PANTRY

Herbs or Herb Cubes
Ice cream/sherbet/ices
Ice cubes
Juice concentrates
Lemon/orange peel
Plain frozen vegetables
Pre-chopped vegetables
Pre-made pie crusts and other frozen
  doughs
Preplanned meals
Sweet (unsalted) butter
Tomato Cubes
Tofu
Tomato paste cubes
Unsweetened frozen fruit

Whole Grain Breads
Biscuits
Crepes
Muffins
Pancakes
Pre-made cake
Rolls
Tortillas
Wholefoods cookies

THE MINIMAL PANTRY

Many who like the idea of wholefoods cuisine are not that interested in doing much cooking. However, eating does have its own imperatives, and whether you are tired, sick, short of time, or only minimally interested in the kitchen arts, you need ample and nourishing food. This is where the pantry again shows its worth. We offer here a list of long-lasting, well-accepted foods that can provide the basis of a no-cook meal, help to round out a meal you bring in, or serve you when you do want to cook.

Bread and Grains
Canned brown bread
Cracked wheat (cooks in 15 minutes)
Hot whole grain cereal of choice
Pasta (cooks in 10 minutes)
Popcorn (better than chips with a sandwich)
Popping corn (kernels keep indefinitely)
Tacos
Tortillas (frozen)
Whole grain breadstuffs (fresh or frozen)
Whole grain cold cereal of choice
Whole grain crackers
Whole wheat pretzels

Nuts, Seeds, Beans
Canned beans
Nuts, seeds, "soynuts" (better than chips with a sandwich)
Peanut butter
Tahini
Unshelled nuts

Cheese and Dairy

Butter
Cottage, pot, or ricotta cheese
Eggs (some hard-cooked)
Hard-grating cheese like Parmesan
Natural slicing cheeses
Nonfat dry milk powder
Yogurt

Fruits and Vegetables

Canned tomatoes
Dried fruit
Fresh fruit (especially apples, oranges, and lemons, which keep longest)
Fresh vegetables (especially onions, celery, carrots, and a few potatoes)
Frozen vegetables (unseasoned)
Fruit butter
Fruit canned in juice or water
Tomato paste
Tomato sauce

Condiments

Basic seasonings like fresh garlic (stick in the freezer), cinnamon, peppercorns, cayenne, oregano, dry mustard
Canned chilies
Capers
Catsup
Dehydrated soup vegetables
Dried Chinese vegetables
Eggplant caponata
Honey
Hot pepper sauce
Maple syrup

Mayonnaise
Mustard
Oil
Pickled peppers
Pimientos
Soy sauce
Stuffed grape leaves
Unflavored gelatin (for quick dessert)
Unsweetened shredded coconut (refrigerate for dessert garnish)
Vanilla extract (used in hot and cold drinks)
Vinegar

Beverages

Bottled water
Cereal grain beverage
Coffee
Fruit and vegetable juices
Leaf and herb teas
Seltzer

Other recommended convenience wholefoods (pre-made foods free of chemical additives, coloring, artificial flavor, left in the whole, unrefined state or processed as little as possible) include:

Buckwheat or whole wheat pancake mix
Canned soup
Falafel or burger mix
Salad dressing
Whole grain baking mix

Food Handling and Storage

One of the most frequent and understandable concerns expressed to us over the last few years had been in regard to food spoilage. Many people apparently believe that foods that have come from a factory are somehow immune to this problem. This point of view is hardly surprising. All of us have heard so much about the need for chemical preservatives, and we know so little about home care of food, that what was once common knowledge is today regarded as a mystery. For example, why is there oil on top of "natural" peanut butter? Is there something wrong with oil that becomes cloudy on refrigeration? Do whole grains need special storage?

Despite what we have been led to believe, the safety of the food we buy depends only minimally on the steps the manufacturer takes to prolong such sensual qualities as texture and flavor. In fact, the cosmetic coloring, flavoring, emulsifying agents, and often even the preservatives only mask actual deterioration. The steps we consumers take at home to keep food fresh and wholesome are much more important. Many food spoilage problems are the result of improper kitchen habits rather than of the actual deterioration of the food itself. The USDA estimates that at least one major error in food handling is committed in over half of the homes in our country.

KITCHEN AND PANTRY STORAGE

Appropriate Storage Places

In addition to the refrigerator, freezer, and pantry shelf, many of us have a "cold spot" in the kitchen or house that may serve better than these more traditional choices for storing certain foods.

The proper temperature for long-term freezing is 0°F. (−18°C.).

Refrigerator temperature should be approximately 40°F. (4°C.).

Suitable room temperature is 55° to 70°F. (7° to 21°C.).

The ideal "cold spot" should be somewhere between 40° and 60°F. (4° to 16°C.). Lacking a cold spot, the refrigerator will generally be your safest bet.

The storage recommendations in this section are based on these ideal temperatures; it would be wise to have a refrigerator/freezer thermometer on hand to monitor these levels. If your kitchen is warmer than normal, as it undoubtedly will be in summer unless it is air-conditioned, you may have to move certain food into the refrigerator or expect a shortened life span.

Note: Recommended storage times may be superseded by the manufacturer's expiration date.

STORAGE AT A GLANCE

Food	Preferred Storage Temperature	Recommended Storage Conditions
Vegetables:		
most varieties	refrigerator	surface dirt removed, but unwashed; in crisper, storage bags, or covered container; 7 days
carrots, beets, radishes	refrigerator	leafy tops removed; in plastic bags; 2 weeks
corn	refrigerator	unhusked; use promptly
fresh peas and pod beans	refrigerator	unshelled; use promptly
greens	refrigerator	pre-wash, if desired; line storage container with paper towels to absorb moisture and provide humidity; 5 to 7 days
mushrooms	refrigerator	loosely wrapped to breathe; 5 to 7 days
avocados	ripen at room temperature	refrigerate when ripe; once cut, bathe surface in lemon juice and leave pit intact to prevent browning; 3 to 5 days
potatoes, onions, winter squash	cold spot	dry in ventilated container away from light; 1 to 4 weeks
sprouts	refrigerator	well drained; covered container; 5 days
sweet potatoes, yams	cold spot	loosely wrapped; 2 weeks
Fruit:		
berries	refrigerator	unwashed, unhulled; cull damaged specimens; 3 to 5 days
apples, citrus	cold spot	bagged to prevent drying; 2 to 4 weeks
others	ripen at room temperature; refrigerator when ripe	thoroughly dried if washed, in crisper (banana skins will darken in cold but fruit will not be harmed); 5 to 7 days
	freezer	see pages 426–428 in "The Food Factory"
Dairy:		
milk, cream	refrigerator	closed, preferably in original or opaque container; 7 days
yogurt, sour cream	refrigerator	closed container; 2 weeks
nonfat dry milk powder	under 68°F.	airtight container; 6 to 9 months
whole milk powder	refrigerator	airtight container; 6 to 9 months
cheese, upripened varieties (soft)	refrigerator	tightly covered; 5 to 7 days
cheese, ripened varieties (hard)	cold spot or refrigerator	surface protected from drying with plastic wrap, butter, or cloth moistened with salt water or vinegar-water solution; trim any surface mold and use promptly; discard if mold penetrates interior
	freezer	airtight packages in ½-pound portions; avoid direct contact with aluminum foil; best used in cooking; 6 to 9 months

STORAGE AT A GLANCE (continued)

Food	Preferred Storage Temperature	Recommended Storage Conditions
Dairy:		
unsalted butter	cold spot	covered; 1 to 2 days
	refrigerator	covered; 2 to 4 weeks
	freezer	airtight wrapping; 6 to 9 months
ice cream	freezer	plastic container or cardboard container wrapped in foil or plastic; 2 to 4 months
Eggs:		
whole	refrigerator	surface dirt removed, unwashed, covered; 2 weeks
	freezer	beaten, airtight container (mark quantity on package); 1 year
yolk	refrigerator	surface covered with water in closed container; 2 to 3 days
	freezer	covered container with amounts marked, or individually in ice cube tray; 1 year
white	refrigerator	covered container; 2 to 3 days
	freezer	covered container with amounts marked, or individually in ice cube tray; 1 year
hard-cooked	refrigerator	unshelled; 10 days
Meat:		
fresh cuts	refrigerator	loosely covered; 5 days
	freezer	airtight package; 9 months
ground	refrigerator	loosely covered; 2 days
	freezer	airtight package; 4 months
variety meats, liver, and stew cuts	refrigerator	loosely covered; 2 days
	freezer	airtight package; 4 months
cooked	refrigerator	chill within 2 hours; 3 to 4 days
	freezer	3 months; reheat to 165°F. before eating
cured meat, unopened	refrigerator	original package; 2 weeks
cured meat, opened, and cold cuts	refrigerator	wrapped; 3 to 5 days
	freezer	not recommended
Poultry (unstuffed):	refrigerator	loosely wrapped; 5 days
	freezer	whole; airtight package; 12 months parts; airtight package; 6 months
cooked	refrigerator	chill within 2 hours; 3 to 4 days
	freezer	3 months; reheat to 165°F. before eating
Fish:	refrigerator	loosely wrapped; 3 to 5 days
	freezer	airtight package; lean fillets, 6 months; fatty fillets, 3 months
Tofu:	refrigerator	submerged in fresh water, changed daily; 5 to 7 days; if slightly soured, refresh by simmering in water for 10 minutes; if pasteurized in sealed package see manufacturer's recommendations
	freezer	freeze as directed (page 503), use within 6 months

STORAGE AT A GLANCE (continued)

Food	Preferred Storage Temperature	Recommended Storage Conditions
Baked Goods:		
bread, rolls, muffins	room temperature or refrigerator	tightly wrapped; 3 to 7 days; refresh as directed on page 326, or dry for crumbs and croutons (page 505)
	freezer	airtight wrapper; 3 to 6 months
crackers	room temperature	airtight container; on staling, recrisp in 300° to 350°F. oven for 5 minutes
cookies, baked	room temperature	airtight container, separate soft and crisp varieties; on staling, recrisp as above
	freezer	cool completely and separate layers in freezer package; 6 months
cookies, unbaked	refrigerator	covered; 2 weeks
	freezer	preshape (see page 371); 6 to 9 months
cakes, uniced	room temperature	covered; 5 to 7 days
	freezer	airtight wrapping; 3 months
coffee cakes, sponge cakes	room temperature	covered; 2 to 3 days, then best toasted
cakes, iced or cream-filled	refrigerator	covered; 5 days
pies, fruit	room temperature	covered; 2 to 4 days
	refrigerator	covered; 1 week
	freezer	airtight wrapper; 6 months
pies, custard, and cheesecake	refrigerator	loosely covered; chill within 24 hours; 3 days
pie crust, uncooked	refrigerator	covered; 2 weeks
	freezer	airtight wrapper; 6 months
pie crust, baked	room temperature	loosely covered; 4 days
	refrigerator	loosely covered; 1 week
	freezer	airtight wrapper; 6 months
Oils:		
olive, peanut	cold spot	opaque or closed container in dark spot; if held in cold place, harmless clouding will occur
corn, soy, safflower, sunflower	cold spot or refrigerator	opaque or closed container in darkness
Sweeteners:		
honey	room temperature	covered container; gentle heating will reverse granulation; variable life span
molasses	room temperature	covered container; variable life span
maple syrup	cold spot	covered container; if fermentation occurs, boil gently for a few minutes to extend life; variable life span

STORAGE AT A GLANCE (continued)

Food	Preferred Storage Temperature	Recommended Storage Conditions
Nuts and Seeds:		
unshelled	below 68°F.	6 to 12 months
shelled	room temperature	airtight container; 4 weeks
	refrigerator	airtight package; 6 months
	freezer	airtight package; 1 year
ground	refrigerator	covered container; 1 month
	freezer	airtight package; 3 months
nut butters	cold spot	covered container; mix well before using; 1 to 2 months
	refrigerator	up to 6 months
Beans:		
dried	room temperature	airtight container; 1 year plus
cooked	refrigerator	covered; 1 week
	freezer	airtight package; 6 to 9 months
Grains:		
whole grains	below 68°F.	airtight container; 6 to 9 months
cooked grains	refrigerator	covered; 1 week
flours	cold spot	airtight container; 2 to 3 months
	refrigerator	airtight container; 6 months
	freezer	airtight container; 1 year
wheat germ	refrigerator	airtight container; 3 months
	freezer	airtight container; 9 months
soy flour	refrigerator	airtight container; 6 months
bran	room temperature	airtight container; 1 year
cornstarch, arrowroot	room temperature	airtight container; 1 year plus
pasta, dried	room temperature	airtight package; 1 year plus
fresh	refrigerator	covered; 1 to 2 days
	freezer	airtight package; 6 months
cooked	refrigerator	covered; 1 week
	freezer	not recommended
dry breakfast cereals	room temperature	airtight package; 3 months
granola-type cereals	room temperature	airtight package; 1 month
	refrigerator	covered container; 3 months
Dried Fruits:	below 70°F.	covered container; variable life span
Canned and Bottled Food (unopened):	room temperature	1 year
Canned and Bottled Food (opened):		
fruits and vegetables	refrigerator	covered container; 3 to 5 days
pickled items, olives	refrigerator	covered with brine; 1 to 2 months

STORAGE AT A GLANCE (continued)

Food	Preferred Storage Temperature	Recommended Storage Conditions
preserves	refrigerator	1 year
mayonnaise	refrigerator	2 to 3 months
catsup	room temperature	1 month
	refrigerator	6 months plus
mustard	cool room temperature or refrigerator	lasts indefinitely
vinegar	room temperature	lasts indefinitely
cooking sherry, salted	room temperature	lasts indefinitely
unsalted	refrigerator	lasts indefinitely
soy sauce	room temperature	lasts indefinitely
flavor extracts	room temperature	tightly closed, out of direct light; 1 year
Dry Staples:		
herbs	cold spot	airtight container, out of direct light; 6 months
spices, unground	cold spot	airtight container; 1 to 2 years
ground	cold spot	airtight container, out of direct light; 6 monhs
salt	warm room temperature	airtight container; storage near stove helps combat moisture; last indefinitely
pepper, unground	room temperature	lasts indefinitely
pre-ground	room temperature	1 month
baking powder	room temperature	airtight container, moisture free; heed expiration date or 18 months
baking soda	room temperature	airtight container, moisture free; 2 years
yeast	refrigerator	heed expiration date
unflavored gelatin, agar	room temperature	lasts indefinitely
cocoa, carob powder	room temperature	airtight container, moisture free; 8 months
baking chocolate	below 80°F.	harmless graying of surface due to cold; long-lasting
tea, leaf	room temperature	airtight container; up to 2 years
herb	room temperature	airtight container; 6 months
coffee, beans	refrigerator	covered container; 1 month
	freezer	airtight package; 6 months
ground	refrigerator	covered container; 2 weeks
	freezer	airtight package; 3 months

Storage Warning Signs

Recognize the warning signs foods give off as they deteriorate. Some merely indicate loss of quality; others are danger signals.

• Pale color in produce is a sign of old age and loss of flavor and nutrients.

• Soft spots and rust on fresh produce indicate rot. Cut them out and use what is left at once.

• Slime on the surface of food is a sign of deterioration; while it may make food unpalatable, it is not dangerous. Wash it off, pat the food dry, and if it does not appear to be otherwise affected, use it at once.

• Mold on food is visible and, while it shouldn't be eaten, it can be removed if it is only on the surface. Just the same, it is a sign that a food is well beyond its prime, and whatever you manage to salvage should be consumed soon.

• A fermented smell in fruit, juice, jam, and wine is your clue that yeast is growing, and while it is not harmful, such food is generally no longer palatable, unless you are making vinegar.

• If a food has an uncharacteristic, obnoxious odor, get rid of it. Never intentionally taste foods that are suspect.

• If a food has an uncharacteristic sour taste, get rid of it.

Foods that are highly acidic like pickles, or highly sweetened like jam, do not support the growth of bacteria, although once they are opened, mold may grow on their surface.

Unfortunately, where harmful bacteria have formed, they remain colorless, odorless, tasteless, and invisible to the naked eye. Those foods preferred by these bacteria include custard; cream-filled pastries; mayonnaise-containing salads; poultry stuffing and gravy; fresh meat, poultry, and fish; high-fat processed meats, and low-acid canned foods. Treat them with respect, and you will not have to worry. And, although it may sound like an unnecessary warning—"When in doubt, throw it out."

FOOD HANDLING DURING COOKING

Proper pantry storage of foods is one important step in maximizing quality. But all this attention is wasted if foods are not handled correctly during preparation.

Bacteria grow best between 40° and 140°F. (4° and 60°C.); thus, exposure within this range should be minimized.

The following points should be considered:

• Unless otherwise directed, don't remove foods from the refrigerator or freezer until you are ready to use them, and return foods to the refrigerator as soon as you are through.

• Thaw frozen foods in the refrigerator; if you need to speed the process, submerge them in a waterproof wrapping in *cold* water.

• Don't sample raw meat, fish, poultry, or egg products.

• Anything that comes in contact with *raw flesh* or *eggs*, including hands, knives, and cutting board, should be flushed with hot soapy water before it is used again.

• The most effective way to destroy bacteria is with the Sanitizing Solution, below. For cleaning a wood cutting board after daily use, however, you might find scrubbing it with coarse salt and a stiff brush more practical. Flush the board with very hot water and air-dry it completely.

• Don't put the utensils from one food into another without washing and rinse the tasting spoon before you put it back into the jar, bowl, or pot.

• All mechanical equipment used for cooking should be sanitized occasionally. Particular offenders are can openers and grinding equipment. Dismantle utensils that come apart so that nothing becomes lodged in the crevices. Use an old toothbrush for the nooks and crannies.

• Rinse the lids of cans before you open them.

• Don't clean the fish tank or your pets' dishes in the same sink you wash

SANITIZING SOLUTION

To destroy bacteria on utensils and work surfaces, rinse with chlorine bleach diluted according to package recommendations, generally 1 ounce per 2 gallons of water. Cracked dishes should be soaked in this solution periodically.

food or family dishes in. Bacteria harbored by animals that are not harmful to them may be to you. If these sort of items do go into the sink, be sure to scrub and sanitize it thoroughly before you use it again.

• Avoid use of cracked or chipped dishes in the kitchen, since bacteria that grow in the open spaces are difficult to reach in cleaning. If they must be used, sanitize them as previously directed.

• Scald sponges and towels between washings by holding with tongs and pouring boiling water over them. Replace them frequently. It is best to clean surfaces either with a cloth that is washed in the sink immediately, or with disposable towels if you are not willing to take the time to keep cloth ones germ-free.

• Once cooked, foods should be kept hot or promptly chilled. If they are kept in between for more than two hours, dangerous bacteria may become abundant.

On Cooking

This section covers all the essential skills that are utilized in wholefoods cooking. The foods that you learn to prepare here will be the foundation of many other recipes; the cooking techniques will be referred to over and over in recipe directions.

HELPFUL HABITS

After spending some time in the kitchen, most people develop habits and pick up tricks that keep them organized and help to make the job quicker, easier, and more rewarding.

Good form makes the difference between having a pleasurable, relaxed time in the kitchen and dashing about madly, using twice the number of utensils necessary or being caught without an ingredient in the middle of a recipe. Cooking habits and shortcuts almost always evolve with experience, but a little bit of advice beforehand can quicken the process and help make you feel comfortable from the first.

You will find this Master Rule the key to minimizing disappointment and failure.

MASTER RULE

Begin each recipe by reading it through completely. Gather all the ingredients and appropriate utensils at your work space and prepare pans and oven if necessary. *Do as much measuring, peeling, chopping, etc., as practical before combining ingredients.* You are now ready to assemble, mix, cook, and concentrate on any unfamiliar techniques—mastering the recipe.

Stock the Pantry

Keep your pantry stocked with a variety of the wholefoods you use. See "The Wholefoods Pantry" for details.

Have a Repertoire

Cultivate some standard family favorites and some special recipes for entertaining. Even professional chefs have a limited number of specialties, which they add to gradually. The list need not be extensive, but it should be made up of dishes you feel at ease with and ones that can be made from ingredients that are generally on hand.

The Bean Pot and Grain Store

To replace the meat in the freezer you might customarily rely on for a meal, some precooked staples should be built in to your meal planning. Having cooked beans and/or grains on hand provides many options for a quickly prepared meal. Thus, when we make beans, we always cook more than we need for that day. The same goes for rice, cracked wheat, kasha, and other favorite grains. All of these will keep well for about a week in the refrigerator. Even if you don't have a particular recipe in mind, cook up a big pot of beans and/or grains when you are home for a couple of hours or while you are preparing another meal. You can decide what to do with them later. Remember, beans can be frozen if you tire of them before you finish the potful.

Just to give you an idea of the Grain Store's potential: (1) Cook up a pot of rice on Monday and use some as a base for a bean or vegetable stew. (2) On Tuesday, reheat some of the rice with mushrooms and onions for a side dish of Dirty Rice. (3) Wednesday, add some fresh vegetables and salad dressing for a rice salad, or throw some of the grain into the soup pot. (4) Thursday, serve Savory Grain Crackers or Rice-Corn Muffins to accompany the meal. (5) On Friday, mix rice with eggs, nuts, and cheese for a main dish of Baked Rice Balls or Italian Rice Croquettes. (6) For a quick Saturday night supper, try Arroz con Queso. (7) If you can stand rice another day, try Top-of-the-Stove Rice Pudding for dessert on Sunday.

Here's how the Bean Pot can simplify your life: (1) Chick-peas can be served the first day as Chick-Pea Gumbo (perfect over rice). (2) Hummus, a chick-pea garlic dip can start off the next day's meal. In the days to come serve (3) an accompaniment of Very Quick Curried Chick-Peas, (4) Chick-Pea and Carrot Puree, (5) Bean Birds or Hawaiian Bean Loaf, (6) Chick-Pea Sandwich Salad in pita bread. (7) Finally, toss any beans that are left into a salad.

Frozen Tofu

With tofu in your freezer at all times, you will have the fixings of many fast meals. One of tofu's more amazing qualities is the wonderful textural changes that occur during freezing. Ordinarily very soft, tofu becomes chewy, more resilient, and quite absorbent after freezing, closer in character to many common protein foods, such as chicken, turkey, fish, and veal. Defrosting takes only about 10 minutes (see "Cooking with Tofu," pages 502–503).

We recommend trying frozen tofu in any recipe in which you find fresh tofu too soft. (See tofu recipes, pages 166–173.) Experiment with your favorite recipes by replacing protein foods, like those mentioned above, with tofu.

Pre-Made Ingredients

Save steps by anticipating future needs. Foods that you use frequently in grated or chopped form can often be prepared more efficiently in quantity if you have a blender or food processor. Grated cheese, nuts, and fresh bread crumbs keep for a week if refrigerated, and for months if frozen. They can be used directly from the freezer without defrosting. Onions, green pepper, carrots, and celery, which you might otherwise find yourself chopping daily for soups and stews, can be prepared en masse and stored in plastic bags in the freezer for a few weeks with no special processing. However, these are mainly suitable for cooked dishes, where they serve as flavoring agents and are not important for texture.

Flavoring Cubes

We have found cooks are enthusiastic about this time- and work-saving device that we have developed to store certain flavoring aids as ice cubes. When we open a can of tomato paste, for example, and use only a bit, the rest gets transferred to a designated ice cube tray where it is frozen into two-tablespoon portions. Later, when we need a little tomato paste for seasoning a soup or a salad dressing or for enriching a sauce, we simply drop in a cube or two. Homemade Tomato Cubes and Herb Cubes (both recipes are given in "The Food Factory") are based on this principle. In addition, small amounts of leftover soup and vegetable purees and sauces, which appear to be of no use in themselves, make excellent flavoring cubes that can be added to a pot of cooking pasta or grains, a bean or vegetable stew, a soup or sauce, or almost any other dish in need of a little change.

Keep Your Food Factory Operating

Turn rinsing sprouts, making fresh yogurt, and other similar jobs such as maintaining a store of hard-cooked eggs in the refrigerator into routine tasks. Posting a sign will help you remember.

Pre-Washed Salad

Although food value is highest when produce is prepared just prior to serving, pre-washed cut-up carrot and celery sticks stored in the refrigerator in plastic bags will make snacking easy. For convenience, greens too can be washed, dried, and kept in a refrigerated lettuce crisper, plastic container, or closed plastic bag. You can even pre-mix the greens with chopped radish, green pepper, carrots, and celery for a standing salad base. A paper or linen towel in the bottom of the container will absorb any moisture, keeping the salad crisp and fresh for about three days. You will be surprised how often you use lettuce on a sandwich or snack on a salad when the fixings are available instantaneously. If the mix becomes too soft for salad, turn it into soup. (Do not add tomatoes, avocado, mushrooms, or other vegetables that wilt or discolor quickly until serving time. Do not add onion or scallion until serving, as their flavors will increase during storage. Do not add dressing either until serving time.)

When preparing salad dressing, make up enough to keep a jarful in the refrigerator. Designating a certain jar (or jars) for this purpose will help remind you to make more when it becomes empty.

Precooked Vegetables

When steaming a pot of vegetables, make extra. Precooked vegetables combined with a thin white sauce make excellent soup; add a thick white sauce and you have the filling for a pot pie. Marinated in oil and vinegar they become an appetizer or salad garnish. Leftover potatoes can be home-fried the next day or mashed and mixed into a potato dough.

Soup is another item easily made in extra volume; what you don't eat the first day can be extended with tomato juice or vegetable broth, enhanced with some cooked grain, pureed for "cream" soup, or simply used as the stock for cooking beans, vegetables, or grains. One pot of soup may actually provide the basis for two or three completely different meals.

Advertising Pays

Stimulate use of leftovers and foods in season by posting a "Now Featuring" list or blackboard on your refrigerator and freezer. This will provide suggestions for those who are browsing, help remind the cook of what is already there, and keep foods, unnoticed at the back of a shelf, from going to waste. In this way, too, cold air will not be wasted as hungry seekers stare into the open refrigerator for inspiration.

Keep a Kitchen Diary

When studying a new subject, many people keep a diary of their progress, mistakes, insights, etc. You might want to try recording your kitchen experiences too.

Have "American Wine" with Every Meal

A waiter in a Dutch restaurant once referred to ice water as "American wine," a notion we particularly like, as we know a bottle of water in the refrigerator and a pitcherful on the table at mealtime promote consumption of this most basic, noncaloric beverage and provide a ready alternative to less desirable drinks. Bottles of cold seltzer or naturally carbonated waters (but not club soda, which contains salt and other unnecessary ingredients) also suit the contemporary table.

Organize the Cooking Schedule

Attempt only one new or complicated dish per meal, keeping the rest simple or familiar. Since timing a meal can be the most complicated part of cooking, you may even find it helpful to write out the menu and post it in the kitchen.

Think through everything that needs to be done. Any items that you store in the refrigerator, which are best served at room temperature, should be removed when you begin meal preparation. Make note of any foods that have to marinate, as you may want to prepare these first. Consider which dishes can be made and held (i.e., kept warm or cold) and which should be served immediately. Foods that can most easily sit should be prepared first, so that last-minute operations can be done without interference. Those that take the longest to cook should be given early consideration too; while they are heating, other parts of the meal can be attended to.

Energy-Saving Tricks

• A pot of water set to boil should always be covered. This conserves time and fuel.

• Unnecessarily fast boiling wastes fuel; keep heat just high enough to maintain a gentle roll. Flames should never emerge around the bottom of a pot.

• Always choose the smallest possible utensil or appliance to do the job. Boiling a little water in a large pot, putting a small pot on a large burner, and lighting the oven to defrost a single slice of bread are frequent violations of this rule.

• When using the oven, try to plan the meal so that the heat will be used for more than one dish.

• If the fuel wasted to preheat an empty oven disturbs you, you will be glad to know that most ovens can be turned off about 10 minutes early, as their insulation will maintain the temperature for at least five minutes. As the oven temperature slowly descends, the heat already trapped within the food will continue to cook it. However, if you suspect longer cooking will be required, leave the oven on; turning it off too soon, only to have to relight it, is less energy-efficient.

BASIC TECHNIQUES

When you're "on" in the kitchen, what you really want to know is the best way to get the job done. Herewith, kitchen know-how to last a lifetime.

How to Measure

Certain utensils are meant to measure dry ingredients and others are designed specifically for liquids. While experienced cooks often judge by their "eye," proper measuring always gives the most predictable results.

Measuring Dry Ingredients

A teaspoon or a tablespoon or a fraction thereof in a recipe refers to standard measuring spoons. The teaspoons and soupspoons you use to eat with are not their equivalents. To measure accurately, dip the measuring spoon into the dry ingredient; then, drag a flat metal spatula or the blade of a knife held on its edge (to prevent packing) across the rim of the spoon to dispose of the excess.

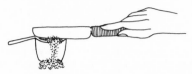

To measure by cup, or fraction thereof, the process is the same. Either dip the measure called for into the dry ingredient or use a spoon to lightly fill the measure. Do not shake, tap, or pat to compress. Gently draw the edge of a knife or spatula across the rim of the cup to "level" the contents.

Measuring Liquid Ingredients

The standard liquid measure is made of transparent material so that you can see when you have the amount called for. Since liquids tend to rise around the edge and drop in the middle, the measurement you seek should be read at the lowest point of the liquid, known as the *miniscus*. For precise results, your eye should be on the same level as the measuring cup.

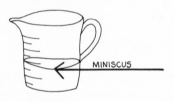

The liquid measuring cup is used for all liquids, including oils and liquid sweeteners. When a recipe calls for oil *and* a liquid sweetener, measure the fat first, then the sweetener in the same utensil; the sweetener will slide right out without sticking. If no oil is needed, wipe the measure first with oil or rinse it in hot water.

When less than a quarter of a cup is specified, liquids should be measured in the same measuring spoons used for dry ingredients. Measure dry ingredients first, then liquid. If you do it the other way around, you will have to wash and dry the spoons first to keep unwanted moisture out of flour, salt, spices, etc.

Displacement Measuring

To measure solid shortening (butter), you can mash it into a dry measuring cup, but you may prefer the "displacement technique" which follows.

(1) Select a liquid measuring cup that holds at least three times the amount you want. (2) Add cold water to measure double the amount of fat you need, for example, if you need ¼ cup butter, pour water into the measuring cup to the ½ cup mark. (3) Now add solid shortening, submerging it completely in the water with your finger or a utensil until the liquid level rises equal to the amount of shortening called for, in this case by ¼ cup to a total volume of ¾ cup. (4) Pour off the water and you'll have the amount of fat that you need.

Measuring by Weight

There are times, of course, when measurements need not be so precise and you will be able to rely on such aids as the markings on a package (butter wrappers, for example, are often marked off in tablespoons) or the amount left in the container (half the yogurt left in a one-pint container, equals 1 cup). You can also measure ingredients by weight. Some countries do all their recipe measuring this way, as opposed to the American use of volume or unit. Measuring by weight actually gives more uniform results, since not every cup of flour is of equal weight, and not every "large" egg weighs the standard two ounces.

When you want to use weights rather than measures, consult the Table of Weights and Measures (page 512) to make the conversions. This approach can be a great time-saver; you can go right from container to mixing bowl without measuring once you know, for example, that an ounce of cheese equals ¼ cup grated, that ¼ pound butter (or one stick) equals ½ cup, and that a 1-pound container of cottage cheese is the same as 2 cups. The Table of Weights and Measures will also help you when a recipe lists ingredients by weight (for example, pound of potatoes) and you do not have a scale or a pre-weighed package.

Cooking with Steam

Steaming, or cooking *over,* rather than *in,* boiling water is the preferred way to cook vegetables. It is a useful technique for heating other foods as well. There are pots specially designed as steamers, but more common are the collapsible baskets that fit inside standard pots, turning anything larger than a 3-quart saucepan into a steaming vessel. No matter what kind of device you use, the same cooking instructions apply.

How to Steam

(1) Fill the pot with about one inch of water; cover and bring to a boil. (2) Arrange the food to be steamed evenly on the steaming surface. (3) Insert the steamer into the pot. The water should be beneath the food and should not touch it. Cover, adjust the heat so that liquid just boils, and steam until food is tender.

The time required will generally be specified in the recipe and will vary slightly, depending on the age of the vegetable, the size of the pieces, and the amount that is being steamed. That is, the older, the larger, or the more crowded the contents, the longer the cooking time. Most foods steam in slightly less time than it would take

them to boil to the tender stage. Properly steamed, they should be just "fork tender," not soft or mushy.

Always turn the heat to the lowest point necessary to keep the liquid boiling. Faster boiling only wastes fuel and accelerates evaporation; it does not speed the cooking process.

When steaming several foods in one pot, put the longer-cooking foods on the bottom, as this layer cooks fastest. Quicker-cooking foods can be added in succession.

If a recipe calls for more than 30 minutes' steaming time, check the water level and replenish it if necessary. When you open the pot to check on the progress, stand slightly back and tilt the lid away from you, allowing the steam to escape. Use caution, as steam can scald.

Foods other than vegetables that are often steamed include dumplings, vegetable and bean balls, fish, and certain breads and puddings. The steamer is also a useful device for reheating grains, softening dried fruit, and even refreshing stale biscuits and muffins. Actually, the steamer has been used for a relatively short period in the western world, and smart cooks should be able to develop dozens of new uses for it.

Stir-Frying

Stir-frying, a refined type of sautéeing, is another technique that both preserves the integrity of food and adds to its taste. Because the foods are cooked quickly in just a small amount of hot fat, nutrients are retained and flavor is enhanced without dramatically adding calories. This method differs from sautéeing, in that foods are kept in constant motion—"stirred" while "frying." Stir-frying is best done in a wok, although it is not imperative to use one. Vegetables, precooked grains, nuts, and strips of tofu, meat, fish, and poultry all lend themselves to this cooking technique.

How to Stir-Fry

(1) Cut like foods in even-sized pieces for uniform cooking. (2) Heat about 1 tablespoon of oil or butter in the utensil, using moderate to high heat. (3) When fat is hot, add the longest-cooking foods first, then the shorter-cooking ones, tossing lightly until tender but still crisp, or as directed in the recipe.

Stir-frying is generally a rapid operation, lasting no more than 5 to 10 minutes. It may be followed by further cooking, most often with the addition of a little liquid, allowing food to simmer with the lid on or off.

A wok, the Chinese cooking vessel constructed particularly for stir-frying, is nothing more than an enormous metal bowl that concentrates the heat at the bottom. As foods cook, they can be pushed up the sides to keep warm, making more room for cooking to continue in the center. A frying pan can be used in a similar manner, but foods that cook in a lesser amount of time cannot be segregated as they can in a wok.

While any utensil can be used for stirring, a wooden spoon, chopsticks, or a long-handled spoon or fork with a heat-resistant handle is best. Regular eating utensils and spoons that transfer heat are not practical, since they are likely to become too warm to hold on to before cooking is completed.

Shallow and Deep-Fat Frying

Frying is a cooking method that is integral to American cookery and to many of the ethnic cuisines that are now a part of it. Although some cultures rely perhaps too heavily on this form of food preparation, often without knowledge of optimal cooking techniques, this abuse does not mean we should deny ourselves the delights of fried food. Rather, we should learn to integrate it intelligently into our cuisine. (If, however, you would like to enjoy some of the aesthetics of frying without going through the motions, you might want to try oven frying, which is described at the end of this section.)

Many people disdain fried foods, declaring them to be indigestible and unhealthy. When the fried foods in question are those that appear in many restaurants, fast-food operations, and take-out stands, we readily agree. However, foods properly fried according to the scientific principles underlying the process possess a flavor and texture that cannot be duplicated by any other form of cooking, and they need not imperil health in the least. The key word in the preceding sentence, of course, is "properly."

The secret of all frying lies in the selection and handling of the fat, and in the preparation of the food. Perhaps the most important fact to keep in mind is that as fat heats, it begins to break down; when it starts to smoke, the decomposition has reached unhealthy (and unaesthetic) levels. The temperature at which fat begins to smoke depends on the kind of fat and how you treat it.

Selection and Care of Fat

Those fats most suitable for frying include peanut, corn, and soy oils. Other common oils, as well as butter, margarine, and lard, break down more readily at 350° to 385°F. (177° to 196°C.), the temperatures that are recommended for frying most foods. The following factors also lower the smoking point:

- The addition of emulsifiers, like mono- and di-glycerides, to the oil
- The length of cooking time
- A large surface area
- The presence of tiny food particles
- The reuse of oil

Thus, if you fry in a narrow pot as opposed to a wide-mouthed utensil, the fat will break down more slowly; if you skim off food particles that accumulate during frying, you will slow the breakdown of fat; if you do not attempt to do too much at one time, and if you do your frying in fresh fat, you will also run less risk of reaching the smoking point. While it is always best to begin with new oil, if you must reuse it, you can slow down the decomposition process by filtering the fat through a fine sieve or cheesecloth after use and storing it in the refrigerator. You can also extend the life of reused oil by adding about one fifth more fresh oil at frying time.

Preparing Food for Frying

Food may be coated or not before frying, depending on the recipe, but either way it must be properly prepared before it is subjected to hot oil.

Breaded fried foods should have a heavy coating, which is achieved by dipping them first into flour or dried bread or cracker crumbs, then into beaten egg, and once again into the crumb mixture. If possible, breading should be applied an hour in advance so it has time to dry and adhere to the surface. A batter can also be used to envelop food, as for tempura. In either case, on contact with hot fat the coating should coagulate quickly and form a protective barrier around the food. A simple dusting of flour does not achieve the same results and is often worse than no covering at all, for particles of flour that fall off into the fat lower the smoking point and cause undesirable flavor changes.

Some foods are fried without a protective covering. Donuts and fritters quickly form their own seal when added to hot fat. Other foods depend on quick cooking of the outer surface to prevent them from soaking up the fat like a sponge. French fries are the best known example, and for this reason french fries and other uncoated foods are often fried at slightly higher temperatures (385° to 395°F. or 196° to 201°C.) than the 350° to 375°F. range used for most other foods.

Deep-Fat Frying

The difference between deep-fat and shallow frying is that in the former the food is immersed in hot fat, while in the latter it is cooked in a generous amount of oil but only enough to cook one side at a time.

A pot that is deeper than it is wide is preferred for deep-fat frying. While cast iron has the advantage of holding heat better than other metals, almost any utensil but glass cookware can be used. One very economical way to deep-fry is in a wok, which, because it is so narrow at the bottom, provides adequate depth with minimal amounts of oil. In wok frying, however, you can only cook three or four pieces at a time to avoid overloading the fat. Thus, the wok is most useful for preparing one or two servings or appetizers.

There are several kinds of equipment that are useful for handling food during frying. A deep-fat fryer, especially designed for the job, comes equipped with a wire basket, which is submerged with the food. When frying is completed, the basket is held above the pot until all the oil drains through. With other pots, use of a long-handled wire spoon allows you to add or remove a single piece at a time and permits the draining of fat back into the pot. The common slotted spoon can also be used, but the fat will not flow off as readily, so that foods may be greasier and will require further draining on removal. Tongs, or chopsticks for the adept, are also good for lifting foods from the cooking oil.

When you are ready to begin, proceed in this manner:

1. Add enough fat to the fryer to comfortably accommodate the food, but do not fill more than two-thirds full.

2. Heat the oil gradually, bringing the fat to the desired temperature before frying begins. Proper temperature helps seal the outside of the food quickly, protecting the interior from grease, a frequent cause of indigestibility. A fat thermometer is the most accurate way to test temperature. Fasten the thermometer in the pot so that the bulb is covered but does not touch the bottom or the sides. If you do not have a thermometer, you can test the fat by the bread-cube test below.

3. Do not crowd the pot; adding too much food lowers the temperature, causing foods to steam and absorb more oil.

4. Deep-fried foods rise to the surface as they brown and must be turned so that all sides brown evenly. Wait until they are almost cooked to perfection but still slightly pale, then gently roll the less cooked area into the fat. When well colored, which will be within a very short time, remove from the pot.

THE BREAD CUBE TEST FOR FAT

A 1-inch cube of bread will turn golden brown in fat:

at	in
345°–355°F.	65 seconds
355°–365°F.	60 seconds
365°–375°F.	50 seconds
375°–385°F.	40 seconds
385°–395°F.	20 seconds

Warning: Hot fat can cause severe burns, so be extremely cautious when frying; stand away from the pot when adding foods in case they spatter, use long-handled utensils, and keep the heat regulated so that fat does not sputter.

Shallow Frying

For shallow frying a large, heavy skillet is best, preferably cast iron. This allows a broad surface so that many pieces can be cooked at once, and the metal, although slow to warm, maintains the heat well during the cooking process.

1. As with deep-fat frying, the oil should be preheated, but this time the fat should be only ⅛ to ¼ inch deep.

2. It is not practical to use a thermometer with such a limited amount of oil. To determine if the pan is sufficiently heated, drop in a little of the crumb mixture or a small piece of food. It should begin to sizzle right away. (Remove the test piece.) Or, sprinkle a few drops of water onto the heating fat. Immediate sputtering indicates that the fat is hot enough.

3. Shallow-fried foods should be turned as soon as the underside is golden; the second side may take a minute or two less to brown. Cook sufficiently on the bottom before flipping, since shallow-fried foods should not be turned more than once.

4. A slotted spatula or tongs is the most appropriate tool to turn the foods and remove them from the hot fat when the time comes. A fork is not recommended, since piercing the outer surface provides a passageway for grease to infiltrate the interior.

Follow-Through

Color is the only guide to doneness in frying. A rich golden hue is the one to aim for and it generally comes within three to five minutes; this should be ample to cook the interior as well. When foods brown too quickly it is an indication that the fat was hotter than recommended.

As soon as food is taken from the pot, it should be blotted to remove any excess fat. Either place it on a double layer of paper toweling or on a surface covered with unglazed paper (brown paper grocery bags, for example). The more closely you have followed the advice in this section, the less paper you will need.

Fried foods are best served right away, so you should prepare the rest of the meal before you begin frying. When necessary, they can be held in a low to moderate oven (300° to 325°F.) or a toaster oven. Do not stack the foods and, if possible, place them on a wire rack so that they do not steep in any oil that drips into the holding pan. Serve as soon as possible so that they do not become limp or dried out.

Oven Frying

Here is the way to get around frying and still enjoy the many recipes that rely on this method of cooking. This approach, which we call oven frying, uses much less oil and offers the convenience of not having to stand guard over a pot of hot fat, especially useful when you are feeding a group. It can be used whenever directions call for frying.

To oven-fry: Place the food on a generously oiled baking sheet or shallow baking pan in a hot oven (375° to 425°F.) for about 20 minutes, or until golden. For even browning, turn pieces about three quarters of the way through or finish cooking in the broiler.

Preparing Vegetables

Historically, vegetables have been one of the most misjudged and mishandled of all foods. While some form of vegetable has been eaten in the wild and eventually cultivated by almost every civilization, a great many were erroneously considered unsuitable for human consumption and even poisonous.

The preparation of vegetables has fared no better. The tradition of lengthy boiling stems from fallacious ideas about disease at a time when medicine was still quite young and foodstuffs easily suspect when illness raged. We now know not only that there are hundreds of vegetables that are safe to eat, but that most are actually much more healthful eaten either raw or only minimally cooked. While some cooking helps break down

the fibrous tissues for easier digestion, most often we cook vegetables for reasons of variety and gastronomy, not safety.

Conserving Flavor and Food Value

The most significant effect of boiling on vegetables is the loss into the surrounding liquid of both the water-soluble nutrients and the flavor oils. As this liquid is generally discarded, the waste is significant.

Exposing vegetables, and particularly the cut surfaces, to liquid as well as air should be minimized to obtain all the nourishment they offer. Baking, stewing in a covered pot in the vegetable's own juices or a small amount of fat, or quick stir-frying all maximize food value. But perhaps the best alternative to boiling—and a process that achieves a similar product is steaming. By cooking the vegetables *over* rather than *in* boiling liquid, both nutrients and natural flavors are conserved. Moreover, this manner of cooking, which renders vegetables crisp, or what is often called "fork-tender" (the point at which they can just be pierced with a fork), makes them more acceptable to those who avoid vegetables, as well as to vegetable lovers. Fresh, steamed, crisp vegetables are a dramatic improvement over the soft, mushlike products of lengthy boiling and are quite a contrast to canned, which are muddied in both taste and texture as a result of the heat of processing.

To Peel or Not

Contrary to popular practice, most vegetables do not require peeling, and since many nutrients are concentrated just below the surface, routine peeling of potatoes, carrots, eggplant, and other vegetables is wasteful. Unless the skins are especially thick and tough, which may happen in older vegetables, a good scrubbing with a vegetable brush is sufficient.

If vegetables are peeled for aesthetic reasons or because of an inedible rind, it is generally best to do so after cooking. Vegetables that are waxed, however, such as rutabaga and turnip, fare better if the waxy coating is cut away before they are exposed to heat. If vegetables are part of a soup, casserole, stew, etc., and thus are cooked in combination with other foods, any peeling will have to be done beforehand.

Cleaning

Unless otherwise directed in the Table of Specific Vegetable Preparation, which follows, wash vegetables quickly under cold running water. If they are especially dirty, scrub them gently but firmly with a vegetable brush. Do not soak them unless this is the only way you can dislodge insects and dirt; this is often the case with cabbage, broccoli, and cauliflower, as their compact heads can conceal insects. For more thorough cleaning, soak these vegetables in cold water to which some salt or vinegar (about 2 tablespoons per quart of water) has been added; this will flush out any tenacious inhabitants. Try not to prolong the soaking; 15 minutes should suffice.

Cutting

Vegetables cooked whole are less susceptible to nutrient loss, but this is not always a practical approach. Most of our recipes give some indication of how vegetables should be cut for best appearance, consistency, and to match the recommended cooking time. Some of the most common methods for cutting vegetables are illustrated below. All instructions are given in relation to the core, or if none exists, in relation to an imaginary "core line" drawn from stem to opposite end.

• To cut vertical slices, or "rounds," "coins," or "rings," make uniform cuts across the "core."

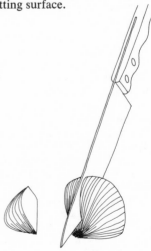

• To slice "lengthwise" or "on the horizontal," cut uniform slices parallel to the "core."

• To cut quarters, eighths, or wedges, cut down through the "core."

• To cut in "crescents" or "half moons," cut in half through the "core," then place flat cut edge on a board and cut narrow, even slices toward the "core." The knife will be held at an angle when cutting the lower ends of the dome but, when the midpoint is reached, it will be perpendicular to the cutting surface.

• To slice "on the diagonal," make uniform cuts at an angle across the "core." (Used frequently in stir-frying as angle cut exposes more surface.)

• To cut in sticks of specified length and width, cut uniform slices of width specified parallel to the "core."

Stack several slices and cut into sticks of desired width.

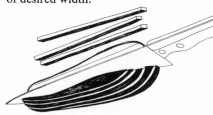

If sticks are longer than required, cut to size.

• To cut in "matchsticks" or "julienne," cut as for sticks, with julienne pieces 2 to 3 inches long and about ⅛ inch wide, and matchsticks only 1 inch long and ⅛ inch wide.

• To cut "cubes," cut slices in either direction (if cube size is specified, make each slice as thick as cube is to be). Stack several slices and cut in a grid. (Space between the cuts should equal the cube size.)

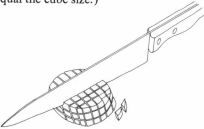

• To "chop coarse," cut thin slices parallel with the "core" but not completely through the vegetable.

Cut thin slices perpendicular to first slices to form a grid, but not through, so they are still attached at one end.

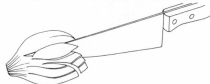

Lay vegetable on work surface, grip with one hand, and slice through grid so that small cubes fall off.

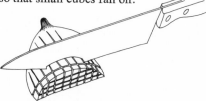

• To "chop fine" or "mince," proceed as above for "coarse chop"; then cut finer by rocking knife back and forth over cut pieces.

• To "shred" soft leaves such as lettuce, roll several pieces together and cut across the bundle in thin slices.

For shorter shred, roll, make a few lengthwise cuts, then proceed as above.

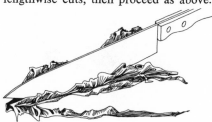

To shred cabbage, cut through the core into halves or quarters. Lay cut edge on a board and make thin slices, holding the knife at an angle. Cut around the stem or incorporate into slices.

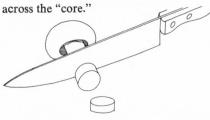

For finer shred, rub quartered cabbage on teardrop side of box grater.

• To cut mushroom "trees," slice downward in a line with the "core."

• To cut mushroom "rounds," cut across the "core."

• To make "flowers" of branched vegetables like cauliflower or broccoli, break off small clusters from the central stem.

• To make free-form slices, cut across the "core."

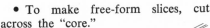

Cooking Time

The cooking time given for vegetables in a recipe is always subject to slight variation. It will be influenced, for example, by the age and size of the vegetables (as logic would have it, the younger the vegetables or the smaller the pieces, the faster they cook), as well as the size of the load (increased volume, especially in a tightly packed vessel, prolongs the cooking).

Rather than relying on recommended times, consider them a gauge and test a little before the anticipated point of readiness to judge for yourself. Either probe with a sharp knife tip or the prongs of a fork, or whenever practical, test by tasting.

Unless recipe directions give other recommendations, here is general advice for preparing vegetables.

Artichoke, Globe: Remove small leaves at base. Cut top half off each leaf with a kitchen scissors. Trim end of stem, but leave stem intact unless artichoke is to be stuffed, in which case stem should be removed so artichoke will stand upright. To remove choke for stuffing artichoke, spread leaves, cut away the small, light leaves in the middle, and scrape off *all* the hairy center with a small paring knife. When trimming is completed, rinse under cold water. If artichoke will not be cooked immediately, place in a bath of cold water to which the juice of a lemon or 1 heaping tablespoon flour has been added. This will prevent discoloration of the leaves. When ready to cook, rinse once again. If recipe requires artichokes to be cut, do so one by one as they are added to the pot.

Artichokes, Jerusalem: Scrub with vegetable brush under cold running water. Peel to use raw or in a casserole or stew. Otherwise cook first, then peel; the skin is not good to eat.

Asparagus: Wash in cold water. Trim stem where it snaps easily when bent. If desired, save the ends for vegetable stock.

Avocado: Prepare as close to serving time as possible. Cut from tip to tip to remove wedges, loosening gently from the pit. To forestall browning, keep pit in contact with unused portion. To use the entire fruit at once, cut in half from tip to tip and twist gently to loosen from pit. Remove skin with a small paring knife; sometimes you will find you can even peel the meat off the skin without a knife, or scoop it out with a spoon. Douse with lemon juice to maintain color.

Beans (green or yellow wax): Wash by sloshing around in basin full of cold water, rubbing to remove any dirt. Then rinse by handfuls under cold running water and drain in colander or salad spinner. Trim ends by snapping. If shorter pieces are desired, section by snapping as well.

Beans (pod): Beans still in the pod should be washed in cold water and cooked either in the shell (the beans will then slip right out) or shelled as for fresh peas.

Beets: Remove tops without cutting into bulb. Scrub surface gently with a vegetable brush under cold water. Peel tough skin before shredding or slicing. To cook whole, leave peel intact and remove after cooking to minimize the beet color bleeding.

Beet Greens: See *Greens.*

Broccoli: Wash in cold running water. If buds are very compact and you suspect the presence of insects, soak up to 15 minutes in a saltwater or a vinegar–water bath. Rinse under cold water and cut as recipe indicates. If stalks seem thick or fibrous, peel with a paring knife or a vegetable peeler to reveal the inner, light green core, which is very sweet and tender. Cut a slit up the stem of wide stalks to shorten cooking time to match that of the quicker-cooking buds.

Brussels Sprouts: Wash under cold running water. Trim tough or discolored stem ends.

Cabbage: For salads or general cooking, cut heads in half through the core and rinse under cold water. If cabbage appears to be buggy, soak up to 15 minutes in saltwater or a vinegar–water bath. Rinse in plain water before use.

To prepare cabbage leaves for stuffing, remove core with a small paring knife and loosen any leaves that easily separate from the head. For leaves that are difficult to separate, heat enough water in a large pot to cover the cabbage, then plunge into boiling water, cover, and cook for three minutes. Remove and rinse immediately in cold running water until cool enough to handle. Gently peel off as many leaves as you can remove easily. When this becomes difficult, plunge cabbage back into boiling water and repeat the process. As the outer leaves are removed, you may have to cut around the stem end again to disconnect leaves. The entire head should be easy to separate leaf by leaf using this method.

For stuffing, each leaf must be pliable enough to roll without cracking the rib. Any leaves that are not flexible should be placed back in boiling water briefly until they can be bent.

Carrots: Wash under cold running water and scrub with a vegetable brush. Peel only if the skin is thick or there are places where dirt cannot be scrubbed free. If desired, save peelings for stock. Trim off any green areas at stem end.

Cauliflower: Remove tough outer leaves; small, tender leaves can be reserved for the soup pot. Soak whole head in saltwater or vinegar–water for up to 15 minutes to drive out insects. If the vegetable is to be divided into "florets," break apart or cut with a small paring knife before washing, then simply rinse under cold water or soak if it appears necessary. The core is quite tasty and can be sliced raw into salads or cooked along with the buds.

Celery: Wash each stalk individually under cold running water, paying particular attention to the dirt at the base. Trim sparingly at the base and reserve, if desired, for soup or stock. If leaves are not to be used, save for soup.

Chard: See *Greens.*

Chicory: See *Greens.*

Chinese Cabbage: The center leaves of this elongated, green leafy vegetable are usually dirt-free; only the cleaning of the outer portions need concern you if the entire head is cut up at once, rather than divided leaf by leaf. Run under cold water and rub gently with hands to clean.

Collards: See *Greens.*

Corn: Don't do anything until just before cooking. Then remove the husk and silk and rinse under cold water only if necessary to remove the silky strands. Corn may be cooked whole, cut into sections still on the cob, or the kernels may be cut away from the cob before cooking. To remove kernels, cut as close to the cob as you can. If you cut into the kernels, you will lose some of the sweet milk. Any of the cob still attached to the kernels can be pulled off with your hands, but it won't hurt you to eat it.

Cucumbers: If cucumber is waxed, as most of those sold commercially are, peel as sparingly as possible before use. Unwaxed cucumbers just need a good rinsing. Seeds need not be removed, but if you are shredding the cucumber and object to the seeds, cut lengthwise and scrape seeds free with the tines of a fork.

Eggplant: Wash under cold running water. Peel with a paring knife or vegetable peeler only if directed.

To char skins for peeling, secure whole eggplant on a skewer, long-handled fork, or a thin, sturdy green branch and hold over a flame, rotating until well blackened on all sides and meat is soft. Remove from heat and, when cool enough to handle, pull peel off by hand. Any pieces that cling can be trimmed with a paring knife.

To bake for peeling, place in a 350° to 375°F. oven in an unoiled pan and bake until quite tender, 30 to 45 minutes, depending on size. When cool enough to handle, remove skin as with charred eggplant.

Salting the eggplant to "extract the bitter juices" is not recommended, although you may encounter a recipe or two here where the eggplant is salted first to soften it for rolling.

Endive: See *Greens.*

Greens (including all lettuce, wild greens, spinach, chard, herbs, etc.): Slosh about in a basin of cold water to loosen dirt. Wash handfuls under cold running water and drain in a salad spinner or colander. Repeat process if any dirt remains. You may sometimes have to rub leaves with your hands to dislodge soil. To dry greens, pat with a towel or give them a whirl in the salad spinner. Or, put them in a mesh basket, take it outside, and rotate quickly with a circular motion to shake off moisture.

Horseradish: Because it is not readily available, you will not find this vegetable included in our recipes. However, if you wish to use it, peeling is advised although it is best left until the last minute to prevent browning.

Jicama: As you might expect from its appearance, the skin is not edible. Remove with a peeler or paring knife, then rinse the portion you are going to use.

Kale: See *Greens.*

Leeks: These can be extremely sandy inside. The best way to get to the sand is to make a long lengthwise slit penetrating just to the center. Then rinse under cold running water, using your fingers to expose the inner surfaces to the water to flush out the sand. Cut away the roots and the dry part of the green end; use all the light portions and the fresh-looking green tops.

Mushrooms: For us the most tedious kitchen job is the cleaning of mushrooms. Mushrooms should never be soaked, as this makes them spongy, and it is best to expose them to water as briefly as possible during cleaning. The preferred method of cleaning is to rub them with a damp paper towel or a soft brush. Peeling is only needed when they are quite discolored or old. No trimming is needed unless the base of the stem is encrusted with dirt or badly damaged.

Okra: Wash under cold running water, rubbing with your hands to dislodge any dirt. Pods can be cooked whole, but if they are cut, discard the stem portion.

Onions: Remove papery outer layers only. Washing is unnecessary. Chill before cutting to reduce tears.

Parsnips: Scrub with a vegetable brush to remove dirt. Although the skins are bitter, and therefore not recommended for eating, it is best to cook them with the skins on whenever possible and then peel with the tip of a paring knife.

Peas: Wash before shelling and shell just before use. Edible pod peas, which do not need shelling, generally require trimming at the ends with a small paring knife.

Peppers, Hot: Hot peppers are prepared in the same manner as sweet ones, but you must be extremely careful, for many are as hot to the touch as they are to the taste. If you are sensitive, wear rubber gloves when you cut them, particularly if the seeds are exposed. (Thin, surgical type gloves are useful.) Roasting and peeling enhances flavor but is not mandatory.

Peppers, Sweet: Rinse in cold water. Cut and remove seeds and any thick white membranes. When blanching is called for (to shorten cooking), steam, or plunge into boiling water for the time specified. When roasting is called for (to remove the skin), hold on a long-handled fork or skewer and rotate over a flame until the skin blisters. When cool enough to handle, rub skin off with fingers. Any difficult spots can be removed with a paring knife. To roast several at a time, char the skins under a broiler.

Plantains: To prevent browning, peel just before cooking as you would a banana. If cooking is delayed, soak in salted water; pat dry before using.

Potatoes: Scrub well with a vegetable brush under cold running water. Do not soak. Cut away any eyes and green portions. Peel only if it is specifically indicated in the recipe or if the skins are very thick or impossible to wash clean. Potatoes discolor rapidly on exposure to air, so, when possible, cut them just before use. Otherwise browning can be reduced by soaking them in cold water, although this is not a nutritionally sound method. A slightly less effective but more wholesome approach would be to keep them in a covered container in the refrigerator.

Pumpkin: The peel is not edible but is best removed after cooking, when practical. If unpeeled, wash before cooking.

Radish: Wash and scrub gently with a vegetable brush or rub with fingers.

Rutabaga: See *Turnips.*

Scallion: Rinse under cold running water to clean, and dry. Trim off the root and unsightly portions at the top. Use both green and white parts unless otherwise instructed.

Shallots: Remove outer papery layers. No need to wash.

Spinach: See *Greens.*

Squash (hard rind): Yellow- and orange-fleshed varieties, as well as patty pan and spaghetti squash, have inedible peels. Once again, it is best to cook these with the peel on and either eat the meat directly from the "shell" or cut it free before use. For stews and soups, however, peeling prior to cooking is necessary; this may be easier to do with a small, sharp paring knife than a vegetable peeler, depending on how thick the rind is and how skilled you are. Try to keep the trimming minimal.

Squash (soft rind): Zucchini and yellow crookneck varieties, with soft, edible rinds, need only rinsing under cold water prior to use. Salting is not recommended except in those recipes where salt is used to extract the moisture from the shredded vegetable for use in salads (when the water content would cause thinning of other ingredients).

Sweet Potatoes and Yams: These potato skins are generally tough. When the vegetable is cooked whole, peel can be removed after cooking if desired.

Tomatoes: Although we do not peel tomatoes for most uses, for canning and some sauces it is best to do so. Charring the skin by holding the tomato on a skewer or long-handled fork over an open flame imparts an outdoorsy flavor as it loosens the skin, but if you have many to peel, this may be too time-consuming a method. In volume, it is easiest to plunge them into a pot of boiling water for a minute until the skins crack, then cool them quickly under cold running water; when they are cool enough to handle, the skin will slip off easily with the help of a fingernail or small paring knife.

Turnips and Rutabagas: These vegetables belong to the same family and are treated similarly. Generally, they are waxed prior to commercial sale. If so, peel them first, whether they are to be used raw or cooked. If they are not waxed, the skins of turnips can be eaten; however, rutabaga skin is too thick and tough to be enjoyable, and so should be removed either before or after cooking.

Basic Bean Cookery

Beans are an important staple in the wholefoods kitchen; the dried form offers the widest variety, best flavor, and greatest economy. Although canned beans are handy as a backup, they do not compare with the home-cooked kind.

So Much Food, So Little Effort

Although beans seem to take a long time to prepare, they require very little of the cook. All varieties are handled in a similar manner and we have included the most common methods of preparation plus a newer, convenient "freezer method," for those with a tight schedule or a small household.

With the exception of split peas, lentils, limas, and special "no soak" brands, dried beans should be pre-soaked to reduce cooking time. There are two standard pre-soaking techniques.

Regular soak: Rinse beans in cool water and drain them. Place in a large pot with two to three times their volume of water and let stand for about eight hours. This effortless task can take place overnight or while you are out during the day. If soaking time will be more than 12 hours, refrigerate beans during soaking to prevent fermentation.

Quick soak: Place the rinsed, drained beans in a pot with two to three times their volume of water. Bring to a boil, simmer for two minutes, cover, remove from heat, and let stand for one to two hours.

Note: Be sure to allow room for expansion in the pot, since dried beans will about triple in volume during cooking.

Cooking is the same after either soaking method; bring the pot of beans and the soak water to a boil, cover, and simmer keeping heat as low as possible until tender. Use the timetable that follows as a guide. Some research has shown that if you drain off the soak water before cooking and replace it with fresh, some of the indigestible carbohydrates (ogliosaccharides) that give beans the reputation of being "gassy" will be eliminated. We believe the soak water should be used in cooking because it also contains same water-soluble B vitamins and minerals. If, however, you have trouble digesting beans you may want to try freshwater cooking and compare the results.

For split peas, lentils, limas and other beans that do not require soaking, just add two to three times their volume of water and cook as for soaked beans.

Low heat will conserve the liquid and also keep beans from splitting, but you should check the water level occasionally and replenish if beans begin to cook dry.

Harmless foam may form on the surface of cooking beans; to reduce it, add a tablespoon of oil.

For flavor, chopped onion, garlic,

herbs, fresh chilies, or crushed hot red pepper can be added at any point. Salt and acid ingredients such as tomatoes, lemon juice, vinegar, and wine tend to toughen the outer skin, slowing the cooking process; these flavoring agents should not be added until the beans are almost tender. When salting, add ½ teaspoon salt per cup of dried beans.

Warning: Many cookbooks, particularly older ones, add baking soda to the bean pot; this should be avoided, as the soda destroys the B vitamin thiamine.

Test for Tenderness

One way to test tenderness is to place a few beans on a spoon and blow on them. If they are done, the skins will split. A better way, of course, is to take a few from the pot and taste them. If you plan to use the beans for salads, or as part of a recipe that requires additional cooking, or for storage in the refrigerator or freezer, cook until they are tender but still hold their shape. If you want to puree them for dips and soups, you may want to cook them a little softer. Note that soybeans and chick-peas remain firm-textured even after lengthy cooking.

TIMETABLE FOR COOKING DRIED BEANS	
Black beans	1½–2 hours
Black-eyed peas	1½ hours
Fava beans	2–3 hours
Garbanzo beans (chick-peas)	2–3 hours
Kidney beans	1½–2 hours
Lentils	45 minutes
Lima beans	45 minutes–1½ hours
Navy and pea beans	1–1½ hours
Pinto beans	1½–2 hours
Small pink beans	1–1½ hours
Soybeans	3–3½ hours
Split peas	45 minutes
White beans (cannellini)	1½–2 hours

The fresher the beans, the faster they will cook.

Pressure Cooking

Dried beans may be pressure-cooked, further reducing the cooking time, but this can be risky if the skins of the beans clog the steam-release valve. Complications can be minimized by oiling the inside of the lid and only filling the vessel half full with water and beans. At any rate, we find slowly simmered beans have a better texture; small limas, lentils, and split peas, in particular, seem to suffer in the pressure cooker where they are easily softened to a mush.

The Freezer Method of Bean Cookery

If you are determined to cut cooking time, there is another method you will appreciate. This technique not only saves time but is excellent for those who wish to cook only a small quantity of beans. It is called the Freezer Method and is accomplished as follows.

Pre-soak beans as previously directed. Drain, pat dry, and place *in a single layer* in a shallow pan. Freeze for a few hours until hard, then transfer to airtight freezer bags and return to the freezer for storage. When you needs beans in a hurry, dump the frozen beans out of the bag into a pot with boiling water to cover. Most varieties will be done in 30 minutes, and even long-cooking beans like soybeans and chick-peas will be ready to eat within 45 minutes. As most of the expansion of beans takes place during soaking, your cooked yield will be only slightly larger than the volume of frozen beans you begin with.

BEAN YIELD
Most dried beans measure 1 to 1⅓ cups per 8 ounces and yield 3 to 3¼ cups cooked beans.

Substituting Canned Beans

Probably the fastest way to get cooked beans is to have someone else do the job. This is what you are doing when you buy canned beans. While these beans are satisfactory for many recipes, there are drawbacks to their use.

1. Canned beans are almost always highly salted. When using these beans, omit the salt in any recipe. Also, avoid those canned with sugar, MSG, hydrolyzed vegetable protein, modified food starch, and EDTA (a chelating agent that traps minerals).

2. The combined effects of processing and cooking make canned beans softer than home-cooked varieties, almost to the point of mushiness. This will affect the texture of the final dish. Certainly purees are easily achieved with canned beans, but while some people find they make other dishes smoother and more palatable, many equate them with baby food. Remember, a cooked dish made with canned beans should only be heated long enough to cook the other ingredients and warm the beans themselves.

Ground Beans (Chopped Beat)

Ground beans are the basis of many economical and imaginative recipes. We have come to call beans in this state "chopped beat" as they are similar to ground meat in terms of versatility and use. Chopped beat can be prepared from cooked beans in minutes; the only requirement is that you have one of the following grinding implements.

• The most basic tools for grinding cooked beans are a small hand (Mouli-type) grater and a food mill. The hand grater works best for small amounts; if you are grinding more than four to six servings, the larger food mill is more practical.

• The quickest way to make chopped beat is with either a meat grinder or a food processor, using the steel blade.

• In some recipes ground beans can be replaced with mashed beans—the result of muscle power applied to soft, cooked beans.

Note: The blender is not a suitable tool for grinding beans; in order to process them, the machine requires liquid and thus you end up with a soft puree rather the desired coarse pulp.

Cooked beans must be drained thoroughly before grinding. When the liquid surrounding them has thickened or congealed (as it may upon storage and often does in canned beans), they should be rinsed through a strainer or colander to remove this adherent "gravy." Pat dry with a cloth or paper towel before grinding.

The ideal texture for chopped beat is dry and crumbly. For more textured dishes, you may allow a few pieces of bean to remain. Canned beans and beans that have been cooked soft, once ground, may require additional binding ingredients (flour, bread crumbs, etc.) in order to be shaped according to recipe directions. This is something you will have to judge by feel.

It is preferable to grind beans for use as needed; however, most ground bean recipes can be prepared in advance and kept in the refrigerator or freezer prior to cooking. Any exceptions will be noted on the recipe itself.

Cooking with Tofu

Although tofu is new to many westerners, there is nothing complicated about cooking with it.

During storage, tofu is kept submerged in water and must be drained before use. Unless otherwise directed, remove from the storage container and blot dry with paper towels.

"Pressing" is frequently recommended to remove additional water for best absorption of seasonings. It also makes tofu firmer for sautéeing or deep-frying. To press tofu:

1. Remove cakes from storage container and pat dry.

2. Slice as directed in the recipe. If cutting is not specified, leave whole.

3. Place several layers of paper toweling or a soft kitchen towel on a plate, cutting board, countertop, or other area where it will not be in your way for at least the next 30 minutes. If you can, slant the pressing surface, so excess water will drain off.

4. Place tofu on toweling, cover with another layer of towels, then top with a plate, baking sheet, or cutting board.

5. Weight the structure with some heavy books, cans, a pot filled with water, or whatever you can locate that will help press the water out of the bean curd and into the towel. Ideally 2 to 5-pound weights should be used.

6. After 30 minutes, remove the tofu. It is now ready for marinating or cooking.

Freezing Tofu

Yet another aspect of tofu's versatility is that it can be frozen for long-term preservation and to change its texture. This process affects the structure to such an extent that frozen tofu is like an entirely different ingredient. Where the fresh variety is dense and tender, frozen tofu is chewy, with an open, coarse texture; it is much like veal or chicken, making it more familiar and welcome. Freezing also increases its spongelike ability to absorb the flavors of the cooking medium.

To freeze, slice tofu cakes so they are about ½ inch thick. If using small 4-ounce cakes (about 2½ x 2½ x 1 inches), slice in half; slice thicker 8- to 10-ounce blocks in fourths. Wrap each piece of tofu in plastic wrapping. This individual packaging will allow removal of pieces as desired. Make a single moisture-proof package of all the tofu, wrapping it in foil or heavy plastic bags. Freeze as you would any food.

For best eating, use frozen tofu within six months.

Reconstituting Frozen Tofu

Frozen tofu must be defrosted before use, and the recommended procedure is quite different from that used with any other frozen food.

Remove all freezer packaging and place tofu in a deep bowl. Cover with *boiling* water. Let stand about 10 minutes and drain. If tofu is still partially frozen, repeat the procedure. When completely thawed, rinse with cool water, then press firmly between your palms to expel all moisture and make it as dry as possible. It is now ready to use.

Basic Grain Cookery

Grains are a mainstay of wholefoods meals; they may be served alone or used as an ingredient in the preparation of more complicated recipes. While similar principles control the cooking of all grains, each has its peculiarities as well.

Grains owe their palatability to the interaction between heat and their starchy kernels. Surrounded by steam or boiling liquid, the grain swells and absorbs moisture. The preferred manner of cooking is to provide only as much liquid as the grain can hold, so that it does not need to be drained. Two parts liquid to one part grain is the standard proportion, although when grains are cooked for cereal or pudding the liquid may be increased to three or four times their volume. Cooking may be done in water, broth, juice, or milk.

Boiling water method: Adding the grains to boiling liquid is said to cause them to swell rapidly, with the effect that when cooking has ended, each grain remains separate. To use this method, sprinkle the grain slowly into the boiling liquid, cover the pot, lower the heat so the liquid barely simmers, and cook until the grain is tender and the liquid absorbed.

Cold water method: Other cooks insist that the Oriental method of preparation is superior. Here the grain is rinsed through a sieve under cold water to remove surface starch, transferred to the cooking vessel, covered with cold water that extends one inch above the grain level (this may be slightly less than twice the grain volume), then brought to a boil, covered, and simmered as in the previous method. To trap the steam around the grain as it cooks, the pot must have a tight-fitting cover.

Regardless of the initial approach, during the cooking process the liquid should barely simmer. Furious boiling will cause the grains to burst.

Do not stir while cooking, unless otherwise directed. Stirring loosens the starch from the outer surface and makes grains gummy.

For most savory dishes, salt is added and, although the amount will vary with personal taste, ½ teaspoon salt per cup of dry grain is a sensible guideline. If the cooking medium is highly seasoned, or if additional flavorings will be added to the grain later on, salt may be omitted. (The addition of salt makes rice and millet firmer, adding to their cooking time. You may wish to allow these grains to cook for 15 minutes before salting them.)

When cooking time is almost over, insert a chopstick or poke with a fork to see if all the liquid has been absorbed at the bottom of the pot. Chew a few top grains to check tenderness. If not done, continue to cook, adding a little liquid, if needed, to prevent scorching. If grains are quite tender but a little liquid still remains, uncover partially and cook until dry. When cooking is completed, remove from heat and, if possible, let stand, covered, for 15 minutes before serving. This allows the grains to "set."

Dry-Roasted Grains

Dry roasting refers to the light toasting of uncooked grains without added fat. This makes them both firmer and fluffier and imparts a nutlike flavor. With most grains this is a matter of taste. With buckwheat groats, however, which are generally mixed with beaten egg and dry-roasted before boiling, the result is so superior that they are almost always cooked this way (see Fluffy Kasha).

To dry-roast, put grains in an unheated, ungreased pot over medium heat. Stir continuously for three to five minutes. You will notice a pleasant aroma and soon a deepening of color in the grains. Do not let them become dark, or the flavor will be burned, not nutty. Add liquid and cook as usual.

Sautéed Grains

Prior to boiling, grains may be sautéed in about 1 tablespoon oil or butter per cup of dry grain. This adds a certain savoriness and often serves as a vehicle for adding other seasonings, including garlic, onion, and small amounts of chopped vegetables (see Viennese Rice and Cracked Wheat Pilaf). Sautéeing is generally reserved for grain dishes that stand on their own during a meal, not for grains that will later be combined with other foods. Once again, stir continuously while sautéeing until grains are golden, then add liquid and cook as usual.

TIMETABLE FOR COOKING GRAINS

These figures are approximate and will vary with the volume of grain, the size of the flame, and the fit of the lid.

Brown rice	50 minutes
Cracked wheat (bulgur)	15–20 minutes
Buckwheat groats (kasha)	20 minutes
Millet	30 minutes
Barley	60 minutes
Oats	10 minutes
Couscous	5–10 minutes

Greater Grains

If you wish to enhance the food value of grains, you can add 1 tablespoon nutritional yeast, or 2 tablespoons wheat germ per cup of dry grain at the end of cooking. Incorporate with a fork, using a light "fluffing" motion.

> **GRAIN YIELD**
>
> One cup dry grain will produce about three times this amount cooked, or enough for four to six servings, depending on use.

Crumbs and Croutons

You will no longer be bothered by staling bread if you think of it not as a food on its way out, but as a crouton or bread crumb about to be born.

To make croutons: Cut bread in cubes, making them uniform in size so that they all dry in the same amount of time. Spread the cubes, leaving space for air to circulate between them, on a screen, wire rack, or other aerated surface to facilitate drying. Leave at room temperature until they are hard. This should take approximately 24 hours but will vary, depending on the bread, the room temperature, and the humidity. In a damp environment, or to speed the process, dry in a low oven (200°F. or less). To conserve energy, use the heat that remains after the oven has been used for cooking. At the lowest setting, 30 minutes is usually adequate to complete the process. Drying at higher temperatures is not recommended—drying should take place from the inside out, not the outside in, or moisture may be trapped and the life span of the crouton shortened. Store in an airtight container to keep dry.

To make soft bread crumbs: Crumble bread that is either fresh or just beginning to stale between fingers to form small particles. For finer bread crumbs or for making crumbs in volume, process in the blender or food processor with the steel blade until evenly grated. Use at once or store in a covered container in the refrigerator or freezer. Soft bread crumbs are also referred to as fresh bread crumbs.

Yield: One ounce (one average slice) bread = ⅓ cup crumbs.

To make dried bread crumbs: Crumb bread as for fresh crumbs. Then dry as for croutons. Store in an airtight container to keep dry.

Yield: One ounce (one average slice) = ¼ cup crumbs.

To make cracker crumbs: Crackers can be ground to a coarse or fine meal in the blender or the food processor, using the steel blade; we find the blender does a more efficient job. Another approach is to place the crackers in a sturdy plastic bag and roll a rolling pin over them until they are finely ground.

Note: All kinds of breads and crackers can be used for crumbs. Corn and rye bread crumbs enhance food flavors, and croutons from raisin or caraway-seeded breads make excellent stuffing as well as soup garnishes.

CRUMB COATING AND STUFFING MIX

Combine the following and store in a covered container.

> **1 cup finely ground dried bread or cracker crumbs**
> **¼ cup finely ground nuts and/or seeds**
> **¼ cup wheat germ**
> **1 tablespoon dried parsley**
> **1 teaspoon nutritional yeast**
> **½ teaspoon salt**

For *Italian Crumb Coating and Stuffing Mix,* add 1 teaspoon oregano and ¼ teaspoon dried basil.

Nut and Seed Meals

Nuts and seeds, ground into a flourlike powder or meal, are often used with bread crumbs as a binder, for a crumb coating, or as a topping. They can generally replace up to ¼ the flour, grain, or other starchy filler in any recipe, adding complementary protein.

To grind meal: Place no more than ½ cup nuts or seeds at a time in the blender container. Run at high speed until finely ground. Stop the machine a few times and loosen the meal that accumulates at the base with a fork to keep the meal fluffy and distribute oils evenly throughout. This is especially important with high-fat nuts like walnuts and pecans, which are apt to become pasty.

Grinding can be done in a food processor fitted with a steel blade, but with less efficiency. A coffee grinder does a good job. The fine drum of a Mouli grater will also process nuts and some seeds into fine, light meal but is impractical for grinding in volume.

Yield: ⅓ cup nuts or seeds produces about ½ cup meal.

Egg Handling

This section covers all the techniques involving eggs that you are likely to encounter in the recipe directions. The reader who wants to learn about the basic cooking of eggs may want to look at our *The Good Breakfast Book.*

To separate eggs: The goal is to crack the egg and allow the white to ooze out while containing the yolk in half of the shell. Start with a cold egg that is as fresh as possible; an old egg with a soft, flattened yolk will be difficult to separate. While a little white in the yolk portion is unimportant, a bit of yolk in the whites will inhibit whipping.

Have a clean bowl ready to catch the white. If whites will eventually be whipped, select a bowl large enough to accommodate the beaten volume. They will almost triple in size once air is incorporated.

• Crack the shell with a knife or on

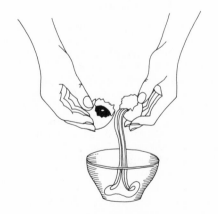

the edge of a bowl with one sharp blow and open upward to contain the egg.

• Holding the halves over the bowl, transfer the yolk, without breaking, from one half of the shell to the other, allowing the white to pour over the edge and into the bowl. Repeat so that all the white runs into the bowl.

If more than one egg is to be separated, use a new bowl for the second white; an accident over the bowl of already separated whites can ruin the lot. The yolks should be gathered together in another bowl.

If any yolk seems in danger of breaking, add immediately to the yolk bowl; it is better to sacrifice a little of the white than to risk ruining the bowl of egg whites. If a piece of shell lands in the whites, scoop it out carefully with a clean utensil. You want to keep the whites as pure as possible to insure maximum whipped volume.

To beat or whip egg whites: Since egg whites balloon several-fold when whipped, be sure to select a big enough bowl. Copper is considered the best medium to beat egg whites in, but glass or stainless steel bowls are perfectly acceptable. Do not use aluminum or plastic, however, as these materials can inhibit volume. Yield is the greatest when the whites are at room temperature, so separate them while still cold at the beginning of cooking and let them sit before whipping until they are needed.

• Using a wire whisk or hand or electric mixer at a low setting, begin beating whites until foamy. If salt is to be added, do so at this point.

• Continue to beat, increasing the speed as whites begin to thicken, much like whipped cream. Move the beater around and scrape the bowl with a rubber spatula if necessary for more even whipping.

• When the whites form soft peaks or little mounds that curl over when the beaters are lifted, it is time to gradually beat in any sweetening that is called for.

• Continue beating at high speed until the beaters drawn up out of the batter leave short, stiff little mountains.

The surface of properly beaten egg whites will still be shiny, like smooth, glistening snow. If the bowl is inverted, the whites will not fall out. Overbeaten whites appear dry and granular and break down quickly.

Egg whites should be whipped in one single operation. Don't walk away before the job is completed. And as the structure they form is not very sturdy, the whipped whites should be used as soon as possible.

Folding egg whites: Because of their delicacy, whipped egg whites must be handled with care. They are combined with other foods using a gentle, vertical mixing motion known as "folding."

• Choose a bowl large enough to accommodate the combined volume.

• Loosen the mixture they will be combined with by carefully stirring in a little bit of the beaten whites, about as much as adheres to the beaters.

• Gently dump the remaining whites on top.

• Using a rubber spatula, wire whisk, or wooden spoon, fold by cutting down into the middle of the bowl with the utensil, turning it flat along the bottom, and slowly bringing it up again a little farther away, using one fluid motion.

• Give the bowl a quarter turn and continue this process until the whites are evenly distributed throughout and only tiny clumps are visible on the surface.

Never stir or treat egg whites harshly. This will cause them to deflate.

Tempering Eggs

When adding raw eggs to anything hot, beat some of the heated mixture into the eggs first by spoonfuls to raise the temperature. Then slowly add the egg mixture to the remaining hot food, gently stirring all the while. This is called *tempering*, and it keeps the eggs from coagulating too rapidly. It is the standard procedure for egg thickening of soups, sauces, and puddings.

Conserving Eggs

If you wish to reduce the number of eggs in a recipe, or use only the whites

or yolks, this can be done without dramatically affecting the flavor and texture.

When eggs are used as a binding agent, as in burgers, loaves, and the filling of ravioli, crepes, and stuffed vegetables, two yolks or two whites can be substituted for one whole egg. This is especially useful if you are dividing a recipe that calls for a single egg, as you can then use either the yolk or the white alone. When a recipe calls for more than one egg however, or when you have a surplus of yolks or whites from a previous recipe, it is best not to replace more than half the eggs in this manner. (Thus, if two eggs are indicated, use one whole and two whites or yolks; if five eggs are specified, use three whole and four yolks or whites, as desired.)

In custards, cakes, pancakes, and similar batters, eggs can be similarly apportioned, using at least one whole egg for every two in the recipe. Here the effect may be slightly more apparent, as egg whites alone tend to make a sturdier custard and a springier cake (angel food cake is a perfect example), while yolks increase tenderness in these foods.

Egg used to moisten foods before a crumb coating is applied may be exclusively whites or yolks.

To reduce the number of eggs or eliminate them in certain recipes, you may apply the following rules:

• As a binder, use 2 tablespoons soy flour mixed to a paste with an equal volume of cold water for each egg omitted.

• In batters, add ½ teaspoon baking powder for each egg omitted. To help compensate for the lost food value, you may want to add 1 tablespoon soy flour per cup of flour, or 1 ounce grated cheese, or 2 tablespoons peanut butter, if appropriate to the recipe.

ENRICHING FOODS

One advantage that wholefoods cooks have is the ability to increase the level of nourishment in the foods they prepare, an attribute no other cuisine has properly developed. Central to this skill of course, is, protein complementation, in which the combining of foods results in greater nourishment than when the same foods are eaten separately. In the wholefoods kitchen we are, thus, actually able to say that "one plus one equals three."

The key ingredients for enriching foods in other ways are discussed below. You may recognize some of them as "health foods," a term that unfortunately has made some people wary and others a bit overenthusiastic. The power of these ingredients lies in the fact that they are very concentrated sources of certain nutrients. They should not be expected to perform miracles, but they can be relied on to enhance many foods—not only in terms of nutrition, but often in terms of flavor and texture as well.

Nutritional yeast, for one, is highly regarded for its B vitamin content and is used regularly by many as a dietary supplement. We have found that it serves us well as a seasoning, imparting a robust and somewhat meaty flavor to many foods, particularly soups and stews. Similarly, soy flour, dry milk powder, and wheat germ—foods that most people use in small amounts, if at all—have the ability to enrich the taste, texture, and nourishment of many dishes. You will find these ingredients are used throughout this book, but sparingly, so as not to overwhelm the recipes. You may choose to make additional use of them in your kitchen.

Soy Flour

Soy flour contains about twice the protein of whole wheat flour and less than one third the starch. While it does not have the elastic properties of wheat flour needed for high-rise baking, it does keep baked goods fresh and moist longer.

In batters, soy flour can be used to replace about 1/12 the flour with excellent results. To accomplish this, take 1½ tablespoons wheat flour out of each cup and replace it with 1½ tablespoons soy flour.

Soy flour also works as a thickener in soups, sauces, and gravies. It takes twice as much soy flour as wheat flour to do the job, or four times as much soy flour as cornstarch, potato starch, or arrowroot. Use it in the same manner, mixing the flour into a paste with an equal amount of cold liquid, then stir this into the hot mixture to be thickened. Simmer gently for five minutes to improve the flavor.

SOY FLOUR, FULL FAT

Amount—¼ cup
Calories—90
Protein—8 grams
Carbohydrate—6 grams
Fat—4.5 grams
Minerals—phosphorus, potassium, iron, and calcium
Vitamins—the B complex

Nutritional Yeast

Nutritional yeast is also known as brewer's or torula yeast. The most effective use of this ingredient is as a thickener for soups, stews, and sauces, or to impart a "meaty" flavor to any dish. Be sure to taste as you add, using the guidelines below, as some brands are stronger-tasting than others.

• Sprinkle 1 tablespoon into each quart of hot soup or stew just before serving.

• Add ½ teaspoon per cup to gravies and sauces just before serving.

• Add to taste to vegetable purees, stewed vegetables, and bean dishes. Begin with 1 tablespoon per 4 servings.

• Mix 1 teaspoon into a bowlful of egg salad, peanut butter, bean spreads, and other sandwich fillings.

• Add 1 tablespoon per cup of dried grain to the grain after cooking.

• In vegetable, bean, and grain burgers and loaves, add 1 tablespoon per 4 servings or 2 cups mixture.

• In baked foods, use 1 teaspoon

nutritional yeast along with each cup flour or meal.

As you become accustomed to its taste, you will be able to increase the amount you use. With highly seasoned foods, especially curries and spicy Mexican dishes, its presence will probably go unnoticed.

NUTRITIONAL YEAST (BREWER'S/TORULA)

Amount—1 tablespoon
Calories—23
Protein—3 grams
Carbohydrate—3 grams
Fat—trace
Minerals—a good source of iron and some calcium value
Vitamins—an abundant source of the B complex

Wheat Germ

This protein fortifier can be used in any place where flour or grains are called for. Pancakes, waffles, bread, cookies, cakes, cereals, crumb toppings and coatings, and grains used alone and as filling all accommodate wheat germ comfortably.

• Replace up to 4 tablespoons per cup of flour or crumbs in toppings and coverings.

• In batters replace up to 2 tablespoons flour per cup with wheat germ.

• Replace up to ¼ the grain or bread crumbs used in fillings, burgers, and loaves with wheat germ.

WHEAT GERM, TOASTED

Amount—¼ cup
Calories—92
Protein—7 grams
Carbohydrate—12 grams
Fat—3 grams
Minerals—phosphorus, iron
Vitamins—B complex

Nonfat Dry Milk Powder

Because nonfat dry milk is not a wholefood, we do not recommend its exclusive use as a beverage. However it is very economical for occasional use in cooking instead of liquid milk. It can also be added dry as a booster to drinks, baked goods, fillings, sandwich spreads, omelets, vegetable purees, and a host of other foods.

There are three common varieties— regular (non-instant), low-density instant (requiring about 1⅓ cups powder per fluid quart), and high-density instant (requiring about ⅞ cup powder per fluid quart). They vary somewhat in terms of nutrition, as indicated on the charts below. Often availability will make the choice for you.

NONFAT DRY MILK POWDER, REGULAR

Amount—¼ cup
Calories—109
Protein—11
Carbohydrate—16 grams
Fat—trace
Minerals—calcium, phosphorus, sodium, potassium
Vitamins—riboflavin, A and D if fortified

NONFAT DRY MILK POWDER, INSTANT

Amount—¼ cup
Calories—62 (low density); 93 (high density)
Protein—6 grams (low density); 9 grams (high density)
Carbohydrate—9 grams (low density); 14 grams (high density)
Fat—trace
Note: Same minerals and vitamins as in "regular."

Some favorite uses follow.

• In any cooked dish calling for milk, use reconstituted dry milk or substitute water for the liquid milk, and for each cup of milk required, add ¼ cup milk powder (high-density types) or ⅓ cup (low-density types) to the dry ingredients. Be sure to try this in baking.

• In addition to its use to replace fluid milk, you can replace up to ¼ the flour in baking with milk powder as well. This is quite a dramatic step, however, and generally we limit it to 1 to 2 tablespoons.

• When you use liquid milk in soups, gravies, sauces, custards, puddings, or hot beverages, add 1 or 2 tablespoons milk powder per cup for increased value.

• When mashing vegetables, beat in milk powder, using ⅓ cup per 2 cups of vegetables. Thin if necessary with a little of the cooking liquid.

• In bean, grain, and vegetable burgers and loaves, milk powder can be added, if not already included, using up to ½ cup per 2 cups mixture.

• Create "cream" soups by pureeing any soup in the blender or food processor along with dry milk powder. The more you add, the thicker the soup will be, but do not exceed ⅞ cup (high density) or 1⅓ cups (low density) per quart.

• When beating eggs for omelets or scrambling, add 1 tablespoon powdered milk per egg.

• When cooking hot cereal, combine uncooked grains with half as much milk powder. Add water and cook as usual.

• Add up to ¼ cup powdered milk (high density) or ⅓ cup (low density) per quart of juice or milk when making blender shakes.

You may also want to experiment with powdered milk as a fortifier in nut and bean spreads. Add enough to make the filling an appealing consistency, but as some people find dry milk tastes gritty or chalky, go easy and see how it's accepted.

Kitchen Math

TABLE OF METRIC EQUIVALENTS

Here are some standard measurements that every cook will find useful.

Measurements by volume

1 teaspoon = ⅓ tablespoon = 5 milliliters
1½ teaspoons = ½ tablespoon
3 teaspoons = 1 tablespoon = 15 milliliters
4 tablespoons = ¼ cup = 59 milliliters
5⅓ tablespoons = ⅓ cup = 79 milliliters
8 tablespoons = ½ cup = 118.4 milliliters
16 tablespoons = 1 cup
1 cup = 8 fluid ounces = .2366 liters (approx. ¼ liter)
2 cups = 1 pint = .4732 liters (approx. ½ liter)
4 cups or 2 pints = 1 quart = .9463 liters (approx. 1 liter)
4 quarts = 1 gallon

Measurements by weight

1 ounce = approx. 28 grams
3½ ounces = 100 grams
16 ounces = 1 pound
1 pound = 454 grams
2.2 pounds = 1 kilogram

All measurements refer to the level amount unless otherwise specified with the adjectives "heaping," "rounded," or "scant."

BAKER'S MATH

Use this as your guide to selecting the proper pan or replacing the one specified in a recipe. Distinction is made here between the manufacturer's listed capacity to the top of the pan, and comfortable capacity, which is generally two-thirds to three-fourths total capacity and really the most useful figure to have.

Dish Description	Capacity
Individual baking dishes	1 to 2 cups comfortably
1-quart casserole	4 to 4½ cups to top; 3 cups comfortably
2-quart casserole	8 cups to top; 6 cups comfortably
4-quart casserole	16 to 17 cups to top; 10 cups comfortably
8-inch square	8 cups to top; 4 to 6 cups comfortably
9-inch layer	same as 8-inch square
9-inch pie tin	4 cups to top; 3 cups comfortably
9-inch square	10 cups to top; 5 to 7½ cups comfortably
deep 9½- to 10-inch pie pan	7 cups to top; 4 cups comfortably
9-inch springform	12 cups to top; 9 cups comfortably

BAKER'S MATH (continued)

Dish Description	Capacity
9-inch tube	11 cups to top; 6 to 8 cups comfortably
9 x 13-inch pan	12 cups to top; 6 to 8 cups comfortably
8½ x 4-inch loaf	6 cups to top; 4 cups comfortably
9½ x 5½-inch loaf	7 cups to top; 4 cups comfortably
11 x 14-inch jelly roll	7 cups to top; 4 cups comfortably
Muffin tin	average 6 tablespoons to top, ¼ cup comfortably per muffin; 2¼ cups to top
	1½ cups comfortably per 6-muffin tin; 4½ cups to top
	3 cups comfortably per 12-muffin tin

TABLE OF FOOD WEIGHTS AND MEASURES

Vegetables

Artichoke, Jerusalem
    1 pound = 3 cups cut in 1-inch pieces
Asparagus
    1 pound = 2⅔ cups cut in 1- to 1½-inch pieces
Avocado
    1 small (12 ounces) = 1½ cups diced
                        = 1 cup mashed
    1 medium (1 pound) = 2¼ cups diced
                      = 1¾ cups mashed
Beans, Green
    1 pound = 4 cups cut in 1- to 2-inch pieces
Beets
    1 2-inch beet = 4 to 5 ounces
    1 pound = 1¾ cups shredded
           = 2 cups diced or sliced
Broccoli
    1 pound = 5 to 6 cups pieces or 4 to 5 cups chopped
           = 2 to 2½ cups flowers, plus 2 to 2½ cups stems
Cabbage, Green and Red
    1 pound = 8 cups cut in strips or 1-inch pieces
           = 5 to 6 cups chopped or coarsely shredded
           = 4 cups finely shredded
Carrot
    1 medium = about 3 ounces
    1 pound = 3 cups shredded
           = 3 cups matchsticks or diced small
           = 3½ to 4 cups coins or large dice
Cauliflower
    1 medium head = 1½ to 1¾ pounds
                = 6 cups florets
    1 pound = 4 cups small pieces
Celery
    1 large outer stalk = ½ cup chopped
    1 small inner stalk = ¼ to ⅓ cup chopped

Vegetables *(continued)*

Corn
    1 7-inch ear = heavy ½ cup kernels
    1 8-inch ear = ¾ cup kernels
Cucumber
    1 medium cucumber = 2 cups large cubes
                      = 1½ cups chopped, diced, or thinly sliced
                        = 1 cup shredded
    1 small cucumber = 4 ounces
                        = ½ cup shredded
Eggplant
    1 medium = 1½ pounds
            = 8 cups large dice
            = 4 cups shredded
    1 pound   = 4 cups small dice
            = 1½ cups cooked, chopped
Garlic
    1 small clove   = ¼ teaspoon minced
    1 medium clove = ½ teaspoon minced
    1 large clove   = ¾ to 1 teaspoon minced
Greens
  Collards
    1 pound = 12 cups cut in 1-inch pieces
  Endive
    6 ounces = 2 cups sliced into rounds
    1 pound = about 5½ cups sliced into rounds
  Escarole
    1 pound = 12 cups loosely packed torn leaves
           = 8 cups shredded, gently pressed into measure
  Lettuce
    1 pound = 10 cups torn leaves
           = 8 cups shredded, gently pressed into measure
  Spinach
    1 pound = 16 cups untrimmed leaves
           = 12 to 14 cups stems and leaves lightly packed into measure
           = 10 cups coarsely chopped, lightly packed into measure
           = 6 cups finely chopped
           = 2 cups salted and pressed
           = 2 cups cooked
Herbs
  Parsley
    ½ ounce = ½ cup gently pressed into measure
           = ¼ cup minced
  Watercress
    1 ounce = 1 cup leaves
Leeks
    4 ounces = 1 cup sliced
Mushrooms
    3 ounces = 1 cup sliced or coarsely chopped
    ½ pound = 3 cups large pieces
           = 2⅓ cups sliced or chopped small
    12 ounces = 4 cups sliced
    1 pound   = 40 medium
           = 32 good stuffing size

TABLE OF FOOD WEIGHTS AND MEASURES (continued)

Vegetables *(continued)*

Okra
    1 pound = 3½ cups sliced into wheels
Olives
    4 ounces pitted = 1 cup sliced
Onions
    1 small   = ¼ cup sliced or chopped
    1 medium = ½ cup sliced or chopped
    1 large   = 1 cup sliced or chopped
    1 pound   = 3 cups sliced
Onions, Green (Scallions)
    1 small to medium = 1 tablespoon chopped or sliced
Parsnips
    1 pound = 4 cups peeled pieces
Peas
    1 pound in shell = 1 to 1½ cups shelled
Peppers, Hot
    1-inch segment = 2 teaspoons minced
Peppers, Sweet Red and Green
    1 medium = 4 to 6 ounces
    1 large   = 6 to 8 ounces
    4 ounces = 1 cup strips
             = ½ cup minced
Potatoes
    1 medium = 6 ounces
             = 1 cup small dice
    1 pound   = 3 cups sliced or cubed
             = 2½ cups small dice
             = 2 cups shredded, pressed
             = about 2 cups, mashed
    10 to 12 small new potatoes =1 pound
Plantain
    1 pound = 2 cups pieces cut in 1-inch sections
Radish
    6 ounces = 1 cup cut up
Sprouts
  Alfalfa
    2 tablespoons seeds = ¾ ounce
                    = 2 cups sprouted
  Mung
    ¼ cup seeds = 2 ounces
              = 1½ cups sprouted
    ½ pound   = 1½ cups
Squash
  Summer
    1 medium zucchini = 10 ounces
    1 medium yellow squash = 6 ounces
    1 pound = 3½ cups sliced or diced
            = 3 cups shredded, lightly packed into measure
            = 1½ cups shredded, salted, and pressed
  Spaghetti
    1½ pounds = 2 cups strands

Vegetables *(continued)*

Winter
1 pound = 3 cups peeled cubes
Sweet Potatoes or Yams
1 pound = 4 cups matchsticks or chunks
        = 3 cups shredded
Tomatoes
1 small   = 4 ounces
        = ⅔ cup chopped
        = ½ cup chopped, drained
        = ¼ cup pureed
1 medium = 6 ounces
        = 1 cup chopped
1 pound = 2⅔ cups chopped
3 canned = 1 cup pulp
6-ounce can paste = ⅔ cup
6-ounce can paste diluted with 1⅓ cups water = 2 cups puree
Turnips
1 pound = 4 cups diced
        = 2⅔ cups shredded

Fruit

Apples
1 medium = 6 ounces
        = 1 cup sliced or diced
1 pound = 2⅔ cups diced or sliced
        = 3½ cups shredded
Bananas
1 medium = ¾ cup sliced
        = ½ cup mashed
Berries
  Blueberries
  4 to 5 ounces = 1 cup
  15 ounces   = 1 pint
        = 3 generous cups
  Strawberries
  8 ounces = 1½ cups cut up
  12 ounces = 1 pint basket
        = 2¼ cups cut up
Cantaloupes
1 medium = 2½ pounds
        = 4 cups diced
Cherries
1 pound = 3 cups
Cranberries
1 pound = 4 to 5 cups
Grapefruit
1 medium = ¾ cup juice
        = 1½ cups segments
Kiwi
1 average = about ⅓ cup sliced
Lemon
1 medium = 3 tablespoons juice
        = 1 teaspoon minced rind

TABLE OF FOOD WEIGHTS AND MEASURES (continued)

Fruit *(continued)*

Lime
    1 medium = 2 tablespoons juice
Orange
    1 medium = ⅓ cup juice
            = 1 tablespoon minced rind
Papaya
    1 medium = 1½ cups diced
Peaches
    1 medium 2-inch peach = 4 ounces
    1 pound = 2 to 2½ cups pieces
           = 1 cup pureed pulp
Pears
    1 pound = 2½ to 3 cups sliced
           = 2⅓ cups diced
Pineapple
    ½ medium = 2 cups
Plums
    1 pound = 2 cups cut up
    1 medium 1½-inch plum = 2½ to 3 ounces
Rhubarb
    1 pound = 4 cups cut in ½-inch dice
           = 2½ cups cooked

Canned Fruit—USDA Figures

8½- to 8¾-ounce can = 1 cup drained fruit
16- to 17-ounce can = 1¾ to 2 cups
20-ounce can = 2¼ to 2½ cups

Dried Fruit

Apples
    8 ounces = 2½ cups diced
Apricots
    8 ounces = 30 moist
          = 2¼ cups
Dates
    1 pound unpitted = 1¾ cups pieces
    1 pound pitted = 3 cups pieces
Figs
    1 pound = 24 figs
Peaches
    8 ounces = 2¼ cups pieces
Prunes
    8 ounces unpitted = 18 medium
                = 1 heavy cup chopped
    8 ounces pitted = 1¾ cups chopped
Raisins
    3½ ounces = ¾ cup
    8 ounces = 1½ heavy cups

Beans

      1 pound dry averages 2⅓ to 2⅔ cups = about 6 cups cooked
      1 cup dry = about 6 to 7 ounces
                = 2½ cups cooked
      1 pound canned =1½ to 1¾ cups beans
      3 cups cooked   = 2 cups ground
      8 ounces tofu = 1½ cups cubes
                = 1 cup pureed or mashed

Grains

Barley
    1 cup dry = 6½ ounces
             = 3½ cups cooked
    1 pound   = 1½ cups
Bread
    1-ounce slice = ⅓ cup fresh crumbs
    1¼ -ounce slice = ½ cup fresh crumbs
    4 ounces = 2 cups cubes
    1 cup fresh crumbs = ⅔ cup dry
Cornmeal
    4 ounces = 1 cup dry
    1 pound = 4 cups
Cracked Wheat
    1 cup dry = 5 ounces
             = 3¾ cups cooked
    1 pound   = 3 cups
Flour
  Buckwheat
    4½ ounces = 1 cup
    1 pound   = 3½ cups
  Rye
    3½ ounces = 1 cup
    1 pound   = 4½ cups
  Soy
    4 ounces = 1 cup
    1 pound = 4 cups
  Whole Wheat
    4½ ounces = 1 cup
    1 pound   = 3½ cups
Millet
    7 ounces = 1 cup dry
            = 5 cups cooked
    1 pound = 2⅛ cups
Oats
    3 ounces = 1 cup dry
    1 pound = 6 cups dry
Pasta
    1 pound spaghetti = 8 cups cooked
    2 ounces = bundle ½ -inch thick
            = 1 cup cooked

TABLE OF FOOD WEIGHTS AND MEASURES (continued)

Grains *(continued)*

> 4 ounces small shells = 1½ cups
> = 2 to 2½ cups cooked
> 4 ounces spirals = 1¾ cups
> = 2¼ cups cooked

Rice
> 6½ ounces = 1 cup dry
> = 3 to 3½ cups cooked
> 1 pound = 2½ cups

Nuts and Seeds

(3 tablespoons nuts or seeds = ¼ cup meal)

Almonds
> 5 ounces = 1 cup
> 1 pound = 3¼ cups

Peanuts
> 5 ounces = 1 cup
> 1 pound = 3¼ cups

Pecans
> 3.5 ounces = 1 cup halves
> 3 ounces = 1 cup chopped
> 1 pound = 5 cups

Pumpkin Seeds
> 5 ounces = 1 cup
> 1 pound = 3¼ cups

Sesame Seeds
> 5 ounces = 1 cup
> 1 pound = 3¼ cups

Sunflower Seeds
> 5 ounces = 1 cup
> 1 pound = 3¼ cups

Walnuts
> 4 ounces = 1 cup
> 1 pound = 4 cups

Dairy

Butter
> 1 ounce = 2 tablespoons
> 4 ounces = ½ cup
> = 1 stick
> 1 pound = 2 cups
> = 4 sticks

Cheese
> 4 ounces = 1 cup shredded or diced
> 1 pound = 4 cups
> 4 ounces blue cheese = ½ cup crumbled
> 1 ounce cream cheese = 2 tablespoons
> 4 ounces cream cheese = ½ cup
> 4 ounces feta cheese = ¾ cup crumbled
> 4 ounces Parmesan cheese = 1⅓ cups grated
> 1 pound cottage or ricotta cheese = 2 cups

Dairy *(continued)*

Eggs

1 large (2-ounce) = scant ¼ cup
= 1 heavy tablespoon yolk
= 2 heavy tablespoons white

Miscellaneous

¼ ounce baking yeast = 1 tablespoon
1 pound honey = 1½ cups
1 pound molasses = 1⅓ cups
10 ounces molasses = 1 cup

Eating Out

A clever diner might never cook and still reap the benefits of wholefoods cuisine. Part of today's way of life includes a number of meals that are eaten away from home; for most, it is breakfast and lunch, Saturday night dinner, and an occasional airplane meal. For others, it is the "21 Club"—all meals eaten out or brought in. What's important is that even these meals can be chosen with the wholefoods concept in mind. Actually, one foolproof way to provide a *varied* diet is to eat as if you were dining in a different country each day; this gives the restaurant-goer an opportunity available at home only to creative cooks.

UNFAMILIAR TERRITORY

The most up-to-date guide to local eateries is the Yellow Pages. By checking the listings under "Health Food" and • "Restaurants" you can quickly narrow down the choices. The heading "Health Food" generally covers both stores and restaurants. You will find that the restaurants frequently are vegetarian and a dependable source of whole grains, fresh vegetables, and a variety of imaginative meals.

The comprehensive list in the "Restaurant" section gives additional clues as to what else you can expect to find. Larger cities often divide restaurants by cuisine, and it is the "ethnic" eateries that really expand the dining-out experience. At the least, Mexican guarantees guacamole, beans, chili rellenos, cheese-topped enchiladas, and corn tortillas; Indian means dahl (beans), yogurt, chapatis and puris (frequently whole wheat), and meatless and light meat entrées. Greek and other Mideastern specialties include hummus, baba ghanouj, tabouli, falafel, yogurt, and fresh salads with feta cheese; Oriental restaurants make good use of the wok and soy products, but because MSG is a common seasoning in these establishments, it is wise to skip the soup and other pre-made dishes and request "no MSG" in everything else. For the traveler trying to escape the "steak and potatoes" or "hamburger–french fries" syndrome, Italian restaurants are a welcome sight. Eggplant Parmesan, stuffed vegetables, and antipasto (without the processed meat) are just some of the dishes which offer a respite from white pasta–white bread dinners. Dairy restaurants cooking in the Jewish kosher tradition offer wholesome choices like kasha, vegetable roasts, bean soups, and diverse salads and vegetables.

Cafeterias provide another viable choice, for in addition to modest prices, there is the obvious advantage of being able to see for yourself what is proffered.

The "salad bar" is the most promising trend in American road food. In the least likely places (diners, steak houses, fast-food operations) you can find an array of fresh vegetables and often chick-peas, a bean salad, cottage cheese, or all three to help create a complete meal at minimum expense and with a minimal amount of processed ingredients.

BEYOND THE MENU

It is not always possible or practical to explore an area long enough to find the perfect place to eat, and hunger often dictates where you stop. For the most part, though, there is always some way to maximize your eating experience.

To attract discriminating diners, many restaurants claim "fresh seafood," "baking done on premises," or "home-cooked vegetables." While this may provide some indication of the kitchen practices, it is somewhat unreliable due to the various interpretations of the English language. Indeed, the "baking" may be from a mix or frozen dough, the "home cooking" from a can, and only one of a dozen of the fish choices may be fresh. The fact that they are making an effort to so advertize their offerings, however, makes such places worth an investigatory phone call or visit.

When you have no choice of restaurant, the best overall advice is to choose those foods closest to their natural state. For example, sliced egg rather than egg salad, or tuna chunks rather than tuna salad, means you don't risk getting a factory-made sandwich filling. With the exception of a real fast-food place, natural Swiss or sometimes even cheddar cheese can be substituted for the standard processed American cheese.

"Broiled" or "baked" is always preferable to "fried," and this is even more important in commercial as opposed to home kitchens. A glance at any restaurant trade magazine will educate you as to one way costs are kept down—reusable fats that last a month or longer. Besides, fried foods are the ones most likely to be made with low-grade materials, chemically seasoned, re-formed, frozen, and purchased from a distributor to be revived as needed.

One should always request 100 percent whole wheat bread, but what you actually get may vary from 100 percent whole wheat to caramel-colored white bread. At least you will help communicate the message that a growing number of restaurant diners would like more whole grain products.

Additional Ordering Suggestions

• Bran muffins offer the rare opportunity to get some natural fiber into your diet on the road.

• If you suspect the eggs are powdered or pre-mixed, stick with poached, fried, or boiled. These still have to come in the shell.

• The same goes for potatoes—french fries almost always come frozen, precut; hash browns often suffer the same abuse. A baked potato, however, is subject to the least processing.

• If you favor sour cream on your potato, be sure to inquire if it's the real thing. More and more restaurants are opting for the less expensive "potato topping," a mixture of water, hydrogenated oil, milk solids, several thickeners and emulsifiers, plus artificial coloring, flavoring, and chemical preservatives. If cottage cheese is on the menu, use it to dress the potato, adding protein to the meal as well.

• When it comes to salad, pry into the kitchen policies. A helpful ploy is to ask which is the "house dressing" and learn that way if any are homemade. If the rest of the menu indicates a low regard for food, simply ask for fresh lemon to squeeze on your salad. If you want to apply real "restaurant guerrilla tactics," ask for cruets of oil and vinegar, a side of mayonnaise, mustard, or catsup, and make your own Russian, French, or creamy dressing right at the table.

• Ground meat is highly susceptible to bacterial contamination and easily adulterated with extenders and flavor enhancers. Thus, whole cuts are a safer bet. When meats are displayed on the counter, avoid them unless they are refrigerated. Precooked roasts left standing at room temperature are a primary source of both mild and serious food poisoning.

• Request honey for sweetening beverages and hot cereal.

• Ask for real milk if nondairy creamer is served.

Finally, one way to determine if your selection is actually fresh from the kitchen or comes from the warehouse is to alter it in some way. A Reuben sandwich consisting of corned beef, sauerkraut, and Swiss cheese on dark bread is a standard on many menus. But try to get Swiss cheese on your cheeseburger, or anything else on dark bread, and you'll often find it can't be done. Similarly, if the "amandine" is reserved only for the trout and can't be had with sole, or the buttered carrots can't be unbuttered, the restaurant is probably using pre-made portion-control meals.

When the public accepts what is offered without question or comment, the restaurateur can assume we are willing to tolerate make-believe foods. Some states, following California's lead, are working toward a "truth-in-menu" law to end this chicanery.

Ordering in a Fancy Restaurant

When you want to visit more elegant dining rooms, do not be intimidated by the surroundings into ordering more than you feel comfortable eating. Often our practice is to order several appetizers and salad and skip the main course. To our astonishment, the headwaiter in a dignified San Francisco establishment made it a point to come to our table and compliment us on our selectivity. He mentioned that the food waste repeated nightly was of great concern to him. Never again have we felt uneasy about ordering with restraint.

You may also find a chef who appreciates a chance to "break out." Calling ahead to make a reservation gives the kitchen time to work out special requests, and a cheese soufflé, as well as a variety of elegant vegetable platters, have awaited us on notice. But even a last-minute appearance can have similar results, especially if you can offer some suggestions, based on other menu choices, as to what you might like to have served. Be sure to suggest some protein—perhaps a poached egg, beans, or cheese wedges.

The Friendly Restaurant

People who eat out regularly find themselves returning to the same places, as much for convenience and comfort as for the quality of the food. If the latter is somewhat lacking where you are a regular customer, one option is to suggest improvements for the sake of all: whole grain breads, crackers, and cereals, steamed vegetables, unrefined sweeteners, pure juices, herb teas, and meatless entrées are all worthwhile goals. Some restaurants we have visited charge a small supplement for some of these costlier items.

Where this strategy fails, ask if you can leave a private stock of any whole-foods you'd like to have on hand. Literature is full of references to the "friendly tavern" where one's usual drink is poured without ordering or a special bottle is set aside. Why not seek that hospitality in favored eating spots?

MEALS EN ROUTE

Airlines today offer many alternatives to their standard menu, including low-salt, low-fat, meatless, (with and without eggs and cheese) and kosher meals. Unfortunately, a common defect in the vegetarian plate is the lack of protein, so for long trips a picnic is the best bet.

When the drink cart comes around, ask for tomato or orange juice. Although liquor and soda pop receive heavy in-flight promotion, juices are generally on hand (if only to be used as "mixers"). If you drink white tea or coffee, be sure to ask for a container of milk; ersatz cream is standard airline fare.

Bring-Alongs

It is more and more common for travelers to carry a few basic supplies with them, either to supplement a restaurant meal or to take the place of one. This approach can be employed just as easily by the daily voyager to school, the workplace, or even on a convivial outing

If you have a small box of raisins or a bag of mixed nuts, there is then no temptation to resort to the ubiquitous candy machines in a rage of hunger. Include a good mix of both nuts and seeds so that it is not only appetizing but also a more balanced source of protein. This mixture is also invaluable for boosting an otherwise dismal salad.

For trips longer than a day, put a supply of herb tea bags in your pocket or purse so that you can enjoy a hot beverage without caffeine.

When space is available, whole grain crackers should fill it. Since they do not spoil, they can be transported with ease and used to complete restaurant meals when it is impossible to find decent bread.

A good granola with added nonfat dry milk powder supplies an instant meal with the simple addition of water.

Peanut butter is a standard traveling staple; a few chopped dates included in the container can take the place of jelly. Spread on crackers or wedges of fresh pear or apple purchased en route, this combination is a satisfying breakfast or snack.

THE WHOLEFOODS RESTAURANT

One of the goals of our earlier book, *The Supermarket Handbook* was to encourage food stores to carry broader lines of wholefoods. To a certain degree we are witnessing this process as supermarkets expand their stock with "health foods," while health food stores include more high-quality wholefoods and even non-food items in order to become one-stop markets.

In a similar vein, we invite those whose profession it is to feed people to adopt *American Wholefoods Cuisine*. By this we mean:

• Use real whole grain breadstuffs, crackers, pasta, grains, and breakfast cereals (not caramel-colored "wheat bread").

• Include an ample selection of meatless (wholefoods) choices on the menu.

• Make unrefined sweeteners, such as maple syrup and honey, available.

• Steam, bake or stir-fry vegetables.

• Provide fresh fruit dishes and unsweetened juices.

• Minimize the use of salt by enhancing flavor with other seasonings.

• Offer only properly fried foods (even if it raises the price).

• Avoid nondairy creamers, toppings and margarine.

• In general, emphasize fresh foods.

Most important, restaurants must provide customers with a choice. In our own area, a Chinese restaurant has accommodated diners, and no doubt increased business, by offering the option of brown rice, "no MSG," and a separate meatless menu. All restaurants, no matter what their fare, can similarly diversify the menu.

Although some of the wholefoods concepts require more labor, the use of basic foodstuffs, particularly in the protein area, should more than compensate for this expense. The reasonable cost of pizza or of falafel (the Mideast "hot dog") illustrates this point. Many eating places also find they are able to afford high-quality ingredients and labor in the kitchen by cutting down on the dining room staff. Self-serve or cafeteria-style service is an ideal way to provide wholesome food at reasonable prices.

Restaurateurs are welcome to add any of our recipes to their menus (hopefully with credit). There are recipes in every section that could easily be adapted to restaurant requirements.

The restaurant trade has always had a legal responsibility to the public in terms of hygiene. But the industry also has another responsibility as well, to provide nourishing, high-quality meals. We hope those who make this their business will take up the challenge to experiment with new ways to feed people in accordance with the traditional wholefoods diet.

Index

A

Acidity required for canning, 431
Acorn squash, *see* squash
Additives, dangers of, 3
Adult party suggestions, 454
African Bean Soup, 103
Agar, 360
  Fruit Juice Gel, 360–61
Aioli with Vegetables, 41
Airplane meals, 522
Alcoholic beverages, 18
Algerian Chick-Peas with Cheese Croquettes, 181
All-Soy Muffins, 329
All-Vegetable Tempura, 172
Almond(s)
  Baked Brie with, 70
  Baked Camembert with, 70
  Baked Rice Balls, 201
  Cookies, Rich, 376
  Crunchy Peach Salad, 305
  Custard, Egg-White, 362
  Drops, 376
  Green Bean Chow Mein, 146
  Mandlebrot, 377
  Sponge Tarts, 383
  Sponge Torte, 383
  Tortoni, 59
  Viennese Plum Tart, 403
Ambassador Pot Pie with Biscuit Crust, 227
American
  Potato Omelet, 131
  Spinach-Feta Pie, 154
  -Style Potato Salad, 46
  Wholefoods
    Broccoli Hollandaise, 235
    Deli Platter, 31
  wine, 487
Anabella's Oatmeal Soup, 97
Animal protein, 2
  adding, 15
  value of, 15
  see also protein
Amino acids, 6, 8
Antipasto
  Heroes, 28

Peppers, 310
Salad, Tofu, 86
Appetizers and hors d'oeuvres, 63–88
  about, 63
  Asparagus in a Blanket, 80
  Avocado Cocktail, 76
  Baba Ghanouj, 68
  Baked
    Brie with Almonds, 70
    Camembert with Almonds, 70
    bean, 86
  Bite-Size Knish, 84
  Broccoli Tropicana, 78
  Carrot Tart, 75
  Cauliflower Rémoulade, 79
  Celery Rémoulade, 79
  cheese and egg, 70
  Corn-Crusted
    Cheese, 71
    Mushrooms, 71
  Dahi Vaddi, 88
  Dip(s), 63
    about, 63
    Blue Cheese, 64
    Curry, 64
    Green, 64
    Herb, 64
    Onion, 64
    Pimiento-Cheese, 47
  Eggplant
    Caponata, 77
    Caviar, 78
    Marinated, 77
  Filled Croustades with Salpicon, 80
  Fried
    Artichoke Hearts, 82
    Camembert, 70
  Greek
    Olives, 65
    Stuffed Cabbage or Grape Leaves, 82
  Green Banana Escabeche, 84
  guidelines for choosing, 16–17
  Hummus, 68
  Israeli Eggplant Spread, 68
  Marinated
    Artichoke Hearts, 65
    Cucumber Salad, 65
    Zucchini Sticks, 66

Appetizers (cont.)
  Mushroom(s)
    Baked, 77
    Cocktail, 76
    in Garlic Butter, 77
    Overstuffed, 76
    Pâté, 67
    Pickled, 66
  Nanette's Vegetable Pâté, 67
  Nikki's Special Kibbi, 87
  Oil-Cured Mozzarella, 70
  Onion Pie, 75
  Party Mousse, 87
  pâtés and spreads, 66
  Pea Pâté, 67
  Poached Spinach-Potato Pâté, 85
  Quiche
    about, 74
    Classic Cheese, 74
    Mushroom, 74
    Spinach, 74
    Vegetable, 74
  Raw Cranberry Relish, 66
  relish tray, 64
  Ricotta Torte, 75
  Rolled Omelet Slices, 73
  Schoolhouse Salad, 79
  Spaghetti Squash Rémoulade, 79
  Spicy
    Cheese Rolls and Cheese Truffles, 72
    Tomato Dressing and Cocktail Marinade, 76
  Spiedini, 71
  Spread(s)
    Celery Cheddar, 30
    Cheese-Nut, 69
    Curry Cashew, 69
    Mild Cheese and Tomato, 30
    Olive and Pimiento Cheese, 69
    Protein, 69
    Sharp Cheese and Tomato, 69
  Spring Lettuce Rolls, 83
  Sprouts Rémoulade, 79
  Steamed
    Artichokes with Dipping Sauce, 81
    Chinese Dumplings, 83
    Egg Rolls, 73
  Stuffed
    Artichokes, 82
    Clam Shells Areganata, 86
    Lemon Eggs, 72
    Squash Blossoms, 71
  Sweet
    and Sour Sprouts, 64
    Stuffed Peppers, Italian Style, 83
  Thousand Island Salad, 78
  Tofu
    Antipasto Salad, 86
    Cream Cheese and Vegetables, 69
  Vegetable(s)
    Derma, 80
    à la Grecque, 78
    White Bean Pâté, 66
    Zucchini Roulade, 73
  see also dips, menu planning, the New
    American menu
Apple(s)
  Babka, 386
  Baked, 355
  -Banana Betty, 356
  -Bean Bake, 260
  Buttered, 61
  -Corn Sticks, 330
  Cream, Frozen, 365
  Crumb Pie, 400
  Crumble, 356
  -Date Tarts, Quick, 406
  Favorite Fruit Salad, 60
  Fruit Curry, 257
  Macaroon-Top, 356
  Mince Filling, 443
  -Oat Muffins, 328
  Onion-Apple-Raisin Sauté, 246
    Curried, 246
  Oriental Soybeans, 259
  Pie, Dutch, 401
  Quick Curried Beans, 258
  Rocks, 378
  Soup, Cold Curry-, 110
  Steamed, 60
  Sweet Noodle Pudding, 278
  Toasted Seeds and Spinach Salad, 298
  -Topped Gingerbread, 385
  Waldorf Salad, 304
Applesauce
  Apple Turnovers, 406
  Cake, 386
    Egg-Free, 386
Apricot(s)
  Canned, 346
  Cake, Orange-, 382
  Dried Fruit Bars, 378
  -Raisin Tart, 403
  Upside-Down Cake, 388
  Vegetables with Apricot Sauce, 146
Arabic
  dinner, 464
  Yogurt Cake, 391
Aromatic Rice with Green Beans, 266
Armenian
  Bean Pies, 280
  Couscous, 192

Arroz con Queso, 189
Artichoke(s)
  Avgolemono, 231
  and Dill, Greek, 231
  globe, preparation, 497
  Hearts
    French Pasta Salad, 278
    Fried, 82
    Marinated, 65
  Jerusalem
    Baked, 231
    preparation, 497
    Smothered, 232
  "noodles," 111
  Paella, 190
  Pasta, Chick-Peas and, with Lemon
      Dressing, 278
  Steamed, with Dipping Sauce, 81
  Stewed, Italian Style, 230
  Stuffed, 82
Asian fare, 466–68
Asopa, Instant, 91
Asparagus
  Baked, 232
  in a Blanket, 80
  with Cashews, 232
  Pan Fried, 51
  preparation, 497
Atlantic Avenue Green Beans, 233
Avocado(s)
  -Bean Salad, 261
  -Cheese Melt, 34
  Cocktail, 76
  Creamy Dinner Fruit Salad, 305
  Dressing, 289
  freezing, 427
  Guacamole, 46
  Mayonnaise, 288
  preparation, 497
  Salad
    Mexican Stuffed, 32
    Stuffed, 32
    Hot, 32
  Tropical Fruit Platter, 305

B

B.O.B (Beans on Board), 43
Baba Ghanouj, 68
Babka, Apple, 386
Bacteria
  effective way to destroy, 482
  growth of, 482
  used in yogurt production, 421
Baguettes, French, 340

Baked
  Apple, 355
  Asparagus, 232
  Bananas and Cheese, 357
  Beans
    about, 259
    Apple-Bean Bake, 260
    Boston Style, 260
    Mexican Lima, 261
  Brie with Almonds, 70
  Broccoli and Cheese Casserole, 152
  Camembert with Almonds, 70
  Cauliflower, 238
  Cheese-Nut Cutlets, 125
  Chocolate/Carob Custard, 362
  Eggs Florentine, 136
  Fruits Alaska, 359
  goods
    about, 366–70
    cake, 381–94
    cookies, 370–81
    flatbreads, 320–22
    pies and individual pastries, 394–410
    quick breads, 325–32
    storage of, 479
    yeast breads, 333–47
  Herbed Eggplant, 241
  Jerusalem Artichokes, 231
  Macaroni and Cheese
    with Egg, 112
    One-Pot, 39
  Meringue Topping, 363
  Mushrooms, 77
  Parsley Tomatoes, 254
  Polenta, 194
  Potato Toppings, 54
  Rice
    Balls, 201
    and Blue Cheese, 189
    Crust, 228
    Pudding, 363
  Spinach
    and Feta, 153
    and Ricotta, 153
  Summer Vegetables with Cheese, 152
  Sweet Potatoes and Yams, 54
  Vanilla Custard, 362
  Vegetable
    Cheese, 127
    entrées, 149–55
    about, 149
    Omelet, 136
    Tofu, 128
  Ziti, 113
Baker, the making of a, 366–67
Baker's math, 511–12

Baking
flour, 367
leavening, 368
liquid ingredients, 368
nuts and seeds in, 368
oven temperatures, 369–70
preparation of pan, 369
shortening, 368
sugar substitutes, 367
techniques, 368–69
Bami-Goreng–Indonesian Fried
    Noodles, 120
Banana(s)
Betty
  Apple-, 356
  Peach-, 356
Bars, 374
Bread, 331
Cake, 387
and Cheese, Baked, 357
Cream, 366
  Pie, Frozen Whipped, 406
Drop Cakes, 374
Escabeche, Green, 84
Favorite Fruit Salad, 60
freezing, 427
Fried Plantains, 248
Fruit Curry, 257
Monkeys in a Blanket, 61
Plantain Cake, 247
Pops, Frozen, 352
Soft-Serve, 59
Bananes aux Pecanes, 357
Barbecue
Sauce
  beans in, 43
  Pineapple, 175
  Quick, 59
suggestions, 455
Barbecued
Corn, 239
Eggplant and Lentils, 179
Tofu and Vegetables, 170
Barley
Bake, Cheese-Vegetable-, 154
Salad, Creamy, 269
  Mushroom and, 264
  Steamed, 263
Soup
  Deluxe Mushroom-, 97
  Vegetable, 92
Steamed, 263
see also grains
Basic
bean cookery, 500
Biscuits, 326

Cookie Dough, 372
cooking techniques, 487–507
grain cookery, 503
Mashed Potatoes, 248
Oil and Vinegar Dressing, 287
Pickles, 439
Rice Salad, 269
Roll Dough, 345
Steamed Spaghetti Squash, 253
Whole Wheat Pasta, 275
Basil
Pasta with Pesto and Slivered Cheese,
    114
Pesto, 318
  Tomato, 319
Basque Country Stew, 180
Batter
Japanese Tempura, 171
No-Egg, 172
Bean(s)
accompaniments, 257–62
  about, 257
Aioli with Vegetables, 41
appetizers, 86
Armenian Couscous, 192
Bake, Apple-, 260
Baked
  about, 259
  Boston-Style, 260
B.O.B., 43
Balls
  Mexican, 198
  Swedish, 199
basic cookery, 500
Basque Country Stew, 180
vs. beef, nutritional breakdown, 10
Birds, 203
Blini, 210
Boston Roast, 44
from Brittany, 180
Burgers, 196
Burger Mix, 445
canned as substitute, 501
-Carrot Stew, 141
Chalupas, 36
-Cheese
  Salad, 261
  Sauce, 37
Chili, 43
Chopped Beat, 502
Chowder, New England, 100
Cold
  Corn, Rice and, 269
  Tahini, 268
and Corn Salad, Mexican, 304

Bean(s) (*cont.*)
Cornish Pasties, 224
Creole Noodles, 116
Egg and Cheese
  Greek, 132
  Italian, 132
  Mexican, 132
Eggplant Rollatini, 162
Empanadas, 282
Fejoida, 184
freezer method of cookery, 501
French-Style Couscous, 192
Fried Mexican Dumplings, 286
and Grain, Peanut-Buttered, 271
and Greens, Italian, 258
ground, 502
Kedgeree, 186
Loaf
  Cottage Cheese and, 204
    Cold, 204
  Hawaiian, 204
Liver, Chopped, 29
mainly, 176–87
  about, 176
in menu planning, 12
Moussaka, 185
Muffin-Topped Deep-Dish Vegetable
    Pie, 226
for minimal pantry, 474
Orange-Wheat Salad, 270
Paella, 190
for pantry, 472
Party Mousse, 87
Pasta
  e Fagioli, 179
  Fagioli Soup, 102
Pastry Turnovers, 282
Pâté
  Sesame-, 29
  Tomato-, 29
  White, 66
Patty Shells, 229
Peppers Stuffed with Corn and, 157
Pies, Armenian, 280
Pistou, 259
Pita
  Indian, 221
  Mexican, 221
  Mideast, 222
Pizzas
  Individual, 34
  Mexican-Style, 177
  -Topped, 176
Porotos Granados, 183
pot and grain store, 484
Pot Pie, 227

pre-soaking
  quick, 500
  regular, 500
pressure cooking, 501
Puerto Rican Rice and, 182
Quick Curried, 258
Refried, 54
Salad
  Avocado-, 261
  Cabbage-Carrot-, 303
  Greek, 262
  Olive-, 29
  Pita, 222
  Three-, 65
  Turkish Country, 301
Sausages, 198
  Onion and Pepper, 198
Sauce, Lasagne with, 123
Sealed Sandwiches, 223
Sloppy, 44
Sopones, 182
Soup
  African, 103
  Black, 102
  Mexican, 103
    Macaroni and, 102
  Pureed, 104
  Quick Creamy, 92
  Senate, 100
with Stewed Onions, 257
storage of, 480
-Studded Pancakes, 210
-Stuffed Pita Pockets, 221
Sweet and Sour Stuffed
  Cabbage, 164
  Lettuce, 165
table of food weights and measures,
    517
Tacos, 36
  Fried, 217
  with Special Bean Filling, 218
Tamale
  Peppers, 157
  Pie, 227
test for tenderness, 501
timetable for cooking, 501
Two-Tone Mexican, 259
Tzimmis, German, 181
uses, 12–13
value of, 13
Vegetables with Curry Cream, 41
yield, 501
see also specific beans
Bean Curd, Spicy, 169
  see also tofu

Bean Sprout(s)
  Salad, Spinach-, 298
  Spiced, 277
  see also sprouts
Bear Claws, 409
Beating, 368
Béchamel, 313
Beer Nuts, 350
Beet(s)
  Borscht
    Cold Creamy, 110
    with Cucumber, 109
    Hot, 93
  Crisp Fried, 234
  Dutch Salad, 304
  Fresh Orange, 234
  Pickled, 310
  preparation, 497
  Russian, 234
  Salad
    with Blue Cheese, 292
    Cold, 292
  Sliced Baked, 234
  Steamed, 234
Berries, freezing, 427
Beverages, 417–19
  about, 417
  alcoholic, 18
  Carob Drink, 418
  Cranberry Juice Cocktail, 418
  Fresh Fruit
    Drink, 418
    Fizz, 418
  Fruit Punch, 417
  Herb Tea and Cereal "Coffee," 419
  Jane's Schlurpy, 418
  Lemon-Limeade, 417
  Lemonade, 417
  for minimal pantry, 478
  Orange Julia, 418
  for pantry, 472
  Party Punch, 418
  Seltzer Fizz, 417
  Sparkling Water, 417
  Thick Shake, 419
  Vegetable Cocktail, 417
  uses, 17–18
  Virgin Sangria, 418
Bialy "Butter," 307
Biscuits, 326–27
  about, 326
  Basic, 326
  Cottage Cheese, 326
  -Crust Pizza, 220
  Greek Feta, 281

Pot of Gold, 327
Quick
  Corn, 449
  Light, 446
  Protein, 448
Soy, 326
Tomato-Cheese, 326
Yogurt, 326
Bite-Size Knish, 84
Black Bean
  Soup, 102
  Fejoida-, 184
Black-Eyed Peas
  Hoppin' John, 178
Blanching, 429
  steam, 429
Blender Salad Soup, 56
Blini, Bean, 210
Blintzes, 214
  assembly and cooking, 215
  Crepes, 214
  fillings
    cheese, 215
    kasha, 215
    potato, 215
Blue Cheese
  Baked Rice and, 189
  Beet Salad with, 292
  Dip, 64
  Dressing, Creamy, 290
    Thick, 57
  Potatoes, Stuffed, 163
Blueberry
  Buckle, Fresh, 356
  Sauce, 412
Borscht
  Cold Creamy, 110
  with Cucumber, 109
  Hot, 93
Boston
  Brown Bread, 332
  Roast, 44
  -Style Baked Beans, 260
Bottom-of-the-Bowl Dressing, 57
Braided Rolls, 338
Braised Red Cabbage, 237
Bran Muffins, 328
Brazilian dinner, 458
Bread-and-Butter Pickles, 439
Bread(s)
  about, 320
  baking, 320–47
  Banana, 331
  Boston Brown, 332
  Brioche, 342
  Broccoli, Bread and Cheese Soup, 95

Bread(s) (*cont.*)
Burger Buns, 346
Buttermilk, 339
Challah, 341
Chapatis, 323
Rye, 324
Spiced, 324
Cheese, 341
Wedges, 341
Cracked Wheat, 338
Cranberry, 332
crumbs, 505
cracker, 505
dried, 505
soft, 505
cube test for fat, 492
Dhal Pouree Roti, 324
Dumplings, 272
French Baguettes, 340
Garlic-Sesame, 49
and Garlic Soup, Portuguese, 55
and grains, for minimal pantry, 474
Herbed Oat, 339
Italian, 340
Meat, 206
Spicy, 206
Native American Seed Cakes, 324
No-Kneading, Fast-Rising Dough, 314
Onion-Cheese Pan, 338
Parmesan Toast, 49
Parsley-Sesame, 49
Pita, 337
Pudding, 363
Date-Nut, 62
Pumpkin, 331
Loaf, 344
Seed, 331
quick bread loaves, 331–33
about, 331
for Sealed Sandwiches, 223
Soft Pretzels, 347
and Spread, 50
Squash Loaf, 344
Sticks, 345
Quick, 446
Rye, 347
Standard Whole Wheat, 337
-Stuffed Peppers, 157
Stuffing, 262
Turnovers with Cheese, 279
whole grain
for pantry, 472
for freezer, 474
Whole Wheat, Standard, 337
yeast, 333–47
about, 333–36

without an oven, 323–25
about, 323
see also biscuits, cornbread, crackers, flatbreads, muffins, rolls, quick breads
Brewer's yeast, *see* nutritional yeast
Brie, Baked with Almonds, 70
Brined Spaghetti Squash, 435
Brioche, 342
Broccoli
Bread and Cheese Soup, 95
Cheese Casserole, Baked, 152
Cold Pasta and, 118
Custard Pie, 225
Hollandaise, American Wholefoods, 235
and Macaroni Soup, 95
Mozzarella, White, 234
Pasta with, 115, 277
preparation, 497
with Peanuts in Sweet and Sour Sauce, 147
Salad, Steamed, 235
Stalk Salad, 235
Steamed, 50
Stir-Fried with Garlic, 233
Tostados, 37
Tropicana, 78
Tuchman's Wheat Berry Bake, 191
Vegetables with Soufflé Sauce, 150
Broiled Orange, 61
Broiler Potato Crisps, 52
Broth
Tamari, 55
Tomato, 430
see also soup
Brown
Cashew Gravy, 314
Gravy, 313
rice; *see* grains, rice
Browned Onion Relish, 57
Brownies, Nikki's New, 379
Brussels Sprouts
Butter-Steamed, 236
preparation, 497
Steamed, 236
Buckwheat groats, *see* kasha
Bulgur
Armenian Couscous, 192
Dumplings, 273
see also cracked wheat
Buns, *see* rolls
Burger(s)
Bean, 196
Buns, 346

Burger(s) (*cont.*)
  Cashew, 197
  Grain, 196
  Mix, 445
    Burgers, 445
    Fritters, 446
  Rice Cheese, 197
  Rye, 36
  Soy, 196
    Onion, 196
  Tempeh, 174
Butter(s)
  Bialy, 307
  Creamy
    Herb, 306
    Lemon, 81
  Fruit, 441
  Nut, 14
    Grains, 49
    Savory, 306
  Seed, 14
  -Steamed Brussels Sprouts, 236
  Sun, 306
Buttercream
  Filling, 383
  Frosting, 414
  Glaze, 414
Buttered
  Apples, 61
  Pears, 61
Butterflies, 346
Buttermilk
  Bread, 339
  Clotted Cream, 411
  Sherbet, 365
Butterscotch Pudding, 361

C

C & C, 27
CLT, 27
Cabbage
  Basque Country Stew, 180
  Beans from Brittany, 180
  Braised Red, 237
  -Carrot-Bean Salad, 303
  Cheese
    Rice with, and, 189
    -Stuffed, 165
  Chinese, *see* Chinese cabbage
  Colcannon, 145
  Cold Cottage Cheese and Bean Loaf,
    204
  Coleslaw
    Cooked, 237

  Country, 292
  Greek, 292
  Pie, 292
  Tangy, 46
  Company, 236
  or Grape Leaves, Greek Stuffed, 82
  Hot Borscht, 93
  Hungarian Vegetable Gulyas, 145
  Noodles
    Hungarian, 119
    in Tomato Broth, 237
  Pan-Fried, 51
  and Potatoes, Indian Style, Fried, 237
  preparation, 497
  Quick Sauerkraut, 236
  Raita, 293
  Salad, Puerto Rican, 292
  and Rice Soup, Italian, 97
  Spiced, 236
  Stroganoff, Stuffed, 165
  stuffing, 164
  Sweet and Sour Stuffed, 164
Caesar Salad, 296
Cake(s), 381–94
  about, 381–82
  Almond Sponge
    Tarts, 383
    Torte, 383
  Apple Babka, 386
  Applesauce, 386
    Egg-Free, 386
  baking guidelines, 381–82
  Banana, 387
    Drop, 374
  Carob and Chocolate Cupcakes, 391
  Carrot, 386
    Cupcakes, 392
  Cheesecake
    Creamy, 393
    Italian, 393
    Pudding, 394
  Coffee
    Fresh Fruit, 389
    Streusel, 390
  cooling, 382
  Country-Fresh Pear, 387
  "Devil Dogs," 384
  Devil's Food, 384
  Double Donuts, 392
  French Nut, 385
  Fresh Peach, 389
  Fruit
    Kuchen Oma, 389
    Shortcake, 388
  Fruitcake, 390
  Gingerbread, 385

Cake(s) (cont.)
  Apple-Topped, 385
  Greek Lenten, 391
  Harvest Corn, 330
  Lemon-Orange Refrigerator Layer, 392
  Marble, 385
  Native American Seed, 324
  Orange-Apricot, 382
  Plantain, 248
  preparation and handling, 381
  Sauce, Rich, 413
  "Twinkies"
    Giant, 383
    Individual, 384
  Upside-Down
    Apricot, 388
    Peach, 388
    Pineapple, 388
  Yogurt
    Arabic, 391
    Pound, 383
    Spice, 382
    Yellow, 382
  Zucchini Loaf, 386
Calzone, 221
  Quick, 33
Camellia Grill Omelet, 39
Camembert
  with Almonds, Baked, 70
  Fried, 70
Campfire Ratatouille, 242
Candied Sweet Potatoes, 252
Canned
  and bottled food, storage of, 481
  Fruit, 436
    Pie or Tarts, 402
  table of food weights and measures, 516
  Peaches
    in Juice, 436
    in Syrup, 436
  Pears and Apricots, 436
  Prune-Plums in Syrup, 436
  Tomatoes, 434
Canner
  steam, 432
  water-bath, 432
Canning, 431–37
  about, 431–34
  equipment for, 432
  preparing, 432
  filling the jars, 433
  heat processing, 433
  jars and lids, 432
  methods of, 431

  selection of food, 431
  signs of spoilage, 443
  storage, 434
  testing the seal, 433–34
Cantaloupe
  Baked Fruits Alaska, 359
  Fruit
    Platter, Tropical, 305
    Salad, Creamy, 305
Caper Sauce, 72
Caponata, Eggplant, 77
Caramel Pears, 359
Caraway
  Cracker Crumb Crust, 46
  Thins, 321
Carbohydrates, 9–10
Carob
  Chip Cookies, 372
    Pecan, 372
  Custard, Baked Chocolate/, 362
  and Chocolate Cupcakes, 391
  "Devil Dogs," 384
  Devil's Food Cake, 384
  Drink, 418
  Frosting, 414
    and Filling, Thick Fudge, 416
  Fudge Sauce, 413
  Pudding, 361
  Syrup, 413
Carrot(s)
  Baked Vegetable Omelet, 136
  -Bean Salad, Cabbage-, 303
  Cake, 386
  and Celery, French, 238
  and Chick-Pea Puree, Mideast, 105
  Company Cabbage, 236
  Cookies, 378
  Cupcakes, 392
  Dressing, Creamy, 291
  Fresh Ginger, 238
  Gravy, 141
  Hungarian Vegetable Gulyas, 145
  Lemon Squash and, 253
  Lima Bean Tzimmis, 180
  Orange-Glazed, 51
  -Peanut Salad, 293
  Peas and Cheese, 303
  Potage Bonne Femme, 92
  preparation, 498
  with Raisins, Sweet Ginger, 238
  Raita, 293
    Sweet, 293
  Soup, 141
    Golden, 100
  Stew, 141
  with Sunflower Seeds, 238

Carrot(s) (*cont.*)
Tart, 75
with Walnuts, 238
and Zucchini Crepes, Creamed, 214
see also parsnips
Cashew(s)
Asparagus with, 232
Burgers, 197
Gravy, 314
Brown, 314
Tomato, 314
Mayonnaise, 289
Spread, Curry, 69
Super-Quick Creamed Green Beans
with, 444
Cassoni, 285
Catsup, 435
Touch-of-Honey, 308
Caucasus Salad, 298
Cauliflower
Baked, 238
-Cheese Chowder, 94
Dinner Salad, 295
freezing, 429
with Peanuts in Sweet and Sour Sauce,
147
preparation, 498
Puff, 150
Rémoulade, 79
Smothered, 232
Steamed Broccoli Salad, 235
Vegetables with Soufflé Sauce, 150
with Yogurt, 239
Caviar, Eggplant, 78
Ceci, Italian Cheese Melt with, 129
Celery
Cheddar Spread, 30
freezing, 427
French Carrots and, 238
preparation, 498
Rémoulade, 79
Soup with Creamy Cheese, 106
Cellophane noodles, 465
Cereal(s)
"Coffee," 419
for pantry, 472
Challah, 341
Chapatis, 323
Rye, 324
Spiced, 324
Stuffed, 284
Cheddar
Pastry, 229
Sauce, Kidney Beans in, 176
Soup, 98
Leek and, 99

Spread, Celery, 30
-Stuffed Sweet Potatoes, 251
see also cheese
Cheese
Ambassador Pot Pie with Biscuit
Crust, 227
appetizers, 70
Arroz con Queso, 189
Bake, Lima Bean, 185
Baked
Bananas and, 357
Eggs Florentine, 136
Ziti, 113
Bean Pot Pie, 227
Beans, Eggs and,
Greek, 132
Italian, 132
Mexican, 132
Biscuits, Tomato-, 326
Blintzes, 214
Boston Roast, 44
Bread, 341
Turnovers with, 279
Wedges, 341
Broccoli Custard Pie, 225
Burgers
Eggplant, 141
Rice, 197
C & C, 27
CLT, 27
Cake
Creamy, 393
Italian, 393
Pudding, 394
Carrots, Peas, and, 303
Casserole, Baked Broccoli and, 152
Cauliflower Puff, 150
Celery Soup with Creamy, 106
Cheeson, 27
Chili Rellenos, 158
for a Crowd, 158
Chowder, Cauliflower-, 94
Colombian Potatoes, 144
Corn
Crusted, 71
Pudding, 137
Cottage, *see* cottage cheese
Creamy Stuffed Baked Potatoes, 163
Crisps, 321
Croque Madame, 124
Croquettes, 128
for Algerian Chick-Peas, 181
Italian Rice, 201
Croutons, 90
Crust, 400
Curry, Vegetable-, 148

Cheese (*cont.*)
  Cutlets, -Nut, Baked, 125
  and dairy products, for minimal pantry, 475
  Danish, 409
  Dip, Pimiento-, 47
  Dressing, Soft, 287
  Dumplings, Fried Italian, 286
  Eggplant
    au Gratin, 241
    Parmesan, 151
    Ratatouille Pie, 150
    Rollatini, 162
  Enchiladas, 217
  entrées, 124–30
    about, 124
  Fettuccine with Spring Vegetables, 117
  Fresh Fruit Tart with Cheese Filling, 402
  and Greens, 296
  Homemade Farmer, 149
  Italian Stuffed Spaghetti Squash, 159
  Lasagne
    with Bean Sauce, 123
    Eggplant, 151
    Matzo, 45
    White, 124
  Layered Tomato Casserole, 45
  Linguine Country-Style, 115
  Macaroni and
    with Egg, Baked, 112
    Italian, 112
    One-Pot Baked, 39
    Salad, 48
    Stove-Top, 112
  Manicotti, 213
    Eggplant, 162
    Omelet, 39
  Melt
    Avocado-, 34
    with Ceci, Italian, 129
    with Corn, Mexican, 128
  Muffins, 328
  Mushroom
    Custard, 128
    Soufflé, 139
    -Spinach Crepes, 213
  Nachos, 279
  Noodle Pudding
    Fruit, 122
    Savory, 122
  -Nut Roast, 126
  Omelet
    Baked Vegetable, 136
    French, 132
  Pan Bread, Onion-, 338

Pancakes
  Corn-, 209
    Quick, 449
  Crisp, 38
Pasta
  Creamy, with, 40
  with Pesto and Slivered, 114
Pastry, Creamy, 400
Pie, 447
Pizza, 219
  Biscuit-Crust, 220
  Fresh Tomato Pita, 33
  Individual Bean, 34
  Mexican, 36
    -Style Bean, 177
  Salad, 47
  -Topped Beans, 176
Plantain Cake, 248
Polenta with Three, 194
Potato(es)
  Niçoise, 143
  Pizzaiola, 142
  Pudding, 155
Pudding, Cornmeal-, 193
Puffs, 284
  Savory Farmer, 284
Quiche
  Classic, 74
  Mexican, 128
Raclette, 129
Rarebit, 37
Ravioli, Red or White, 121
Refried Beans with, 54
Rice
  with Cabbage and, 189
  -Nut Loaf, 205
  Pancakes, 38
  with Stuffed Chilies, Green, 188
Rolls and Truffles, Spicy, 72
Rumanian Mammaliga, 194
Salad
  Bean-, 261
  with Walnut Dressing, 296
Sandwich
  French-Toasted, 34
  Souffléed, 34
Sauce, 313
  Bean-, 37
  Double, 58
  No-Cook Cold, 319
  for Peruvian Mountain Potatoes, 145
  Quick, 444
    Tomato-, 444
Skillet
  Corn, Chilies, and, 43
  Stew, 42

Cheese (*cont.*)
Soufflé, 138
Soup, Broccoli, Bread and, 95
Spiedini, 71
Spinach Noodle Casserole, 121
Spread(s), 69
  Celery Cheddar, 37
  -Nut, 69
  Olive and Pimiento, 69
  and Tomato
    Mild, 30
    Sharp, 69
Steak, 125
Sticks, Quick, 450
-Stuffed
  Cabbage, 165
  Mushrooms, 52
  Zucchini with Cheese and Raisins, 160
Stuffing Balls, Italian, 127
Super Spanish Wheat, 270
Surprise Mashed Potatoes, 248
Tamale
  Peppers, 157
  Pie, 227
Tempeh Parmesan, 174
Tofu with Onions and, 167
Tortilla Pyramid, 37
Turnovers
  Bean Pastry, 282
  Hot Potato, 283
Vegetable(s)
  Baked, 127
    Summer with, 152
  -Barley Bake, 154
  Casserole, Italian, 154
  Julienne, and, 303
  Mexican, 147
  with Soufflé Sauce, 150
  Steamed, with, 41
  Tempura, 172
  with Yogurt and, Skillet, 140
Veggie Reuben, 35
Ziti with, 40
  see also specific cheese
Cheeson, 27
Chef's Special Salad or Salad Bar, 31
Cherry Pie, Sour, 402
Chestnuts, Roasted, 350
Chèvre, Tomatoes with, 254
"Chicken"
  Salad, Tofu, 30
  -Style Gravy, 314
Chick-Pea(s)
  with Cheese Croquettes, Algerian, 181

Falafel
  I, 199
  II, 200
  with Feta, Spinach and, 153
  with Gravy, 258
  Greek Stuffed Tomato, 255
  Gumbo, 177
  on the Half Shell, 161
  Italian Cheese Melt with Ceci, 129
  Nanette's Vegetable Pâté, 67
  Nikki's Special Kibbi, 87
  Pan Bagnia, 222
  Pasta with Artichokes, and, with Lemon Dressing, 278
  Puree, Mideast Carrot and, 105
  Roasted, 349
  Salad, 29
    Mideast, 261
  Spanish-Style, 177
  Stewed Artichokes, Italian Style, 230
  Tunisian Sandwiches, 222
  Very Quick Curried, 54
Children('s)
  adequate diets for, 9
  party suggestions, 454
Chili, 43
  Nuts, 350
  Rellenos, 158
    for a Crowd, 158
  Sauce, 309
Chilies
  Arroz con Queso, 189
  and Cheese, Skillet Corn, 43
  Green Rice with Stuffed, 188
Chili
  Rellenos, 158
    for a Crowd, 158
Chinese
  cabbage, preparation, 498
  dinner
    I, 466
    II, 466
    III, 466
  Dipping Sauce, Sweet, 307
  Fried Noodles—Lo Mein, 119
  Greens in Broth, 91
  Hot and Sour Soup, 107
  Mustard, 307
  Radish Salad, 297
  -Style Fried Rice, 120
Chocolate
  /Carob Custard, Baked, 262
  Cupcakes, Carob and, 391
  "Devil Dogs," 384
  Devil's Food Cake, 384
  Frosting, 414

Chocolate (*cont.*)
and Filling,
Cream, 415
Thick Fudge, 416
Nikki's New Brownies, 379
Nut Squares, 380
Pecan Chip Cookies, 372
Pudding
Honey-, 361
Pie, 361
Syrup, 413
Toll-Free Cookies, 372
Chop Suey, Vegetable, 119
Chopped
Bean Liver, 29
Beat, 502
Eggplant Steak, 195
Chow Mein, Green Bean, 146
Chowder
Cauliflower-Cheese, 94
New England Bean, 100
Okra, 94
see also soup
Chunky
Cottage Cheese Dressing, 288
Pasta Sauce, 58
Chutney
Fresh Plum, 442
Pineapple, 442
Raisin
Cooked, 309
Raw, 309
Cinnamon
Buns, 407
Rolls, 345
Citric acid, 431
Clam Shells Areganata, Stuffed, 86
Classic Cheese Quiche, 74
Clotted Cream, 411
Cloverleaf Rolls, 340, 345
Cobbler, Summer Fruit, 360
Cocktail
Avocado, 76
Cranberry Juice, 418
Marinade, Spicy Tomato Dressing and, 76
Mushroom, 76
Sauce, Quick, 308
Vegetable, 417
Coconut
Cookies, 372
Custard Pie, 404
freezing, 427
Kisses, 352
Sambal, 310
Tropical Fruit Platter, 305

Coffee
Cake
Fresh Fruit, 389
Streusel, 390
Cereal, 419
Colcannon, 145
Cold
Beet Salad, 292
Corn, Rice, and Beans, 269
Cottage Cheese and Bean Loaf, 204
Creamy Borscht, 110
Curry-Apple Soup, 110
Dilled Pea Soup, 101
Eggplant and Yogurt, 243
Ginger Eggplant, 243
Pasta
and Broccoli, 118
with Tomato Dressing, 48
sandwiches and salad platters, 27–33
soups, 108–10
Stuffed Tomato, 47
Tahini Beans, 48
Coleslaw
Cooked, 237
Country, 292
Greek, 292
Pie, 292
Tangy, 46
Veggie Reuben, 35
Colombian Potatoes, 144
Company Cabbage, 236
Complement, Protein, 6, 8, 23, 111
Compote, Dried Fruit, 60
Condiments, 306–11
about, 306
Antipasto Peppers, 310
Bialy Butter, 307
Browned Onion Relish, 57
Chili Sauce, 308
Chinese Mustard, 307
Coconut Sambal, 310
Cranberry
Jelly, 418
Relish
Crunchy, 309
Raw, 66
Sauce, 309
Creamy Herb Butter, 306
Dipping Sauce
Oriental, 307
Sweet Chinese, 307
"Duck" Sauce, 307
Fiery Sauce, 30
Gomasio, 306
Greek Olives, 65
Italian Vegetable Marinade, 311

Condiments (*cont.*)
  Marinated Artichoke Hearts, 65
  for minimal pantry, 475
  Namasu, 311
  pantry, 473
  Pickled
    Beets, 310
    Mushrooms, 66
  Quick
    Cocktail Sauce, 307
    Mexican Hot Sauce, 58
    Pickles, 310
    Turnip, 311
  Raisin Chutney
    Cooked, 309
    Raw, 309
  Raw Creole Sauce, 309
  Salsa Cruda, 308
  Savory Nut Butter, 306
  Spicy
    Salsa, 308
    Tunisian Sauce, 30
  Tartar Sauce, 308
  Touch-of-Honey Catsup, 308
  see also chutney, relish
Confetti Pasta, 118
Conserve, Summer, 442
Consum, 285
Convenience
  mixes, 443–50
  soups, 90–92
Cooked
  Coleslaw, 237
  Raisin Chutney, 309
Cookies, 370–81
  about, 370–71
  Almond
    Drops, 376
    Rich, 376
  Apple Rocks, 378
  baking, 371
  Banana
    Bars, 374
    Drop Cakes, 374
  batters, 370–71
  Carob Chip, 372
  Carrot, 378
  Chocolate Nut Squares, 380
  Coconut, 372
  Cottage Cheese, 373
  Date Bars, 379
  Dough
    Basic, 372
    Crust, 398
    storing and freezing, 371, 479
    Tart Shells, 399

Dried Fruit Bars, 378
Ginger, 375
Great Big Honey-Molasses, 375
Hamentaschen, 380
Honey Grahams, 372
Lemon-Nut, 372
Light Spice, 372
Mandlebrot, 377
Mr. Bill, 375
Nikki's New Brownies, 379
Orange, 372
Peanut, 372
Butter
  -Oat, 377
  Traditional, 377
Pecan Chip, 372
Rugelach, 380
  Fruit-Nut, 380
  Poppy Seed, 380
Shortbread, 373
  Scotch Oat, 373
  Squares, Walnut Date-Topped, 374
Soft Oatmeal, 378
Spritz, 376
Sunflower-Date, 372
Toll-Free, 372
Vanilla, 372
Walnut
  Jumbo, 375
  Rich, 376
Corn
  Barbecued, 239
  and Beans, Peppers Stuffed with, 157
  Biscuits, Quick, 449
  Bread, 330
    about, 330
    House, 330
    Savory Onion, 330
  Cake, Harvest, 330
  -Cheese Pancakes, 209
    Quick, 449
  Chilies, and Cheese, Skillet, 43
  Chips, 321
  on the Cob, 50
  Confetti Pasta, 118
  Crisps
    and Pones, 322
    Quick, 449
  -Crusted
    Cheese, 71
      Sticks, Quick, 450
    Mushrooms, 71
      Quick, 450
    Tofu Sticks, Quick, 450
    Tomatoes, Quick, 450

Corn (*cont.*)
Curried, 239
Dodgers, 273
Flats, 449
freezing, 427
Fritters, Quick, 450
Gnocchi, Italian, 273
Italian Spaghetti Stew, 113
Mexican
  Beans and Pasta Bake, 185
  Cheese Melt with, 128
Mix, 448
Muffins, 328
  Double, 330
  Golden Temple, 329
  Quick, 449
  Rice-, 329
  Sweet, 329
O'Brien, Creamed, 239
Oysters, 240
Pierogi, 273
Popped, 348
preparation, 498
Pudding
  Cheese-, 137
  Fresh, 137
Rice, and Beans, Cold, 269
Salad, Mexican Bean and, 304
Soup
  Creamed, 56
  Mexican, 98
Succotash, 240
Sticks, Apple-, 330
Tamale Peppers, 157
Cornish Pasties, 224
Cornmeal
-Cheese Pudding, 193
Crust, 228
Filled English Pancakes, 209
Indian Pudding, 364
Polenta, 194
  Baked, 194
  Italian-Style, 194
  with Three Cheeses, 194
Rumanian Mammaliga, 194
Tamale Pie, 227
Tortillas, 323
see also corn
Cottage Cheese
Baked Summer Vegetables with Cheese,
  152
and Bean Loaf, 240
Cold, 204
Biscuits, 326
C & C, 27

Cheese
-Nut Spread, 69
-Stuffed Mushrooms, 52
Coffee Cake
  Fresh Fruit, 389
  Streusel, 390
Cookies, 373
Cottage Pie, 155
Creamy Herb Dressing, 290
Cucumber(s)
  with Creamy, 294
  Mousse, 294
Curry Cashew Spread, 69
Cutlets, 38
Dip
  Blue Cheese, 64
  Curry, 64
  Green, 64
  Herb, 64
Dressing, Chunky, 288
Fluffy Stuffed Baked Potatoes, 163
German-Style New Potatoes, 144
Hi-Protein Crepes, 213
Hungarian Cabbage Noodles, 119
Marinated Green Beans with, 291
Matzo Lasagne, 45
Mushroom Paprikash, 142
Noodle Pudding
  Fruit, 122
  Savory, 122
Polish Pierogi, 207
Protein Spread, 69
Pudding Cheesecake, 394
Quick Creamy Onion Pie, 45
Sloppy Beans, 43
Spaghetti with Eggplant Sauce, 116
Spinach-Noodle Casserole, 121
Stuffed
  Avocado Salad, 32
  Hot, 32
  Tomato Salad, 32
Vegetable, 47
Whipped Cottage Cream, 56
Zucchini Roulade, 37
Country
Coleslaw, 292
Fresh Pear Cake, 387
Couscous, 191–93
about, 191–92
Armenian, 192
French-Style, 192
Moroccan, 193
dinner, 464
Cracked Wheat
Bread, 338

Cracked Wheat (*cont.*)
  Crackers, 320
  Greek Stuffed Tomato, 255
  Orange-Wheat Salad, 270
  Pilaf, 48
  Spanish
    -Style Chick-Peas, 177
    Wheat, 270
  Tabouli, 302
  Vegetable Crumb Sauté, 256
  see also bulgur
Cracker(s)
  Bread, Quick Protein, 448
  Caraway Thins, 321
  Cheese Crisps, 321
  Corn
    Chips, 321
    Crisps
      and Corn Pones, 321
      Quick, 449
    Flats, 449
  Cracked Wheat, 320
  crumbs, 505
  Flatbreads, 320–22
    about, 320
    Rye, 321
  Oatcakes, 322
  Rye-Wheat Thins, 321
  Savory Grain, 271
  whole grain, for pantry, 472
Cranberry
  Bread, 332
  Crunch, 357
  Jelly, 418
  Juice Cocktail, 418
  Pudding, 357
  Relish
    Crunchy, 309
    Raw, 66
  Sauce, 309
Cream
  Banana, 366
  Clotted, 411
  Cheese
    C & C, 27
    Curry Cashew Spread, 69
    Frosting, 415
    Fresh Fruit Tarts with Cheese Filling, 402
    and Vegetables, Tofu, 69
  Frozen Apple, 365
  of Mushroom Soup, 99
  Peach, 366
  Puffs, 283, 406
  of Spinach Soup, 99
  Strawberry, 366
  of Tomato Soup, Quick, 444
  Whipped
    Cottage, 56
    Orange-Sesame, 412
    Real, 412
    Soy, 411
    Yogurt, 411
Creamed
  Carrot and Zucchini Crepes, 214
  Corn
    O'Brien, 239
    Soup, 56
  Soups, Quick, 444
Creamy
  Barley Salad, 269
  Blue Cheese Dressing, 290
  Carrot Dressing, 291
  Cheese Pastry, 400
  Cheesecake, 393
  Dinner Fruit Salad, 305
  Dressing, 287
  French Tomato Vinaigrette, 288
  Herb
    Butter, 306
    Dressing, 290
  Lemon Butter, 81
  Lima Bean Soup, 104
  Mushrooms and Onions, 245
  Nut Dressing, 290
  Orange-Honey Dressing, 291
  Pasta with Cheese, 40
  Peanut Butter, 31
  Pimiento Sauce, 315
  Rice Salad, 269
  Stuffed Baked Potatoes, 163
  Tahini Rice, 268
  Tofu Garlic Dressing, 290
  Tomato Dressing, 290
Creole
  Noodles, 116
  Okra, 245
  Sauce, Raw, 309
  Tomato and Peanut Soup, 107
Crepes
  about, 210–12
  batter for, 211
  for Blintzes, 214
  cooking, 211
  Creamed Carrot and Zucchini, 214
  Dinner, 212
  Egg, 212
  flipping, 211
  Fresh Tomato-Filled, 214
  Hi-Protein, 213
  Manicotti, 213
  preparation in advance, 212

Crepes (*cont.*)
  Spinach, 212
    Mushroom-, 213
  value of, 212
Crescents, 346
Crisp
  Cheese Pancakes, 38
  Fried
    Beets, 234
    Onions, 246
  Shredded Salad, 304
Croissants, 410
Croque Madame, 124
Croquettes
  Cheese, 128
  for Algerian Chick-Peas, 181
  Italian Rice, 201
Croustade, 80
Croutons, 505
  Cheese, 90
Crumb(s)
  Coating and Stuffing Mix, 505
  Italian, 505
  and croutons, 505
  Crust, 398
    Nut and, 398
  -Crusted Pears, 359
  Pie
    Apple, 400
    Fruit, 401
Crunchy
  Cranberry Relish, 309
  Peach Salad, 305
  Pretzels, 351
Crust
  Baked Rice, 228
  Cornmeal, 228
  for Pizza, 219
    Biscuit-, 220
  Savory
    Cracker Crumb, 46
    Soy, 228
  see also dough, pastry, pie crust, shells
Crusty
  Rolls, 345
  Sandwich, 343
Cubes
  Flavoring, 485
  Herb, 428
  Soup 'n' Greens, 428
  Tomato, 430
Cucumber
  Borscht with, 109
  Blender Salad Soup, 56
  Caucasus Salad, 298
  with Creamy Cottage Cheese, 294

Cuchumber, 294
  freezing, 427
  Italian Sautéed, 240
  Mideast Relish, 294
  Mold, Pineapple, 295
  Moroccan Yogurt Soup, 109
  Mousse, 294
  Pickles
    Basic, 439
    Bread and Butter, 439
    Quick, 310
    preparation, 498
  Salad
    Greek Tomato and, 300
    Marinated, 65
    Ricotta-, 46
    with Spicy Dressing, 294
    Yogurt-, 293
  Sautéed, 240
  White Gazpacho, 108
  Yogurt Salad Puffs, 284
Cumin, fresh ground, 299
Cupcakes
  Carob and Chocolate, 391
  Carrot, 392
Curry(ied)
  -Apple Soup, Cold, 110
  Beans, Quick, 258
  Cashew Spread, 69
  Chick-Peas, Very Quick, 54
  Corn, 239
  Cream, Vegetables with, 41
  Dip, 64
  Dressing, India Salad with, 302
  Eggplant and Potato, 242
  Fruit, 257
  Kedgeree, 186
  Nuts, 350
  Onion-Apple-Raisin Sauté, 246
  Pakistani, 148
  Parsnip, 247
  Popcorn and Nuts, 348
  Powder, Homemade, 445
  Vegetable
    -Cheese, 148
    -Potato, 242
    -Tofu, 149
Custard
  Baked
    Chocolate/Carob, 362
    Vanilla, 362
  Egg-White Almond, 362
  Mushroom, 128
  Pie
    Broccoli, 225
    Coconut, 404

Custard (cont.)
Pumpkin, 404
Quick-Cooking, 60
Sauce, Foamy, 413
Tahini, 362

D

Dahi Vaddi, 88
Dahl, 258
Dairy products
cheese and, for minimal pantry, 475
in menu planning, 14–15
storage of, 477–78
table of food weights and measures, 518–519
value of, 15
Danish, Cheese, 409
Darwinian diet, 3
Date(s)
Apple Rocks, 378
Bars, 379
Cookies, Sunflower-, 372
Dried Fruit Bars, 378
Favorite Fruit Salad, 60
Fudge, 352
-Nut Bread Pudding, 62
Tarts, Quick Apple-, 406
-Topped Shortbread Squares, Walnut, 374
David's Pan Fries, 53
Decorative Pastry Cutouts, 226
Deep Dish Pie(s), 226–29
about, 226
Strawberry Rhubarb, 401
Vegetable, Muffin-Topped, 226
see also pies
Defrosting, 431, 482
tofu, 503
Deli
Platter, American Wholefoods, 31
-Style Health Salad, 301
Deluxe Mushroom-Barley Soup, 97
Derma, Vegetable, 80
Dessert Cream Puffs, 406
Desserts, 59–62, 354–416
about, 354–55
Apple(s)
Baked, 355
-Banana Betty, 356
Buttered, 61
Cream, Frozen, 365
Crumble, 356
Macaroon-Top, 356
Steamed, 60

Baked
Fruits Alaska, 359
goods, 366–410
about, 366–70
Banana(s)
Cream, 366
and Cheese, Baked, 357
Soft Serve, 59
Bananes aux Pecanes, 357
Broiled Orange, 61
Cranberry
Crunch, 357
Pudding, 357
Custard
Baked
Vanilla, 362
Chocolate/Carob, 362
Egg-White Almond, 362
Tahini, 362
Quick Cooking, 60
Date-Nut Bread Pudding, 62
Dried Fruit Compote, 60
Favorite Fruit Salad, 60
Fresh Blueberry Buckle, 356
frozen, and puddings, 361–66
about, 361
Fruit, 355–61
about, 355
Juice Gels, 360–61
about, 360
Agar, 361
Gelatin, 360
Ice Cream
Fresh Strawberry, 366
Maple-Walnut, 366
Peach, 366
Mango Jam, 358
Marinated Figs, 358
Monkeys in a Blanket, 61
Peach(es)
-Banana Betty, 356
Cream, 366
and Cream, Poached, 358
Pears
Buttered, 61
Caramel, 359
Crumb-Crusted, 359
in Vanilla Syrup, 358
Pudding
Bread, 363
Butterscotch, 361
Carob, 362
Honey
-Chocolate, 361
-Vanilla, 361
Indian, 364

Pudding (*cont.*)
Lemon Sponge, 363
Pie, Chocolate, 361
Rice
Baked, 363
Top-of-the-Stove, 363
Roast Pineapple, 359
Sherbet
Buttermilk, 365
Honey-Lemon Milk, 365
Peach, 365
Pineapple, 59
short order, 59–62
Strawberry
Cream, 366
Ice, 364
Yogurt, Frozen, 364
Summer Fruit Cobbler, 360
Tortoni, 59
uses of, 17
Winter Fruit Salad, 359
see also cookies, cakes, pies, pastries, tarts
Dessert toppings, 410–16
Baked Meringue Topping, 363
Blueberry Sauce, 412
Carob Fudge
Sauce, 413
Syrup, 413
Chocolate Syrup, 413
Clotted Cream, 411
Foamy Custard Sauce, 413
Fresh
Peach Sauce, 412
Strawberry Sauce, 412
Hot Wet Nuts, 413
Raisin Sauce, 413
Rich Cake Sauce, 413
Whipped
Cream
Orange Sesame, 412
Real, 412
Soy, 411
Ricotta Topping, 411
see also frosting, icing
"Devil Dogs," 384
Deviled Tofu, 30
Devil's Food Cake, 384
Dhal Pouree Roti, 324
Diary, kitchen, 486
Dijon Potato Salad, 250
Dilled
Green Beans, 440
Pea Soup, Cold, 101
Dinner Crepes, 212

Dips, 63–64
about, 63
Baba Ghanouj, 68
Blue Cheese, 64
Curry, 64
Green, 64
Herb, 64
Hummus, 68
Onion, 64
Pimiento-Cheese, 47
see also appetizers, pâtés, spreads
Dipping Sauce
Oriental, 307
for Steamed Artichokes, 81
Sweet Chinese, 307
Dirty Rice, 267
Displacement measuring, 488
Donuts, Double, 392
Double
Corn Muffins, 330
Donuts, 392
Dough
Basic Roll, 345
Foundation Sweet, 406
No-Kneading, Fast-Rising, 344
Potato, 206
for Russian Vegetable Turnovers, 281
for Vegetable Strudel, 224
see also bread, biscuits, chapatis, pastry shells
Dressing(s), 286–91
about, 286–87
Avocado, 289
Basic Oil and Vinegar, 287
Bottom-of-the-Bowl, 57
Chunky Cottage Cheese, 288
Creamy, 287
Blue Cheese, 290
Thick, 57
Carrot, 291
Herb, 290
Nut, 290
Tofu Garlic, 290
Tomato, 290
Garlic, 287
Green Goddess, 289
Herb, 287
Italian, 287
Lemon-Tahini, 290
Light Tomato
French, 57
Italian, 57
Mexican, 57
Mayonnaise
Avocado, 288
Cashew, 289

Dressing(s) (*cont.*)
  Fresh, 288
    in a Machine, 288
  Tofu, 289
  No-Oil Tomato Juice, 288
  Orange-Honey, 291
    Creamy, 291
  Peanut Cream for Tropical Fruit Platter, 305
  Revisionist, 57
  Rich Parsley, 288
  and sauces, 56–59
  Soft Cheese, 287
  Soy-Sesame, for Spinach-Bean Sprout Salad, 298
  Spicy Tomato and Cocktail Marinade, 76
  Sweet and Spicy, 288
  Thousand Island, 289
  Tofu Sour Cream, 289
  Tomato Vinaigrette
    French, 288
      Creamy, 288
    Italian, 288
    Mexican, 288
  Whipped Cottage Cream, 56
Dried
  Chinese mushrooms, 465
  Fruit
    Bars, 378
    Compote, 60
    for pantry, 473
    storage of, 480
    see also specific fruit
Dry
  pantry, 471–73
  -Roasted Nuts, 350
  staples, storage of, 481
"Duck" Sauce, 307
Dumpling(s), 271–74
  about, 271–72
  Bread, 272
    Meat, 206
      Spicy, 206
  Bulgur, 273
  Cassoni, 285
  Corn
    Dodgers, 273
    Gnocchi, Italian, 273
    Pierogi, 273
  Egg, 272
  Fried, 285
    Chinese, 286
    Italian, 286
    Mexican, 286
  Garnish for Polish Pierogi, 208

  Matzo Balls, 272
  Polish Pierogi, 207
  Ricotta-Spinach, 127
  Steamed Chinese, 83
Dutch
  Apple Pie, 401
  Salad, 304

E

Eastern European table, 462
Easy NFDM Yogurt, 422
Eating out, 520–23
Egg(s)
  appetizers, cheese and, 70
  Baked Macaroni and Cheese with, 112
  Cheese-Corn Pudding, 137
  Cheese and Beans
    Greek, 132
    Italian, 132
    Mexican, 132
  conserving, 507
  Crepes, 212
  Drop Soup, 55
    Italian, Stracciatella, 91
  Dumplings, 272
  entrées, 130–39
    about, 130
  Farmer's, 130
  Florentine, Baked, 136
  -Free Applesauce Cake, 386
  Fresh Corn Pudding, 137
  Frittatas, 134
    Italian Spinach, 134
    Spaghetti, 134
    Zucchini, 135
  Fu Yung, 136
  Hero, Pepper and, 35
  Huevos Rancheros, 131
  and Lemon, Rice with, 276
  Marseilles Spinach Stew, 143
  in menu planning, 14
  Noodles, 276
  Omelet
    American Potato, 131
    Baked Vegetable, 136
    Camellia Grill, 39
    Fines Herbes, 132
    Fluffy, 133
      Mushroom, 133
    French
      Cheese, 132
      Tomato, 133
    Manicotti, 39
    Mexican, 135

Egg(s) (*cont.*)
  Parmentier, 130
  Slices, Rolled, 73
  Spanish, 133
  and Potatoes, 130
  Roll(s)
    Steamed, 73
    for Zucchini Roulade, 73
  Salad
    Lima Bean-, 28
    Tofu, 30
  Soufflés
    about, 137
    Cheese, 138
    Mushroom, 139
  separating, 506
  storage of, 478
  Stuffed Lemon, 72
  techniques for handling and cooking,
    506–507
  tempering, 507
  with Tomatoes, Scrambled, 131
  Tortilla
    de Patatas, 130
    Pyramid, 37
  use in cooking, 25
  value of, 15
  White(s)
    beating or whipping, 506
    folding, 507
    Almond Custard, 362
Eggplant
  Appetizer, Marinated, 77
  Baba Ghanouj, 68
  Baked Herbed, 241
  Bean Moussaka, 185
  Caponata, 77
  Caviar, 78
  Cheeseburgers, 141
  Cold Ginger, 243
  Cutlets, 140
    Parmesan, 141
    Provolone, 141
  au Gratin, 241
  Lasagne, 151
  and Lentils, Barbecued, 179
  Manicotti, 162
  Noodles, Steamed, 243
  Outdoor Mixed Grill, 173
  Parmesan, 151
  and Potato Curry, 242
  preparation, 498
  Ratatouille, 242
    Campfire, 242
  Pie, 150
  and Rice, Greek, 266

  Rollatini, 162
  Sauce, Spaghetti with, 116
  Spread, Israeli, 68
  Steak, Chopped, 195
  Stuffed, 161
  and Yogurt, Cold, 243
Egyptian Pickled Turnips, 440
Emergency Mexican Tomato Sauce, 58
Empanadas, 282
English
  farmhouse supper, 461
  Muffins, 343
  Pancakes, Filled, 209
  wholefoods dinner, 461–62
Enchilada(s)
  Cheese, 217
  Sauce, 317
Energy-saving tricks, 487
Enriching foods, 507–10
Equipment
  canning, 432
  home freezing, 426
  pickling, 438
Escabeche, Green Banana, 84
Everyday soups, 92–104
Extra
  Flaky Pastry, 406
  Light Mix, 446

F

Falafel I, 199
  II, 200
Family and company dinners, 452–53
Far East Sweet Potatoes, 251
Farmer('s)
  Cheese, Homemade, 149
  Eggs, 130
Fat
  use in cooking, 24
  selection and care of, for frying, 491
Favorite Fruit Salad, 60
Fejoida, 184
Feta
  Baked
    Potato Toppings, 54
    Spinach and, 153
  Biscuits, Greek, 281
  Casserole, Top-Crusted Spinach-, 154
  Greek
    Country Salad, 32
    Tomato and Cucumber Salad, 300
  Israeli Salad, 302
  Main Dish Spinach Salad, 298

Feta (*cont.*)
Pie
American Spinach-, 154
Greek Spinach-, 153
Spinach and Chick-Peas with, 178
Turkish Country Salad, 301
Zucchini Pancakes, 195
Fettuccine
with Spring Vegetables, 117
see also pasta
Fiery Sauce, 309
Red Pepper, 318
15-Minute Italian Tomato Sauce, 58
Figs
Dried Fruit Bars, 378
Marinated, 358
Filled
Croustades with Salpicon, 80
Pancakes, 208–18
about, 208–209
English, 209
Filling(s)
for Blintzes, 215
for Fried Tacos, 218
Kasha, for Bite-Size Knish, 84
Mince, 443
Potato, for Bite-Size Knish, 84
for Russian Vegetable Turnovers, 281
for Sealed Sandwiches, 223
Finger Rolls, 345
Finishing touches, 410–16
about, 410–11
Fish
storage of, 478
value of, 15
Flan, 362
Flash freezing, 426
Flatbreads, 320–22
about, 320
Rye, 321
see also crackers
Flavor extracts, for pantry, 473
Flavoring Cubes, 485
Flour
Mixes, Multi-Purpose
about, 446
Corn, 448
Extra-Light, 446
High Protein, 448
for pantry, 471
sifting, 367
use in baking, 367
whole wheat vs. white, 10
Fluffy
Kasha, 264
Omelet, 133

Mushroom, 133
Spanish, 133
Stuffed Baked Potatoes, 163
Foamy Custard Sauce, 413
Food
factory, 420–50
about, 420
handling
during cooking, 482–83
and storage, 476–83
spectrums, 4–5
Fork-tender, 493
Foundation Sweet Dough, 406
Freezer pantry, 474
Freezing
direct, 426, 427–28
foods suitable for, 426
equipment for, 426
flash, 426
labeling packages, 426
need for pre-freezing processing, 429
French
Baguettes, 340
Carrots and Celery, 238
Cheese Omelet, 132
country dinner, 460
cuisine, 459–61
about, 459–60
dining, gourmet, 460
Fries, 249
Left Bank street fare, 461
Mediterranean meal, 460
Mushroom
Salad, 297
Soup, 105
Nut Cake, 385
Onion Soup, 96
Country Style, 96
Pasta Salad, 278
-Style Couscous, 192
tart tins, 396
toast
Croque Madame, 124
-Toasted Cheese Sandwich, 34
Tomato
Dressing, Light, 57
Omelet, 133
Vinaigrette, 288
Creamy, 288
Fresh
Blueberry Buckle, 356
Chinese Fried Noodles, 276
Corn Pudding, 137
Fruit
Coffee Cake, 389
Drink, 418

Fresh Fruit (*cont.*)
Fizz, 418
Tart, 402
with Cheese Filling, 402
Ginger Carrots, 238
Mayonnaise, 288
in a Machine, 288
Orange Beets, 234
Peach
Cake, 389
Sauce, 412
Plum Chutney, 442
Strawberry
Ice Cream, 366
Sauce, 412
Tomato
Filled Crepes, 214
Pita Pizza, 33
Pizza, 220
Soup, 93
Fried
Artichoke Hearts, 82
Cabbage and Potatoes, Indian Style, 237
Camembert, 70
Dumplings, 285
Chinese, 286
Italian, 286
Mexican, 286
Green Tomatoes, 254
Noodles
Chinese, 119
Indonesian, 120
Plantains, 248
Rice
Chinese-Style, 120
Indonesian, 121
Tacos, 217
Zucchini, 253
Frittata
about, 134
Italian Spinach, 134
Spaghetti, 134
Zucchini, 135
Fritters
Burger Mix, 446
Quick Corn, 450
Frosting
about, 414
Buttercream, 414
Carob or Chocolate, 414
Cream Cheese, 415
and Filling
Chocolate Cream, 415
Thick Fudge, 416
Orange, 415

Spice, 414
see also glaze, icing
Frozen
Apple Cream, 365
Banana
Pops, 352
Soft-Serve, 59
desserts, puddings and, 361–66
about, 361
foods, homemade, 426–31
Juicicles, 353
Pineapple, 352
Strawberry Yogurt, 364
Whipped
Banana Cream Pie, 406
Peach, 406
Strawberry, 405
Fruit(s)
Alaska, Baked, 359
Bars, Dried, 378
Butter, 441
-Cake, 390
Canned, 336
about, 336
for pantry, 472
Pie or Tarts, 402
Cobbler, Summer, 360
Coffee Cake, Fresh, 389
Crumb Pie, 401
Curry, 257
desserts, 355–61
about, 355
Dried
Compote, 60
for pantry, 473
storage of, 480
Drink, Fresh, 418
Fizz, Fresh, 418
fresh
for pantry, 472
for refrigerator pantry, 474
Juice Gels, 360–61
about, 360
Kuchen Oma, 389
Noodle Pudding, 122
-Nut Rugelach, 380
Platter, Tropical, 305
Purees, 436
Punch, 417
Salad
Creamy Dinner, 305
Favorite, 60
Winter, 359
Shortcake, 388
storage of, 477
Summer Conserve, 442

Fruit(s) (*cont.*)
 table of food weights and measures, 515–16
 Tart(s)
  Fresh, 402
   with Cheese Filling, 402
  Quick, 61
 Thick Shake, 419
 Twist, 408
 and vegetables, for minimal pantry, 475
 see also specific fruit
Frying
 bread-cube test for fat, 492
 deep-fat, 491
 oven, 493
 preparing food for, 491
 selection and care of fat, 491
 shallow, 492
 and deep-fat, 490–93
Fu Yung Sauce, 136
Fudge, 352
 Frosting and Filling, Thick, 416
 Sauce, Carob, 413

G

Gado Gado, 149
Garden Rice, 267
Garlic
 Dressing, 287
 -Sesame Bread, 49
 Soup
  Portuguese Bread and, 55
  Spanish, 91
 Spaghetti with, 277
Gazpacho, 108
 White, 108
Gelatin, about, 360
 see also gel(s)
Gel(s), Fruit Juice
 Gelatin, 360
  Fruited, 361
 Agar, 361
German
 Bean Tzimmis, 181
 Potpourri, 462
 -Style New Potatoes, 144
Giant "Twinkie," 383
Ginger
 Carrots
  Fresh, 238
  with Raisins, Sweet, 238
 Cookies, 375
 Eggplant, Cold, 243

Gingerbread, 385
 Apple-Topped, 385
 Mr. Bill Cookies, 375
Glaze, Buttercream, 414
 see also frosting, icing
Glazed Onions, 246
Globe artichoke, *see* artichoke, globe
Gnocchi, Italian, 207
 Corn, 273
Goldbecks' Masala, 445
Golden
 Carrot Soup, 100
 Temple Muffins, 329
Gomasio, 306
"Gorp," *see* "snacks"
Gourmet French dining, 460
Grahams, Honey, 372
Grain(s)
 Balls, Mixed, 201
 basic cookery, 503–505
  boiling water method, 503
  cold water method, 503
 breads and, for minimal pantry, 474
 Burgers, 196
 Butter Nut, 49
 Crackers, Savory, 271
 dry-roasted, 504
 dumpling and pasta accompaniments, 262–79
 enhancing food value, 504
 fragmentation of, 3
 leftover, 262
 mains, 188–94
 in menu planning, 12
 for pantry, 471
 Peanut-Buttered, 271
  Beans and, 211
 sautéed, 50
 seasoning, 262
 storage of, 480
 store, bean pot and, 484
 table of food weights and measures, 517–18
 timetable for cooking, 504
 value of, 12
 yield, 505
 see also specific grains
Granola Bars, 351
Grape Leaves, Greek Stuffed Cabbage or, 82
Gravy
 Brown, 313
 Carrot, 141
 Cashew, 314
  Brown, 314
  Tomato, 314

Gravy (*cont.*)
  Chicken-Style, 314
  Mushroom, 314
  Tahini, 314
  see also sauce
Great Big Honey-Molasses Cookies, 375
Greater grains, 504
Greece and the Middle East, cuisine of, 463–64
  about, 463
Greek
  Artichokes and Dill, 231
  Bean Salad, 262
  Beans, Eggs and Cheese, 132
  Coleslaw, 292
  Country Salad, 32
  dinner, 463
  Eggplant Rice, 266
  Feta Biscuits, 281
  Lenten Cake, 391
  Lentil Soup, 101
  Olives, 65
  Spinach
  -Feta Pie, 153
  Rice, 266
  Stuffed
    Cabbage or Grape Leaves, 82
    Tomato, 255
  Tomato and Cucumber Salad, 300
Green
  Banana Escabeche, 84
  Bean(s)
    Aromatic Rice with, 266
    Atlantic Avenue, 233
    with Cashews, Super-Quick Creamed, 444
    Chow Mein, 146
    Colombian Potatoes, 144
    with Cottage Cheese, Marinated, 291
    Dilled, 440
    with Garlic, Stir-Fried, 233
    Pasta with, 115
    preparation, 497
    Quick Creamed, 233
    Salade Niçoise, 301
    Spiced, 232
    and Tomato Salad, 291
  Dip, 64
  Goddess Dressing, 289
  Linguine with
    Red Mushroom Sauce, 114
    White Mushroom Sauce, 113
  pepper, *see* peppers, green
  Rice with Stuffed Chilies, 188
  Tomatoes, 430

Fried, 254
  Mince Filling, 443
  Quick Corn-Crusted, 450
  Relish, 440
  Sauce, 431
Greens
  in Broth, Chinese, 91
  Cheese and, 296
  Chinese Style, Stir-Fried, 244
  Consum, 285
  Fejoida, 184
  Italian Beans and, 258
  Lemon, 295
  Potato and, 94
  preparation, 498
  "Soup 'n Greens" Cubes, 428
  Steamed, 244
Grilled Open-Face Tofu Sandwich, 35
Groats, buckwheat, *see* kasha
Ground beans (Chopped Beat), 502
Guacamole, 46
Gulyas, Hungarian Vegetable, 145
Gumbo, Chick-Pea, 177

H

Halvah, 352
Hamentaschen, 380
Harvest Corn Cake, 330
Hash Browns, 250
Hawaiian Bean Loaf, 204
Heat processing, for canning, 433
Herb(s)
  Butter, Creamy, 306
  Cubes, 428
  Dip, 64
  Dressing, 287
    Creamy, 290
  freezing, 427
  and spices, for pantry, 473
  Tea and Cereal "Coffee," 419
Herbed
  Eggplant, Baked, 241
  Oat Bread, 339
  Squash, 253
Hero(es)
  Antipasto, 28
  Pepper and Egg, 35
  Rolls, 340
Hi-Protein Crepes, 213
High Protein Mix, 448
Hindu Pulao, 266
Holiday entertaining suggestions, 455–56

Hollandaise, American Wholefoods
　Broccoli, 235
Home Fries, 249
Homemade
　Farmer Cheese, 149
　frozen foods, 426–31
　　equipment, 426
　　selection of foods, 426
Honey, 354–55, 367
　-Chocolate Pudding, 361
　Grahams, 372
　-Lemon Milk Sherbet, 365
　Molasses Cookies, Great Big, 375
　-Vanilla Pudding, 361
Hoppin' John, 178
Hors d'oeuvres, see appetizers
Horseradish, preparation, 498
Hot
　Borscht, 93
　Dressed Vegetables, 51
　Leek and Potato Soup, 109
　Open-Faced Sandwiches
　　Tempeh, 174
　　Tofu "Turkey," 168
　Potato Turnovers, 283
　sandwiches and entrées, short order,
　　33–46
　Sauce for Porotos Granados, 183
　and Sour Soup, Chinese, 107
　Stuffed Avocado Salad, 32
　Wet Nuts, 413
House Corn Bread, 330
Huevos Rancheros, 131
Hummus, 68
Hungarian
　Cabbage Noodles, 119
　Vegetables Gulyas, 145

I

Ice cream
　Fresh Strawberry, 366
　Maple-Walnut, 366
　Peach, 366
　Strawberry, 364
Icing
　Buttercream Glaze, 414
　Whipped White, 415
　see also frosting
Ilse's Vegetables in Cream Sauce, 142
India Salad with Curry Dressing, 302
Indian
　Bean Pita, 221
　Dinner, 467
　Lentils, 258
　Pudding, 364

Individual
　Bean Pizzas, 34
　"Twinkies," 384
Indonesian
　dinner, 468
　Fried
　　Noodles–Bami Goreng, 120
　　Rice–Nasi Goreng, 121
Ingredients, pre-made, 485
Instant
　Asopa, 91
　Sauce Balls, 315
　Soup, 54
International dinners, 456–68
　about, 456
　Arabic, 464
　Brazilian, 458
　Chinese I, 466
　　II, 466
　　III, 466
　Eastern European table, 462
　English
　　farmhouse supper, 461
　　wholefoods dinner, 461–62
　French
　　country dinner, 460
　　gourmet dining, 460
　　Left Bank street fare, 461
　　Mediterranean meal, 460
　German potpourri, 462
　Greek, 463
　Indian, 467
　Indonesian, 468
　Irish farm dinner, 462
　Israeli "tourist special," 463–64
　Italian feast I, 458
　　II, 459
　　III, 459
　Japanese, 465–66
　Lebanese, 464
　Mexican feast, 457
　Moroccan Couscous, 464
　Puerto Rican, 457
　South American medley, 458
　Spanish supper, 457
Irish farm dinner, 462
Israeli
　Eggplant Spread, 68
　Salad, 302
　"tourist special," 463–64
Italian
　Beans
　　Eggs and Cheese, 132
　　and Greens, 258
　Bread, 340
　Cabbage and Rice Soup, 97

Italian (*cont.*)
  Cheese
    Melt with Ceci, 129
    Stuffing Balls, 127
  Cheesecake, 393
  Crumb Coating and Stuffing Mix, 505
  Dressing, 287
  Egg-Drop Soup, 91
  feast I, 485
    II, 459
    III, 459
  Gnocchi, 207
    Corn, 273
  kitchen, 458
  Lentil Soup, 101
  Macaroni and Cheese, 112
  Mushroom Soup, 105
  Omelet (Frittata), 134
  Rice Croquettes, 201
  Sautéed Cucumber, 240
  Spaghetti Stew, 113
  Spinach Frittata, 134
  Stuffed Spaghetti Squash, 159
  -Style Polenta, 194
  Tofu Balls, 127
  Tomato
    Dressing, Light, 57
    Salad, 299
    Sauce, 317
      15-Minute, 58
    Vinaigrette, 288
  Vegetable
    Casserole, 154
    Marinade, 311

J

Jam, Mango, 358
  see also jelly, preserves
Jane's Schlurpy, 418
Japanese
  dinner, 465–66
  Tempura Batter, 171
Jelly, Cranberry, 418
  see also jam, preserves
Jerusalem artichokes, *see* artichokes,
    Jerusalem
Jicama, preparation, 498
Juice, for pantry
  fruit, 472
  vegetable, 472
  see also beverages
Juicicles, Frozen, 353
Julienne Vegetables and Cheese, 303
Jumbo Walnut Cookies, 375

K

Kanten, 360
Kasha
  Blintzes, 214
  filling for Bite-Size Knish, 85
  Fluffy, 264
  Knishes, 264
  Mushroom, 264
  Onion, 264
  Protein-Enriched, 264
  Varnishkas, 264
Kebabs
  Tempeh, with Pineapple Barbecue
    Sauce, 175
  Vegetable, 172
Kedgeree, 186
Kibbi, Nikki's Special, 87
Kidney Bean(s)
  Bean-Studded Pancakes, 210
  in Cheddar Sauce, 176
  Cold Pasta and Broccoli, 118
  Luncheon Salad, 28
  Sopones, 182
  see also beans
Kisses
  Coconut, 352
  Peanut, 352
Kitchen
  American Wholefoods, introduction,
    1–19
  diary, 486
  math, 511–19
  and pantry storage, 476–81
  short order, 26
  utensils for, 26
Kitchree, 187
Kiwi, Tropical Fruit Platter, 305
Kneading yeast breads, 334
Knish(es)
  Bite-Size, 84
  Kasha, 264
  Miniature, 265
  Potato, 283
Kolache, 407
Kosheri, 187
Kuchen Oma, Fruit, 389

L

Lasagne
  about, 122
  with Bean Sauce, 123
  Eggplant, 151
  Matzo, 45
  White, 124

Latin influence, 456
Layered Tomato Casserole, 45
Leavening, in baking, 368
Leban, Macaroni and, 279
Lebanese dinner, 464
and Cheddar Soup, 99
and Potato Soup, Hot, 109
preparation of, 498
Vichyssoise, 109
Left Bank street fare, 461
Leftovers, stimulating use of, 486
Lemon
Butter, Creamy, 81
Greens, 295
-Limeade, 417
Meringue Pie, 405
Milk Sherbet, Honey-, 365
-Nut Cookies, 372
-Orange Refrigerator Layer Cake, 392
Rice with Egg and, 268
Sponge Pudding, 363
Squash and Carrots, 253
-Tahini Dressing, 290
Lemonade, 417
Lenten Cake, Greek, 391
Lentil(s)
Barbecued Eggplant and, 179
Dahi Vaddi, 88
Indian, 288
Kitchree, 187
Kosheri, 187
Mulligatawny Soup, 102
Sauce, Pasta with, 117
Soup, Greek, 101
Italian, 101
see also beans
Lettuce
Rolls, Spring, 83
Sweet and Sour Stuffed, 165
see also salad
Light
Fresh Tomato Sauce, 316
Spice Cookies, 372
Tomato Dressing
French, 57
Italian, 57
Mexican, 57
Lima Bean(s)
Baked Mexican, 261
Basque Country Stew, 180
Cheese Bake, 185
-Egg Salad, 28
Soup, Creamy, 104
Succotash, 240
Tzimmis, 180
see also beans

Linguine
Country-Style, 115
with Red Mushroom Sauce, Green, 114
with White Mushroom Sauce, Green, 113
see also pasta
Liquid ingredients in baking, 368
Liver, Chopped Bean, 29
Liverish, 202
Lo–Mein—Chinese Fried Noodles, 119
Luncheon Wheat Germ Loaf, 205

M

Macaroni
and Cheese
with Egg, Baked, 112
Italian, 112
One-Pot, Baked, 39
Salad, 48
Stove-Top, 112
Kosheri, 187
and Leban, 279
Salad, 48
Soup, Broccoli and, 95
see also pasta
Macaroon-Top Apples, 356
Main course, 111–229
about, 111
Main Dish, 16
Stir-Fry, 42
Spinach Salad, 298
Mainly beans, 176–87
Major Protein, 6, 23, 111
Mammaliga, Rumanian, 194
Mandarin Pancakes, 216
Mandelbrot, 377
Mango Jam, 358
Manicotti, 213
Eggplant, 162
Omelet, 39
Maple
syrup, 367
-Walnut Ice Cream, 366
Marble Cake, 385
Marinade
Italian Vegetable, 311
Spicy Tomato Dressing and Cocktail, 76
for Vegetable Kebabs, 172
Marinara Sauce, 316
Marinated
Artichoke Hearts, 65
Cucumber Salad, 65

Marinated (cont.)
  Eggplant Appetizer, 77
  Figs, 358
  Green Beans with Cottage Cheese, 291
  Zucchini Sticks, 66
Marseilles Spinach Stew, 143
Masala, Goldbecks', 445
Mashed
  Combination Vegetables, 256
  Potato(es)
    Basic, 248
    Soup, 94
Master rule, 25, 484
Math, kitchen, 511–19
Matzo
  Balls, 272
  Lasagne, 45
Mayonnaise
  Avocado, 288
  Cashew, 289
  Fresh, 288
    in a Machine, 288
  Tofu, 289
Meals for one, 18–19
Measure, how to, 487–89
Measuring
  displacement, 488
  dry ingredients, 487
  liquid ingredients, 488
  by weight, 488
Meat
  adding to recipes, 15
  Bread, 206
    Spicy, 206
  storage of, 478
  value, 15
Menu(s)
  New American, 11–19
  planning, 11, 451
    course approach, 16–18
    family and company dinners, 452–53
    food approach, 11–16
    need for diversity, 11
    simple wholefoods dinners, 451–52
  sample, 451–68
  suggestions
    adult party, 454–55
    barbecue, 454
    children's party, 454
    holiday entertaining, 455–56
Meringue
  Baked Fruits Alaska, 359
  Pie, Lemon, 405
  Topping, Baked, 363
Metric equivalents, table of, 511

Mexican
  Bean
    Balls, 198
    Corn Salad, 304
    Eggs and Cheese, 132
    and Pasta Bake, 185
    Pita, 221
    Soup, 103
  Cheese Melt with Corn, 128
  Corn Soup, 98
  feast, 457
  Omelet, 135
  Pizza, 36
  Quiche, 128
  Stuffed Avocado Salad, 32
  -Style Bean Pizza, 177
  Tomato
    Dressing, Light, 57
    Vinaigrette, 288
  Vegetables, 147
Middle East, Greece and, cuisine of,
    463–64
Mideast
  Bean Pita, 222
  Carrot and Chick-Pea Puree, 105
  Chick-Pea Salad, 261
  Relish, 294
  Smorgasbord, 200
Milk
  in cooking, 24
  powder, nonfat dry, 509
  Sherbet, Honey-Lemon, 365
  value of, 15
  for yogurt making, 421
Millet
  Cheese Stuffed Cabbage, 165
  Moroccan Couscous, 193
  Stuffed Chapatis, 284
  see also grains
Mince Filling, 443
Minestrone, 96
  Genovese, 96
Miniature Knishes, 265
Minimal pantry, 474–75
Miniscus, 488
Minor Protein, 6, 23, 111
Mr. Bill Cookies, 375
Mix(es)
  Burger, 445
  Corn, 448
  Extra Light, 446
  High Protein, 448
  Mushroom Sauce, 444
  for pantry, 472, 475
  Pocket Soup, 444
  White Sauce, 443

Mixed
  Fry, 450
  Grain Balls, 201
  Grill, Outdoor, 173
  Vegetable Pickles, 439
  Vegetable Soup, 434
Mock Pumpkin Pie, 404
Molasses, 367
  Cookies Great Big Honey-, 375
Mom's Thick Split-Pea Soup, 100
Monkeys in a Blanket, 61
Mornay Cheese Sauce, 313
Moroccan
  Couscous, 193
  dinner, 464
  Yogurt Soup, 109
Moussaka, Bean, 185
Mousse
  Cucumber, 294
  Party, 87
Mozzarella
  Oil-Cured, 70
  -Stuffed Tomato, 52
  Vegetables, 140
  White Broccoli, 234
  see also cheese
Mu Shu Vegetables with Mandarin Pan-
  cakes, 216
Muffin(s), 327–30
  about, 327
  All-Soy, 329
  Apple-Oat, 328
  Bran, 328
  Cheese, 328
  Corn, 328
    Double, 330
  English, 343
  Golden Temple, 329
  Peach, 328
  Quick
    Corn, 449
    Light, 446
    Protein, 448
  Rice-Corn, 329
  Spiced Pear, 328
  Sunflower-Rye, 329
  Sweet Corn, 329
  -Topped Deep-Dish Vegetable Pie, 226
  Wheat Germ, 328
  Whole Wheat, 327
Mulligatawny Soup, 102
Multi-purpose flour mixes
  about, 446
  Corn Mix, 448
  Extra Light Mix, 446
  High Protein Mix, 448

Mushroom(s)
  Baked, 77
  and Barley Salad, 264
  -Barley Soup, Deluxe, 97
  Burger Sauce, Tomato-, 318
  Cheese-Stuffed, 52
  Cocktail, 76
  Confetti Pasta, 118
  Corn-Crusted, 71
    Quick, 450
  Croque Madame, 124
  Custard, 128
  Dirty Rice, 267
  dried Chinese, 465
  in Garlic Butter, 77
  Gravy, 314
  Kasha, 264
  Omelet, Fluffy, 133
  and Onions, Creamy, 245
  Overstuffed, 76
  Pakistani Curry, 148
  Paprikash, 142
  Pâté, 67
  Peas and, 247
  Pickled, 66
  Pilaf, 49
  preparation, 499
  Rissoles, 202
  Salad
    French, 297
    Tomato-, 297
  Sauce, 314
    Mix, 444
    Red, Green Linguine with, 114
    Quick, 444
    Tangy, 444
    White, Green Linguine with, 113
  Sautéed, 245
  Soufflé, 139
  Soup
    Cream of, 99
    French, 105
    Italian, 105
  -Spinach Crepes, 213
  Spinach Salad, 298
  Stuffed Cabbage Stroganoff, 165
  Tofu à la King, 168
  Tofu Stroganoff, 170
  -Vegetable Stew, 314
  White Lasagne, 124
Mustard, Chinese, 307

N

Nachos, 279
Namasu, 311

Nanette's Vegetable Pâté, 67
Nasi Goreng, 121
Native American Seed Cakes, 324
National Academy of Sciences, 1, 8
New American
  Creamy Tomato Sauce, 317
  menu, 11–19
New England Bean Chowder, 100
Nikki's
  New Brownies, 379
  Special Kibbi, 87
No-Cook Cold Cheese Sauce, 319
No-Egg Batter for Tofu-Vegetable Tempura, 172
No-Kneading, Fast-Rising Dough, 344
No-Oil Tomato Juice Dressing, 288
Nonfat dry milk powder, 509
  value of, 509
Noodle(s)
  Bami Goreng, 120
  "bean thread," 465
  Casserole, Spinach, 121
  cellophane, 465
  Creole, 116
  Egg, 276
  Fresh Chinese Fried, 276
  Hungarian Cabbage, 119
  Lo Mein, 119
  Pudding
    Fruit, 122
    Savory, 122
    Sweet, 278
  Ricotta, 276
  with Sesame Paste, 277
  Soy-Whole Wheat, 276
  Steamed Eggplant, 243
  Toasted, 52
  Yogurt, 276
  see also pasta
Northern and eastern Europe, cooking
    of, 461–62
  about, 461
Nuts
  Apple Rocks, 378
  Aromatic Rice with Green Beans, 266
  Beer, 350
  Bread Pudding, Date-, 62
  Butter, Savory, 306
  Cake, French, 385
  Cheese
    Steak, 125
    Truffles, 72
  Chili, 350
  Cookies, Lemon-, 372
  Creamy Tahini Rice, 268
  and Crumb Crust, 398

Curry, 350
  Popcorn and, 348
Cutlets, Baked Cheese-, 125
Date Bars, 379
Dirty Rice, 267
Dressing, Creamy, 290
Dry-Roasted, 350
Grains, Butter-, 49
Granola Bars, 351
Hot Wet, 413
Liverish, 202
Loaf
  Luncheon Wheat Germ, 205
  Rice, 205
Mushroom
  Pâté, 67
  Rissoles, 202
Roast, Cheese-, 126
Rugelach, Fruit-, 380
and seeds
  in baking, 368
  and beans for minimal pantry, 474
  butters, for pantry, 473
  meals, 505
    grinding, 505–506
    yield, 506
  in menu planning, 13
  for pantry, 472–73
  storage of, 480
  table of food weights and measures,
    518
  value, 14
Soy, 349
  -Roasted, 350
"Snacks," 349
Spaghetti
  Fantasy, 118
  Roast, 205
Spread, Cheese-, 69
Squares, Chocolate, 380
see also specific nut
Nutritional
  needs, guidelines, 4–5
  yeast, 508–509
  value of, 509
Nutted
  Baked Onions, 246
  Rice with Raisins, 265

O

Oat(s)
  Apple
    Crumble, 356
    Rocks, 378
  Bread, Herbed, 339

Oat(s) (*cont.*)
  Cookies, Peanut Butter-, 377
  Cranberry Crunch, 357
  Dried Fruit Bars, 378
  Granola Bars, 351
  Muffins, Apple-, 328
  Pastry, Rye-, 229
  Pilaf, 265
  -Vegetable, 265
  Rolls, Herbed, 339
  Shortbread, Scotch, 373
  Vegetable Roast, 203
Oatcakes, 322
Oatmeal
  Cookies, Soft, 378
  Soup, Anabella's, 97
Oil(s)
  -Cured Mozzarella, 70
  for pantry, 473
  storage of, 479
  use in cooking, 24
Okra
  Chick-Pea Gumbo, 177
  Chowder, 94
  Creole, 245
  preparation, 499
Olive(s)
  -Bean Salad, 29
  Caper Sauce, 72
  Eggplant Caponata, 77
  Greek, 65
  Mexican Bean and Corn Salad, 304
  and Pimiento Cheese Spread, 69
  Salade Niçoise, 301
  Spaghetti Fantasy, 118
  Sweet Stuffed Peppers, Italian Style, 83
  Zucchini Roulade, 73
Omelet(s)
  American Potato, 131
  Baked Vegetable, 136
  Camellia Grill, 39
  for Egg Fu Yung, 136
  Fines Herbes, 132
  French
    Cheese, 132
    Tomato, 133
  Fluffy, 133
    Mushroom, 133
  Italian, 134
  Manicotti, 39
  Mexican, 135
  Parmentier, 130
  Slices, Rolled, 73
  Spanish, 133
  see also frittata

One-Pot Baked Macaroni and Cheese, 39
Onion(s)
  -Apple-Raisin Sauté, 246
  Curried, 246
  Bialy Butter, 307
  -Cheese Pan Bread, 338
  Creamy Mushrooms and, 245
  Crisp Fried, 246
  Dip, 64
  for Fejoida, 184
  freezing, 428
  Glazed, 246
  Kasha, 264
  Kosheri, 187
  Milk Soup, Raw, 56
  Nutted Baked, 246
  Pie, 75
  Quick Creamy, 45
  Pissaladière Niçoise, 282
  Polish Pierogi, 207
  Potato Knishes, 283
  preparation, 499
  -Radish Relish, 297
  Relish, Browned, 57
  Rings, Quick-Fried, 447
  Sauce, 314
    Pasta with, 114
  Sausages and Pepper and, 198
  Semel Bresel, 207
  Shortcake, 225
  Soup
    French, 96
      Country Style, 96
    Quick, Tomato-, 90
  Soyburgers, 196
  Spiced, for Peruvian Mountain Potatoes, 145
  Stewed, Beans with, 257
  Tofu with Onions and Cheese, 167
Orange
  -Apricot Cake, 382
  Beets, Fresh, 234
  Broiled, 61
  Cookies, 372
  Frosting, 415
  -Glazed
    Carrots, 51
    Parsnips, 51
  Honey Dressing, 291
    Creamy, 291
  Julia, 418
  Preserves, Pineapple, 442
  Refrigerator Layer Cake, Lemon-, 392
  -Section Salad, 296
  -Sesame Cream, Whipped, 412

Orange (*cont.*)
-Sweet Potato Casserole, 251
-Wheat Salad, 270
Orient, cuisines of, 465–66
about, 465
Oriental
Dipping Sauce, 307
Salad Platter, 302
Soybeans, 259
Outdoor Mixed Grill, 173
Oven
Fried Tofu, 173
Fries, 249
frying, 493
temperatures in baking, 369
Overstuffed Mushrooms, 76
Oysters, Corn, 240

P

Pachadi, Tomato, 300
Paella, 190
Soyfood, 190
Pakistani Curry, 148
Pan Bagnia, 222
Pancakes
Bean-Studded, 210
Corn-Cheese, 209
Quick, 449
Crisp Cheese, 38
Filled, 208–18
English, 209
Mandarin, for Mu Shu Vegetables, 216
Potato, 37
Quick Light, 447
raised, about, 208
Rice, 38
Zucchini, 195
see also crepes
Pan
-Fried
Asparagus, 51
Cabbage, 51
-Roasted Potatoes, 248
Pantry
condiment, 473
dry, 471–73
freezer, 474
minimal, 474–75
refrigerator, 474
wholefoods, 473–75
Paprikash, Mushroom, 142
Parker House Rolls, 346
Parmesan
Eggplant, 151
Cutlet, 141

Tempeh, 174
Toast, 49
Parsley
Dressing, Rich, 288
-Sesame Bread, 49
Tabouli, 302
Tomatoes, Baked, 254
Parsnip(s)
Curry, 247
Orange-Glazed, 51
preparation, 499
see also carrots, squash
Party
Mousse, 87
Punch, 418
suggestions
adult, 454
children's, 454
Pasta
accompaniments, 274–79
Artichoke(s), 111
and Chick-Peas with Lemon Dressing, 278
Bami Goreng, 120
Basic
cooking, 274
Whole Wheat, 275
Broccoli
and Cold, 118
and Macaroni Soup, 95
with, 115, 277
Brown "Rice-a-Roni," 49
with Cheese, Creamy, 40
Confetti, 118
with Creamy Spinach, 113
entrées, 111–24
about, 111–12
e Fagioli, 179
Fagioli Soup, 102
Fettuccine with Spring Vegetables, 117
Fresh Chinese Fried Noodles, 276
with Green Beans, 115
Alfredo-Style, 115
homemade, general directions for, 274
Lasagne
with Bean Sauce, 123
White, 124
with Lentil Sauce, 117
Linguine
Country-Style, 115
Green
with Red Mushroom Sauce, 114
with White Mushroom Sauce, 113
Lo Mein, 119
Mexican Beans and Pasta Bake, 185
with Onion Sauce, 114

Pasta (cont.)
for pantry, 474
Peanut Butter, 277
with Pesto and Slivered Cheese, 114
Red or White Cheese Ravioli, 121
Salad, French, 278
Spinach-Noodle Casserole, 121
substitute
Basic Steamed Spaghetti Squash, 253
Cabbage Noodles in Tomato Broth, 237
Steamed Eggplant Noodles, 243
with Tomato Dressing, Cold, 48
Tomato Shells, 40
Vegetable Chop Suey, 119
whole grain, 111
Ziti
Baked, 113
with Cheese, 40
with Zucchini, 115
see also macaroni, noodles, spaghetti
Pasties, Cornish, 224
Pastry(ies)
accompaniments, savory, 279–86
about, 279
Apple Turnovers, 406
Bear Claws, 409
Cheddar, 229
Cheese Danish, 409
Cinnamon Buns, 407
Cream Puffs, 406
Creamy Cheese, 400
Croissants, 410
Cutouts, Decorative, 226
Extra Flaky, 406
Foundation Sweet Dough, 406
Fruit Twist, 408
Kolache, 407
leftover, 398
making in advance, 397
pies and, 394–410
about, 394–98
Plus, 399
Rye-Oat, 229
savory, 218–29
about, 218–19
Snails, 408
Standard, 399
yeast, about, 398
see also crust, dough, pies, savory
pastry, shells, tarts
Pâté(s)
Mushroom, 67
Nanette's Vegetable, 67
Pea, 67
Poached Spinach-Potato, 85

Sesame-Bean, 29
and Spreads, 66–70
Tomato-Bean, 29
White Bean, 66
see also spread
Patties, balls and loaves, 194–208
about, 194
Bean
Balls
Mexican, 198
Swedish, 199
Birds, 203
Burgers, 196
Loaf
Cottage Cheese and, 204
Cold, 204
Hawaiian, 204
Sausages, 198
Boston Roast, 44
Bread Meat, 206
Spicy, 206
Burgers
Bean, 196
Cashew, 197
Grain, 196
Rice Cheese, 197
Soy, 196
Chopped Eggplant Steak, 195
Falafel I, 199
II, 200
Italian Gnocchi, 207
Liverish, 202
Luncheon Wheat Germ Loaf, 205
Mixed Grain Balls, 201
Mushroom Rissole, 202
Peanut Butter Loaf, 44
Polish Pierogi, 207
Potato Dough, 206
Rice
Balls, Baked, 201
Cheese Burgers, 197
Croquettes, Italian, 201
-Nut Loaf, 205
Semel Bresel, 207
Soyballs, 199
Spaghetti Roast, 205
Vegetable Roast, 203
Zucchini Pancakes, 195
Pea(s)
Black-Eyed, Hoppin' John, 178
and Cheese, Carrots, 303
and Mushrooms, 247
Pakistani Curry, 148
Pâté, 67
preparation, 499

Pea(s) (*cont.*)
 Split
  Basque Country Stew, 180
  Deluxe Mushroom Barley Soup, 97
  Dhal Pouree Roti, 324
  Pocket Soup, 445
  Puree Mongole, 101
  Soup
   Cold Dilled, 101
   Mom's Thick, 100
Peach(es)
 -Banana Betty, 356
 Cake, Fresh, 389
 Canned
  in Juice, 436
  in Syrup, 436
 Cream, 366
  Pie, Frozen Whipped, 406
 and Cream, Poached, 358
 "Duck" Sauce, 309
 freezing, 428
 Ice Cream, 366
 Muffins, 328
 Pie, Walnut-, 401
 -Plum Preserves, 442
 Salad, Crunchy, 305
 Sauce, Fresh, 412
 Sherbet, 365
 Upside-Down Cake, 388
Peanut
 Butter
  Cookies
   -Oat, 377
   Traditional, 377
  Complements, 31
  Creamy, 31
  Gado Gado, 149
  Loaf, 44
  Pasta, 277
  value of, 14
  -Vegetable Sauce, 319
 -Buttered
  Beans and Grain, 271
  Grain, 271
 Cookies, 372
 Cream Dressing for Tropical Fruit
   Platter, 305
 Kisses, 352
 Rice, 265
 Salad, Carrot-, 293
 Sauce, Spicy, 319
 -Sesame Butter, 31
 Soup, Creole Tomato and, 107
 -Sunflower Crunch, 31
 in Sweet and Sour Sauce
  Broccoli with, 147

 Cauliflower with, 147
 see also nuts, seeds
Pear(s)
 Buttered, 61
 Cake, Country-Fresh, 387
 Caramel, 359
 Crumb-Crusted, 359
 German Bean Tzimmis, 181
 Muffins, Spiced, 328
 Salad, 304
 in Vanilla Syrup, 358
Pecan(s)
 Bananes aux Pecanes, 357
 Chip Cookies, 272
 Pie, 403
Pepper(s)
 Antipasto, 310
 Chili Rellenos, 158
  for a Crowd, 158
 and Egg Hero, 35
 freezing, 428
 Pickled Hot, 440
 preparation
  hot, 499
  sweet, 499
 Sausages, Onions, and, 198
 Sauce
  Fiery Red, 318
  Sweet Red, 318
 Stuffed
  Bread-, 157
  with Corn and Beans, 157
  Ricotta-, 156
  Italian Style, Sweet, 83
  stuffing, 156
  Tamale, 157
 see also pimiento
Peruvian Mountain Potatoes, 145
Pesto, 318
 and Slivered Cheese, Pasta with, 114
 Tomato, 319
Pickle(s)
 Basic, 439
 Bread and Butter, 439
 Dilled Green Beans, 440
 Italian Vegetable Marinade, 311
 Mixed Vegetable, 439
 Namasu, 311
 Quick, 310
  Turnip, 311
 Sweet Summer Squash, 439
 see also relish
Pickled
 Beets, 310
 Hot Peppers, 440

Pickled (*cont.*)
  Mushrooms, 66
  Turnips, Egyptian, 440
  Vegetables
    Raclette, 129
Pickling, 437–40
  about, 437–38
  equipment, 438
  ingredients, 437
  packing and processing, 438
  produce, 437
Pie(s) and pastries, 394–410
  about, 394–98
  Armenian Bean, 280
  Broccoli Custard, 225
  Canned Fruit Pie or Tarts, 402
  Cheese, 447
  Chocolate Pudding, 361
  Coconut Custard, 404
  Coleslaw, 292
  Cottage, 155
  Crumb
    Apple, 400
    Fruit, 401
  Crust
    basic instructions, 395–96
    Cheese, 400
    Cookie Dough, 398
    Crumb, 398
     Nut and, 398
    Tender, 400
    see also crust
  deep-dish or pot, 226–29
  Dutch Apple, 401
  Eggplant Ratatouille, 150
  Frozen Whipped
    Banana Cream, 406
    Peach Cream, 406
    Strawberry Cream, 405
  lattice, 396
  Lemon Meringue, 405
  Onion, 75
  Quick Creamy, 45
  Pecan, 403
  Pumpkin, 404
    Mock, 404
  single-crust, 395
  Sour Cherry, 402
  Spinach-Feta
    American, 154
    Greek, 153
  Tamale, 227
  two-crust, 396
  Walnut-Peach, 401

  see also deep-dish pies, pastries, pot pies, tarts
Pierogi
  Corn, 273
  Polish, 207
Pilaf
  Cracked Wheat, 48
  Mushroom, 49
  Oat, 265
    -Vegetable, 265
  see also pulao
Pimiento(es)
  Antipasto Peppers, 310
  -Cheese
    Dip, 47
    Spread, Olive and, 69
  Red Pepper Sauce
    Fiery, 318
    Sweet, 318
  Sauce, Creamy, 315
Pineapple
  Barbecue Sauce for Tempeh Kebabs, 175
  Buttermilk Sherbet, 365
  Chutney, 442
  -Cucumber Mold, 295
  freezing, 428
  Frozen, 352
  Hawaiian Bean Loaf, 204
  -Orange Preserves, 442
  Roast, 359
  Sherbet, 59
  Tropical Fruit Platter, 305
  Upside-Down Cake, 388
Piroshki, 281
Pissaladière Niçoise, 282
Pistou Soup, 97
Pita
  Bean
    Indian, 221
    Mexican, 221
    Mideast, 222
    Pies, Armenian, 280
    Salad, 222
    -Stuffed Pita Pockets, 221–22
  Bread, 337
Pizza
  Fresh Tomato, 33
  Individual Bean, 34
  Quick Calzone, 33
  Tempeh, 36
  Tofu, 35
Pizza(s), 219–21
  Biscuit-Crust, 220
  dough, Calzone, 221

Pizza(s) (*cont.*)
 Individual Bean, 34
 Mexican, 36
 -Style Bean, 177
 Salad, 47
 Tomato
  Fresh, 220
  Pita, Fresh, 33
  Regular, 220
 ·Topped Beans, 176
Pizzaiola, Potatoes, 142
Plain Rolls, 346
Plantain(s)
 Cake, 248
 Fried, 248
 preparation, 499
 Sopones, 182
Plum
 Chutney, Fresh, 442
 Preserves, Peach-, 442
 Tart, Viennese, 403
 see also prune-plums
Plus Pastry, 399
Poached
 Peaches and Cream, 358
 Spinach-Potato Pâté, 85
Pocket Soup, 445
Polenta, 194
 Baked, 194
 Italian-Style, 194
 Rumanian Mammaliga, 194
 with Three Cheeses, 194
Polish Pierogi, 207
Popcorn
 Balls, 349
 and Nuts, Curry, 348
Popped Corn, 348
Poppy Seed Rugelach, 380
Porotos Granados with Hot Sauce, 183
Portuguese
 Bread and Garlic Soup, 55
 Stew, 169
Pot
 of Gold Biscuits, 327
 Pie(s)
  Bean, 227
  with Biscuit Crust, Ambassador, 227
  Quick, 447
  see also deep-dish pies
Potage Bonne Femme, 92
Potato(es)
 Aioli with Vegetables, 41
 Blintzes, 214
 Colcannon, 145
 Colombian, 144

Cornish Pasties, 224
Cottage Pie, 155
Crisps, Broiler, 52
Curry
 Eggplant and, 242
 Vegetable-, 243
David's Pan Fries, 53
Dough, 206
Eggs and, 130
filling for Bite-Size Knish, 85
French Fries, 249
Fried Cabbage and, Indian Style, 237
German-Style New, 144
Greek Artichokes and Dill, 231
and Greens, 94
Hash Browns, 250
Home Fries, 249
Hot Borscht, 93
Hungarian Vegetable Gulyas, 145
Ilse's Vegetables in Cream Sauce, 142
Italian Gnocchi, 207
Knishes, 283
 Kasha, 264
 Miniature, 265
Marseilles Spinach Stew, 143
Mashed
 Basic, 248
 Surprise, 248
Mountains, 163
New England Bean Chowder, 100
Niçoise, 143
Omelet
 American, 130
 Parmentier, 131
Oven Fries, 249
Pakistani Curry, 148
Pancakes, 37
Pan-Roasted, 248
Pâté, Poached Spinach-, 85
Peruvian Mountain, 145
Pizzaiola, 142
Portuguese Stew, 169
Potage Bonne Femme, 92
preparation, 499
Pudding, 155
Raclette, 129
Salad
 American-Style, 46
 Dijon, 250
 Dutch, 304
 Ricotta, 250
Salade Niçoise, 301
Semel Bresel, 207
Soup
 Hot Leek and, 109

Potato(es) (*cont.*)
  Mashed, 94
  Senate Bean, 100
  Standard Baked, 53
  Stuffed
    Baked
      Creamy, 163
      Fluffy, 163
    Blue Cheese, 163
  sweet, *see* sweet potatoes
  Tortilla de Patatas, 130
  toppings, baked, 54
  Tunisian Sandwiches, 222
  Turnovers, Hot, 283
  Vichyssoise, 109
Poultry, storage of, 478
Pound Cake, Yogurt, 383
Preparation and cooking time, 23–24
Preservatives, chemical, 3, 476
Preserves, 441–43
  about, 441
  Fruit Butter, 441
  Peach-Plum, 442
  Pineapple-Orange, 442
  Summer Conserves, 442
Pretzels
  Crunchy, 351
  Soft, 347
Processed foods, dangers of, 3
Produce
  need for fresh, 11
  putting up, 425–43
    about, 425
    selection, 426, 431, 437
  see also fruit, vegetables
Protein
  animal vs. vegetable, 8
  Biscuits, Quick, 448
  Complement, 6, 8, 23, 111
  complementation, 7, 8, 508
    classic examples, 9
  complete, 6
  content, 23
  continuum, 7
  Cracker Bread, Quick, 448
  Crepes, Hi-, 213
  definition, 6
  -Enriched Kasha, 264
  high quality, 6
  Major, 6, 23, 111
  Minor, 6, 23, 111
  Mix, High, 448
  Muffins, Quick, 448
  need for, 6–7
  nonanimal, 7
    combining, 7–9

  principle, 5–9
  Spread, 69
  twentieth century, 6
  values
    animal, 15
    bean, 13
    grains, 12
    nuts and seeds, 14
Provolone
  Cheeson, 27
  Eggplant Cutlet, 141
  see also cheese
Prune(s)
  Dried Fruit Bars, 378
  Hamentaschen, 380
  Lima Bean Tzimmis, 180
  -Plums, Canned, in Syrup, 436
Pudding, 361–64
  about, 361
  Bread, 363
  Butterscotch, 361
  Carob, 362
  Cheese-Corn, 137
  Cheesecake, 394
  Cornmeal-Cheese, 193
  Cranberry, 357
  Date-Nut Bread, 62
  Fresh Corn, 137
  Honey-
    Chocolate, 361
    Vanilla, 361
  Indian, 364
  Lemon Sponge, 363
  Noodle
    Fruit, 122
    Savory, 122
    Sweet, 278
  Pie, Chocolate, 361
  Potato, 155
  Rice
    Baked, 363
    Top-of-the-Stove, 363
Puerto Rican
  Cabbage Salad, 292
  Dinner, 457
  Rice and Beans, 182
Puffs
  Cheese, 284
  Cream, 283, 406
  Savory Farmer, 284
  Yogurt Salad, 284
Pulao, Hindu, 266
Pumpkin
  Bread, 331
  Custard, 404
  freezing, 429

Pumpkin (*cont.*)
  Loaf, 344
  Pan Rolls, 344
  Pie, 404
  preparation, 499
  Seed Bread, 331
  Soup, 106
Punch
  Fruit, 417
  Party, 418
Puree
  Fruit, 436
  Mideast Carrot and Chick-Pea, 105
  Mongole, 101
Pureed Bean Soup, 104
Putting up produce, 425–43
  about, 425

Q

Quiche, 74
  Classic Cheese, 74
  Mexican, 128
  Mushroom, 74
  Spinach, 74
  Vegetable, 74
Quick
  Apple-Date Tarts, 406
  Barbecue Sauce, 59
  Bread(s), 325–33
    about, 325–26
    loaves, 331–33
      about, 331
    Sticks, 446
  Calzone, 33
  Cheese
    Sauce, 444
    Sticks, 450
  Cocktail Sauce, 308
  -Cooking Custard, 60
  Corn
    Biscuits, 449
    -Cheese Pancakes, 449
    Crisps, 449
    -Crusted
      Mushrooms, 450
      Tomatoes, 450
    Fritters, 450
    Muffins, 449
  Cream of Tomato Soup, 444
  Creamed
    Green Beans, 233
    Soups, 444
    Vegetables, 233
  Creamy
    Bean Soup, 92

  Onion Pie, 45
  Curried Beans, 258
  -Fried Onion Rings, 447
  Fruit Tarts, 61
  Light
    Biscuits, 446
    Muffins, 446
    Pancakes, 447
  Mexican Hot Sauce, 58
  Mixed Vegetable Soup, 90
  Mushroom Sauce, 444
    Tangy, 444
  Pickles, 310
  Pot Pie, 447
  Protein
    Biscuits, 448
    Cracker Bread, 448
    Muffins, 448
  Sauerkraut, 236
  Tofu Sticks, 450
  Tomato
    -Cheese Sauce, 444
    -Onion Soup, 90
  Turnip Pickles, 311
  Vegetable Medley, 255
  White Sauce, 444

R

Raclette, 129
Radish
  Caucasus Salad, 298
  Crisp Shredded Salad, 304
  preparation, 499
  Relish, Onion-, 297
  Salad, Chinese, 297
Raised pancakes, 208–210
Raisin(s)
  Chutney
    Cooked, 309
    Raw, 309
  Nutted Rice with, 265
  Sauce, 413
  Sauté, Onion-Apple-, 246
    Curried, 246
  Stuffed Zucchini with Cheese and, 160
  Sweet Ginger Carrots with, 238
  Tart, Apricot-, 403
Raita
  Cabbage, 293
  Carrot, 293
  Sweet, 293
Rarebit, Cheese, 37
Ratatouille, 242
  Campfire, 242
  Pie, Eggplant, 150

Ravioli, Red or White Cheese, 121
Raw
  Cranberry Relish, 66
  Creole Sauce, 309
  Onion Milk Soup, 56
  Raisin Chutney, 309
Real Whipped Cream, 412
Red
  cabbage, see cabbage
  or White Cheese Ravioli, 121
Refried Beans, 54
  with Cheese, 54
Refrigerator pantry, 474
Regular Tomato Pizza, 220
Relish
  Browned Onion, 57
  Cabbage Raita, 293
  Carrot Raita, 293
    Sweet, 293
  Chutney
    Fresh Plum, 442
    Pineapple, 442
    Raisin
      Cooked, 309
      Raw, 309
  Cranberry
    Crunchy, 309
    Raw, 66
  Green Tomato, 440
  Mideast, 294
  Onion-Radish, 297
  tray, 64
  Zucchini, 440
  see also condiments, salads, pickles
Rémoulade
  Cauliflower, 79
  Celery, 79
  Spaghetti Squash, 79
  Sprouts, 79
Restaurant(s)
  choosing, 520
  the friendly, 522
  health food, 520
  ordering suggestions, 521
  wholefoods, 523
Reuben, Veggie, 35
Revisionist Dressing, 57
Rhubarb
  freezing, 428
  Pie, Deep-Dish Strawberry-, 401
Rice
  Arroz con Queso, 189
  Balls, Baked, 201
  and Beans
    Cold Corn, 269
    Puerto Rican, 182

and Blue Cheese, Baked, 189
  with Cabbage and Cheese, 189
Cheeseburgers, 197
Cheese-Stuffed Cabbage, 165
Chinese-Style Fried, 120
-Corn Muffins, 329
Creamy Tahini, 268
Croquettes, Italian, 201
Crust, Baked, 228
Dirty, 267
with Egg and Lemon, 268
Fejoida, 184
Fried Dumplings
  Chinese, 286
  Italian, 286
Garden, 267
Greek
  Eggplant, 266
  Spinach, 266
  with Green Beans,
    Aromatic, 266
Hindu Pulao, 266
Hoppin' John, 178
Kedgeree, 186
Kitchree, 187
Kosheri, 187
Nasi Goreng, 121
-Nut Loaf, 205
Paella, 190
  Soyfood, 190
Pancakes, 38
Patties, 268
Peanut, 265
Peanut Butter Loaf, 44
Pudding
  Baked, 363
  Top-of-the-Stove, 363
  with Raisins, Nutted, 265
-a-Roni," Brown, 49
Salad
  Basic, 269
  Creamy, 269
  with Snow Peas, 267
Soup
  Italian Cabbage and, 97
  Thick Tomato, 93
Spanish, 270
-Style Chick-Peas, 177
Stuffed
  Cabbage Stroganoff, 165
  Chapatis, 284
  with Chilies, Green, 188
Sushi, 268
and Vegetables, Woodstock, 188
Viennese, 265
see also grains

Rich
  Almond Cookies, 376
  Cake Sauce, 413
  Parsley Dressing, 288
  Walnut Cookies, 376
Ricotta
  American Wholefoods Broccoli Hol-
    landaise, 235
  Baked Spinach and, 153
  Calzone, 221
    Quick, 33
  Confetti Pasta, 118
  Cream
    Banana, 366
    Peach, 366
    Strawberry, 366
  -Cucumber Salad, 46
  Frozen Whipped
    Banana Cream Pie, 406
    Peach Cream Pie, 406
    Strawberry Cream Pie, 405
  Green Linguine
    with Red Mushroom Sauce, 114
    with White Mushroom Sauce, 113
  Noodles, 276
  Pasta
    with Creamy Spinach, 113
    with Green Beans Alfredo-Style, 115
  Potato Salad, 250
  Ravioli, Red or White Cheese, 121
  -Spinach Dumplings, 127
  -Stuffed Peppers, 156
  Topping, Whipped, 411
  Torte, 75
  Tortoni, 59
  see also cheese, cottage cheese
Rising
  of yeast bread, 335
  warm water bath, 335
Rissoles, Mushroom, 202
Roast(ed)
  Chestnuts, 350
  Chick-Peas, 349
  Pineapple, 359
Rollatini, Eggplant, 162
Rolled Omelet Slices, 73
Rolls and Buns
  Braided, 338
  Burger Buns, 346
  Butterflies, 346
  Cinnamon, 345
    Buns, 407
  Cloverleaf, 338, 345
  Crescents, 346
  Crusty, 345
    Sandwich, 343

Dough, Basic, 345
  English Muffins, 343
  Finger, 345
  Herbed Oat, 339
  Hero, 340
  Parker House, 446
  Plain, 346
  Pumpkin Pan, 344
  Spicy Cheese, 72
  Spring Lettuce, 83
  Squash, 344
  Steamed Egg, 73
  Vegetable, 280
Roulade, Zucchini, 73
Rugelach
  Fruit-Nut, 380
  Poppy Seed, 380
Rumanian Mammaliga, 194
Russian
  Beets, 234
  Vegetable Turnovers, 281
Rutabagas, turnips and, preparation,
  499
Rye
  Bread Sticks, 347
  Burgers, 36
  Flatbreads, 321
  Muffins, Sunflower-, 329
  -Oat Pastry, 229
  -Wheat Thins, 321

S

Salad(s), 291–305
  Avocado
    Bean, 261
    Stuffed, 32
      Hot, 32
      Mexican, 32
  Bar, 31
  Barley
    Creamy, 269
    Steamed, 263
  Bean
    -Cheese, 261
    and Corn, Mexican, 304
    Greek, 262
    Pita, 222
    Three-, 65
  Beet
    with Blue Cheese, 292
    Cold, 292
  Broccoli
    Stalk, 235
    Steamed, 235

Salad(s) (cont.)
  Cabbage
    Puerto Rican, 292
    Raita, 293
  Caesar, 296
  Carrot
    -Cabbage-Bean, 303
    -Peanut, 293
    Peas, and Cheese, 303
    Raita, 293
    Sweet, 293
  Caucasus, 298
  Cauliflower Dinner, 295
  Cheese
    and Greens, 296
    with Walnut Dressing, 296
  Chef's Special, 31
  Chick-Pea, 29
  Chinese Radish, 297
  Cold Corn, Rice, and Beans, 269
  Coleslaw
    Country, 292
    Greek, 292
    Pie, 292
    Tangy, 46
  Crisp Shredded, 304
  Crunchy Peach, 305
  Cucumber(s)
    with Creamy Cottage Cheese, 294
    Cuchumber, 294
    Marinated, 65
    Mousse, 294
    with Spicy Dressing, 294
  Deli-Style Health, 301
  and dressings, 286–305
    about, 286–87
  Dutch, 304
  fine points in making, 286–87
  French Pasta, 278
  Fruit
    Creamy Dinner, 305
    Favorite, 60
    Platter, Tropical, 305
    Winter, 359
  Greek Country, 32
  Green Beans
    with Cottage Cheese, Marinated, 291
    and Tomato, 291
  Guacamole, 46
  India, with Curry Dressing, 302
  Israeli, 302
  Julienne Vegetables and Cheese, 303
  Kidney Bean Luncheon, 28
  Lemon Greens, 295
  Lima Bean-Egg, 28

  Macaroni, 48
    and Cheese, 48
  Mideast
    Chick-Pea, 261
    Relish, 294
  Mushroom
    and Barley, 264
    French, 297
  Niçoise, 301
  Olive-Bean, 29
  Onion-Radish Relish, 297
  Orange
    -Section, 296
    -Wheat, 270
  Pasta
    Artichokes and Chick-Peas with
      Lemon Dressing, 278
    Cold with Tomato Dressing, 48
  Pear, 304
  Pineapple-Cucumber Mold, 295
  Pizza, 47
  Platter(s), 31–32
    Oriental, 302
  Potato
    American-Style, 46
    Dijon, 250
    Ricotta, 250
  pre-washed, 486
  Puffs, Yogurt, 284
  Rice
    Basic, 269
    Creamy, 269
  Ricotta-Cucumber, 46
  Schoolhouse, 79
  Soup, Blender, 56
  Spinach, 298
    -Bean Sprout, 298
    Main Dish, 298
    Toasted Seeds and, 298
    Wilted, 299
    -Yogurt, 299
  Steamed, 296
  Sweet and Sour Sprouts, 64
  Tabouli, 302
  Tempeh Sandwich, 175
  Thousand Island, 78
  Tofu
    Antipasto, 86
    "Chicken," 30
    "Egg," 30
  Tomato
    and Cucumber, Greek, 300
    Italian, 299
    -Mushroom, 297
    Pachadi, 300

Salad(s) (*cont.*)
  Slices with Sweet-and-Sour Onion
      Dressing, 300
  Stuffed, 32
  Turkish Country, 301
  Turnip Slaw, 300
  uses of, 17
  Vegetable Cottage Cheese, 47
  Vegetables à la Grecque, 78
  Virgin Mary, 300
  Waldorf, 304
  Yogurt
    -Cucumber, 293
    Squash, 299
  Zucchini Sticks, Marinated, 66
Salad dressing, *see* dressings
Salade Niçoise, 301
Salpicon, Filled Croustades with, 80
Salsa Cruda, 308
  Spicy, 308
Salt, cooking with, 24
Sambal, Coconut, 310
Sandwich(es)
  Antipasto Heroes, 28
  Avocado-Cheese Melt, 34
  Bean-Stuffed Pita Pockets, 221–22
  C & C, 27
  CLT, 27
  Cheese Rarebit, 37
  cold, 27–31
  Curried Vegetable, 42
  French-Toasted Cheese, 34
  Grilled Open-Face Tofu, 35
  hot
    and entrées, 33–46
  Open-Faced
    Tempeh, 174
    Tofu "Turkey," 168
  Pan Bagnia, 222
  Pepper and Egg Hero, 35
  Quick Calzone, 33
  Salad, Tempeh, 175
  Sealed, 223
  Sloppy Beans, 44
  Souffléed Cheese, 34
  Spiedini, 71
  Tempeh Pita, 36
  Tofu Pita, 35
  Tunisian, 222
  Veggie Reuben, 35
  see also spreads
Sangria, Virgin, 418
Sanitation of kitchen utensils, 482–83
Sanitizing solution, 482
Sauces and gravies, 312–19
  about, 312

Balls, Instant, 315
Bean-Cheese, 37
Béchamel, 313
Blueberry, 412
Caper, 72
Carob Fudge, 413
Cheese, 313
  Double, 58
Chili, 308
Chunky Pasta, 58
Cranberry, 309
Creamy
  Lemon Butter, 81
  Pimiento, 315
Dipping, for Steamed Artichokes, 81
"Duck," 307
Enchilada, 317
Fiery, 309
  Red Pepper, 318
Foamy Custard, 413
Fresh
  Peach, 412
  Strawberry, 412
Hot, for Porotos Granados, 183
Marinara, 316
Mix
  Mushroom, 444
  White, 443
Mushroom, 314
  Quick, 444
  Tangy, 444
New American Creamy Tomato, 317
No-Cook Cold Cheese, 319
for Noodles with Sesame Paste, 278
Onion, 314
Oriental Dipping, 307
Peanut Butter-Vegetable, 319
Pesto, 318
  Tomato, 319
Pineapple Barbecue for Tempeh
    Kebabs, 175
Quick
  Barbecue, 59
  Cocktail, 308
  Cheese, 444
  Mexican Hot, 58
  Tomato-Cheese, 444
Raisin, 413
Raw Creole, 309
Rich Cake, 413
Salsa Cruda, 308
Spicy
  Peanut, 319
  Salsa, 308
starch-thickened, 312–15

Sauces and gravies (*cont.*)
 Sweet
  Chinese Dipping, 307
  Red Pepper, 318
 Spicy Tunisian, 309
 Tahini, 200
 Tartar, 308
 Tomato
  about, 315
  Emergency Mexican, 58
  15-Minute Italian, 58
  freezing, 430
  Green, 431
  Italian, 317
  Light Fresh, 316
  -Mushroom Burger, 318
 Velouté, 313
 White, 313
  Quick, 444
 Yogurt
  for Dahi Vaddi, 88
  -Tahini, 319
 see also gravy
Sauerkraut, Quick, 236
Sausages, Bean, 198
 Onions and Peppers, 198
Sautéed
 Cucumbers, 240
 Mushrooms, 245
Savory
 Cracker Crumb Crust, 46
 Farmer Puffs, 284
 Grain Crackers, 271
 Noodle Pudding, 122
 Nut Butter, 306
 Onion Corn Bread, 330
 pastry(ies), 218–29
  about, 218
  accompaniments, 279–86
   about, 279
 Smoky Tofu, 169
 Soy Crust, 228
Scallion, preparation, 499
Schoolhouse Salad, 79
Scotch Oat Shortbread, 373
Scrambled Eggs with Tomatoes, 131
Sealed Sandwiches, 223
Seasoning(s)
 about, 24
 grains, 262
 savory, for pantry, 473
Seed(s)
 Cakes, Native American, 324
 mail order suppliers for sprouts, 425
 and Spinach Salad, Toasted, 298
 see also nuts and specific seeds

Seltzer Fizz, 417
Semel Bresel, 207
Senate
 Bean Soup, 100
 Select Committee on Nutrition and Human Needs, 1
Senegalese Soup, 110
Sesame
 -Bean Pâté, 29
 Bread
  Garlic-, 49
  Parsley-, 49
 Butter, Peanut-, 31
 Cream, Whipped Orange-, 412
 Gomasio, 306
 Paste, Noodles with, 277
 see also tahini
Shallots, preparation, 499
Sharp Cheese and Tomato Spread, 69
Shells, Bean Patty, 229
 see also crust, dough, pastry
Shepherd's Pie, 155
Sherbet
 Buttermilk, 365
 Honey-Lemon Milk, 365
 Peach, 365
 Pineapple, 59
Shish Kebab in a Bag, 242
 see also kebabs
Shortbread, 373
 Scotch Oat, 373
 Squares, Walnut Date-Topped, 374
Shortcake
 Fruit, 388
 Onion, 228
Shortening, in baking, 368
Short-order
 cooking, 26–62
  about, 26
 kitchen, 13
 utensils for, 13
Side dishes, 230–305
 about, 230
 short order, 46–50
Simple
 Vegetable Stir-Fry, 255
 wholefoods dinners, 451–52
Skillet
 Corn, Chilies, and Cheese, 43
 Stew, 42
 Vegetables with Yogurt and Cheese, 140
Sliced Baked Beets, 234
Sloppy Beans, 44
Smorgasbord, Mideast, 200

Smothered
  Cauliflower, 232
  Jerusalem Artichokes, 232
Snacks, 348–53
  about, 348
  Coconut Kisses, 352
  Crunchy Pretzels, 351
  Frozen
    Banana Pops, 352
    Juicicles, 352
    Pineapple, 352
  Fudge, 352
  Granola Bars, 351
  Halvah, 352
  Nuts
    Beer, 350
    Chili, 350
    Curry, 350
    Dry-Roasted, 350
    Soy, 349
      Roasted, 350
  Peanut Kisses, 352
  Popcorn
    Balls, 349
    and Nuts, Curry, 348
  Popped Corn, 348
  Roasted
    Chestnuts, 350
    Chick-Peas, 349
  "Snacks," 349
Snails, 408
Snowpeas, Rice with, 267
Soft
  Cheese Dressing, 287
  Oatmeal Cookies, 378
  Pretzels, 347
Sopones, 182
Soufflé(s)
  about, 137
  Cheese, 138
  Mushroom, 138
Souffléed Cheese Sandwich, 34
Soup(s), 54–56, 89–110
  about, 89
  African Bean, 103
  Anabella's Oatmeal, 97
  Black Bean, 102
  Blender Salad, 56
  Borscht
    Cold Creamy, 110
    with Cucumber, 109
    Hot, 93
  Broccoli
    Bread and Cheese, 95
    and Macaroni, 95

Carrot, 141
  Golden, 100
Cauliflower-Cheese Chowder, 94
  with Creamy Cheese, Celery, 106
Cheddar, 98
Chinese
  Greens in Broth, 91
  Hot and Sour, 107
Cold, 108–110
  Curry-Apple, 110
  Dilled Pea, 101
convenience, 90–92
Cream of
  Mushroom, 99
  Spinach, 99
Creamed Corn, 56
Creamy Lima Bean, 104
Creole Tomato and Peanut, 107
Deluxe Mushroom-Barley, 97
Egg Drop, 55
everyday, 92–104
French
  Mushroom, 105
  Onion, 96
    -Country Style, 96
Fresh Tomato, 93
Gazpacho, 108
  White, 108
Greek Lentil, 101
" 'n Greens" Cubes, 428
Instant, 54
  Asopa, 91
Italian
  Cabbage and Rice, 97
  Chilled Tomato, 108
  Lentil, 101
  Mushroom, 105
Leek
  and Cheddar, 99
  and Potato, Hot, 109
Mashed Potato, 94
Mideast Carrot and Chick-Pea Puree,
  105
Mexican
  Bean, 103
  Corn, 98
  Macaroni and Bean, 102
Minestrone, 96
  Genovese, 96
Mixed Vegetable, 434
Mom's Thick Split-Pea, 100
Moroccan Yogurt, 109
Mulligatawny, 102
New England Bean Chowder, 100
Okra Chowder, 94
Pasta Fagioli, 102

Soup(s) (*cont.*)
Pistou, 97
Pocket, 445
Portuguese Bread and Garlic, 55
Potage Bonne Femme, 92
Potato and Greens, 94
Pumpkin, 106
Puree Mongole, 101
Pureed Bean, 104
Quick
Cream(ed), 444
of Tomato, 444
Creamy Bean, 92
Mixed Vegetable, 90
Tomato-Onion, 90
Raw Onion Milk, 56
Senate Bean, 100
Spanish Garlic, 91
specialty, 105–107
Stracciatella, 91
Tamari Broth, 55
thickeners, 89–90
Thick Tomato Rice, 93
Vegetable, 92
Barley, 92
Vichyssoise, 109
Watercress, 109
Wild Green, 109
Sour
Cherry Pie, 402
Cream
Fresh Tomato-Filled Crepes, 214
Ilse's Vegetables in Cream Sauce, 142
Tofu, 289
South American medley, 458
Southern-Fried Tofu, 167
Soy
Biscuits, 326
Crust, Savory, 228
flour, 508
nutritional components, 508
Muffins, All-, 329
Nuts, 349
-Roasted, 350
-Sesame Dressing, for Spinach-Bean
Sprout Salad, 298
Whipped Cream, 411
-Whole Wheat Noodles, 276
Soyballs, 199
Soybeans
Chopped Eggplant Steak, 195
Oriental, 259
Party Mousse, 87
Soyburgers, 196
Onion, 196

Soyfood Paella, 190
Spaghetti
with Eggplant Sauce, 116
Fantasy, 118
Frittata, 134
with Garlic, 277
Roast, 205
Squash
Basic Steamed, 253
Brined, 435
Italian Stuffed, 159
Rémoulade, 79
Stew, Italian, 113
with Zucchini Sauce, 116
see also pasta
Spanish
Garlic Soup, 91
Omelet, 133
Rice, 270
-Style Chick-Peas, 177
supper, 457
Wheat, 270
Super, 270
Sparkling water, 417
Specialty soups, 105–107
Spice(s)
Cake, Yogurt, 382
Cookies, Light, 372
Frosting, 414
herbs and, for pantry, 473
Spiced
Bean Sprouts, for Noodles with Sesame
Paste, 277
Cabbage, 236
Green Beans, 232
Onions, for Peruvian Mountain Pota-
toes, 145
Pear Muffins, 328
Spinach, 250
Spicy
Bean Curd, 169
Bread Meat, 206
Cheese Rolls and Cheese Truffles, 72
Peanut Sauce, 319
Salsa, 308
Tomato Dressing and Cocktail Mari-
nade, 76
Tunisian Sauce, 309
Spiedini, 71
Spinach
Baked Eggs Florentine, 136
-Bean Sprout Salad, 298
and Chick-Peas with Feta, 178
Crepes, 212
Mushroom-, 213

Spinach (*cont.*)
  Dumplings, Ricotta-, 127
  and Feta, Baked, 153
  -Feta
    Casserole, Top-Crusted, 154
    Pie
      American, 154
      Greek, 153
  Frittata, Italian, 134
  -Noodle Casserole, 121
  Pasta with Creamy, 113
  -Potato Pâté, Poached, 85
  Quiche, 74
  Rice, Greek, 266
  and Ricotta Baked, 153
  Salad, 298
    Main Dish, 298
    Toasted Seeds and, 298
    Wilted, 299
  Soup, Cream of, 99
  Spiced, 250
  Stew, Marseilles, 143
  White Lasagne, 124
  -Yogurt Salad, 299
Split peas, *see* peas
Spoilage, signs of in home-canned foods,
    443
Sponge
  method in yeast bread, 334
  Tarts, Almond, 383
  Torte, Almond, 383
Spread
  Bread and, 50
  Celery Cheddar, 30
  Cheese
    -Nut, 69
    and Tomato
      Mild, 36
      Sharp, 69
  Curry Cashew, 69
  Israeli Eggplant, 68
  Olive and Pimiento Cheese, 69
  Protein, 69
  Tofu Cream Cheese and Vegetables, 69
  Vegetable Cottage Cheese, 47
  see also pâté, dips
Spring Lettuce Rolls, 83
Spritz Cookies, 376
Sprouts
  growing, 422–25
    about, 422–23
    equipment, 423
    jar sprouting, 424
    mail order seed suppliers, 425
    step-by-step, 423
    strainer, 424

Rémoulade, 79
  Sweet and Sour, 64
  using, 425
Squash
  Basque Country Stew, 180
  Blossoms, Stuffed, 71
  and Carrots, Lemon, 253
  Chick-Peas on the Half Shell, 161
  Herbed, 253
  Loaf, 344
  Pickles, Sweet Summer, 439
  preparation
    hard rind, 499
    soft rind, 499
  Rolls, 344
  Stuffed Winter, 252
  Sunflower, 252
  Sweet Baked, 252
  Turkish, 159
  Yogurt, 299
  see also zucchini, spaghetti squash
Standard
  Baked Potato, 53
  Pastry, 399
  sauce base for starch-thickened sauces,
    313
  Whole Wheat Bread, 337
Staples, dry, storage of, 481
Starch-thickened sauces, 312–15
Steak
  Cheese, 125
  Chopped Eggplant, 195
Steam
  canner, 432
  blanching, 429
  cooking with, 489
Steamed
  Apples, 60
  Artichokes with Dipping Sauce, 81
  Barley, 263
    Salad, 263
  Beets, 234
  Broccoli, 50
    Salad, 235
  Brussels Sprouts, 236
  Chinese Dumplings, 83
  Egg Rolls, 73
  Eggplant Noodles, 243
  Greens, 244
  Salad, 296
  Vegetables
    with Cheese, 41
    with Salsa Cruda, 256
Sterilizing equipment for canning, 432
Stew
  Basque Country, 180

Stew (cont.)
Carrot, 141
Bean-, 141
Hungarian Vegetable Gulyas, 145
Italian Spaghetti, 113
Marseilles Spinach, 143
Mushroom-Vegetable, 314
Portuguese, 169
Skillet, 42
Sopones, 182
Stewed
Artichokes, Italian Style, 230
Frozen Tomatoes, 429
Stir-
Fried
Broccoli with Garlic, 233
Greens, Chinese Style, 244
Green Beans with Garlic, 233
Fry(ing), 490
Main Dish, 42
Steamed Vegetables, 50
Storage
appropriate places, 476
at a glance, 477–81
food handling and, 476–83
of home-canned foods, 434
kitchen and pantry, 476–82
warning signs, 482
Stove-Top
Macaroni and Cheese, 112
Stuffing, 263
vegetables, 139–49
about, 139
Stracciatella, 91
Strawberry
Cream, 366
Pie, Frozen Whipped, 405
Ice, 364
Cream, Fresh, 366
-Rhubarb Pie, Deep-Dish, 401
Sauce, Fresh, 412
Yogurt, Frozen, 364
Streusel Coffee Cake, 390
Stroganoff
Stuffed Cabbage, 165
Tofu, 170
Strudel, Vegetable, 224
Stuffed
Artichoke, 82
Avocado Salad, 32
Hot, 32
Mexican, 32
Baked Potatoes
Fluffy, 163
Creamy, 163

Blue Cheese Potatoes, 163
Cabbage
Cheese-, 165
or Grape Leaves, Greek, 82
Stroganoff, 165
Sweet and Sour, 164
Chapatis, 284
Chick-Peas on the Half Shell, 161
Chili Rellenos, 158
for a Crowd, 158
Clam Shells Areganata, 86
Eggplant, 161
Manicotti, 162
Rollatini, 162
Lemon Eggs, 72
Lettuce, Sweet and Sour, 165
Peppers
Bread-, 157
with Corn and Beans, 157
Ricotta, 156
Sweet, Italian Style, 83
Tamale, 157
Squash
Blossoms, 71
Spaghetti, Italian, 159
Turkish, 159
Tomato
Cold, 47
Salad, 32
vegetable entrées, 156–66
Winter Squash, 252
Zucchini
with Cheese and Raisins, 160
Rounds, 160
Stuffing
Bread, 262
cabbage, 164
Mix, 263
Crumb Coating and, 505
Italian, 505
peppers, 156
Stove-Top, 263
Succotash, 240
Sugar substitutes in baking, 367
Summer
Conserve, 442
Fruit Cobbler, 360
Squash Pickles, Sweet, 439
Vegetables
with Cheese, Baked, 152
Stir-Steamed, 50
Sun Butter, 306
Sunflower
Crunch, Peanut-, 31

Sunflower (*cont.*)
-Date Cookies, 372
-Rye Muffins, 329
Seeds
  Carrots with, 238
  Cheese Croquettes, 128
  Overstuffed Mushrooms, 76
  Pear Salad, 304
  Vegetable Crumb Sauté, 256
  Waldorf Salad, 304
Squash, 252
Super
-Quick Creamed Green Beans with
    Cashews, 444
Spanish Wheat, 270
Surprise Mashed Potatoes, 248
Sushi Rice, 268
Swedish Bean Balls, 199
Sweet
  Baked Squash, 252
  Carrot Raita, 293
  Chinese Dipping Sauce, 307
  Corn Muffins, 329
  Ginger Carrots with Raisins, 238
  Noodle Pudding, 278
  Potatoes and/or Yams
    Baked, 54
    Candied, 252
    Casserole, Orange-, 251
    Cheddar-Stuffed, 251
    Far East, 251
    preparation, 500
  Red Pepper Sauce, 318
-and-Sour
  Onion Dressing, Tomato Slices with,
    300
  Polynesian Tofu, 171
  Sauce, with Peanuts
    Broccoli in, 147
    Cauliflower in, 147
  Sprouts, 64
  Stuffed
    Cabbage, 164
    Lettuce, 165
  and Spicy Dressing, 288
  Stuffed Peppers, Italian Style, 83
  Summer Squash Pickles, 439
Sweeteners
  in baking, 367
  for pantry, 473
  storage of, 479
Syrup
  Carob, 413
  Chocolate, 413

T

Table of
  Food Weights and Measures, 512–19
    beans, 517
    dairy products, 518–19
    fruit, 515–16
    grains, 517–18
    nuts and seeds, 518
    vegetables, 512–15
  Metric Equivalents, 511
  Specific Vegetable Preparation, 497–
    500
Tabouli, 302
Tacos
  Bean, 36
  Fried, 217
  with Special Bean Filling, 218
Tahini
  Baba Ghanouj, 68
  Beans, Cold, 48
  Bread and Spread, 50
  Chick-Peas with Gravy, 258
  Custard, 362
  Dressing, Lemon-, 290
  Garlic Sesame Bread, 49
  Gravy, 314
  Greek Lenten Cake, 391
  Halvah, 352
  Hummus, 68
  Noodles with Sesame Paste, 277
  Peanut-Sesame Butter, 31
  Protein Spread, 69
  Rice, Creamy, 268
  Sauce
    for Falafel, 200
    Yogurt, 319
  Sesame Bean Pâté, 29
  value of, 14
  see also sesame
Tamale
  Peppers, 157
  Pie, 227
Tamari Broth, 55
Tangy
  Coleslaw, 46
  Quick Mushroom Sauce, 444
Tart(s)
  about, 397
  Almond Sponge, 383
  Apricot-Raisin, 403
  Canned Fruit Pie or, 402
  Carrot, 75
  Fresh Fruit, 402
    with Cheese Filling, 402
  Filled Croustades with Salpicon, 80

Tart(s) (*cont.*)
Quick
Apple-Date, 406
Fruit, 61
Shells, Cookie Dough, 399
tins, French, 396
Viennese Plum, 403
Tartar Sauce, 308
Tea, Herb, 419
Techniques
basic
bean cookery, 500–502
cooking, 487–507
grain cookery, 503–505
cooking with
steam, 498
tofu, 502–503
crumbs and croutons, 505
egg handling, 506–507
how to
measure, 487–89
stir-fry, 490
nut and seed meals, 505–506
preparing vegetables, 493–500
proper, for baking, 368–69
shallow and deep-fat frying, 490–93
Tempeh, 173–75
about, 133
Burgers, 174
Kebabs
with Pineapple Barbecue Sauce, 175
with Tomato Barbecue Sauce, 175
Main Dish Stir-Fry, 42
Parmesan, 174
Pita, 35
Sandwich
Hot Open-Face, 174
Salad, 174
Soyfood Paella, 190
Tempura
All-Vegetable, 172
Cheese-Vegetable, 172
Japanese Batter for, 171
No-Egg Batter for, 172
Tofu-Vegetable, 171
Tender Pie Crust, 400
Thick
Creamy Blue Cheese Dressing, 57
Fudge Frosting and Filling, 416
Shake, 419
Tomato Rice Soup, 93
Thickeners for soup, 89
Thousand Island
Dressing, 289
Salad, 78
Three-Bean Salad, 65

Timetable for cooking
dried beans, 501
grains, 504
Toast, Parmesan, 49
Toasted
Noodles, 52
Seeds and Spinach Salad, 298
Tofu, 166–73
about, 166, 502–503
Antipasto Salad, 86
Baked Vegetable, 128
Balls, Italian, 127
"Chicken" Salad, 30
Confetti Pasta, 118
Cream Cheese and Vegetables, 69
Curry, Vegetable-, 149
Deviled, 30
"Egg" Salad, 30
freezing, 503
reconstituting, 503
frozen, 485
Gado Gado, 149
Garlic Dressing, Creamy, 290
Hot Open-Faced Tofu "Turkey" Sandwiches, 168
à la King, 168
Main Dish Stir-Fry, 42
Mayonnaise, 289
with Onions and Cheese, 167
Onion Shortcake, 225
Outdoor Mixed Grill, 173
Oven-Fried, 167
Pita, 35
Portuguese Stew, 169
pressing, 502–503
Sandwich, Grilled Open-Face, 35
Savory Smoky, 169
Shish Kebab in a Bag, 242
Sour Cream, 289
Soyfood Paella, 190
Southern-Fried, 167
Spicy Bean Curd, 169
Sticks, Quick, 450
storage of, 478
Stroganoff, 170
Sweet and Sour Polynesian, 171
and Vegetables, Barbecued, 170
value of, 13
Vegetable
Kebabs, 172
Tempura, 171
Toll-Free Cookies, 372
Tomato(es)
Atlantic Avenue Green Beans, 233
Baked Parsley, 254
-Bean Pâté, 29

Tomato(es) (*cont.*)
Blender Salad Soup, 56
Broth and Drained Tomato Pulp, 430
Canned, 434
Carrot
Gravy, 141
Soup, 141
Stew, 141
Cashew Gravy, 314
Casserole, Layered, 45
Catsup, 435
Touch-of-Honey, 308
-Cheese Biscuits, 326
with Chèvre, 254
Cold Stuffed, 47
Cubes, 430
and Cucumber Salad, Greek, 300
Dressing
and Cocktail Marinade, Spicy, 76
Cold Pasta with, 48
Creamy, 290
Light
French, 57
Italian, 57
Mexican, 57
Eggplant Ratatouille Pie, 150
-Filled Crepes, Fresh, 214
freezing, 428
Frozen
Stewed, 428
Whole, 428
Gazpacho, 108
Greek Stuffed, 255
Green, 430
Fried, 254
Mince Filling, 443
Relish, 440
Sauce, 431
Green Linguine with Red Mushroom
Sauce, 114
Huevos Rancheros, 131
Italian
Cheese Melt with Ceci, 128
Macaroni and Cheese, 112
Spaghetti Stew, 113
Juice
Cabbage Noodles in Tomato Broth,
237
Dressing, No-Oil, 288
Mexican
Cheese Melt with Corn, 129
Vegetables, 147
Mixed Vegetable Soup, 434
Mozzarella-Stuffed, 52
-Mushroom
Burger Sauce, 318

Salad, 297
Omelet, French, 133
-Onion Soup, Quick, 90
Pachadi, 300
Pasta with Green Beans, 115
and Peanut Soup, Creole, 107
Pesto, 319
Bean Pistou, 259
Pizza
Biscuit-Crust, 220
Fresh, 220
Pita, 33
Regular, 220
Portuguese Stew, 169
Potatoes
Niçoise, 143
Pizzaiola, 142
preparation, 500
Puree, 429
Mongole, 101
Quick Corn-Crusted, 450
Ratatouille, 242
Campfire, 242
Salad
Green Bean and, 291
Italian, 299
Stuffed, 32
Sauce, 315–18
about, 315
Cheese, Quick, 444
Chunky Pasta, 58
for Eggplant Rollatini, 162
Emergency Mexican, 58
Enchilada, 317
Fiery, 309
15-Minute Italian, 58
freezing, 430
Italian, 317
Light Fresh, 316
Marinara, 316
Mushroom-, 316
New American Creamy, 317
Raw Creole, 309
Salsa Cruda, 308
Spicy
Peanut, 319
Tunisian, 309
Scrambled Eggs with, 131
Shells, 40
Slices with Sweet-and-Sour Onion
Dressing, 300
Smothered Jerusalem Artichokes, 232
Soup
Fresh, 93
Italian Chilled, 108

Tomato(es) (*cont.*)
  Quick Cream of, 444
  -Rice, Thick, 93
Spanish
  Rice, 270
  -Style Chick-Peas, 177
  Wheat, 270
    Super, 270
Spread
  Mild Cheese and, 30
  Sharp Cheese and, 69
Tamale Peppers, 157
Vegetables Mozzarella, 140
Virgin Mary Salad, 300
Top
  -Crusted Spinach-Feta Casserole, 154
  -of-the-Stove Rice Pudding, 363
Topping(s)
  Baked Meringue, 363
  for Baked Potatoes, 54
  Rich Crumb, Vegetables with, 51
Torte
  Almond Sponges, 383
  Ricotta, 75
Tortilla(s)
  Broccoli Tostados, 37
  Chalupas, 36
  Cheese Enchiladas, 217
  Cornmeal, 323
  Mexican
    Omelet, 135
    Quiche, 128
  de Patatas, 130
  Pyramid, 37
  Tacos
    Bean, 36
    Fried, 217
    with Special Bean Filling, 218
Tortoni, 59
Torula yeast, *see* nutritional yeast
Tostados, Broccoli, 37
Touch-of-Honey Catsup, 308
Traditional Peanut Butter Cookies, 377
"Trail Mix," *see* "Snacks"
Traveling, bring-along food, 522
Tricks, energy-saving, 487
Tropical Fruit Platter, 305
Truffles, Cheese, 72
Tunisian
  Sandwiches, 222
  Sauce, Spicy, 309
"Turkey" Sandwiches, Hot Open-Faced
    Tofu, 168
Turkish
  Country Salad, 301
  Squash, 159

Turnip(s)
  Crisp Shredded Salad, 304
  Egyptian Pickled, 440
  Pickles, Quick, 311
  and rutabagas, preparation, 500
  Slaw, 300
Turnovers
  about, 397
  Apple, 406
  Bean Pastry, 282
  Bread, with Cheese, 279
  Consum, 285
  Cornish Pasties, 224
  Empanadas, 282
  Russian Vegetable, 281
  Sealed Sandwiches, 223
  Stuffed Chapatis, 284
  "Twinkie"
    Giant, 383
    Individual, 384
Two-Tone Mexican Beans, 259
Tzimmis
  German Bean, 181
  Lima Bean, 180

U

U.S. Surgeon General, 1
Upside-Down Cake
  Apricot, 388
  Peach, 388
  Pineapple, 388
Utensils
  for short-order kitchen, 26

V

Vanilla
  Cookies, 372
  Custard, Baked, 362
  Pudding, Honey-, 361
Variety, need for, 4
Vegetable(s)
  accompaniments, 230–57
    about, 230
  Aioli with, 41
  with Apricot Sauce, 146
  appetizers, 76
  Barbecued Tofu and, 170
  Casserole, Italian, 154
  Cheese
    Baked, 127
    with, Baked Summer, 152
    Curry, 148

Vegetable(s) (*cont.*)
  and, Julienne, 303
  with, Steamed, 41
  -Vegetable-Barley Bake, 154
  Chop Suey, 119
  cleaning, 494
  Cocktail, 417
  cookery, short order, 50–54
  cooking time, 496
  Cottage Cheese, 47
  in Cream Sauce, Ilse's, 142
  with Curry Cream, 41
  Crumb Sauté, 256
  cutting, 494–496
  Derma, 80
  Eggplant Ratatouille Pie, 150
  entrées
    baked, 149–56
    stove-top, 139–49
    stuffed, 156–66
  Filled Croustades with Salpicon, 80
  Gado Gado, 149
  à la Grecque, 78
  Hollandaise, 235
  Hot Dressed, 51
  Gulyas, Hungarian, 145
  Kebabs, 172
  Main Dish Stir-Fry, 42
  with Mandarin Pancakes, Mu Shu, 216
  Marinade, Italian, 311
  Mashed Combination, 256
  Medley, Quick, 255
  Mexican, 147
  for minimal pantry, 475
  Mozzarella, 140
  Omelet, Baked, 136
  Pakistani Curry, 148
  for pantry
    canned, 472
    fresh, 472
  Pâté, Nanette's, 67
  peeling, 493
  Pickles, Mixed, 439
  Pie, Muffin-Topped Deep-Dish, 226
  Pilaf, Oat-, 265
  -Potato Curry, 242
  precooked, 486
  preparation, 493–500
    conserving flavor and food value, 493
    general directions for, 494–96
    table of specific, 497–500
  Quick Creamed, 233
  Ratatouille, 242
    Campfire, 242
  for refrigerator pantry, fresh, 474
  with Rich Crumb Topping, 51
  Roast, 203
  Rolls, 280
  with Salsa Cruda, Steamed, 256
  Sauce, Peanut Butter-, 319
  Shish Kebab in a Bag, 242
  Skillet Stew, 42
  with Soufflé Sauce, 150
  Soup, 92
    Barley, 92
    Mixed, 434
    Quick, 90
  Stew, Mushroom-, 314
  Stir
    -Fry, Simple, 255
    -Steamed, 50
  storage of, 477
  Strudel, 224
  table of food weights and measures, 512–19
  Tempura
    All-, 172
    Cheese-, 172
    Tofu-, 171
  Tofu
    Baked, 128
    Cream Cheese and, 69
    Curry, 149
  Turnovers, Russian, 281
  Woodstock Rice and, 188
  with Yogurt and Cheese, Skillet, 140
  see also specific vegetables
Veggie Reuben, 35
Very Quick Curried Chick-Peas, 54
Velouté, 313
Vichyssoise, 109
Viennese
  Plum Tart, 403
  Rice, 265
Vinaigrette
  French Tomato, 288
  Creamy, 288
  Italian Tomato, 288
  Mexican Tomato, 288
Virgin
  Mary Salad, 300
  Sangria, 418

W

Waldorf Salad, 304
Walnut(s)
  Apple Rocks, 378
  Bear Claws, 409
  Cake
    French Nut, 385

Walnut(s) (*cont.*)
  Fruit, 390
  Greek Lenten, 301
  Streusel Coffee, 390
  Carrots with, 238
  Carrot Cupcakes, 392
  Cookies, Jumbo, 375
    Rich, 376
  Date
    Bars, 379
    -Topped Shortbread Squares, 374
  Dressing, Cheese Salad with, 296
  Favorite Fruit Salad, 60
  Ice Cream, Maple-, 366
  -Peach Pie, 401
  Snails, 408
  Stuffed Zucchini Rounds, 160
Warm water-bath rising, 335
Warning signs of food deterioration, 482
Water
  benefits of, 18
  sparkling, 417
  -bath canner, 432
Watercress Soup, 109
Weight control, 2, 9–10
Wheat
  Berry Bake, Tuchman's, 191
  Germ, 508
    Loaf, Luncheon, 205
    Muffins, 328
    nutritional value, 509
  Salad, Orange-, 270
  Spanish, 270
  Super, 270
  Thins, Rye-, 321
  see also cracked wheat, whole wheat
Whipped
  Cottage Cream, 56
  Cream
    Real, 412
    Soy, 411
  Orange-Sesame Cream, 412
  Ricotta Topping, 411
  White Icing, 415
Whipping, 368
White
  Bean Pâté, 66
  Broccoli Mozzarella, 234
  Gazpacho, 108
  Lasagne, 124
  Sauce, 313
    Mix, 443
    Quick, 444
Whole grain
  breads, for pantry, 472
  crackers, for pantry, 472

Whole Wheat
  Bread, Standard, 337
  Muffins, 327
  Noodles, Soy-, 276
  Pasta, Basic, 275
  Sticks, 337
Wholefoods
  cooking, skills and techniques, 484–510
  definition, 3
  dinners, simple, 451–52
  fragmentation of, 3
  pantry, 471–75
  restaurant, 523
Wild Green Soup, 109
Wilted Spinach Salad, 299
Wine, "American," 487
Winter
  Fruit Salad, 359
  squash, *see* squash
  Stir-Steamed Vegetables, 50
Wok, use of, 490
Woodstock Rice and Vegetables, 188

Y

Yams
  Baked Sweet Potatoes and, 54
  preparation, 500
  see also sweet potatoes
Yeast
  bread, 333–47
    about, 333–37
  nutritional, *see* nutritional yeast
  pastries, about, 398
Yellow Yogurt Cake, 382
Yogurt
  about, 420
  Aioli with Vegetables, 41
  American-Style Potato Salad, 46
  Baked
    Mushrooms, 77
    Rice and Blue Cheese, 189
  Banana Cake, 387
  Basic Mashed Potatoes, 248
  Biscuits, 326
  Braised Red Cabbage, 237
  Broccoli
    Custard Pie, 225
    Tropicana, 78
  Cabbage Raita, 293
  Cake
    Arabic, 391
    Yellow, 382

Yogurt (*cont.*)
Carrot
-Peanut Salad, 292
Raita, 292
Caucasus Salad, 298
Cauliflower
with, 239
Puff, 150
Rémoulade, 79
Celery Rémoulade, 79
and Cheese, Skillet Vegetables with, 140
Cold
Beet Salad, 292
Curry Apple Soup, 110
Eggplant and, 243
Coleslaw
Cooked, 237
Country, 292
Cottage Pie, 155
Cream, 411
Creamy
Barley Salad, 269
Cheesecake, 393
Dinner Fruit Salad, 305
Mushrooms and Onions, 245
Pasta with Cheese and Herbs, 40
Peanut Butter, 31
Rice Salad, 269
Cucumber
Mousse, 294
Salad, 293
Crunchy Peach Salad, 305
Dip
Green, 64
Herb, 64
Onion, 64
Pimiento-Cheese, 47
Double Donuts, 392
Dressing
Avocado, 289
Creamy, 287
Blue Cheese, 290
Thick, 57
Carrot, 291
French Tomato Vinaigrette, 288
Herb, 290
Nut, 290
Orange-Honey, 291
Green Goddess, 289
Peanut Cream, 305
Revisionist, 57
Thousand Island, 289
Easy NFDM, 422
Eggplant and Potato Curry, 242

Fluffy
Mushroom Omelet, 133
Stuffed Baked Potato, 163
French Pasta Salad, 278
Fresh
Fruit Tart with Cheese Filling, 402
Peach Cake, 389
Strawberry Ice Cream, 366
Tomato Filled Crepes, 214
Fruit Kuchen Oma, 389
Frozen
Apple Cream, 365
Strawberry, 364
generations of, 422
House Corn Bread, 330
Hungarian Vegetable Gulyas, 145
Ilse's Vegetables with Cream Sauce, 142
India Salad with Curry Dressing, 302
Kidney Bean Luncheon Salad, 28
Lima Bean Egg Salad, 28
Macaroni
and Cheese Salad, 48
and Leban, 279
Salad, 48
making, about, 420–22
step-by-step, 421
Maple-Walnut Ice Cream, 366
Marble Cake, 384
Mideast Relish, 294
Noodle(s), 276
Pudding
Savory, 122
Sweet, 122
Onion Pie, 75
Party Mousse, 87
Pasta, Artichokes, and Chick-Peas with Lemon Dressing, 278
Peach Sherbet, 365
Pound Cake, 383
Protein-Enriched Kasha, 264
Ricotta Potato Salad, 250
Russian Beets, 234
Rye-Wheat Thins, 321
Salad
Puffs, 284
Spinach-, 299
Sauce
for Dahi Vaddi, 88
No-Cook Cold Cheese, 319
Mushroom, 314
Onion, 314
Peanut Butter-Vegetable, 319
-Tahini, 319
Tartar, 314
Soup, Moroccan, 109

Yogurt (*cont.*)
  Spice Cake, 382
  Spinach Quiche, 74
  Squash, 299
  Steamed Vegetables with Salsa Cruda,
    256
  Stuffed
    Cabbage Stroganoff, 165
    Lemon Eggs, 72
  Tempeh Sandwich Salad, 175
  Tender Pie Crust, 400
  Tofu
    "Chicken" Salad, 30
    Stroganoff, 170
  Tomato Pachadi, 300
  Tuchman's Wheat Berry Bake, 191
  Turkish Squash, 159
  Vegetables
    with Curry Cream, 41
    with Soufflé Sauce, 150
  Waldorf Salad, 304
  Whipped Ricotta Topping, 411
  White Gazpacho, 108

Z

Ziti
  Baked, 113
  with Cheese, 40
Zucchini
  Baked Vegetable Omelet, 136
  Cold Curry-Apple Soup, 110
  Crepes, Creamed Carrot and, 214
  Fried, 253
  Frittata, 135
  Italian Sautéed Cucumber, 240
  Loaf Cake, 386
  Pancakes, 195
  Pasta with, 115
  Ratatouille, 242
    Campfire, 242
  Relish, 440
  Roulade, 73
  Sauce, Spaghetti with, 116
  Sticks, Marinated, 66
  Stuffed
    with Cheese and Raisins, 160
    Rounds, 160
  Yogurt Squash, 299